Yearbook of Islamic and Middle Eastern Law

Volume 4

1997–1998

Yearbook of Islamic and Middle Eastern Law

Volume 4
1997–1998

General Editors

Eugene Cotran, LLD
Circuit Judge, Visiting Professor of Law, SOAS
Chairman, CIMEL

Chibli Mallat, PhD
Attorney and Professor of Law
St Joseph University, Beirut

Published for
the Centre of Islamic and Middle Eastern Law
at the School of Oriental and African Studies
University of London

CIMEL

SOAS

KLUWER LAW INTERNATIONAL
THE HAGUE · LONDON · BOSTON

Published by
Kluwer Law International Ltd
Sterling House
66 Wilton Road
London SW1V 1DE
United Kingdom

Kluwer Law International incorporates the
publishing programmes of
Graham & Trotman Ltd,
Kluwer Law & Taxation Publishers
and Martinus Nijhoff Publishers

Sold and distributed
in the USA and Canada
by Kluwer Law International
675 Massachusetts Avenue
Cambridge MA 02139
USA

In all other countries sold and distributed
by Kluwer Law International
P.O. Box 322
3300 AH Dordrecht
The Netherlands

© Eugene Cotran and Chibli Mallat 1998
First published in 1998

ISBN 90 411 0593 X

British Library Cataloguing in Publication Data and Library of Congress Cataloging-in-Publication Data is available

This publication is to be cited as *Yearbook of Islamic and Middle Eastern Law*, Volume 4 (1997–98)

Typeset by On Screen, West Hanney, Oxfordshire
Printed and bound in Great Britain by MPG Books Ltd, Bodmin, Cornwall

Contents

v

Biographical Notes

Richie Alder is a Solicitor of the Supreme Court of England and Wales, and has worked for Trowers & Hamlins, Oman, since 1995 specializing in commercial litigation, including banking, shipping, construction and bankruptcy.

Shaheen Sardar Ali is a Professor of Law, University of Peshawar, Pakistan, where she chaired the Department of Constitutional and International Law and was Director, Women's Study Centre at the same university. She is currently a lecturer at the School of Law, University of Warwick, UK. Her main areas of research include Islamic law, human rights, women's studies and international law, where she has published extensively. Professor Ali has received a number of national and international awards for teaching and research including a UNESCO award for development of teaching of human rights (1992), the Aizaz-i-Fazilat (Presidential Award) for contribution to higher education in Pakistan (1992), and the Star Woman of the Year Award in Law (1996).

Abd al-Amir al-Anbari (PhD Law (Harvard)), has been Ambassador of Iraq to UNESCO, an ex-Ambassador to London and Iraq Permanent Representative to the United Nations. He negotiated the Memorandum of Understanding of UNSCR 986 (Oil for Food).

Husain M. Al-Baharna gained a doctorate in international law from the University of Cambridge, and is a Barrister-at-Law of Lincoln's Inn and a member of the Bahrain Bar Association. He is a member of both the UN International Law Commission and the International Council for Commercial Arbitration (ICCA). He is the former Minister for Legal Affairs in the State of Bahrain, and is now an attorney and legal consultant in Bahrain. He is also a registered arbitrator.

Sabah Al-Mukhtar (LLB, LLM) is a member of both the Iraqi Bar and of the Arab Lawyers Federation. He is a legal consultant in Iraqi, Arab and Islamic laws, a fellow both of the British Institute of Management and the Institute of Petroleum, and a founding member and partner of the Arab Lawyers Network, London.

Najeeb Al-Nauimi (LLB, PhD) is a Qatari lawyer with degrees in law gained in Egypt and the United Kingdom. He is a former Minister of Justice for the State of Qatar and is Professor of Public Law at Qatar University. He is the Agent and Counsel of the Government of Qatar to the International Court of Justice in the case *Qatar v. Bahrain*, Qatar's representative to the International Court of Justice on Request for Advisory Opinion on the Legality of the Threat or Use of Nuclear Weapons, Vice-Chairman of the Working Group of Experts focusing on Liability and Compensation for Environmental Damage from the Iraqi Military Activities against Kuwait organized by the United Nations Environment Programme, National President of the World Jurist Association, current President of the Asian African Consultative Committee and Chairman of the Committee of Arab Legal Experts of the Arab League on the Law of the Sea. He has been head of the Qatari delegations to various international seminars and conferences. He is a writer, author and co-editor of books, and a member of various lawyers' associations, the Cairo Regional Centre for International Commercial Arbitration and the World Commission for the Oceans.

Anis Al-Qasem (LLM, PhD), a Barrister-at-Law of Lincoln's Inn, was formerly Legal Adviser to the Government of Libya and Chairman of the Libyan Petroleum Commission during the monarchy. He is presently a practising lawyer and consultant in London in the laws of the Middle East, a licensed legal consultant in Dubai, a visiting examiner and Associate Fellow of the Institute of Advanced Legal Studies, University of London, and Chairman of the Legal Committee of the Palestine National Council.

Lu'ayy Minwer Al-Rimawi holds a Master's degree in law from Cambridge University and a Master of Science in international relations from the London School of Economics. He is a doctoral researcher in the regulation of Arab securities markets, a Tutorial Fellow and teaches public international law at the LSE. He has had contributions on a wide range of legal and socio-political issues published in the *European Business Law Review*, *Journal of Financial Regulation and Compliance*, *The Company Lawyer*, *Millennium: Journal of Business Studies*, *CCH: Financial Services Law Reporter*, the *International Herald Tribune*, the *Guardian*, the *Guardian Manchester Weekly*, the *Independent*, the *Independent on Sunday*, the *Yorkshire Post*, the *Jordan Times*, the *Jerusalem Post*, *Al-Quds Al-Arabi*, *Al-Hayat*, *Al-Sharq Al-Awsat*, *El Rai*, and *Ed Dostour*. He is currently the principal Middle Eastern correspondent to the *European Financial Services Law Journal*.

Eugene Cotran (LLD) has been a circuit judge in England since 1992. He is a Visiting Professor of Law at the School of Oriental and African Studies, University of London, and the Chairman of the Centre of Islamic and Middle Eastern Law within the School. He was formerly a practising Barrister-at-Law in England and the Commonwealth, a Law Commissioner and High Court judge in Kenya and an international arbitrator. He is also a Board Member of the Palestinian Independent Commission for Citizens Rights. He has numerous publications on the laws of Africa, the Commonwealth, the Middle East and international and immigration law.

Michael Dark (MA) is an English solicitor on secondment from the international law firm of Graham & James to the Law Firm of Salah Al-Hejailan in Riyadh.

Abdul Hamid El-Ahdab (LLD) is a lawyer and a member of the Paris and Beirut Bars who resides in Paris. He is also president of the Arab Association for International Arbitration (AAAI) and secretary general of the Euro–Arab Council for International Arbitration.

Mustafa El-Alem (LLB, LLM) is a Libyan practising lawyer and legal adviser and a member of the Libyan Bar Association. He is a member of the Board of Directors of the Arab Association for International Arbitration and the Libyan member of the Alliance of Arab Lawyers and a full Member of the Euro–Arab Arbitration Board in London.

Jacques el-Hakim (LLD) is *agrégé* from the French Faculties of Law and has graduated in law in Syria, Lebanon and the USA. He is a member of the Damascus Bar and is currently a Professor and Head of the Commercial Law Department, Faculty of Law of Damascus University and an Attorney-at-Law. He has produced several publications on Syrian and other laws and on economics.

Salah El-Hejailan is the founder of the leading Law Firm of Salah El-Hejailan in Saudi Arabia and is the President of the Arbitration Board of the Euro–Arab Arbitration System.

Nicholas Foster was educated at Trinity Hall, Cambridge, and the University of Aix-Marseille. After qualifying as a solicitor he practised company, commercial and banking law with Clifford Chance and Nabarro Nathanson. He now lectures in Middle Eastern and comparative African Studies, University of London.

Afif Gaigi gained a degree in private law from the University of Tunis and went on to receive postgraduate diplomas in general private law and criminal science from the University of Paris. He is an attorney at the Tunis Court of Cassation, a member of the Tunis Bar and a university lecturer.

Salem A. Gammed (PhD) is Assistant Professor of Private Law, Faculty of Law, Gar Younis University, Benghazi, Libya.

Hamzeh Haddad was educated at Cairo University, from which he graduated as a Doctor of Laws, and the University of Bristol, where he gained a doctorate. He is the author of numerous books and articles and a speaker at many regional and international conferences. He is a member of the Jordan Bar Association and of the Arbitration Board of the Arab-Swiss Chamber of Commerce, and a practising attorney and arbitrator.

Vernon Handley (BA) is an attorney with the Law Firm of Salah Al-Hejailan ("LFSH"). Since 1994 Mr Handley has been based in the Middle East and, before joining LFSH, worked for Clifford Chance, a leading London-based law firm, first on secondment to Clifford Chance's associate office in Bahrani and, latterly, on secondment to Clifford Chance's Dubai office. Vernon Handley is a British subject. He holds a BA from Durham University.

Sibel Inceoglu (LLM) is Associate Professor of Constitutional Law, Faculty of Law, Marmara University. She has studied at Istanbul and Marmara universitites, and has been a visiting scholar in the Faculty of Law, University of California, Los Angeles.

Mohammad Hashim Kamali is a professor of Islamic law and jurisprudence at the International Islamic University Malaysia where he has been since 1985. Previously he lectured in Islamic law at McGill University, Montreal, and later at Capital University in Columbus Ohio. He has published several books and numerous articles on Islamic law, including *Principles of Islamic Jurisprudence* (Cambridge 1991) and *Freedom of Expression in Islam* (Cambridge, 1997).

Yamina Kebir is a practising attorney at the Court and the Supreme Court of Algeria. She is a member of the Algiers Bar. She graduated in law and English literature and holds a postgraduate degree in business law from the University of Paris II. She has published several articles on Algerian law in English.

The Law Firm **Kosheri, Rashed & Riad** was established in 1974 by Professor Dr Ahmed El-Kosheri and Professor Dr Samia Rashed. The firm has a strong commercial and litigation practice which includes investments, international business contracts, construction, banking, mining and petroleum concessions, patents and trademarks, business litigation and transnational arbitration. The firm is composed of seventeen lawyers, including two partners who are members of the New York Bar (Tarek Riad and Hala Riad), in addition to the support staff.

Martin Lau is a Barrister and lecturer in law at the School of Oriental and African Studies, University of London, where he teaches South Asian law. He studied at the University of Heidelberg, Germany, and at the University of London. He has published extensively on South Asian law and frequently acts as an expert in proceedings for the International Chamber of Commerce and English courts.

John Wuol Makec is a Justice of the Supreme Court of the Sudan. He has an LLB, University of Khartoum (1964–1969) and an LLM, University of London (SOAS) (1978–1980). He was formerly Minister of Cooperative and Rural Development of the High Executive Council Juda — Southern Sudan and Speaker of Bahr el Ghazal Regional Assembly. He has published extensively on the Customary Laws of the Sudan, in particular of the Dinka people.

Chibli Mallat (PhD) is a practising attorney and a professor of law at St Joseph University, Beirut. He is the author or editor of some fifteen books, including most recently *Presidential Choices* (Beirut, in Arabic, English and French, 1998) and *The Middle East into the 21st Century* (Reading, 1996 (paperback, 1997)).

Hyam Mallat is Chairman of the Board, National Security Fund, Lebanon. He is a lawyer and legal advisor, and teaches at St Joseph University, Beirut. He is the author of several books, including most recently *Droit de l'Urbanisme, de la Construction, de l'Environnement et de l'Eau au Liban* (Beirut, Paris and Brussels, 1997).

Fadi B. Nader is Partner and Legal Counsel of The International Investor KCSC, an Islamic Investment Bank based in Kuwait which is currently managing US$3.2 billion of local and international investment products, and is widely considered as one of the leading players in Islamic finance. He qualified in 1985; was an associate 1986–1988 with Samir Saleh and Associates, London; a company secretary 1988–1992 UB (Suisse) SA, Geneva; in private banking 1992–1993 with Crédit Commercial de France, London; and a Partner since 1987 in Moghaizel Law Offices, Beirut. He is a member of the Beirut Bar Association and the International Bar Association. He was educated at College des Frères Mont La Salle, Lebanon; St Joseph University, Beirut (LLB, June 1985); Queen Mary College, London (LLM, September 1997).

Sebastiaan Pompe (PhD) was formerly associated with the Jakarta law firm Ali Budiard jo Nugrobo Reksodiputro and is presently a senior lecturer at the Faculty of Law, University of Leiden. He completed his doctorate on the Indonesian court system. He specializes in Indonesian investment law and international commercial transactions.

Richard Price is the Gulf Resident Partner of Clifford Chance based in Dubai. Since 1982 he has spent much of his career in the UAE and Saudi Arabian offices of Clifford Chance specializing particularly in international maritime and trade law. He is the author of *The Maritime Laws of the Arabian Gulf Cooperation Council States* (Graham & Trotman) and numerous articles on all aspects of Gulf shipping and commercial law appearing in various legal and business journals.

Nageeb Shamiri (LLD) is a member of the Supreme Judicial Council of Yemen and of the Constitutional Division of the Supreme Court of Yemen. He was formerly the Chief Justice of South Yemen. He is the Chairman of the Judicial Inspection Commission, the Secretary of the Law Reform Unit at the Ministry of Legal and Parliamentary Affairs and contributed to the drafting of the Republic's main unified laws. He is a member of the National Committee regarding the Arbitration with Eritrea, and of the Joint Commission with Saudi Arabia regarding Maritime Boundaries.

David Wilson is a Solicitor of the Supreme Court of England and Wales, and has worked for Trowers & Hamlins in Dubai and Oman since 1991, specializing in international trade, agency and distribution, taxation, banking and project finance, air transportation and oil and gas.

Mamman A. Lawan Yusufari lectures in Islamic law at Bayero University, Kano. He is currently a postgraduate student at the Faculty of Law, University of Lagos.

Michèle Zirari-Devif is a Professor at the Faculty of Juridical, Economic and Social Sciences, University Mohammed V, Rabat, Morocco.

Preface

This year's volume 4 of the *Yearbook* deals not only with 1997 but also with the developments in the law until contributors wrote their country surveys in May 1998, hence it becomes volume 4 (1997–8) and will continue in this fashion in future years i.e. volume 5 (1998–9) etc.

Part I is a bumper year for articles, both as to length and quality. The first three deal with commercial and financial laws, viz. "Commercial securities and movables in the UAE" by Nicholas Foster, "Libyan joint venture investments" by Salem Gammed and "Jordan's financial and securities laws" by Lu'ayy Minwer al-Rimawi. There is then an article by Dr al-Anbari on the case for Iraq in regard to the UN sanctions regime, followed by four articles dealing with Islamic law – on women's human rights (Shaheen Sardar Ali), Islamic law in Malaysia (Mohammed Hashim Kamali), Indonesia (Sebastiaan Pompe) and in Nigeria (Mamman Lawan Yusufari). Finally, Professor Hyam Mallat surveys the social security and social insurance laws of nine Arab states: Saudi Arabia, Bahrain, Iraq, Jordan, Kuwait, Lebanon, Oman, Syria and Yemen.

In Part II, contributors survey, as before, developments in the various countries, but this year and in future years until May of the year of writing. These of course vary in length according to legislative activity. Jordan, for example, is short, but we hope that is made up by the article of Mr al-Rimawi and his comment on Jordan's recent Association Agreement with the European Union.

We regret that it has not been possible to have a full survey for Kuwait, or any survey for Iran, but we hope to include them next year in volume 5 to cover the position from 1997 to 1999.

In Part III we have included all UN Resolutions on Iraq, the UN Memorandum of Understanding and the US Congress Resolutions, which complement the article by Dr al-Anbari and Sabah Al-Mukhtar's survey. Selected documents include (a) the new Rules of Conciliation, Arbitration and Expertise of the Euro–Arab Arbitration System, which has now moved its headquarters and Secretariat from Paris to the premises of the Arab–British Chamber of Commerce at 6 Belgrave Square, London SW1X 8PH, and (b) the two papers of the Palestinian National Authority Ministry of Justice on the Rule of Law Strategic Development Plan and the Legal Project Advisory Board.

The legislation section of Part III has the full text of (a) two new laws from Egypt on investment guarantees and incentives, companies and partnerships, (b) the text of the new law of arbitration in Oman, based on the UNCITRAL Model Law, with a commentary by Dr Abdul Hamid El-Ahdab and (c) the text of the Malaysian Syariah Criminal Offences (Federal Territories) Act of 1997 which deals with the interesting offences relating to worship (*'aqidah*), to the sanctity of Islam, to decency and miscellaneous others.

Part IV contains the full International Court of Justice judgment on the preliminary issue in the *Lockerbie* case, and a Yemeni case, which received wide publicity, involving the alleged "spying" by the three BBC correspondents, Baron, Smith and Omar.

Finally, Part V has a variety of book reviews and the obituary of Dr Norman Calder.

We have omitted the list of transliteration included in previous volumes. We feel that subject to some standardization of more common terms contributors prefer to use their own, especially where such is included in legislation.

We wish to thank all who have helped us in producing this fourth volume of the *Yearbook*, in particular all contributors, the staff of CIMEL and SOAS and last but not least Hilary Scannell of Kluwer International and her assistant Rachel Amphlett.

Eugene Cotran and Chibli Mallat
October 1998

Part I

Articles

Commercial Security over Movables in the UAE: A Comparative Analysis in the Light of English Law, French Law and the *Shariʿa*

*Nicholas Foster**

1 INTRODUCTION

The UAE Commercial Code of 1993[1] greatly affected the law of the United Arab Emirates[2] relating to security over movables in the commercial field.[3] This is a topic of some importance for banks. Historically, banks operating in the UAE have

---

* School of Oriental and African Studies, London University. Ian Edge, Sabah Mahmoud of Gulf Legal Services, Peter O'Brien of Clifford Chance, Dubai and Luma Saqqaf of Allen & Overy, Dubai were kind enough to comment on a draft and provided valuable information. Ruchdi Maalouf provided very helpful assistance in research. The usual disclaimer applies. Any comments or corrections would be gratefully received. Passages from publications which are divided into numbered paragraphs are cited both by the paragraph number (indicated by the symbol §), and by the page numbers, which immediately follow the paragraph number. References to articles without more are references to articles of the Commercial Code. Translations which are otherwise unacknowledged are the author's.

1 *Qanun al-muʾamilat al-tijariyya* (the Law of Commercial Transactions), enacted by Federal Law No. 18 of 1993, UAE Official Gazette dated 20 September 1993, came into force on 20 December 1993. For an English translation, see Dawoud S. Al-Alami (trans.) *The Law of Commercial Procedure of the United Arab Emirates*, London, Graham and Trotman, 1994; for an overview see Neil McNeill, foreword to Al-Alami; Richard Price, "United Arab Emirates", in volume 1 of this *Yearbook* (1994), pp. 307–329; and Clifford Chance, "The UAE Commercial Transactions Law", *Middle East Commercial Law Review*, 2, 1995, p. 41. There is little consistency in the name of the law in English; it is referred to *inter alia* as "the Commercial Transactions Law" (or CTL), "the Law of Commercial Procedure" and "the Commercial Code". This article will refer to it as "the Commercial Code". The translation used here is that prepared for Clifford Chance, Dubai.

2 "The UAE". For introductions to the UAE and its legal system, see Price, "United Arab Emirates", 1994; Butti Sultan Butti Al-Muhairi, "The development of the UAE legal system and unification with the judicial system", *Arab Law Quarterly*, 1996, p. 116; and S. Mahmoud, *UAE Company Law and Practice*, 3rd edn, London, Medina, pp. 1–5.

3 Some aspects of the law are yet to be made effective, for example the registration system for pledges of commercial undertaking was only set up in Dubai in 1997.

contented themselves mainly with trade financing and so did not suffer unduly from the pre-Commercial Code deficiencies of the laws on security over movables, but do need an effective regime if they are to expand their activities.

This article examines this area in comparative perspective in the light of English[4] law, French law and the *shari'a*, the initial viewpoint being that of an (English) common lawyer. There are two reasons for a comparative, rather than a purely descriptive, approach: first, the intrinsic academic interest of a comparative approach to this subject, which affords good opportunities for analysis of the way in which four legal systems deal with the issues; secondly, the practical consideration that in explaining any aspect of Middle Eastern law, a comparative approach is very helpful for proper understanding. In the Middle East, such a comparative approach necessarily involves looking at the law of the European jurisdiction (in this case, France) which has been received in the Middle East jurisdiction concerned, together with the *shari'a*, in addition to the actual rules of the Middle East jurisdiction. In such a study, an indication of the common law approach can be useful for lawyers of the Romano-Germanic tradition[5] who wish to understand common law security techniques, as well as for common lawyers who can look at the common law approach in a new, comparative, light. Hence the choice of jurisdictions.

On the comparative level, the question of the degree to which the UAE regime of security over movables will succeed as a "legal transplant" is an underlying theme of the article. Put very briefly, academic opinion is sharply divided as to the effectiveness of a transplant of one legal system's concepts to another legal system. At the risk of caricaturing the complex arguments, one might sum up one side's argument as follows: law is culture, cultures do not travel well, therefore law does not travel well. The other side takes the opposite view and points to what it claims to be many instances of successful legal borrowing.[6] Whatever the situation may be in other regions, in the Middle East the acceptability of law as measured by its "cultural" aspects (the word culture as used here includes religious considerations) is a significant factor. By the inclusion of a comparison throughout the article of the Commercial Code provisions with the *shari'a* as a manifestation of "culture" in this broad sense, the article attempts to provide a tentative indicator (even if that

---

[4] With apologies to any Welsh readers for the inaccuracy, for the sake of brevity the words "England" and "English" are used to refer to the jurisdiction of England and Wales.

[5] It is usual practice for common lawyers to use the term "civil law" in two quite different senses: first, to refer to legal systems deriving from the continental European legal tradition, secondly to refer to that branch of the law which relates to non-business actors and transactions between individuals as opposed to, for example, commercial law. In order to avoid confusion, this article will use the term "civil law" only in the sense of the law relating to non-business actors and transactions, and René David's term "Romano-Germanic" will be used when referring to the legal systems. For basic concepts of the Romano-Germanic law tradition, see *inter alia* Konrad Zweigert and Hein Kötz, Tony Weir trans., *An Introduction to Comparative Law*, 2nd edn, Oxford, Clarendon Press, 1992, Chapter 6 ("The history of French law"), Chapter 7 ("The spirit and essential features of the Code Civil"), Chapter 8 ("The reception of the Code Civil") and Chapter 9 ("Courts and lawyers in France and Italy"); and M. Vranken, *Fundamentals of European Civil Law*, London, Blackstone Press, 1997, Part A ("Historical overview and conceptual framework").

[6] A rather less cursory discussion (although still a brief treatment of a very complex and controversial topic) is to be found in the conclusion (section 11.2.2, "The UAE regime in the light of legal transplant theory").

indicator is only one element of a very complex picture) of the likelihood of a successful reception of the movable security regime, and by extension of the present commercial law generally.

The article concentrates on the "classical" forms of security provided by the Commercial Code, together with the related topics of assignment and priority rights, which are of particular interest in the comparative context, as well as providing a short treatment of set-off and mentioning very briefly sale-related mechanisms and promissory notes as security. It also deals with possible limitations on the effectiveness of security on the insolvency of the debtor. For reasons of space it does not deal with the more specialized area of security over ships and aircraft, nor with security associated with letters of credit. Although from the point of view of strict logic guarantees and bank guarantees do not belong in a discussion of security over movables, they are briefly referred to for the sake of convenience.[7]

2 THE *SHARI'A* IN THE COMMERCIAL CONTEXT AND THE CIVIL LAW/COMMERCIAL LAW DIVIDE

Although the Commercial Code provisions relating to security over movables show striking similarities in form and content to those of French law, they operate in an environment influenced by the *shari'a*.[8] It is therefore necessary to examine not only the French-influenced statutory regime, but also the role of the *shari'a*, its relationship with that regime, and the method used to try to reconcile the two influences.

2.1 The *shari'a* in the commercial context

Even when the *shari'a* was regarded as at best of marginal importance in most Middle Eastern jurisdictions in the commercial context, and many considered the only relevant source of commercial law to be Romano-Germanic style statutes, the *shari'a* was in fact of considerable importance. As a religious law and an important part of the culture of the region, it exercises a considerable influence on the practice and interpretation of the law, as well as the behaviour of parties to a transaction. To take the example of one of the commonest commercial transactions in the region, that of agency, "the civil law concept of 'an agency made for the mutual benefit of the parties' is often transformed in practice into a permanent form of partnership

---

[7] For an overview of UAE security law before the enactment of the Commercial Code, which includes accounts of those matters not dealt with herein, see R. Horsfall Turner, "Security and enforcement in Dubai and other United Arab Emirates", *Arab Law Quarterly*, 1991, p. 311.

[8] For a history of the introduction of Western-style laws into the Gulf states, see S. E. Rayner, *The Theory of Contracts in Islamic Law*, London, Graham and Trotman, 1991, Chapter 2 ("The modern dichotomy"). For Egyptian law on the subject, see 'Abd al-razzaq Al-Sanhuri, *Al-wasit fi sharh al-qanun al-madani al-jadid,* vol. XI (*Al-ta'minat al-shakhsiyyat wa al-'ayniyyat*), Cairo, name of publisher not indicated, 1950–1969.

between the principal and his agent, thus explaining the local sensitivity and social stigma attached to termination of agencies".[9]

Consequently, the difference between "law in action" and "law in the books" (which exists in any legal system) may be greater than that to which Western lawyers are accustomed – statutes which closely resemble Romano-Germanic laws in both form and content may be interpreted and enforced in unexpected ways. Samir Saleh refers to this potentially misleading dichotomy between the words of statutes and what actually happens in practice as "the dual reality in which the *shari'a* and secular law do not necessarily exclude but often complement each other".[10]

In addition to this background importance of the *shari'a* which has always existed, the resurgence in Islamic thinking of the last twenty years has to a considerable extent rolled back the former modernizing, Westernizing trend. In this climate the legislator cannot ignore the *shari'a*, which therefore informs the content of many statutory provisions themselves.[11]

2.2 The Commercial Code and the Civil Code: a compromise solution

This situation presents Middle Eastern legislators drafting commercial legislation with a difficult task, because some basic principles of the *shari'a* (such as the prohibition of *riba* and *gharar*) cannot, on anything but a very liberal, and minority, interpretation of the *shari'a*, be reconciled with many important international business practices (such as the charging of interest and speculation). However, these international practices are so important to the economy of the region that they cannot be ignored. The French distinction between civil and commercial law has been adopted as a compromise solution in an attempt to reconcile the demands of the newly resurgent *shari'a* and those of international business.

French law formally distinguishes commercial from civil (non-commercial) law, with a separate Commercial Code and separate courts of first instance. English law does not make such a distinction, although in certain important respects it takes a different approach to commercial causes from that adopted in non-commercial matters.[12] Originally, the French distinction arose out of historical accident and is "not

---

[9] Samir Saleh, *Commercial Agency and Distributorship in the Arab Middle East*, The Hague, Kluwer Law International, 1995, 1-1–1-2.

[10] *Ibid.*; see also W. Ballantyne, "The Shari'a and its relevance to modern transnational transactions", in International Bar Association (ed.), *Arab Comparative Commercial Law: The International Approach*, vol. 1, London, Graham and Trotman, 1987; and Noel Coulson, *Commercial Law in the Gulf States: The Islamic Legal Tradition*, London, Graham and Trotman, 1984: introduction, pp. 1–8.

[11] See Coulson, *Commercial Law in the Gulf States*, especially the conclusion (pp. 105–108); W. Ballantyne, "The new Civil Code of the United Arab Emirates: a further reassertion of the Shari'a", *Arab Law Quarterly*, 1986, p. 245; and Ballantyne, "The Shari'a and its relevance to modern transnational transactions".

[12] On the position in English law, see R. Goode, *Commercial Law*, 2nd edn, Harmondsworth, Penguin, 1995, pp. 1205–1206; R. Goode, "The codification of commercial law", *Mondale Law Review*, 14, 1988, p. 135; and L. S. Sealy and R. J. A. Hooley, *Text and Materials in Commercial Law*, London, Butterworths, 1994, Chapter 1 ("An introduction to commercial law"), especially pp. 23–31. For a comparative study, see G. Samuel, "Civil and commercial law: a distinction worth making?", *Law Quarterly Review*, 102, 1986, p. 56. Discussion of this issue in English law

the result of any positive rationalization".[13] It has its origins in the Middle Ages, when, as a result of the deficiencies of the legal systems of the time, there arose a body of international law and practice, independent of national legal systems, the *lex mercatoria*. The *lex mercatoria* was gradually absorbed into both the French and the English legal systems, but whereas in England the *lex mercatoria* became part of the "mainstream" legal system, in France a formal distinction was preserved. The preservation of the distinction was partly a consequence of the way in which French law tends to divide and categorize and partly a consequence of historical and social factors. It also stemmed from the belief that private individuals, being unsophisticated, needed a high degree of protection, whereas commerce needed an environment with far fewer restrictions, and that the best way to satisfy these contradictory needs was to have two distinct systems.

The distinction permeates various areas of the law, including that of security over movables. As well as leading to significant differences in the legal rules,[14] the distinction has also been instrumental in creating certain commercial concepts, such as that of "commercial undertaking",[15] a specified class of property which is used in business, in respect of which special rules exist as to, *inter alia*, its purchase, sale and the grant of security interests over it.

For various reasons, such as the development of sophisticated consumer law, some challenge whether it is worth keeping the distinction and many other Romano-Germanic law jurisdictions, such as Italy and Switzerland, have abolished it. However, the UAE, in common with nearly all other Arab jurisdictions, has adopted it in an attempt to reconcile the conflicting demands of the *shari‘a* with those of international commerce, with the result that it is an essential part of the structure of commercial law in the UAE. The UAE Civil Code[16] incorporates *shari‘a* ideas for non-business transactions between individuals in order to satisfy the need for a *shari‘a* element in the law; the Commercial Code incorporates international commercial practice for business transactions.

---

cont.
  is often put as the search for the answer to a question: does English law distinguish between civil and commercial law in the same way as French law? This is in fact misleading – English law has never looked at the matter in this way and attempting to find an answer to this question produces rather unsatisfactory results. It is more helpful to consider English and French law as inhabiting different mental and historical worlds, leading them inevitably to take different approaches to the way in which commercial and non-commercial matters are dealt with by the legal system.

[13] Samuel, "Civil and commercial law", p. 570.

[14] "The formation of such contracts, their proof, and their effects may differ according to whether or not they are subject to commercial law rules. Similarly, problems of capacity are seen differently by civil law and commercial law" (René David, quoted in J. H. Merryman, D. S. Clark and J. O. Haley, *The Civil Law Tradition: Europe, Latin America and East Asia*, Charlottesville, Virginia, The Michie Company, 1994, p. 1140).

[15] The *fonds de commerce*.

[16] *Qanun al-mu’amilat al-madaniyya* (the Law of Civil Transactions), enacted by Federal Law No. 5 of 1985, UAE Official Gazette, December 1985, came into force on 29 March 1986. Sources of the legislation include the Maliki and Hanbali schools, other Arab civil codes, and customary applications of the *shari‘a*. See also amendment enacted by Law No. 1 of 1987. For an English translation, see J. Whelan and M. J. Hall, *The Civil Code of the United Arab Emirates: The Law of Civil Transactions of the State of the United Arab Emirates*, London, Graham and Trotman, 1987; for an overview see Ballantyne, "The new Civil Code". This article will refer to it as "the Civil Code". The translation used herein is Whelan and Hall's.

An example of the difference between the two regimes in the movable security field can be seen in the area of the enjoyment of the fruits of pledged property: Article 1474(1) Civil Code provides that the pledgee may not enjoy the use of the property without the consent of the pledgor, whereas Article 169 Commercial Code reverses the situation.[17]

However, this simple picture needs qualification. As mentioned above, a Romano-Germanic style statute such as the Commercial Code will be used and enforced in the UAE by people who may, consciously or unconsciously, interpret it in a way influenced by the *shari'a*. One should also note that it is neither self-contained nor comprehensive.[18] It is not self-contained because, following the French model, UAE commercial law is not a separate system: commercial law rules are additions to, or variations from, the "normal" rules contained in the Civil Code.[19] It is not comprehensive for various reasons: in commercial matters, contract and commercial custom have a considerable impact on the law, and the Commercial Code recognizes this;[20] there is always some overlap between civil and commercial rules, and where an overlap does occur it would make little sense to repeat in the Commercial Code rules already enunciated in the Civil Code;[21] and specialized areas of commerce need their own specialized legislation.[22]

2.3 Scope of the Commercial Code

The Commercial Code follows the example of French law and uses the concepts of "merchant" and "commercial transaction" to determine its scope.[23] Article 1 provides: "The provisions of this Code shall apply to merchants and to all commercial business undertaken by any person whether or not a merchant." Where there are mixed parties, one non-commercial and one commercial, then Article 10 takes a more draconian attitude than French law (which has an extensive case law in this area) and provides that the Commercial Code "shall apply to the obligations of both parties unless the law provides or the parties agree otherwise". Articles 4–9 define commercial business and Articles 11–25 deal with the status of merchant. Generally the definition of commercial business is what one would expect, however one

---

[17] Also contrast Art. 1474(2) Civil Code with Art. 169 Commercial Code on the question of the application of the fruits of the pledged object in repayment of the principal and interest.

[18] Although it is far more complete than the French Commercial Code, which is virtually an empty shell.

[19] One result of this is that, as the Commercial Code builds on a foundation laid by the *shari'a* based Civil Code, it itself undergoes thereby the influence of the *shari'a*, which provides not only a very significant part of the content of the civil law rules but also numerous fundamental and important matters such as the sources of law (which include the *shari'a* as a backstop – Art. 1 Civil Code) and general, Islamic, rules of interpretation – Art. 2 Civil Code.

[20] Art. 2(1) and Art. 2(2).

[21] Guarantees, for example, are relevant in both civil and commercial matters, and the main rules thereon are contained in Arts. 1056–1105 Civil Code. Some specialized guarantees, such as bank guarantees, are only relevant in commerce and are dealt with in the Commercial Code.

[22] Art. 3 specifically contemplates such specialized laws.

[23] See Price, "United Arab Emirates", pp. 308–312. The equivalent French provisions are Art. 1 French Commercial Code (merchants) and Arts. 632 and 633 French Commercial Code (commercial transactions).

should note that the liberal professions, organs of the state and clubs are excluded,[24] as is artistic work, the work of authors[25] and general farming activities.[26]

3 VARIATIONS WITHIN THE UAE

The UAE is a very new, federal, state in which differences of approach exist between emirates, reflected notably in the fact that the federal court system does not apply in all seven of the emirates, the exceptions being Dubai and Ras al Khaimah. Such differences may lead to an uneven application of federal legislation such as the Commercial Code[27] and the lack of judicial precedent could contribute to the survival of such differences.[28]

4 ENGLISH, FRENCH AND *SHARI'A* APPROACHES TO COMMERCIAL SECURITY OVER MOVABLES

4.1 Comparing regimes of commercial security of movables

Like other areas of comparative law, the comparison of different legal regimes of security over property owes more to art than to science.[29] However, a (non-exhaustive) checklist of the most important considerations, used with discretion, can be helpful as a guide through the complexities.[30] To take the example of the pledge, the topics covered in such a list might include: the formal basis of the pledge;[31] the

---

[24] Art. 15.

[25] Art. 8.

[26] Art. 9.

[27] See generally Horsfall Turner, "Security and enforcement", p. 311 and *passim*.

[28] For precedent in the UAE see below (section 6.1, "General characteristics of the UAE system").

[29] For general comparative considerations and a survey of the major jurisdictions of the world, see Philip R. Wood, *Comparative Law of Security and Guarantees*, London, Sweet and Maxwell, 1995, Chapter 1 ("Principles of security"), Appendix I:1 and I:2, pp. 405–407 and Chapter 2 ("Universal business charges").

[30] The list which follows is by no means comprehensive; for a fuller list see Wood, *Comparative Law*, Chapter 1, Appendix I:1 and I:2, pp. 405–407.

[31] In French law (or more accurately, the antecedent Roman law), the *shari'a* and English law, the pledge antedates notions of contract and is only categorized as a contract at quite a late date. The way in which this categorization takes place and its importance differ from system to system. In French law, the pledge, although it has its distinct characteristics, is formally defined by statute as a contract (Art. 2071 and Art. 2072 French Civil Code). In the *shari'a* the pledge forms one of the list of nominative contracts and is also formally defined by reference to contract (Art. 706 *Majalla* and see references below (section 4.4, "The *shari'a* approach to the law of commercial security over movables")), although not by statute and in quite a different theoretical environment. For the *Majalla* (*Majalat al-ahkam al'adiya*), the Ottoman code based on the Hanafi school, see the English translation in C. A. Hooper, *The Civil Law of Palestine and Trans-Jordan*, Jerusalem, Azriel Printing Works 1933. This translation is serialized in *Arab Law Quarterly*, vols. 1–5 (1986–1990). In English law, as is usual, there is no statutory or other definitive definition, but the unofficial definitions available show evidence of the traces of the pledge's origin as a *sui generis* mechanism antedating contract: *Halsbury's Laws of England*, 4th edn, London, Butterworths, 1981, vol. 36, §101, p. 65 makes no reference to contract, the word "contract" is only found in a later description of pledge in §103, 66.

essential characteristic of a pledge (transfer of possession in England and France, but extended in different ways in the two jurisdictions); the debts which can be secured (interest, future debts and sums lent over a specified maximum amount may be excluded); the assets which can be pledged (can land, after-acquired property, receivables,[32] property other than the pledgor's, or all the assets of a business be pledged?); the identity of the secured creditor (some jurisdictions limit the classes of persons who may take security); the means of perfection of the pledge (actual or constructive transfer of possession is always required, but one or more of writing, notarization, registration and tax may also be necessary); the type of enforcement regime in place (enforcement remedies vary widely[33] and sometimes practical restrictions exist);[34] and the priority given by the security (some other creditors such as the tax authorities or the employees may have a higher priority on insolvency than the secured creditor).

Having used such a list in order to examine the issues in a reasonably systematic way, one can then proceed to some broader tests in order to attempt to reach some general conclusions.[35]

One such test is the degree to which the system does or does not favour secured creditors. This test is sometimes expressed as a contrast between "pro-debtor" and "pro-creditor" systems, but this is rather misleading, since a system which is not particularly pro-creditor may favour other actors (such as employees and the holders of preferential rights) as much as, if not more than, the debtor.

Another such test, related to the first, is the degree of generalization and abstraction in the system. Systems of security over movable property all originate with the concrete, with the physical transfer of possession of the asset (the pledge). The pledge has its advantages (simplicity, avoiding the false wealth problem), but also serious drawbacks (such as storage and maintenance responsibilities for the creditor, deprivation of the asset for the debtor, limitation to tangible assets, limitation to one secured creditor).[36] Simplifying greatly, systems which wish to solve these problems can take either a "generalist" or "particularist" approach. In the generalist approach, associated with "pro-creditor" regimes, generalized, abstract devices, such as the English charge, are more prominent, as are general principles. In the particularist approach, associated more with "pro-debtor" regimes, particular types of property and actors are dealt with piecemeal and generalized, abstract devices and general principles are less important.

---

[32] Analysis of the often difficult issues involved with debts, especially with their assignment, tends to be confused in English by the terminology, since the word "debt" is used to denote both the debtor's obligation to pay (French *dette*) and the creditor's right to receive payment (French *créance*). In order to avoid confusion the factoring term "receivable" will be used to denote the creditor's right to receive payment, the term "obligation to pay" will be used to denote the debtor's obligation to pay, and the term "debt" will be used to refer to the obligation being secured.

[33] England allows quite draconian, and private, enforcement whereas other regimes, less severe on the debtor, require public involvement (through the courts and public auctions).

[34] E.g. in Saudi Arabia land may only be owned by a Saudi national, or by a GCC national for a dwelling, so the disposal of land pursuant to security enforcement procedures will be more difficult.

[35] Any such conclusions are "bound to be impressionistic and unreliable" (Wood, *Comparative Law*, pp. 5–9) but are none the less useful within their limits.

[36] Some intangible assets can be pledged if there is some tangible asset which the law regards as embodying that asset, for example bearer shares and negotiable instruments.

Without taking a mechanistic approach, the following sections will examine the general approaches of the English, French and *shari'a* regimes in the light of the list of considerations and the two tests set out above.

4.2 The English approach to the law of commercial security over movables[37]

4.2.1 Underlying attitudes

The English approach to security over movables reflects the general English approach to commercial law, the encouragement of commerce at the expense of other considerations, a system in which little allowance is made for the weak or foolish.[38]

As there is no formal distinction between civil and commercial matters, the starting point is that the same rules on security over movables apply in theory to private and commercial transactions.[39]

4.2.2 Sources and overview of mechanisms

This apparently simple position rapidly gives way to complication. One's first impression is that the system is fragmented, complex, disorganized and confusing. Based on (sometimes ancient) case law, with few statutory provisions, an initially bewildering array of mechanisms of different types jostle for attention.[40] In addition to various classes of securities created by operation of law, consensual security (security created as such by the agreement of the parties) comprises four mechanisms: the pledge, the mortgage, the charge and the contractual lien. The pledge is effected by a transfer of actual or constructive possession. The mortgage was originally effected by a transfer of title and this is still the case with mortgages of movables. The charge is a "proprietary interest granted by way of security".[41] The contractual lien is a right to retain property which is already in the custody of the creditor for some other purpose. Specialized types of property, such as shares, create particular problems.[42] Numerous indirect mechanisms[43] exist,

---

[37] See Goode, *Commercial Law*, Part 4 ("Secured financing"), especially pp. 642–674. For short introductions written for lawyers trained in the Romano-Germanic tradition, see Edward Miller, "Les garanties portant sur des biens situés en Angleterre", *Banque*, 546, 1994, pp. 50–51, and Michael Elland-Goldsmith, "Les suretés réelles mobilières du droit anglais: real security over personal property in English Law", *Revue de droit des affaires internationales – International Business Law Journal*, 2, 1995, pp. 145–170.

[38] Goode, *Commercial Law*, p. 1206.

[39] With notable exceptions, e.g. those transactions governed by consumer protection legislation such as the Consumer Credit Act 1974.

[40] See Goode, *Commercial Law*, p. 729. Despite some calls for reform, there does not seem to be any consensus that codification or statutory intervention is needed.

[41] Lord Hoffmann in *Re Bank of Credit and Commerce International SA (No. 8)* [1998] AC 214, at 226, [1997] 4 All ER 568, at 576, HL.

[42] E.g. title to shares in a company incorporated in England is transferable only upon registration of the transfer in the books of the company.

[43] Security mechanisms can be divided into two broad categories – those which have been "specifically designed in order to achieve a precise aim" and those which are not so specifically

such as the assignment (a method of transferring title to intangible property), retention of title clauses, receivables financing mechanisms, leasing contracts and set-off agreements.[44]

The registration system is also worth mentioning, in that registration, which is in a central registry and which lasts for the lifetime of the security, exists primarily to protect the public, rather than to validate the security[45] or determine priorities. Priority is basically determined by the time of creation of the security.[46]

4.2.3 *Enforcement*

Upon enforcement, fixed security has absolute priority over unsecured creditors to the extent of the sale proceeds of the secured asset, only floating security ranks behind preferential creditors. Enforcement can take place immediately upon default and the commonest English law enforcement procedure, that of sale by receiver, is private.[47]

4.2.4 *Conclusion*

The initial impression of confusion is deceptive, for despite the many problems (particularly in the interaction of these mechanisms in the matter of priority), the system both works efficiently and has a definite general direction or philosophy: the encouragement of lending by facilitating the creation of security interests and by the easy, cheap and rapid enforcement of those interests in priority to other creditors.

This situation has been achieved by leaving both the creation of the security regime and its enforcement largely in the hands of the business community and their lawyers who, by a long process of extension and increasing abstraction of the consensual forms of security, the use of numerous indirect mechanisms and the development of general principles, have ensured that security interests can be granted over

---

cont.

designed but which "manifest sufficient elasticity to be adapted to [a certain aim], according to practical needs": J. Mestre, E. Putman and M. Billiau, *Traité de droit civil: droit commun des suretés réelles: théorie générale*, Paris, Librairie Générale de Droit et de Jurisprudence, 1996, §11, pp. 9–10. Examples of the former in English law include the mortgage and the charge, examples of the latter include the assignment and the retention of title clause.

There is no generally accepted terminology for these categories. The terms "security" to denote the first category and "quasi-security" to denote the second are reasonably common in English practice, but are not entirely satisfactory, since the effect of "quasi-security" is usually to grant rights to the grantee which are quite as effective as those granted using "security". Mestre *et al.*, *Traité de droit civil*, fix on the terms "specific" for the first and "indirect" for the second category: *ibid*. These terms will be used in this article.

[44] See Goode, *Commercial Law*, pp. 646–666. The complication produced by the existence of so many indirect mechanisms of different types has been criticized, but it does provide great flexibility.

[45] Although if not registered within the prescribed time limits, the security may be invalid, either under the Bills of Sale Acts or s. 395 Companies Act 1985.

[46] But this is a complex area and difficult questions can arise; see Goode, *Commercial Law*, Chapter 24 ("Principles of perfection and priorities").

[47] The English attitude is that private sale is efficient and speedy and concords well with the English dislike of bureaucracy and what is perceived as public interference in private affairs.

any property,[48] present or future, real or personal, tangible or intangible, by any person[49] with legal capacity in favour of any other person, in respect of any debt (present, future or conditional, with no maximum), with minimal interference from the state (whether judicial or statutory)[50] in either the creation of the rules or their enforcement. Levels of formality for execution of documents are very low,[51] there are no requirements for notarization. Standard documentation usually circumvents the theoretical possibility of prolonged negotiation. The very diversity of the legal mechanisms, although it can create other problems, gives a great amount of choice to the parties and this, combined with the great emphasis placed on freedom of contract and enforceability of obligations, allows parties considerable flexibility in new situations.

In terms of the tests referred to above, the English system is pro-creditor, generalist and quite abstract.

4.3 The French approach to the law of commercial security over movables

In addition to the formal separation between commercial and non-commercial matters the French system is markedly different from the English approach in many other ways, including the general attitude towards security, the sources of the law, the mechanisms available (which include rights granted under the preferential regime) and enforcement.[52]

---

[48] Illustrative of the attitude of the English legal system in this regard is the fierce debate concerning the validity of charges granted by lenders over money deposited with a bank in order to secure obligations owed by the lenders to that bank, with those arguing for the validity of such charges proceeding on the assumption that all types of asset should be capable of being used in order to secure lending. See *Re Charge Card Services Ltd* [1987] Ch 150, [1986] 3 All ER 289, affd [1988] Ch 497, [1988] 3 All ER 702, CA; and *Re Bank of Credit and Commerce International SA (No. 8)* [1998] AC 214, [1997] 4 All ER 568, HL. Lord Hoffmann's dictum (at [1998] AC 228, [1997] 4 All ER 578) is of particular interest: "In a case in which there is no threat to the consistency of the law or objection of public policy, I think that the courts should be very slow to declare a practice of the commercial community to be conceptually impossible. Rules of law must obviously be consistent and not self-contradictory ... But the law is fashioned to suit the practicalities of life and legal concepts like 'proprietary interest' and 'charge' are no more than labels given to clusters of related and self-consistent rules of law." See also the judgment of the Court of Appeal [1996] Ch 245, [1996] 2 All ER 121; Anu Arora, *Practical Banking and Building Society Law*, London, Blackstone Press, 1997, pp. 320–322; and Goode, *Commercial Law*, pp. 659–660.
[49] Only companies and farmers (s. 5 Agricultural Credits Act 1928) can grant floating charges. Charges granted by individuals fall under the registration requirements of the Bills of Sale Acts, which make floating charges impracticable.
[50] One aspect of the French system which strikes an English lawyer most forcibly is the use of not only civil, but also criminal sanctions to achieve what in England would (in the absence of fraud) be solely a matter of agreement between the parties – it is a criminal offence (*détournement de gage*) to destroy property given as security or otherwise put the property beyond the reach of the creditor (Arts. 314–315 French Penal Code).
[51] Even the procedure for executing deeds has been simplified by (for companies) s. 36A Companies Act 1985 (as inserted by s. 130(2) Companies Act 1989) and by (for individuals) s. 1 Law of Property (Miscellaneous Provisions) Act 1989.
[52] See generally Mestre *et al.*, *Traité de droit civil*; Dominique Legeais, *Sûretés et garanties de crédit*, Paris, Librairie Générale de Droit et de Jurisprudence, 1996: §1–29, pp. 1–17 (especially for historical aspects); and Philippe Simler and Philippe Delebecque, *Droit civil: les sûretés, la publicité foncière*, 2nd edn, Paris, Dalloz, 1995, §2–20, pp. 5–26. Works in English include Robert Pennington, "The financing of current transactions by companies under English, French and

4.3.1 Underlying attitudes

The underlying attitude of French law is rather suspicious towards commerce in general and security in particular, and tends to be more protective of the debtor. For example, old French law viewed the pledge with disfavour and the draftsmen of the French Civil Code considered that pledge was "an operation smelling of want exploited by usurers".[53] In addition to this general hostility, movables were regarded as a second class asset in comparison to land. This attitude, summed up in the Latin tag: *res mobilis, res vilis* ("a movable asset is a lowly asset": a maxim of which Napoleon I apparently approved) has left a legacy the effects of which can still be discerned.

4.3.2 Sources

The classical view is that true security can only be given by the legislator, a view encapsulated in the maxim *pas de privilège sans texte*, which one can translate/paraphrase as "no priority without [legislative] authority".[54] In accordance with this view, all specific security mechanisms derive their existence from statute.[55] This attitude has important theoretical and practical consequences. It is not possible, for example, to create a pledge without transfer of possession in the absence of legislation, nor to create anything equivalent to the floating charge simply by agreement between the parties. To do so would be to "undermine credit and so enter into an agreement contrary to public policy".[56] It is common, even where a contractual/property mechanism is initially recognized by case law, to legitimize (and sometimes strengthen) it by statute.[57] However, the classical view has been challenged in recent years, which have seen the courts give effect to numerous indirect mechanisms. The conflict between these two viewpoints is an important theoretical debate in the area.[58]

---

cont.

  German law", in Robert R. Drury and Peter Xuereb (eds), *European Company Laws*, Aldershot", Dartmouth, 1991; and Michael G. Dickson, Wolfgang Rosener and Paul Storm, *Security on Movable Property and Receivables in Europe: The Principal Forms of Security in the European Community (except Greece) and Switzerland*, Oxford, ESC Publishing, 1988, chapter on France.

[53] Malaurie and Aynès, cited in Simler and Delebecque, *Droit civil*, §505, 420.

[54] The word *texte* is commonly used to mean legislation. Mestre *et al.*, describe this maxim as "a heritage of our legal tradition": Mestre *et al.*, *Traité de droit civil*, §237, 220.

[55] This is not to underestimate the importance of case law (which has more importance in France than generally recognized by common lawyers) in relation both to indirect mechanisms and to the interpretation of the statutory provisions relating to specific mechanisms.

[56] Simler and Delebecque, *Droit civil*, §258, 239–240. See Civ 3 May 1973 (1975) *Journal du droit international*, 74, note Fouchard, where a pledge without transfer of possession over a movable situate in France was held to be invalid on the grounds that French law was the sole law applicable to property rights over movables situate in France.

[57] For example, reservation of title clauses were initially recognized by case law, but without effect in the insolvency of the buyer until given this effect by legislation: Law of 13 July 1967, Law of 12 May 1980, as amended by Law of 25 January 1985 and Law of 10 June 1994.

[58] See Mestre *et al.*, *Traité de droit civil*, §15–18, 14–16; and Simler and Delebecque, *Droit civil*, §258–261, 239–244. The present uncertain state of the law, which is subject to considerable pressure to conform to international business practices, is discussed in Guy Chauvin, "Le droit des suretés à l'épreuve de la modernité" (1995) *La semaine juridique édition notariale* (JCP N) Pratique 635, 1995.

4.3.3 Overview of mechanisms

An overview of the mechanisms available gives, at least to common lawyers who think of French law as coherent and logical, a rather surprising impression. There is a confusing array of specific security mechanisms, which include the general commercial pledge[59] (*gage commercial*),[60] various specialist pledges for different types of property (extending the concept of *gage/nantissement* to various categories of property, including intangibles such as receivables, shares and intellectual property, creating separate regimes with different rules but with some common threads running through them);[61] various kinds of warrant;[62] and a simplified procedure for security over commercial/professional receivables *(Loi Dailly)*.[63] The *hypothèque*, which is conceptually very close to the concept of a charge and in another cultural context might have been used as a general security mechanism, is restricted to land.

This "particularist" approach runs through all parts of the law of security, with numerous consequences, one of which is that it is not possible to tell in advance whether a class of property can be the subject of a particular type of security, or at all. For example, stock and land may not be the subject of a pledge of commercial undertaking. Another such consequence is that one cannot assume that a particular class of parties is permitted to be the grantee of security – an illustration of this is the monopoly enjoyed by the *caisses de crédit municipal* (government-owned credit organizations) in pledge-based transactions.[64]

---

[59] The French terms cannot be completely accurately translated, since two words exist (*nantissement* and *gage*) where English only has one ("pledge"). *Nantissement* is defined in Art. 2071 French Civil Code. Gage is defined in Art. 2072 French Civil Code as a *nantissement* of movable property. Unless otherwise indicated, "pledge" will be used to translate both terms. Where they need to be distinguished, the French terms will be used.

[60] Defined in Art. 91 French Commercial Code (as inserted by Law of 23 May 1863).

[61] Including the pledge of commercial undertaking (*nantissement du fonds de commerce*), the pledge of tools and material (*nantissement de l'outillage et du matériel*), the pledge of motor vehicles (*gage sur véhicules automobiles*), the pledge of cinema films (*nantissements sur films cinématographiques*), the pledge of immovables (*antichrèse*), the pledge of shares (*nantissement de parts sociales* (accurate translation is impossible of the single word "shares", since two types exist in French law, *parts sociales* for certain types of companies and "*actions*" for others)), the pledge of securities (*nantissement de valeurs mobilières*) and the pledge of sums of money (*gage sur sommes d'argent*). Specialized pledges are still being created, such as the new pledge over software – see Hervé Croze, "Le nantissement du droit d'exploitation des logiciels: Décret n° 96-103, 2 févr 1996. Etude", *La Semaine Juridique édition notariale* (JCP N) (1996) Pratique, 304–307, 1996, pp. 904–907, which shows some of the problems inherent in the system.

[62] Warrants give the secured creditor an instrument constituting the security. Either possession and control remain with the debtor or the assets are put into public warehouses. Examples include general warehouse warrants (*warrant des magasins généraux*), agricultural warrants (*warrants agricoles*), hotelier's warrants (*warrants hôteliers*), oil warrants (*warrants pétroliers*) and industrial warrants (*warrants industriels*).

[63] Law of 2 January 1981.

[64] The monopoly was originally granted to religious, charitable organizations called *Monts de piété*. The present monopoly is contained in the Law of 15 June 1992 concerning *caisses de crédit municipal* and is backed up by Art. 411 French Penal Code (see also Art. 16–1 of the Law of 28 December 1966 on usury (as amended)). The monopoly only relates to tangible goods. See Simler and Delebecque, 1995: $505, 420, $509, 421.

Writing is usually required, as is notice in certain cases, such as security over receivables. Registration is essential to give effect to non-possessory specific mechanisms; it acts as a priority point and is only valid for a limited time.[65]

There is also an array of contractual/property based indirect mechanisms (*propriété-sureté*), such as transfer of title (*cession fiduciaire* (or *fiducie*)), rights of retention (similar to some liens in English law), retention of title, leasing and assignment of receivables. These are the result of commercial practice and the case law (and sometimes the statutory) recognition of that practice.[66] Such indirect mechanisms have grown in number and importance as a result of the influence of international (mainly American and English law) practices, the restrictive attitude of the French judiciary towards specific mechanisms and the great stress laid by the 1985 insolvency legislation on the rehabilitation of the corporate enterprise, which considerably reduced the status of the creditor secured by specific mechanisms.[67]

The complication is exacerbated by the regime of *privilèges*.[68] These are roughly equivalent to the rights of English law preferred creditors on insolvency, but (and this is the reason for their inclusion among the categories of security mechanisms) in contrast to English preferential rights they are secured on the assets of the insolvent.[69] They include employees' remuneration (to which much greater importance is attached than in England), tax and social security contributions, but a confusingly large number of other rights exist.

4.3.4 Enforcement

Enforcement is markedly different from English law. The debtor is automatically allowed a grace period before realization is allowed.[70] French law generally frowns on

---

[65] Ten years in the case of the *nantissement de fonds de commerce*.

[66] See Mestre *et al.*, *Traité de droit civil*, §14–48, 12–48; and Simler and Delebecque, *Droit civil*, §258–259, 239–241.

[67] Law of 25 January 1985, as significantly amended by Law of 10 June 1994, *inter alia* to grant a more realistic position to secured creditors. See Legeais, *Suretés et garanties de crédit*, §13–16, 7–9; Yves Chaput, "L'apport du droit de l'entreprise au droit des suretés (1996)", *Cahiers de droit de l'entreprise, La semaine juridique entreprise et affaires* (JCP E), supplément 2/97 23, 1997; Fernand Derrida, "La réforme du droit des enterprises en difficulté (premier aperçu)", *Recueil Dalloz*, 34, 1994, p. 267; and Philippe Delebecque, "La propriété en tant que sureté dans les procédures collectives", *Revue de jurisprudence commerciale*, 3, 1994, p. 385. See below (section 10, "The effect of insolvency on security").

[68] See J. Grandmoulin, *Traité élémentaire de droit civil égyptien indigène et mixte, comparé avec le droit français: suretés personnelles, suretés réelles, publicité des droits réels immobiliers*, Rennes, Librairie Thanoux, 1912: §602–604, 170–171 (especially for the history of the institution); Simler and Delebecque, *Droit civil*, §613–660, 506–538; Mestre *et al.*, *Traité de droit civil*, §482, 449–440; and below (section entitled "Liens, priority rights and rights of retention"). Translation of the term poses various difficulties, in this article Whelan and Hall's translation of the Arabic equivalent term as "priority right" will be used. Under French law, a priority right can only be established by statute and provisions which establish them must be restrictively interpreted: Soc 30 November 1951, D 1952 121, note Voirin, see also Mestre *et al.*, *Traité de droit civil*, §237, 220 for the more general implications of this principle.

[69] Another difference between the two jurisdictions is that English preferential debts rank equally amongst themselves, whereas French preferential debts have different rankings.

[70] For example, a grace period of eight days is provided for commercial pledges in Art. 93 French Commercial Code. There is no grace period for commercial debts themselves – Art. 86 French

private enforcement procedures, with self-help not only forbidden in most circumstances, but regarded as anathema.[71] Simler and Delebecque, when commenting on Article 2078(1) French Civil Code (which provides that the creditor may either obtain a court order that title be transferred to him in satisfaction of the debt or obtain a court order that the property be sold at auction) refer to:

the well-known principle according to which no-one may take the law into their own hands and its legal corollary that the implementation of means of enforcement is the sole province of judicial tribunals.[72]

They add, commenting on Article 2078(2) French Civil Code, which provides for the nullity of the *pacte commissoire* (a clause allowing the appropriation of the asset in satisfaction of the debt, a kind of contractual foreclosure) and the *voie parée* (a clause allowing the creditor to sell the asset without following the procedures laid down by the law),[73] that:

[these clauses] are indeed dangerous for the debtor, who, cornered, might suffer the worst sort of pressure from his creditor. Their voidness is necessary, because of the moral violence that they imply.[74]

Possession of the secured asset is therefore normally effected through the court[75] and the sale of the asset is effected at public auction presided over by public officials.

4.3.5 Conclusion

The general impression is that of a relatively incoherent web of *ad hoc* solutions to situations as they arise, with the legislator keeping a tight control over all aspects.[76] General principles informing the legislation and the case law on the subject do exist, but these are nowhere specifically stated and must be teased out by theorists, who

---

cont.

Commercial Code provides: "The Courts may not grant a person obligated by a commercial debt a grace period to fulfil it or to meet it by instalments without the consent of the obligee or in generally exceptional circumstances."

[71] A degree of self-help is allowed in commercial pledges. See Art. 93, which provides: "In the absence of payment on the due date, the creditor may, eight days after simple notice given to the debtor and to the third-party bailee of the pledge, if any, proceed to the public sale of the pledged assets."

[72] Simler and Delebecque, *Droit civil*, §524, 431.

[73] Such clauses are only voidable if this is agreed at the time of the grant of the security. If such a clause is agreed afterwards, it is allowed, since it gives the debtor an opportunity to reduce the expenses of realization and there is less opportunity for pressure on the debtor.

[74] Simler and Delebecque, *Droit civil*, §528, 433.

[75] This is the case even for the *gage commercial*, although an application to court is not necessary where the property is already in the possession of the secured creditor. Simler and Delebecque, *Droit civil*, §534, 438.

[76] Writers vary in their estimation of the magnitude of the problem. See Jean-François Riffard, *Le "security interest" ou l'approche fonctionnelle et unitaire des sûretés mobilières (contribution à une rationalisation du droit français)*, unpublished thesis, Université de Clermont-Ferrand I, 1995, pp. 9–12 for a trenchant criticism of the state of the modern French law.

attempt to bring some sort of classificatory order into a very disordered situation.[77] In certain respects, the situation is the mirror image of the English system: there is no overlap between mechanisms, but at the same time there is no English generalist approach as described above.[78] Security mechanisms are kept within strict bounds.[79]

However, the effective difference between the two systems should not be over-stated. The multitude of mechanisms covers very nearly the same range of property as that covered by English law (with the notable exception of the floating charge over stock)[80] and there is no objection in principle to accumulating different kinds of security over different kinds of property.[81]

In terms of the tests referred to above, the French system is less pro-creditor than the English system, less abstract and less generalist.

4.4 The *shariʿa* approach to the law of commercial security over movables[82]

Although the main influence on the content of the UAE rules regarding security over movables derives from French law, the *shariʿa* attitude to this area is also of considerable significance, for the reasons mentioned above.

---

[77] See for example the rather forced classification of disparate statutory forms of security into the categories of *gage* and *hypothèques*, such as the classification of *hypothèques mobilières* (mortgages over movables), used in connection with ships and aircraft, as a kind of *gage* without transfer of possession (Simler and Delebecque, *Droit civil*, §261, 243). Academic writers differ in their view of the possibility of finding general principles. Contrast Legeais, *Sûretés et garanties de crédit*, §24, 14 ("The law of securities seems intractable to any general theory") with Mestre *et al.*, *Traité de droit civil*, p. 6 ("It is possible to consider the rules governing each security as a unit of provisions of specific law, obeying general principles, a common law").

[78] See Mestre *et al.*, *Traité de droit civil*, §160–170, 143–155 for an analysis of the freedom of the creditor to take security and the restrictions thereon. The English lawyer would probably just assume this freedom and would be very unlikely even to embark on such a discussion.

[79] The differences between the two jurisdictions have emerged in a striking way when an attempt was made to enforce an English floating charge in France, and enforcement was refused. See Mestre *et al.*, *Traité de droit civil*, §180, 162–164 and §238, 223–225; and Frédérique Dahan, "La floating charge: reconnaissance en France d'une sureté anglaise", *Journal du droit international*, 123, 1996, p. 381 (especially at pp. 397–404), who examines this issue in depth. Dahan also provides an insight into the way in which a Romano-Germanic lawyer views the common law mechanisms, as well as showing the degree to which basic assumptions need to be challenged in order to understand another system.

[80] The lack of a mechanism giving security over all the assets of a debtor, including stock and land, combined with the court-based enforcement procedures, results in the impossibility of an equivalent to the English receiver, a private individual who enforces the security and, if appointed under a floating charge over all the property of the debtor company, has the special status of an administrative receiver and can take over the management of the company with the possibility of rehabilitating it. See R. Goode, *Principles of Corporate Insolvency Law*, 2nd edn, London, Sweet and Maxwell, 1997, Chapter 9 ("Administrative receivership").

[81] Mestre *et al.*, *Traité de droit civil*, §167, 148. Such an accumulation of securities cannot be used to circumvent public policy rules.

[82] See Sélim Jahel, "L'adéquation du droit musulman classique aux procédés modernes de financement et de garantie", *Revue trimestrielle de droit commercial et de droit économique*, 38, 1985, p. 483. Also see Nicholas Dylan Ray, "The medieval Islamic system of credit and banking: legal and historical considerations", *Arab Law Quarterly*, 1997, p. 43 on medieval Islamic credit and banking. This article contains (at pp. 81–90) a useful bibliography on Islamic commercial law and its historical background. Purely for the sake of convenience within the

4.4.1 Underlying attitudes

The *shari'a* regards commerce generally in a favourable light,[83] but the prohibition of *riba* and *gharar* influences the theory and practice of commercial security over movables as it does financial transactions generally.[84] However, so long as neither prohibition is contravened,[85] for example by the lender deriving an unfair advantage from the loan, or the security relating to an uncertain amount such as future or conditional indebtedness, the *shari'a* has no objection to the lending of money or the taking of security.[86] Security is mentioned in the Qur'an[87] and a *hadith* relates that the Prophet pledged his armour in exchange for food.[88]

---

cont.

    limited compass of this article, the *Majalla* is used as the primary reference point for the *shari'a* rules on *rahn*.

[83] See Frank E. Vogel and Samuel L. Hayes, *Islamic Law and Finance: Religion, Risk and Return*, The Hague, Kluwer Law International, 1998, Chapter 3 ("Qur'an and Sunna on contract and commerce"), pp. 53–69. Indeed, some important terms of "Western" commercial law have their origin in *shari'a* mechanisms, such as *aval* (from *hawala*, see below (section entitled "Assignments")) and cheque (from *sakk*, "document", itself originally from the Persian, see E. W. Lane, *An Arabic-English Lexicon*, London, Williams and Norgate, 1867, reprinted New York, Frederick Ungar Publishing, 1956), see J. Schacht, *An Introduction to Islamic Law*, Oxford, Clarendon Press, 1964, p. 78.

[84] Neither term has a clear definition, but one can think of *riba* as an unearned, and therefore unfair, advantage, and *gharar* as socially unacceptable risk or speculation. For *riba*, see *inter alia* Qur'an 4:160–161 and the list of sources in Nabil Saleh, *Unlawful Gain and Legitimate Profit in Islamic Law: Riba, Gharar and Islamic Banking*, London, Graham and Trotman, 2nd edn, 1992, pp. 42–43; *Mahmood-ur-Rahman Faisal and Others v. Secretary, Ministry of Law, Justice and Parliamentary Affairs, Government of Pakistan and Others* PLD [1992] FSC 1, Federal Shariat Court, including the last sermon of the Prophet at 70–71; Vogel and Hayes, *Islamic Law and Finance*, Chapter 4 ("Islamic laws of usury, risk, and property"), especially the section headed "Plumbing the rules of *Riba*" at pp. 77–87; C. Mallat, "The debate on riba and interest in twentieth century jurisprudence", in C. Mallat (ed.), *Islamic Law and Finance*, London, Graham and Trotman, 1988, p. 27; Schacht, *An Introduction to Islamic Law*, pp. 119, 145–146 and 153; Nabil Saleh, *Unlawful Gain and Legitimate Profit*, Chapter 1 ("Riba (Unlawful advantage by way of excess or deferment)"); and Rayner, *The Theory of Contracts*, Chapter 6.7 ("*Riba, Gharar* and *Maysir*"). For *gharar* see the list of sources in Nabil Saleh, *Unlawful Gain and Legitimate Profit*, 106; Nayla Comair-Obeid, *The Law of Business Contracts in the Arab Middle East: A Theoretical and Practical Comparative Analysis (with Particular Reference to Modern Legislation)*, The Hague, Kluwer Law International, 1996, p. 57; and Rayner, *The Theory of Contracts*, Chapter 6.7 ("*Riba, Gharar* and *Maysir*").

[85] And the contract is valid in other respects, for example neither the loan nor the security contract may concern or involve forbidden commodities such as wine or pork.

[86] See Qur'an 2:282, which provides a procedure for recording a debt; Vogel and Hayes, *Islamic Law and Finance*, p. 61; Khalil Ben Ishaq, *Al-mukhtasar fi al-fiqh*, sub nom Code Musulman par Khalil. Rite Malakite – Statut réel, texte arabe et nouvelle traduction par N. Seignette, Algiers, Constantine, 1878, §386, 120; and Ibn Qudama, (trans. Laoust, Henri 1950 – the author lived from 1146 to 1223); *Le précis de droit d'Ibn Qudama*, Beirut, Institut français de Damas, p. 101: "It is forbidden to stipulate an advantage in favour of the lender; however the lender may demand the grant of a pledge (*rahn*), or the designation of a surety (*kafil*")."

[87] Qur'an II:283. Indeed, rules existed concerning *rahn* before the coming of Islam. A *hadith* relates that the former custom was for the pledgee to keep the pledged property even where the pledgor would have been able to obtain its release except for having failed to comply with a time limit, and that Islam (in a similar spirit to that shown by the Court of Chancery in respect of the equity of redemption) changed this to allow for the release to the pledgee even where the time limit had not been complied with. See the entry for *rahn* in Lane, *An Arabic-English Lexicon*, col. 2.

[88] Bukhari (trans. Muhammad Muhsin Khan), *The Translation of the Meanings of Sahih Al-Bukhari*, Lahore, Kazi Publications, 6th edn, 1986, vol. III, Nos. 685 and 686. There is also a

4.4.2 Overview of mechanisms

Compared to modern English and French law, the *shariʿa* has quite a limited range of mechanisms. These are constituted by one specific mechanism, the pledge (*rahn*),[89] which can be given over both movables and immovables, and several indirect mechanisms.

The *shariʿa* has an extensive corpus of rules concerning pledge, among which there was significant variation between schools and jurists.[90] This corpus contain both general principles and detailed rules.

The definition of pledge in the *Majalla* refers to the "setting aside [of] property from which it is possible to obtain payment or satisfaction of some claim".[91] Pledge is a contract, concluded by offer and acceptance.[92] Both parties must have full capacity[93] and need to show a clear intention that a pledge is intended, although the actual word does not have to be used.[94] Pledge involves a transfer of possession, and the lack of such transfer leads to the pledge being "incomplete and revocable",[95] but possession can be constructive,[96] even through the pledgor.[97]

---

cont.

  hadith according to which the Prophet said that pledged animals may be ridden because of what is spent on them, and that the milk of a milch animal may be drunk during the period of the pledge (*ibid.*, vol. III, Nos. 688 and 689).

[89] See Arts. 701–761, Book V *Majalla*; Choucri Cardahi, "Les suretés réelles et la vente forcée dans le droit des pays sous mandat du levant (aperçu historique, critique et de droit comparé)", *Bulletin de la société de législation comparée*, 1929, pp. 564–568, at p. 563, who discusses the differences between the different schools; Schacht, *An Introduction to Islamic Law*, p. 138 and pp. 139–140; Georges-Henri Bousquet, *Précis de droit musulman, principalement malekite et algérien*, Tome I, Algiers, La Maison des Livres, 2nd edn, 1947, §146, pp. 231–233; Georges-Henri Bousquet, *Le droit musulman par les textes (Précis de droit musulman, Tome II)*, Algiers, La Maison des Livres, 2nd edn, 1947, §37, pp. 72–74; *Encyclopédie de l'Islam*, 1994: tome VIII, 414, entry on *rahn*; ʿAbd al-Rahman Al-Jaziri, *Kitab al-fiqh ʿala al-madhahib al-arbaʿa*, Cairo, Matbaʾat al-istiqama, 1963–1972 Vol. 2, pp. 219–237; Al-Shirazi, *Kitab al-tanbih*, (Georges-Henri Bousquet, trans.), Algiers, La Maison des Livres, 1949, §127–128, 24–27; and Khalil, *Al-mukhtasar fi al-fiqh*, §368–431, 115–134. There was also the *garouka*, a special type of pledge relating to land; see Grandmoulin, *Traité élémentaire de droit civil égyptien indigène et mixte*, §230–§239, 61–64. Bousquet, *Le droit musulman par les textes*, §79, 172–173 sets out an Algerian model pledge document relating to land. The primary meaning of the root *rahana*, as set forth in Lane, *An Arabic-English Lexicon*, is that of continuance, permanence and lasting.

[90] See Al-Jaziri, *Kitab al-fiqh ʿala al-madhahib al-arbaʿa*, vol. 2, pp. 319–327 for a discussion of some of the differences.

[91] Art. 701 *Majalla*.

[92] Art. 706 *Majalla*.

[93] Art. 708 *Majalla*.

[94] Art. 707 *Majalla*.

[95] Art. 706 *Majalla*.

[96] Art. 722 *Majalla* and Arts. 752–755 *Majalla*.

[97] Art. 749 *Majalla*, which expresses this idea as a loan by the creditor to the debtor of the property, granting the creditor a "right of preference over other creditors of the pledgor in respect to the pledge".

The obligations which can be secured have to be certain and in existence; security over future debts is not permitted.[98] The property capable of being given in security must be "something which may be validly sold".[99] Detailed rules exist as to whether borrowed property may be given in security,[100] the care of the asset, its loss, its use by the pledgee, the ownership of the fruits of the property, and their possible application in satisfaction of the debt and enforcement.

An account of pledge is not, however, the whole story. Some priority rights existed.[101] Various types of contractual/property indirect mechanisms (classified as "stratagems" – *hila*, plural *hiyal*) were extensively used in the Middle Ages in order to circumvent the prohibition on *riba*, the need for transfer of possession and the court enforcement mechanisms.[102] These mechanisms were more effective than, and to a large extent supplanted, the pledge.[103] Among the most well-known of these were the double sale (*'ina* or *mukhatara*), the sale with right of redemption (*bay' al-wafa'* or *bay' bil-wafa'*)[104] and the sale with right of redemption plus lease or borrow back by the "vendor" (*bay' bil-istighlal*). Despite their general use, opinion was divided at the time, and still is today, on their acceptability.[105] The *shari'a* also knew the right of retention.[106]

In addition, Islamic banking techniques, developed in order to respect the prohibition on *riba* and *gharar*, can complicate the picture. Some techniques can themselves involve the effective taking of security, so making formal security irrelevant in at least one part of the transaction. In other techniques, the taking of security can be prohibited as being contrary to the spirit of the transaction.

---

[98] Mahiudin Abu Zakaria Yahya Ibn Sharif Al-Nawawi (E.C. Howard, trans. from 1882 French edition of *L. W. C. Van Den Berg*; *Minhaj Et Talibin: A Manual of Muhammadan Law according to the School of Shafii*, Lahore, Law Publishing Company, 1914, Book 11 ("Pledge or Security"), 153; and Shirazi, *Kitab al-tanbih*, §127, 24: "[the pledge] is not valid if it relates to a non-compulsory debt, or for which one does not find a cause making it compulsory, for example, a *rahn* for a loan which will take place tomorrow"; *contra* see Khalil, *Al-mukhtasar fi al-fiqh*, §368, 116. The *Majalla* allows the exchange of one piece of property for another (Art. 712), the increase of the property given in security (Art. 713) and the increase of the debt (Art. 714).
[99] Art. 709 *Majalla*.
[100] Arts. 726–728 *Majalla*.
[101] See below (section 7.6, "Liens, priority rights and rights of retention").
[102] On the relationship between (particularly commercial) practice and theory in the *shari'a*, see Schacht, *An Introduction to Islamic Law*, Chapter 11 ("Theory and practice").
[103] Art. 3 *Majalla* provides: "a contract for sale subject to a right of redemption has the force of a pledge".
[104] The original form of the *bay' al-wafa'*, the circumstances in which it arose and the aim of the transaction are all remarkably similar to those of the mortgage. See Nicholas Dylan Ray, *Arab Islamic Banking and the Renewal of Islamic Law*, London, Graham and Trotman, 1995, p. 68.
[105] See e.g. Art. 3, Art. 119 and Arts. 396–403 *Majalla*; Schacht, *An Introduction to Islamic Law*, pp. 78–82; Vogel and Hayes, *Islamic Law and Finance*, 39–40; Rayner, *The Theory of Contracts*, pp. 23–25, 118–121, 276; Ray, *Arab Islamic Banking*, pp. 55–57, 68–69; Sélim Jahel, "L'adéquation du droit musulman classique aux procédés modernes de financement et de garantie", 1985, pp. 498–499; Cardahi, "Les sûretés réelles et la vente forcée dans le droit des pays sous mandat du levant", pp. 568–571; and Grandmoulin, *Traité élémentaire de droit civil égyptien indigène et mixte*, §187–§199, 50–54.
[106] See Schacht, *An Introduction to Islamic Law*, p. 140; and Bousquet, *Précis de droit musulman*, §130, pp. 208–209.

Islamic banking techniques fall into two categories: participation financing and trade financing.[107]

In participation financing, the lender shares the risk by investment. One such mechanism, the *'inan sharikat mal* (the finance limited investment partnership), provides an example of the prohibition of security: in this mechanism, security cannot be taken from the partners (apart from security against the risk of negligence or wilful wrongdoing of the partner or non-compliance with the partnership contract), because it is of the essence of the mechanism that the "lender" share the "business risk inherent in the partnership and its outcome".[108]

In trade financing the lender trades in goods which the "lender" wishes to buy and makes a profit out of selling the goods to the "borrower". For example, in *murabaha* (mark-up financing), if a "borrower" needs finance to buy goods, the "lender" buys goods on his own account and then sells the goods to the "borrower". The "lender" becomes in law the owner of the property, which cannot therefore be given in security.[109] However, the "borrower" will have promised to buy the goods on their coming into the ownership of the "lender", and security can be, and is commonly, taken in respect of this obligation.[110]

4.4.3 Enforcement

The difficulties of accurately summing up *shari'a* rules, where differences of opinion are common, are very evident in the area of enforcement of the pledge. Some jurists allowed the power of sale, whereas others denied it, only allowing retention of the asset by the creditor until satisfaction of the debt.[111]

4.4.4 Conclusion

Compared to the English and French regimes, the *shari'a* rules are, as one would expect from the nature of the *shari'a*, quite pro-debtor (although the debt obligation is taken very seriously).[112] They also are more limited, reflecting as they do a less

---

[107] See *inter alia* Vogel and Hayes, *Islamic Law and Finance*, Chapter 6 ("The law of Islamic financial institutions and instruments"); and Saleh, *Unlawful Gain and Legitimate Profit*, Chapter 4 ("A financial system based on Islamic ethics").

[108] Saleh, *Unlawful Gain and Legitimate Profit*, pp. 116–117. See also Ray, *Arab Islamic Banking*, p. 63, where he states: "The Islamic bank cannot indemnify itself against normal business loss."

[109] If entered into in the UAE, the unpaid seller's lien contained in Art. 107 would be relevant, as would be the provisions concerning sale by instalments in Arts. 114–121.

[110] See Ray, *Arab Islamic Banking*, pp. 54, 58 and, on delayed payment security, p. 183.

[111] See Cardahi, "Les suretés réelles et la vente forcée dans le droit des pays sous mandat du levant", pp. 584–585 and compare Art. 757 *Majalla* (on which see Emile Tyan, "Iflas et procédure d'éxécution sur les biens en droit musulman (madhab hanafite)", *Studia Islamica*, 21, 1964, pp. 161–162) and Khalil, *Al-mukhtasar fi al-fiqh*, §409, 127 with Al-Nawawi, *A Manual of Muhammadan Law*, Book 11 ("Pledge or Security"), pp. 152–160; and Ibn Qudama, *Le précis de droit d'Ibn Qudama*, pp. 101 and 105–106.

[112] Vogel and Hayes, *Islamic Law and Finance*, pp. 61–62. The Qur'an contains specific provision encouraging the humane treatment of debtors, including indulgence (2:280). The prohibition of *riba* and *gharar* also forms part of this general picture.

complex commercial environment. Some degree of abstraction does occur, but is relatively restricted.

5 GENERAL CHARACTERISTICS OF THE UAE COMMERCIAL CODE SYSTEM OF SECURITY OVER MOVABLES

The UAE regime is modelled on the French,[113] and we encounter many of the same concepts, such as the commercial undertaking and the commercial pledge. The system is statute based in a similar way, the insolvency regime is the same as the old French law, and so on. Restrictive attitudes similar to those found in the French system prevail towards the classes of property capable of being given as security, the actors and enforcement: for example Article 49(2) provides: "If the details of the mortgage (of commercial undertaking) are not prescribed, it shall apply only to the trade name, the right to let, contact with clients and commercial standing"; Article 49(1) provides that grantees of a pledge of the commercial undertaking can only be banks and finance houses; and Article 172 provides for a French-style grace period of seven days before realization is allowed, as well as for enforcement through the court. As in France registration (in the trade register of the Emirate) grants effect to the security[114] and is only valid for a limited time (five years for pledges of commercial undertakings).[115]

However, there are significant differences.

In the UAE, the complication and fragmentation of French law have been mitigated, producing a fairly clear system, with a smaller range of specific security mechanisms.

More importantly perhaps, the French-inspired provisions function in the *shari'a* influenced environment referred to above.

6 SOME CONSEQUENCES OF THE *SHARI'A*-INFLUENCED ENVIRONMENT

6.1 Precedent and statutory interpretation

One notable consequence of this *shari'a* influenced environment is that, although UAE legislation closely resembles French statutes in style,[116] the attitude towards

---

[113] Al-Sanhuri, *Al-wasît fi sharh al-qanun al-madani al-jadid*, vol. X was presumably consulted by the draftsman and should be useful in helping to resolve difficulties of interpretation.

[114] For example French Law of 17 March 1909, Art. 10(2); compare Art. 50(1) UAE Commercial Code: "A mortgage shall only be made by notarized contract or a contract certified by a notary and entered in the trade register."

[115] Art. 51.

[116] Unlike English legislation which attempts to cover every situation in detail, French legislation is couched in quite general terms. This is less of a problem than it might appear to a common lawyer, since the general principles enunciated in the Civil Code and other generalist legislation provide a substratum of basic law to which one can look for help with interpretation, and the judges have considerable freedom of interpretation.

precedent as an aid to statutory interpretation is different. In France lawyers rely heavily upon case law for the detail of interpretation, whereas in the UAE the role of judicial precedent is more problematic.[117] Article 101 UAE Constitution provides that "the judgments of the federal Court of Cassation shall be final and binding on all". The better interpretation of this wording is that a judgment of the Court of Cassation is binding on lower courts in a particular case, rather than that such a judgment has any formal precedential value. This view is supported by the fact that in the *shari'a* (which the UAE Constitution declares to be a principal source of law in the UAE),[118] precedent was frowned upon,[119] as well as by the fact that the federal Court of Cassation has on several occasions departed from its previous decisions. This formal position is tempered somewhat by the fact that decisions do in practice have persuasive value,[120] but there is little case reporting, none of which is systematic. This leads to more uncertainty than either a common lawyer or a French lawyer is used to experiencing. On the other hand, however, if a matter is clearly covered by a statute, there is, in theory, no room for discretionary interpretation. This is a principle of Islamic law which is enacted into UAE law – "There shall be no innovative reasoning (*ijtihad*) in the case of provisions of definitive import."[121]

6.2 Background law (including the law of contract)

Other important aspects of the *shari'a* environment are the general background law and the law of contract. Examples of the general background law are to be found in Article 2 Civil Code, pursuant to which the interpretation of legislative provisions is to be conducted according to the rules of Islamic jurisprudence, and in Article 3 Civil Code, which provides that the references to "public order or morals" in legislation are references to Islamic concepts.[122] As regards the law of contract, without entering into a detailed discussion of the differences between French and UAE contract law, the Civil Code includes such *shari'a*-inspired provisions as the requirement that the property the subject of a contract must be

---

[117] See Mahmoud, *UAE Company Law and Practice*, p. 5; and Essam Al-Tamimi, "Rulings of the Courts of Cassation in the United Arab Emirates", *Middle East Commercial Law Review*, 5, 1995, p. 176.

[118] Art. 7 UAE Constitution. Also relevant are Art. 75 Federal Law No 10 of 1973 and Art. 8 Federal Law No. 6 of 1978; see W. Ballantyne, *Commercial Law in the Arab Middle East: The Gulf States, London*, Lloyd's of London Press, 1986, pp. 57–58.

[119] See e.g. Art. 16 *Majalla*: "One legal interpretation does not destroy another." Case law did in fact have some significance, despite the clear position of the jurists: see Noel Coulson, "Muslim custom and case-law", *Welt des Islams*, new series 6, 1959, pp. 20–24.

[120] "[A]lthough the decisions of the Federal Supreme Court are not considered to be part of the legislative process they are extremely important, and definitely serve as an indicator to the Law and its interpretations in this jurisdiction." Mahmoud, *UAE Company Law and Practice*, p. 5.

[121] Art. 1 Civil Code.

[122] An example of the use of the concept of public order or morals is to be found in Art. 205(2) Civil Code, which provides that a contract is void if "the law prohibits dealing in a thing or if it is contrary to public order or morals".

"property which may lawfully be dealt in"[123] and various requirements as to certainty.[124]

6.3　Future property and future advances in the UAE system

Such requirements of certainty are particularly important in a *shari'a* context in view of the great stress laid upon this concept in *shari'a* contract law, and are relevant to the law of security in respect of two questions. Firstly, may future property (property not in the ownership of the security grantor at the time of the execution of the contract) be granted as security? Secondly, may security validly be granted in respect of future advances (advances not made at the time of the execution of the contract)?

English law permits both the grant of future property as security and the grant of security in respect of future advances.[125]

French law does not provide a definitive answer to the question of whether future advances may be secured.[126]

French doctrine has some difficulty with the concept of granting security over future property; for example the *hypothèque* of future property is in principle forbidden.[127] As far as pledge is concerned, where the transfer of possession is of the essence of the pledge in question, then the pledge of future property is impossible. However, where a pledge may validly be created without transfer of possession, then, although the matter is not free from difficulty or controversy, the better view is that future property may validly be pledged,[128] but the property must be capable of being determined with sufficient precision to meet the requirements of Article 1129 French Civil Code. A good example of the view taken of what constitutes sufficient precision for the purposes of Article 1129, and of the difference between English and French law on this point, is to be found in the pledge of future receivables – cautious French practice is only to pledge future receivables if they will result from contracts which have been concluded but not yet performed, whereas the granting of security over all future receivables of a business is very common in English law and is undoubtedly valid.[129]

---

[123] Art. 200(1) Civil Code and Art. 96 Civil Code, e.g. not wine or pork.

[124] These include Art. 129(b), Art. 202 and Art. 203 Civil Code. On certainty in *shari'a* contracting, see Rayner, *The Theory of Contracts*, pp. 131–141, Ballantyne, "The Shari'a and its relevance to modern transnational transactions", pp. 14–18; and Comair-Obeid, *The Law of Business Contracts*, pp. 18–31.

[125] Future property has long been capable of being granted as security, thanks to the equitable mortgage and its descendant, the charge. Future advances do not pose a problem since they can be defined with sufficient precision for the purposes of English contract law, although the requirements of the rule in *Clayton's* case (*Devaynes v. Noble, Clayton's* case (1816) 1 Mer 572) need to be borne in mind: see Goode, *Commercial Law*, p. 688; and Arora, *Practical Banking and Building Society Law*, pp. 103–105.

[126] Mestre *et al.*, *Traité de droit civil*, §334, 307–308.

[127] *Ibid.*, §167, 148 and §321, 294.

[128] *Ibid.*, §321, 294 take this position and base it on their claim that "the possibility of a real security attaching to a future asset is the principle, and that its prohibition is the exception". See also *ibid.*, §146, 127. Discussion of this point also leads to a consideration of the basic nature of the pledge, on which opinions are divided in France; see Simler and Delebecque, *Droit civil*, §514, 425.

[129] Mestre *et al.*, *Traité de droit civil*, §321, 295–296.

The *shari'a* does not permit the pledge of future property.[130]

In the UAE one also needs to distinguish between those pledges with transfer of possession and those without.

As regards pledges with transfer of possession, one reaches the same conclusion as in French law: pledges entailing transfer of possession (such as the commercial pledge) cannot validly be constituted over future property.[131]

As regards pledges without transfer of possession, property needs to be divided into two categories for these purposes, registrable and non-registrable. Registrable property such as boats and aircraft must be in existence when the pledge is made. This is a result of Article 1405 Civil Code, which requires that "real property pledged by way of security pledge must be present and in existence when the pledge is made", and which is made applicable to "movable property which the special laws provide must be registered" by Article 1411 Civil Code.

Whether other future property may validly be the subject of a pledge without transfer of possession depends on the Civil Code provisions on certainty. The starting point is Article 202(1) Civil Code, which contains the general rule, similar to that in French law (Article 1130 French Civil Code), that future property may be the subject of a contract, and which requires that *gharar* be absent.[132] Article 129(b) Civil Code requires that the subject matter of a contract be "possible and defined" and "capable of being defined", Article 203(1) Civil Code that "the subject matter must be specified in such a way as to avoid gross uncertainty by reference to it or to the place where it is if it is in existence at the time of the contract or a statement of its distinguishing characteristics" and Article 203(3) renders the contract void if the subject matter is not so specified.[133] Article 204 Civil Code deals with the requirement of certainty where either "the subject matter of the disposition of the consideration therefor is money", if this is the case then "its amount and type must be specified".

Given these requirements, it is clear that, for a valid pledge to be constituted over future property, the property must be described with a fair degree of precision. What is not so clear is the exact degree of precision required.[134] The Civil Code

---

[130] Art. 709 *Majalla*. However, Art. 712 *Majalla* does allow the replacement of the pledged property by other property.

[131] The legislator has alleviated the disadvantages of this somewhat by following the *Majalla* and providing that the pledged property may be replaced with other property: Art. 171.

[132] Whether the word as used here refers to the rather restricted provisions on *gharar* in Arts. 1012–1055 Civil Code or the general *shari'a* concept is itself uncertain.

[133] An examination of these provisions demonstrates the difficulties of legal translation. Art. 202(1) Civil Code refers to *gharar*, which is translated as "uncertainty". Art. 203(1) Civil Code refers to *jahala* (literal translation: ignorance) which is also translated as "uncertainty". Both translations are quite justified and no criticism is intended – the translation of *gharar* as "uncertainty" stresses what is probably the most important aspect of *gharar*, and using the same word to translate the two concepts is probably unavoidable; indeed it rightly emphasizes the link between the *shari'a* "uncertainty" concept of *jahl* and that of *gharar*. Clearly, however, any attempt at detailed interpretation of the provisions based on the translation alone is doomed to failure.

[134] It may well also depend on the type of pledge concerned. The very nature of the pledge of commercial undertaking, for example, contemplates that a certain amount of future property will come within its ambit.

provisions, especially as interpreted in a *shari'a* influenced environment, may well lead to more stringent specifications than those required by French law.

Assignments merit separate consideration. Under UAE law assignments are transfers by debtors of obligations to pay, rather than transfers by creditors of receivables.[135] They are also subject to quite stringent requirements as to certainty. Therefore the assignment of future receivables *en bloc* is not possible.[136]

In respect of future advances, the Civil Code provisions referred to above will need to be considered, as will Article 1409 Civil Code (pledge by way of security) and Article 1452 Civil Code (possessory pledge).[137] These articles require the consideration for pledges to be "an ascertained debt owed or promised, specified at the time of the pledge". There would therefore be no problem regarding specific advances in respect of which the security was granted and which are made shortly after the conclusion of the transaction. In respect of other advances much would depend on the degree of precision with which they are described. A very general "all monies" clause such as commonly occurs in English security documentation would not be adequate. Other types of clause would need to be examined individually, but the cautious view is to take new security in respect of any specific further advances.[138]

Security over current accounts is dealt with separately. Article 396(1) provides that, if it is agreed to credit a current account with an amount secured by a consensual security, the security secures the balance of the account on closure, notwithstanding transactions on the account between the entering of the secured amount and closure of the account (unless otherwise agreed).

7 THE MAIN CATEGORIES OF MECHANISM PROVIDING SECURITY OVER MOVABLES IN THE UAE

If one excludes purely civil law security mechanisms, the list of commercial security mechanisms over movables in the UAE is relatively simple, consisting of the specific security mechanisms of the commercial pledge (with special rules relating to instruments, promissory notes and receivables),[139] the pledge of commercial undertaking[140] and the pledge of securities (together with priority rights (preferential debts secured by operation of law))[141] as well as the indirect mechanisms of set-off, the retention of title clause[142] and the right of retention.

---

[135] Except where there is antecedent liability between the principal creditor and the transferee of the obligation or where the transferee is in possession of property by way of trust or guarantee: Art. 1108(2) Civil Code.

[136] See below (section entitled "Assignments").

[137] Art. 1409 Civil Code concerns pledges by way of security, Art. 1452 Civil Code possessory pledges.

[138] See Horsfall Turner, "Security and enforcement in Dubai", pp. 317–318 (regarding both pledges of shares under the Commercial Companies Law and other movable assets).

[139] Arts. 164–177 Commercial Code.

[140] Arts. 49–56.

[141] Arts. 1504–1528 Civil Code.

[142] Art. 118.

7.1 Pledges

7.1.1 *Terminology*

The terminology of real security in UAE law can be confusing. The word *rahn*, which as seen above refers in the *shari'a* simply to the pledge, has been used to denote the pledge (adjectivally qualified to become *rahn hiyazi*, literally possessory pledge) and the French *hypothèque* (becoming *rahn te'mini*, literally security pledge), as well as the pledge of commercial undertaking.

In this situation, there are no ideal translations. In the absence of generally accepted practice, it is probably most convenient to translate the Arabic literally. Accordingly, *rahn hiyazi* will be translated as "possessory pledge" and *rahn te'mini* will be translated as "pledge by way of security".[143] When used in other contexts, such as in the grant of security over debts or securities, *rahn* will be translated simply as "pledge".

7.1.2 *Pledges in general – the Civil Code*

As mentioned above, the Commercial Code is a collection of additions and amendments to the basic Civil Code rules, which therefore provide a starting point for any discussion of pledge.[144]

7.1.3 *Pledges by way of security*

Although pledges by way of security mainly fulfil the function of English mortgages over real property or French *hypothèques*, and as such are beyond the scope of this article, the provisions relating to them are relevant for two reasons. In addition to providing the basic rules for non-possessory security, such as the pledge of commercial undertaking, these provisions do apply, by virtue of Article 1411 Civil Code, to "movable property which the special laws provide must be registered", which is interpreted to include durable movable assets such as boats and vehicles.

Article 1399 Civil Code defines a pledge by way of security as follows:

A pledge by way of security is a contract whereby an obligee acquires, over real property[145] allocated for the satisfaction of his debt, a right *in rem* whereby he shall take precedence

---

[143] Both these translations are those used by Whelan and Hall in their translation of the Civil Code. Some translate *rahn te'mini* as "mortgage", which is quite accurate in relation to land, but less so in relation to movables, since an English law mortgage over movables still entails a transfer of title, which is not the case with a *rahn te'mini*.

[144] The Civil Code rules on pledge are to be found in Arts. 1399–1447 (pledges by way of security) and Arts. 1448–1500 (possessory pledges: Arts. 1484–1486 relate to land, Arts. 1487–1490 to movable assets and Arts. 1491–1500 to debts). Art. 1490 Civil Code provides specifically for exceptions to the Civil Code: "The foregoing provisions shall apply to the extent that they do not conflict with commercial laws and special laws consistent with the Islamic *shari'a*."

[145] In Arabic *'aqar*, i.e. immovables.

over ordinary obligees and obligees subsequent in rank to him in the satisfaction of his
right out of the proceeds of such land, in the possession of whomsoever it may be.

Article 1400 Civil Code provides that a pledge by way of security "may only be made
by registration thereof".[146] Transfer of possession is not necessary and the pledgor
has the right to manage the property until "compulsorily divested of ownership upon
his failure to pay the debt".[147] The pledgor "is liable in full for its safety until the date
the debt is paid".[148]

In accordance with *shari'a* principles, future land cannot be granted as security,[149]
but Article 1407 Civil Code permits growing things and "any new buildings erected
on the land after the contract was made" to be included. Under Article 1406(2) Civil
Code, the court may set aside a pledge if the land is not "sufficiently described".[150]

Article 1422 Civil Code provides that the pledge takes full effect as against third
parties only from the date of registration, which also determines priority.

7.1.4 *Possessory pledges*

The provisions relating to possessory pledges provide the basic rules for such mechanisms as the general commercial pledge. Article 1448 Civil Code defines a possessory pledge as:

a contract giving rise to a right to retain the property[151] in the hands of the obligee or the
hands of a stakeholder by way of security for a right which may be recovered thereout in
whole or in part in priority over other obligees.

Article 1449 Civil Code requires that the assets must be capable of delivery (i.e. capable of transfer) and capable of sale at public auction. Interestingly from the point
of view of a common lawyer, a possessory pledge of land is possible.[152] Transfer of
possession[153] is required, although possession may be in the hands of a trustee.[154]
(In the case of receivables, transfer of possession of "the instrument proving such

---

[146] Emphasis added.

[147] Art. 1413 Civil Code.

[148] Art. 1414 Civil Code.

[149] Art. 1405 Civil Code provides: "The real property pledged by way of security pledge must be
present and in existence when the pledge is made", which also applies to registrable movable
property by virtue of Art. 1411 Civil Code. See section 6.3, "Future property and future
advances in the UAE system".

[150] Art. 1406(2) Civil Code.

[151] In Arabic, *mal*. See Arts. 95–103 Civil Code for the general rules on property, Arts. 104–111
Civil Code for the general rules on, and categories of, rights.

[152] Arts. 1484–1486 Civil Code.

[153] Art. 1307 Civil Code defines possession and Arts. 1308–1316 provide rules regarding
possession. The property must be ascertained and separated from other assets, and it is unlikely
that devices meant to enable the taking of pledges over stock and plant and machinery are valid:
see Horsfall Turner, "Security and enforcement in Dubai", p. 318.

[154] In Arabic, *'amin*. Art. 1472 Civil Code.

debt"[155] is also needed, together with notice to the debtor or his consent.)[156] As in French law (and unlike English law) a document is required in order to perfect the transaction.[157]

7.1.5 *Enforcement*

In respect of both mechanisms Article 1419 Civil Code (concerning pledges by way of security but made applicable also to possessory pledges by Article 1479 Civil Code), permits the pledgee to "satisfy his debt out of the land pledged … after taking the steps laid down in the law of procedures before the civil courts, and special laws". Those steps will be some form of enforcement through the court and sale by public auction. Contracting out of the enforcement procedures is forbidden, whether by attempting to agree to vest ownership of the asset in the pledgee upon default by the pledgor or by any condition "that it be sold regardless of the legal procedures".[158] In other words, the French prohibition of both the *pacte commissoire* and the *voie parée* has been adopted.

7.1.6 *Execution*

Although the legislation does not specify a general method of execution of pledge documents, the cautious view is that it is prudent to have the documents notarized.[159] If they are so notarized, they will need to be translated into Arabic.

7.1.7 *Commercial Pledges*[160]

Taking a French-style piecemeal approach, the legislation provides rules for the grant of a commercial pledge over general property,[161] with special rules for the grant of pledges of instruments, promissory notes and receivables.

   Article 164(1) restricts the commercial pledge to movable assets by defining it as follows:

A commercial pledge is that which is agreed concerning movable property as security for a commercial debt.[162]

---

[155] Art. 1491 Civil Code.
[156] Art. 1492(1) Civil Code. Notification or consent also fixes the priority point (Art. 1492(3) Civil Code). Note the similarity to s. 136 Law of Property Act 1925.
[157] Art. 1487 Civil Code.
[158] Art. 1480 Civil Code, which refers back to Art. 1420 Civil Code (concerning pledges by way of security).
[159] Horsfall Turner, "Security and Enforcement in Dubai", pp. 318–319 and Clifford Chance (undated); Memorandum on UAE Security, p. 6.
[160] See generally Price, "United Arab Emirates", pp. 315–316, at p. 303.
[161] Arts. 164–177.
[162] Author's translation.

As one might expect in a Romano-Germanic statute, "commercial debt"[163] is not defined. By relying on the general provisions contained in Articles 4 and 5 (which define commercial business) one can conclude that it means an obligation to pay money incurred in the course of commercial business as defined by those articles.

A commercial pledge is a possessory pledge, as it requires a transfer of possession. This is made clear by Article 165(1) which provides:

A commercial pledge shall be implemented vis-à-vis the obligor or other parties *only by transfer of possession of the pledged object from the pledgor to the pledgee*[164] or to a third party designated by the contracting parties [and the pledged object must remain] in the possession of the person taking receipt ... until the pledge is extinguished or until it is placed in common possession in a manner which makes the pledgor unable to dispose of it in isolation from the pledgee.[165]

Article 165(2) defines transfer of possession by providing that:

The pledgee or the third person shall be deemed to be the possessor of the pledged object *when it is placed at his disposal in a manner leading others to believe that the pledged object has come into his safekeeping.*[166]

This provides some degree of constructive possession, which is extended for practical purposes by the system of deposit in public depositories.[167] Pledged goods may be kept in these depositories for the account of the owner or the person who deposited them. The public depository issues a storage receipt to the deposited goods.[168] This system is also convenient if there might be difficulties in physically transferring possession of the goods upon entering into a pledge. However, constructive possession does not go as far as English law, under which in theory even possession by the pledgor is permissible, since in the UAE the pledgor must be "unable to dispose of [the pledged asset] in isolation from the pledgee".[169]

Writing is specifically required for various specialized types of property, but no mention is made of it in the general provisions, which seems to imply that the general necessity for a document has been dispensed with in the commercial context, as in French law.[170] It is obviously advisable, however, to document the transaction.

---

[163] The word here translated by "debt" (*dein*) could also mean "obligation", but this seems not to be the case in the Commercial Code, as the draftsman has consistently differentiated between debt (*dein*) and obligation (*iltizam*).

[164] Emphasis added.

[165] Compare Art. 2076 French Civil Code: "The priority only subsists in respect of the pledged property insofar as this pledged property has been placed and has remained in the possession of the creditor, or in that of a third party agreed upon by the parties."

[166] Emphasis added.

[167] Arts. 178–195. See below (section 7.1.13, "Deposit in public depositories").

[168] If it is a depository licensed to do so by the relevant authority in accordance with a resolution issued by the Ministry of Economy and Commerce, it may also issue negotiable instruments of title in respect of the goods – Art. 178(2).

[169] Art. 165(1). French law has certain categories of pledge with no transfer of possession, such as the pledge of commercial undertaking, the pledge of tools and equipment, the pledge of cinematographic films and the pledge of motor vehicles.

[170] Art. 109 French Commercial Code. This conclusion also seems to follow from the wording of Art. 165(1). Examples of property the pledge of which do necessitate writing include nominative instruments (Art. 166(1)) and debts (Art. 167(1)).

Article 170 obliges the pledgee to provide a receipt upon request of the pledgor and Article 168 obliges him to take care of the property. Under Article 169 the pledgee may take receipt of any profits accruing to the property, such as interest, and then, unless otherwise agreed, set them first against expenses paid by him on the pledgor's behalf; secondly against the interest on the secured debt; and thirdly against the principal of the secured debt.

The pledgee is protected against diminution in value of the property by Article 174. If the value of the pledged assets goes down to such an extent that their value is no longer sufficient to secure the debt, then the pledgee may require the pledgor to add to the assets granted as security in order to cover the amount secured. If the pledgor does not do so, then the pledgee can realize the security, even if the due date of the secured debt has not arrived. This is an illustration of the different approaches taken by Romano-Germanic inspired legal systems and English law, in which a similar effect, if desired, would be achieved by a provision contained in the security document.

The realization of security must take place through the court.[171] The creditor must serve a notice on the debtor giving him at least seven days to pay,[172] and once this seven-day grace period has expired, the creditor applies to the court for leave to sell the pledged object, which must, under Article 172(1), examine the application "as a matter of urgency". The court determines how the sale is to take place. Contracting out of this procedure is not allowed, and Article 176(1) renders any agreement to do so invalid; however, once the debt (or an instalment of the debt) has fallen due, "it may be agreed that the obligor cede all or part of the pledged object to his obligee in settlement of all or some of the debt".[173] In other words, as in French law, contractual foreclosure (the *pacte commissoire*) is allowed once the debt has fallen due.

A question which immediately arises in the mind of an English lawyer is whether the general commercial pledge allows anything like the English floating charge.[174] Given the requirement for possession by the pledgee or the pledgee's agent, the impossibility of a possessory pledge over future property and the doubtful validity of a contractual obligation to pledge future property,[175] a floating charge as such is not possible. The replacement procedure contained in Article 171 provides some flexibility in a way which is distantly similar to that given by the floating charge in England, but this should not be exaggerated. In addition to other important differences between the commercial pledge and the floating charge, the floating charge

---

[171] Art. 172. Art. 189 sets out the order of satisfaction of debts with a higher priority than that of the principal sum secured, i.e. (1) "taxes and charges due on the goods", (2) "judicial charges expended in the common interests of the obligees" and (3) "the expenses of keeping, storing and selling the goods". Presumably this provision has general application, despite being found in the section dealing with public depositories.

[172] Contrast the situation under English law, where no grace period is implied by law (although it can be negotiated into the Event of Default clause of the loan agreement) and where, when monies become payable upon demand, they must be paid immediately: see Arora, *Practical Banking and Building Society Law*, pp. 289–291.

[173] Art. 176(2). This reflects the French law position.

[174] See Goode, *Commercial Law*, Chapter 25 ("Floating charge"); and Romer LJ's often quoted description of the floating charge in *Re Yorkshire Woolcombers Association Ltd* [1903] 2 Ch 284, CA at 295.

[175] On the grounds of lack of certainty. (See section 6.3, "Future property and future advances in the UAE system".)

allows automatic replacement of property, whereas under Article 171 the parties must go through the replacement procedure, and a floating charge allows all property charged to be used in the normal course of business until crystallization, whereas under Article 171 property of sufficient value to cover the loan will remain permanently out of the possession of the pledgor.

7.1.8 Instruments

The Commercial Code provides separate rules for instruments (documents of title to money or goods).[176] Instruments are of two types: bearer and nominative.

Nominative instruments are those which are made out to a named person, usually called in English terminology "order" instruments. The pledge of nominative instruments requires a document. Article 166(1) provides that:

pledging of them shall be done in writing by an assignment of the instruments stating that it is as a guarantee, and the instrument itself shall be endorsed [and the assignment] shall be entered in the records of the party who issued the instrument.

Article 166(2) allows pledging of bearer instruments[177] by endorsement, which must indicate "the value for pledge or security or any other information to this effect".

Article 165(2) provides that the pledgee, or the third party taking possession on behalf of the pledgee, is deemed to come into possession of pledged property represented by an instrument: "if he takes receipt of an instrument representing the pledged object and giving its possessor the sole right to take receipt of it" and Article 165(3) provides that possession of the rights to such pledged property passes "upon delivery of the instruments thereto".

Article 165(3) provides that if the instrument is on deposit with another party, delivery may be effected by delivery of the deposit receipt, so long as the receipt clearly describes the instrument and the depositary is willing to remain in possession on behalf of the pledgee.

7.1.9 Receivables

The granting of receivables as security poses particular problems in all four systems under consideration. It is probably easier to examine these issues under the heading of assignments, so suffice it to say here that the Commercial Code follows French law and extends the concept of the pledge to receivables. Article 167(1) provides that the pledge must be effected in writing and that the pledgor must deliver an instrument confirming that receivable to the pledgee, Article 167(2) provides that the pledge document itself must be served on, or accepted by, the principal debtor and that without possession of the instrument, the pledge is invalid as against third

---

[176] Art. 482 defines bearer instruments. The Commercial Code does not contain a definition of nominative instruments.

[177] The actual expression used is "promissory instruments" (*al-sukuk al-idhniyya*) but apparently this means bearer instruments in this context, although Art. 482 uses a different term (*al-sened li hamilihi*) when defining bearer instruments.

parties, and Article 167(3) provides that priority is determined by the date of service on, or acceptance by, the pledgor of the pledge document. This procedure is of limited practical ambit, as the receivable must be in existence at the time of the pledge and the procedure itself is cumbersome, involving documentation and notice to the debtor in respect of each receivable pledged.[178]

7.1.10 Perishable goods

Article 175 allows the sale of goods before the due date of the loan secured by the pledge if the goods are "liable to destruction or deterioration or [their] possession becomes costly" and they are goods for which "the pledgor is unwilling to provide a replacement object". Either the pledgor or the pledgee may apply to the court for leave. The pledge then attaches to the proceeds of sale.

7.1.11 Pledges of commercial undertakings

The very idea of commercial undertaking, which does not exist in English law, comes from France, as does the idea of having a separate body of rules regarding dealings in the commercial undertaking. However, the UAE law is different in various ways from modern French law.

As to the commercial undertaking itself, UAE law, unlike French law, contains a statutory definition. Article 39 provides a general definition – the commercial undertaking is:[179]

the whole of the material and intellectual property designated for the practice of commercial business.

Article 40 lists the elements making up this "whole":

tangible elements such as goods, stores, machinery and tools, and intangible elements such as contact with clients,[180] commercial standing,[181] trade name, the right to let, rights of industrial, intellectual and technical ownership, and licences.

Notable omissions are land, stock and receivables.

---

[178] Therefore it cannot be used for receivables financing. A procedure does exist whereby the lender is obliged to pay all trade debts into a special account, with a specific right of set-off being taken against that account, but it is doubtful whether this is effective: see Horsfall Turner, "Security and enforcement in Dubai", p. 320. In French law the deficiencies of the pledge over debts have led to the statutory alternative provided by the *Loi Dailly* and to a debate over whether assignments under the general law are, and whether they should be, acceptable. See Mestre *et al.*, *Traité de droit civil*, §36–48, 36–48.

[179] In Arabic, *mahall al-tijari*.

[180] The translation of *clientèle*, which denotes the current clients of the business.

[181] The translation of *achalandage*, which refers to those clients of the business who become clients because of the location of the business. The combination of *clientèle* and *achalandage* approximate to the English concept of goodwill.

Articles 49–56 relate to the pledge of commercial undertaking itself. These provisions are quite sparse. This by itself would not cause a problem if one knew where to look for general principles, but unfortunately the Commercial Code contains no indication of the category into which pledges of commercial undertaking fall, so it is uncertain which basic rules apply. Article 50(1) does not require a transfer of possession, so it seems that pledges of commercial undertaking cannot be categorized as commercial pledges, which by Article 165(1) require such transfer. It would seem logical, and it may be the better view, to categorize them as pledges by way of security, but Article 1411 Civil Code only extends the ambit of the relevant provisions from land to "movable property which the special laws provide must be registered" and, although transactions relating to the commercial undertaking need to be registered under Article 42, the commercial undertaking itself does not.

Article 50 does not define the pledge, but simply states that:

A [pledge] shall only be made by notarised contract or a contract certified by a notary and entered in the trade register.

Transfer of possession is not necessary and future assets come within the ambit of the pledge of commercial undertaking,[182] so, unlike the commercial pledge, possession and control of the assets remain with the debtor. Thus the pledge of commercial undertaking is a pledge in name only and resembles an English-style charge; indeed French authors regard the French equivalent as more of a *hypothèque* of movables than a true pledge.[183]

Article 50 requires that the pledge be made by "notarized contract or a contract certified by a notary and entered in the trade register", that entry in the trade register ensures priority for a period of five years and that it may be renewed during that period. Presumably more than one renewal may occur, but this is not expressly stated. Article 42 lays down the minimum information that must be set out in the contract.

In keeping with the particularist trend of French law, any assets which do not form part of the commercial undertaking cannot be pledged by a pledge of commercial undertaking (although presumably they can, as in French law, be given as security separately by other means). If it is wished to include all the elements of the commercial undertaking in the pledge, this must be expressly stated in the pledge contract, otherwise only the trade name, the right to let, contact with clients and commercial standing will be included.[184] Article 55 expressly extends the pledge to insurance proceeds.

Also in line with the particularist attitude of French law, and modelled on the French law provisions now restricting the provision of pledge-based finance to the *caisses de crédit municipal*,[185] Article 49(1) allows the pledge of commercial undertaking to be made only "to banks and finance houses". The UAE provision, by restricting the donors of such finance to institutions whose activities are relatively

---

[182] The provisions in the Commercial Code assume that future property is included in the commercial undertaking on realization.

[183] Simler and Delebecque, *Droit civil*, § 591, 486.

[184] Art. 49(2).

[185] See above (section 4.3.3, "The French approach to the law of commercial security over movables").

easily controllable by the authorities, fits well with the policy of striking a balance between on the one hand the perceived need for allowing security to be granted in respect of interest-based transactions and on the other the desire to prevent interest-based lending spreading throughout society. In practical terms, little is lost by imposing such a restriction, as in the great majority of cases such a pledge would only be made to such institutions.

The Commercial Code makes no mention of the question of whether the pledgee may dispose of all or part of the commercial undertaking during the life of the pledge, and whether, if this is permissible, the pledge attaches to the proceeds of sale.[186]

The enforcement procedure, contained in Article 53, is similar to that pertaining to commercial pledges, but there are some differences. The pledgee must give eight days' notice to the pledgor, on expiry of this period the pledgee may ask leave for permission to sell the property. The pledgee petitions the summary magistrate, who does not determine the modality of sale, since this is laid down in the Commercial Code as being public auction. These provisions are, like those for commercial pledges, mandatory,[187] therefore, as in French law,[188] the *pacte commissoire* is effectively forbidden.

7.1.12 Lending against securities[189]

The *shari'a* had no techniques for dealing with the modern Western invention of securities.[190]

English law applies the concepts of pledge, mortgage and charge to the relevant instruments, taking account of their legal status and the ways in which possession and title may be transferred – for example, a legal mortgage of shares can only be effected by transfer of title to the mortgagee in the books of the company.

French law has a complex regime, based on three different statutes.[191] The Law of 3 January 1983 deals specifically with securities as opposed to shares in personal companies. Article 29 of this law provides that the pledge of securities is effected by a declaration dated and signed by the owner. The securities are placed in a special account either with the company itself or with a third party financial institution.

In the UAE the Commercial Code deals with security over securities in a separate section constituted by Articles 450–466 (called herein "the securities section"), providing a specialized form of pledge inspired generally by French law.

Article 450 distinguishes between nominative instruments and bearer instruments. The pledge of nominative instruments is effected by an assignment in writing evidenced both on the instrument itself and in the records of the issuer.[192] No

---

[186] In French law the separate sale of an element of the commercial undertaking constitutes the offence of *détournement de gage* (Arts. 314–315 French Penal Code).
[187] Art. 54.
[188] Art. 8 Law of 17 March 1909, Simler and Delebecque, *Droit civil*, §594, 489.
[189] See Clifford Chance (undated); Memorandum on Taking Security over Securities in the UAE, and Price, "United Arab Emirates", pp. 325–326.
[190] Islamic banking has had to confront the very difficult problems associated with securities – see Vogel and Hayes, *Islamic Law and Finance,* p. 13 and pp. 165–178.
[191] Law of 4 January 1978, Law of 3 January 1983 and Law of 9 July 1991. See Simler and Delebecque, *Droit civil*, §540–544, 443–447.
[192] Art. 450(1).

special procedure is provided for bearer securities, which are declared to be "material movables", so presumably they may be pledged by commercial pledge.[193] Article 451 provides that possession of the pledged instruments passes to the pledgee, who has the right to withhold the instruments.

Article 452 obliges the pledgee to apply any sums received by it in respect of the instruments against the principal of the secured debt. Article 453 provides the enforcement procedure, which is by application to the Court for authorization to sell the instrument, either at public auction or at the "stock exchange price" (if any).

Unfortunately there are some problems of interpretation.

There is no definition of the word "security". One difficulty which has already arisen from this omission is the question of whether shares in a UAE limited liability company[194] can be granted as security pursuant to the securities section. Such shares resemble in some respects interests in an English partnership, are not usually represented by share certificates and are not freely transferable, being subject to statutory pre-emption rights. It would seem therefore that they are not securities at all[195] and cannot be granted as security under the Commercial Code. This view is now generally accepted.[196] Clearly, freely transferable shares of companies incorporated in jurisdictions other than the UAE will be classified as "securities", but one can easily imagine similar questions to those concerning shares in UAE limited liability companies arising in relation to shares in foreign companies which have some restriction on transfer.

It is not entirely clear whether the procedures set out in the securities section only apply to loans by banks. The placing of the section in Book III, which is entitled "Banking Transactions", strongly implies that this is the case, but it is nowhere specifically stated and the drafting is inconsistent: Article 450(1) (which provides that "lending secured by securities is a loan guaranteed by a pledge") implies, but does not state, that the "loan"[197] is made by a bank; the securities section contains references in some Articles to "banks"[198] and in others simply to "pledgees".[199]

---

[193] Art. 450(2).

[194] A particular form of company which can be incorporated under the Commercial Companies Law (equivalent to a French *société à responsabilité limitée*), to be distinguished from the English use of this term. For Limited Liability Companies generally, see Mahmoud, *UAE Company Law and Practice*, pp. 61–68. Shares in public and private joint stock companies can be granted as security pursuant to the securities section as well as pursuant to Art. 164 Commercial Companies Law, on which see below (section 7.2, "Shares").

[195] For the statutory restrictions on transfer, see Mahmoud, *UAE Company Law and Practice*, pp. 63–64.

[196] This view is consistent with the French approach, in which securities (*valeurs mobilières*) are dealt with by a different statute from that which provides a security regime for shares in personal companies.

[197] For loans generally, see Arts. 710–721 Civil Code (loans of fungibles, the word translated by "loan" is *qard*) and Arts. 849–871 Civil Code (loans of non-fungibles, the word translated by "loan" is *i'ara*). Art. 409 defines a bank loan (*qard masrafi*) on which see Dubai Court of Cassation Case No. 87/97, where the court concluded that the intention of the parties must be taken into consideration when deciding whether a guarantee related to a specific loan or to banking facilities generally.

[198] Art. 451(2), Art. 452 and Art. 453.

[199] Art. 455, Art. 456 and Art. 457. Cf Art. 49(2) which expressly provides that "A firm may be mortgaged only to banks and finance houses."

Also not entirely clear is the relative status of the securities section. Is it subject to the rules governing commercial pledge or is it free-standing, and therefore subject only to the general rules of the Civil Code concerning possessory pledge?[200] Various problems arise from this uncertainty. For example, can the pledged securities be replaced? There is no specific provision in the securities section, but Article 171 allows the replacement of assets pledged by a commercial pledge. Does Article 171 apply to securities? A second example is that of contracting out of the statutory enforcement procedures. Contracting out of the commercial pledge enforcement procedure is expressly forbidden by Article 176(1), with Article 176(2) providing an exception by allowing application of the pledged object to the debt without recourse to the court if this is agreed after the due date for payment of the principal. There is no equivalent provision in the securities section. Does Article 176(2) apply or do the Civil Code rules on possessory pledges apply, which do not provide this exception?[201] A third example is provided by the establishment of the priority point. Article 166 provides that the transfer of possession necessary to perfect a commercial pledge of nominative instruments "shall be entered in the records of the party who issued the instrument … and the category of pledgee shall be determined from the date of that entry". Article 450(2) provides for the same procedure, but does not mention the question of priority. Does this mean that securities which are nominative instruments are governed by Article 166 as well as by Article 450(2)?

The argument for the securities section being subject to the rules on commercial pledge runs as follows: given its position in Book III, which is entitled "Banking Transactions", one can argue that it concerns only bank loans; Article 410 defines bank loans as commercial under all circumstances; Article 164 defines commercial pledges by reference to "commercial debt"; ergo the securities section is subject to the rules on commercial pledge. However, one can produce counter-arguments at every step of this sequence and there are no cross-references or other clues to help us determine the relationship, if any, between the two sections.[202]

Article 460, although not contained in the securities section, is also relevant, in that it provides that the depositary may not dispose of the deposited securities, pledge them or exercise rights deriving from them without the special authorization of their owner. In other words, the depositary may so dispose, pledge or exercise if such authorization is obtained, and this article potentially provides another, flexible, means of providing security over securities by simple deposit plus agreement.[203]

---

[200] Presumably the rules on possessory pledges apply rather than those on pledges by way of security, since Art. 451 requires the transfer of possession.

[201] Art. 1420 Civil Code as applied to possessory pledges by Art. 1480 Civil Code.

[202] Cf. the provisions regarding carrier's liens in Arts. 303 and 332, which specifically cross-refer to commercial pledge enforcement procedures.

[203] But one could also argue, on the analogy of some French law thinking, that this should not be possible as such a use, especially given the existence of an express statutory procedure, would be trespassing upon the domain of the legislator and would therefore be illegitimate.

7.1.13 Deposit in public depositories

As mentioned above, the Commercial Code provides for a system of public depositories, which forms an integral part of the pledge regime.[204] For example, such aspects of the pledge regime as constructive possession and the replacement of pledged goods depend upon the existence of the depository system.

Article 178(1) envisages documents of title to goods and other instruments being used and Article 178(3) the use of the depository in relation to pledges.[205] Article 183 requires the storekeeper to give a storage receipt to the depositor, together with an instrument of pledge, which must contain the same details as the storage receipt. If the documents are to the depositor's order, they can be assigned, either by delivery if he assigns them together, or by endorsement if assigned separately, thus permitting easy transfer of constructive possession for the purposes of a pledge and for the purposes of on-sale of goods subject to a pledge. Article 187 provides that the holder of both storage receipt and instrument of pledge has the right to receive the deposited goods. In order for such documents to be assignable, Article 185 requires them to be "issued in the name of the depositor or to his authorization". If a person only holds the instrument of pledge, he may only pledge the goods.[206] If a person holds only the storage receipt, then he may recover the goods, but only on payment of the sum secured by the instrument of pledge (if that sum has fallen due) or upon payment to the depositary of the total sum payable (if that sum has not yet fallen due).[207] Thus the ultimate purchaser of the goods may satisfy the amount due to the lender and receive the goods by using this system.

7.2 Shares

As discussed above,[208] shares in public and private joint stock companies incorporated under the Commercial Companies Law, as well as transferable shares in companies incorporated in other jurisdictions, can be pledged under the Commercial Code, but it is generally thought that shares in UAE limited liability companies and other non-freely transferable shares cannot be so pledged.

Shares in public and private joint stock companies can also be "pledged" under Article 164 Commercial Companies Law. Article 164 in fact provides for a transfer of title pursuant to Article 162 Commercial Companies Law. This procedure is therefore similar to that of an English legal mortgage of shares. The company may refuse to register the transfer for a variety of reasons, such as violation of the company articles and prior pledging of the shares by court order, so it is essential for the transfer to be registered before any funds are advanced against the security of the shares.

---

[204] This derives from the French system of *magasins généraux*; see Grandmoulin, *Traité élémentaire de droit civil égyptien indigène et mixte,* §211, 56–57 and Simler and Delebecque, *Droit civil,* p. 438, notes 5 and 6.

[205] A depository which issues negotiable instruments must have a licence from the competent authority in the Emirate concerned: Art. 178(2).

[206] Art. 187(2).

[207] Art. 187(3).

[208] Section 7.1.12, " Lending against securities".

Unless otherwise agreed, the pledgee is entitled "to receive the dividends and utilise the rights related to the share".[209]

7.3 Assignments

Before discussing assignment, it is perhaps useful to examine some of the general considerations affecting the transfer of "debts", which are the commonest subject of assignments as security.[210]

The substantive difficulties arise from various factors. Receivables are pure intangibles (although documents may exist, such documents will be no more than evidence of the receivables' existence) and are therefore only enforceable by action. Being pure intangibles, transfer of possession is not possible, creating the problems of potential fraud on third parties (who would be unaware that receivables apparently due did not form part of the assets of the debtor), and disputes arising therefrom. The value of receivables is uncertain, as it is conditional upon various factors which are difficult to evaluate and predict. These include the ability of the principal debtor to pay (and pay on time), the possible existence of counterclaims and possible fraud affecting the amount or the very existence of the receivable. Receivables involve a relationship between the debtor and the creditor which may involve personal factors such as trust and confidence, and the moral aspects of this relationship make the satisfactory resolution of the problems more complicated than might otherwise be the case. Receivables entail all the ideological and moral baggage attached to the concept of money-lending and debt and consequently they may not be regarded in the same way as other kinds of property, or indeed may not be regarded as property at all.

The legal systems under study have all dealt differently with these problems.

English law has arrived at a situation where receivables are easily granted as security, by assignment (which can be either legal, if the procedures set out in section 136 Law of Property Act 1925 are followed, or equitable, if they are not) or by charge (which can be fixed or floating). Traces of the courts' disquiet with the idea of transferring a relationship with personal elements can be seen both in the distinction between legal and equitable assignments (deriving from the refusal of the courts of law to countenance the assignment of receivables), and the absolute refusal of both the courts of law and equity to allow the transfer of obligations otherwise than by a novation involving all three parties.

In contrast to English law, French law was and remains hostile to transfers of title by way of security generally, the lack of transfer of possession and the concomitant risk of fraud being regarded as fatal flaws.[211] The *Loi Dailly* is viewed as an exceptional case of statutory intervention.

---

[209] Art. 164 Commercial Companies Law.

[210] This is a discussion postponed from (section 7.1.9, "Receivables"). As in other parts of this article, the factoring term "receivable" will be used to denote the creditor's right to receive payment, the term "obligation to pay" will be used to denote the debtor's obligation to pay, and the term "debt" will be used to refer to the obligation being secured.

[211] See Simler and Delebecque, *Droit civil*, §551, 455–456; and Mestre *et al., Traité de droit civil*, §43–45, 40–45 and §47, 47. The latter refer to the transfer of title by way of security as a "regression in legal technique" (*ibid.,* §47, 47, which also contains a discussion

The *shari'a* transfer mechanism (*hawala*) contrasts strongly with the English approach.[212] It allows the transfer of the obligation to pay, something which is not possible under English law except by novation of the contract.[213] The *shari'a* encourages such transfers, as it favours the release of debtors from their obligations by transferring that obligation to someone likely to be able to satisfy it. A transfer of receivables, on the other hand, is of something uncertain, therefore aleatory and invalid.[214] In addition, the receivable is viewed not as an asset like any other but as, at best, abstract property and, at worst, as not constituting property at all. In this view, the debt concerns the conscience of the debtor rather than his property, so the debt is "a quality which affects the state of the person [the debtor]" and "it seems inconceivable that the creditor could alienate the [receivable] to a third party".[215] It follows that a receivable may not be pledged, that the *shari'a* does not allow the transfer of receivables, except where the transferor thereby extinguishes a second debt which he owes to the transferee[216] and that *hawala* may not be used for financing purposes.[217] Indeed, the importance of the *hawala* lies just as much, if not more, in its use as an alternative to the traditional *shari'a* guarantee as in its use as a transfer mechanism.[218]

---

cont.

of a case where the French Court of Cassation ruled that the transferor of a receivable remained its owner despite the transfer).

[212] See *Majalla* Book IV, Arts. 673–700; Schacht, *An Introduction to Islamic Law*, p. 149; Ray, "The medieval Islamic system", pp. 60–65; Jahel, "L'adéquation du droit musulman classique aux procédés modernes de financement et de garantie", pp. 488–497 ("Le transport de l'obligation"); Al-Bukhari, *The Translation of the Meanings of Sahih Al-Bukhari*, §486, 269–270; Al-Nawawi: 174–175; Al-Shirazi, *Kitab al-tanbih*, §135, 34–35; Al-Jaziri, *Kitab al-fiqh 'ala al-madhahib al-arba'a*, vol. 3, pp. 210–220; and Bousquet, *Le droit musulman par les textes*, §53, pp. 109–110.

[213] The *Majalla* sets out various ways in which a valid transfer may be made: Art. 682 and Art. 683 provide for tripartite arrangements, consisting of a bipartite contract plus agreement of the third party; Art. 681 however provides for a bipartite contract only, between the creditor and the transferee.

[214] See Vogel and Hayes, *Islamic Law and Finance*, pp. 114–124 on the general prohibition of the exchange of "abstract" property for "abstract" property (*dein* for *dein*) and specifically p. 117 on the implications of this rule for the trade of obligations. However, an invalid transfer could be construed as a contract of agency, with the would-be assignor being the principal and the would-be assignee being the agent, appointed to collect the money due from the debtor: see Coulson, "Muslim custom and case law", pp. 29–30.

[215] Jahel, "L'adéquation du droit musulman classique aux procédés modernes de financement et de garantie", p. 489.

[216] If A owes B £100, and C owes A £100, then C can transfer his obligation to pay A to B, which cancels out the receivable owed to B by A. B has a right of recourse against C. The effect is therefore the same as a transfer to B of the receivable owed by C to A. The jurists accepted that a true assignment of receivables was taking place in this place. See Jahel, "L'adéquation du droit musulman classique aux procédés modernes de financement et de garantie", p. 495; and Shirazi, *Kitab al-tanbih*, §135, 34. Such an assignment was called "restricted" (*muqayyada*), because it was limited to the second debt or other property, as opposed to a normal assignment (*mutlaqa*, usually translated as "absolute", but probably better translated as "unrestricted" or "unlimited") which was made without reference to any other obligations.

[217] Vogel and Hayes, *Islamic Law and Finance*, p. 235.

[218] Similar problems with guarantees under Western legal systems have been solved by on-demand instruments, and in this connection see Jahel's suggestion to use *hawala* in order to create an Islamic equivalent to demand guarantees in Jahel, "L'adéquation du droit musulman classique aux procédés modernes de financement et de garantie", pp. 490–494.

The UAE provisions on assignments[219] derive from the *shari'a*. Article 1106 Civil Code defines assignment as "the transfer of a debt and claim from the liability of the transferor to the transferee", "debt" meaning obligation to pay. The *shari'a* division between "limited" assignments and "absolute" assignments appears in Article 1108 Civil Code. Common lawyers, who might be tempted to draft documents in which the creditor is given the role of the transferor of a receivable, should note that in fact the debtor should be the transferor of the obligation to pay.[220] Article 1109 Civil Code requires the consent of all three parties.

The assignment mechanism can be useful, providing a way of taking security over intangibles the possession of which cannot be transferred, such as money owing under leases or insurance policies.[221] However, to an English lawyer accustomed to the flexibility given by English law assignments, UAE assignments are quite narrow in scope and practical application. In addition to the general Civil Code requirements as to certainty,[222] Article 1113 Civil Code sets out a list of requirements for a valid assignment. In respect both of an absolute and a limited assignment, these include the following: it must be "completed and dependent on no condition other than an appropriate or customary condition"[223] (which raises the question of whether an assignment by way of security is "completed"); its performance "must not be deferred to an unknown future date"[224] and "it must be limited in time to a specific time limit"[225] (so there is no scope for a parallel process to the "perfection" of assignments under English law); and the obligation transferred "must be a known debt".[226]

For limited assignments, there is an additional requirement in Article 1113(e) Civil Code that the property transferred to the transferee "must be a debt or specific property which cannot be compounded, and both types of property must be equal in type, amount and description".

The consequence of non-compliance with any of these requirements is the voidness of the assignment.[227] Consequently, any assignment needs to be carefully considered in the light of the stringent requirements imposed. It goes almost without saying that this procedure is not usable for receivables financing, which depends upon the mass transfer of future receivables.

---

[219] Arts. 1106–1132 Civil Code.
[220] This follows not only from the definition contained in Art. 1106 Civil Code, but also from Art. 1110 Civil Code which provides that "for an assignment to be valid, the transferor must be indebted to the creditor".
[221] Clifford Chance, Memorandum on UAE Security, p. 3. It should be noted that ownership of an asset can bring onerous obligations with it, such as the performance of the covenants of a lease.
[222] Art. 129(b), Art. 202, Art. 203 and Art. 204 Civil Code, discussed above (section 5, "General characteristics of the UAE system").
[223] Art. 1113(a) Civil Code.
[224] Art. 1113(b) Civil Code.
[225] Art. 1113(c) Civil Code.
[226] Art. 1113(d) Civil Code.
[227] Art. 1114 Civil Code.

7.4 Set-off and combination of accounts

7.4.1 Set-off

Set-off is one of the most commonly used indirect security mechanisms and therefore, although it is not one of the specific security mechanisms contained in the Commercial Code, and is strictly speaking outside the ambit of this article, a brief account is set out below.[228]

The English rules of set-off[229] derive from case law, although Rule 4.90 Insolvency Rules 1986 lays down the rule for set-off in insolvency. Various kinds of set-off exist and constitute an important and effective security mechanism.

Set-off is recognized by the *shari'a*.[230] Where the two debts are in the same amount and in the same specie, they can be set off against each other even if one of them may no longer be demanded.

French law set-off derives from Article 1289–1290 French Civil Code and from case law thereon.[231] As in England, set-off is important and effective.[232] Set-off is divided into three categories: legal (arising by operation of law), contractual and judicial. The basic rules are contained in those relating to legal set-off; contractual set-off is used when the parties wish to exclude the operation of some of the requirements necessary for a legal set-off; judicial set-off allows the judge, in his or her absolute discretion, to disregard the requirements of legal set-off if justice demands it. It is also necessary to bear in mind that current and other accounts have a body of law to themselves, which has no real equivalent in English law: set-off in this context is dealt with as an issue related to, but slightly separate from, the general rules on set-off.[233]

UAE law derives from French law.[234] The basic rules are contained in Articles 368–377 Civil Code and apply to commercial matters by virtue of Article 2(2) Commercial Code.[235] The Commercial Code also contains some relevant provisions.

---

[228] Although set-off is subject to various disadvantages as a security mechanism, such as the relevant funds being vulnerable to attachment at the instance of other creditors: see Horsfall Turner, "Security and enforcement in Dubai", p. 319.

[229] The English law position is too complex to be summarized in the space available here without misleading distortion. See Goode, *Principles of Corporate Insolvency Law*, Chapter 8 ("Set-off and netting"); Goode, *Commercial Law*, pp. 657–659; and Sealy and Hooley, *Text and Materials in Commercial Law*, pp. 565–566.

[230] For the *shari'a* position see Khalil, *Al-mukhtasar fi al-fiqh*, §363–367, pp. 111–113.

[231] Simler and Delebecque, *Droit civil*, §15, 19 and §451, 381–382.

[232] *Ibid.*, §15, 19–20; and Legeais, *Suretés et garanties de crédit*, §23, p. 13. French law also has the *action directe*, which enables certain categories of creditor to proceed directly against the debtor of their debtor: Legeais, *Suretés et garanties de crédit*, §23, p. 13; Mestre *et al.*, *Traité de droit civil*, §130, pp. 114–115; and Simler and Delebecque, *Droit civil*, §11, 14–15.

[233] The concept of current account is not restricted as in English law to dealings between banks and their customers, but extends to dealings between non-bank parties; see Barthélémy Mercadal, *Droit des affaires 1991: Mémento pratique Francis Lefebvre*, Paris, 1991, §1100–1139, pp. 211–222.

[234] See Al-Sanhuri, *Al-wasît fi sharh al-qanun al-madani al-jadid*, vol. III, pp. 873–943.

[235] Horsfall Turner, "Security and enforcement in Dubai", p. 319.

Set-off is defined by Article 368 Civil Code as "the satisfaction of an obligation of the obligee by an obligation to be performed by the obligor", and is therefore substantive (a defence which justifies the obligee in withholding payment rather than only coming into operation upon judgment). As a result of Article 688 Commercial Code, set-off is valid in commercial insolvency so long as there is an "association" between the right and the obligation of the insolvent, and it is specifically provided that such an association arises if "the right and the obligation arise from one cause or they are included in a current account".

However, Article 377 Civil Code provides that, where a counterparty can either rely on set-off, or satisfy the obligation that he owes and rely on security[236] existing in relation to the obligation owed to him, that counterparty "may not rely on the guarantees of that right to the detriment of third parties"; in other words he must first rely on the set-off, rather than satisfy the obligation and then enforce the third-party security. Article 377 Civil Code excuses him from this requirement if he is unaware of the existence of the right of set-off and has a reasonable excuse for that ignorance.

The Civil Code has three categories of set-off: mandatory, voluntary and judicial.

Mandatory set-off is equivalent to French "legal" set-off.[237] It is defined in Article 369 Civil Code as "occurring by operation of law". Article 370 lays down the conditions for mandatory set-off:

each of the parties must be both the obligor and the obligee of the other, and the obligations must be of the same type and description, must be equally due and of equal strength or weakness, and the making of the set-off must not be prejudicial to the rights of third parties, whether the cause of the arising of the obligations is the same or different.

There are some difficulties of interpretation here, but it seems clear that contingent and future obligations are not of the same type as present obligations, nor would unliquidated damages be the same type as liquidated damages (although in both cases voluntary set-off could be used).

Voluntary set-off is permitted by Article 371 Civil Code "if any of the conditions for a mandatory set-off is not satisfied".

Judicial set-off is defined in Article 369 Civil Code as set-off "by order of the court" and can take place pursuant to Article 372 Civil Code by order by a judge "if the conditions thereof are satisfied, either upon an original application or upon an objection".

7.4.2 *Combination of accounts and accounts generally*

English law grants a bank an implied contractual right to combine a customer's account with one or more others in the name of that customer. It is debatable whether

---

[236] The word used in the Civil Code is *damanat*, which Whelan and Hall translate as "guarantees". This word is probably used to mean securities in general, rather than both securities and guarantees in the English sense. A different word, *kafala*, is used to mean guarantee in the English sense in, for example, Art. 73 and Art. 74 Commercial Code.

[237] The difference in terms is a result of differences in translation into English.

this right is truly a right of set-off. One can take the view that an account is normally a mere record of one credit or debit position of the depositor with the bank, not a separate obligation, and that therefore set-off is not possible, since only one overall obligation exists, made up of the combined credit and debit positions of the depositor. In this view, combining accounts is no more than the calculation of the true extent of this obligation. Others however maintain that combination is truly set-off.[238]

A somewhat similar situation exists in French law, although one should also note the existence of a regime regulating the existence of accounts, particularly the current account, in which the effect of debit and credit entries in the account is regarded as set-off.[239]

The UAE legislation specifically provides for "set-off" in two situations: cash deposits and current accounts. Article 390, in its definition of current account, provides that rights and obligations arising from the relationship of the parties "are converted to account entries which are offset against each other, whereby the final balance on closing the account itself is a debt due for payment".[240] Article 373 provides that a cash deposit (unless it is a "deposit designated for investment") is a debt which may be set off by the bank against monies owed to the bank by the depositor, and contracting out of this article is forbidden.

Article 379(3) allows joint accounts to be set off against other accounts held in the name of only one of the joint account holders if written consent has been given.

7.5 Cash deposits

When considering security over cash deposits,[241] one needs to discuss separately two situations: that where A charges to bank B a deposit made by A with B in respect of a loan made by B to A (an "own bank security"); and that where A charges to bank C a deposit made by A with bank B in respect of a loan made by C to A ("a third-party bank security").

In England the question of whether it is possible to create a valid own bank security has given rise to a great deal of difficulty and controversy, largely caused by the analysis of a cash deposit as an obligation by the bank to pay the amount of

---

[238] See Goode, *Commercial Law*, p. 176; and Arora, *Practical Banking and Building Society Law*, pp. 106–107. On combination of accounts under English law generally, see Arora, *ibid.*, pp. 105–111.

[239] This would be regarded by an English lawyer as no more than a statement of the obvious: see Goode, *Commercial Law*, p. 173. Current accounts are defined in Art. 390 and general provision is made for them in Arts. 390–408 Commercial Code. On banking operations generally in the Commercial Code, see Price, "United Arab Emirates", pp. 323–326.

[240] And indeed payments entering the account "must be in cash or replaceables of common kind so that there can be an offset between them": Art. 392(1).

[241] "Cash deposit" denotes a certain sum of money in an account, as opposed to the credit balance of an account for the time being. This discussion is limited to the former, since taking security over the balance of an account for the time being falls foul of the requirements of certainty discussed above (section 6.2, "Background law"), although Art. 396(1) does provide for an amount already secured and placed in an account to vary (including the law of contract").

that deposit to the customer.[242] This sort of difficulty has not arisen in France, since French law takes quite a different approach to the analysis of cash deposits, treating them as property, possession of which is transferable by entry from one account to another.[243] A deposit can therefore be pledged by the depositor to the bank by agreement and transfer from one account to another, the pledge being enforceable by set-off.

In the UAE, Article 373, as noted above, creates essentially the same starting point for the discussion as in English law: a cash deposit (other than one designated for investment) is a receivable. As such, it can be pledged to third parties. In other words, a third party bank security is possible. Given this theoretical basis, it is legitimate to ask whether the same problems might arise as in England concerning own bank securities.

Some of the arguments used in the English discussions could be useful in this context. Briefly, those who argue against the enforceability of a charge over own bank deposits maintain that a receivable is not "property" as between the debtor and creditor. It is an obligation, which is enforceable only by action by the creditor against the debtor. A charge of an obligation owed to himself by the debtor is therefore a transfer of the right to sue and this is impossible, since one cannot sue oneself. The only way in which the creditor can enforce the charge is by set-off. In addition to these technical arguments, Goode argues that such a charge should not be allowed as a matter of policy, since it would constitute an illegitimate extension of the rights of set-off such as is not permitted in relation to set-off *per se* in insolvency.[244]

Contra, one can say that such a charge is not in fact a transfer of a right to sue, but a grant of a right in respect of a chose in action, and the fact that enforcement can only take place by transfer of the credit balance, i.e. set-off, is irrelevant – it just so happens that the set-off is the only way in which the creditor can take possession of the property. As for the policy argument, the way in which the law classifies a credit balance is highly technical and in practical terms a credit balance is almost cash, so why should the set-off rules apply to it?

Whether all, or any, such arguments would be used in the UAE is a matter of conjecture. All one can do at this stage is look at the definition of possessory pledge contained in Article 1448 Civil Code, which provides that a possessory pledge "is a contract giving rise to a right to retain the property", not, as with an English charge, a grant of a right over the property. Receivables are specifically included as a par-

---

[242] See *Re Charge Card Services Ltd* [1987] Ch 150, [1986] 3 All ER 289, affd [1988] Ch 497, [1988] 3 All ER 702, CA; *Re Bank of Credit and Commerce International SA (No. 8)* [1998] AC 214, [1997] 4 All ER 568, HL. See also the judgment of the Court of Appeal at [1996] Ch 245, [1996] 2 All ER 121, CA; Arora, *Practical Banking and Building Society Law*, pp. 320–322; and Goode, *Commercial Law*, pp. 659–660. Third-party bank security does not pose such problems.

[243] This is inherent in the terminology – such security is called either *gage-espèces* (cash pledge) or *gage sur sommes d'argent* (pledge over sums of money). See generally Simler and Delebecque, *Droit civil*, §545, 447–448, and in particular §547, 450–451. However, a pledge of debts is not possible over an ordinary account with varying balances, because here the obligation of the bank to the customer is analysed as a debt, which cannot be pledged to the person who owes the debt. See Simler and Delebecque, *Droit civil*, §547, 450–451.

[244] Goode, *Commercial Law*, pp. 659–660.

ticular kind of asset which can be the subject of a possessory pledge.[245] A pledge of an own bank cash deposit could be said to be granting "a right to retain", but is an own bank cash deposit "property" *vis-à-vis* the debtor and the creditor? Article 1458 Civil Code provides that the pledgor of a receivable must be "the owner of the property pledged and be competent to make dispositions over it". Can the pledgor properly be described as the "owner" of an own bank cash deposit? Given the French ancestry of most of the security provisions of the Commercial Code, it may be that the French attitude will be adopted of considering the deposit property and therefore a potential subject of a pledge.

One should also note that a combination of blocking the account and the use of the express right of set-off is an effective security mechanism. In this procedure the depositor and the bank create a blocked account, with the depositor agreeing that the account will only become available to him after the date on which the principal obligation owed by him to the bank has become payable[246] (the depositor also agrees that the contents of the account cannot be charged or assigned to any other party). The deposit becomes safe and, if enforcement becomes necessary, this can be effected by set-off.

7.6 Liens, priority rights and rights of retention

The word "lien" can cause problems in comparative context. In English usage, the word has a confusingly wide range of meanings, including rights to retain, but not sell, property as security for a debt and rights of various kinds granted by case law or statute over property.[247] However, this wide range of meanings does not include preferential debts, which are quite different from liens. Preferential debts are certain categories of receivables (such as those due to the tax authorities) which rank on insolvency ahead of ordinary creditors and holders of floating charges,[248] but they do not have the status of secured debts, and they rank after fixed security.

As seen above,[249] French law also accords preferential status to certain classes of receivables, the list of which is somewhat similar to that existing in English law, but accords secured rights[250] to them (some of which rank above all other security). One might therefore call such rights a lien, but they are quite different from most English concepts of lien. In particular, they can only be created either directly by statute or if specific statutory authorization is given for their creation by contract. Accordingly, particular care needs to be taken when translating "privileges" as "lien", if one does so at all.[251]

---

[245] Art. 1458 Civil Code.
[246] Art. 371 provides that the bank is "obliged to return the sum on demand or *in accordance with the agreed terms*" (emphasis added).
[247] Goode, *Commercial Law*, pp. 668–670; and Halsbury's Laws: §701, p. 352.
[248] S. 115 Insolvency Act 1986, rule 4.180(1) Insolvency Rules 1986 (expenses of liquidation) and s. 175(2)(b) Insolvency Act 1986. S. 175(1) Insolvency Act 1986 provides for the priority status of preferential debts. The categories of preferential debts are set out in Sch. 6 Insolvency Act 1986.
[249] See above (section 4.3.3, "Overview of mechanisms").
[250] *Privilèges*.
[251] Hence the use herein of Whelan and Hall's translation "priority right" both for the French and the Arabic terms.

The *shari'a* had some notions of priority rights, such as that attached to a debt incurred in respect of funeral expenses, the right of the carrier over transported goods and the right of the artisan over the product of his labour.[252] There is no general principle to be discerned in the rules (and often there is disagreement among the jurists). For example, in a conflict between a pledgee and the beneficiary of a priority right, for example, the conflict is sometimes resolved in favour of one, sometimes in favour of the other, depending on the case.[253]

7.6.1 UAE priority rights

In the UAE, the Civil Code[254] provides the general rules on priority rights, the general structure of which derives from French law, although there is also some evidence of *shari'a* influence.[255] A priority right is defined as "a specific right over property following (such property), conferring upon the obligee priority status in obtaining his right in accordance with his bargain and as acknowledged by law".[256] Priority rights are divided into general (applicable to all the assets of the obligor) and particular (applicable to specific property).[257] Although not formally so defined by the legislation, they are also divided into those arising by operation of law and those which take effect only upon registration,[258] and these two categories are in fact dealt with in separate sections of the Civil Code. The rights of those in possession of movable property in good faith are not affected by priority rights.[259] Some priority rights take precedence over secured rights.[260]

Various parts of the rules applicable to possessory pledges are made applicable also to priority rights: in the case of real property, those rules are made applicable in their entirety, apart from where the rules "do not conflict with the nature" of the priority rights;[261] in the case of both movable and immovable property, those

---

[252] See Bousquet, *Précis de droit musulman*, §131, pp. 209–210; Grandmoulin, *Traité élémentaire de droit civil égyptien indigène et mixte,* §605, p. 171; Khalil, *Al-mukhtasar fi al-fiqh*, §475–491, pp. 146–151. It is noteworthy that, in the case of priority rights over movables, the right only exists over the movable itself and, apart from exceptional cases, there is no right to trace.

[253] Bousquet, *Précis de droit musulman,* §131, pp. 210.

[254] Arts. 1504–1528.

[255] On the Egyptian law, see Al-Sanhuri, *Al-wasît fi sharh al-qanun al-madani al-jadid,* vol. X, pp. 918–1008.

[256] Art. 1504 Civil Code. Compare Art. 2095 French Civil Code: "the priority right is a right which the quality of the receivable gives to a creditor to be preferred to other creditors, even those benefiting from a mortgage".

[257] Art. 1506 Civil Code.

[258] Art. 1526, Art. 1527 and Art. 1528 Civil Code, relating respectively to the sale price of land, amounts due to contractors and amounts due to co-owners upon division of the land.

[259] Art. 1507(1) Civil Code.

[260] For example, Art. 1512 Civil Code provides that judicial costs "expended for the common benefit of creditors in preserving the property of the debtor and selling the same ... shall be recovered before any other right notwithstanding that it may be ... secured by way of a pledge by way of security".

[261] Art. 1508(1) Civil Code.

provisions relating to destruction or damage to property[262] and those relating to termination (unless there is a specific provision to the contrary) are applicable.[263]

It is not specified precisely what the "priority status" accorded to priority rights by Article 1504 Civil Code is, but working on the analogy of French law, and Article 794(1) Commercial Code referred to below, it would seem reasonable to conclude that the priority is mainly relevant on the insolvency of the debtor in determining the priority of claims against the insolvent debtor's assets. If this is the case, it would explain the absence of a right of sale, although it should be noted that Article 1507(3) Civil Code does entitle the holder of a priority right over movable property to require that it "be placed under protection" if he "fears that it will be lost or disposed of".

As in French law, the ranking of a priority right is determined specifically by statute, usually in the provision granting that right. As between rights of equal rank, claims are settled *pari passu*.[264] Article 1505 Civil Code contains a "sweep-up" provision, pursuant to which priority rights whose status is not specified by law rank below those set out in this chapter of the Civil Code.

The priority rights set out in the Civil Code include such things as judicial costs relating to the preservation and sale of property (absolute priority in respect of the property concerned),[265] taxes (absolute priority after judicial costs),[266] rent over agricultural property,[267] a hotelier's claims for board and accommodation[268] and the price of real property owing to a seller.[269] In each case it is specified whether the priority right is general or specific and whether it needs to be registered in order to be effective.

Low down the ranking list, after the other priority rights over movables, but significant nevertheless for commercial transactions, is the priority right of the seller of movable property for the price of goods.[270] The goods must retain their identity and the rights of persons who have acquired their rights over the goods in good faith cannot be affected.[271] The article is specifically made subject to commercial laws.

As far as the Commercial Code is concerned, Article 794(1) states the general principle that the expenses of the insolvency and priority rights are to be paid out first and the remainder to the other creditors. Article 703 provides that the holders of particular priority rights, along with the holders of security, are not to be included in the list of creditors of the insolvent.[272]

---

[262] Art. 1509 Civil Code.
[263] Art. 1510 Civil Code.
[264] Art. 1511 Civil Code.
[265] Art. 1512 Civil Code.
[266] Art. 1513 Civil Code.
[267] Art. 1517 Civil Code. Art. 1520 grants a right to trace the property if removed without the landlord's knowledge or consent and there are insufficient assets, so long as the person in possession did not act in good faith.
[268] Art. 1522 Civil Code.
[269] Art. 1526 Civil Code.
[270] Art. 1524 Civil Code.
[271] Art. 1524(1) Civil Code.
[272] Art. 703 uses the same expression as Art. 1506(1) Civil Code (*imtiyaz khas*, translated herein as "particular priority right") and there is no reason to believe that the use of this expression is different in Art. 703 from its use in Art. 1506(1) Civil Code. However, some have been perturbed by the use of different English translations in the two articles as well as by the rendering by some translators of *imtiyaz* as "lien" (e.g. Whelan and Hall's translation of Art. 110(2) Civil Code).

The Commercial Code also sets out various priority rights additional to those set out in the Civil Code, as well as some amendments of the Civil Code general provisions. Examples of additional rights include the right of the seller of a commercial undertaking to exercise a priority right in the insolvency of the buyer over the commercial undertaking so long as that priority right was set out in the contract of sale and advertised by newspaper publication,[273] the right of an auctioneer in respect of the goods he sells[274] and the right of an agent in respect of his principal's goods.[275] Article 716 limits the amount of taxes given priority to two years' worth.

Article 713 deals with employees' remuneration by providing a procedure which effectively gives priority to employees for thirty days' remuneration – a priority right as such is not granted, but the insolvency trustee is required, having obtained leave from the court, to pay this remuneration out of available assets within ten days of the issue of the insolvency declaration in priority to all other debts.

7.6.2 *UAE rights of retention*

The English law "lien" constituted by a right of retention has equivalents both in French law and the *shari'a*. In all the systems under study, there is not a great deal of theoretical coherence, the various categories of right having grown up empirically to meet practical needs.

The French *droit de rétention* is an important form of indirect security which is valid against third parties, even in an insolvency situation, indeed it gives the retainer a super-preferred position.[276]

The *shari'a habs* gives a right to retain property to various actors, such as the vendor of such property until payment therefor and the workman for work done on such property, but not to others, such as the pledgee who has incurred expense on the pledged property.[277] The right of the pledgee to retain the property is considered to be a *habs*.

The UAE rules on rights of retention (*haq al-ihtibas*) are to be found in the Civil Code.[278] The Civil Code authorizes the retention of property – Article 414 Civil Code gives a general dispensation to obligors from performance of their obligations if connected obligations have not been performed; Article 415 Civil Code authorizes retention in contractual, Article 416 Civil Code in non-contractual, situations where the retainer has incurred "necessary or beneficial expense"; and Article 419 Civil Code gives a retaining party who no longer retains possession the right to require the return of property within thirty days of learning of it having passed out of his possession. The retainer is obliged to preserve the asset and give an account

---

[273] Art. 48.

[274] Art. 127.

[275] Art. 237.

[276] Simler and Delebecque, *Droit civil*, §500, pp. 417–418, §660, p. 538; and Mestre *et al.*, *Traité de droit civil*, §49–84, 48–75, §482, 449–457.

[277] Arts. 278–284 *Majalla*; Schacht, *An Introduction to Islamic Law*, p. 140; Bousquet, *Précis de droit musulman*, §130, pp. 208–209; and Grandmoulin, *Traité élémentaire de droit civil égyptien indigène et mixte*, §805, p. 226.

[278] Arts. 414–419 Civil Code. On the Egyptian law, see Al-Sanhuri, *Al-wasît fi sharh al-qanun al-madani al-jadid*, vol. 2, pp. 1124–1190.

for any benefit deriving from it.[279] Article 418 Civil Code grants to the retainer a "prior right over other competing creditors for the satisfaction of rights". Presumably this means that, as in French law, a right of retention "trumps" all other competing creditors, even priority rights.

The Commercial Code has various rights of retention dotted through it. These include those granted to agents,[280] sellers,[281] carriers of goods[282] and those granted to banks in respect of documentary credits,[283] deposited securities[284] and the contents of deposit boxes.[285]

8 STATUTORY PROTECTION IN SALE CONTRACTS

In the non-consumer context, English law characteristically allows sellers in contracts of sale to protect themselves by contractual devices (mainly the retention of title clause) with the result that there is only limited statutory provision.[286] In the UAE, such matters are regulated by the Commercial Code, which provides various mechanisms. A detailed analysis of these mechanisms lies outside the scope of this article, but a sketch is provided below.

The UAE provides various statutory rights which create effects similar to security. In particular, retention of title is not left to the general law, but is created by statute.[287] The Commercial Code contains various other mechanisms: it grants rights of sale over goods and other rights to an unpaid seller of those goods; it provides a regime resembling security, independent of the parties' agreement, for sales with payment by instalments;[288] in a dispute where the purchaser refuses to take delivery of the goods, it permits the seller to apply to the court for permission to sell the goods under the supervision of the court;[289] and it provides various protections in the sale of a commercial undertaking.[290]

---

[279] Art. 417(1) Civil Code.
[280] Art. 213.
[281] *Inter alia*, Arts. 118 and 731.
[282] Art. 303.
[283] Art. 439.
[284] Art. 462(2).
[285] Art. 475.
[286] On English law retention of title clauses, see Goode, *Commercial Law*, pp. 637, 642, 652, 654–656. On the *shari'a* position, see Jahel, "L'adéquation du droit musulman classique aux procédés modernes de financement et de garantie", pp. 500–504. On French law, see Mestre *et al., Traité de droit civil,* §20–21, 16–20; and Simler and Delebecque, *Droit civil,* §604–609, 496–503.
[287] Art. 557 Civil Code. This is similar to the French approach. Also see Arts. 725–732 Commercial Code, which deal with recovery of property on insolvency.
[288] The seller has a right, subject to the discretion of the court, to rescind the contract if the purchaser fails to meet one of the instalments – Art. 116(1). The buyer may not dispose of the goods before all instalments are paid in full, unless the seller has allowed such disposal in writing – Art. 120. It is also noteworthy that Art. 117 allows a seller to reserve the right to accelerate the instalments on non-payment of an instalment, but only after notice is served and a grace period of seven days has elapsed.
[289] The net proceeds of sale are deposited with the court cashier pending resolution of the dispute.
[290] See for example Art. 45(5) and Art. 48.

9 GUARANTEES, BANK GUARANTEES AND PROMISSORY NOTES

This article does not deal with guarantees, bank guarantees or promissory notes in any detail, but a brief mention is made of the relevant provisions for the sake of convenience.

9.1 Guarantees

The word "guarantee" is used here in the English sense, i.e. a personal obligation of a third party to satisfy the obligation of the principal obligor (usually a simple debt owed to a bank) if the principal obligor fails to satisfy that obligation.

The Civil Code contains the fundamental rules concerning guarantees.[291] Article 73 Commercial Code provides that a guarantee is commercial if it is granted in respect of a debt which is commercial *vis-à-vis* the obligor, or the parties agree that the guarantee is to be commercial, or the guarantor himself has the status of merchant and has an interest in guaranteeing the debt.

9.2 Bank guarantees

The rules on bank guarantees are to be found in Articles 411–419. Such a guarantee can take "numerous" forms, three of which are given as specific examples, namely:

–   the bank's signature to commercial paper as reserve guarantor, or the provision of such a reserve guarantee by way of a separate instrument which allows several commercial papers to be guaranteed at one time;[292]
–   the conclusion of a separate contract of suretyship;[293] and
–   the forwarding of a letter of guarantee by the bank to the customer's obligee, in which the bank guarantees that the customer will meet his obligations.[294]

Of these three example mechanisms, the "letter of guarantee" is what English practice would call a "bank guarantee" or "demand guarantee". It is defined as being "an undertaking given by the guarantor bank at the request of a customer (the orderer) unconditionally to pay a specified or specifiable sum to another person (the beneficiary)".[295] Such a letter can be made conditional if it must states the purpose for which the bank is providing it[296] and it is only assignable with the consent of the bank.[297]

---

[291] Arts. 1056–1105 Civil Code.
[292] Art. 412(1).
[293] Art. 412(2).
[294] Art. 412(3).
[295] Art. 414.
[296] Art. 414.
[297] Art. 416.

Prima facie, letters of guarantee are independent of the underlying transaction, but in "exceptional cases" the court may prevent payment and attach the amount of the guarantee in the hands of the bank "provided that the orderer bases his case on good and firm grounds".[298] Article 419 provides express subrogation of the bank to the rights of the orderer for any sum paid out in respect of the letter of guarantee.

9.3 Promissory notes

Articles 591–594 set out the rules for promissory notes. Article 593(1) provides that a writer of a promissory note is bound in the same way as an acceptor of a draft. Promissory notes can be used as security and can be guaranteed.[299]

10 THE EFFECT OF INSOLVENCY ON SECURITY

The most important reason why security is taken is to ensure payment in the insolvency of the debtor, in preference to other creditors; therefore it is vital to be aware of the relationship between the insolvency regime and the law of security. It is the insolvency regime which determines the ranking of security, and the way in which that security can be enforced, in an insolvency. The insolvency regime (especially those parts of it which attempt to prevent the abuse of security) may also impose limitations on the effectiveness of security[300] and although such limitations are necessary, they can work to the unexpected detriment of the honest, but ill-advised, secured creditor.

England on the one side and France and the UAE on the other take quite different attitudes towards insolvency generally and, as a result of these differing attitudes, different approaches to the relationship of security and insolvency rules.

English insolvency law is typical of the general English approach to commerce. A large number of company insolvencies are dealt with privately, with no court involvement; indeed the usual reason for court involvement is the lack of enough assets to pay a private person to act as liquidator. Insolvency was decriminalized in the nineteenth century, coming to be regarded more as a misfortune than a crime, so that before the 1985 reforms the role of criminal law was minimal (even now it is far from primary), and the legislature took a trusting, *laissez-faire* attitude. This attitude allowed considerable abuses, resulting in the 1985 reforms, which produced a substantial body of anti-abuse provisions.[301] These provisions are particularly important in view of the absolute priority given to fixed security over all other creditors.

---

[298] Art. 417.

[299] Art. 594(3).

[300] Real security carries with it the possibility of abuse on insolvency, as any person who is on the brink of insolvency can all too easily grant security over assets to persons ready to collude with that person in an attempt to deprive unsecured creditors of those assets.

[301] See J. Lingard, *Bank Security Documents*, 3rd edn, London, Butterworths, 1993, Chapter 6 ("Inherent defects"); and Goode; *Commercial Law*, pp. 856–861.

Before 1985, French insolvency law proceeded on the assumption that insolvency must have involved blameworthy conduct and therefore attached great importance to criminal law. Modern French law has mitigated the old severity towards the debtor, but it still bears traces of this approach.[302] The court's involvement is far greater than in England; for example all company insolvencies start with a petition to the court. As far as anti-abuse provisions are concerned, the greater general role of the criminal law is still evident, but there is also a general civil action (the "Paulian action")[303] also exists, as do specific civil anti-abuse provisions.[304]

The *shari'a* did not have an exact equivalent to modern insolvency regimes, but by combining rules allowing execution against goods, the removal of a debtor's legal capacity and imprisonment for recalcitrant, but solvent, debtors, provided solutions considerably in advance of those available until modern insolvency regimes were first enacted in Europe in the nineteenth century.[305] However, until the *Majalla* the removal of capacity was not retroactive; in other words the law did not contain anti-abuse provisions.[306]

In the UAE, the Civil Code contains a section governing non-commercial insolvency, the main philosophy of which derives from the *shari'a*. It provides for the imposition of a restriction on the debtor whose assets exceed his liabilities, an attachment order over his assets and the sale of those assets by order of the court.[307] The Commercial Code provisions, governing commercial insolvency, are derived ultimately from old French law on the subject and provide a regime for commercial insolvency for both individuals and companies.[308] A person may be declared insol-

---

[302] French law since 1985 attaches great importance to the rehabilitation of the business and accords a high priority to the claims of employees as against those of general creditors. Law of 25 January 1985, as significantly amended by Law of 10 June 1994, *inter alia* to grant a more realistic position to secured creditors. See Arnold Gewelbe, "France" in Dennis Campbell, *International Corporate Insolvency Law*, London, Butterworths, 1992, pp. 177–205 on the 1985 French legislation and Legeais, *Sûretés et garanties de crédit*, §13–16, pp. 7–9; Chaput, "L'apport du droit de l'entreprise au droit des suretés"; Derrida, "La réforme du droit des enterprises"; and Simler and Delebecque, *Droit civil*.

[303] The Paulian action (Art. 1167 French Civil Code) entitles a person harmed by any of a range of dispositions by an insolvent debtor, including dispositions by way of security, to seek a declaration of the unenforceability of such a disposition against the petitioner. See Mestre *et al., Traité de droit civil,* §3, 2–3 (which also refers to other anti-abuse provisions) and §150–151, 129–132.

[304] Art. 107 Law of 25 January 1985. Mestre *et al., Traité de droit civil,* §153, 132–136.

[305] See Al-Nawawi: 161–166; Khalil, *Al-mukhtasar fi al-fiqh*, §432–491, pp. 135–151; Shirazi, *Kitab al-tanbih*, §129–130, pp. 27–29, §131, 29; Art. 959 and Arts. 998–1002 *Majalla*; and Tyan, "Iflas et procédure d'éxécution sur les biens en droit musulman (madhab hanafite)". The *shari'a* operated the rule of *pari passu* distribution, pp. 163–164. The first modern insolvency regime was introduced into the region by the Ottoman Commercial Code of 1850, a French translation of which is to be found in George Young, *Corps de droit ottoman*, vol. VII, Oxford, Clarendon Press, 1906, p. 54.

[306] Tyan, "Iflas et procédure d'éxécution sur les biens en droit musulman (madhab hanafite)", pp. 159–160. Contrast Art. 1002 *Majalla*, which does contain such provisions.

[307] Arts. 401–413 Civil Code (Restrictions on bankrupt obligors). Note also Arts. 394–395 Civil Code (Claims under sham contracts) and Arts. 396–400 Civil Code (Claims against a debtor not to make dispositions detrimental to the creditor).

[308] Arts. 645–900 Commercial Law. The modern French law has greatly modified its former approach. For an overview of the UAE law, see Price, "United Arab Emirates", pp. 326–329; and Clifford

vent by the court upon "cessation of payments",[309] a concept which is used throughout the legislation and which also serves to define the "suspect period" (the period between cessation of payments and the declaration in bankruptcy, used frequently in both criminal and civil anti-abuse provisions).[310] The declaration may be sought by the trader, his creditor, the public prosecutor or the court of its own motion.[311] Upon the declaration of insolvency, the creditors are automatically formed into a "body of creditors" which has separate legal personality[312] and is represented by an administrator. However, the group of creditors does not include secured creditors, except to the extent that they are, or become, unsecured. The UAE insolvency procedures are entirely administered by the court and public officials.

10.1 Enforcement of security in insolvency

The Civil Code lays down two general principles, both of which derive from French law, but which have their counterparts in the *shari'a*. Article 391(1) provides that "the property of the obligor stands as security for the performance of his obligations". This article, derived from French law, simply means that the property of the obligor is available to creditors through execution processes if the obligor fails to satisfy his obligations.[313] Article 391(2) provides that "[a]ll creditors stand pari passu in respect of such security", but, as in most systems, "all creditors" must be understood to mean "all creditors of the same class", this article does not prevent secured creditors from exercising prior rights to unsecured creditors.

Article 704(3) allows the enforcement of security in insolvency, which will take place through the court as described above.[314] All creditors, including secured creditors, must hand over to the trustee in bankruptcy the documents proving their debts.[315] The trustee in bankruptcy then lodges a list with the court,[316] and the judge draws

---

cont.
   Chance "The UAE Commercial Transactions Law", *Middle East Commercial Law Review*, 2, 1995, pp. 53–54.
[309] Art. 645 (individuals), Art. 802 (companies). See Art. 655, Art. 658 and Art. 659 for the procedures for fixing the date of cessation of payments, which may not be fixed beyond two years before the date of adjudication of insolvency (Art. 659(2)). The difference between this test and the assets over liabilities test of Art. 401 Civil Code is noteworthy.
[310] In French the *période suspecte*. The present French legislative provision is Art. 9 Law of 25 January 1985. See Pascal Diener, "Du caractère suspect de l'absence de période suspecte", *Recueil Dalloz Sirey, Chronique LXVIII*, 1993, p. 255, for a brief history of this concept and a criticism of the present practice.
[311] Arts. 647 and 650. Art. 649(1) obliges the trader to do so within thirty days of the cessation of payments.
[312] Art. 703 and Art. 787, the French *masse des créanciers*, abolished by the French reforms of 1985.
[313] The French equivalent is Art. 2092 French Civil Code. See Mestre *et al.*, *Traité de droit civil*, §108–121, pp. 100–107.
[314] This applies even to goods which have been borrowed by the debtor in order to pledge them, so long as the pledgee was unaware that the goods did not belong to the pledgor – Art. 726(4). Under Art. 706, interest due on the secured debt may only be paid from the proceeds of realisation, not from the proceeds of other assets.
[315] Art. 752.
[316] Art. 755. Contingent debts are provable – Art. 707.

up a list of uncontested debts[317] which includes the names of creditors with security over movable property.[318] The trustee may, with leave of the court, "settle a debt secured by a pledge and recover the pledged objects on account of the group of creditors".[319] Predictably, Article 712(1) provides that any surplus achieved by realization of the security comes into the pot of assets available to general creditors and that the secured creditor becomes an unsecured creditor in respect of any shortfall.

The trustee may require the secured creditor to enforce his security.[320] Article 746(1) provides that property may not be sold during the preliminary procedure period. It is not specified whether this article relates to property subject to security and, if this is the case, there may be some delay on enforcement.[321]

Valid contractual quasi-security arrangements based on title retention or transfer are enforceable in insolvency, Article 725 specifically provides that the owners of property in the possession of the insolvent may recover that property, so long as ownership can be proved.

The Commercial Code also contains various provisions designed to protect sellers of goods to insolvent purchasers.[322]

Article 688 deals with set-off on insolvency, providing that set-off is possible on insolvency only between connected debts. Specific examples given of connected debts are those which arise from one cause or one current account.[323]

10.1.1 Anti-abuse provisions – criminal

The Commercial Code resembles the pre-1985 French legislation in according great importance to criminal sanctions.

Three categories of individual insolvency (fraudulent, seriously negligent and negligent) give rise to criminal liability, with maximum possible imprisonment terms of five years, two years and one year respectively.[324] An insolvency will fall into one of these categories if one of a list of elements is present. Those elements include various matters which may be relevant to security, such as: the misappropriation or concealment of property;[325] making "a special award to one of his creditors for the purpose of obtaining acceptance of a composition" after cessation of payments;[326] the disposition by the management of a company "of company prop-

---

[317] Art. 757.
[318] Art. 711.
[319] Art. 711.
[320] Art. 711(2).
[321] Art. 746.
[322] Arts. 731–732 and Art. 48.
[323] On current accounts, see above (section 7.4, "Set-off and combination of accounts"). On set-off in a current account (or, more accurately, combination) see Mercadal, *Droit des affaires 1991*, §1115, p. 216.
[324] Art. 878, Art. 880 and Art. 881. A fine is also possible in the latter two cases. Art. 879 and Art. 882 provide equivalent offences for company insolvencies. In addition, the UAE Penal Code (Federal Law No 3 of 1987) contains provisions concerning fraudulent bankruptcy and fraud in trade generally.
[325] Art. 878(2).
[326] Art. 881(5).

erty after ceasing to make payments, in order to distance this property from the creditors";[327] and the grant of securities in a corporate insolvency after cessation of
payments in order to prefer creditors.[328]

Other relevant offences include the fraudulent increase by any creditor of the
bankrupt of the bankrupt's debts to him[329] and the making of any "secret agreement
with the bankrupt after he has ceased payments which knowingly gains him special privileges to the detriment of the other creditors".[330] These offences have civil
consequences, in that the court is obliged to "rule of its own accord that such agreements are invalid with respect to the bankrupt and to any other person, and [to]
require the creditor to return what he acquired through the invalid agreement even
if he is found not guilty of the offence". The court may also grant damages upon
being requested to do so.

10.1.2 Anti-abuse provisions – civil

Article 396 Civil Code relates to gifts and disposals "by way of commutative contract", whether there is preference or not, and forbids an obligor whose obligations "exceed or are equal to [his] assets" from making disposals "which he is not
bound to make or which custom does not dictate that he must", and entitles an
obligee of the obligor to request an order that any such disposition be deemed ineffective against the petitioning obligee, as well as entitling such obligee to request
an order for the sale of the obligor's property. It is not specified whether the word
"disposals" includes the granting of security.

Article 701 provides that in commercial insolvencies only the trustee can apply
under Civil Code rules for a declaration that the disposals are ineffective if the disposal took place before the adjudication in bankruptcy. Article 701 also provides
that a declaration of ineffectiveness renders a disposal ineffective *vis-à-vis* all creditors, irrespective of whether their interest arose before or after the relevant disposal.

Article 1454 Civil Code renders a contract of pledge void if, before the pledgee
takes possession of the asset to be pledged, the pledgee becomes subject to a restriction on making dispositions of his property.[332]

Under Article 111 Commercial Companies Law:

> The chairman of the board of directors and the directors shall be liable towards the
> company, the shareholders and third parties for all acts of fraud, abuse of authority and any
> violation of the Law or the company articles as well as mismanagement.

Also relevant in this context is Article 808, pursuant to which the court may declare bankrupt "any person who carried out business on his own account in the company's name and disposed of its property as though it were his own", as is Article

---

[327] Art. 882(3).
[328] Art. 882(4).
[329] Art. 886(1).
[330] Art. 886(3) and Art. 890(3).
[331] Art. 886.
[332] Under Arts. 401–413 Civil Code.

809 which provides that, if after realization of the assets at least 20 per cent of the debts of a company are not satisfied, then the directors may be ordered by the court to contribute to payment of the company's debts.

Article 696 renders void with respect to the group of creditors certain disposals made "after the date of cessation of payments but before the declaration in bankruptcy", including, under Article 696(4), "[a]ny pledge or other security prescribed for the funds of the debtor as a guarantee for a previous debt". Article 697 adds to the list "any disposals other than those aforestated in the preceding Article made by the bankrupt during the period referred to … if the disposal is harmful to [the group of creditors] and at the time of the disposal the alienee was aware that the bankrupt had ceased making payment". In all such cases, the group of creditors may institute an action for recovery.[333]

Security rights may be declared ineffective under Article 699(1) if registered after the date of cessation of payments.

10.1.3 Composition

Articles 831–877 provide for the possibility of composition proceedings as an alternative to insolvency proceedings. The requirements for such proceedings make it unlikely that they will be used in a great many cases, since the distribution proposed must be not less than 50 per cent of the debts outstanding, the period for payment must not exceed three years[334] and the proposals must be approved by a majority of creditors present at the creditors' meeting holding two-thirds of the debts owed to those creditors present.[335] Secured creditors are excluded from voting in the creditors' meeting unless they waive their security.[336] Application must be made through the court, which supervises the procedure.[337] Once approved, the composition arrangement binds all "ordinary" debtors.[338]

Two major consequences follow from the initiation of composition proceedings, one relating to the grant of security during the procedure and the other to its enforcement.

Concerning the grant of security, if the composition is approved, then Article 846(2) forbids the debtor from granting a pledge or making any disposition "involving transfer of ownership" except those either "required by his commercial business" or approved by the court. It is therefore important before taking security to ensure that the debtor is not in composition.

Concerning enforcement, any enforcement proceedings are suspended under Article 847(1) from the date of initiation of the composition proceedings. As to whether this suspension expires at the end of the composition proceedings, Article 867 pro-

---

[333] Art. 698.
[334] Art. 837(1).
[335] Art. 861(1).
[336] Art. 862.
[337] Art. 841(1).
[338] Art. 867. Art. 868(1) provides that joint debtors and guarantors do not benefit from the composition and Art. 868(2) that certain creditors are not bound by it.

vides that the composition applies to all creditors with debts "considered ordinary under the bankruptcy provisions". Presumably "ordinary" debts exclude secured debts, but this is not specifically stated.

11 CONCLUSION

A comparative study such as that attempted in this article provides material for re-flection, both as regards the regime of substantive law under examination and in the area of comparative law.

11.1 An assessment of the UAE regime of security over movables

The UAE regime of security over movables provides a useful range of devices for taking security over movables covering a reasonably broad range of assets and oblig-ations. It is quite coherent (more so than either French or English law). It is a wel-come addition to the commercial law of the UAE and should enable a broader range of financing transactions to take place, so encouraging commerce generally.[339]

Certain criticisms might be made. Some problems of interpretation, compounded by the difficulties associated with case law in the UAE, lead to a degree of uncer-tainty.[340] The regime is very new and therefore less sophisticated than either of the French or English law regimes. It is particularist, with a relatively low degree of abstraction and generalization (traits inherited from French law), which results in it being less favourable to secured creditors than, say, England, with: a less broad range of property available to be granted as security (e.g. future receivables); a less broad range of debts capable of being secured (e.g. further advances); a less broad range of mechanisms available; a lack of flexibility to deal with new situations and new types of property; the absence of a real equivalent to the floating charge; and an absence of self-help, with a consequent dependence on the courts and public auc-tion system.[341]

Such criticisms may, however, be ethnocentric, based on the assumptions of com-mon lawyers steeped in the English approach to commerce that in the commercial context it is desirable to allow the greatest range possible of types of property to be given as security in respect of the greatest range possible of debts, that it is proper

---

[339] For the moment, registers for the pledge of commercial undertaking exist only in Dubai and the Jebel Ali Free Zone.

[340] Such uncertainty can be a significant hindrance to commerce, since businessmen can plan around most unfavourable regimes, but find it more difficult to plan around uncertain ones.

[341] In English law, French law and medieval practice in the Middle East, aspects of the law of security over movables rather similar to the above considerations led the mercantile community to devise indirect mechanisms, based on a combination of contract and property concepts. It remains to be seen whether this will take place in the UAE. If parties do attempt to go this route, then they should be aware *inter alia* of various Civil Code provisions regarding the construction of contracts, sham contracts and so on. These provisions include Art. 106(2)(b), Art. 126, Art. 129(c), Art. 258(1), Art. 265(2), Art. 394(2), Art. 395, Art. 424, Art. 583 and Art. 613(c) Civil Code. Also see section 6, entitled " Some consequences of the *shari'a* influenced environment".

to allow the commercial community (aided by their lawyers and the courts) great freedom to create new methods of security in the interests of flexibility, that a system of security should favour the extension of credit through the strengthening of the position of the secured creditor at the expense of other groups in society and that self-help is usually the better way to effect enforcement. Others might challenge these assumptions, and take the view that even in the commercial context credit needs to be carefully controlled at all stages, that it is right to examine carefully on a case by case basis the justification for allowing a particular type of property to be given in security and for allowing a particular type of debt to be secured, that a proper balance between the interests of the various parties involved necessarily entails quite a high degree of restriction of the secured creditor's rights, that the creation of new types of security is the proper province of the legislator and that the involvement of the public authorities is preferable to self-help.

11.2 Comparative aspects[342]

11.2.1 The interaction of society and commercial law in a comparative context

As between France and England, the differences in the systems show that an apparently technical area of the law, in two societies which one might imagine to be substantially similar in their basic commercial needs, is to a great extent a reflection of, and influence upon, the culture of the societies concerned. The more a common lawyer studies the French system, the more aware he or she becomes of the deep differences in assumptions, philosophy and approach underlying the particular rules. End results are often reasonably similar, but there are also significant differences.[343] Mestre, Putman and Billiau comment on the differences between the two systems in the following terms:

Is this to say that credit needs are so different from one country to another? In truth, the aim pursued in both cases is the same: to encourage credit while providing as security company assets without transfer of possession. But a credit policy is not conceived simply in terms of economics or banking practice. It is also a function of the historical vicissitudes of the law of credit itself. The law of credit is not just a product of the evolution of the economy of credit: the opposite can also be true ... What is practical and self-evident in one legal security tradition can be a doubtful combination in another: legal cultures are not easily conciliable.[344]

---

[342] For a recent discussion of comparative law theory, see Mark Van Hoecke and Mark Warrington, "Legal cultures, legal paradigms and legal doctrine: towards a new model for comparative law", [1998] *International and Comparative Law Quarterly*, 1998, p. 495.

[343] See for example the problems which have occurred concerning the recognition of the floating charge in France referred to above: Mestre *et al., Traité de droit civil*, §180, 162–164 and §238, 223–225; and Dahan, "La floating charge". In addition to causing problems when an attempt is made to enforce the mechanism of one system in a jurisdiction belonging to another system, such differences can lead to misunderstandings and mistakes when a lawyer of one tradition attempts to understand another's system. Some such mistakes were made in the drafting of this article, and were pointed out by those kind enough to review it. No doubt others remain.

[344] Mestre *et al., Traité de droit civil*, §180, 163–164.

When the comparative net is cast further to encompass not only France and England but also the *shari'a* and the UAE, a similar conclusion is reached. When starting to study this area, one might be forgiven for expecting commerce to be reasonably uniform the world over, but in fact societies differ in their attitudes to it to a significant degree, and those differences are reflected in their law. The radical difference between the *shari'a* and English law attitudes to assignments of debts, discussed above, is a good example.

11.2.2 The UAE regime in the light of legal transplant theory

The system of UAE commercial law, of which the system of security over movables forms a part, presents an intriguing example of the transplantation of rules and institutions from one jurisdiction to another, an area of comparative studies where controversy abounds.[345] On one side are ranged such writers as Legrand (who states boldly and baldly that "legal transplants are impossible")[346] and the Seidmans (who have formulated a "Law of non-transferability of law").[347] On the other side, Watson declares that "legal rules may be very successfully borrowed where the relevant social, economic, geographical and political circumstances of the recipient are very different from those of the donor system",[348] and indeed that "transplanting is, in fact, the most fertile source of development. Most changes in most systems are the result of borrowing."[349]

The question of which of the two sides is right is of particular relevance in the Middle East. The jurisdictions of the region received a foreign system of law which was quite different in basic conception from their "indigenous" system, the *shari'a*. The sentiment of cultural distance from the secular law felt by some Muslims, and their desire to return to the *shari'a* in some form or other, is manifest in various ways, including the high *shari'a* content of the Civil Code.[350] This would seem to indic-

---

[345] See Gunther Teubner, "Legal irritants: good faith in British law or how unifying law ends up in new divergences", *Modern Law Review*, 61, 1998, pp. 14–18 for a summary of the main arguments.

[346] Pierre Legrand, "The impossibility of 'legal transplants'", *Maastricht Journal of European and Comparative Law*, 4, 1997, p. 114.

[347] Abbreviating the Seidmans' original formulation gives us: "the same rules of law in different times and places, with different physical and institutional environments, will not likely induce the same behavior in their respective role-occupants" (Ann Seidman and Robert B. Seidman, *State and Law in the Development Process: Problem Solving and Institutional Change in the Third World*, Basingstoke, Macmillan, 1994, pp. 44–46). Montesquieu is often cited: "The political and civil laws of each nation ... must be so specific to the people for which they are made, that it is a great chance if those of one nation can suit another." Quoted in Otto Kahn-Freund, "Uses and misuses of comparative law", *Modern Law Review*, 37, 1974, p. 6.

[348] Alan Watson, "Legal transplants and law reform", *Law Quarterly Review*, 92, 1976, p. 81.

[349] Alan Watson, *Legal Transplants: An Approach to Comparative Law*, 2nd edn, Athens, University of Georgia Press, 1993, p. 95. Teubner expresses this as follows: "Alan Watson ... provides rich historical evidence showing that transferring legal institutions between societies has been an enormous historical success despite the fact that these societies display a bewildering diversity of socio-economic structures"; Teubner, "Legal irritants", p. 15.

[350] One notable general example is that of the 1982 Egyptian project to produce a *shari'a*-based corpus of legislation, see Bernard Botiveau, *Loi islamique et droit dans les sociétés arabes*, Paris, Karthala-IREMAM, 1993, Chapter 8 ("Le fardeau de la politique législative"). Sufi Abu Talib,

ate that the "culturalist" view put forward by Legrand is more relevant to legal transplants, at any rate in the Middle East, than Watson's view.[351]

If this conclusion is correct, then in order to see whether the Commercial Code security regime will survive and prosper, one needs to investigate not only the legal rules but also the cultural context in which they operate, as well as the degree to which the regime is regarded as imposed by a foreign culture.[352] An investigation into all the aspects of the cultural context goes beyond the ambit of this article. However, at least some of the answer to the question will lie in the degree of acceptability of the regime in terms of one "cultural" aspect which can be studied, the *shari'a*.

Looked at from one viewpoint, it might be difficult for the regime to fulfil the requirement of compatibility with the *shari'a*. Although the *shari'a* had various security mechanisms, the present-day UAE provisions are designed for a commercial environment which is based on *riba* and *gharar* and is therefore quite foreign to the *shari'a*.

However, the legislator has made a valiant attempt to minimize this difficulty. The very aspects referred to above as limitations of the system presumably result largely from a desire to reconcile the system with the *shari'a*. He has also used various devices, including the separation of the Civil Code from the Commercial Code, the dependence (to some degree) of the Commercial Code on the *shari'a*-based Civil Code and the use of some *shari'a* terminology and concepts, such as the preservation of the basic pledge concept rather than any system based essentially on registration. His task has been made easier in that the attitudes of the imported French system are not too distant from *shari'a* ideas. The rather suspicious attitude to security of French law, deriving ultimately from the same cultural influences that produced the prohibition on *riba* and *gharar*,[353] the general philosophy behind the French system of attempting to strike a fair balance between secured creditors, unsecured creditors and debtors, the tenor of the French rules (quite similar to those of the *shari'a*, for example the French and the *shari'a* definitions of pledge are far more similar to each other than either is to the English definition), all help to create a regime that its protagonists can at least argue is not too far removed from its *shari'a* counterpart.

---

cont.
the president of the special commission in charge of the project, referred to "the alienation which we have experienced in the shadow of foreign laws for more than a century" and to "the contradiction between ... what the Egyptian man believes and the laws which govern him" (cited in Botiveau, *Loi islamique et droit dans les sociétés arabes*, p. 285).

[351] Sir Otto Kahn-Freund stated that comparative law "becomes an abuse ... if it is informed by a legalistic spirit which ignores [the] context of the law". Kahn-Freund, "Uses and misuses of comparative law", p. 27, quoted by Legrand, "The impossibility of 'legal transplants'", p. 124.

[352] Legrand quotes FSC Northrop: "in introducing foreign legal and political norms into any society, those norms will become effective and take root only if they incorporate also a part at least of the norms and philosophy of the native society": Legrand, "The impossibility of 'legal transplants'", p. 118, note 22.

[353] The general common ancestry of the mistrust of interest and moneylenders is clear, and is present in all three "religions of the book", but the degree to which the similarities arise from evolutionary convergence or a common ancestry is beyond the scope of this article. On the relationship of Islamic law with other systems of law, see the bibliography in Schacht, *An Introduction to Islamic Law*, pp. 222–223 and N. Seignette's introduction to Khalil, pp. xxxvi–xlviii.

Libyan Economic Policy and Joint Venture Investments

*Salem A. Gammed**

1 INTRODUCTION

The rapidly increasing number of joint ventures established between Libya and foreign capital, state owned and private, represents a salient new feature in the Libyan economy. The turn towards joint ventures with foreign participation has been a result of gradual changes in Libyan economic policy. However, an investment in or with Libya is, in many instances, a special case that has to take into account the characteristics of the Libyan economy and the lack of experience with joint business relationships of this sort.

In is inevitable that any study dealing with Libya begins with a statement that the Libyan system after the revolution is unique. No other country has a socio-economic structure that resembles the Libyan *Jamahiriya*.[1] The principles on which this system is based can be summarized in two words: mass government. However, this varnish of simplicity begins and ends with the definition. In fact the Libyan system is very complicated, and in constant evolution – a never-ending process of experiments and continuing changes for improvement. Although the political and economic situation of socialism is one of great delicacy after the collapse of socialism in Eastern Europe, the Libyan government insists on adopting what is being called a new version of socio-economic system.[2]

---

* Assistant Professor of Private Law, Faculty of Law, Gar Younis University, Benghazi, Libya.

[1] *Jamahiriya* has been the official name of Libya since 2 March 1977. The General Mass Conference (the Libyan Parliament) passed a most important constitutional document which was entitled the "Declaration of People Authority and First *Jamahiriya*".

[2] From being a carbon copy of the eastern states, the Libyan system developed into its new *Jamahiriya* which, it was said, is a new version of socialism. The basic principles of this system were laid down in the teachings of the School of the Sun. The system is also influenced by the cooperative inspired by Robert Owen (1777–1858), the Phalansteres of Charles Fourier (1772–1837), the Paris Commune of 1871, the Russian Soviets of 1905–1917 and the Yugoslav worker self-management, which all contained important elements which became incorporated in Libyan *Jamahiriya* and mass government. See A. Mehoub, *Lectures in Libyan*

Having taken power on 1 September 1969, the revolutionary government advanced itself with two declared broad tasks. First, to free the country from foreign military bases and what was described as foreign imperialism; second, to reorganize the economy according to the Universal Third Theory.[3] The great waves of nationalization generated by the liberation created a momentum of sizeable force. Many measures such as nationalization, cessation and prohibition of foreign investments were adopted in many sectors.

2 TAKING OVER THE NATIONAL MEANS

There was a process of "Libyanization", that is that Libyan citizens and firms should, to the extent possible, replace foreigners and foreign-owned firms in trade, government and related activities. In 1970, the government embarked upon a programme of progressive nationalization. The nationalization programme included sequestration of all Italian assets, socialization of the banking and insurance business and the placing of all forms of trade under government control. In addition, a progressive substitution of Libyans for foreign administrative and management personnel in resident foreign concerns was another aspect of the government's policy in replacing foreigners and foreign-owned firms with Libyans.

In the banking system, as a first step, the government required that all banks be Libyan controlled and it bought out 51 per cent control of banks that had not converted to Libyan control. In July 1970 the government took 100 per cent control of four of the major banks that had foreign minority ownership. In December 1970 the government purchased outright all banks that still had some foreign minority participation. By a process of merging, the number of commercial banks was reduced to five. The result was a banking system not only nationalized but also socialized.[4] At the same time, insurance companies were required to have 60 per cent government participation. In 1971 they were totally taken over by the government and merged from four to two and afterwards in only one company.[5]

In the petroleum sector a constantly increasing financial squeeze was put on the companies, and the threat of widescale, if not overall, nationalization of their con-

---

cont.

Civil Law, Theory of Possession, typescript, officially unpublished, Faculty of Law, Benghazi, 1982, pp. 15–18.

[3] The second goal was clearly declared in the interim Constitutional Proclamation of 11 December 1969. Art. 9 stated that: "The state relies on a national comprehensive socio-economic system. In order to achieve national development goals, cooperation between private and public sectors shall be considered for the purpose of economic plans."

[4] See the Act 153/1970, 6 LOG (Libyan Official Gazette) Year 9, 17 February 1971. The first article of this Act stated that: "From the date of which this Act comes to force, all non totally Libyan-owned companies are prohibited from engagement in any banking business. All foreign participation in the existing banks shall be owned by the state."

[5] See M. S. Sharkawi, "Legal aspects of public sector in Libya" (article in Arabic), 1 *Derasat Kanonia*, Gar Younis University (yearly law review published by the Faculty of Law), Benghazi, Libya, 1971, pp. 251–259. K. Shawi, "Nationalization of foreign shares in commercial banks and State's participation in insurance companies" (in Arabic), *Derasat Kanonia*, 1, 1971, p. 285.

cessions, production and transport facilities was a growing spectre. In 1970 LINOCO (Libyan National Oil Corporation) was created for petroleum policy implementation. In July 1970 LINOCO's jurisdiction was expanded by legislation that nationalized the foreign-owned Esso, Libya Shell, ENI marketing subsidiaries and Petro Libya (a small local company) and transferred their operations to LINOCO.[6] These operations included managing companies in importation, distribution and sale of refined petroleum production in Libya. In 1971 the companies were merged into a single countrywide marketing enterprise.[7] In December 1971 the government nationalized the shares of British Petroleum (BP) in Nelson Bunker Hunt Serir field.[8] In 1973 Nelson Bunker Hunt itself was nationalized.[9] In 1972 Libya was in the forefront of OPEC in addressing itself to the question of government participation in the capital structures and decision-making processes of the oil companies. The companies vigorously opposed the proposal, and from the moment when OPEC settled for the 20 per cent participation in first the Arabian American Oil Company (ARAMCO) to when most of the other major companies agreed in 1972, Libya was already either increasingly insisting on majority partnerships or taking over projects entirely. In 1972, the Libyan government reportedly had a 51 per cent interest in a fifteen-year agreement with the ENI subsidiary and other ENI (Italian organization) ventures in Libya. The government in its settlement with Esso, on the pricing of natural gas exported to Italy and Spain in 1972 had obtained an option of 50 per cent of Esso's liquefication plant at Marsa al Burayqah. In September, an agreement for 50 per cent participation in ENI's concession and profits was signed.[10] One year later, a partnership agreement was signed between LINOCO and Amerada Libya.[11] This was followed by many other partnerships such as the agreements with Continental Petroleum Libya, Marthoun Petroleum Libya and Occidental Petroleum Limited.[12]

Briefly, by mid-1972, the government's role in the economy was overwhelmingly predominant. Mineral rights were vested in the state, as were water rights, for all practicable purposes. Basic infrastructure facilities (for instance motorways, communications, ports, airlines, airports and electric power) were directly or indirectly owned and operated by the government. After the expulsion of the Italian colonists, the government became a major landowner. It directly controlled the money market and, though its exchange control mechanism, it controlled the movements of foreign and domestic trade. In other words, the government was progressively

[6] See the Act 69/1970, 44 LOG, 11 August 1970.
[7] R. F. Nyrop, *Area Handbook for Libya*, 2nd edn, US Government printing office, Washington, 1973, p. 249.
[8] See Act 115/1971, 6 LOG, 10 February 1972. It was said that this nationalization was made in response to the British government's failure to intervene to prevent Iran from taking possession of islands in the Persian Gulf. Nyrop, *Area Handbook*, p. 250.
[9] Act 42/1973, 32 LOG, 12 February 1973.
[10] See the Act 131/1972 concerning approval of the contract of partnership between Libyan National Oil Company and Agip Oil company. A memorandum related to the subject submitted by the Libyan Petroleum Minister; 57 LOG, Year 10, 12 February 1972.
[11] 41 LOG, Year 11, 1 October 1973.
[12] See Act 8/1974 concerning contracts of partnership and investments between LINOCO and these companies in 47 LOG, Year 12, 2 July 1974.

becoming the proprietor, or senior participant in, an ever larger proportion of the country's productive activities.[13]

As a result of nationalization and Libyanization, the government had super-abundant capital resources. The problem facing it was how to use these to create the non-petroleum physical resources, human resources and domestic production that the country lacked. Clearly, the country would have to import in the short run and probably in the medium as well, most of its management, technical expertise and large though decreasing amounts of its skilled manpower. This, of course, would run fully counter to the government's policy of placing Libyans at the upper level of management and giving Libyans control of enterprises, a policy that formed a major building block of the revolutionary government's policy edifice. The decision, in the beginning, was political rather than economic; in addition to inviting foreign capital, the government adopted a policy of joint venture investments.

3 JOINT INVESTMENTS

In spite of nationalization that extended to most economic fields, Libya like any other developing country, is in need of foreign investments to obtain management skills, knowhow and transfer of technology. Therefore, in addition to inviting numerous foreign and multinational companies to invest their capital in the country, a number of joint ventures with foreign investors were created.[14] The formation process of joint ventures in Libya began in 1972. The first Libyan foreign joint company (Arab Libyan Algerian Shipping Company) was established and registered in Tripoli.[15] In addition to domestic investments, great care has been given to investment of national capital abroad, and numerous agreements concerning economic cooperation[16] and establishment of corporations with other states were signed. From 1972 over three hundred joint companies have been established or joined.[17] No specific policies or rules were followed in joining or establishing joint investments.

---

[13] In addition to the infrastructures mentioned earlier, the government has monopolies in the production of sugar, salt, tobacco and matches, marketing of petroleum products, petrochemicals, steel, cement, pipes, leather and footwear, textile, floor milling, food production and pharmaceutical trade. In short, all the economic sectors were socialized. See the Cabinet decision concerning transaction and business which can only be carried out by state-owned companies and public enterprises: 1 LOG, Year 16, 19 January 1978.

[14] Such as civil construction, oil production, electricity projects, agriculture and land reclamation, machinery and the like.

[15] See the text of the agreement providing on establishment of this company in 42 LOG, Year 10, 1972.

[16] It would be too arduous to list all the legislation and treaties related to investments abroad. Some examples, however, could be given, such as the Act 23/73 concerning investments of national capital abroad (see 21 LOG, Year 11, 22 May 1973); the Treaty of encouraging transfer of capital between Libya and Malta (see 30 LOG, Year 11, 30 June 1970) and the Treaty of Arab Capital Investments and settlement of investment disputes between host states and investors of other Arab states (see 23 LOG, Year 15, 18 April 1977).

[17] The exact number of joint investments cannot be given because some of them have not been declared or their official documents have not yet been published. However, most of the joint investments abroad are listed in the annual reports of LAFICO (Libyan Arab Foreign Investment Company) and LAEB (Libyan Arab Foreign Bank).

3.1 Internally

Some investments are directly partnered by the government[18] while others are indirectly partnered through state-owned companies.[19] In the mid-1970s, the Libyan legislator started to include in the Articles of Association of state-owned companies provisions to enable them to participate in joint companies either with national or foreign partners.[20] This policy was followed by creating a Development Bank to invite and participate with foreign capital to create productive projects according to national economic policy.[21]

3.2 Externally

In early 1972, the Libyan government established the Libyan External Bank[22] to serve as a vehicle for Libyan assistance to other countries and to establish jointly with them banks and monetary institutions. The bank was entrusted with the task of financing development and investment operations on a commercial basis. It may participate in, purchase and create joint institutions and banks whenever necessary to achieve its goals.[23] The activities of the bank extended to many countries – by 1992, it either owned, or had participated in, thirty operational banks (see Table 1). In 1975 an Act concerning investments of national capital abroad was passed to organize not only government investments, but also any private investments. This Act may be regarded as the first attempt to build a legal infrastructure for the investment of national capital abroad. It established what was called the "Investment Council". This Council was authorized to draw up a policy for the state's investments, taking into consideration the proper economic factors. The government, because of its enthusiasm to support developing countries or for some other reasons, disregarded the Act and ignored the council.[24] However, this Act was clearly invalidated

---

[18] For instance, the Act 20/1970 authorized the Minister of Agriculture to participate with the Tunisian National Council of Fishing to establish the Libyan Tunisian Fishing Company. The Act authorized the minister to pay the Libyan government contribution from the third division of mining and industry budget. See 18 LOG, Year 10, 27 April 1972.

[19] For instance, the Act 9/74 concerning permission to the Public Company for Land Reclamation to participate with the Aberotious Company (a Greek engineering company) to establish the National Company for Land Reclamation and Erosion Resistance. See 16 LOG, Year 12, 16 April 1974.

[20] See for example Act 9/1974, 16 LOG, Year 12, 16 April 1974. The Cabinet decision of 24 April 1975, concerning the Articles of Association of the National General Company for Maritime Carriage, 14 LOG, Year 14, 17 February 1976; Cabinet decision of 21 May 1975, concerning the Articles of Association of the General Company for Electrical Constructions and the decision of 26 May 1975, concerning the Articles of Association of the National General Company of Textile and Weaving, 21 LOG, Year 14, 20 March 1975.

[21] See the Act 8/1981 concerning the Development Bank, 19 LOG, Year 19, 30 April 1981.

[22] This bank was established according to the Act 18/1972. 18 LOG, Year 10, 1972.

[23] Article 2/12 of the Articles of Association. See 47 LOG, Year 10, 28 September 1972.

[24] For example, the Cabinet made a decision on 12 December 1975 which agreed and approved Libyan participation with the Turkish government in establishing the Ammonia Farnlik Factory (a Turkish company). It authorized the Libyan External Bank to pay the government contribution, the partnership agreement. See 49 LOG, Year 14, 4 September 1976. See also the first article of the Cabinet decision concerning the establishment of a pharmaceutical company

Table 1 The geographical distribution of LEAB participation

No	Location	Name of the joint ventures
1	Arab	North African Commercial Bank
2	countries	Arab Libyan Mauritianian Bank
3		Arab Latin American Bank ARLK
4		Western Arab Bank for Investment and International Trade
5		Arab International Bank UBAF
6		Tunisian Economic Development Bank
7		Arab Financial Service Company
8		Arab Jordanian Investment Bank
9		Arab Bank for Investments and International Trade
10		Tunisian Libyan Bank for International Trade and Development
11		Arab International Bank
12		ABC Bank
13		International Trade and Finance Bank
14	Africa	Arab Libyan Nigerian Bank for Trade and Development
15		Arab Libyan Chad Bank
16		Arab Libyan Togo Bank for International Trade
17		Arab Libyan Uganda Bank for International Trade and Development
18		Assahel Commercial Bank
19		Arab Libyan Borcaina Bank for International Trade
20	Europe	Arab Greece Bank
21		Arab Italian Bank UBAI
22		Inter Continental Arab Bank
23		Arab Spanish Bank
24		UBAF Limited Bank
25		Arab Turkish Bank
26		UBAF Paris Bank
27	America	Arab American Bank UBAF
28	and Far	UBAK KERSOA Company
29	East	Petroleum Investments Company
30		Panama–Mexico Corporations
31		UBAF Hong Kong Limited

Source: *Annual Report of the LEAB* 1992.

as a result of the passing of a new Act concerning investments abroad. This was Act 6/1981 concerning the establishment of the Libyan Arab Foreign Investments Co (LAFICO) which, apart from banking, became responsible for most of the government's investments abroad.[25]

---

cont.
jointly with Malta and the Netherlands. This decision was made according to a memorandum submitted by the Minister of Health who was not a member of the Investment Council. See 21 LOG, Year 16, 19 January 1978.
[25] 13 LOG, Year 19, 31 March 1981. The annual report of the company for 1990 stated that: "The Libyan Arab Foreign Investment Company 'Joint Stock' is a Libyan incorporated

According to the Act 6/1981 LAFICO was created to gather and control most of the investments which were participated in and owned by ministries, public institutions, public organizations and state-owned companies. However, Article 6 exempted investments of the Central Bank of Libya, investments of the Libyan Insurance Company related to its objectives, external deposits of commercial banks, investments of the Arab Libyan External Bank, and government contributions in some international financial organizations.[26] Article 23 of the Act clearly provided the objectives of the company and it stated that:

1) The company, in order to vary income resources and develop national economy, invest Libyan capital abroad in sectors of agriculture, industry, tourism, shipping, fishing, mining, transportation and all other sectors on economical and commercial basis.
2) The company may carry out any activities which support achieving all or part of its objectives. It may in particular: establish, participate or possess, partly or entirely, projects in fields linked with its goals, carry out any other business according to the government's orders within the scope of cooperation with other states and, in order to fulfil its objectives, the company may establish projects and enter into agreements with other partners who organize or carry out similar business.

Having incorporated the company, LAFICO became responsible for most of the government's investments abroad. Therefore, the functions of the company became extremely wide and its activities extended to twenty-two countries in Africa, nine countries in Asia, seven countries in Europe and two countries in Latin America. The number of operational companies owned by the company or in which it has participated at 1990 was eighty-eight at the end of 1989. The paid up capital in these companies have reached approximately LD211 million (approximately US$700 million). Tables 2 to 5 show the participation according to the various economic sectors and the geographical distribution for LAFICO's participation.

---

cont.
company with a capital of 500,000,00 Libyan dinars. The company was established in accordance with law number (6) of 1982 issued by the General Peoples Congress dated 29 Rabi el Awal 1390 ADP (After the Death of the Prophet, which is one of the Libyan calendars) corresponding to 4 February 1981 as a joint stock company enjoying the nationality of the Socialist People's Libyan Arab *Jamahiriya* having a legal status and independent financial responsibility. The objective of the company is to invest Arab Libyan Funds outside the Socialist People's Libyan Arab *Jamahiriya* in all economic fields on a sound economic basis.

The company's capital was set at LD500 million (approximately US$1.7 billion) divided into five million shares totally owned by the state.

The company in achieving its objectives is to establish and enter into partnership in totally or partly owned projects in the sectors related to its objectives and lending and borrowing funds and taking all legal functions within what it owns of moveable or immovable property or other rights". *LAFICO Annual Report*, 1990, p. 4.

[26] These organizations are the International Bank for Reconstruction and Development (IBRD), the International Monetary Fund (IMF), the Arabic Monetary Fund (AMF), the Islamic Development Bank (IDB), the Arab Economic and Social Development Fund, the Arabic Bank for African Economic Development, the African Development Bank, and the Arab International Bank for International Trade and Development.

Table 2 Libyan majority participation in companies established abroad

No. Company	Location	Libyan %
1 LIBMA Construction Company	London	80
2 Kalabely Jamaynder Company	Bangkok	75
3 Libyan Rwanda Company for agriculture development	Kigali	70
4 Arab Company for Real Estate ARESCO	Beirut	66.67
5 Libyan Maltese Co for agricultural chemicals	Malta	65
6 Libyan Borondese Holding Company	Bojambora	60
7 Libyan Rwanda Tourist Development Company	Kigali	60
8 Arab Libyan Maltese Investment Company	Malta	60
9 Libyan Greece Investment Company Libyan	Athens	60
10 Malli Company for animals, agriculture and property	Kigali	60
11 Libyan Chad Company for animal production and marketing	N'djamena	60
12 Libyan Chad Company for agriculture development	N'djamena	60
13 Metrovia Commercial Company	Geneva	60
14 Conteremix Commercial Company	London	60
15 Meditex Commercial Company	Tunis	55
16 Libyan Uganda Holding Company	Kampala	51
17 Libyan Maltese Holding Company	Malta	51
18 Arab Turkish Bank	Istanbul	51
19 Libya Uganda Bank for foreign trade and development	Kampala	51
20 Veba Petroleum Operation Company	The Hague	51

Source: *Annual Report of LAFICO*, 1993; *Annual Report of LEAB*, 1993.

Table 3 LAFICO's investment distribution according to economic sector

	Sectors	No. of companies	Paid up capital (LD million)
1	Holding and investment companies	22	87.142
2	Marine transport companies	6	33.351
3	Industrial companies	12	24.476
4	Tourist companies	9	22.501
5	Mining companies	6	15.450
6	Agricultural companies	14	14.745
7	Fishing companies	3	6.536
8	Other companies	6	6.185
9	Real estate companies	2	0.552
10	Commercial companies	8	0.419
	Total	88	211.357

Source: *LAFICO Annual Report*, 1990.

Table 4 Geographical distribution of LAFICO's investments

Geographical distribution	Participation	%	LD invested	%
Arab world	32	36.6	11,933,272	53.0
European countries	18	20.4	34,457,802	16.3
African countries	18	20.4	26,281,093	12.4
Asian countries	4	4.5	20,986,354	9.9
State of Malta	14	15.9	15,073,644	7.1
Latin American countries	2	2.5	2,625,512	1.3
Total	88	100.0	211,357,677	100.0

Source: *LAFICO Annual Report*, 1990.

Table 5 Libyan foreign 50-50 joint companies

No.	Company	Location
1	Pak-Libya Holding Company	Karachi
2	Libyan Liberia Holding Company	Monrovia
3	El Hambra Holding Company	Madrid
4	Libyan Morocco Holding Company	Casablanca
5	Libyan Sudanese Holding Company	Khartoum
6	Libyan Algerian Shipment Company	Algiers
7	Libyan Turkish Shipping Company	Istanbul
8	Libyan Tunis Shipping Company	Tunis
9	Astrises Industrial Company	Athens
10	Libyan Mauritanian Fishing Company	Nouadhibou
11	Libyan Togolese Fishing Company	Lorne
12	Libyan Maltese Fishing Company	Malta
13	Corntia Limited Company	Malta
14	Libyan Syrian Company for Industrial Investments	Damascus
15	Libyan Centra-African Mining Copmany	Bangui
16	Libyan Guinea Co for Agriculture Company	Conakry
17	Libyan Turkish Agriculture Company	Ankara
18	Libyan Togo Agriculture Company	Lorne
19	Libyan Liberian Development Bank	Monrovia
20	Libyan Tunisian Development Bank	Tunis
21	Libyan Niger Company for Agricultural Development	Niamey
22	Libyan Centra-African Company for Agricultural Production	Bangui
23	Libyan Cameroon Company for Agricultural Production	Yaounde
24	Libyan Sierra Leone Agriculture Company	Freetown
25	The Mediterranean Airlines Company	Malta
26	Libyan Maltese Engineering Company	Malta
27	Libyan Centra-African Trade Company	Bangui
28	Swan Washer Company	Malta
29	Arab Fishing Company	Alexandria
30	African Investment Company	Tripoli
31	Arab Book Press	Tripoli

Sources: *LAFICO Annual Report*, 1993; *LEAB Annual Report*, 1993; Ministry of Economy, Government of Libya.

It is understood that many joint corporations were exempted from LAFICO's control company because they carry out their activities on a non-commercial basis but it is not clear why other commercial enterprises were exempted. On the other hand, Act 6/1981 authorized the Cabinet to exclude other projects without providing any criteria for this power. This Cabinet may withdraw all LAFICO's functions either by exempting the existing companies or creating new exempted ones. It would have been better if the Act excluded only the government's contributions to international organizations and non-commercial enterprises and provided specific criteria for excluding any project in the future.

It is worth mentioning that the Libyan legislator, even after the creation of LAFICO, still provides state-owned companies with the ability to participate with other legal institutions, by any means, in joint business. This simply means that these companies can create joint ventures outside the control of LAFICO or any other specialized corporation. Apparently the legislator, instead of harmonizing with previous laws, disregards them when composing new ones. It also seems, in creating new state-owned companies, he copies old articles in spite of their discrepancy with the law.[27]

---

[27] Many examples can be given, such as the Garyan Building and Constructions Company and the Jdabya Construction Company, which were created by the Housing Minister decision No. 161/82 and 166/82 respectively, 32 LOG, Year 20, 27 October 1982. In fact, many joint investment companies were created and controlled jointly by these companies. For instance, see Cabinet decision No. 70/1989 concerning permission to Elgabel Algharbi Company for Agricultural Production to participate with Elbostan Company (a Lebanese company) to create a joint venture company. See 8 LOG, Year 27, 17 April 1989.

Jordan's Financial Laws: An Introduction to an Arab Model in Securities Regulation*

*Lu'ayy Minwer Al-Rimawi***

1 PREFACE

This article looks briefly at Jordan's financial laws as an Arab model in securities regulation. Special attention will be given to its securities laws as Jordan is viewed as one of the first Arab countries to have issued a specific securities Act. In order to give a fuller picture, Jordan's banking, company and investment regulations will be briefly examined. This article will not touch directly on issues relating to *shari'a* law in regard to general concepts of finance and other related matters. Much scholarly work has already been done on the position of Islam *vis-à-vis* modern issues like banking and the concept of *riba* or interest,[1] insurance,[2] contract law,[3] commercial litiga-

---

* This paper is also part of an academic presentation which the author delivered before the annual Cambridge International Symposium on Economic Crime held on 13–19 September 1998 at Jesus College/University of Cambridge.
** LLB (Jordan University), LLM (Cambridge University), MSc (LSE). The author lectures in public international law and researches financial regulation at the London School of Economics and Political Science/University of London.

[1] See for example, C. Mallat, "The renaissance of Islamic law: constitution, economics and banking in the thoughts of Muhammad Baqer As-Sadr", PhD thesis, London University, 1990. S. Madi, "The concept of unlawful gain and legitimate profit in Islamic law", PhD thesis, London University, 1989; N. Thani, "Legal aspects of the regulatory framework of the Malaysian financial system", PhD thesis, London University, 1993, especially pp. 278–320. For articles, see for example A. Mayer, "The regulation of interest charges and risk contracts: some problems of recent Libyan legislation", *The International and Comparative Law Quarterly*, 28 (4), 1979, especially pp. 541–553; N. Cagatay, "Riba and interest concepts and banking in the Ottoman empire", *Studia Islamica*, 32, 1970; M. Parker, "The rise and rise of Islamic banking", *The Middle East*, October 1987.
[2] See for example, F. Moghaizel, "Insurance in the light of Islamic legal principles", PhD thesis, London University, 1991.
[3] See for example, S. Al-Kuhaimi, "Contract law and the judicial system in Saudi Arabia", PhD thesis, London University, 1982.

tion,[4] etc. In particular, the article will present a general perspective on securities regulation, account for the Arab world's recent interest in its securities markets; and advance a critique of the Jordanian definition of the term "financial security" after having briefly looked at the American and English definitions of the term.

2 GENERAL PERSPECTIVE

Although Arab countries did not participate in the 1980s intense global financial deregulation, it is highly apt that they should now stress tackling their financial services regimes and securities markets regulation. Yet despite Arab governments' recently proclaimed interest in developing regional securities markets, Arab representation in international regulatory debates remains noticeably absent. Throughout the various EBRD conferences related to securities markets in emerging economies, one has rarely come across any Arab delegation.[5]

Stable macroeconomic conditions, orderly exchanges, competent financial and banking systems, coupled with effective legal corporate structures underpinned by efficacious legal procedures, are all among the prerequisites for well-functioning securities markets. Nevertheless, if Arab securities markets are to prosper domestically and attract substantial foreign portfolio investments, more attention must be paid to current global regulatory debates. We live now in an era of integrated and globalized securities markets, where highly complex legal mechanisms are constantly evolving and passed from one jurisdiction to another. Recent globalization of the securities markets is enabling issuers to raise capital outside their own countries. In 1985, US$4.3 billion in international equity issues were completed worldwide. This market grew to US$20.9 billion in 1987 and US$22.5 billion in 1992.

2.1 The domestic economic rewards of orderly securities markets[6]

For their parts, securities markets are often a composite of many different components: broker-dealers, physical or electronic exchanges, clearance and settlements organizations, agents for issuing the securities, institutional underwriters of securities, etc. It is also often advocated that proposed securities laws for emerging economies should include incentives to increase the supply and demand of securities and promote liquidity in the market. However, the aims of securities regulations include governing public and private issues of securities, corporate listing, disclosure requirements, defining and facilitating the contributions of investment companies, pension funds and insurance companies, all of which are often said to be sub-

---

[4] See for example, I. Ghanem, "The role of Islamic law in commercial litigation in North Yemen", PhD thesis, University of London, 1987

[5] Though, during the second Amman MENA economic summit, senior businessmen, fund managers and regional market operators and officials held very constructive workshops on regional capital market developments.

[6] For example, annual average net private portfolio equity flows to developing countries increased from US$1.3 billion in 1983–1990 to US$39.5 billion in 1994 only. On the other hand, annual average net loans made to developing countries dropped from US$42.3 billion in 1977–1982 to US$3.6 billion in 1993.

ject to prudential regulation which aims at maintaining systemic stability and the avoidance of concomitant moral hazards. (For example, the collapse of Barings Bank because of systematic abuse in derivatives trading has raised considerable implications for systemic stability repercussions in securities firms.)

Evidently, the structure of regulation depends largely on the existing institutional financial structure, the sophistication of the economy, reactions to notable financial scandals[7] and the financial and legal philosophy of any given country. In addition, the system of financial regulation can also depend on the historical-political relationship between the central government and the financial sector, as was evident in the traditionally self-regulatory system of the City of London before the Big Bang.[8] Here the unique importance of the City as a financial centre which has even often helped provide finance for expensive Crown activities throughout the centuries, has effectively meant a balance of power tilting towards the City and its operators.[9] However, after the Big Bang, the self-regulatory structure became two-tiered.[10] Under that structure the Securities and Investment Board (SIB) delegated its regulatory responsibility to self-regulatory organizations (SROs). Here the SIB (like the British Panel on Mergers and Acquisitions) was considered a public body, whose decisions were amenable to judicial review. Originally, five SROs obtained recognition from the SIB. These were: the Securities Association (TSA), the Financial Intermediaries Managers and Brokers Regulatory Association (FIMBRA), the Life Assurance and Unit Trust Regulatory Organization (LAUTRO), the Investment Management Regulatory Organization (IMRO) and the Association of Futures Brokers and Dealers (AFBD). After a shake up in British SROs, largely resulting from functional overlapping, three SROs were in operation: the Securities and Futures Authorities (SFA), IMRO and the Personal Investment Authority (PIA). However, in light of new regulatory changes in the UK, the SROs will remain in charge until the passage of the regulatory reform legislation, though enforcement and

---

[7] Well-known historical English examples in this sense are the 1697 Act to Restrain the Numbers and Practices of Brokers and Stock Jobbers (which was passed after a damning report of the Royal Commission of Trade in England) and the 1720 Bubble Act (enacted after the disastrous collapse of the share price of the South Sea Company). See George Gilligan, "The origins of UK finanacial services regulation", *The Company Lawyer*, 18(6), 1997, pp. 171, 174. See also generally G. Robb, *White-Collar Crime in Modern England: Financial Fraud and Business Morality, 1845–1929*, Cambridge University Press, 1992.

[8] The financial self-regulatory system of the City of London is also often attributed historically to decentralization and lack of strong state interference. Local administration of economic, political and legal matters (civil and criminal), which persisted until the nineteenth century, had strongly influenced the development of English markets and industries. This was also underpinned by a local and national culture which believed that "commerce is a domain of private transactions". The City's poweful international financial clout had also guaranteed its historically autonomous position *vis-à-vis* all other cities of England. In more recent times, the lobbying efforts of City professionals, its developed internal structures, which were averse to public models of regulation, together with its unique links with the Treasury and the Bank of England, have all helped maintain the City's regulatory independence. See Gilligan, "The origins of UK financial services regulation", pp. 167–174.

[9] *Ibid.*, p. 169.

[10] For the impact of the Big Bang on regulation in the UK see, for example, L. Gower "Big Bang and City regulation", *Modern Law Review*, 51, 1988. See also on UK financial regulation generally, B. Rider, C. Abrams and E. Ferran, *Guide to the Financial Services Act 1986*, 2nd edn, CCH Publications, 1989. For general books on the subject of securities regulations see L. Loss, *Fundamentals of Securities Regulations*, Boston, Little Brown and Company, 1983.

authorization decisions will be taken by the staff of the newly established Financial Services Authority. It is also expected that the SROs will continue their regulatory responsibilities until the regulation transferring their responsibilities to the Financial Services Authority becomes a law in early 2000.[11]

In its 1995 report entitled *Regulation of the United Kingdom Equity Markets*, the SIB stated that in order to achieve and retain investor confidence, a regulatory system must meet three basic criteria.[12] First, market users must be confident that they are treated equitably in the sense that no one group of market participants should use the market to the disadvantage of another. Second, there should be confidence in the integrity of the price formation process. This means that regardless of the method by which market users choose to deal, they must be able to do so in the confidence that quoted prices, so far as practicable, reflect the full extent of market activity at the time of the transaction. Third, market users should always be confident that all reasonable steps will be taken to maintain the safeguards against market abuse and that adequate measures (effective and timely) will be undertaken in order to punish abusers. It is also worth mentioning here that the SIB report dealt in detail with many regulatory issues such as transparency, the market-making system, market conduct and regulation in a diverse marketplace (i.e. centralized markets in an economic sense when the market has ceased to be centralized organizationally, especially OTC and overseas trading of UK equities). The report extolled the virtues of high quality and timely trade information, as the best assurance for continued integrity of the price formation process, especially following the SIB's agreement with the London Stock Exchange to significantly increase the Exchange's post-trade transparency requirements.[13] Moreover, the SIB report highlighted the increasing importance of international regulatory dimensions and pointed out that domestic regulation was becoming marginalized or an ever-smaller part of the whole scheme of securities regulation.[14]

3 INCREASING ARAB ATTENTION TO THEIR SECURITIES MARKETS[15]

3.1 Introduction

It is pertinent to start by mentioning that most Arab equity markets have recovered noticeably following the peaceful resolution of the February stand-off between

---

[11] See *CCH Financial Services Newsletter*, No. 4, April 1998, p. 1.
[12] See generally *Regulation of the United Kingdom Equity Markets: Report by the Securities and Investment Board*, The Securities and Investment Board, June 1995, London.
[13] For a follow-up on this report, see also *Regulation of the United Kingdom Equity Markets, Market Views: A Digest of Responses to SIB's Discussion Paper*, The Securities and Investment Board, June 1995, London.
[14] In this regard, the SIB also set up a working party drawn from the SROs, the Bank of England, the Treasury, British industry and academia to identify and address the implications for international regulation of the increasing internationalization of securities business.
[15] See p.2, http://www.fsa.gov.uk/launchdc/appl.htm.

the US and Iraq.[16] Gulf equity markets have especially rallied in the immediate aftermath of the UN brokered deal with Iraq.[17] In Saudi Arabia, for example, the stock exchange has halted its downward trend since the beginning of 1998.[18] Bahrain's stock exchange also experienced tentative buoyancy when the market, in late February, rallied by 1.8 per cent compared with the previous week. The situation in Kuwait was similar, where the market over the same period saw an increase of 1.6 per cent. Capital markets in Lebanon, Jordan and the Palestinian self-rule areas also appreciated in that period, though to lesser degrees.[19] Recent figures provided by the Amman financial market also indicate that, compared to the previous year, 1997 witnessed an overall increase in trading of up to 40 per cent. Moreover, the value of shares held by non-Jordanians rose to JD100 million,[20] compared to JD26 million in 1996.

The sovereign bond market has also been receiving increasing attention from Arab countries.[21] For example, in late February 1998, domestic banking sources in Qatar reported that Qatar was preparing to make its debut in the international sovereign bond market to raise US$200 million. Several banks are competing to lead manage the issue including France's Société Générale and JP Morgan.[22] For its part, Moody's has rated Qatar at BAA2 with a short-term rating of P-2. Standard and Poor's has given Qatar a sovereign BBB rating with a stable outlook. Qatari banking sources, however, attribute Qatar's enthusiasm for bonds market to the success of Oman's $225 million bond issued in 1996. Qatar has so far borrowed more than $2.7 billion from syndicated loans and raised over $10 billion through non-recourse loans for various gas-related projects, as Qatar is keen to cash in on its sound

---

[16] However, in late August 1998, "Qatar's DSM Index, up 42 percent for the year, gained 3.6 percent to close at 141.88. Kuwait's KSE Index (added) 2.5 percent to close at 2,191.00. Morocco's CSE Index (added) 1.2 percent (to finish) at 875.25. Bahrain's BSE Index gained 0.7 percent to close at 2,557.36. Lebanon's BLOM closed at 913.63, while the AFM finished at 182.76. Tunisia's BVM Index inched ahead 0.1 percent, closing at 460.59. Oman's faltering MSM Index, down 40 percent so far this year after a 140 percent increase in 1997, was the big loser among the Arab bourses this week, dropping 4.7 percent to close at 285.84. Egypt's ESE Index down 1.6, (closing) at 349.88. The Saudi NCFEI All Index down 0.8 percent at 169.81." For full report see http://www.arabia.com/content/business/8_98/Bourse.30.8.98.shtml.

[17] This appreciation should be treated with considerable caution. It should be seen in the context of recent forecasts which estimate that Arab Gulf countries stand to lose as much as 25 per cent of their annual income due to steeply plummeting international oil prices (though admittedly this may produce a twin effect of massive privatization of publicly held corporations, concomitant with large scale lay-offs).

[18] By the end of February 1998 the index registered 181.78, an increase of almost 2 per cent from its average the previous week. In the same period the volume of trading increased by 5 per cent.

[19] See *Al-Sharq Al-Awsat* (a London-based Arabic daily) "Weekly Report on the Performance of Arab Stock Exchanges", 27 February 1998. However, at the end of August 1998 AFM's index reached 183 points.

[20] The Jordanian dinar exchange rate to the dollar is roughly about JD1: US$0.70.

[21] This relates to private, public and joint private/public Arab corporations.

[22] The same sources (quoting the corporate manager for finance at Qatar General Petroleum Corporation) also added that the corporation would be raising US$500 on the bond market. In addition, one of the Qatari corporations which is certain to raise finance from the international bond market (before December 1998) will be the Qatar Vinyl Company (QVC). See http://www.arabia.com/content/business/2_98/qatar26.2.98.shtml.

credit ratings. For example, a $1.2 billion bond issued by one of Qatar's three gas projects, Ras Laffan LNG Company (Rasgas), in December 1996 was well received. Moody's, however, has since downgraded the Rasgas bonds to BBB+ following the economic meltdown in South Korea, which has contracted to buy 80 per cent of the project's output. But the bonds are still rated investment grade because of the project sponsors' strength – mainly Mobil and QGPC.[23]

In addition, varying degrees of interest have recently been exhibited by many UK investment houses in the emerging markets of the Arab world. Such funds include: Flemings Securities, Barings, Foreign and Colonial, Merrill Lynch, JP Morgan and many more. In addition, specialized Middle Eastern mutual funds are currently set or being set up for the purpose of investing in the region. They include the Arab Countries Fund (Fleming), the Emerging Middle East Fund (Foreign and Colonial), Atlas Maroc (Financiers Atlas/France), the Maghreb Fund (Framlington), the Maroc Privatization Fund (GP Banque/France), the Middle East Opportunities Fund (Alliance Capital/Luxembourg).[24] However, Arab emerging markets can only represent a fraction of the market capitalization and sophistication evident in other emerging markets in Eastern Europe, Latin America and Asia Pacific. It has recently been estimated that total capitalization of Arab stock markets amounts to US$89 billion against the US$1,000 billion shared by the rest of the emerging markets. However, the region as a whole is believed to attract less than 1 per cent of the total capital flows into developing countries, and about 0.3 per cent of foreign portfolio investment.

3.2 Macroeconomic reasons for increased interest in Arab financial markets

Although one must emphasize that the economies of the region differ sharply in their per capita incomes and underlying economic structures, a combination of factors is responsible for the recent upsurge in Arab interest in securities markets.

The first factor is the spiralling expenditure costs of the Iran–Iraq war and the 1991 Gulf war; dwindling export revenues and oil global overproduction have forced many of the rich Arab Gulf countries to offset budget deficits by raising funds through issuing domestic debt securities.[25] As market-orientated treasury debt instruments provide a non-inflationary source of deficit financing, it was estimated

---

[23] *Ibid.*

[24] For useful general information on finance and investment aspects in the Arab world, see for example http://www.arabiaweb.com/business/financebanking.shtml (it covers information on a number of Arab investment corporations). For useful general information on Arab stock exchanges see also: http://www.embofleb.org/stock.htm (on the Beirut Stock Exchange), http://www.eyi.com/mideast/MEBBqart.htm (on the Doha Securities Market), http://accessme.com/AFM/ (on the Amman Financial Market) and http://www.alsadon.com/profile.html (on the Kuwait Stock Exchange).

[25] However, recent oil price projections are viewed pessimistically by Arab Gulf countries. Such projections indicate that the average price will not exceed US$17 a barrel. This makes the price US$2 less than the prices of 1996 and 1997 which were US$20.2 and US$19 respectively. In turn, this constitutes to a loss of more than US$10 billion a year to Arab Gulf countries. Financial sources also estimate that GCC states need to cut 20 per cent of their current spending in the coming three years in order to keep budget deficits to acceptable levels in

that Saudi Arabi's domestic public debt (mostly in the form of debt securities) had in the last four years risen from 50 per cent of GDP to 80–85 per cent.[26] However, Saudi Arabia's intentions to issue bonds to redress its fiscal imbalances dates back to 1987. King Fahed, in a television broadcast, then justified this on grounds relating to drastic decrease in state revenue.[27] In addition, many of the Gulf countries are gradually becoming less dependent on oil as their main export and are diversifying their economies by building petrochemical industries with significant potential for private sector contribution.

The second factor is that external borrowing is also becoming less accessible to poorer Arab countries. Foreign direct investment and, to a lesser extent, foreign portfolio investments are instead being viewed as the panacea for the region's deficits in financing requirements (which the World Bank says is the highest of any developing region). Indeed, the World Bank and the IMF have been instrumental in pushing for structural and fiscal reforms which aimed at ultimately rendering the region more attractive to foreign investment. Many Arab countries complied and took substantial measures to balance their budgets and current account deficits while simultaneously fostering privatization and reducing public expenditure. Since 1985 Jordan, Morocco and Tunisia have embarked on programmes of macroeconomic stabilization and structural reform.[28] Despite the fact that Syria's and Egypt's economies are characterized by pervasive public ownership, they too, have nevertheless embarked since the early 1990s on economic liberalization programmes. Securities markets in most Arab countries are currently experiencing considerable structural reforms. These reforms are being underpinned by the increasingly stable macroeconomic conditions in many Arab countries. In the last two years or so, inflation and budget deficits have been dropping steadily while GDP and financial markets capitalization have generally been on the increase. Algeria's GDP, for example, rose to 4.3 per cent in 1995 and about 4 per cent in 1996. Inflation, which reached 29 per cent in 1994 and 1995, dropped to 14 per cent in 1996. Egypt growth rate reached about 5.5 per cent in 1996. Lebanon also increased its fiscal revenue from 6.5 per cent of GDP in 1990 to 17 per cent in 1996. In Morocco the budget deficit fell from 12 per cent of GDP in the 1982 to 3.1 per cent in 1994. In Tunisia, GDP growth rate was 5 per cent, inflation rate was less than 5 per cent and budget deficit was 3 per cent (1995).[29] Jordanian macroeconomic

cont.
comparison with last year's spending which was more than US$88.4 billion. See for example http://www.arabia.com/content/business/8_98/GCCcover.2.8.98.shtml.

[26] It was also estimated that the collective average fiscal deficits of Bahrain, Kuwait, Oman, Qatar, Saudi Arabia and the UAE widened from 1.5 per cent of GDP in 1981–85 to 8 per cent of GDP in 1986–90, while rising to 9 per cent of GDP in 1991–95.

[27] See for example, Barry Finn's article in the *Financial Times* "Saudi Arabia plans first sale of bonds", 31 December 1987.

[28] According to some analysts, the tightening of fiscal policies in these countries lead to a "steep" decline in budget deficits from an average of 14 per cent of GDP in 1981–1985 to about 5 per cent of GDP in 1986–90 and 3 per cent of GDP in 1991–95. Average inflation decline was also estimated to have fallen from 9 per cent in 1981–85 to abount 6 per cent in 1986–95.

[29] See generally *Euro-Mediterranean Partnership: Forging New Links in the Miditerranean*, vol. 2, CCL Commerce, London, 1997.

figures have, however, been recently subject to controversy.[30] The IMF still cautions about the, until very recently, annual average decline of 0.5 per cent of per capita growth in Middle East and North African (MENA) countries. Moreover, on the eve of the third MENA economic summit in Cairo in November 1996 the IMF warned the region of continued dependability on favourable external factors to sustain high growth rates and financial balance improvements.

The third factor is the MENA economic summits. Various Euro–Mediterranean agreements, coupled with the Arab countries' desire to join multinational treaties like the WTO, EFTA and GATT, has also added considerable impetus to the momentum of privatization and economic openness.[31] Many Arab countries are now competing in outperforming each other in the provision of best conditions favourable to attracting foreign capital. Tax relief packages,[32] new anti-trust laws, unregulated foreign currency movement and convertibility, corporate ownership and freedom to lease and contract have all been provided to cater for foreign demand. Indeed, one may justifiably say that these events acted initially as a catalyst for a regional entrepreneurial culture which is also highly appreciative of the benefits of foreign investment.[33] It is no exaggeration to say that authoritarian Arab economics is gradually giving way to decentralization and genuine readiness to embrace the role of the private sector.[34]

The fourth reason is the general trend towards privatization is placing large amounts of equity at the disposal of foreign and domestic investors. Privatization plans are currently being implemented rigorously in Jordan, Egypt,[35] Morocco and Tunisia since the mid-1980s and early 1990s. In particular, Egypt has recently been highly commended by the IMF for its privatization drive. The IMF stated in its latest report that "Egypt's current privatization effort ranks among the top four

---

[30] The Jordanian government had initially announced that the growth rates for 1996 and 1997 were 5.2 per cent and 5.3 per cent, respectively. However, more recent figures produced by the Jordanian Department of Statistics pointed to 1 per cent and 2.5 per cent growth rates for 1996 and 1997.

[31] The Arab world in general is implementing serious steps towards institutionalizing the concept of the rule of law in its modern civic sense. For example, 1994 heralded the introduction of a Basic System of Rules (constitution) to the solidly *shari'a*-based country of Saudi Arabia. In equally progressive moves, Saudi Arabia acceded to the Universal Copyright Convention and the NY Convention on the Recognition and Enforcement of Foreign Arbitral Awards, and since 1996, has had a new set of Anti-Bankruptcy Regulations. See Salah Hejailan, "Legal Developments in Saudi Arabia", in this volume at p. 338.

[32] For example, around 250 new projects have recently benefited from tax exemptions in Jordan totalling more than JD 300 million (US$270 million). Projects cited to have benefited from these exemptions are in the sectors of industry, agriculture, hotels, hospitals, maritime transport and railways.

[33] This burgeoning culture is also being underpinned by attempts to create financing institutions such as the Middle East Development Bank capitalized at US$5 billion, with a paid-up capital of US$1.2 billion.

[34] For example, Egypt's Parliament recently amended the Companies Law to ease bureaucratic procedures. Such amendments now allow investors to set up firms ten days after submitting the required paperwork. The required subscription of authorized capital at the time of establishment has also been lowered to 10 per cent from 25 per cent, providing subscription takes place in three months. See http://www.arabia.com/content/business/9_98/Egypt.2.9.98.shtml.

[35] It is also estimated that foreign interest in large-scale non-oil projects in Egypt's lesser developed areas has this year grown up to US$1.00 billion (from January until August 1998). *Ibid.*

countries. Its privatization rate of about 1.5 per cent of GDP a year, is bettered only by Hungary, Malaysia and the Czech Republic." However, so far, eighty-four public companies have been sold with a market value of $US5.21 billion, accounting for about 7 per cent of Egypt's GDP.[36] Calls for privatization are now being voiced publicly and vociferously in many Gulf Arab countries. For example, the Chief of the Kuwait Economic Society was quoted as calling for full privatization of all public institutions. On the official level, the Kuwaiti National Assembly's legal experts, after months of deliberations, have examined the new privatization draft law, which attempts to regulate the sale of state-owned utilities and services. Kuwaiti officials had earlier confirmed that government planners and lawmakers would be meeting in late May 1997 in order to iron out potential problems expected to surface in the new privatization draft law. It has also been recently reported that Oman is conducting a feasibility study to privatize the management of its naval base at Wudam on the Arabian Sea. It is generally estimated that proceeds of selling state-owned corporations in the Gulf Co-operation Council can reach up to US$100 billion.[37]

The fifth reason is that a very important development with regard to equity and debt acquisition has taken place in the formerly sensitive area of foreign corporate ownership. Foreign individual and institutional investors are now allowed to purchase equities and bonds in some government and many private companies. Egypt, Tunisia, Jordan, Lebanon, Morocco, Oman, Bahrain (and the Palestinian Stock Exchange, currently capitalized at around $700 million) are among the Arab countries whose national laws allow foreign corporate ownership. However, Arab countries do vary considerably in their tolerance of foreign corporate ownership. While Oman allows foreign mutual funds to own up to 49 per cent of listed companies, Jordanian legislation, for example, last year scrapped the 49 per cent restriction on foreign ownership. In a landmark development Faroise de Consentre, a French division of Coca Cola International, and the American United Soft Drinks Production became one of the first wholly foreign-owned companies operating in Jordan after having finalized a deal to buy all the shares of Coca Cola Jordan. However, following the recent abolition of the non-Jordanian equity ownership ceiling in the AFM, foreign capital flows into the country are expected to increase substantially. Sectors which have recently been completely liberalized include transportation, insurance, banking, telecommunications and agriculture. Construction, retail, trading and metallurgy sectors were, however, excluded from this recent liberalization.[38] In addition, it is also generally estimated that foreign investment[39] in Jordanian companies rose to 43 per cent of market capitalization from 36 per cent in 1997 following the lifting of the 49 per cent ceiling on foreign ownership of Jordanian

---

[36] See http://www.arabia.com/content/business/8_98/Egypt.5.8.98.shtml. However, it is estimated that privatization has earned Egypt (from January 1996 to the end of June 1997) around $US1.53, with 40 per cent of the money paying off debts owing to banks, 55 per cent to the Treasury and 5 per cent as early retirement pensions. *Ibid.*

[37] See http://www.arabia.com/content/business/8_98/GCCover.30.8.98.shtml.

[38] Moreover, around 250 new projects have benefited from tax exemptions totalling more than JD 300 million (US$270 million). Projects cited to have benefited from these exemptions are in the sectors of industry, agriculture, hotels, hospitals, maritime transport and railways.

[39] Arab investments in the banking sector reached 48 per cent. Foreign investment in Jordan also doubled from $54 million between 1986 to 1990 to $112 million from 1991 to 1995.

enterprises.[40] Recent reports from Amman have indicated that non-Jordanian equity purchase increased to JD29.2 million ($41.7 million) in 1997[41] (although this twelve-fold increase was mostly from Arab countries).[42]

4 OUTLINE OF JORDANIAN BANKING, COMPANY, INVESTMENT AND SECURITIES REGULATIONS

4.1 General legal setting in Jordan

Given its small size and high receptiveness to external regional influences one cannot fully understand the Jordanian legal and financial systems without grasping Jordan's geo-political setting. Broadly speaking, Jordan's financial system is akin to that of neighbouring Arab countries, though one must hasten to add that it has traditionally been less liberalized than the Lebanese system and freer than the semi-centralized economies of Egypt and Syria. However, as in most LDCs, economic decisions in Jordan have often been made on political grounds. This fact is important especially when one attempts to understand the rationale behind many Jordanian economic decisions, financial, commercial and company laws.

As a civil-law country, Jordan's legal system has been influenced heavily by other regional civil-law states such as Syria, Egypt and Lebanon. These countries were, during different historical periods, under direct French colonial rule and subsequently heavily influenced by the French legal system (Syria and Lebanon until the late 1940s and Egypt during the late eighteenth century). In this respect, one can easily discern almost identical similarities between Jordanian commercial, shipping, penal and administrative codes and their Egyptian, Syrian and Lebanese counterparts. Yet, although historically Jordan was under British rule from 1921 until 1946, its tribal laws and Ottoman codes were almost kept intact. This, however, can be contrasted to British mandated Palestine where the British pursued domestic policies which substantially influenced its legal system.

---

[40] The issuance of Jordan's first GDR in London by the Arab Potash Company (APC), is also deemed as one the reasons to have initially stimulated foreign interest in Jordanian corporations. However, in early September 1998, APC shares, which on 2 September fell by the daily limit of 5 per cent to 4.28 dinars ($6.0), were still reacting to a slump in the value of their GDRs on international markets after poor half-year results. By early September 1998 the AMF Index plummeted to 177.18 points to its lowest level since mid-July. See the *Jordan Times* 1 September 1998 and 3 September 1998.

[41] Also between January and June of 1997, non-Jordanian investors bought shares worth JD39.5 million ($56.4 million).

[42] For example Arab investments in the banking sector reached 48 per cent: 57 per cent of this was in the Arab Bank, 61 per cent in the Arab Banking Corporation, 41 per cent in the Housing Bank, 19 per cent in the Jordan National Bank, 21 per cent in the Arab Jordan Investment Bank. In the industrial sector foreign stake totalled 22 per cent. Arab investments accounted for 10 per cent in the tobacco and cigarette company, 3.6 per cent in the cement factories, 41 per cent in the Arab potash and 27 per cent in the paper and cardboard factories. Foreign investment in Jordan also doubled from $54 million between 1986 to 1990 to $112 million from 1991 to 1995.

4.2 Outline of Jordan's banking regulations[43]

Prior to the establishment of the Central Bank of Jordan (CBJ) the 1925 agreement between the then Emirate of Trans-Jordan and the Ottoman Bank authorized the latter to act as the government's bank. The Jordanian Currency Act No. 35 of the year 1949 established the Jordanian Currency Council. Article 6 mandated that the Council should comprise from a President and four members. However, currency matters were earlier dealt by the Currency Act of April 1923 which was published in the Official Gazette of June 1923.[44] This Act was subsequently repealed by the Substitution of Egyptian and Ottoman Currencies by the Palestinian Currency Act of the year 1927, which replaced the Egyptian currency by the Palestinian pound. Article 2 mandated that the wording "Palestinian pound" should replace the expression "Egyptian pound" or "Ottoman Lire". The promulgation of this Act did not prohibit using Egyptian and Ottoman currency in Jordan. However, the Palestinian Currency Act of the year 1928 mandated specifically that Egyptian and Ottoman currencies in Jordan were no longer legal tender.[45] The Jordanian Currency Act No. 35 of the year 1949, which repealed all former Currency Acts, mandated that the Jordanian dinar should become the legal tender. It also pegged the Jordanian dinar to the pound sterling.

The Central Bank of Jordan Act No. 4 for the year 1959 mandated that a central bank should be established. In addition, the Jordanian government also issued the Supervision of Banks Act No. 5 of the year 1959 extending the supervisory role of the CBJ to all other operating banks in Jordan. The Control of Foreign Currency Act No. 6 of the year 1959 gave the supervision of all matters related to foreign currency to the executive committee of the CJB.[46] This Act was amended by the Act No. 33 of the year 1960. The official creation of the legal personality of the CBJ ensued after the Jordanian Council of Ministers gave effect to the Central Bank of Jordan Act No. 4 of the year 1959. The CBJ started its work officially in 1964. In addition to its monetary role, the CBJ exercises regulatory and supervisory regulation over commercial banks and other financial institution in Jordan.

Evidently, Arab central banks have traditionally played a crucial role in directing monetary and wider economic policies in the majority of Arab countries. This is nowhere clearer than in Saudi Arabia with its powerful Saudi Arabian Monetary Authority (SAMA). SAMA has traditionally enforced the views of the incumbent finance minister, strongly encouraged banks to give loans to local citizens at subsidized rates and heavily supported many domestic industries. *Inter alia*, SAMA also issues debt instruments for different maturity periods and non-negotiable deposits

---

[43] See article by Lu'ayy Minwer Al-Rimawi "Middle Eastern review: recent company and financial legal reforms in selected Arab jurisdictions", in the *European Financial Services Law*, 5, 1998, pp. 40–44.

[44] Art. 1 of the 1923 Currency Act replaced Syrian currency by Egyptian currency. Art. 4 mandated that government salaries must also be paid in Egyptian currency. For a general discussion on this matter, see *The Encyclopaedia of the Historical Development of the Jordanian Banking System*, vol. 1, 1996 (in Arabic).

[45] *Ibid.*

[46] All these acts were published in the Official Gazette No. 1413 issued in April 1959. *Ibid.*, p. 33.

to commercial banks. Yet, as a tool of central government planning, the CBJ has been instrumental in, on the one hand injecting funds into the Amman Financial Market (AFM), and on the other setting up financial institutions undertaking public services.[47] This can be seen through its demanding that commercial banks invest at least 20 per cent of their paid-up capital and reserves in stocks, 4 per cent of their deposits in bonds of public holding companies, and 4 per cent of their deposits in government bonds and bills. In addition, CBJ regulations allow banks to grant loans for the purpose of investing in the AFM.[48] However, the most important current banking acts and regulations in Jordan include the following: the Central Bank of Jordan Act No. 23 of the year 1971;[49] the Banking Act No. 24 of the year 1971;[50] the Public Debt Act No. 1 of the year 1971;[51] the Foreign Exchange Control Provisional Act No. 95 of the year 1966;[52] the Money Exchange Business Act No. 26 of the year 1992[53] and the Representative Offices Regulation No. 11 of the year 1977.[54]

Islamic banking in Jordan has also recently received a significant boost, especially after the Islamic International Arab Bank launched its banking services in February 1998. However, most recent lending activities that have involved Islamic banking in Jordan include the February 1998 agreement between the Jordanian Electric Power Company and the Islamic Bank (Jordan's most influential Islamic banking institution). Under the agreement, which is worth JD 10 million, the Islamic Bank will provide finance for the Jordanian Electric Power Company's purchases upon the guarantee of the company's assets. The agreement is subject to the Murabaha system.[55] For its part, the Housing Bank, Jordan's second largest financial institution, obtained in May 1997 a licence for commercial banking transactions. The CBJ allowed the Housing Bank to invest in projects and offer commercial loans to businesses and individuals in Jordan. This was largely due to an increase in activities,

---

[47] The CBJ has also been instrumental in setting up the Housing Bank, which is the largest bank in Jordan specializing in giving loans for housing purposes. The CBJ has also been instrumental in setting up the Jordanian pension fund, the Social Security Corporation.

[48] For example, from 30 December 1995 the CBJ raised the level of credit facilities granted to individuals for investment in the AFM from JD150,000 to JD500,000 (US$135,000 to US$450,000). With regard to corporations and other juristic legal personalities , the ceiling was raised from JD300,000 to JD1 million (US$270,000 to US$910,000). Should the amount requested exceed JD150,000 or JD300,000, the prior consent of the CBJ is required. See the *Central Bank of Jordan Annual Report* No. 31 for the year 1994, p. 48.

[49] Published in the Official Gazette No. 2301 dated 25 May 1971 and its many amendments, latest of which was Law No. 16 of the year 1992 published in the Official Gazette No. 3817 dated 1 April 1992.

[50] Published in the Official Gazette No. 2031 dated 25 May 1971, as amended by Law No. 11 of the year 1992 published in the Official Gazette No. 3808 dated 1 March 1992.

[51] Published in the Official Gazette No. 2283 dated 16 February 1971, as amended by Provisional Law No. 59 of the year 1976 published in the Official Gazette No. 2658 dated 5 October 1976.

[52] Published in the Official Gazette No. 1958 dated 22 October 1966.

[53] Published in the Official Gazette No. 3823 dated 30 April 1992.

[54] According to Art. 1, this Regulation is cited as "The Licensing and Control of Business of Representative Offices of Foreign Bank Regulations of 1977". It was issued in accordance with Art. 30 of the Banking Act No. 24 of the year 1971 and was amended by Regulation No. 85 of the year 1981.

[55] Since 1986, the Islamic Bank and the Jordanian Electric Power Company have signed lending agreements worth JD 70 million.

especially as the bank doubled its capital to 50 million Jordanian dinars (US$70 million).[56] However, the Arab Bank remains the most heavily capitalized Jordanian bank and by far the leading deposit-taking financial institution. It has in particular experienced intense foreign interest in its shares following recent Jordanian reforms, which have allowed for foreign acquisition of Jordanian equities. Moreover, the non-Jordanian share in Jordan's banking equities traded on the Amman Financial Market (especially following recent attempts at privatizing key national institutions) has reached new heights. It has recently been reported in Amman that the ratio of the non-Jordanian share in local shareholding companies by the end of November 1997 was 38.27 per cent compared with 32.43 per cent in October and 32.80 per cent in the end of 1996.[57] However, foreign stake in the services sector dropped below 8 per cent against 8.68 per cent in 1996. The size of non-Jordanian investments in 1997 was nearly JD 57 million.[58]

4.3 Jordanian company laws[59]

Many of early Jordanian company laws have their roots in corporate legislation enacted in neighbouring Arab countries. For example, the Companies Act No. 12 of the year 1964, in its provisions dealing with limited liability and foreign companies, re-enacted earlier Palestinian company law. In respect of publicly held companies, this Act followed rules adopted by the Syrian Trade Law. Before the Companies Act of 1964, companies in Jordan were subject to the Provisional Companies Act No. 33 of the year 1962, which replaced the Ottoman Trade Law which in itself was adapted from the French Trade Law of 1807.[60] Company law in Jordan is considered part of commercial regulations. However, Articles 2, 4 and 5 of the Jordanian Trade Act No. 12 of 1966[61] state that sources of commercial legislation in Jordan include commercial codes, the Civil Code[62] and trade custom. With regard to the Civil Code being a legislative source of commercial practice, Article 2/1 of the Jordanian Trade Act states that, if there is no adequate legislation available, then the rules of the Civil Code should be applied.

---

[56] The bank, which is owned by the governments of Jordan, Iran, Oman, Qatar, Kuwait and Arab businessmen, has assets estimated at US$1.6 billion.

[57] Recent monthly statistics of the Amman Financial Market also revealed that non-Jordanian share in the banking and financial sector recorded a growth in the same month from 47.72 in 1996 to 52.67.

[58] See *The Star* (a Jordanian English weekly) quoting an Amman *Financial Market Bulletin*, 12 February 1998.

[59] See article by Lu'ayy Minwer Al-Rimawi, "Corporate, financial and investment legislation in Jordan", in *The Company Lawyer*, 19 (1), 1998, pp. 28–31. See also article by the author "Jordan's recent Association Agreement with the EU and the latest reforms in Arab company and financial laws", *European Business Law Review*, 9, 1998, pp. 30–37.

[60] See Aziz Akili, *Commercial Companies under Jordanian Legislation: A Comparative Study with Company Laws in Iraq, Lebanon, Saudi Arabia and Egypt, Amman*, 1995 at p. 23 (in Arabic).

[61] This Act which comprised 480 articles was published in the Official Gazette No. 1910, 30 March 1966.

[62] The Jordanian Civil Law Code is also known as Act No. 43 of the year 1976.

The most important Company Acts in Jordan are the Companies Act No. 12 of the year 1964, the Provisional Companies Act No. 1 of the year 1989 and the Companies Act No. 22 of the year 1997.[63] This new Act comprises 286 Articles and is subdivided into 15 parts. Article 6 divides Jordanian companies into the following categories: general partnerships (Articles 9–40), limited partnerships (Articles 41–48), limited liability companies (Articles 53–76), limited partnerships in shares (Articles 77–89), and public shareholding companies (Articles 90–203). These forms of company are also found in company laws in a number of Arab countries including Egypt, Syria, Lebanon and Saudi Arabia. In addition, Part 8 deals with holding companies (Articles 204–208), Part 9 deals with mutual fund companies or joint investment companies (Articles 209–210) and Part 10 deals with offshore companies or exempt companies. The new Jordanian Companies Act No. 22 of the year 1997 became effective on 15 June 1997, one month after it was published in the Official Gazette.

However, the main highlights of the new Act centre around its "decentralization concepts", limiting routine procedures and facilitating the process of registering companies. For example in order to register a general partnership company, Article 11 of the 1989 Companies Act stipulated that "an application for registration shall be submitted to the controller together with original partnership agreement, signed by all the partners, and with a memorandum signed by each of them before the controller or the person authorized by him in writing". The same article stipulated that the partnership agreement and its memorandum must include the following: title of the partnership; names of partners, age and nationality; the partnership's capital and each partner's share therein; objectives of partnership; duration if limited, etc.[64] However, Article 11/b gives the controller the right to reject registering the partnership and in such an event, the partners may submit an appeal to the Minister within thirty days. Should the Minister dismiss the appeal, the appellants have the right to resort to the Higher Court of Justice within thirty days of their notification of the Minister's decision.

In this respect, it has also been estimated that it could take up to four months to register a public shareholding company.[65] Under the 1989 Act, the registration of these companies could take up to six months. Foreign companies are allowed to open branch offices in Jordan, but the majority will resort to this only in order to

---

[63] The Companies Act No. 12 of the year 1964, all its subsequent amendments, and all other legislation which may contravene it were abrogated by Art. 285 of the Companies Act No. 22 of the year 1977 and Art. 320 of the Provisional Companies Act No. 1 of the year 1989. The Provisional Companies Act No. 1 of the year 1989 was published in the Official Gazette No. 3596 dated 1 January 1989. The Companies Act No. 22 of the year 1997 was published on page No. 2038 of the Official Gazette No. 4204 dated 15 May 1997.

[64] Other information includes the name of partners authorized to manage and sign on partnership's behalf and the position of the partnership in the event of death of any or all of its partners.

[65] The registration of foreign companies or non-operating regional offices have also been organized. However, Art. 2 of the Representative Offices Regulation No. 11 of the year 1977 defines "Foreign Financial Companies" as: "foreign financial companies non-resident in the kingdom and not having any licensed branch operating therein". It also defines the "Representative Office" as "any office licensed with the provisions of this Regulation to carry on business stipulated therein".

execute a particular project by contract. Accordingly, they must close the branch when the contract is completed, though they may continue if they obtain a new contract. A regional office, on the other hand, may not conduct business in Jordan. Its duties are limited to promoting its company's business in the region, collecting information and examining the feasibility of obtaining contracts.

Article 281 of the 1989 Companies Act used to stipulate that application by a non-operating foreign company for the purpose of registration should be submitted to the controller with a number of documents, translated into Arabic and duly certified. These documents include the registration certificate of the company in its home country; the company's Memorandum and Articles of Association which indicates its capital and objective; a certified balance sheet of the company's latest fiscal year in its home country, etc. However, other documents include a copy of the power of attorney by which a resident person in the kingdom is authorized to deal with the company's affairs and any other data or information which the controller deems relevant. Article 281/b has incorporated what it terms "fundamental information". This includes the name of the foreign company and its headquarters; type of company and its nationality; the capital of the company and the name of its promoters or partners and any other information the controller deems relevant.

The abrogation of the Issuing Committee is deemed to be a main change. Such a measure was undertaken in a bid to speed up the registering of public shareholding companies and simplify raising capital through public or private shares offerings. In addition, double taxation has also been remedied. Companies are no longer required to pay a 15 per cent capitalizing charge and no more than 20 per cent of the net profit of public holding companies could be allocated to companies' special reserve funds. New changes also include introducing provisions which aim at promoting more simplified mechanisms for public shareholding companies which seek to increase their capital. The authority for approving premiums was given to the board of directors of the company concerned and the underwriter instead of the Issuing Committee. The criteria would ultimately depend on market forces rather than rigid bureaucratic interpretations.[66] Legal questions associated with mergers and the protection of shareholders' rights as well as other parties have also been addressed. Other important improvements brought about by the 1997 Jordanian Companies Act include:

- organizing a new breed of companies called "civil companies", which basically refer to parterships between professionals such as lawyers, doctors, accountants, etc. (Article 7);
- simplifying the registration procedures for lawyers who organize companies' Memoranda of Association (Articles 11, 57 and 92);
- devolving a number of responsibilities, originally undertaken by the Company Controller, to junior employees in order to speed up company registration (Article 248); and
- providing special provisions to register companies working within the Free Zones Area (Article 7).

---

[66] Prices of a new share offering were originally determined by an Issuing Committee at the Ministry of Industry and Trade in cooperation with the AFM.

Finally, under the most recent regulations in Amman, when attempting registration, Jordanian public shareholding companies have to pay JD3 per every thousand dinars of the authorized capital (instead of the previous limit of JD1 per every thousand). Added to this amount is stamp duty at a rate of JD3 per every thousand, which should be affixed to the application. Accordingly, newly established public shareholding companies have now to pay a gross fee of JD6 per thousand (instead of the overall former limit of JD3 per thousand). It is the present writer's view, however, that by indirectly double-taxing them on their authorized capital (as opposed to tax on their paid-up capital), the Jordanian legislature may have placed unnecessary burdens on newly established companies. Moreover, with the additional corporate listing fee (stock exchange regulations state that it must not exceed JD10,000), newly registered Jordanian public shareholding companies are likely to be discouraged from declaring high and ambitious authorized capital.

4.4 Jordanian investment laws[67]

4.4.1 *The investment setting in Jordan*

Jordan was one of the first Arab countries to opt for credit rating. It has recently been rated at the speculative grade (BB-) by S&P (on a par with Argentina, Kazakhstan, Romania and Russia and outperforming Brazil, Turkey and Venezuela). For its part, Moody's has also rated Jordan the speculative grade (BA3) (on par with Kazakhstan, Romania and Turkey and outperforming Argentina, Brazil, Peru and Bulgaria).[68] Yet some leading investment banks in the UK remain neutral in recommending Jordan for foreign investment.[69]

Jordan has also recently been paying considerable attention to increasing the share of the private sector in the economy. The share of the private sector in Jordan is expected to rise from 61 per cent in 1993 to 67 per cent by 1997. In 1995 Jordan achieved 30 per cent investment rate and in 1996 this increased to 31 per cent. Moreover, sharp increases in foreign currency held at the CBJ are also attributed to the improved performance of the economy and large inflows of foreign capital. The CBJ announced recently that foreign reserves have risen to a sharp 36 per cent in the first half of 1997 to a record $950, compared to $697 million for 1996. A recent statement issued by the CBJ has completely abolished all restrictions on money movement from within and without Jordan. This move has been interpreted by domestic observers as a strong sign of confidence in the Jordanian economy. Furthermore, although the CBJ's liberalizations have come as a formality, they are expected to provide a psychological boost for domestic investors. It is expected that they will encourage Jordanian investors to bring back into the country substantial amounts

---

[67] See article published by Lu'ayy Minwer Al-Rimawi, "An Overview of Jordanian Investment Laws Set in a Larger Regional Context", *European Business Law Review*, 8 (9), 1997, pp. 198–201.

[68] Over the past four years Jordan's budget deficit, which was 20 per cent of GDP, fell below 4 per cent and the balance of payments deficit fell to lower than 3 per cent.

[69] See Banque Paribas, *Emerging Markets Research Quarterly Strategist*, Winter 1996/97.

of their savings abroad. Around fifty projects have benefited from tax exemptions in the first few months of 1997 totalling JD60 million (US$52 million).

In May 1997 the Paris Club agreed to reschedule $400 million of the debt which should have been paid by 1999, for eventual payment over twenty-two years. However, the contributions of six countries account for 40 per cent of the total aid that Jordan receives from donor nations.[70] Yet, the US still remains by far Jordan's largest provider of foreign aid. Since 1990 it is estimated that Jordan has received a total of $2 billion in grants from the United States. American aid for the fiscal year of 1997 is likely to reach $146 million. However, one must hasten to add that Jordan has had a number of import/export laws and regulations, the most important of which is the Import and Export Act No. 14 of the year 1992. This Act took effect on 26 March 1992.[71]

4.4.2 Jordan's investment laws

Historically, Jordan has had a number of laws which aimed at promoting domestic investment. These include the Encouragement and Guidance of Manufacturing Act No. 27 of the year 1955; the Encouragement of Foreign Capital Act No. 28 of the year 1955; the Provisional Act for Investment Promotion No. 1 of the year 1967; the Investment Promotion Act No. 53 of the year 1972 and the Encouragement of Investment Act No. 11 of the year 1987. Jordan also has a number of specific laws which aim at promoting Arab and foreign investment in Jordan. For example, the Act Regulating Arab and Foreign Investments of the year 1992, has been instrumental in faciliating foriegn and Arab investment in Jordan.[72] Article 2 of this Act defines the investor as "Any non-Jordanian natural or juristic person". The same article defines the project as "Any investment activity in the fields allowed by this Act whether in the form of an individual establishment or a company". However, this Act distinguishes between Arab and foreign investors. Article 4/a, for example, states that Arab investors can invest their "capital", or "share" or "shareholding" in industry, tourism, health, agriculture, housing and construction projects.[73] Non-Arab investors may invest in these projects, but only upon recommendations by the Minister and with the approval of the Council of Ministers.[74] Article 9 protects the investor from having his investment confiscated.[75] Article 11 repeals earlier regulations issued in 1978 and 1986.[76] A follow-up to this Act were

---

[70] Namely, Japan, Canada, Switzerland, Norway, Australia and South Korea.

[71] Art. 14 abrogated the following regulations: Import Regulation No. 78 of the year 1976 and all its amendments; the Export Regulations No. 66 of the year 1979 and all its amendments; the Export and Import Control Act No. 50 of the year 1960 and all its amendments and the Minister of Finance/Customs Authorities Act of 1960 and all its amendments.

[72] This Act is also known as Act No. 27 of the year 1992.

[73] Art. 4/a also stipulates that the capital invested "shall not be less than the amount specified in the Regulations issued by virtue of this Act".

[74] Art. 4/c. However, Art. 2 defines the "Minister" as the Minister for Trade and Industry.

[75] Art. 9 reads "Neither Project subject to the provisions thereof shall be confiscated, nor its Funds attached or frozen or confiscated except through the court."

[76] These are the Regulations of Foreign Business Activities No. 51 of the year 1978 and the Regulations for the Facilitation of Investment of Arab Nationals No. 27 of the year 1986.

the Regulations Organizing Arab and Foreign Investments of the year 1992.[77] Article 2/a of these regulations states that the "capital" or "share" or "shareholding" of an Arab investor shall not be less than JD30,000. Article 2/b states that for non-Arab foreign investors the minimum shall be no less than JD50,000.[78] Article 6 of these regulations states that they do not apply to investors who invest in the free trade zone, where "specific laws", "regulations" and "instructions" apply.

The Investment Promotion Act No. 15 of the year 1995 was modified and offers customs and income tax exemptions. An Investment Promotion Corporation was established in according to the provisions of this Act, where Article 13 states that: "According to the provisions of this Act, a corporation called Investment Promotion Corporation shall be established and shall have a juristic personality with financial and administrative independence ...". According to this Act, no customs duties are levied on all fixed assets of the project for three years and only 15 per cent duty is levied on spare parts. Income tax exemptions have been divided into three categories: category A which entails tax exemptions totalling to 25 per cent, category B which entails tax exemptions of up to 50 per cent and category C which entails tax exemptions of up to 70 per cent. Article 2 defines the investor as: "The natural or legal person who invests in the Kingdom according to the provisions of this law". The same article defines the project as: "Any economic activity falling within the provisions of this Act and the regulations and instructions thereof."

Article 3 identifies the sectors which are liable to exemptions. These are industry, agriculture, hotels, hospitals, maritime transport and railways and "any other sector or its branches where the Cabinet decides to add according to a recommendation by the council". Article 30 states that non-Jordanian investors have the right to transfer abroad their foreign capital and any money resulting from the liquidation of their investments without delay. Article 33 gives foreign investors equal footing with Jordanian government institutions and sets a maximum time for the resolution of disputes.[79] Jordan is a member of the Amman Arab Agreement on Commercial Arbitration, which was entered into in Amman on 28 November 1987. Signatories include Jordan, Tunisia, Algeria, Djibouti, Sudan, Syria, Iraq, Palestine, Lebanon, Lybia, Morocco and Yemen. In addition, Jordan has an arbitration law, the Arbitration Act No. 18 of the year 1953. However, Article 22 of this Act has abrogated the following laws and regulations: the Sixth Chapter of the Palestinian Laws of the year 1933; the Amended Arbitration Act of the year 1946;[80] the Foundations

---

[77] These Regulations, known as Regulations No. 25 of the year 1992, were issued by virtue of Art. 12 of the Act Regulating Arab and Foreign Investments No. 27 of the year 1992.

[78] However, Art. 3 states that the share or shareholding of an Arab or foreign investor in sea, land and air transport shall not be less than JD100,000. Art. 4 also states that for commercial or contracting projects, the contribution by Arab or non-Arab foreign investors should not be less than JD200,000.

[79] Art. 33 reads: "Investment disputes between the investor of foreign capital and the Jordanian Governmental Corporations are friendly settled between the two parties, and if this dispute could not be settled in this way within a period of not more than six months, both parties may resort to the judicial authorities or refer the dispute to 'The National Centre for Settlemetn of International Disputes', to settle it either by agreement or by arbitration . . .".

[80] Published in the issued No. 1536 of *The Palestinian Documents* on 20 October 1946.

of Arbitration of the year 1935 and all Jordanian and Palestinian Acts and regulations which were issued before and contravene the provisions of the Arbitration Act No. 18 of the year 1953.

However, one of the cited drawbacks of Jordanian investment laws is the relative slowness in implementing their provisions. It has also been estimated that obtaining licensing for projects and registration of public holding companies could take up to 325 days. Moreover, the process of registering new projects can be complicated by the need to obtain different licences from various departments.

4.5 Jordanian Securities Markets Laws[81]

4.5.1 Introduction

Before the establishment of the Amman Financial Market (AFM), trading in stock took place through brokers and estate agents. The need to establish a stock exchange was recognized in the 1964 National Development Plan and was highlighted in the development plans of 1973 and 1976. The AFM, which started its operations on 1 January 1978, was initially set up jointly by the CBJ and the IFC. Since its establishment, the number of listed companies traded on the AFM has almost doubled. In 1978 there were only 66 listed companies, while now there are more than 125. Since 1980, the AFM has also had a share price index. This indicator was developed to represent market trends. In 1992, the index was revised and updated in cooperation with the IFC. Companies in the index are listed on their market capitalization, liquidity and price. The index currently comprises the sixty top Jordanian companies. Jordan also has a parallel market which was established in 1982. Trading on the parallel market started on 20 February 1982. However, by the end of the same year (1982), the parallel market was capitalized at JD16 million. Regional financial analysts have often observed that the AFM is highly sensitive to regional political instability. In order to limit speculation and stem price fluctuations, the value of daily quoted companies must not exceed 5 per cent up or down. In this respect, two main adverse factors have been important: first, the sharp decline in making progress in the Middle East peace process, and second, the continued dithering over the UN economic embargo over Iraq.[82] However, dealing on the AMF is expected to become fully automated by October 1998. There are also plans to privatize the AMF, something which is expected to draw more foreign investors. In

---

[81] For discussions on Jordanian securities laws, see article by Lu'ayy Minwer Al-Rimawi, "Middle Eastern review: regulation in the Jordanian and Palestinian securities markets", *European Financial Services Law*, 4, 1997, pp. 158–161. See also the article by the author "Jordan's recent attempts at modernising its securities regulations correspond to a wider regional setting", *The Company Lawyer*, 18 (9) 1997, pp. 282–285. See also feature article by the author "Jordan's New Securities Act", *CCH: Financial Services Reporter*, Issue No. 10, November 1997.

[82] For example, following the implementation of UN–Iraqi oil-for-food deal, the official indicator rose to 150, its highest level in nine months. Recent reports from Amman have indicated that the index of the P/E ratio was reduced from 18 to 13. It has also recently been estimated that P/E ratio shall be a multiplier of 10 in 1997 and that it is expected to decrease further to 7.5 in 1998. The P/E average according to the IFC is 21. Recent Jordanian estimates are more bullish, however.

addition the privatization of state-owned companies such as the JTC and JCFC is expected to increase the depth of the AFM, which has thus far been heavily reliant on trading in the equities of the Arab Bank.

4.5.2 Relevant legislation

Traditionally, the AFM has been subject to the Articles of Associations of the AFM, the Amman Financial Market Act No. 31 of the year 1976 and its amendments and the Amman Financial Market Act No. 1 of the year 1990 as amended by the Act No. 31 of the year 1992. The AFM is also governed by other directives and regulations. These include:

–   The Directives for Listing and Suspension of Jordanian Public Shareholding Companies. These directives comprise thirty-nine articles. Part 1 defines a number of terms including "The Regular Market", "The Parallel Market", "The Trading Floor", "Delisting" and "Suspension". These directives also deal with "Listing Requirements for Public Shareholding Companies at the Regular and Parallel Markets" (Part 2), "Transfer and Delisting of Public Shareholding Companies at the Regular Market" (Part 5) and "Suspension of Public Shareholding Companies from the Parallel Market and the Regular Market" (Part 6).
–   The Rules Covering Trading in Financial Papers on the Amman Financial Markets.[83] These Rules comprise over 255 articles. Part 1 deals with definitions. Part 2 deals with "Procedures for Trading in Financial Papers on the Floor of the Market"; this is subdivided into three chapters and thirteen sections dealing with management and administrative procedures, execution procedures and procedures for fellow-up on the execution of purchase and sale orders. Part 3 deals with "Procedures Regarding the Transfer of Title and the Trading of Financial Papers outside the Market Floor". It is subdivided into two chapters and four sections dealing with transfer of title of financial papers which are not subject to trading on the market floor through the legal department and trading shares issued by companies which are not listed on the market. Part 4 deals with "Settlement Procedures", subdivided into four chapters dealing with settlement procedures between brokers, settlement procedures for returned agreements, settlements' procedures between brokers and clients and settlement procedures between brokers and the AFM.
–   Regulations No. 26 of the year 1980[84] which were issued in accordance with Articles 34 and 51 of the Amman Financial Market Act No. 31 of the year 1976. These regulations comprise eighty-seven articles. Part 1 deals with various definitions. It defines financial paper as "Negotiable shares, bills and bonds issued in the Kingdom by the Government, governmental institutions, municipalities, or public and private Jordanian shareholding companies, or any other negotiable financial papers". It also defines securities transactions as "Buying and selling financial papers directly or through brokers". Part 2 deals with

---

[83] Issued in accordance with Arts. 3 and 87 of the Articles of Association of the Amman Financial Market.
[84] Known also as the Internal Regulations of the Amman Financial Market.

the "Management of the AFM". Part 3 deals with "Membership" "Duties of Public Shareholding Companies" and "Conditions for Membership of Public Shareholding Companies." Part 4 deals with "Brokers" and "Conditions of Admission". Part 5 deals with "Functions of Brokers", "Duties and Rights of Brokers", "Actions by Persons and Brokers" and "Securities Transactions on the Floor". Part 6 deals with "Market Resources", "Membership and Brokers Fees" and "Market Commissions". Part 7 deals with "The General Assembly". Part 8 deals with "Authorities of the Disciplinary Council".

– The Draft Regulations on Listing and Accounting Principles of the year 1998 (Disclosure and Transparency Regulations).[85]

4.5.3 *New Securities Act (Financial Papers Act 1997)*

Jordan has recently undertaken serious measures, which aim at modernizing its securities markets. It has also become one of the first Arab countries ever to issue a separate Act dealing with securities. Two days after the announcement of the approval of the Securities Act the index of the AFM went up by 2 points to close at 152 (a far cry from its high rallying points in 1995 when the index reached more than 175 points).[86] In addition, the new Securities Act separates the supervisory role of the AFM from its management branch. Traditionally, the AFM has been given mandate to regulate the activities of member firms dealing in securities such as underwriters, brokers and investment advisors. Yet it is interesting to note that the English translation of the title this Act is somewhat misleading. The translation does not warrant naming this Act as the "Securities Act". A literal translation would read as "the Provisional Financial Papers Act No. 23 of the year 1997". However, this new Act comprises eighty-two articles. These eighty-two articles are subdivided into nine chapters dealing with matters relating to setting up a Securities Exchange Commission; setting up a Securities Deposit Centre (Articles 29–34); financial services companies (Articles 35–43); investment funds and investment companies (Articles 44–52); disclosure (Articles 53–66) and violations and penalties (Articles 67–72).

Article 6 of the new Securities Act sets up a new Securities Exchange Commission, which enjoys administrative and financial autonomy. Article 7 states that the SEC is designed to achieve an environment conducive to sound trading in securities, develop and monitor the securities market. Article 7 also states that the Securities Exchange Commission shall undertake to regulate and monitor the issuance and dealing in securities; regulate and monitor the business operations of the entities which fall under its supervision; regulate the disclosure of information concerning securities and issuers and dealing of insiders; and regulate public tenders to purchase joint stock companies. Article 9 states that the Board of Commissioners shall exercise a number of duties including preparing draft securities laws and

---

[85] This draft comprises thirty-eight Articles.

[86] Art. 77 of this Act abrogates (after the passing of the specified period mentioned in Art. 73) the Amman Financial Market Law No. 1 of the year 1990 and all its amendments. In addition, Art. 80 also abrogates all other laws and regulations which may contravene this Act.

regulations; preparing, amending or revoking directives for the management of the SEC; approving bylaws and rules of the SEC; granting licences pursuant to the Act. However, Article 20 states that the following are subject to the monitoring of the SEC: the Exchange, The Securities Deposit Centre, financial services companies, joint stock companies, investment funds and certified financial professionals.

Article 29 establishes the Securities Deposit Centre for depositing and transferring ownership of securities traded on the Exchange and settling of the prices of such securities among financial brokers. Article 35 states that financial services companies can invest as trustees, practise investment management, act as financial advisers and financial brokers. They may also manage primary issues. Article 46 divides investment funds companies into "variable-capital investments funds" (open-ended), or "fixed-capital investment funds" (closed-ended). Article 50, states that an "investment company" is a public joint stock company which primarily undertakes or intends to undertake the business of investing and trading in securities, or owns or intends to own securities equal in value to more than 50 per cent of its total assets. The definition also excludes banks, insurance companies, financial services and holding companies. Article 55 stipulates that an issuer or an affiliate of an underwriter may not sell a security before the approval of the prospectus. Article 56 states that the prospectus shall contain the following: adequate description of the issuer, adequate description of the security, the financial position of the issuer and any other information required by the SEC or authorized by it.

Article 67 defines inside information as any information which has not been made public and that if advertised is expected to affect the price of one security or more. Article 68 prohibits insiders including members of the Board of Directors of the SEC, and members of the Securities Deposit Centre and the executive managers and staff from exploiting inside information. Paragraph (d) also prohibits a number of practices. These include giving the public a false information of real or factitious dealing in securities, to influence the prices of securities and adversely affect the capital market in any shape or form.

Article 70 imposes hefty penalties on violations of the provisions of the Act. These vary between up to JD 20,000 and/or of a fine no less than twice and not more than five times the profit made or loss avoided by the violator. In addition to the fine, violators of Article 68 can expect an imprisonment sentence of up to three years and up to one year for violating provisions 35b, 36b and 45c.

5 CRITICAL REMARKS ON THE JORDANIAN DEFINITION OF THE TERM "SECURITIES" IN LIGHT OF BRITISH AND AMERICAN DEFINITIONS

Despite the progressive Jordanian attitudes *vis-à-vis* this nascent area of legislation, its securities laws are still lacking in sophistication. This lack, however, is not only an outcome of the letter of the new Jordanian Securities Act. Rather, it is a result of an underdeveloped local securities jurisprudence and dearth of underlying legal infrastructure. An advanced legal infrastructure concomitant with competent legal experts needs to be in place if a country envisages the orderly functioning of its securities markets. More importantly, a full understanding of the legal implications of the letter of securities laws needs to be ascertained. It is axiomatic in international comparative law that legal grafting from one jurisdiction into another can often prove futile and counterproductive. It is this important aspect of financial regulation which the concluding remarks of this article attempt to address. Accordingly, some of the legal implications of the new Jordanian Securities Act's definition of the term "securities" will be briefly examined. This examination will be seen in light of other relevant Jordanian definitions of financial securities and contrasted with statutory definitions in the US and UK. It will, subsequently, be demonstrated that Jordanian definitions of the term "securities" fall far short of encompassing the statutory and jurisprudential definitions adopted in these two countries.

5.1 Definition of the term "securities" in the UK

In the UK, the Financial Services Act 1986 (the FSA) has introduced wide-ranging changes in regulating British financial services industries. However, the FSA uses the term "investment" to refer to securities instruments and defines the term as "any asset, right or interest falling within any paragraph in Part I of Schedule I of the Act". To go a step further, we observe that the Schedule referred to lists the following instruments as "securities":[87]

-   shares and stock in the share capital of a company (Part I, Sch. 1, para. 1);
-   debentures (Part I, Sch. 1, para. 2). This, however, includes debenture stock, loan stock, bonds, certificates of deposit and other instruments creating or acknowledging indebtedness, not being instruments falling within the next category;
-   government and public securities (Part I, Sch. 1, para. 3). This refers to loan stock, bonds and other instruments creating or acknowledging indebtedness issued by or on behalf of a government, local authority or public authority;
-   instruments entitling to shares or securities (Part I, Sch. 1, para. 4). In this category we find warrants or other instruments entitling the holder to subscribe for investments falling within para. 1, 2, 3 above;
-   certificates representing securities (Part I, Sch.1, para. 5). Here we can assume that this includes: property rights in respect of any investment falling within paras. 1, 2, 3 and 4 above; any right to acquire dispose of, underwrite or convert an instrument, being a right to which the holder would be entitled if he/she held any such instrument to which the certificate or instrument relates; contractual rights, excluding options, to acquire any such investment otherwise than by subscription;
-   units in a collective investment scheme (Part I, Sch. 1, para. 6). This encompasses shares in, or securities of an open-ended investment company;
-   options (Part I, Sch. 1, para. 7). This would be to acquire or dispose of: an investment falling within any other paragraph of the Schedule; currency of the UK or any other country; gold or silver; and an option to acquire or dispose

---

[87] As quoted from the enumeration mentioned in R. Hameed, "Some Comparative Aspects of Securities Regulation in the United Kingdom and the United States", PhD thesis, London University, 1991, pp. 69–70.

of an investment falling within this paragraph by virtue of some of the above mentioned;
–   futures (Part I, Sch. 1, para.8);
–   contracts for difference (Part I, Sch. 1, para.9);
–   long-term insurance contracts (Part I, Sch. 1, para.10); and
–   rights and interests in investments (Part I, Sch. 2, para.11).

5.2 Definition of the term "securities" in the US

According to s. 2/1 of the Securities Act 1933 "security" refers to:

–   any note; stock; treasury stock; bond; debenture;
–   evidence of indebtedness;
–   certificate of interest or participation in any profit-sharing agreement;
–   collateral-trust certificate; preorganization certificate or subscription;
–   transferable share; investment contract;
–   voting-trust certificate; certificate of deposit for a security;
–   fractional undivided interest in oil, gas or other mineral rights;
–   any put, call, straddle option;
–   any privilege on any security; certificate of deposit or group of index of securities (including any interest therein or based on the value thereof);
–   any put, call, straddle option or privilege entered into on a national exchange relating to foreign currency;
–   in general, any interest or instrument commonly known as "security";
–   any certificate of interest or participation in temporary or interim certificate for, receipt for guarantee of, or warrant or right to subscribe to or purchase any of the foregoing.

In the US the definition of securities can be assumed to be broader than in the UK due the fact that the US Securities Act 1933 and the US Securities Exchange Act 1934 have occasionally used generic, open-ended definitions. Moreover, the definitions mentioned thereon were also repeated in the US Investment Advisers Act 1940 and the Investment Company Act 1940. The occasional generic definition of US securities and their apparent outdatedness has spurred American courts to develop a somewhat elaborate system of jurisprudence in order to deal with evolving definitional challenges. This has enabled US courts to add their own interpretations of the term "securities". Accordingly, US courts have deployed a variety of tests in order to determine whether or not a transaction involves a security. Most important American cases are: *SEC v. Joiner Leasing Corporation* (1943), *SEC v. Howey & Co.* (1946), *Silver Hills Country Club v. Sobieski, United Housing Foundation v. Forman* (1975), *Landerth Timber Co. v. Landerth* (1985).[88] For its part, the 1934 Securities Exchange Act introduced amendments which included deleting, *inter alia*, any reference to "evidence of indebtedness" and an exclusion of "currency or any

---

[88] *Ibid.*, pp. 72–80.

note, draft, bill of exchange, or banker's acceptance which has a maturity at the time of issuance" However, these federal definitions (found in the 1933 and 1934 Acts) should be examined in conjunction with the very complex blue-sky regulations which pertain to the respective jurisdictions of individual American states.

5.3 The Jordanian legal definition of the term "securities"

Various Jordanian Acts and regulations previously gave less adequate definitions of securities. For example, Article 2 of the Rules Covering Trading in Financial Papers on the Amman Financial Markets defines "securities" as "Shares, bonds and debentures issued in the Kingdom by government corporations or municipalities or Jordanian public or private shareholding companies, or any negotiable financial paper". Article 2 of the Internal Regulations of the Amman Financial Market also gives a an identical definition. The same definition is also repeated by Article 2 of the Amman Financial Market of the year 1976. And again the same definition is given in Article 2 of the Amman Financial Market Law No. 31 of the year 1992.

Article 3 of the new Securities Act defines financial securities as:

–   investment units issued by investment funds; convertible shares;
–   securities deposit receipts issued by financial services companies;
–   equity option bonds; futures contracts and call and put options; and
–   any other local or international security which is internationally considered as such.

It must be noted that Article 3 of the new Securities Act has substantially enlarged the definition of financial papers or "securities". However, it is quite apparent from this fleeting examination of the definition of the term "securities" in the UK and US, that the Jordanian definition is somewhat hesitant and lacking in detail. It has also paradoxically left the definition too wide relying on so-called "international" definitions, which may in themselves be subject to interpretational controversy abroad. Moreover, despite the fact that there is currently a global trend aimed at harmonizing securities regulation (and the many European directives in this field), highly complex financial instruments are evolving in a rapid manner which often eludes definition even in advanced economies. (Relevant European directives in this context are: the Admissions Directive,[89] the Listing Particulars Directive,[90] the Interim Reports Directive,[91] the Prospective Directive,[92] the Capital Adequacy Directive,[93] the Insider Dealing Directive,[94] the UCITS Directive,[95] and the Directive on Investor Compensation Scheme.)[96]

---

[89] Regulation No. 79/279/EEC.
[90] Regulation No. 80/390/EEC.
[91] Regulation No. 82/121/EEC.
[92] Regulation No. 89/298/EEC.
[93] Regulation No. 93/6/EEC.
[94] Regulation No. 89/592/EEC.
[95] Regulation No. 85/611/EEC.
[96] Regulation No. 97/9/EEC.

Given also the different legal traditions and conceptual framework between com-mon-law-countries and civil-code ones, problems are likely to arise when dealing with cross-jurisdictional admissibility of evidence. Even among Anglo-American jurisdictions *inter se*, there has been noticeable difference in judicial leeway in interpreting the term "securities". For, while there has been inchoate British judicial contribution in delineating the boundaries of the term "securities" (though, Part II of Sch. 1 of the British FSA details the definition of "investment business"), US jurisprudence has centred around the notion of "investment contracts". Moreover, relying on "international" interpretations to determine what may retrospectively constitute a Jordanian security could be further compounded by the fact that sophisticated financial instruments require more advanced capital markets. Needless to say, the majority of Jordanian judges, for the time being, lack the necessary expertise in order to make their own jurisprudential contributions in providing dynamic exegeses of the term "securities".[97]

Finally, the present author concludes by calling for more sophistication in Arab securities laws in a manner which will render them able to embody regulatory advances in insider-dealing prohibitions, public offerings and private placements rules, corporate disclosure, companies' stock exchange listings requirements, corporate take-over and mandatory bids provisions, institutional underwriting of securities, market policing and enforcement, civil and criminal corporate liabilities, common-law corporate remedies, market manipulation prohibitions, rules, etc. The present writer also looks forward to Arab countries structuring effective regulatory bodies akin to the American SEC or the newly established British Financial Services Authority. Moreover, it is also hoped that Arab jurisprudence will evolve to catch up with international standards in regulating capital adequacy of securities firms, authorization, licensing, conduct of business rules, conflict of interest problems, Chinese walls, cold-calling, investment advertisement, compensation funds for investors, market fraud and manipulative practices, etc. Yet, having concluded the article with this definitional critique, the present writer also hopes that he has outlined the highly complex nature of securities regulations and the further need for more specialized Arab legal studies in this important field.

---

[97] To the author's knowledge, so far, no Jordanian court has dealt with cases which involved defining the term "securities".

The UN Sanctions Regime: The Case of Iraq

*Abd al-Amir al-Anbari**

As the Soviet Union was on the verge of collapse and the cold war between the Eastern and Western blocks came to an end, the United States of America began to tighten its grip on international and regional organizations, particularly the Security Council of the United Nations, to secure its strategic interests against its political opponents and reinforce its economic competitiveness *vis -à-vis* its Western and Asian allies.

As a consequence, the imposition under one pretext or another of collective economic sanctions through the UN Security Council on various Third World countries, including three Arab countries, i.e. Iraq, Libya and Sudan, has become one of the most conspicuous international phenomena of the post-cold war era. In addition, the US resorted to unilateral sanctions through American legislation directly against such "rogue" countries as Cuba, Iran and others and indirectly, on other countries which trade or deal with them. Hence the question of international and unilateral economic sanctions has became of great concern to a number of statesmen, diplomats, academicians and international humanitarian organizations particularly as regards the proper use and possible abuse of such sanctions in international relations and their impact on world peace and security. Indeed, the United Nations Secretary General, the UN General Assembly and the majority of the members of the Security Council have called for the reform and humanization of the UN sanctions.

In his report on the work of the organization (S/1995/1) 25 January 1995, the Secretary General cautioned against the temptation to use sanctions to achieve objectives other than those declared, as this could impair rather than promote world peace and stability. The Secretary General recalled that the authority and validity of such sanctions rests on Article 41 of the Charter, hence the purpose of the sanctions "is to modify the behaviour of a party that is threatening international peace

---

* Ambassador of Iraq to UNESCO, Ex-Ambassador to London, Iraq Permanent Representative to the UN, negotiated the Memorandum of Understanding of UNSCR 986 (Oil for Food).

99

and security and not to punish or otherwise exact retribution" (*ibid.*, p. 16). One can hardly dispute such an approach to international sanctions, but one cannot deny that in practice the use, or rather the abuse, of international sanctions to achieve purposes other than those that were declared when sanctions were imposed is at the present more often the rule than not. Such abuses are all the more frequent in view of the "combination of imprecision and mutability [which] makes difficult for the Security Council to agree on when the objectives can be considered to have been achieved and sanctions can be lifted" (*ibid.*). Apart from peace and security, the Secretary General noted that "sanctions . . . are a blunt instrument. They raise the ethical question of whether suffering inflicted on vulnerable groups is a legitimate means of exerting pressure on political leaders" (*ibid.*). He further noted that sanctions "can complicate the work of humanitarian agencies . . . conflict with the development objectives . . . and can have a severe effect on other countries" (*ibid.*).

The sanctions regime imposed on Iraq on 6 August 1990 has metamorphosed since March 1991 into a modern Pandora's box out of which has come all the harm and damage which the Secretary General cautioned against, and much more.

1 THE INITIAL PHASE OF THE SANCTIONS REGIME

The UN sanctions against Iraq originated in Security Council Resolution 661 (6 August 1990) which was passed under Chapter VII of the Charter. The main features of those sanctions are as follows:

(a) They were imposed to achieve a specific objective as determined by paragragh 2 of Resoultion 661, i.e. "To secure compliance of Iraq with paragraph 2 of Resolutions 660 (1990) and to restore the authority of the legitimate government of Kuwait". It will be recalled that paragraph 2 of Resolution 660 demanded that Iraq withdraw all its forces to the points in which they were located on 1 August 1990.

(b) The sanctions imposed were total, prohibiting all states from importing to or exporting from Iraq any and everything, including foodstuffs, civilian requirements, educational materials, technical services, health and sanitary materials, fertilizers, all production and construction supplies and financial transactions. The only exception made was "supplies intended strictly for medical purposes and, in humanitarian circumstances, foodstuffs".

Since all Iraqi assets were frozen, the exception made for payments exclusively for medicine and foodstuffs was left to the discretion of the states where such assets were located, with the result that very little use was made by Iraq of such restrictive exceptions. Furthermore, the expression "humanitarian circumstances" was not a clearly defined term with an established meaning. Hence the Security Council passed another Resolution, 666 (13 September 1990), emphasizing that the determination as to whether such circumstances had arisen was for the Council alone or acting through its "Committee". In this respect the Council or some of its members seem to view the "human circumstances" as implying the spread of starvation throughout the country. Hence the Council introduced new conditions for the distribution of foodstuffs, requiring that it be carried out through the UN and the international committee of the Red Cross, thereby trying to reduce Iraq to a refugee camp and turn 20 million Iraqis into refugees. This is a modification of paragraph 4 of Resolution 661 which envisaged payment by Iraq for such foodstuffs. Resolution 666 was supposed to provide the Iraqi population with "humanitarian aid", mainly food and medicine, but in relation to the size of Iraq and its population few humanitarian supplies were actually delivered. Thus the sanctions were so sweeping, denying the Iraqi civilian population of all basic necessities for civilized life, that they became virtually a collective and inhumane punishment rather than a measure to secure the two specific objectives set out in paragraph 2 of Resolution 660 and paragraph 2 of Resolution 661.

(c) The sanctions were applied to Iraqis abroad as well. For the sanctions overrode all international contracts and commitments with Iraq, humanitarian international conventions, all foreign national laws and required all states to enact new laws or take other measures necessary for their implementation. Such national measures were not uniform, and were sometimes ill informed, which created a state of confusion and arbitrary measures and in many cases subjected Iraqi nationals living abroad to financial and political restrictions depriving them of their means of living, studying or obtaining medical treatment and in many cases exposed them to deportation without legal safeguards, contrary to basic human rights.

(d) The monitoring of the sanctions was entrusted to a Committee consisting of all the members of the Security Council. However, the Council did not indicate the procedures to be followed by the Committee. Nor did it authorize the Committee to make exception of the sanctions in any emergency, epidemics or natural disasters. On its part, the Committee (henceforth referred to as the "661 Committee") decided that the consensus required for its decision should mean unanimity of all its fifteen members, thereby enabling any one member to block any decision supported by all the other members. In this respect the Committee became the only UN organ to act on unanimity rather than majority or consensus basis. Further, the procedures adopted by the Committee did not require a dissenting member to explain or justify its dissent. Nor did the procedure provide for any form of transparency or require any deadline for its decisions. (At a later stage the Committee required, to no avail, that a dissenting members had to explain its position but in practice any member could veto any decision, no matter how arbitrary its position might be.)

(e) Although the sanctions were imposed to secure specific and concrete objectives no reference was made in Resolution 661 as to when or how the sanctions would be lifted once the said objectives had been achieved. One thing is clear; they were not originally meant to remain effective after the achievement of their objectives, let alone to remain in perpetuity. As will be seen later, subsequent Resolutions escalated the sanctions, changed their nature and transformed their now objectives and broadened their sphere.

2 FROM ECONOMIC SANCTIONS TO BLOCKADE

Soon after the passing of Resolution 661, which required all states to implement the sanctions and entrusted the 661 Committee with the tasks of monitoring their implementation, the Security Council introduced a new mechanism for the enforcement of the sanctions. This was done through Resolution 665 (1990) which called upon:

Those member states cooperating with the Government of Kuwait which are deploying maritime forces to the area to use such measures commensurate to the specific circumstances as may be necessary under the authority of the Security Council to halt all inward and outward maritime shipping in order to inspect and verify their cargoes and destination to ensure strict implementation of the provisions related to such shipping laid down in Resolution 66 (1991).

Although the same Resolution requested the states concerned to coordinate their actions, and their forces were commonly referred to as the multinational interception force, in practice there was widespread chaos and abuse of force verging on piracy. More often than not, suspected vessels were intercepted for inspection several times by various maritime forces or forced to divert to far away ports to unload their cargoes for inspection. Naval forces from Argentina, Australia, Belgium, the United States, France and the UK and other states participated in and carried out more than 22,000 interceptions, resulting in nearly 10,000 boardings and more than 550 diversions of ships, according to the 661 Committee's report to the Security Council dated 26 August 1996. The Committee's report did not make any reference as to whether any embargoed cargoes were seized, which seems to imply that none were. Such sweeping authorization to various national and unlimited numbers of maritime forces to halt all inward and outward shipping without clear and enforceable guidelines and without actual coordination with the 661 Committee and with no accountability *vis-à-vis* the military staff Committee or members of the Security Council highlights the dangerous consequences of such forceful means of enforcement to international maritime trade and to the other members of the international community. By enforcing the economic sanctions through the use of maritime force as each maritime power chose to exercise it, the Council relinquished its power and responsibility to ensure the proper implementation of its Resolutions. Indeed, in a number of cases peace and order and maritime safety were in great jeopardy and human lives were at clear risk.

The most dangerous aspect of the Resolution, however, is that by changing the means of enforcement from diplomatic and political to the arbitrary use of various national maritime forces, the Council brought about a drastic mutation in the nature of economic sanctions. The maritime blockade, coupled with air blockades under another Resolution 670 (1990), amounted to an act of war, thereby making the economic sanctions an act of war as well. Although such blockades were authorized by the Security Council "under its authority", the Council did not spell out which provision in the Charter gave the Council the authority to use force to implement economic sanctions. Article 41 of the Charter, which authorizes the Council to impose economic sanctions, does not authorize blockades. It is Article 42 which authorizes the use of force including blockades, subject to the conditions specified in Articles 42–49 of the Charter. It follows that the Council does not have the power to delegate such authority to a diverse and unspecified number of states which acted at liberty and on their own authority without being responsible for any excessive use or abuse of power by their maritime forces and without being accountable to any international authority. Such use of force "under the authority" of the Council raises the troubling and very complex question of the scope of the authority of the Security Council under the Charter or, even worse, whether the Council power is absolute and subject to no rule of law.

3 THE USE OF ALL NECESSARY MEANS

In the third phase of the sanctions, the Security Council combined the use of force with the existing economic sanctions. For this purpose the Council passed Resolution 678 (29 November 1990) authorizing "States cooperating with Kuwait to use all necessary means to uphold and implement Resolution 660 (1990)". The Resolution did not mention the use of force expressly, but that was to avoid the conditions and mechanisms required by the UN Charter once the Council decides to use force, in accordance with Article 42 on the Charter and subsequent articles, which determined the mechanism for the use of force and the necessity of consultation and supervision by the Security Council. However, use of force was what every member of the Council understood the Resolution to authorize, despite the semantic fictions employed. But the question remains of what "all necessary means" means. Does it include mass destruction weapons, such as nuclear weapons or weapons involving the use of heavy shells made of spent uranium, which on impact release nuclear radiation, as was extensively used in Iraq by the coalition forces?[1]

Thus on further reflection, "all necessary means" as intended by Resolution 678, creates a worldwide dangerous precedent whereby anything could be used, including conventional and mass destruction weapons. With hindsight, it means that no "proportionality" need be observed and that the law of war as embodied in the Geneva Conventions and Protocols might be ignored. Such absolute use of all "necessary means" by one or more power has become the cornerstone of what is labelled as "the world new order" under which none of the provisions of the Charter concerning the use of force, the rules of humanitarian law or indeed previous Security Council Resolutions need be seriously respected.

The Resolution made such authorization conditional, i.e. if Iraq failed to fully implement Resolution 660 and all the subsequent relevant Resolutions on or before 15 January 1991. On the face of it, such a condition could have made force unnecessary, but in reality it was more tactical window dressing than a genuine opportunity to solve the crisis by peaceful measures. For now the Council attached a short, seemingly benign, rider, to the objectives of the use of all necessary means that made the use of force unavoidable. For the first time since the beginning of the Gulf crisis, and without any new development, the Council added a new objective, i.e. "To restore international peace and security in the area", thereby changing not only the objectives of the sanctions but the territorial, temporal, material and personal spheres of the crisis extending to the whole region of the Gulf as well as the Middle East including, presumably, the Arab–Israeli conflict.

It is to be recalled that throughout the deliberations preceding the adoption of Resolution 678, some permanent members of the Council made persistent pleas for the use of force under Article 51 of the Charter regarding "the inherent right of individual or collective self-defence". This article, however, conditions the resort to force in self-defence "until the Security Council has taken measures necessary to maintain international peace and security". The eventual use of force by the coalition

---

[1] See for example the findings of Dr Siegwart Horst Gunther as reported by Amy Henderson in the *Jordan Times*, 4–5 May 1995.

ignored this time limit as well as the requirement under international law that the use of force in the exercise of the right of self-defence should be proportionate.

What followed was nothing less than a Third World War, in which more than thirty countries led by the US attacked first in Iraq by air, land and sea, and then in Kuwait for a total of forty-three days which ended at midnight on 27–28 February 1991.[2] A provisional end to hostilities was declared in accordance with a new Resolution, 686 (2 March 1991), until a "definitive end to the hostilities" was established as anticipated in the Resolution's final paragraph.

On the same day, the President of the Council issued a statement on behalf of the Council urging the 661 Committee "to pay particular attention to the findings and recommendations on critical medical/public health and nutritional conditions in Iraq". Such a statement confirms the ineffectiveness of the exceptions to the sanctions in Resolution 661 and the lack of seriousness in the application of Resolution 666, as well as the disproportionate devastation which the coalition inflicted on Iraq.

4 PERMANENT CEASEFIRE, PERMANENT SANCTIONS?

More than a month after the adoption of Resolution 686, the Council adopted Resolution 687 which, through another metamorphosis, did not provide for a definitive end to the hostilities, as prescribed in Resolution 686. Instead it declared in paragraph 33 that upon official notification by Iraq of its acceptance of the provisions of the Resolution "a formal ceasefire is effective". On 6 April Iraq officially notified the Security General and the President of the Council that it had no choice but to accept the Resolution. On 11 April, the President of the Council declared that the formal ceasefire was in effect.

In the words of the United Nations Secretary General Mr Boutros Boutros Ghali, the 687 Resolution "represents one of the most complex and far reaching sets of decisions ever taken by the Council". The longest text ever adopted by the Council, it sought to involve Iraq cooperatively in post-war measures to built lasting peace and stability in the region. At the same time, enforcement measures remained in effect, including the sanctions regime and the Council's authorization to Member States to use "all necessary measures" to uphold Iraqi compliance.[3]

The ceasefire declared by the Council upon formal acceptance by Iraq (as required by paragraph 33 of the Resolution) is supposed to be between Iraq and "Kuwait and the Member Sates cooperating with Kuwait in accordance with Resolution 678 (1990)", yet the other parties involved were not required to accept the ceasefire, nor did they declare that they would respect the ceasefire. This is an odd and bewildering innovation since a ceasefire had to be accepted and respected by all parties to the conflict otherwise it would be a unilateral act, which raises questions that could lead to unpredictable consequences:

---

[2] A comprehensive assessment of the damage inflicted on Iraq by the coalitions bombardment prepared for the Pentagon remains classified, but a summary was published in the *International Herald Tribune* on 4 June 1991, pp. 1 and 2.

[3] *The United Nations and the Iraq Kuwait Conflict 1990–1996*, p. 29.

(a) Since ceasefire does not, strictly speaking, bring a "definitive end to the hos-
     tilities", will such hostilities remain indefinitely, unless the Council one day de-
     clares a formal end to them?
(b) If the other parties to the conflict violated the ceasefire, as indeed some of them
     did, would Iraq be legally entitled to retaliate or declare the ceasefire null and
     void?
(c) In paragraph 8 of Resolution 686 the Council committed itself "that in order to
     secure the rapid establishment of a definitive end to the hostilities, the Council
     remains actively seized of the matter," yet six years have lapsed and the Council
     has failed to establish that it did commit itself to do. Again one wonders whether
     the Council is totally free to ignore its own commitments and Resolutions?
(d) Could the Council legally force one party to abide by the ceasefire but keep
     its economic sanctions against it in force and leave the other parties to the con-
     flict free to use force and maintain their maritime and air blockades?
(e) Given the realization of the specific objectives for which the original sanc-
     tions were imposed, what legal ground could be claimed for the continuing
     enforcement of the sanctions and the imposition of new ones for the achieve-
     ment of new objectives, including restoration of peace and stability in the re-
     gion? Is it feasible that such an objective can be achieved through the imposi-
     tion of sanctions against one country in the region while the other countries
     of the same region are not required to accept the restoration of peace and
     stability in the region nor were they called upon to do so?

As noted earlier, Resolution 687 kept the old sanctions of Resolution 661 but has
changed their objectives, conditions and mechanism.

The Council cited no legal ground for continuing the old sanctions or for requiring the achievement of the new objectives. Instead it resorted to a variety of
events and statements most of which took place before the outbreak of the Gulf
crisis on 2 August 1990. Ironically the second paragraph of the preamble simply
welcomed "the restoration to Kuwait of its sovereignty, independence and territorial integrity and the return of its legitimate Government". These were the objectives for which the sanctions were imposed and of the launching of a war that first
destroyed much of Iraq before moving to achieve the objectives of Resolutions
660 and 661. Yet the total realization of the objectives for which the sanctions
were imposed and the war against Iraq was launched was acknowledged, but reduced to a mere preamble. The rest of the preamble referred to a variety of national and regional events and objectives such as *"the need to be assured of Iraq's
peaceful intentions"* (italics added). The preamble then referred to the use by Iraq of
a number of ballistic missiles during the coalition's devastating attack on Iraq, de-
scribing such use as "unprovoked attacks" and calling for specific measures in regard
to such missiles located in Iraq. A question thus needs to be considered, namely,
could a country which is devastated by attacks that go beyond the scope and objectives of the Security Council Resolutions resort to the use of force in self-defence or should it be required to stand still? The preamble further referred to Iraq
in a statement threatening to use chemical weapons which Iraq made long before
the Gulf crisis in the event of it being attacked by nuclear weapons. The preamble
ignored the fact that the statement was conditional and that the unconfirmed use
of chemical weapons was reported during the war between Iran and Iraq in which

the Council was seized with, but made no references to, such reported attacks – the sources of which were controversial at best.

The preamble then called for four regional objectives:

(a) the establishment of a nuclear weapon-free zone in the region of the Middle East;
(b) the establishment in the Middle East of a zone free of mass destruction weapons;
(c) the achievement of balanced and comprehensive control of armaments in the region; and
(d) the achievement of the objectives noted above through "all available (sic) means", including a dialogue among the states of the region.

Noble as these regional objectives may seem, anyone familiar with the peace process in the region and the complexity of the issues involved, could have no difficulty in categorizing them as utopian at best compared to the authoritative, arrogantly condescending language used in the provisions relating to the mechanisms, sanctions and enforcement measures applied in reference to Iraq; yet such utopian objectives have been used to perpetuate the sanctions regime against Iraq – country, government and people.

We now turn to the operational paragraphs of Resolution 687 whereby the materials and services subject to the sanctions regime were classified into four categories:

(a) civilian exports to Iraq;
(b) arms embargo;
(c) mass-destruction weapons and technology; and
(d) petroleum and other imports from Iraq.

4.1 Civilian exports to Iraq

For the first category of civilian exports, paragraph 20 of Resolution 687 provided implicitly for the continuing use of the sanctions by removing the prohibitions against the sale or supply to Iraq of foodstuffs, in which case the 661 Committee need only to be notified by the exporting state. The same paragraph provided for a rather simpler procedure of "no-objection" within a given period of time for the approval of sale or supply of "materials and supplies for essential civilian needs" as identified in the report of the Secretary General of 20 March 1991 (S/22366) as well as any other findings of humanitarian need by the Committee. To enable Iraq to purchase such basic civilian requirements, the Resolution removed the previous prohibition against financial transactions related to in paragraph 20.

The Resolution provided for another important exception from the embargo on imports of petroleum and other products originating in Iraq in paragraph 23. This paragraph authorized the sanctions Committee to approve such imports to enable Iraq to pay for its imports of foodstuffs, medicine and essential civilian supplies. Such an exception was not made as a matter of course but was a condition some members of the Council insisted upon for their approval of the Resolution. However, some members acting through the Sanctions Committee vetoed all requests made by Iraq to make use of the exception claiming that such authorization by the Committee is a last resource to be used only after Iraq exhausts all other available means. This practice by some permanent members in the Sanctions Committee illustrated the manipulative tactics used by such members to cancel out practically what they conceded to other members of the Council to secure their votes in favour of a given Resolution.

Consequently the utility of the above exception and the new procedures have been greatly diminished for lack of financial resources available to Iraq on the one hand and the practice of the 661 Committee, or some members thereof, of considering any item for the repair or rehabilitation of the infrastructure of Iraq, including reparation of electrical plants, dams and bridges, grain silos, etc. as being not supplies for essential civilian needs but supplies for the rehabilitation of Iraq's economy, a category which is nowhere prohibited by any Resolution.

Apart from the above modifications, Resolution 687 kept the embargo on civilian supplies without fixing a time for the lifting of such an embargo and without specifying the conditions necessary for its lifting. Instead the Resolution provided in paragraph 21 that the Council will review paragraph 20 every sixty days in light of the policies and practices of the government of Iraq, including the implementation of all relevant Resolutions, for the purpose of determining whether to reduce or lift the prohibition referred to them. The fact that a periodical review, every sixty days, was required to reduce or remove the prohibitions gives the impression that the Council intended to relax the prohibitions as the implementation of the Resolution progressed with time. Yet despite all that has been done, particularly in the field of mass destruction weapons, the Council could not agree on such relaxation to the point that the periodical review has become a proforma meeting that ends with a ritualistic statement to the effect that no agreement was reached as to the need for a change in the sanctions, as if the relaxation of sanctions imposed by the Resolution adopted by majority required the agreement of all members of the Council. The political interests of one or more permanent members have certainly played a major role in preventing the Council from relaxing or lifting the sanctions.

It should be noted, however, that removal of such sanctions is complicated by the multiplicity of the relevant Resolutions which so far number more than thirty-two – and more may be implemented. The laxity and overlapping of provisions and the complexity of the conditions and objectives of the various Resolutions, together with the mercurial nature of expression such as "practices and policies of the Iraqi government", create difficulty for any *bona fide* attempt to bring such sanctions to an end as long as the political interests of some permanent members *vis-à-vis* Iraq and their oil interests in the Gulf region remain, as they have since the Gulf crisis.

4.2 Arms embargo (conventional weapons)

Resolution 687 (in paragraph 24) prohibited all states from selling, supplying or transporting to Iraq arms and related material of all types, including conventional military equipment, spare parts and their means of production as well as technology, personnel or materials for training or technical support services, etc.

Such a prohibition was construed as continuation of the prohibition stipulated in Resolution 661 and subsequent Resolutions. But the objectives for the sanctions under those Resolutions had been achieved, and their *raison d'être* has ceased to exist. Nevertheless Resolution 687 expressly stated that such prohibition will continue "until a further decision is taken by the Council". Shortly after the adoption of Resolution 687, the Council adopted Resolution 700 on 17 June 1991, which elaborated further on the scope and frequency of the reports to be submitted by Member States to the Secretary General indicating the procedures and measures they adopted as required by Resolution 687. The new Resolution 687 provided that the Council should review its guidelines, periodically referring to paragraph 28 of Resolution 687 which refers to Iraq's compliance with the Resolution and *the "general progress towards the control of armaments in the region"* (italics added). The Council entrusted the 661 Committee with the responsibility of monitoring the prohibition against the sale or supplying of arms to Iraq.

Under Resolution 700 the 661 Committee was mandated to supervise and report on the implementation of the arms embargo in accordance with the guidelines approved by the same Resolution. The Resolution called for the implementation of such sanctions at three levels – by all states, by international organizations and through intergovernmental cooperation.[4] In its first report to the Council, the 661 Committee reported that "during the period under review, no allegations of violations of sanctions, particularly with regard to paragraph 24 of Resolution 686 (1991) have been reported to the Committee".[5]

In effect, the Council, by maintaining the embargo until a further resolution is passed, decreed that with the passing of time Iraqi conventional military force should be reduced to a bare minimum, if not virtually disarmed. Given the delicate balance of power in the region such a unilateral disarmament of a major country as Iraq could create an extremely dangerous power vacuum, which is bound to promote territorial expansions, armed conflicts not only between Iraq and other powers in the region but throughout the Middle East, which runs contrary to the declared objective of Resolution 678 (1990), i.e. "to restore peace and security in the area", as well as the fundamental principles of the UN Charter.

4.3 Prohibition of mass destruction weapons

Resolution 687 provided for a comprehensive prohibition against Iraq's possession of nuclear, chemical, biological weapons and ballistic missiles of a range beyond 150 km and all related technology, materials and equipment as detailed in section (c) paragraphs 8, 9, 10, 11, 12 and 13 (hereinafter referred to collectively as WMD). The resolution also required that Iraq "shall unconditionally accept the destruction removal, or rendering harmless" supervision plus ongoing long-term monitoring and verification.

These sanctions seem to be at the core of Resolution 687 but they concern us here for one main reason, i.e. their full implementation as a condition for the lift-

---

[4] See Doc. S/22660, 2 June 1991.
[5] Doc. S/23036, 13 September 1991.

ing the embargo on Iraqi oil and other Iraqi commodities pursuant to other paragraphs of that Resolution.

The military and political objectives of these provisions are self-evident. Of no less significance, for our purpose, is that the ways and means for the implementation of these provisions and the international organs entrusted with the task of destroying and monitoring of such weapons are all technical rather than political.

The Council constituted a technical Commission for the above purpose, composed of experts in the fields of mass destruction weapons from various countries including states which are not members of the Security Council. The Special Commission, called UNSCOM, is chaired by a diplomat from a neutral country in his personal capacity. UNSCOM was asked to draw up a working plan to be submitted to the Council for approval, which it did by Resolution 699 (1991). The Council granted UNSCOM complete power to execute the plan at its discretion with comprehensive diplomatic privileges and immunities.

The same authorities and privileges were likewise given to the International Atomic Energy Agency (IAEA) with respect to nuclear materials and related matters.

On the other hand the obligations imposed on and the cooperation required from Iraq regarding the prohibited weapons and activities were very comprehensive; but unlike other prohibitions and requirements, they were not vague and general but very specific. This was emphasized by the President of the Council in his statement issued on 11 March 1992 (S/23699) in which he distinguished between Iraq's commitments of general nature and those of specific nature relevant to (WMD).

In a previous statement, dated 19 February 1992 (S/23609) the President of the Council confirmed that Iraq has accepted unconditionally Resolutions 707 (1991) and 715 (1991).

The task entrusted to UNSCOM and IAEA involved three main phases:

(a) collecting and analysing all data relevant to the procurement, specifications, location and development of the prohibited weapons and materials;
(b) the destruction, removal or rendering harmless of all such weapons, materials, equipment and facilities;
(c) propose a plan and, after approval by the Security Council, install and man ongoing monitoring and verification facilities inside Iraq and at the headquarters of UNSCOM and IAEA.

Phases (a) and (b) have, over a period of more than six years, almost been completed. In fact the only controversial issue which is still outstanding is UNSCOM's claim that Iraq has not been able to satisfy it about the destruction or the whereabouts of some sixteen missiles of a range more than 150 km. Iraq claims that such missiles were destroyed soon after the ceasefire. It is this writer's view that whatever the case may be, it is a false issue in view of the elaborate ongoing monitoring and verification operations authorized by unconditionally in 1992. Subsequently Iraq fully cooperated in extending and securing all surveillance and communication facilities by air and on land, and naturally expected that such cooperation would lead UNSCOM and IAEA to report to the Council that Iraq had completed the implementation of its obligations under section (c) of Resolution 687. Thus even if UNSCOM is genuinely sceptical of Iraq's claim that the missiles unaccounted for had been destroyed, the fact that UNSCOM would continue to have the authority and power required to ensure Iraq's compliance through its ongoing monitoring and verification operations should assure UNSCOM and the Security Council that such missiles, if they were still hidden somewhere inside Iraq, would sooner or later be located and destroyed and until then they could not be used without being immediately identified and located through satellites and other means of surveillance under the disposal of UNSCOM.

Furthermore, the 661 Committee, in cooperation with UNSCOM and IAEA, finalized a plan in accordance with paragraph 7 of Resolution 715 for a worldwide mechanism for "monitoring any future sales or supplies by other countries to Iraq of items relevant to the implementation of section (c) of Resolution 687 and other relevant Resolutions".[6] The plan not only covers the prohibited materials and technologies but also long categories of dual purpose items. The Council adopted Resolution 1051 (1996) approving the plan and the mechanism proposed by the 661 Committee, UNSCOM and IAEA and entrusting to them the task of supervising its implementation and requiring them to report periodically to the Council and to propose any modification necessary to ensure the effectiveness of the ongoing monitoring and verification of Iraq's compliance with section (c) of Resolution 687 and Resolutions 707, 715 and 1051. The export–import mechanism approved by Resolution 1051 is not yet operational since all the sanctions imposed on Iraq are still in force. However, the ongoing monitoring and verification activities currently being carried out consist of the following types of activities as detailed in the seventh report of the Secretary General to the Council:

(a)   inspection to verify the completeness of the list of sites monitored and of the inventories, to verify declarations as to activities conducted and any information that "might question Iraq's compliance";
(b)   aerial surveillance from high-altitude (the U-2) and the Commission's helicopters;
(c)   maintenance of the site monitoring and verification protocols by the experts at the Baghdad monitoring centre;
(d)   monitoring activities conducted by experts dispatched to Iraq for a specific purpose;
(e)   review and analysis of the product of the sensors installed at the various sites.[7]

The report states in paragraph 133 that "the Commission wishes to place on record that it has received full cooperation from Iraq in the setting up and operation of the monitoring system". Typically, the Commission added "some issues, however, still remain". But even if all outstanding issues are settled, UNSCOM tends to bring up new issues. The most recent one is its decision to have approximately 130 missile engines which have been destroyed and buried inside Iraq removed to the United States to verify the origin of the materials used in making the missiles. Such a request by UNSCOM reflects on its efficiency if nothing else. It virtually makes its initial task open ended and the ultimate judge to confirm the completion of Iraq's obligations under section (c) of Resolution 687 the government of the United States,

---

[6]   Doc. S/1995/1017 dated 7 December 1995.
[7]   See Doc S/1995/284, 10 April 1995.

rather than UNSCOM as the technical and neutral organ entrusted by the Security Council to carry out exclusively the requirements of section (c) of that Resolution. For its part, the government of Iraq suggested that Iraqi experts should participate in the verification but UNSCOM deemed such a requirement an infringement on its authority. Iraq also proposed that since the missiles were of Russian origin their remnants should be examined by Russian experts. For some reason, the chairman of UNSCOM refused. Such open-ended requests by UNSCOM and the somewhat arbitrary refusal of any Iraqi request seem to render futile all efforts on the part of Iraq to cooperate with UNSCOM.

It should be noted that despite the critical and complex task entrusted to UNSCOM, the United Nations has failed to provide the Commission with the required financing. So far it depends on donations and loans from the USA, Saudi Arabia, Kuwait and few others. Likewise, most of the Commission's inspectors and experts are on temporary secondment mainly from the USA, UK, Germany, Russia and few other countries. Thus the financing and expertise of UNSCOM could compromise its independence and objectivity; but unless proved otherwise it has to be assumed that UNSCOM and IAEA are technical and non-political organs whose loyalty is exclusively to the United Nations which, through the Security Council, entrusted them exclusively with the task of eliminating the prohibited weapons and operating the ongoing monitoring and verification system.

4.4 The prohibition against the importation of petroleum and other products originating in Iraq

Of all the obligations and sanctions imposed on Iraq none requires the full cooperation of Iraq more than those related to WMD. Without such cooperation and willingness it could be impossible to implement the requirements of Resolution 687 relevant to WMD. Hence the Resolution specifically linked the removal of the prohibition against the importation of Iraqi petroleum and other products to the completion of all the requirements relating to WMD. The linkage is specifically stipulated in paragraph 22 of Resolution 687 which states as follows:

[The Council] decides that . . . upon Council agreement that Iraq has completed all actions contemplated in paragraphs 8, 9, 10, 11, 12 and 13, the prohibitions against the import of commodities and products originating in Iraq and the prohibitions against financial transactions related thereto contained in Resolution 661 (1391) shall have no further force or effect.

The critical issue here is whether the Council or any of its members can insist on keeping the prohibitions against the importation of petroleum and other Iraqi commodities when UNSCOM and IAEA confirm that Iraq has completed all actions required of it under paragraph 22 above. It is the opinion of this writer that once such confirmation is presented to the Council it follows that neither the Council nor any of its members, including those who enjoy the privilege of veto, can legally insist on maintaining the embargo on oil and other Iraqi products. The embargo should then be automatically come to end without the need for a new Resolution. Such a construction of the said paragraph does not deprive the Council or its members of any of their power under the Charter.

In fact the Council itself had decided in advance, as stated in paragraph 22, that once Iraq's obligations were fulfilled then the relevant prohibitions "Shall have no further force or effect". It is true that paragraph 22 stipulates that "upon Council agreement that Iraq has completed all actions". Such an agreement, however, does not concern the lifting of the embargo; rather it is related to a factual and technical matter for the determination of UNSCOM and IAEA. Once such determination is finally made the Council must formally agree to it, which would automatically render the relevant prohibitions without any "further force or effect".

Although it is rare for the Council to decide in advance to terminate the enforcement of one of its decisions pending the occurrence of certain event or fact, there are precedents for it, one of which is in paragraph 33 of Resolution 687 itself. In that paragraph the Resolution stated that the Council "declares that upon official notification by Iraq of its acceptance of the provisions above a formal cease-fire is effective".

It is worth noting that the language of paragraph 22 must have been chosen deliberately in order to ensure the cooperation of Iraq with UNSCOM and IAEA in carrying out the required destruction and long-term monitoring and verification; otherwise, if the conditions for the lifting of the embargo on Iraqi petroleum and other commodities were as vague and political as the conditions for the lifting of the other sanctions, Iraq would have no incentive or interest in agreeing and carrying out such cooperation. Nor would the Council or the coalition have any viable alternative to Iraq cooperation. Now that Iraq has gone a long way in its cooperation without obtaining any relaxation of the oil embargo one has to question the good faith of the parties concerned.

It is submitted, however, that whatever merits the above interpretation of paragraph 22 may have, it is presently a theoretical one and will continue to be so until UNSCOM and the IAEA present their final reports to the Council confirming Iraq's fulfilment of all its obligations under section (c).

In the meantime the Council adopted in 1991 Resolutions 706 and 712 authorizing, all states to import from Iraq petroleum and petroleum products worth not more than $1.6 billion for a period of six months. Although the two resolutions were adopted for humanitarian purposes to enable Iraq to purchase foodstuffs, medicine and essential civilian needs, they required that 30 per cent of the above stated sum should go to the compensation fund, and that a further amount should be allocated to cover the full costs of carrying out the tasks authorized by section (c) of Resolution 687 as well as other operations carried out by the United Nations under relevant Resolutions. Furthermore, the two Resolutions provided for a far reaching monitoring of contracts for the sale oil and for the purchase of food, medicine and civilian supplies beginning from the export ports to the final destination. For unknown reasons, the two Resolutions fixed one outlet for the export of Iraqi oil via the Turkish Cehan sea port, even though the Iraqi port of Al-Baker at the Gulf was operational.

Five rounds of technical negotiations between the Iraqi government and the United Nations Secretariat were carried out in Vienna and New York but no final agreement on the practical arrangements was reached.

In April 1995 a new Resolution (986) was passed authorizing the sale of petroleum and petroleum products worth $2 billion for six months renewable. Most of the conditions imposed by Resolution 986 were similar to those of 706 and 712.

After six rounds of technical negotiation between Iraq and the Secretariat over a period of four months a Memorandum of Understanding for the implementation of Resolution 986 was signed on 20 May 1996. A distribution plan was later approved by the Secretary General, followed by the 661 Committee approval of new procedure to expedite its approval of contracts, then a pricing formula for oil sales presented to the Committee approved by fourteen members; but, at present the USA is still withholding its approval.[8]

5 IMPACT OF SANCTIONS ON IRAQ

The first United Nations mission sent to Iraq after the ceasefire described the destruction inflicted by the coalition bombardment on Iraq as having pushed Iraq back to the pre-industrial stage. Be that as it may, the continuing enforcement of the sanctions for over more than six years has brought about a slow but steady destruction of the Iraqi people and civilian society far greater than the coalition's bombardment. The shattering impact on the population at large, particularly on children, women and the elderly, has been well documented by UN agencies such as UNICEF, WHO, FAO and many NGOs. Few references may be sufficient here. A report prepared by the WHO[9] concluded, *inter alia*, as follows: "Financial constraints as a result of the sanctions have prevented the necessary import of food and medicine." The vast majority of the country's population has been on a semi-starvation diet for years. This tragic situation has tremendous implications for the health status of the population and not only for the present generation but for the lives of the future generation as well.

The reduction in the import of medicines, owing to a lack of financial resources, as well as a lack of minimum health care facilities, insecticides, pharmaceutical and other related equipment and appliances, have crippled the health care services, which in pre-war years were of a high quality. Assessment reports rightly remarked that the quality of health care in Iraq, due to the six week war in 1991 and the subsequent sanctions imposed on the country, has been put back by at least fifty years. Diseases such as malaria, typhoid and cholera which were once almost under control, have rebounded since 1991 at epidemic levels, with the health sector as a helpless witness.

Very rarely has the impact of sanctions on millions of people been documented. Severe economic hardship, a semi-starvation diet, high levels of disease, scarcity of essential drugs and, above all, the psycho-social trauma and anguish of a bleak future, have led to the break up of numerous families, leading to distortion in social norms.

The impact of this unfortunate situation on the infant and child population in particular in Iraq needs special attention. It is not only the data on morbidity and morality that tell the story, but equally important are the crippling effects of many

---

[8] The Resolution eventually came into effect on 10 December 1996 following the submission by the Secretary General of a report to the Council that all the preparatory steps needed for the implementation of the Resolution had been completed.

[9] EHA/96.1, March 1996, *The Health Conditions of the Population in Iraq since the Gulf Crisis*.

of these morbidities which are often forgotten. The psychological trauma of the six-week war in 1991 and the terrible hardships endured with the sanctions since then can be expected to leave indelible marks on the mental health and behavioural patterns of these children when they grow to adulthood. This tragic aspect of the impact of the war and conditions surrounding the sanctions is rarely articulated, but the world community should seriously consider the implications of an entire generation of children growing up with such traumatized mental handicaps, if of course, they survive at all.

As recently as October 1996, a spokesperson for UNICEF, Ms Caral Bilami, announced at a press Conference at the UN Headquarters that 4,500 Iraqi children die every month because of hunger and disease. Similar conclusions were arrived at by the FAO in its report No. TCP/IRQ/4552 concerning food and agriculture in Iraq in which FAO estimated that an amount of US$2.7 billion would be necessary to import food to meet the shortage for 1995–1996. Another report prepared for UNESCO's periodical sources described the impact of the war and sanctions on the education system in Iraq as follows:

During the Gulf War and its aftermath, some 40 percent, or more than 5,500 of Iraq's educational institutions were badly damaged . . .

The embargo imposed . . . has meant that materials cannot be imported to carry out the necessary repairs – unless they come in as humanitarian aid – and their use is strictly supervised . . . However, the sanctions Committee . . . has to approve any material or equipment . . . The system is cumbersome and slow, while degradation on the spot is increasing exponentially. Thus hungry children, whose parents cannot afford adequate food and clothing for them, must work in draughty classrooms, with leaky roof and broken windows . . . sitting on either damp or flooded floors with no lighting. Teachers work with few materials – often without even a blackboard – paper is rare and text books few.

The report further noted that "the terrible conditions, both in and out of school, are also seriously affecting the children's health. Communicable diseases and malnutrition are the main problems."[10]

Even worse destruction has befallen the economy structure and productivity, and lead to the semi-collapse of the local currency, hyperinflation and the disintegration of the social fabric and moral traditions.

6 IMPACT OF SANCTIONS ON THIRD COUNTRIES

Iraq, with its rich and balanced natural and human resources, used to be one of the most viable economies in the region. It was inevitable that many countries, particularly neighbouring countries and trading partners would and did suffer great losses. Article 50 of the UN Charter gave such countries the right to apply to the Security Council to remedy their situation. Turkey alone announced recently that it had suffered losses amounting to US$20 billion because of the embargo. A great many other countries applied to the Security Council but received only a little help.

---

[10] UNESCO's sources, No. 49, 1993 p. 29.

Ironically, many other countries, particularly oil exporting countries and weapons exporters, made great fortunes thanks to the embargo.

This article will focus attention, briefly, on the impact of the embargo on international oil prices and the future supply of crude oil.

Prior to the embargo, oil prices were diving downward to a level as low as US$10 per barrel. The pre-Gulf crisis conditions caused a limited reduction in oil production of the Gulf countries causing a rise in prices to US$18 pb. However, as the embargo continued, particularly after the stalemate facing the implementation of the so-called oil for food Resolution 986 (1995), prices have soared to US$25 pb and the prospect for further increases is almost certain. The main beneficiaries of the price increase have of course been the oil producing countries. Saudi Arabia alone had its oil revenue increased in 1996 by U5$10 billion. Thus, as long as the oil embargo is in force, price fluctuation is bound to continue mainly upward in view of the lack of any spare capacity outside OPEC and the limited production spare capacity within OPEC and mainly in Saudi Arabia, which is estimated to be less than 3 mbpd representing, according to recent study by the Centre for Global Energy studies, less than 4 per cent of global consumption of oil. It is in this context that the dangerous impact of the embargo on Iraqi oil is greatest. The security of world oil supply depends on reasonable spare production capacity, diversity of sources of supply and on an economically acceptable level of prices. On all these accounts the present world oil supply is vulnerable. Any interruption of oil supplies because of natural disaster or political act, even for a short period, would cause such a panic that prices would shoot upward, sending the world global economy into deep recession. The world will not be spared such a risk as long as the present situation of supply and demand prevails. Only by relaxing and eventual lifting of the embargo on Iraqi oil would the world be assured of the security of supply at an acceptable level and a healthy rate of economic growth. The sooner the embargo is lifted the better and safer Iraq and the rest of the world would be.

8 CONCLUSIONS AND RECOMMENDATIONS

To many observers, the continuing imposition of sanctions against Iraq for more than six years amount to a slow but inevitable genocide of 20 million Iraqi people. But there is at least one positive impact of the embargo as it has generated a strong movement within the Security Council and the General Assembly for a drastic reform of international sanctions as concerns their objectives, scope, duration and protection of civilian population, as reflected in Secretary General's report entitled "Supplement of an Agenda for peace" of 3 January 1995 (S/1995/1) and the provisional thirty-nine recommendations of the working group of the General Assembly on an Agenda for Peace 10 July 1996.

It is hoped that the thirty-nine recommendations would be approved by the General Assembly and respected by the Security Council. Given the genocidal impact the sanctions imposed on Iraq, as attested by UNICEF, WHO and FAO and quoted earlier, such recommendations should apply to Iraq as well as other countries subjected to sanctions by the Security Council.

The following recommendations are of utmost urgency:

(a)   No open-ended sanctions should be allowed. Reasonable deadlines must be specified in the light of the relevant circumstances. On the date specified sanctions should be lifted unless renewed or relaxed by another resolution. The adoption of such a recommendation is the only way to prevent any permanent member forcing its will on the Council and the world, thereby jeopardizing world peace and order.

(b)   Foodstuffs, medicine and basic civilian supplies and the financial resources needed for their procurement should always be exempt from any regime of sanctions.

(c)   No regime of sanctions should be permitted to violate the Geneva Conventions, the Human Rights Charter and other humanitarian international conventions.

(d)   The Sanctions Committee should not act on the basic of unanimity; only a simple majority of its members should be required for adoption of a decision.

(e)   Finally, the Security Council and any of its permanent members should not be conceded absolute authority above the Charter and international law. A check and balance mechanism must be introduced in the UN system by allowing the International Court of Justice the jurisdiction to review the constitutionality of the Security Council's Acts and Resolutions. Indeed, many intentional law scholars believe that by virtue of its statute the ICJ already has such power and should not shy away from applying it for the sake of maintaining the integrity of the Council, promoting the efficiency of the UN system and above all replacing the tendency to "be above the law" by the cardinal principle of "the due process of law" at the core of the new world order.

Women's Human Rights in Islam: Towards a Theoretical Framework

*Shaheen Sardar Ali**

1 INTRODUCTION

The purpose of this article is to highlight the gap between what may be described as the Islamic "ideal" of women's human rights as opposed to the contextual realities of the status of women in various Muslim jurisdictions today. As indicated in section 2 of the present study, rights afforded to women in the Islamic tradition emanate from its main sources, i.e. the Qur'an,[1] *hadith*,[2] *ijma*[3] and *qiyas*.[4] Yet, the body of principles informing Islamic law, collectively known as the *shari'a*, do not form a homogeneous entity as these depend on interpretations of the sources, particularly the Qur'an and *hadith*, influenced by cultural and ethical differences, historical contexts, colonial pasts, the sect or school of jurisprudence (*madhab*) that a particular community subscribed to, as well as the political and economic policy of Muslim states.

It has been argued that the basic tone and complexion of Islam is reformative, enjoining upon people equity and justice for all. The ethical voice of the Qur'an is egal-

---

* Professor of Law, University of Peshawar, Pakistan; lecturer, School of Law, University of Warwick.

[1] The Qur'an, believed by Muslims to be the word of God, is the primary source of Islamic law. It is based upon revelations made to the Prophet Muhammed through the angel Gabriel over a period of twenty-two years, two months and twenty-two days. Of the 6,666 verses of the Qur'an, about 500 have a legal element, the vast majority of which deal with worship rituals, leaving only eighty verses of legal subject matter in the strict sense. See, A. R. Doi, *Shariah: The Islamic Law*, Ta Ha Publishers, London, 1984, at pp. 21–22; A. Rahim, *Muhammadan Jurisprudence*, Mansoor Book House, Lahore, 1995, pp. 58–65.

[2] *Hadith*, meaning the record of the words and deeds of the prophet Muhammad that was compiled after his death and form the second source of Islamic law.

[3] *Ijma* denotes consensus of opinion among the Muslim jurists in a particular age on a certain question of law.

[4] *Qiyas*, or analogical deduction as the fourth source of Islamic law comes into operation in matters not expressly covered by a text of the Qur'an or *hadith*, nor determined by *ijma*.

itarian and non-discriminatory.[5] At the same time, it concedes to resourceful, adult Muslim men, as the privileged members of society, responsibility to care for (and exercise authority over), women, children, orphans and the needy. The Qur'an therefore contains verses validating the creation and reinforcement of hierarchies based on gender and resources. However, these verses are very few, not exceeding 6 out of a total of 6,666 that make up the text of the Qur'an. Yet it is difficult to understand why and how these six verses outweigh the remaining 6,660, and the position of women in Islam appears to be determined solely on rules derived from a literal and restrictive reading of these verses.[6]

A number of scholars have challenged the restrictive interpretations of the religious text in Islam. They argue that norms of the Islamic tradition, which are discriminatory to women, are a result of the fact that historically it was men who acted as commentators and interpreters of the religious texts as well as being legislators, jurists and judges and those in power.[7] Latter day legal, political and economic developments in the Muslim world also contributed to a perpetuation of an Islamic legal tradition seeking to uphold gender inequality as the dominant theme of the Qur'an.[8] These scholars have attempted to present alternative interpretations of the Qur'anic verses that declare the inherent superiority of Muslim men, by arguing for a radically different construction to be placed on them. This article explores this pluralistic Islamic legal tradition based on varying interpretations of the religious text in an attempt to develop a theoretical framework for analysing women's human rights in Islam.

2 FROM THE SAINTLY TO THE EVIL: CONFLICTING IMAGES OF WOMEN IN QUR'AN AND *HADITH* LITERATURE AND IMPLICATIONS FOR WOMEN'S HUMAN RIGHTS IN ISLAM

Developing an analytical framework of women's human rights in Islam implies going beyond the textual sources of law to capture the perception of the "feminine" in

---

[5] For this line of argumentation, see F. Rahman, "Status of women in Qur'an", in G. Nashat (ed.), *Women and Revolution in Iran*, Westview Press, Boulder, Col., 1983; J. L. Esposito, *Women in Muslim Family Law*, Syracuse, Syracuse University Press, 1982; A. Al-Hibri, "A study of Islamic herstory: or how did we ever get into this mess?", vol. 5, *Women Studies International Forum*, 1982; B. Ultas (ed.), *Women in Islamic Societies*, London, Curzon Press, 1983; F. Hussain (ed.), *Women and Islam*, trans. M. J. Lakeland, Oxford, Basil Blackwell, 1991; L. Ahmed, *Women and Gender in Islam: Historical Roots of a Modern Debate*, New Haven, Yale University Press, 1992; A. A. An-Naim, *Toward an Islamic Reformation*, Syracuse, Syracuse University Press, 1990; R. Hassan, "An Islamic perspective", in J. Belcher (ed.), *Women, Religion and Sexuality*, Geneva, WCC Publications, 1990.
[6] These Qur'anic verses include the following: 2:221; 2:228; 2:282; 24:30; 4:3; 4:34 and will be dealt with below.
[7] *Op. cit.*, note 5.
[8] The Muslim world has had more than its fair share of authoritarian regimes where the voice of the people was rarely heard. Traditionally, women were confined to the home and public life, i.e. matters of state, government and making interventions in public life were considered outside her domain. The last three centuries also saw the vast majority of Muslim countries colonized and hence suppressed and under alien rule. The post-colonial era brought its own political and economic problems. It is not surprising therefore that, in countries where the male population found itself unable to share in governance, women's participation and empowerment was far more problematic.

the Islamic tradition.[9] However this tradition, it may be argued, was not and indeed could not have been a complete break with the immediate past and was in fact accompanied by the historical and cultural baggage of pre-Islamic Arabia. Thus, despite an entirely new ideological perspective, Islam's view of the feminine was influenced by the very culture it had come to change.[10]

There can be no doubt that generally speaking, the Qur'anic images of women are favourable, particularly when studied against the background of the *jahilliyya*.[11] Both social status and legal rights were imposed by express injunctions in the Qur'an, some granting women's complete equality with men, others aimed at protecting women in a predominantly male environment as well as correcting practices which affected the position of women adversely.[12] It must also be acknowledged, however, that Qur'anic laws, while improving the status of women, do not establish political, social or economic equality of the sexes, as "men are a degree above women".[13]

The tone of these verses does not represent women in any derogatory manner; rather kindness and fairness of treatment is enjoined. The only concept in the Qur'an relating to a woman that may be construed as negative is that of her potential for becoming *nashiz* (disobedient). This term occurs prominently in verse 4:34 of the Qur'an, where men are permitted to "lightly beat" women who are disobedient. There is no comparable injunction regarding a "disobedient" man, hence the question as to why only women have been singled out for disobedience? The wider implications of this concept are evident from commentaries of this verse validating restrictions upon women, keeping them "in control", lest they become disobedient. The dictates of the Qur'an were thus made the basis of interpretation and hence accommodation, adaptation and adjustment to later reality and contexts of a rapidly changing Islamic society.[14]

Hadith literature mirrors and further heightens this tension and conflict regarding where images of women span "the whole spectrum from the saintly to the evil and unclean".[15] At one end of the spectrum are images of saintly, extraordinary women, favoured by God and blessed with unusual powers and extraordinary

---

9 For a detailed discussion on the subject, see R.W.J. Austin, "Islam and the feminine", in
   D. MacEoin and Al Al-Shahi (eds.), *Islam in the Modern World*, St Martin's Press, New York, 1983.
10 *Ibid.* Al-Hibri believes that by preaching the equality of all human beings, Islam struck at the
   heart of patriarchy, but that through a process of cooption, patriarchy was able to devour Islam
   and quickly make it its own. Thus the position of women suffered a setback. See Al-Hibri, "A
   study of Islamic herstory", pp. 207–219. Other Muslim feminists agree with Al-Hibri, for
   example, Fatima Mernissi and Leila Ahmed. Modernist Muslim scholars, Fazlur Rahman and
   Abdullahi Ahmed An-Naim, also subscribe to the view that a clean break with the pre-Islamic
   Arab tribal culture was not possible; hence the advancement in the position of women was not
   achieved to the optimum levels as envisaged by Islam.
11 The term *jahilliya* denotes ignorance, and is used to describe the period immediately preceding
   Islam.
12 See the section below.
13 Qur'an, verse 2:228. Other verses pointing towards male superiority include verse 4:34,
   highlighting the fact that men are in charge of women; verse 2:282, that the evidentiary value of
   a women's testimony is half that of a man's; verse 24:30 that women should remain inside their
   houses in seclusion, and veil themselves when they had to venture out of their houses; verses
   regulating dissolution of marriage where, despite a number of safeguards for women, inequality
   between men and women remains, as the husband can repudiate his wife, whereas she cannot
   do the same.
14 B. Stowasser, "The status of women in early Islam", in F. Hussain (ed.), *Muslim Women*, St
   Martin's Press, New York, 1984, at p. 25.
15 *Ibid.*, at p. 29; Austin, "Islam and the feminine".

experiences. These are the wives of the Prophet Muhammad to whom the term "*Ummahat al-Mu 'minin*" (Mothers of the Believers) is applied as a finite group. It is important to note that *hadith* literature lays emphasis on the fact that by virtue of this title, the wives of the Prophet are elevated to a position above male believers. As regards ordinary women, Stowasser is of the view that the general attitude reflected in the *hadith* is a positive one. She states that:

It [*Hadith*] elaborates on the *Qur'anic* teachings regarding spiritual equality of women and men, and provides detailed information on women who perform all the religious duties enjoined by Islamic doctrine, thereby proving their full membership to the faith, such as prayer, almsgiving, the freeing of a slave, ritual slaughtering of sacrificial animals, and fasting (although the latter, according to some, should be done with the husband's permission except during *Ramadan* when the husband's consent is not necessary). As for the holy war, its equivalent is the blameless pilgrimage. Regarding martyrdom, the woman who dies in childbirth is a martyr. Women also build mosques, and can even act as prayer leaders.[16]

Marriage is advocated by the Prophet Muhammad in numerous *ahadith* and declared a meritorious institution. A wife should be given her full share of sexual pleasure by her husband, while the wife must not shun her husband's bed, and if she denies herself to him and he is annoyed because of her denial, "the angels curse her till dawn". *Hadith* literature also declares that women should be cared for and treated with kindness by their husbands. They should be given the right to indulge in their own idiosyncrasies, since a "woman is like a rib which will snap if one tries to straighten her natural crookedness".

But the framework of an essentially patriarchal social order affected the positive images of women and women came to be perceived in a different light. This perception is also highlighted in *hadith*. Thus some *hadith* describe women as morally and religiously defective; women, houses and horses are ominous; prayer is interrupted if dogs, donkeys and women pass too closely by the place of prayer. Women make up the larger inhabitants of Hell, because of their unfaithfulness and ingratitude towards their husbands; a people that entrust their leadership to a woman will not prosper. At the same time, women are committing a sin if they leave the mannerisms and confine of their sex. Thus the Prophet Muhammad is supposed to have pronounced a curse on women who behave and act like men.[17]

The above description of women in *hadith* literature is only a brief but representative sample of the conflicting images of women in the religious texts of Islam. The relevance of these conflicts for women's human rights cannot be overstated as it shows that accommodating the principle of equality in an Islamic human rights scheme involves dealing with two aspects in the Islamic tradition, one egalitarian and the other mandating sexual and religious discrimination, as well as mixed reactions of contemporary Muslims to these two aspects.[18] The question that Mayer and other writers on Islamic law pose, is why Muslims (and probably other religious and

---

[16] *Ibid.*, at p. 30.

[17] *Ibid.*, at p. 32.

[18] A. E. Mayer, *Islam and Human Rights: Tradition and Politics*, Boulder, CO: Westview Press, at p. 79; S. Mahmassani, "Adaptation of Islamic jurisprudence to modern social needs", in J. Donohue and J. Esposito (eds.), *Islam in Transition: Muslim Perspectives*, New York, Oxford University Press, at pp. 181–187; Al-Hibri, Mernissi, Fazlur Rahman, Hussain, Stowasser, Sayeh and Morse Jr. and many others.

cultural traditions as well) have made such selective and scarce use of the ethical dimension of regulatory norms favouring equality and non-discrimination for women.
For instance, nowadays, there is general agreement among Muslims that slavery is
unacceptable, and the large body of the *shari'a* regulating it has been effectively
discarded.[19] Why is it then, that Muslims are so deeply divided on the question of
whether legal distinctions based on sex and religion have become similarly superseded, and need to be addressed in the light of changing circumstances and needs
of the community? Why do they so vigorously disagree about whether a legal system in which women and non-Muslims were given equal rights with Muslim men
would be compatible with the requirements of Islam? There are no easy or straightforward answers to these questions. But an analysis of women's human rights in
Islam grounded in the two basic sources of Islamic law, the Qur'an and *hadith*, in
conjunction with the science of exegesis (*tafsir*) of the Qur'an, may be employed in
developing a theoretical framework leading to the view that the various categories
of rights and privileges are not immutable but subject to an evolutionary process.
This perception in turn may provide space for the argument that equality between
the sexes is possible within the Islamic legal tradition.

3 *IBADAT* AND *MUAMALAT*: ESPOSITO'S HIERARCHICAL NOTION OF RIGHTS IN THE ISLAMIC TRADITION

In this section it is proposed to look into women's human rights in Islam based on
a hierarchical notion of rights as developed by John Esposito. As the very word of
God, the Qur'an is the fundamental textual source of Islamic law. Esposito states
that the primary legal value of the Qur'an stems from the fact that it is an ethico-
religious revelation and acts as the source book of Islamic values from which specific
regulations of substantive law (*furu-al-fiqh*) are derived through human effort.[20]

Esposito believes that this task may be achieved through Muslim exegesis which is
a systematic study of the value system of the Qur'an and the hierarchization of its ethico-
religious values.[21] This method would resolve the problem of *naskh* (abrogation, the
suppression of one *shari'a* rule by a later one where divergent regulations exist) as well
as supplying a reasonable explanation for the comprehensiveness of the Qur'an. Most
importantly, it would provide a context within which one could understand the value
of specific Qur'anic regulations by shifting the emphasis beyond the specific regulation to its intent, to the value it sought to uphold.[22] Thus Qur'anic prescription has
two levels of importance – the specific injunction or command, whose details may be
relative to its space and time context, and the ideal or Qur'anic value, whose realization the specific regulation intends to fulfil. Since the task of the Muslim community
is the realization of these Qur'anic verses, the goals of jurists is to ensure that *fiqh* regulations embody these *shari'a* values as fully and perfectly as possible.

---

[19] One would find it extremely difficult to come across any constitution or law in any part of the
Muslim world sanctioning slavery today, despite the fact that the Qur'an contains clear texts
regulating the practice.
[20] Esposito, *Women in Muslim Family Law*, at p. 106.
[21] Ismail Ragi al-Faruqi, "Towards a new methodology of Qur'anic exegesis", *Islamic Studies*,
1962, p. 35.
[22] Esposito, *Women in Muslim Family Law*, at p. 107.

Verses from the Qur'an have been used by different factions to both support a woman's subservience to a man and to defend her rights to equality. This seeming contradiction can therefore be resolved by an analysis of the relevant Qur'anic verses through a system of "hierarchization of Qur'anic values" used by John Esposito to deal with human rights of women in Islam. This method, it is stated, is reminiscent of the process by which Qur'anic values were first applied to newly encountered social situations in the formative period of Islam by differentiating between the socio-economic and the ethico-religious categories in Qur'anic legislation.[23] While women's status is inferior to men in the former, they are full equals in the latter as to the spiritual and moral obligations imposed upon them, in their relationship to their Creator, and in the compensation prepared for them in the Hereafter.[24] While the status difference of men and women in the socio-economic sphere belongs to the category of *muamalat* (social relations), which are subject to change, their moral and religious equality belongs to the category of *ibadat* (religious duties towards God), which are immutable.[25] By applying the principle of "hierarchization" of Qur'anic values, the Muslim reformers argue that the moral and religious equality of men and women "represents the highest expression of the value of equality"[26] and therefore constitutes the most important aspect of the Qur'anic paradigm on the issue. Keeping this scheme of "hierarchization" in mind, it is possible then to categorize women's human rights in Islam.

A word of caution needs to be included here. Although Esposito's attempt at hierarchization of rights within the Islamic tradition is an important step in his endeavour to develop a modern framework for achieving equality for the sexes, we must not lose sight of the fact that in his attempt to realise the legislative value of Qur'anic verses, he places emphasis on exegesis or *tafsir*. This, Esposito believes, is due to the necessity to get at the motive, intent, or purpose behind Qur'anic passages. This approach reasserts the original influence of Qur'anic values in the early development of law and, as such, seeks to renew the process by which Qur'anic values were applied to newly encountered social situations in the first centres of Islamic legal history.[27] But it is submitted that the process of exegesis itself (as will be discussed below) resulted in some restrictive interpretations to Qur'anic verses regarding the status of women.

4 WOMEN'S HUMAN RIGHTS IN ISLAM AS CATEGORIES OF ENTITLEMENTS

Alongside the "hierarchization" of women's human rights in Islam, it is also proposed to use a method of "categorization" of these rights. Hevener classifies international human rights instruments relating to women as having undergone a progressive journey through three stages, each representing international consensus on women's human rights.[28] These categories are protective, corrective and non-

---

[23] *Ibid.*
[24] E.g. as stated in Qur'anic verses 33:35; 9:71; 40:40; 9:72; 48:5; 57:12; 3:195 and others.
[25] Esposito, *Women in Muslim Family Law*, p. 108.
[26] *Ibid.*
[27] *Ibid.*
[28] See N. Hevener, *International Law and the Status of Women*, Westview Press, Boulder, Col., 1983.

discriminatory. The protective category is one where laws are formulated which reflect a societal conceptualization of women as a group which either should not or cannot engage in specified activities. They imply that women are a subordinate, weak and disadvantaged group in society; hence the need to extend protection of unlimited duration.[29] The second category is the corrective category which also identifies women as a separate group who need separate treatment. However, the aim of the corrective provisions is "to alter and improve specific treatment that women are receiving, without making any overt comparison to the treatment of men in the area. They may be of limited duration, depending on the time period required to achieve the alteration desired."[30]

Finally, the non-discriminatory, sex-neutral category includes provisions which reject a conceptualization of women as a separate group, and rather reflect one of men and women as entitled to equal treatment. The concept is one which holds that biological differences should not be a basis for the social and political allocation of benefits and burdens within a society. These provisions treat women in the same manner as men.[31] For the purpose of analysing women's human rights in Islam, it is proposed to add here a fourth category, i.e. the discriminatory category wherein one may place certain injunctions, rules and regulations of the Qur'an and *hadith* literature where women and men clearly appear unequal. In the remaining part of this section, it is proposed to use a combination of the methods of "hierarchization" and "categorization" of women's human rights to discuss these within the Islamic tradition.

4.1 The non-discriminatory category of rights, *ibadat* and women's human rights

A number of writers on Islamic law[32] believe that the basic ethical norm of the Qur'an is equality between the sexes. This equality comes across most prominently in issues such as the creation of man and women, moral and spiritual obligations, and reward and punishment. The Islamic tradition is clear that God created men and women from one fundamental substance. As the Qur'an says: "He created you from one being, then from that (being) He made its mate."[33] *Hadith* literature also presents instances where the principle of complete equality has been espoused. The Prophet Muhammad is reported to have said: "All people are equal, as equal as the tooth of a comb. There is no claim of merit of an Arab over a non-Arab or of a white over a black person: only God-fearing people merit a preference with God. Thus men and women are equal."[34]

---

[29] *Ibid.*, at p. 4.
[30] *Ibid.*
[31] *Ibid.*
[32] Including Esposito, Fazlur Rahman, Riffat Hassan, Ustadh Taha, Abdullahi Ahmed An-Naim, Mernissi, Al-Hibri and Stowasser.
[33] The Qur'an, verse 39:6.
[34] The last address of the Prophet Muhammad to the Muslims on the occasion of the *Hajjat-ul-Wida* (the last pilgrimage).

In the Qur'an, Adam and Eve are held jointly responsible for the transgression and consequent expulsion from paradise.[35] Verse 7:18–26 is self-explanatory in this regard:

He (God) said (to Iblis): Go forth from hence, degraded banished. As for such of them as follow thee, surely I will fill hell with all of you. And (unto man): O Adam! Dwell thou and thy wife in the Garden and eat from whence ye will, but come not nigh this tree lest ye become wrongdoers. Then Satan whispered to them that he might manifest unto that which was hidden from them of their shame, and he said: Your Lord forbade you from this tree only lest ye should become angels or become immortals. And he swore to them (saying): I am a sincere adviser unto you. Thus did he lead them on with guile. And when they tasted of the tree, their shame was manifest to them and they began to hide (by heaping) on themselves some of the leaves of the Garden. And their Lord called them (saying): Did I not forbid you from that tree and tell you: Lo! Satan is an open enemy to you? They said: Our Lord! We have wronged ourselves. If Thou forgive us not and have not mercy on us, surely we are of the lost! He said: Go down (from hence), one of you a foe to the other. He said: There shall ye live, and there shall ye die, and thence shall ye be brought forth. O Children of Adam! We have revealed unto you raiment to conceal your shame, and splendid vesture, but the raiment of restraint from evil, that is best. This is of the revelations of Allah, that they may remember.

On the ethico-religious level (or *ibadat* on Esposito's hierarchy of rights), the position of men and women is on an equal standing, "both as to their religious obligations toward God and their peers as well as their consequent reward or punishment".[36] In support of this argument, Esposito cites verses 9:71–72 of the Qur'an which state thus:

The Believers, men and women, are protectors one of another; they enjoin what is just, and forbid what is evil; they observe regular prayers, practice charity, and obey God and His Apostle. On them will God pour his mercy . . . God hath promised to believers men and women, gardens under which rivers flow, to dwell therein, and beautiful mansions to dwell in gardens of everlasting bliss.

Similarly, the following verses also reflect equality in moral and spiritual obligations:

For Muslim men and Muslim women, for believing men and believing women, for devout men and devout women, for true men and true women, for men and women who are patient and constant, for men and women who humble themselves, for men and women who give charity, for men and women who guard their chastity, and for men and women who engage in God's praise, for them has God prepared forgiveness and great reward.[37]

---

[35] Stowasser, "The status of women in early Islam", at pp. 22–23.

[36] Esposito, *Women in Muslim Family Law*, p. 107; M. M. Taha, *The Second Message of Islam*, translated by A. A. An-Naim, Syracuse University Press, Syracuse, 1987, at p. 139 where he argues that "Islam's original precept is complete equality between men and women".

[37] The Qur'an, verse 33:35. Ustadh Taha, in support of the equality argument also cites other Qur'anic verses. These include: 40:17 "Today each soul is rewarded for what it earned, without unfairness. Surely, God is swift at reckoning"; verse 74:38 "Every soul is pledged for what it has earned"; verse 6:164 "Nor does any bearer of burden bear the burden of another, no matter how overburdened and not even of a kin. You are to warn [those] who sincerely fear God and perform the prayer. And who pay alms [*zakah*] is cleansing himself, and to God [you] shall return."

Whoever doeth right, whether male or female, and is a believer, him verily We shall
quicken with good life.[38]

Along with equal rewards in the hereafter, equality in punishment is enjoined for violating divine laws. So, for instance indulging in sexual relationships outside marriage brings with it severe punishment for both men and women as stated in verses
24:2–4 below:

The adulterer and the adulteress,
Scourge each one of them
(with) a hundred stripes.
And let not pity for the
Twain withhold you from
Obedience to Allah, if ye
believe in Allah
And the last day.
And let a party of believers witness their punishment.
The adulterer shall not
marry save an adulteress
Or an idolatress, and the
adulteress none shall marry all
Save an adulterer
or an idolater.
All that is forbidden unto believers.

Some *Hadith* literature and a few Qur'anic verses, however, in many areas tend to
deviate from, and consequently undermine, the non-discriminatory Qur'anic norms.
For instance, as opposed to Qur'anic verses (cited above), where both men and
women have been mentioned separately as being absolutely equal in virtue and piety,
in a very famous and important *hadith*, contained in the most authoritative *hadith*
collections, the Prophet is quoted as having said to some women that they were
inherently inferior to men both in matters of religion and intelligence. Asked how
they were weak in religion, he allegedly replied, "Because when you menstruate, you
are required neither to pray nor fast". Fazlur Rahman states that this *hadith* is contradictory to the Qur'anic verses on equality of the sexes in matters of piety and religious merit.[39] In response to the further question as to why they (women) were
inferior in intelligence, the Prophet is reported to have said, "Is not your evidence
(in a court) half of the value of men's evidence?" The women replied "Yes".[40]

Even though the Qur'anic verse 2:282 has been used to lay down a rule that
the value of the testimony that a woman gives in court in financial transactions has
to be corroborated by another woman, thus leading to the commonly held notion
that the evidence of two women is equal to that of a single male, yet there are instances where the evidence of one women outweighs that of a man. A woman's oath
in cases where her husband accuses her of adultery is enough to avert punishment.
Verses 24:6–9 state the following:

---

[38] The Qur'an, verse 16:97.
[39] Rahman, "Status of women in the Qur'an", at p. 41.
[40] *Ibid*.

As for those who accuse their wives but have no witnesses except themselves; let the testimony of one of them be four testimonies, [swearing] by Allah that he is of those who speak the truth; and yet a fifth, invoking the curse of Allah on him if he is of those who lie. And it shall avert the punishment from her if she bear witness before Allah four times that the thing he saith is indeed false. And a fifth [time] that the wrath of Allah be upon her if he speaketh the truth.

Islam has accorded women civil and property rights, including rights of inheritance. Women have been guaranteed complete control over what they earn and possess:

And their Lord hath heard them (and He sayeth): Lo! I suffer not the work of any worker, male or female, to be lost. Ye proceed one from another.[41]

Unto the men belongeth a share of that which parents and kindred leave, and unto the women a share of that which parents and near kindred leave.[42]

Unto men a fortune from that which they have earned, and unto women a fortune from that which they have earned.[43]

The afore-mentioned Qur'anic verses thus create a hierarchy of non-discriminatory rights. Some other examples of non-discriminatory laws granting Muslim women complete equality with men are: that she is *sui juris* (legal person) and can make independent decisions as regards entering into a contract, and the acquisition, disposal and alienation of property. The property laws of the Qur'an guarantee women the right to have full possession and control of their wealth including dower, during marriage and after divorce.[44] In the sphere of family law, too, certain provisions afford women complete equality; for example, the right to enter marriage of their own will, on attaining adulthood, without an intermediary (*wali*).[45]

Contrary to popular belief, there is nothing in any verse of the Qur'an barring women from participation in public and political life, including the right to vote, holding public office such as Head of State, judicial office, etc. Many *ahadith* however, declare some professions as out of bounds for women, one such being that of Head of State. For instance, one of the most oft-quoted *hadith* runs thus: "Those who entrust their affairs to a woman will never know prosperity."[46] This *hadith* barring women from public life first appeared on the Muslim political scene about twenty-five years after the death of the Prophet and was narrated by one Abu Bakra. He recollected this *hadith* at a highly opportune moment – the entry into Basra of the Caliph Ali after defeating Aisha (wife of the Prophet Muhammad) at the Bat-

---

[41] The Qur'an, verse 3:285.
[42] The Qur'an, verse 4:7.
[43] The Qur'an, verse 4:32.
[44] The Qur'an, verse 4:7; 4:11; and 4:12 as regards inheritance and bequeathal rights of women, and 4:4;4:24; 4:20; and 2:229 for full possession and control over their wealth.
[45] This, however, is a controversial right since under Shafei law a women always needs a guardian to contract her in marriage even when she has attained puberty. Even under Hanafi law it is subject to debate, as seen in the recent Pakistani case *Asma Jehangir v. Abdul Waheed*, PLD 1997 Lah. 301.
[46] Bukhari, *Sahih*, vol. 4, p. 226. The *Sahih* by Nukhari, along with five other *hadith* collections, rank as the "Six" authentic compilations of the words and deeds of the Prophet Muhammad.

tle of the Camel! Abu Bakra was among the notables of Basra who had refused to participate on either side in the civil war and feared reprisal from the Caliph Ali. Conveniently recalling such a *hadith* obviously meant soliciting political favour with a victorious leader at the cost of the vanquished foe. But this seemingly benign act of political expediency had a far reaching effect on the status of women and how they would henceforth be perceived, for in this case the defeated insurgent leader happened to be a woman. *Hadith*, being a source of Islamic law, have to be compiled scientifically along stringent rules to sift the authentic ones from those that have been fabricated or those that do not fulfil the rules laid down for determining the authenticity of traditions.[47] One such role is uprightness of character of the narrator. Applying this rule to Abu Bakra, he stands disqualified as he was convicted and flogged for false testimony (*qadhf*), by the second Caliph, Umar Ibn-Al-Khattab.[48] Despite this questionable background, many Muslims quote this *hadith* as "authority" for excluding women from decision-making and public life.

The historical context of the *hadith* under discussion is reported to have been the occasion when the Prophet Muhammad received news that Khusuro's daughter had succeeded to the throne. It is said that this woman was known to be highly authoritarian, and the comment in all likelihood was specifically in relation to her. Scholars like Dr Abdul Hameed consider this *hadith* as being informative and certainly not an immutable injunction for Muslims at all times and in all ages.[49]

In contradistinction to the above *hadith* one finds that in Chapter 27 of the Qur'an entitled *Naml* or the Ants, Bilquis, the Queen of Sheba, and her rule is mentioned with great commendation. Verses 32–34 of that chapter in particular described Bilquis as a ruler enjoying great wealth and dignity, and the full confidence of her subjects. She administers the country in consultation with her Council who in turn are committed to her and carry out her bidding. Might we not therefore argue, that if Islamic injunctions were set against women as Head of State or holding any other political office, the Queen of Sheba would not have found such honourable mention in the Qur'an? That women were an important constituent of the Muslim community and indeed expected to participate in political life is borne out by the fact that women as a group participated in the initial pledge of allegiance (*bay'a*) extended to the Prophet Muhammad by the Muslims.[50] This practice was continued in later years as well, making it an integral part of the political process.[51]

---

[47] For a comprehensive discussion on classification of traditions (*hadith*), and rules for authenticity see A. Rahim, *The Principles of Muhammadan Jurisprudence*, All Pakistan Legal Decisions, n.d., Lahore, first edition published 1911.

[48] Ibn al-Athir, *Usd al-Ghabra*, vol. 5, p. 38. For a detailed discussion of the circumstances surrounding narration of this *hadith*, see F. Mernissi, *Women and Islam*, translated by M. J. Lakeland, Basil Blackwell, Oxford, 1991. For a critique of Mernissi's analysis, see R. Afshari, "Egalitarian Islam and misogynist Islamic tradition: a critique of the feminist reinterpretation of Islamic history and heritage", *Critique*, 1994, pp. 13–33.

[49] A. Hameed, *Mabadi-e-Nazam ul Hukum Al Islami*, at pp. 876–878.

[50] Stowasser, "The status of women in early Islam", at p. 34.

[51] L. P. Sayeh and A. M. Morse Jr., "Islam and the treatment of women: an incomplete understanding of gradualism", 30 *Texas International Law Journal*, 30, 1995, p. 311 at p. 323 and accompanying footnotes.

It is important to make the point here that Ayesha, wife of the Prophet Muhammad, actively participated in political and public life. She is one of the most renowned and credible narrator of *hadith*, and is known to have completed and corrected many *ahadith* reported inaccurately or inadequately.[52]

4.2 The protective and corrective category, *muamalat* and women's human rights

In order to appreciate the protective and corrective category of women's human rights in Islam, it is important to study these against the background of the *jahilliyya*. The basic teachings of the Qur'an focus on efforts to improve the condition of, and strengthen, the weaker segments of society in pre-Islamic Arabia – orphans, slaves, the poor, women, etc. – segments which had been abused by the stronger elements in society.[53] Therefore Qur'anic verses aimed at ameliorating the plight of the down-trodden classes, and women in particular, stand out prominently. At the same time it has to be conceded that no matter how revolutionary the philosophy of Islam may have been, in order to take root among a tribal, patriarchal society, an outright break with the past would not have served any useful purpose. It is perhaps diffi-cult to appreciate today, in the closing years of the twentieth century, the extent of reform brought about by Islam fourteen hundred years ago in laying the foun-dations of an egalitarian society based on the principles of social justice. There-fore a number of rights discussed in this section will no doubt come across as half-measures and incapable of according women the same degree of importance as men.

Using Esposito's "hierarchization" of Qur'anic values, we come to the second cat-egory of women's human rights, i.e. rights that deal with *muamalat* or the socio-economic sphere of life. Here we discern some verses that accord more rights to men but have been framed so as to appear as corrective of wider forms of discrimina-tion in pre-Islamic Arabia and/or seen as protecting women along with other dis-advantaged sections of society. One would like to argue that these categories are not immutable as they are susceptible and sensitive to changing perceptions of society.[54] As Fazlur Rahman argues, "although women's inferior status has been written into Islamic law, it is by and large the result of prevailing social conditions rather than of the moral teaching of the Qur'an".[55]

Changing social conditions may therefore propel protective and corrective rights into the non-discriminatory category.[56]

---

[52] *Ibid.*, at pp. 322–323 and accompanying footnotes. For a very interesting account of the life and personality of Ayesha, wife of the Prophet Muhammad, see N. Abbot, *Aishah The Beloved of Muhammad*, Arno Press, New York, 1973 (reprint). For a more recent account, see D. A. Spellberg, *Politics, Gender and the Islamic Past: The Legacy of Aisha Bint Abi Bakr*, New York, Columbia University Press, 1994.

[53] Rahman, "Status of women in the Qur'an", p. 32.

[54] In Hevener's categorization of rights, the protective category is deemed of unlimited duration whereas rights placed in the corrective category may be of limited duration and no longer required when men and women achieve complete equality.

[55] Rahman, "Status of women in the Qur'an", p. 32.

[56] It is here that my views on Hevener's categorization differ to the extent that in applying these I perceive all four as a continuum flowing one from the other.

Among many Arab tribes, the girl child was an unwelcome intruder and was buried alive for reason of poverty and honour.[57] The Qur'an describes the situation in the following words:

When one of them is given the glad tiding of (the birth of) a female, his face darkens as he tries to suppress his chagrin. He hides from people out of a sense of disgrace of the news he has been given and he ponders whether to keep her in disgrace or shove her under the earth. Evil is, indeed, what they judge.[58]

In the corrective category of women's human rights therefore, perhaps the most important piece of Qur'anic injunction is the prohibition on female infanticide and hence the right to life for the girl child. In this respect, the Qur'an enjoins thus:

Slay not your children,
Fearing a fall to poverty.
We shall provide for
them and for you.
Lo! the slaying of them
Is a great sin.[59]

Hadith literature also contains a number of incidents and sayings of the Prophet Muhammad that reflect of the concern about female infanticide. Since pre-Islamic Arabia regarded the birth of a girl child as a punishment and humiliation from the gods, it was important that pronouncements be made to enforce the Qur'anic statements prohibiting the practice and removing the prevalent misgivings entrenched in the Arab mind. These *ahadith* were corrective of the social norm of female infanticide by engendering sentiments of love, affection and mercy for the girl child in the hearts of their parents.[60]

The pre-Islamic practice of *zihar* whereby an Arab husband would make a pronouncement of divorce upon his wife by comparing her with the back of his mother (and therefore prohibited to him), was also abolished.[61] This prohibition came in the light of the humiliation caused to the woman as a result of this particular form of divorce. Verse 33:4 of the Qur'an states: "God has not put two hearts in any man's breast: He has not made your wives with whom you do *zihar* your mothers, nor has He made your so-called (i.e. adopted) sons your real sons."

---

[57] Rahman, "Status of women in the Qur'an", at p. 37; Rahim, *Muhammadan Jurisprudence*.

[58] The Qur'an, verse 16:58–59.

[59] The Qur'an, verse 17:31. Similarly, in verse 6:151, the same commandment is repeated in these words: "Kill not your children On a plea of poverty We provide for you and For them".

[60] It is related from Ayesha, wife of the Prophet Muhammad, "If daughters are born to a parent and he treats them benevolently and beneficially, he will be secured from the fire of Hell." Anas bin Malik reports, "He who brings up two girls and they attain puberty, will come of the day of judgement and he and I will be like this." Saying this the Prophet joined his fingers. Abdullah reports, "If a girl child is born to someone and he brings her up well and educates and trains her well and whatever mercy is shown to him by Allah is showered by him on his daughter, that girl will be a screen and curtain for him from the fire of Hell."

[61] For a discussion of the various kinds of divorce in pre-Islamic Arabia, see Rahim, *Muhammadan Jurisprudence*, at pp. 8–9; Rahman, "Status of women in the Qur'an" , at pp. 38–39.

Another corrective measure in the Qur'anic text relates to a pagan custom whereby a son inherited his stepmother as part of his father's legacy. The son could either force her to marry him or debar her from remarrying anyone else for the rest of her life. In the absence of a son, the next male kin of the deceased had the same power over her.[62]

Another example of a protective/corrective right in the *muamalat* hierarchy is the right of inheritance granted to women which is invariably half that granted to men in comparable situations. The Qur'an states: "God thus directs you as regards your children's (inheritance). To the male a portion equal to that of two females."[63]

Although the right to inheritance is corrective of pre-Islamic custom of exclusion of women from any form of inheritance whiles also being protective of her vulnerable economic position, the half share is in any case discriminatory of her equal rights. But many writers on Islamic law have argued that this law does not discriminate against women. Perveen Shaukat Ali, for instance, argues thus:

> In their opinion this is against the basic rules of justice to give women half of the male's share. It may, however, be pointed out that a woman is in no way a loser in this bargain. She gets her part of property from three different sources, i.e. father, husband and son, and this makes her share almost equal to [that of the] man.[64]

It is submitted with respect to Perveen Shaukat Ali's argument, that men too inherit from other sources. They inherit from the mother, wife and daughter and in most cases their share is double that of the woman's.[65] Inheritance rights of women may be placed in the protective category by virtue of the fact that Qur'anic injunctions ensure to women a basic minimum share, recognizing the reality that they will always be a class of persons in need of protection. This is borne out by centuries of oppression where women have not and in all likelihood, will not in the foreseeable future be able to attain substantive economic parity with their male counterparts. At the same time, however, this minimum share does not preclude an enhanced share or a share equal to or more than that of a male. A parent, spouse or any other person may, by executing a valid gift deed, give away his/her entire wealth to a woman to the exclusion of all expectant male heirs.

Similarly, a husband may, under a stipulation in the marriage contract, be divested of his entire possessions by way of dower, as there is no maximum limit to what may be given as dower to a wife.

In the area of family law, human rights of women are for the most part of the corrective/protective category although, as mentioned above, the initial premise of entering into the marriage contract is one of complete equality. However, once the contract is made, then inequality between the contracting parties emerges. For instance, under the "protective" right of dower as a "consideration" for the marriage contract, the husband becomes the protector and the wife the protected. She re-

---

[62] Rahim, *Muhammadan Jurisprudence*, pp. 7–9; Rahman, "Status of women in the Qur'an", pp. 38–39. The prohibition came in verse 4:19 of the Qur'an.

[63] The Qur'an, verse 4:11.

[64] P. S. Ali, *Human Rights in Islam*, Aziz Publishers, Lahore, 1980, at p. 120.

[65] For example, as a wife who has children, a wife inherits one-eighth of her husband's estate; one-fourth if she is childless. A husband on the other hand inherits one-fourth from his wife if they have children, one-half if they are childless. For a detailed exposition of the Islamic law of inheritance see M. A. Mamman, *Principles of Muhammadan Law*, Lahore, PLD Publishers, 1995, Chapters 6, 7 and 8.

tains the dower (or the right over it if not paid already), so long as she remains the wife or the husband dissolves the marriage tie by *talaq*.[66] But if the wife is desirous of terminating the contract,[67] then this protection of dower money or property must be returned to the husband to "ransom herself from her husband".[68]

The Qur'an also introduced significant changes in the concept of dower. In contrast to the pre-Islamic notion of dower as a form of bride-price to be appropriated by the father or other male relative of the woman, the wife became the sole recipient of this sum of money or other property. Furthermore, verse 4:20 also prohibited the practice of forcing one's wife to make a will in one's favour that remitted the dower or any other gifts the husband had given to her.

But if you do want to take another wife in her place (i.e. by divorcing her) and if you have gifted to her a heap of gold, do not take anything back from it; will you take it back as a stunning lie and a clear sin? And how will you take it back when you have been intimate with each other and they have had solemn promises from you?[69]

Haeri sums up this reform in family law in the following words:

In the seventh century AD the Prophet Muhammad unified the multiplicity of pre-Islamic modes of sexual mores of sexual unions by outlawing all but one form of marriage, namely marriage by contract. Fundamental to this rearranging of the existing social structure was the realignment of the role of the husband and wife into that of the principal transacting parties. As distinct from the pre-Islamic form of "marriage and dominion", Islamic law recognised the wife – not her father – to be the recipient of the brideprice. Implicit in this act is a recognition of a degree of women's autonomy and violation. As a party to the contract, it is the woman herself who has to give consent – however nominally – for the contract to be valid. And it is the woman herself, not her father (custom aside), who is to receive the full amount of brideprice, be it immediate or deferred.[70]

It is an established fact that traditional Islamic law accords the Muslim male a unilateral right to dissolve the marriage tie (*talaq*) without assigning any cause[71] and without the interference of the court.[72] On the other hand, it confers on a woman the right to seek dissolution of the marriage tie by forgoing her dower, with the difference that the woman has to convince the court of her fixed aversion and the

---

[66] The unilateral right to terminate the marriage contract belongs to the husband under Islamic law which is technically known as *talaq*. The husband has to pay the wife the dower on pronouncement of *talaq*.

[67] The concept of the wife being able to "buy" her freedom by returning her dower is technically known as *khula* which affords a woman the right to get out of an undesirable union.

[68] The Qur'an, verse 2:229.

[69] The Qur'an, verse 4:20.

[70] S. Haeri, "Divorce in contemporary Iran: a male prerogative in self-will", in *Islamic Family Law*, Graham and Trotman, London, 1990, at p. 56.

[71] In a famous Pakistani case, *Khurshid Bibi v. Muhammad Amin*, PLD 1967 SC 97, their Lordships were of the view that *talaq* is not an unfettered right of the husband, as the Qur'an in 4:35 provides for the appointment of arbiters to curtail the unbridled exercise of this right. These fetters are hardly effective if the husband is determined to go ahead with the pronouncement of the divorce.

[72] Despite this privilege accorded to the husband in traditional Islamic law, many Muslim countries have legislated certain procedural requirements that have to be undertaken to finalize the divorce. See for instance, the Muslim Family Laws Ordinance, 1961 of Pakistan.

irretrievable breakdown of the marriage (*khula*).[73] Although some leading judgments from the superior courts of Pakistan have tried to equate the right to pronounce *talaq* by the husband with the right of *khula* available to the woman,[74] yet it is submitted that there are major differences between these two modes of dissolution of marriage. No matter what obstacles one places in the husband's right to give *talaq*, at the end of the day by its very definition *talaq* may be pronounced with or without the intervention of a court of law. On the other hand, if a woman fails to convince the judge of the genuineness of her case for *khula*, she cannot unilaterally terminate the marriage contract.[75] It is with these drawbacks in mind that I have placed *khula* in the protective/corrective category of women's human rights rather than in the non-discriminatory one.

Another protective right as regards dissolution of marriage is *talaq-i-tafwid*, or delegated right of divorce given to the wife in the contract of marriage. Muslim women may take advantage of the fact that marriage is a civil contract and stipulations limiting or even prohibiting the husband from dissolving the marriage tie can be incorporated in it. An effort at achieving some measure of equality may thus be successful.[76]

The right of the wife to be properly fed and clothed at the husband's expense is another protective right afforded to the woman.[77] This right is available to her even though she may be wealthier than the husband and capable of maintaining not only herself but him as well.[78]

The divorce laws stipulating a waiting period (*iddat*) during which the marriage is suspended, but not terminated, may also be seen in a protective/corrective framework. In the pre-Islamic laws of divorce, husbands were not required to follow any particular procedure for terminating the marriage contract. They could at will marry, divorce and remarry the same woman. By laying down a waiting period before which the divorce became irrevocable, the unilateral right of divorce allowed to men (and not to women) was toned down and chances of reconciliation kept alive until the period of waiting expired.[79]

---

[73] PLD 1967 SC 97.

[74] For example in *Safia Begum v. Khadim Hussain* 1985 CLC 1869 and *Syed Muhammad Rizwan v. Mst. Samina Khatoon* 1989 SMCR 25.

[75] For instance, see *Aali v. Additional District Judge* I, Quetta: 1987 CLC 27, *Raisa Begum v. Muhammad Hussein* 1986 MLD 1418 and many others.

[76] Here a note of caution as regards these stipulations favourable to women. Societal pressure strongly discourages use of these rights afforded to women. For details, see S. S. Ali, "An analysis of the trends of the superior courts of Pakistan in matters relating to marriage, dower, divorce", working paper for the Women and Law project, *Women Living Under Muslim Laws*, 1993.

[77] For example as enjoined in the Qur'an, verse 4:34.

[78] But this protective right to be maintained ceases as soon as the woman is divorced or is widowed. For the issue of post-divorce maintenance, see the famous Indian case of *Muhammad Ahmed Khan v. Shah Bano Begum* and others, AIR 1985, SC 945.

[79] There are three modes of pronouncing *talaq*: *talaq-i-Ahsan*, *talaq-i-hasan* and *talaq-ul-biddat*. The first two offer some scope for reconciliation as the divorce does not become irrevocable for some time. The time afforded before the divorce becomes irrevocable is the first kind of waiting period. Then there is the period of *iddat*, which is a period during which a woman whose marriage has been terminated either by death or divorce may not remarry. *Talaq-ul-biddat* (the third mode), is an irrevocable divorce as soon as it is pronounced and there is no chance of reconciliation. This mode is not the one sanctioned by the Prophet and hence is rejected by some Muslims.

As regards the rights and privileges of a woman in her capacity as mother, the concept of child care as a joint parental and social responsibility has deep roots within the Islamic tradition. While breastfeeding and its duration are recommended, the modalities are to be decided by "mutual consultation" of both parents. If the mother is unable to fulfil her duty, the father is under an obligation to make alternate arraignments, e.g. hiring a wet nurse, etc. Where the parents are divorced and the mother has custody, the father is bound to feed, maintain and pay the mother as he would any wet nurse for performing this job.[80] This placing of the monetary responsibility for the welfare of the child and the nursing mother, although within the protective category of human rights, reinforces the stereotype roles of men as providers and women as passive consumers and men's liability.

Regarding custody and guardianship of children, in cases of divorced parents, a mother is entitled to *hizanat* or custody of a boy up to the age of seven and a female child until she attains puberty.[81] After that period , custody reverts to the father who is generally known as the "natural guardian" of his children. The mother cannot, under traditional Islamic law, be recognized as the legal guardian of her own children. There is no verse of the Qur'an establishing the father as the sole legal guardian of his children to the exclusion of the mother. However, there is a saying of the Prophet, which is an extract of his sermon on the occasion of the Last Pilgrimage (*Hajjat-ul-Wida*), to the effect that "the child belongs to him/her on whose bed it is born". In the patriarchal social organization it is the man who has to provide the household effects (including the bed on which the child is born). It has thus been inferred over the centuries that the child "belongs" to the father. This is also in line with the above mentioned principle of Islamic law where the father is made to pay for feeding and rearing the child, even if it is by the child's own mother. But what is very important to realize is that these recommendations/injunctions are always prefaced by the economic superiority of the man. The question posed here is what the position would be if one were to reverse the situation and the woman/mother was the breadwinner/provider of the family.

---

[80] Nor should he [father] to whom the child is born
   [be made to suffer] because of his child.
   (An heir shall be chargeable in the same way
   if they both decide on weaning)
   if they desire to wean the child by mutual consent,
   And, [after] consultation, it is no sin for them,
   And if you wish to give your children out to
   Nurse, it is no sin for you provided ye pay
   [the nursing woman as hired].
   What is due from you [i.e. money that has been either
   fixed or according to common practice]
   Observe your duty to Allah, and know that Allah
   Is Seer of what ye do
                                    The Qur'an, verse 2:233.

[81] These are not uniformly applicable rules, as only the Hanafi Sunni school of thought adheres to them. Under Shia law, a mother is only entitled to custody of her minor children up to the age of two years in the case of a male child and seven years in the case of a female.

4.3 Discrimination category of rights: the verse 4:34 debate

In the hierarchization and categorization of rights, we now come to an area where the male is provided status, control and authority over the woman (although in recent years, some male and female scholars and theologians[82] have challenged the male-orientated interpretation of some of these verses). In this section it is proposed to analyse these Qur'anic verses that arguably establish and reinforce gender hierarchies within the Islamic tradition. Although the most oft-quoted verse in this regard is verse 4:34 of the Qur'an, male dominance and priority is also determined by this verse used in conjunction with verse 12:282 (testimony of women), verses permitting polygamy, the superior right of the male to terminate marriage, etc. Each of these verses used over the centuries as sources of positive law on the subject in various Muslim jurisdictions is open to diverse interpretations to the point where they have even been used to promote women's rights (see discussion below).

Some Qur'anic laws that regulate the structure of authority in the Muslim household stipulate that within the context of marriage and as a member of the husband's household, the wife is his responsibility and hence under his authority. The Qur'an thus endows the man both with authority over the woman in the family setting, coupled with the obligation to provide for her by way of material support.[83] The classic verse confirming male superiority (or at least perceived as such by most Muslims) is the following:

Men are the protectors
And maintainers of women,
Because God has given
The one more (strength)
Than the other, and because
they support them from their means.
Therefore the righteous women
are devoutly obedient, and guard
In (the husband's) absence
What God would have them guard.
As to those women
On whose part ye fear
Disloyalty and ill-conduct,
Admonish them (first)
(Next), refuse to share their beds,
(And last) beat them lightly

---

[82] See for instance the work of Riffat Hassan, who is to the author's knowledge the first and one of the very few female theologians in the Muslim world and has written prolifically on the subject. Some of the more relevant to our present discussion are "The role and responsibilities of women in the legal and ritual tradition of Islam", paper presented at a biannual meeting of a trialogue of Jewish-Christian-Muslim scholars at the Joseph and Rose Kennedy Institute of Ethics, Washington DC, on 14 October 1980; "On human rights and the Qur'anic Perspective" in A. Swidler (ed.), *Human Rights in Religious Traditions*, Pilgrim Press, New York, 1982; and "An Islamic perspective", in J. Becher (ed.), *Women, Religion and Sexuality*, WCC Publications, Geneva, 1990, at p. 93.

[83] B. F. Stowasser, "Religious ideology, women and family", in B. F. Stowasser (ed.), *The Islamic Impulse*, Croom Helm, London, 1987, at p. 293.

But if they return to obedience,
Seek not against them
Means (of annoyance)
For God is Most-High
Great (above you all).[84]

As mentioned above, a number of scholars have taken up the challenge of reinterpreting verse 4:34. Riffat Hassan, for instance, argues that:

While Muslims through the centuries have interpreted Sura An-Nisa:34 as giving them (men) unequivocal mastery over women, a linguistically, and philosophically/theologically accurate interpretation of this passage would lead to radically different conclusions. In simple words what this passage is saying is that since only women bear children (which is not to say either that all women should bear children or that women's sole function is to bear children) – they should not have the additional obligation of being breadwinners whilst they perform this function. Thus during the period of a woman's child-bearing, the function must be performed by men (not just husbands) in the Muslim "Ummah" . . . It enjoins men in general to assume responsibility for women in general when they are performing the vitally important function of child-bearing.[85]

It is submitted however with respect to Riffat Hassan's interpretation of verse 4:34 of the Qur'an that, although by virtue of her innovative interpretation, one may succeed in placing this verse in the protective category of rights for women, her argument cannot be used to acquire non-discriminatory status for women. What is perhaps possible is to emphasize that verses where wealth has been described as the sole determinant of superiority, such as verse 4:34, we may assume that were women to achieve that measure, they would be accorded the same status as men in a similar position.[86]

A further point with regard to Riffat Hassan's interpretation lies in the fact that she fails to come up with a plausible explanation of why men (in that particular superior position) are justified in beating the woman (women) in their charge. According to her view, all three stages of admonishment are invokable only if women (*en masse*) refuse to procreate. However, it has to be said that neither a textual reading of the verse nor any contextual evidence leads one to this inference.[87]

Aziza Al-Hibri, another Muslim scholar, analyses verse 4:34 in the following manner: "Men are *qawwamun* over women in matters where God gave some of them more than others, and in what they spend of their money." Al-Hibri argues that the problematic concept here is *qawwamun*, which is difficult to translate. She says that while some writers translate it as "protectors" and "maintainers" (i.e. A. Y. Ali's translation), this is not quite accurate as the basic notion involved here is one of moral guidance and caring.[88] The "standard" interpretation of the above passage declares men as being in charge of women's affairs because men were created by God as superior to woman (in strength and reason) and because they provided for women

---

[84] The Qur'an, verse 4:34.
[85] R. Hassan, extract from a paper present at a Qur'anic interpretation held in Karachi, Pakistan (8–13 July 1990), under the auspices of *Women Living Under Muslim Laws*.
[86] This argument needs further research and refinement.
[87] Hassan "An Islamic perspective", at pp. 110–112.
[88] Al-Hibri, " A study of Islamic herstory", p. 217.

(they spent their money on them). Al-Hibri challenges it on two counts – that it is unwarranted and that it is inconsistent with other Islamic teachings.[89] She concludes therefore that:

nowhere in the passage is there a reference to the male's physical or intellectual superiority. Secondly, since men are *qawwamun* over women in matters where God gave *some* of the men more than *some* of the women, *and* in what the men spend of their money, then clearly men *as a class* are not *qawwamun* over women as a class. The conditions of being *qawwamun* as specified in the passage are two:
(1)   that the man be someone whom God gave more in the matter at hand than the woman and
(2)   that he be her provider
If either condition fails, then the man is not *qawwamun* over that woman. If both obtain, then all it entitles him to is caring for her and providing her with moral guidance. For, only under extreme conditions (for example insanity) does the Muslim woman lose her right to self-determination, including entering any kind of business contract without permission from her husband . . . It is worth noting that the passage does not even assert that *some* men are inherently superior to *some* women. It only states that in certain matters some men may have more than some women.[90]

Al-Hibri also makes the point that according to her interpretation of verse 4:34, no one has the right to counsel a self-supporting woman and since "Islam emphasises democracy and enjoins Muslims to counsel each other in making decisions, this resolution falls totally within the spirit of Islam."[91]

The second line of argument pursued by Al-Hibri in support of her alternate explanation is to state that the traditional interpretation is inconsistent with other Islamic teachings. She cites verse 9:71 of the Qur'an which declares that: "The believers, men and women, are *awliya*, one of the another". *Awliya* may be translated as meaning protectors, in charge, guides. In fact, conceptually it is quite similar to the term *qawwamun*. Al-Hibri then poses the question:

How could women be *awliya* of men if men are superior to women in both physical and intellectual strength? And, how could women be in charge of men who have absolute authority over them?[92]

Esposito, arguing in the same vein as Riffat Hassan and Al-Hibri, initiates the discussion by stating that in the socio-economic sphere, scholars of Islam agree that a major concern of the Qur'an was the betterment of woman's position by establishing their legal capacity, granting their economic rights (dower, inheritance, etc.) and thus raising their social status.[93] However, the traditional interpretations of Qur'anic verses such as 4:34 only support what today would be deemed an inequitable position for women. This verse has been interpreted as indicating men's priority over women. According to Pickthall's translation of the Qur'an, verse 4:34 states that

---

[89] *Ibid.*
[90] *Ibid.*, at p. 218.
[91] *Ibid.*
[92] *Ibid.*
[93] Esposito, *Women in Muslim Family Law*, at p. 107.

"Men are in charge of women, because Allah hath made one to excel the other, and because they spend their property (for the support of women)."[94]

However, the "priority" attributed to men over women is best understood as originating from their greater responsibility as protectors and maintainers within the socio-economic context of Arabian society during the Prophet's time. Men, by virtue of their duty to defend and support their extended family members, enjoyed more rights and subsequently a different status in Muslim society. This understanding of a man's role is illustrated by another possible translation of the same Qur'anic verse: "men are the guardians (i.e. protectors and maintainers) over women because God made some of them (to excel) over others and because they (men) provide support from their wealth."[95]

Esposito, too, appears to be in agreement with the view that it is primarily the economic superiority and responsibility for the household that accords to the male a degree of excellence, but only to those men who fulfil this task, and not all men.

Barbara Stowasser, in her study of the status of women in early Islam, states that verses such as 4:34 have fallen prey to the Qur'anic interpreters who, in their enthusiasm to ensure maximum application of Qur'anic provisions, attempted to place "a fence about the law by requiring a precautionary margin in order to ensure the entire fulfilment of its dictates, so the interpreters of the Qur'an demanded more than the original".[96]

As a justification of her argument, Stowasser cites a number of commentaries of the Qur'an and shows how each successive commentator became more restrictive of women's rights. Consequently, by the time one reaches the seventeenth century, women have been completely excluded from all spheres of public life and made "invisible".

The earliest comment on verse 4:34 cited by Stowasser is taken from Abu Jafar Muhammad Jarir al-Tabari's (d. 923) work. He says that:

Men are in charge of their women with respect to disciplining (or chastising) them, and to
providing them with restrictive guidance concerning their duties towards God and
themselves (i.e. the men); by virtue of that by which God has given excellence (or preference)
to the men over their wives: i.e. payment of their dowers to them, spending of their wealth
on them, and providing for them in full. This is how God has given excellence to (the men)
over (the women), and hence (the men) have come to be in charge of (the women) and hold
authority over them in those of their matters with which God has entrusted them.

Tabari's interpretation of this verse is very literal and specifically endow men with authority over their women in the family setting coupled with the obligation to provide for their women by way of material support.[97]

The second commentary of verse 4:34 is taken from Nasir al-Din Abu al-Kyahr'Abd Allah idn Umar al-Baydawi (d. 1286). This interpretation following some 350 years after Tabari, becomes more detailed and restrictive, sanctioning the view of women as creatures incapable of and unfit for public duties:[98]

---

[94] M. Marmaduke Picktall, trans., *The Meaning of the Glorious Koran* n.d., Mentor, New York, p. 83.
[95] Esposito, *Women in Muslim Family Law*, at p. 108.
[96] Stowasser, "The status of women in early Islam", at p. 25, quoting R. Levy, *The Social Structure of Islam*, p. 126.
[97] *Ibid.*, at p. 26.
[98] *Ibid.*

Men are in charge of women, i.e. men are in charge of women as rulers are in charge of their subjects . . . God has preferred the one (sex) over the other, i.e. because God has preferred men over women in the completeness of mental ability, good counsel, complete power in the performance of duties and the carrying out of (divine) commands. Hence to men have been confined prophecy, religious leadership (*'imama*), saintship (*wilaya*), the performance of religious rites, the giving of evidence in law courts, the duties of the Holy War, and worship (in the mosque) on Friday, etc. the privilege of electing chiefs, the large share of inheritance, and discretion in matters of divorce, by virtue of that which they spend of their wealth, in marring (the women) such as their dowers and cost of their maintenance.[99]

It is clear therefore that verse 4:34 has been used to bring within its ambit the entire legal personality of a woman, denying to her independent personhood. Ahmad ibn Muhammad al-Khafaji (d. 1659) further "refined" the restrictive detail provided by Baydawi's exegesis by stating that religious leadership (*imama*) (which is inaccessible to women) is understood to include both the *imama kubra* and the *imama sughra*. He understands *wilaya* not as "saintship" but as "assuming of responsibility (*tawallin*) for the woman in matters of marriage, which means the power to make decisions" (which in any case by this time was no longer theirs).[100]

The religious rites (*sha'a'ir*) from which women are barred according to Baydawi, are the call to prayer (*adhan*), the second call to prayer (*iqama*), the Friday sermon, Friday worship (in the mosque) and the *takbirat al-tashriq* (certain rites during the Pilgrimage).[101]

The foregoing discussion on the varying interpretations of verse 4:34 clearly outlines its importance in creating gender hierarchies within the Islamic tradition. But the most far reaching implications for women's human rights lies in the justification of this verse for physically chastising a "disobedient" woman. Very little comment in this regard has been offered by any of the writers mentioned above including Riffat Hassan, Al-Hibri or Esposito.[102] Fazlur Rahman however, does take up the issue and offers the jurisdiction that:

the Qur'an appears to be saying is that since men are the primary socially operative factors and bread-winners, they have been wholly charged with the responsibility of defraying household expenditure and upkeep of their womenfolk. For their duties and economic struggles and experiences they have become entitled to manage women's affairs and, in case of recalcitrance on the part of women, to admonish them, leave them alone in their beds and as a last resort, beat them.[103]

---

[99] *Ibid.*
[100] *Ibid.*
[101] *Ibid.*
[102] Mernissi has dealt with the issue at some length in her book entitled *Women and Islam*, where she argues that the verse was revealed at a point in tie when the newly formed Muslim (male) community feared that the Prophet Muhammad by prohibiting violence against women, was encouraging a "female rebellion". Verse 4:34 seems to have quelled those fears forever and reinstated male superiority.
[103] Rahman, "Status of women in the Qur'an", p. 44.

4.4 Evidentiary value of women's testimony

Verse 2:282 of the Qur'an provides another example where pronouncements of arguably restricted application have been used as justification for creating gender hierarchies within the Islamic tradition. A number of Muslim jurisdictions, including Pakistan, have legislated on the basis of this verse, thus legally reducing the status of women.[104] The verse states that the testimony of a woman is worth half that of a man in financial transactions reduced to writing:

And get two witnesses
Out of your own men,
And if there are not two men,
Then a man and two women,
Such as ye choose,
For witnesses,
So that if one of them errs,
The other can remind her.[105]

Hadith literature has further presented this inequality in the value of evidence of a woman as reflecting an innate inferiority of women as opposed to superiority of men. As mentioned above, a *hadith* quotes the Prophet Muhammad as having stated that women were inferior both in matters of religion and intelligence. The reason the Prophet Muhammad is supposed to have cited for a woman's inferiority in intelligence is that the value of her evidence is half that of a man's.[106] Fazlur Rahman, in analysing this *hadith* appears to be questioning its authenticity when he argues that it (*hadith*) presupposes the development of the law of evidence in early Islam.[107] As regards verse 2:282, he is of the opinion that the Qur'an is not stating any general law of the evidentiary value of male and female statements as the law.

If the Qur'an really regarded a woman's evidence as half that of a man's, why should it not allow the evidence of four females to be equivalent to that of two males, and why should it say that only one of the males may be replaced by two females? The intention of the Qur'an apparently was that since it was a question of a financial transaction and since women usually do not deal with such matters or with business affairs in general, it would be better to have two women rather than one – if one had to have women – and that, if possible at all, one must have at least one male.[108]

Fazlur Rahman then goes on to state that one simply cannot deduce from verse 2:282 a general law to the effect that under all circumstances and for all purposes, a

---

[104] Section 17 of the *Qanoon-i-Shahadat* Order, 1984.

[105] The Qur'an, verse 2:282.

[106] But some writers have stated that the intellectual status of a Muslim woman is "neither marred nor degraded by the commandments of the Qur'anic verse". R. El-Nimr, "Women in Islamic Law", in M. Yamani (ed.), *Feminism and Islam*, at p. 95. El-Nimr's views appear to be representative of many Muslim writers including Mawdudi who argue in a defensive, apologetic vein. She described reasons of emotional, physical and psychological strain as disabling women from acting as competent witnesses.

[107] It may be pertinent to point out with reference to this statement of Fazlur Rahman that while he is not explicitly setting it out, he appears to be challenging the authenticity of this *Hadith*.

[108] Rahman, "Status of women in the Qur'an", at p. 42.

women's evidence is inferior to a man's. He is convinced that this verse does not have the slightest intention of proving any rational deficiency in women *vis-à-vis* men. As an example, Fazlur Rahman cites the example of classic Islamic law regarding women with knowledge of gynaecology as the most competent witnesses in cases involving gynaecological issues.[109] Finally, he also puts forward the suggestion that even if a law could be formulated on the basis of such a generalization, then may we not change the law when social circumstances so change that women are not only educated equally with men but are also conversant with business and financial transactions?[110]

With respect to the arguments presented by Fazlur Rahman, it is submitted that looking at the formulation of the verse under discussion in its socio-economic perspective, one is inclined to argue that against the background of the social milieu of seventh-century tribal Arabia, involving a woman as witness in an activity that clearly lay within the public sphere of life and was until that time out of bounds for women, may be regarded as an important first step. It was without doubt corrective of complete non-recognition of women as legal persons capable of participating in financial transactions reduced to writing. However, what is a matter for concern is the fact that this step towards according women greater autonomy and legal personality was frozen in time and not taken forward towards achieving equality. Furthermore, one has to acknowledge that this incapacity (of women to given evidence) is not only confined to commercial transactions reduced to writing. In fact in cases wherever *hadd* punishment[111] may be inflicted, the testimony of women and non-Muslims is not even accepted.[112] A further example is that of the contract of marriage in Islam, which is also in the nature of a financial transaction, and here too, women who witness signing of the marriage deed suffer from the same disability.[113]

But it may be argued that verse 2:282 is not necessarily of general universal application. This may be inferred from verse 24:6–9 of the Qur'an where a woman's oath by which she defends herself against her husband's accusation of adultery outweighs that of the man's (her husband's) in the absence of witnesses.

4.5 Inheritance rights of women: a fixed, unchangeable share, or the basic minimum?

Another sensitive issue concerning rights of women in the sphere of family law is that of inheritance. As mentioned above, women generally inherit half of what men in comparable situations would inherit. While this was a progressive initial step in a society where, as Fatima Mernissi remarks, the newly converted Meccan

---

[109] *Ibid.*

[110] *Ibid.*

[111] *Hadd* means limit. In legal terms it means mandatory punishment limits for which have been laid down in the Qur'an.

[112] For details, see for example, the Hudood Ordinances, 1979 promulgated by General Zia of Pakistan. For adverse implications and human rights violations of women as a result of these laws, see A. Jehangir and H. Jilani, *The Hudood Ordinances: A Divine Sanction?*, Rohtas Books, Lahore, 1990 and R. Mehdi, "The offence of rape in the Islamic law of Pakistan" *International Journal of the Sociology of Law*, 18, 1990, pp. 19–29 and S. S. Ali, "Gender, Islamic fundamentalism and human rights: a case study of Pakistan", *Women Against Fundamentalism Journal*, 1991.

[113] C. Hamilton, *Hedaya*, Karachi, Darol-Ishrat, 1989 edn, p. 74.

aristocrats did not mind sharing Heaven and the rewards of the Hereafter with their Muslim sisters, what hurt their egos (and economic interests) was that they were being required to share their worldly possessions with women who until the dawn of Islam were little more than the chattels and property of these very men.[114] Over the centuries, this entitlement of women to half the share of a man in a comparable situation became the fixed, unchangeable and only share that she was entitled to.[115]

Of the many justifications advanced by Muslims (men and women) regarding the half share in inheritance rights for women, the following may be mentioned as the most repeated:[116]

(a) women are not providers for households, while men are; hence a greater burden requires a greater share;

(b) Qur'anic injunctions do not require a Muslim wife to share her resources with her spouse or spend it on household expenses even though the husband may be destitute. On the other hand, a wife may seek a decree for dissolution of her marriage on the grounds that her husband is incapable of, or will not maintain her;

(c) a husband is required to pay his wife a sum of money or other property as dower as part of the marriage contract, therefore in addition to her half share in inheritance, she also receives a further share as dower.

With regard to the above arguments, it is submitted that the situations described above are subject to changing realities of society, as well as the socio-economic circumstances of the present day and are therefore weak justifications. Thus, for instance, are men always the "bread winners" of families? Is it not a fact that there are millions of families around the world where women are heads of households and have had to take on responsibility for meeting the entire household expenses? As to the second line of argument, while women are not legally required to share responsibility for the household, yet one would have to look very hard indeed to find a family where the woman, despite having the resources, goes hungry and places her spouse and children in a similar predicament. As to (c), it may be argued that the amount of dower stipulated in the marriage contract is invariably less than an equivalent share in inheritance. Furthermore, if a woman seeks dissolution of marriage from her husband, she will have to forgo this amount.

4.6 Polygamy: an acknowledgement of "different needs" or statement of male superiority?

The third issue to be addressed in the discriminatory category of rights is that of restrictions imposed on women within the institution of marriage without corresponding limitations on men. Thus Qur'anic injunctions enjoin strict monogamy on women and also confine her to a Muslim spouse, while men may marry up to

---

[114] Mernissi, *Women and Islam*, at p. 120.

[115] F. Rahman, "Status of women in the Qur'an", at p. 45.

[116] These views are based on personal communications with a wide range of people as well as readings on the subject. For a recent empirical study on the subject, see S. S. Ali, "Using law for women in Pakistan" in A. Stewart (ed.), *Gender, Law and Justice*, Blackstone, forthcoming, 1998.

four wives at any one time from among *kitabia*[117] women.[118] Polygamy is permitted in Islam although as the Qur'anic verse allowing states, it is with certain provisos: "Marry women of your choice, two, three or four, but if you fear that you shall not be able to deal justly (with them) then only one."[119]

The debate around polygamy raises a number of questions. Does, for instance, the Qur'anic verse create an obligation for all male Muslims to emulate the practice or, is it a qualified "right" to be exercised under certain "controlled" circumstances set out in the verse above?[120] Al-Hibri is of the opinion that the mere fact that the Prophet Muhammad was polygamous in his later life is no evidence of a "right" of Muslim men to also be polygamous. She argues on the basis of the Qur'anic verses that state quite clearly that neither the Prophet nor his wives were like other men and women.[121] Secondly, the passage in the Qur'an which has been used to justify polygamy attaches a condition for such action, i.e. requiring the man to make an undertaking to deal justly with all his wives. Reinforcing this condition is the Qur'anic statement (verse 4:129) that "Ye are never able to be fair and just among women even if you tried hard." "Modernist" Muslim scholars are of the opinion that for evolving a rule of law relating to polygamy, these two Qur'anic verses must be read and interpreted together.[122] The implication of the combined passages in the opinion of Al-Hibri would be as follows:

(a)   If you can be just and fair among women, then you can marry four wives.
(b)   If you cannot be just and fair among women, then you may marry only one.
(c)   You cannot be just and fair among women; from which follows: i.e. you may marry only one wife.

---

[117] *Kitab* literally means book. *Kitabia* means women of the book. Here it implies women professing one of the revealed religions, i.e. Christianity, Judaism, etc.

[118] The Qur'an, verse 2:221 and 5:5.

[119] The Qur'an, verse 4:3.

[120] A. R. I. Doi, in his book entitled *Shariah: The Islamic Law* at p. 146 outlines the various circumstances for which he considers polygamy to be the "best solution". These situations include the wife suffering from a serious disease; where the wife is barren; is of unsound mind, where the wife is old and infirm; where the wife is of "bad character" and cannot be reformed; where the wife moves away from her husband's place of residence, is disobedient and difficult to live with; as a result of many men dying during war leaving behind a large number of widows. The final reason that Doi advances is that if the husband feels that he simply cannot do without another wife and is capable of providing equal support to the existing wife(ives), then he is justified in doing so. Doi has, in effect, provided a *carte blanche* to the man to marry if he feels like it. This hardly appears in consonance with the contextual rationale behind the Qur'anic verse.

[121] The Qur'an, verse 33:32, 50. For example, while the Prophet encouraged widows and divorcées to remarry, his own wives were not to be remarried after his death. They were considered the "mothers of all believers" and no believer may marry his mother. However, as the Prophet grew older he gave his wives the choice to leave and marry another male more fulfilling perhaps of husbandly duties. All but one wife refused to leave him. See Al-Hibri, "A study of Islamic herstory", at p. 216 citing J. Al-Afghani, 1945, p. 79.

[122] Al-Hibri, "A study of Islamic herstory", p. 216; Rahman, "Status of women in the Qur'an" at pp. 45–49; Mernissi, *Beyond the Veil: Women and Islam*, and Hassan, "An Islamic perspective". Muslim law reform in the twentieth century has relied upon this interpretation. See the discussion in section 3 of this article.

Furthermore, given (c) the condition for (a) is never satisfied, so that we can never conclude: you may marry four wives.[123]

In response to the above argument, it has to be said that some Muslim thinkers claim that the words "justly" and "just" occurring in the two Qur'anic passages above have two different meanings; hence the view that these cannot be combined to draw an inference.[124] Abdur Rahman Doi also challenges the view of the modernists who consider verse 4:129 as a legal condition attached to polygamous union;[125] citing Shaikh Muhammad bin Sirin and Shaikh Abubakr bin al-Arabi, he makes the point that the inability to do justice between women referred to in the Qur'an is in respect of love and sexual intercourse only, which is beyond the control of the man. Justice required of man is, in the opinion of these scholars, confined to matters of providing equality in residence, food and clothes to co-wives. So long as a man can provide these, he is seen as being just between women.[126]

4.7 *Hijab* (veiling of women): a prescription for female modesty or symbolic division of Muslim space on the basis of gender?

In the Islamic tradition, veiling represents the ultimate dichotomy between the public and private spheres of life, with the woman being confined to the private sphere. However, there exists a wide range of views among scholars of Islam regarding this institution and its implication for women's human rights. General and vaguely phrased Qur'anic verses regarding modesty in behaviour for men and women have been interpreted in a variety of ways by male Muslim scholars, a process that many writers believe led to an ever-increasing exclusion of Muslim women from the public sphere of life.[127] Stowasser is of the view that Qur'anic exegesis prescribed veiling in absolute and categorical fashion and the wide degree of difference between the commentaries of Tabari, Baydawi and al-Khafaji go to show how Muslim women were forced to disappear behind the veil, not only physically but as a symbol of their invisibility from public life.[128] While Tabari argued that veiling did not include covering the face, half the forearm, eye make-up, rings, bracelets and dyes, Baydawi's interpretation of verse 24:30 reads as follows:

Let them lower their gaze before the men at whom it is not lawful to look, and let them *guard their private parts* by veiling them, or by bewaring of (or: guarding against) fornication. The lowering of the glances is presented because the glance is the messenger of fornication. And let them not display of their adornment such as jewellery, dress, make-up – let alone the

---

[123] Al-Hibri, "A study of Islamic herstory", p. 216. Ustadh Taha's arguments follow a similar line. He states that polygamy is not an original precept in Islam and a combined reading of verse 4:3 and 4:129 leads to an implied prohibition of polygamy. For Taha's views see his work *The Second Message of Islam*, trans. A. A. An-Naim, Syracuse University Press, 1987, at p. 140.

[124] *Ibid.*, citing Mahmassani, *The Principles of Law-Making in Islam*, at p. 470.

[125] Doi, Chapter 8, especially pp. 147–150.

[126] *Ibid.*

[127] For a "feminist" interpretation of Qur'anic verses enjoining veiling and segregation, see Mernissi, *Beyond the Veil: Women and Islam*; Ahmed, *Women and Gender in Islam*.

[128] Stowasser, "The status of women in early Islam", at p. 27.

parts where they are worn or applied – to those to whom (such display) is not lawful . . . what is meant by adornment is the place where adornment is put (or worn) . . .[129]

As to the opinion that the prohibition to display does not include the face and hands, because they are not pudendal, Baydawi argues clearly:

this applies to prayer only, not appearance, because the whole body of a free women is pudendal, and it is illicit for anyone (except the husband or the *dhawu mahram*)[130] to look at any part of her except by necessity such as (medical) treatment, or the bearing of witness.

In later commentaries such as al-Khafaji's *Hashiya* on al-Baydawi, this restrictive interpretation is further heightened. Al-Khafaji justifies the complete "disappearance" of women behind the veil on the authority of al-Shafei declaring categorically "the whole body of the women is pudendal, even face and hand, without exception (absolutely)".

Since this interpretation so obviously contradicts the Qur'anic expression "except that which is apparent", al-Khafaji and others deal with it by interpreting this verse as "a command of exception from the established rule, which applies to such exceptional circumstances as the giving of evidence in law courts and medical treatment only".

Among twentieth-century Muslim scholars, Mawdudi is perhaps the most vocal in his restrictive treatment of veiling as an "Islamic" institution. In his much-read and publicized book entitled *Purdah*,[131] he argues vociferously for the institution on the basis the segregation will prevent "loose Western morals" from creeping into Islamic society, and keep the family intact.[132] In the discussion on the sphere of operation of women and segregation, he initiates the debate by stating that women are rulers of their household and accountable for their actions within it. They (women) have been released from certain religious obligations (that men must fulfil). As examples, Mawdudi cites the Friday congregation as not being obligatory on women, neither is participating in the holy war (*jihad*) compulsory. A woman may not travel without her *mahram*. In short, he states that Islam abhors the venturing out of the home of a woman unless it is absolutely imperative, such as to earn a living.[133]

However, modernist Muslim writers challenge this restrictive and literal interpretation of the Qur'anic verses on veiling and segregation. Fazlur Rahman puts forward the view that the Qur'an advocates neither the veil nor segregation of the sexes; rather it insists on sexual modesty.[134] He further states that it is also certain on historical grounds that there was no veil in the Prophet's time, nor was there segrega-

---

[129] *Ibid.*, at pp. 26–27.

[130] A male within the prohibited degrees of relationship with whom a Muslim women cannot lawfully enter into contract of marriage. In addition to the husband who is her *mahram*, these include a father, brother, son, uncle, whether paternal or maternal, grandfather, whether paternal or maternal.

[131] A. A. Mawdudi, *Purdah*, Islamic Publications, Lahore, 1997.

[132] *Ibid*. This study uses the Urdu version and all page numbers referred to are taken from this edition.

[133] Mawdudi, *Purdah*, at pp. 235–239.

[134] Rahman, "Status of women in the Qur'an", at p. 40.

tion of the sexes in the sense that Muslim societies have developed it. In fact the Qur'anic statements on modesty imply that neither the veil nor segregation of the sexes existed.[135] Hence the need to impose some ground rules for male–female interaction. If segregation of the sexes existed, there would have been no point in asking the sexes to behave with modesty. The Qur'an states in verse 24:31:

> Say (O Muhammad) to believing men that they should observe modesty of the eye and guard their sexual parts – this is purer for them, but God knows well what they do. And say to believing women that they should observe modesty of the eyes and guard their sexual parts and let them not display their attractions except those naturally exposed – and let them cast down their head-scarves onto their bosoms.

It is pertinent to make the point here that "modesty of the eye" spoken of in the verse above is in connection with both sexes and not only with regard to women. Secondly, this injunction would have no meaning at all if the sexes were segregated or if *hijab* (veiling) as we know it today were observed.[136] The injunction to "not display their attractions except those naturally exposed" have been interpreted in various ways, some restrictive, others liberal. However, it is generally presumed that attractions as are commonly exposed include the face, half the forearm, and any cosmetic or jewellery on these such as rings, bangles, henna or other colouring for hands and nails.[137] The words "and let them cast their head-scarves down their bosoms" also prove that covering the face is not required by this verse.

Other verses of the Qur'an laying down guidelines to women for venturing outside the house appear in Chapter 33. Verses 59–60 of Chapter 33 state that Muslim women, including women of the Prophet Muhammad's household must "draw tight their outer garments" when they go out at night "so that they can be recognized as Muslim women and not molested" and the "Hypocrites"[138] who are said to have molested women are threatened with exile if they do not refrain from such actions. Fazlur Rahman is of the opinion that there is nothing in these verses that calls for the veil as such.[139] In the same chapter, verse 33:30 warns the wives of the Prophet against any suggestions of immodesty and are threatened with a "double punishment" if they are immodest; verse 33:32 states that the "Hypocrites" are eager to spread rumours about the Prophet's wives who are advised "not to speak in an inaudible voice to any male – if you are God-fearing – lest he in whose heart there is sickness covets to exploit the opportunity". This verse however, is a special case addressed to the Prophet's wives, whom the Qur'an declares to be "Mothers of the Faithful" in verse 33:6. On the strength of these Qur'anic verses it may be argued that segregation and veiling has roots deeper and preceding Islam and is also strongly linked to class, acting primarily in its present manifestation as a symbol of honour or status.[140]

---

[135] *Ibid.*
[136] *Ibid.*
[137] *Ibid.*
[138] The "Hypocrites" were certain inhabitants of Medina who had reluctantly converted to Islam, but were engaged in subverting it.
[139] *Ibid.*, at p. 41.
[140] *Ibid.*

Ustadh Taha differentiates between the conceptual parameters of *al-hijab*, which requires covering of all the woman's body except her face and hands and *al-sufur*, which permits more exposure, provided modest dress is maintained in general.[141] He believes that Islam's original precept is *al-sufur* because in his opinion the "purpose of Islam is chastity, emanating from within men and women, and not imposed through closed doors".[142]

The veil, Taha further argues, was imposed as a transitional requisite and would become redundant when inner chastity was achieved through education and discipline.[143] Female Muslim scholars in recent years have questioned the restrictive interpretation of Qur'anic injunctions on veiling and segregation of the sexes.[144] Nazirah Zein-Ed-Din sums up the feeling of outrage and frustration of the Muslim women in her excellent work entitled *As-Sufur wal Hijab* in the following words:

What is this unjust law (of veiling) which is permeated with the spirit of tyranny and oppression? It is in violation of the Book of God and His Prophet may God bless his soul. This law is the law of the victor, the man who subdued the woman with physical force. Man tampered with God's book to make this law. He prided himself on his tyranny and oppression, even as those hurt him too. He made the law independently, not permitting the women to share in a single letter. So, it came out in accordance with his desires and contrary to the will of God.[145]

5 GRADUALISM AS A METHOD OF INTERPRETATION FOR WOMEN'S HUMAN RIGHTS IN ISLAM

As mentioned earlier, Islamic jurisprudence consists of an interplay between the Qur'an, *hadith* and its subsidiary sources, including *ijma, qiyas* and *ijtihad*.[146] Although Muslims accept the Qur'an as the primary and authoritative textual source containing the word of God and *hadith* as an inspired secondary source that can shed light on the interpretation of the verses of the Qur'an,[147] yet when it comes to deriving laws from these sources, serious differences of opinion between the various schools of juristic thought arise, as will have become more evident from the preceding sections of this paper. These differences emanate from a major, and irreconcilable difference in perspectives regarding the injunctions laid down in the Qur'an. The view of conservative, "literalist" Muslim scholars is that whatever is considered permissible in the Qur'an is valid action for all times, and the changing perception of concepts, institutions and actions is no justification for modification in

---

[141] Taha, *The Second Message of Islam*, at p. 141.

[142] *Ibid.*

[143] *Ibid.*

[144] Mernissi, *Women and Islam* and Ahmed, *Women and Gender in Islam*.

[145] N. Zein-Ed-Din, *As-Sufur wal Hijab*, Beirut, 1928 at p. 140 cited in Al-Hibri, "A study of Islamic herstory", at p. 219.

[146] Rahim, *Muhammadan Jurisprudence*, and Mahmassan, *Principles of Law-Making in Islam*, p. 7; F. Rahman, *Islam and Modernity: Transformation of an Intellectual Tradition*, Chicago, University of Chicago Press, 1982 and F. Rahman, "Islam: challenges and opportunities", in A. Welch and P. Cachia (eds.), *Islam: Past Influence and Present Challenge*, Edinburgh, Edinburgh University Press.

[147] Sayeh and Morse, "Islam and the treatment of women", p. 317.

the law. The modernist view on the other hand argues for taking account of the historicity of Islamic law based on Qur'anic text that spoke to the times, claiming that legal rules of Islam are subject to rationalisation, and changes in interpretation of its rules are permissible, indeed inevitable.

These scholars argue that the *shari'a*, or principles of Islamic law, is meant to have an in-built dynamism and receptivity to change and was developed by jurists in the early years of Islam to administer appropriate rulings in a new factual setting.[148] It is said that *shari'a* allows different interpretations of existing precedent in at least three situations as laid down in the Qur'an and *Sunna*: necessity or public interest, change in the facts which originally gave rise to the law and change in the custom or usage on which a particular law was based.[149] If one of the three conditions given above is present, the jurist may adapt existing law to the new situation, and his ruling then becomes a part of the *shari'a*, provided it does not contradict the Qur'an. Sayeh provides an illustration of the process where he explains how the Prophet Muhammad's rule of a volumetric measurement for wheat and barley was changed to measurement by weight.[150]

Gradualism draws upon these principles and implies a method of interpretation that proceeds by degrees over time, advancing slowly but regularly.[151] It is a conceptual framework that is said to have the potential of highlighting the overall pattern in the evolution of the status of Muslim women beginning with the rights of women in the partriachal society existing prior to the Prophet, followed by the rights enumerated for women in the Qur'an, and ending with the treatment of women in Muslim society today.[152]

A Tunisian scholar, Al-Tahir al-Haddad, also argues for using gradualism as a method for interpretation of the Qur'an in order to achieve equal rights of women in the Islamic tradition.[153] In his controversial book entitled *Our Women in the Law and in Society*, al-Haddad uses the methodological premise employed by some other Muslim reformists, (in his case Muhammad Abduh), namely that Islamic law is not immutable and was not revealed all of a piece but developed as the historic Islamic community developed. Al-Haddad not only argues for the temporality of the *shari'a*, his "daring audacity" is to claim that the precepts of the Qur'an itself were not eternal but subject to historical contingency.[154] Norma quotes al-Haddad thus:

---

[148] *Ibid.*, p. 317; Rahman; Riffat Hassan, Al-Hibri and Mahmassani.

[149] *Ibid.*, p. 317, citing A. al-Hibri, "Islamic constitution and the concept of democracy" 24 Case W. Res, *Journal of International Law*, 1, 2 and n. 2 1992; also Mahmassani, *The Principles of Law-Making in Islam*, 1961, p. 7.

[150] Sayeh and Morse, "Islam and the treatment of women", p. 317 citing Mahmassani.

[151] As a methodology, gradualism holds a particular appeal to modernist Muslim scholars including Muhammad Abduh, Fazlur Rahman, Muhammad Iqbal, Tahir al-Haddad, Esposito, Al-Hibri, Riffat Hassan and many others, although various scholars writing on the subject differ in the exact formulation for application to specific situations. However, with reference to this particular example used, it is submitted that the issue is fairly non-controversial. One would be hard put to identify similar departures from earlier Islamic norms. Moreover, one wonders how and to what extent this principle may be employed in the area of women's human rights as arguably the rules in this area are based on clear express verses of the Qur'an, to which this principle (and indeed all others) are subservient.

[152] Sayeh and Morse, "Islam and the treatment of women", p. 318.

[153] N. Salem, "Islam and the status of women in Tunisia", in F. Hussain (ed.), *Muslim Women*, St Martin's Press, New York, 1984, p. 143.

[154] *Ibid.*, at p. 144. Al-Haddad distinguishes between the eternal principles in Islam such as the creed of unity, ethical requirements, justice and equality, and those precepts dependent upon

Islam is the religion which holds to the principle of gradualism in legislating its laws according to (limiting) capacity. There is nothing which states or indicates that the state achieved during the Prophet's lifetime was the hoped-for final (stage) after which there would be no end since gradual (evolution) is linked to the difficulties of those issues for which gradual steps are to be taken . . .[155]

Sayeh and Morse argue that gradualism is ideally suited to Islam because, while the Qur'an does enumerate certain legal standards, it consists primarily of very broad and general moral directives that may be used as indicators of evolution and growth of the community.[156] As a process applied to Islamic law, it presupposes two main elements; one, that the end result one is attempting to achieve does not contradict a clear Qur'anic injunction on the subject, and secondly, that each succeeding stage of Islamic society identified with and internalized the (proposed) evolving principle. In addition to the above, applying the methodology of gradualism also appears to use examples of a succession of Qur'anic verses on a subject that progressively moved from recommendatory discontinuance of a practice before imposing a final mandatory position. Finally, how does one justify application of the process to practices/norms in respect of which no final prohibition exists in the Qur'anic text?

Sayeh and Morse[157] cite two examples during the lifetime of the Prophet Muhammad, one identifying application of gradualism and the other where it was not required. It is argued by them that for practices less central to the basic characteristics of society such as the practice of charging interest on loans, there appeared no reason to slowly acclimatize people to effect this change, therefore a clear directive and final admonition against the practice was pronounced in the Qur'an in verse 2:275–276.[158] By contrast there were less amenable to instant change and had to be modified slowly and gradually. For example, Arabs were accustomed to drinking alcohol and gambling, and initially the Qur'an did not prohibit the practice outright but issued a recommendation (verse 2:219). Later a verse was revealed which imposed a moratorium on drinking alcohol during the hour of prayer.[159] The final stage was an outright and absolute interdiction of all intoxicants and of gambling in all circumstances.[160] This change of practice was brought about by a series of verses revealed over a period of years.[161]

---

cont.

human contingencies; particularly as they related to conditions in the *jahiliyya* period of Arabia. According to al-Haddad, the basic tendency within Islam, actually within the Qur'an itself, is to take a gradualist approach such that its precepts are suited to its historic reality and thus effective.

[155] Al-Haddad thus believes that the texts of Islam tend to "take woman along with man on the road of equality in all aspects of life". He acknowledges that the social situation of women should be improved and encouraged towards equality since mere laws without a conducive environment will not make men and women equal in real life.

[156] Sayeh and Morse, "Islam and the treatment of women", at p. 318, quoting Esposito.

[157] At p. 319.

[158] Despite the fact that it was a very important practice affecting adversely a few rich merchants of Meccah, yet by and large the community benefited and resistance was not high.

[159] The Qur'an, verse 4:43.

[160] *Ibid.*, verses 5:90–92.

[161] Sayeh and Morse, "Islam and the treatment of women", at p. 320.

It has been argued that the same method my be used in relation to women's human rights and in the gradual "phasing out" of practices adverse to equal rights for women. Examples of areas where gradualism may be used include dower, polygamy and right to education. The concept of dower underwent a process of change after the promulgation of Islamic norms. Starting from a position where it (dower) was the bride-price paid by the husband to the male members of the woman's family, it was modified to become a sum of money or other property paid by the husband to the wife as a mark of respect to her and to be held by her as her property.[162] As regards polygamy, Islam restricted the practice of virtually marrying as many women as a man was inclined to, to up to four, with provisos but also with arguably, sufficient space to abolish the practice by gradualism (as discussed above). Sayeh is of the view that verse 4:129 read in conjunction with 4:3 permitting polygamous unions, "upon closer analysis appears as a microcosm of the gradualism inherent in Islam".[163] In this regard, however, it is submitted that the potential for polygamy to be declared redundant in the Islamic legal tradition through gradualism appears a difficult proposition for the following reasons. While in the case of gambling and alcohol, clear Qur'anic verses may be cited in support of complete prohibition of these practices, the same cannot be said about polygamy, as one does not come across verses that present a comparable finality to that of verses on gambling and alcohol. In response to this argument, one may mention here that the institution of slavery is perhaps the classic example of gradualism. While slavery is no doubt recognized in the Qur'an, strong regulatory verses are also present – the tone of which is towards abolition of the practice. Despite the fact that there is no final injunction for its abolition, there would be few Muslims in the world today who would argue that slavery as an institution should be maintained on the basis that the Qur'an does not expressly prohibit it. How then might we explain the strong and persistent resistance to applying the gradualist approach to the position of women?

The strongest and most workable example provided by Sayeh and Morse of the process of gradualism is that of education as an effective tool for empowerment of women. The argument made by Sayeh and Morse is that in comparison to the pre-Islamic society, Islam improved the status of women. This process of improvement was arrested soon after the death of the Prophet Muhammad and steadily after the last of the Rightly-Guided Caliphs.[164] The various schools of interpretation

---

[162] For a discussion of the modification of the concept of dower within the Islamic tradition, see Rahim, *Muhammadan Jurisprudence*; Sayeh and Morse, "Islam and the treatment of women", pp. 326–327; Rahman, "Status of women in the Qur'an"; Haeri and others. The case of dower as the sole property of the wife however needs to be distinguished here because the relevant verses of the Qur'an sanctioning dower clearly identify the stage at which the practice has arrived, i.e. that the family of the wife have no right over the dower as it belongs to her.

[163] Sayeh and Morse, "Islam and the treatment of women", pp. 328–330.

[164] One may perhaps be able to concede that were this tradition of progressive interpretations to have continued it may have brought within its ambit issues addressing women's position as well, and issues addressing women's position, but Islamic history took a contrary course in that after the era of the first four Caliphs, the prestige of rulers rested in sheer force rather than on successorship to the Prophet Muhammad. Because of this development, later day Islamic rulers required doctrinal legitimacy. Therefore, in addition to retreating to patriarchal interpretation as a result of political necessity, rulers attacked the roots of independent thinking, causing a retreat of critical thought. The threat of individual violence against Muslim scholars advocating free will in the interpretation of Islam and the imposition of an official dogma effectively

that developed over the centuries had one thing in common – a patriarchal value system. A further contributing factor was that soon after the death of the Prophet Muhammad, men alone began to assume the role of interpreting the Qur'an.[165] These schools began to disallow the participation of women in public life, and as a result, Qur'anic scholarship and the interpretation of Islamic law became the province of men, with predictable results for the rights of women in society. It is argued therefore that the principle of gradualism that could not be taken to its logical conclusion of complete equality, rights and dignity of men and women alike was arrested as a result of these factors. Starting from the premise that pre-Islamic custom did not provide adequate opportunities for equal acquisition of knowledge to men and women, Islam declared it as a religious obligation and incumbent for every Muslim whether man to woman, to be educated.[166] The position of women in the Muslim world today bears testimony to the fact that wherever women have been afforded the opportunity of education, other rights have followed suit. Thus the practice of child marriage, denial of access to resources, lack of participation in public life and employment, and a host of other areas of discrimination have receded and encroached on women's rights.

Application of the principle of gradualism to women's human rights poses a number of problems. The most crucial of this is the prerequisite for a genuine belief among Muslims that Islam was not intended to freeze human history at a point in time at which God's word (the Qur'an) was revealed to the Prophet Muhammad and that a contextual approach to law-making based on Qur'anic injunctions does not entail relinquishing its status as the primary source of Islamic law.

6 EVOLUTIONARY APPROACH TO WOMEN'S HUMAN RIGHTS IN ISLAM

The late Sudanese reformer, Ustadh Mahmood Muhammad Taha, adopted a very revolutionary approach in dealing with issues such as women's rights within Islam. In his work, *The Second Message of Islam*, he outlines his novel technique for reformulating *shari'a*.[167] He calls for the shifting of legal efficacy from one set of Qur'anic verses to another in keeping with the needs of societies today.[168] He believes that the inferior status of women[169] and practices such as the wearing of the veil (*hijab*),[170]

---

cont.

limited religious interpretation. See Hamid Enayat, *Modern Islamic Political Thought* 13 (1988); Sayeh and Morse, "Islam and the treatment of women", p. 318. Finally, in the tenth century, the Sunni religious leadership decided that henceforth only accepted schools of interpretation would delineate the meaning of the Qur'an and the *Hadith* based on their earlier *Ijtihad*. This is known as the closing of the door of *ijtihad*. Today, Sunni Islam judges are therefore severely limited in their authority to engage in *ijtihad*, and accordingly their flexibility and adaptability in applying principles of interpretation such as *shari'a* is limited. Mahmassani at pp. 7–8. M. Iqbal, *Reconstruction of Religious Thought in Islam*.

[165] Sayeh and Morse, "Islam and the treatment of women", p. 321; see also Al-Hibri, Esposito, Fazlur Rahman, Leila Ahmed and Mernissi.

[166] Sayeh and Morse, "Islam and the treatment of women", p. 324.

[167] For a comprehensive treatment of Taha's approach, see *The Second Message of Islam*.

[168] *Ibid.*, at p. 23.

[169] *Ibid.*, at p. 139.

[170] *Ibid.*, at p. 143.

polygamy,[171] and segregation of men and women,[172] are not original precepts of Islam. Rather, these discriminatory practices were imposed only for a transitory period as immediate change from the *jahilliya* to complete equality was considered too drastic a step for seventh century Arabian society to adopt and imbibe.[173] The true message of Islam, according to Taha, is one of complete equality.[174] He suggested that the fundamental and universal message of Islam is to be found in the Qur'an and *Sunna* texts of the earlier stage of Mecca. These earlier verses were not lost forever despite subsequent superseding texts. Their implementation was merely postponed until such time as it would be possible to enact them into law.[175]

Taha's approach has been taken up by his followers and students, among them Professor Abdullahi Ahmed An-Naim. He believes that by conceding the basic premise of Taha's revolutionary thinking, a whole new era of Islamic jurisprudence, compatible with international human rights law can begin. For instance, the fact that "traditional" *shari'a* does not treat women and non-Muslims equally with male Muslims is beyond dispute. Besides seeking to justify such discrimination in apologetic terms, modern Muslim scholars claim that some of the objectionable rules may now be reformed by reviving the techniques of *ijtihad*. But *ijtihad* has its limitations since it is not permitted in any matter governed by an express and definite text of the Qur'an or *Sunna*. Within the context of women's human rights, this becomes problematic as some of the most obviously discriminatory texts are in fact based on them.[176] The only way out of this dilemma is to "evolve Islamic law on a fresh plane rather than waste time in piecemeal reform that will never achieve the moral and political objective of removing all discrimination agasint women".[177]

An-Naim has applied Taha's approach in his writings on religious minorities under *shari'a* as well as women's human rights.[178]

7 EQUAL BEFORE ALLAH, UNEQUAL BEFORE MAN? DILEMMA OF WOMEN IN THE MUSLIM WORLD

Attempting to develop a theoretical framework of women's human rights in the Islamic tradition poses insurmountable difficulties, the basic and most crucial of these

---

[171] *Ibid.*, at p. 140.

[172] *Ibid.*, at p. 145.

[173] The justification for these changes was that the latter injunctions were not suitable for the people at the earlier time. Even the Qur'an states in 3:159 that "It is part of the Mercy of God that thou dost deal gently with them. Wert thou severe or harsh hearted, they would have broken away from about thee."

[174] Taha, *The Second Message of Islam*, at p. 139.

[175] *Ibid.*, at p. 23.

[176] The Sunnah which provides authority for the exercise of *ijtihad*, the Prophet's instructions to *Ma'adh ibn Jabal* when he appointed him governor of Yemen, described *ijtihad* as a last resort, to be exercised only when no explicit and definite ruling can be found in the Qur'an or Sunnah.

[177] An-Naim *Toward an Islamic Reformation*.

[178] See An-Naim's writings, e.g. "A modern approach to human rights in Islam: foundations and implications for Africa" in C. E. Welch Jr. and R. I. Meltzer (eds.), *Human Rights and Development in Africa*, State of New York Press, Albany, 1984; "Religious minorities under Islamic law and the limits of cultural relativism", *Human Rights Quarterly*, 9, 1987; and "The rights of women and international law in the Muslim context", *Whittier Law Review*, 9, 1987, 491.

being, how and to what extent, might religious texts be employed as sources of positive law and rights? Are competing sets of norms in the Qur'anic text equally valid, and if so, might we base a rule of law on either, in the light of the general principles of *naskh* (abrogation) laid down by Muslim jurists regarding the order of revelation of the Qur'an? A book of divine revelation such as the Qur'an coming together over twenty-three years is by its very nature open to varying interpretations. But how much space is one afforded to discuss and critique laws derived by jurists taking account of the historicity of events, particularly norms that may be completely out of line with contemporary needs of society? Finally, where does one seek legitimation for alternative human rights schemes and categories within the Islamic framework, such as those discussed in the present article?

It is also evident that restrictive rules of interpretation of the Qur'an, *hadith* literature and the process of law making based on these sources have combined to push into the background whatever norm of equality and egalitarianism Islam represented. Leila Ahmed presents the view that:

Even as Islam instituted, in the initiatory society, a hierarchical structure as the basis of relations between men and women, it also preached, in its ethical voice (and this is the case with Judaism and Christianity as well), the moral and spiritual equality of all human beings. Arguably, therefore, even as it instituted a sexual hierarchy, it laid the ground, in its ethical voice, for the subversion of the hierarchy.[179]

It is this principle of "subversion" present in the ethical Qur'anic norms that may be employed to justify a framework for women's human rights in Islam today.

A common feature of the various frameworks of women's human rights discussed above have one common factor: they highlight the fact that no matter what methodology one attempts to employ, there appears no escape from certain clear Qur'anic verses creating gender hierarchies. When we concede to every word of the Qur'an law-making authority, how can one deny to one group of Muslims the right to legislation on the basis of verses that discriminate against women, just as another group would aspire to invoke the non-discriminatory verse in order to create laws affording complete equality between the sexes?

Whether it is Esposito's hierarchizaiton of Qur'anic values, Hevener's catagorization of rights, Taha's evolutionary approach or the modernists' method of gradualism, complete equality as the term has come to be understood in modern day usage is difficult to infer from any of these schemes. It might be strategically opportune to seek a rigorous implementation of all the protective/corrective category of rights before embarking upon the "equality" and non-discrimination path. By applying the Islamic paradigm of equality to human dignity and worth, and requiring "those in authority", i.e. men and the state, to accept responsibility for fulfilling the material needs of women, children and other disadvantaged sections of society in their charge, and provide them access and control over resources, a move towards substantive as opposed to mere formal equality for all may be possible.

---

[179] Ahmed, *Women and Gender in Islam*, at p. 238.

Islamic Law in Malaysia: Issues and Developments

*Mohammad Hashim Kamali**

1 INTRODUCTORY REMARKS

One of the growing concerns of Malaysian administrators and Muslim leaders in the post-war period has been a marked marital instability among Malay Muslims that has been characterized by high rates of divorce and polygamy, especially in Kelantan and Kedah in the north and Melaka and Johore in the south. Numerous explanations were given, e.g. disparities between state legal and administrative systems, wide-ranging socio-economic differentials of the Malay Muslims encompassing bilateral and matrilineal systems of kinship, and disparities between poorly educated fishermen and farmers on one hand and urban professionals and business executives on the other.

The reformist elite and women's groups saw the problems over the high rates of polygamy and divorce as a main consequence of the ways in which the *shari'a* provisions were understood and applied in Malaysia, but it proved extremely difficult to address them. It was in adjacent Singapore (which has a substantial Muslim minority population but no entrenched Islamic establishment) that a Muslim Ordinance was passed in 1957 (amended in 1960) stipulating that only divorces by mutual consent may be registered by a *qadi*, that only the chief *qadi* may solemnize a polygamous union, and that a consolatory gift, or *mut'ah*, may be payable by a divorcing husband. The Ordinance also provided for the creation of a *shari'a* court which would exercise jurisdiction in matrimonial disputes among Muslims. The effects of these measures were considerable.

In peninsular Malaysia, separate state administrations and the subordination of the *shari'a* court to civil courts hampered the prospects of substantive reforms, and it was not until the rise to prominence of the Muslim revivalist and *da'wah* movements in the 1970s and early 1980s that circumstances became more favourable for marriage law reforms.

Family law reforms in Malaysia were introduced within the general framework of *siyasah shar'iyyah*, or *shari'a*-oriented policy, which encouraged adoption of judi-

---

* Professor of Islamic law and jurisprudence at the International Islamic University Malaysia.

cial measures which secured benefit for the people and were not contrary to the *shari'a*. Salient among these were statutory restrictions on polygamy and divorce with the expressed purpose of ensuring the Qur'anic requirements of justice therein. The Islamic Family Law (IFL) (Federal Territories) Act 1984 was a landmark legislation which addressed, in about 135 sections, issues pertaining to the administration of Islamic law on registration and solemnization of marriage, guardianship, maintenance, custody and dissolution of marriage. The two most significant reforms that were introduced related to polygamy and divorce. In a series of substantially similar enactments passed between 1984 and 1990 most of the other states in Malaysia adopted the provisions of the IFL 1984 with a measure of enthusiasm that was, however, short lived. Within a decade, the religious leaders challenged the modernist interpretations of the *shari'a* as being too radical and in disharmony with the traditional *shari'a*. Some of these reforms were consequently revoked and amendments were introduced by many states that were indicative of a conservative comeback in the administration of *shari'a* in Malaysia.

Since the second half of the 1980s and throughout the 1990s the religious authorities and departments in several states have allowed and even encouraged the practice of polygamy and ignored the restrictions that were in force under the existing enactments. A clear manifestation of this conservative reaction was the Islamic Family Law (Federal Territories) (Amendment) Act 1994, which effectively overruled some of the earlier reforms. This article elaborates on these developments and the concerns that they have caused over the status of Islamic law in Malaysia.

This article begins with a section on historical developments affecting the application of *shari'a* in Malaysia and limitations that were imposed on it in the Federal Constitution and other laws. This section also provides background information on the issuance of fatwas (rulings or verdicts) by the Mufti and Islamic Religious Councils, their scope and binding force under the state enactments. This is followed, in section 3, by a discussion of polygamy and restrictions that were imposed on it under the IFL 1984 and then the relaxation of those restrictions through subsequent amendments in 1994. A similar pattern of discussion is presented in section 4 pertaining to divorce. Section 5 discusses the fatwas and recent legislation that demands strict adherence to fatwas, making, for the first time in the Malaysian legal history, the violation of a fatwa into a punishable offence. Section 6 reviews the continuing impasse over the *shari'a* Criminal Code of Kelantan, known as the *Hudud* Bill, which was passed by the state legislature but has remained in abeyance for about five years owing to the federal government's refusal to ratify it. The last two sections discuss specific cases over apostasy, and participation in beauty pageants by Muslim girls, both of which became media topics and have attracted much public attention since mid-1997. The last section concludes.

2   LIMITATIONS AND SCOPE

A glance at the pre-colonial history of Malaysia indicates that the law applied in peninsular Malaysia was the Islamic law which had absorbed certain elements of Malay custom. In some parts of Malaysia, as in Negeri, Sembilan and Melaka and in the Borneo states, the influence of Malay custom was stronger. Islamic law was mainly administered by the *qadi* with an appeal to the ruler. From the early years of the colonial era, the Malay states in the peninsula had by statute empowered the *qadi* courts to exercise jurisdiction over matters of Muslim matrimonial and other personal law. Though there existed a broad outline of uniformity among the states, they nevertheless reflected the religious authority of the state rulers and displayed certain differences that were jealously guarded.

Under British colonial administration, English law was introduced by legislation to replace the Islamic law, and civil courts were established to take over the functions of the *qadi* courts. These latter were pushed to the bottom of the hierarchy of courts and their powers were curtailed.[1]

After the Federation of Malaya was constituted in 1948, the Courts Ordinance 1948 established a judicial system for the Federation which omitted the *shari'a* courts. The judicial power of the Federation was vested in the Federal Court, the two High Courts in Malaya and in Borneo, and the inferior courts comprising of session courts, magistrate courts and penghulu courts. The *shari'a* courts were relegated to the position of state courts and their jurisdiction was limited by the Federal Constitution (Ninth Schedule, List II, State List). In a similar vein, the definition of law under the Federal Constitution did not mention Islamic law.[2]

Islamic law in Malaysia applies to Muslim citizens only and is basically confined to matters as specified in the State List of the Federal Constitution. The State List specifies matrimonial law, charitable endowments (*awqaf*), bequests, inheritance and offences that are not governed by federal law such as matrimonial offences, *khalwat* (intimate proximity between a male Muslim and a woman, whether Muslim or non-Muslim, to whom he is not married) and offences against religion. These are to be regulated by the state enactments and the power to legislate on these matters is vested in the state legislature and the sultan. Federal Parliament can only legislate on matters dealing with Islamic law and religion for the Federal Territories of Kuala Lumpur and Labuan, and has no power to legislate for the rest of Malaysia. Article 76 of the Federal Constitution thus stipulated that Parliament can legislate on matters pertaining to the State List in order only to realize "uniformity of law and policy", and in matters of Islamic law and the Malay custom "if so requested by the legislative assembly of any state". Even when Parliament makes law at the request of the state legislative assembly on personal law matters, such law "shall not come into operation in any state until it has been adopted by a law made by the legislature of that state". Such a law is then deemed to be a state law and not a federal law, and "may accordingly be amended or repealed by a law made by that legislature".[3] It is thus clear that even when Parliament passes a law on *shari'a*-related matters, the state legislature has powers to amend or repeal it as it deems fit. This may be said to be a recipe for disparity and divergence as it is now seen in the application of Islamic law in Malaysia, so much as to prompt observers to note that "there are various family laws practised in Malaysia",[4] and that "Malaysia is the

---

[1] Ahmad bin Mohamed Ibrahim, "Justice in the *shari'a* court", in Aidit Ghazali (ed.), *Islam and Justice*, Institute of Islamic Understanding Malaysia, Kuala Lumpur, 1993, p. 92.

[2] Article 160(2)(b) of the Constitution provides: "Law includes written law, the common law in so far as it is in operation in the Federation or any part thereof, or any custom or usage having the force of law in the Federation or any part thereof."

[3] Federal Constitution, Art. 76(3).

[4] Hamid Jusoh, *The Position of Islamic Law in the Malaysian Constitution*, Dewan Bahasa dan Pustaka, Kuala Lumpur, 1993, p. 63.

only country in the Muslim world where each state has independent jurisdiction over religion leading to inconsistencies and contradictions in the provisions of law, in interpretation and in implementation, state by state".[5] In response to the question as to "why should Malaysia, a relatively small country, have fourteen different religious authorities", another observer noted that religion provided the "basis for our Monarchy's legitimacy", that religion was "among the few things left", and that the Malay rulers had otherwise surrendered the power to rule either to federal or state authorities.[6]

In each state in Malaysia, Islamic law is administered according to the administration of Muslim law enactments or ordinances. The enactments are similar in content, yet there are differences between them, often important enough to give them unique features of their own. Each enactment establishes a Council of Religion of Islam (*Majlis Agama Islam*) for the state. The *Majlis* can make rules on administrative matters such as collection, administration and division of *zakat* (legal alms), appointment of committees such as the Legal Committee, the Mosque Committee and the *Zakat* Committee, and it is vested with powers to issue fatwas on religious matters. Under the Selangor Administration of Islamic Law Enactment 1989, the Islamic Legal Consultative Committee consists of the Mufti as Chairman, the Deputy Mufti, the State Legal Advisor of Selangor, an officer of the Islamic Religious Department of Selangor to be appointed by the *Majlis*, and at least two, but not more than five, experts on *shari'a* to be appointed by the *Majlis* (section 34(1)). The *shari'a* court in each state operates separately from the *Majlis*; it is presided over by a *qadi* who is appointed by the sultan, or by the *Yang di-Pertuan Agong* (king) for the Federal Territory, Penang, Melaka, Sabah and Sarawak, states which do not have a ruling sultan of their own.

In issuing a fatwa, the Mufti, Legal Committee and the *Majlis* are required ordinarily to follow the orthodox tenets of the *shafi'i* school, but where the public interest so requires the fatwa may be given according to the tenets of the other schools of Islamic law. However, a fatwa of this kind, that is, a fatwa based on other than the orthodox views of the *shafi'i* school, often requires the approval of the sultan. Section 39 of the Administration of Islamic Law (Federal Territories) Act 1993 authorizes the Mufti, if he considers that none of the reliable positions of "the four *madhhabs* may be followed without leading to a situation which is repugnant to public interest", to resolve the question according to his own judgment without being bound by the prevailing doctrines of any of the four *madhhabs* (for more detail see section 5 below). A fatwa may also relate to customary *adat* matters, and in some states the Mufti must have regard to *adat* in the performance of his functions.[7] The administration of Islamic law in every state is thus subject to modification by the *Majlis* in the light of Malay custom and public interest.

---

[5] Sisters in Islam, letter to the Prime Minister Datuk Seri Dr Mahathir Mohamad in thirteen pages, dated 8 August 1997, p. 9. This unpublished letter bears ten names of Sisters in Islam. I would like to thank Zainah Anwar, one of the ten signatories, for providing me with a copy.

[6] Abdul Aziz Bari, "Beauty contests and the Syariah laws", *The Sun*, Kuala Lumpur, 27 July 1997, p. 12.

[7] See for details Ahmad Ibrahim, "The position of Islam in the Constitution of Malaysia", in Ahmad Ibrahim (ed.), *Readings on Islam in Southeast Asia*, Institute of Southeast Asian Studies, Singapore, 1986, p. 218.

The Selangor Administration of Muslim Law Enactment 1952 (revised in 1983 and 1989) specified a procedure whereby the state Mufti, who usually became chairman of the Legal Committee of the *Majlis Agama Islam*, could entertain requests for the issuance of a fatwa. This according to section 41 of the said enactment:

(1)   Anyone may, by letter addressed to the Secretary, request the *Majlis* to issue a fatwa or ruling on any point of Muslim law or doctrine or Malay customary law. On receiving any such request, the Secretary shall forthwith submit the same to the Chairman of the Legal Committee.

(2)   The Legal Committee shall . . . prepare a draft ruling. If such a draft ruling is unanimously approved by the Legal Committee . . . the Chairman shall on behalf and in the name of the *Majlis* forthwith issue a ruling in accordance therewith.

The text continues in section 41(2) to stipulate for the eventuality where the Legal Committee is not unanimous, in which case the issue must be referred to the *Majlis*, which may issue a ruling based on the support of the majority of its members.

As for the legal effect of such a fatwa, the Selangor Enactment provided in section 42(3) that any ruling passed by the *Majlis*, whether directly, or through the Legal Committee, if the *Majlis* so determines, or if the sultan so directs, be published by notification in the Gazette and "shall thereupon be binding on all Muslims resident in the state". The Administration of Islamic Law (Federal Territories) 1993 (and its equivalent enactments, in other states), adopted the substance of the above procedure with minor modifications that gave greater prominence to the Mufti himself. Section 34(1) thus provided:

The Mufti shall, on the direction of the Yang di-Pertuan Agong, and may, on his own initiative, or on the request of any person made by letter addressed to the Mufti, make and publish in the Gazette, a fatwa or ruling on any unsettled or controversial question of or relating to Islamic law.

It is generally agreed that a valid fatwa normally binds the *shari'a* court in the state in which it is concluded. The question, however, arose as to whether the fatwa binds the civil courts, which are courts of general jurisdiction in Malaysia. An answer to this is provided in the case of *Tengku Mariam v. Commissioner for Religious Affairs*[8] and *Commissioner for Religious Affairs v. Tengku Mariam*.[9] The issue here was over the validity of *waqf* (charitable endowment) wherein the disputing parties had agreed to submit the *waqf* document to the Mufti of Terengganu and to abide by his decision. The Mufti issued a fatwa declaring the validity of the *waqf* and the fatwa was gazetted. But the aggrieved heirs took the matter to the High Court of Terengganu. Justice Wan Sulaiman gave judgment to the effect that the fatwa was of no effect. He cited section 25(4) of the Terengganu Administration of Muslim Law Enactment which upheld the superiority of the civil court over the *shari'a* court. He stated that the Enactment did not make the fatwa binding on the civil court, regardless of whether the court itself or another interested party might have solicited the fatwa. Justice Sulaiman thus wrote: "I . . . am of the view that even if it had been this

---

[8]   [1969] 1 MLJ 110.
[9]   [1970] 1 MLJ 220.

court which had sought the fatwa, the court yet retains unfettered discretion as to how much of such fatwa it should accept, and may decline to be bound by it."[10]

The case was appealed to the Federal Court, and its judgment, based on majority opinion, was delivered by Suffian J, with the concurrence of Lord President Azmi. While confirming the High Court decision, Suffian J wrote : "In my judgment, Wan Sulaiman J was right in ruling that he was not precluded by the gazetted fatwa from himself determining the validity of the *waqf*."

It thus seems likely that the fatwa, even if gazetted after approval by the Religious Council and the Mufti, does not bind the High Court, although it does bind the Muslim residents of the state concerned as well as the *shari'a* court judges in that state. It is too early yet to determine whether the provisions of the *Shari'a* Criminal Offences (Federal Territory) Act 1997 (discussed below) would affect the position of the High Courts *vis-à-vis* the fatwa of the State Religious Council.

The fact that every state in Malaysia acted separately from other states has led to disparities at various levels, and it was felt that a central organization should be created to coordinate the administration of Islamic law at the national level. A step in this direction was taken in October 1968 by the Conference of Rulers to establish the National Council for Islamic Affairs. Its members are:

(a) a chairman appointed by the Conference of Rulers (the Prime Minister is usually appointed);
(b) a representative of each state in peninsular Malaysia appointed by the ruler concerned; and
(c) five persons appointed by the king with the consent of the Conference of Rulers.

The functions of the National Council are to advise and make recommendations to the Conference of Rulers, state government and State Religious Council on the administration of Islamic law with a view to encouraging uniformity among the various states of Malaysia. The Council has a Fatwa Committee that comprises the Muftis of all the member states and five other Muslim scholars appointed by the king.[11]

A certain improvement in the status of the *shari'a* courts took place as a result of a 1988 amendment to Article (121) of the Federal Constitution. Article 121 provides for the jurisdiction of the High Courts, the Court of Appeal, the Federal Court, but then adds: "(121A) The courts referred to in clause (1)[12] shall have no jurisdiction in respect of any matter within the jurisdiction of the *Syariah* Courts".[13] Article 121 has thus demarcated the jurisdictional spheres respectively of the civil courts and *shari'a* courts. This has meant recognition of an independent status for the *shari'a* courts, which, however, "needs to be supplemented by amendments to the existing laws, so that the *shari'a* courts will be better able to apply the Islamic law . . . much remains to be done to bring up the *shari'a* courts and their officers to the status and position of the civil courts and their officers".[14]

---

[10] *Ibid.*, p. 227.
[11] Ibrahim, "The position of Islam", at p. 218.
[12] I.e. the High Courts and Subordinate Courts.
[13] The Constitution (Amendment) Act 1988 (Act A 704).
[14] Ahmad Ibrahim, "The introduction of Islamic values in the Malaysian legal dystem", *IKIM Journal*, 2 (1), 1994, Kuala Lumpur, p. 41.

According to Harun Hashim, a Supreme Court judge (as he then was) "what Article 121(1A) has done is to grant exclusive jurisdiction to the *shari'a* courts in the administration of Islamic law. In other words, Article 121(1A) is a provision to prevent conflicting jurisdiction between the civil courts and the *shari'a* courts."[15] More recently Syed Hamid Albar, the Law Minister (as he then was) commented that the constitutional amendment to Article 121 was designed "to put a stop to civil court intervention in matters pertaining the *shari'a* law", and enable the *shari'a* courts to issue conclusive decisions in matters that fall under their jurisdiction.[16] The new amendment thus seeks to ensure that decisions made within jurisdiction by the *shari'a* courts are not reversed by the civil courts. It does not, however, overrule the general jurisdiction of the High Court to review decisions of the *shari'a* courts, for it merely says that civil courts cannot exercise the *shari'a* court's jurisdiction. The new amendment, in other words, articulates what would normally be expected in matters of jurisdiction: no court may exercise the jurisdiction of another court. This by itself did not envisage any new development in the overall structure of the judiciary, and subsequent developments seem to endorse this.

3 POLYGAMY

Reforms in the Islamic law of polygamy were mainly introduced under the Islamic Family Law (IFL) (Federal Territory), Act 1984 which required that an application for polygamy shall fulfil at least five conditions: the proposed marriage is "just and necessary"; the applicant has the financial means to support his existing and future dependants; the consent of the existing wife, the applicant's ability to accord equal treatment to his wives "as required by *Hukum Syara'*"; and the proposed marriage would not cause *darar syar'i* (harm under the *shari'a*) to the existing wife or wives. The law also stipulated that the proposed marriage would not directly or indirectly lower the standards of living of the existing wife and dependants.[17]

On receipt of the application, the *shari'a* court summons the applicant and his existing wife or wives to be present at the hearing of the application, "which shall be *in camera*". The court may grant permission when the required conditions have all been met. A copy of the completed application is then served together with the summons on each of the existing wives.[18]

To show that the proposed marriage is "just and necessary" regard must be had to circumstances such as sterility or physical infirmity of the existing wife, "physical unfitness for conjugal relations", wilful avoidance of an order for restitution of conjugal rights, or insanity.[19] As a result of that legislation, the decision to marry a

---

[15] *Mohamed Habibullah v. Faridah* [1992] 2 MLJ 793 at p. 803.

[16] Syed Hamid Albar, "The *Syari'a* and *Syariah* courts in Malaysia", in Abdul Munir Yaacob (ed.), *Undang-Undang Keterangan di Mahkamah,* Institute Kefahaman Islam Malaysia, Kuala Lumpur, 1995, p. 34.

[17] S. 23, Islamic Family (Federal Territories) Act 1984 (Act 303) published by International Law Book Services, Kuala Lumpur, 1987.

[18] *Ibid.*, s. 23(5).

[19] *Ibid.*, s. 23(4)(a).

second or subsequent wife no longer rested on the Muslim male in Malaysia. The state authorities and *shariʿa* courts were thus entrusted with the responsibility to ensure that the application for polygamy met the requirement of justice that is stipulated in the Qurʾan (al-Nisaʾ, 4:3).

The IFL 1984 clearly saw the necessity of consultation with the existing wife. Her experience of married life and cohabitation with her husband would inform and assist the court in ascertaining the character of the husband and his ability, or lack of it, to fulfil the stipulated conditions. The provisions of IFL 1984 are followed in most of the states in Malaysia, with the exception of Kelantan, Terengganu and Perak. The Islamic family law enactments in these three states do not contain the conditions that are stipulated in the IFL 1984 and the enactments of the other ten states.

The Kelantan Islamic Family Law Enactment 1983 merely provided, in section 19, that "No male person shall marry another woman at any place while he is married unless he has obtained a prior written consent of the Court of *Qadhi*", without, however, specifying any conditions under which such consent may be granted or refused. Section 21 of the Terengganu Administration of Islamic Family Law Enactment 1985 contains a provision similar to that of the Kelantan enactment. The Perak Islamic Family Law Enactment 1984 merely provides that "no man shall, during the subsistence of a marriage, contract another marriage except with the prior certification in writing of a judge", to the effect that the applicant had made a declaration before the judge that "he shall be fair toward his wives". This provision does not even require the consent of the judge but merely a declaration before the judge. The equivalent provisions of the Kelantan and Terengganu enactments do require a judicial consent but do not stipulate the detailed conditions that are adopted in the Federal Territories Act and the enactments of the other ten states.

In contrast, we may note the Johor Islamic Family Law Enactment 1990, which has an additional provision that applies to a neglectful husband in a polygamous marriage:

127(2): any person who has more than one wife and has failed to give justice to the wives on maintenance, clothing, place of abode and other entitlements according to *hukum syarak* commits an offence and shall be punished with a fine not exceeding one thousand ringgit or with imprisonment not exceeding six months or with both such fine and imprisonment.

The original substance and sprit of the family law reforms of the early 1980s were, however, largely eroded as a result of the amendments that were subsequently introduced.[20] Instead of reinforcing the original intention of the IFL 1984, the various states of Malaysia have introduced amendments which have either changed or deleted the proposed conditions for polygamy. These amendments have had the effect generally of leaving the *shariʿa* court judge to use his discretion to decide whether or not a husband is eligible to take another wife. Selangor and the Federal Territory of Kuala Lumpur were two jurisdictions which had remained faithful to the original terms of the IFL reforms. Yet in 1988 Selangor deleted section 23(4)(e) of its IFL enactment which had provided that the proposed marriage should not directly or indirectly lower the standard of living enjoyed by the existing wife and dependants.

---

[20] A total of thirty-nine amendments and new additions were introduced as a result of coming into force of the IFL (Federal Territories) (Amendment) Act 1994.

In 1994 Federal Territories followed suit by introducing a series of amendments to the 1984 Act, which are specified, in reference to polygamy, as follows.

Section 23(1) of the 1984 Act had declared categorically that: "No man, during the subsistence of a marriage, shall, except with the prior permission in writing of the *Syariah* judge, contract another marriage, nor shall another marriage contracted without such permission be registered under this Act."

Then came the Islamic Family Law (Federal Territories) (Amendment) Act 1994, which added to the above text the following: "Provided that the court may, if it is shown that such marriage is valid according to *Hukum Syara'* order it to be registered subject to Section (123) (Amendment 9, of the 1994 Act)."

Section 123 of the IFL 1984 makes a polygamous marriage that is contracted without the court permission liable to a fine of up to RM1,000 or a maximum of six months imprisonment or both. The court may, in other words, approve a polygamous union, even when contracted without the court's permission, to be in accordance with the *Hukum Syara'* and order it to be registered, on the one hand, and penalize it under Section 123 on the other. To declare a polygamous marriage valid and in conformity with the *Hukum Syara'*, the judge would basically ascertain that the parties were in possession of their faculties to conclude a valid contract, ascertain the just character of the husband, and his financial ability to support another wife. Under the 1994 amendment, it would appear that the character evaluation of the intending polygamist, and his financial capability, are open to the discretion of the presiding judge. The more specific and detailed provisions of the 1984 Act have, in other words, been effectively set aside.

The 1994 amendment also deleted altogether one of conditions that was laid down in section 23 of the principal Act that the proposed marriage would not, "directly or indirectly, lower the standard of living that the existing wife or wives and dependants had been enjoying and would reasonably expect to continue to enjoy were the marriage not to take place".

Since the 1994 amendment removed the ban on the registration of polygamous marriages without the court order, it has likewise deleted certain sections of the principal Act (parts of sections 108 and 109) concerning registration of marriages that are contracted outside the Federal Territories and in Malaysian embassies and consulates abroad. These can now be registered even when concluded without the permission of the court if they are otherwise in conformity with the *shari'a*.

Applications for polygamy can, as a result of these amendments, proceed without the court permission and without the consent of the first wife. Critics have called these amendments "retrogressive" and contrary to the spirit of the original reform. For they assume that polygamy is a right of every Muslim male, and that what was needed was to ensure that it is more easily accessible. Sisters in Islam took a leading role in criticizing the IFL amendments and demanded that they should be revised if the ruling authorities believed that Islam stood for justice and fair treatment for all.[21] In a joint letter addressed to the Prime Minister Dr Mahathir, Sisters in Islam and the Association of Women Lawyers recorded their protest as they wrote that "through amendments made by the various states, the original substance and

---

[21] Sisters in Islam, "Ideal state of marriage in Islam", *The Star*, Kuala Lumpur, 22 October 1996, p. 19.

spirit of this law reform has been violated".[22] In some states, such as in Perak, these amendments had the result that "the decision to contract a polygamous marriage rests solely on the husband". In Kelantan and Terengganu "the specific conditions for polygamy have also been deleted, leaving the Shariah judge to use his own discretion to decide on whether a husband is eligible to take another wife".[23]

Attention was also drawn to the enforcement of the penalties for violations: section 123 of the IFL 1984 penalizes with imprisonment and fine the offence of practising polygamy without the court permission. In practice, however, this penalty has not been utilized: "As far as we know no man has been imprisoned for contracting a polygamous marriage without the court's permission. It is also rare for the maximum fine of RM1,000 to be imposed."[24] A more common practice is to impose a fine of RM300. It is then added that these random amendments to section 23(1) had also encouraged husbands intending to practise polygamy to contract their proposed marriages outside their own states, if the state to which they belonged happened to apply a stricter regime on polygamy.

Experience further shows that in granting permission for polygamy, *shari'a* judges in Malaysia emphasize, more than anything else, a man's capacity to support a second wife, at the expense of almost all the other conditions which are stipulated under section 23 of the IFL 1984. This situation was addressed in a 1990 judgment of the Selangor *shari'a* Appeals Court in the case of *Aishah Abdul Rauf v. Wan Mohamad Yusof Wan Othman*.[25] In this case the Appeal Court unanimously set aside the lower court's decision to permit Wan Yusof to take a second wife on the ground that he was able to maintain a polygamous household. The *shari'a* court had approved the husband's application on that basis alone. The appellant, the existing wife, appealed to the *shari'a* Appeal Court, which passed judgment to the effect that all conditions for polygamy set out in the Selangor Islamic Family Law Enactment were of equal importance and should be proven independently. In this case the respondent-husband had not given evidence to show that the conditions were satisfied, and that the marriage was just and necessary. The court stated that failure to fulfil one condition alone would have been sufficient for the lower court judge to reject the husband's application.

It is commonly known that the first wife is often threatened with divorce unless she gives consent before the judge. After the court appearance, she would return to the court to express her disagreement to the proposed polygamous marriage. It thus becomes all the more advisable for the judge to ensure that the consent of the existing wife is not obtained under duress.

Judicial attitudes tend to differ. It is of interest to note, for instance, that the chief *qadi* of Kelantan issued a circular in November 1991 to all the *qadis* in Kelantan drawing their attention to unsatisfactory implementation of section 19 which had affected family harmony in the state. In that circular, the chief *qadi* directed

---

[22] Unpublished five-page letter (and seven pages enclosure) entitled "Memorandum on reform of the Islamic family laws on polygamy submitted to the Prime Minister Datuk Seri Dr Mahathir Mohamad", 11 December 1996, p. 3.

[23] *Ibid*.

[24] *Ibid*., p. 6.

[25] [1990] 3 MLJ ix.

the *qadis* to carefully scrutinize the application for polygamy before granting their consent, particularly regarding the financial means of the husband, and giving proper notification to the existing wife or wives.[26] On the other hand in Perlis, where the statutory provisions follow the Federal Territories Act 1984, all applications for polygymy had been granted permission since 1993.[27]

With a view to overcoming these issues, the Association of Women's Lawyers and Sisters in Islam have made the following recommendations.

(a)   An integrated approach to the implementation of all the conditions for polygamy as are stipulated in the IFL 1984.

(b)   The applicant must be required to enclose specific supporting documents and provide responsible witnesses to attest to his character and ability to be fair and just and that the proposed marriage "would not cause *darar syarie* (harm affecting the wife in respect of religion, life, body, mind, moral integrity and property)". A mere verbal declaration that the applicant would be fair, without supporting evidence, is not sufficient. The existing wife must also be called to testify concerning the character of her husband.

(c)   The court should solicit medical and other evidence to prove that the wife is sterile, physically infirm, unfit for conjugal relations, insane or wilfully avoiding an order for restitution of conjugal relations.

(d)   The court should consider the applicant's statement of income, his income tax statement and other financial documents, including any source of income from his proposed second wife, to show that the living standard of the existing wife and children will not be adversely affected.

(e)   The applicant's intended wife should also be summoned to the court "to meet with the first wife for consultation to help her consider the realities of a polygamous marriage and whether the applicant can really fulfil the conditions required for such a marriage".

(f)   All states must adopt uniform laws on polygamy, using the Islamic Family Law Act 1984 in its original form before it was amended. "Perak, Perlis, Terengganu and Kelantan, in particular, must be advised to amend their enactments immediately to grant women better protection."[28]

These reforms can be carried out at the initiative of the states themselves or by Parliament in order to ensure uniformity in the law. The Federal Constitution (Article 76) confers power on Parliament to "... make laws with respect to any matter enumerated in the State List ... for the purpose of promoting uniformity of the laws of two or more states".[29]

Article 76 has, in the past, been invoked in the formulation of the National Land Code, the National Forestry Act and the Local Governments Act. In the

---

[26] Circular 1/91 of the chief *qadi*, Eng. trans. appears in Nik Noriani Nik Badli Shah, "Controversial areas in the law relating to marriage and divorce in modern times: possible reforms within Islamic framework", Master of Comparative Law Dissertation 1996/97, International Islamic University, Malaysia, p. 88.

[27] *Ibid.*

[28] Sisters in Islam *et al.* "Memorandum on reform", pp. 9–11.

[29] Federal Constitution 1957 (Art. 76(1)(b)).

same manner, Parliament can pass legislation for a uniform law of polygamy for the whole of the federation. This approach is not, however, without drawbacks, one of which is that any law passed by Parliament under Article 76 does not come into force until adopted by the state legislative assembly. The latter may or may not adopt it, or indeed adopt it with amendments. Thus even after promulgating a uniform law, Parliament cannot prevent a state from making whatever amendments it deems fit.

One way to deal with this drawback may be for the government to advise the king to use his position under Article 3(3) of the Federal Constitution as the head of the religion of Islam in the Federal Territories of Kuala Lumpur and Labuan and in the states of Melaka, Penang, Sabah and Sarawak and His Majesty's home state of Negeri Sembilan, to influence these five states and the two Federal Territories to adopt the uniform law passed by Parliament. This will, it is hoped, set a persuasive precedent for other states to follow.

4 DIVORCE

Under the IFL 1984, a Muslim man wishing to divorce his wife has to apply on a prescribed form on which he must state his reasons and say whether reconciliation has been attempted. Only if this is unsuccessful may the *shari'a* court permit the husband to pronounce one *talaq* and record the divorce. A *talaq* pronounced outside the court has no juridical value and could incur a fine. The IFL enactments also made provisions for initiation of divorce proceedings by the wife through nullification (*faskh*) on appropriate grounds, through claiming non-observance of prenuptial conditions that the spouses had agreed for a suspended (*ta'liq*) divorce, and through divorce by mutual consent (*khul'*). The IFL enactments also regulate in some detail other aspects of breakdown relating to maintenance, disposal of joint property, and custody of children, all of which are subject to court intervention and will be referred to in the following pages.

Reform of the divorce law in Malaysia, according to Professor Ahmad Ibrahim, manifested an attempt at implementing the Qur'anic requirement, addressed to the husband, of "kindness and equitable treatment" that he must grant to his estranged wife (Sura al-Baqarah, 2:231). This would naturally mean that the husband should avoid exercising his power of *talaq* so as to injure or take advantage of the wife. To realize this objective, it was highly recommended that "all pronouncement of *talaq* should be made before the *shari'a* court and with the permission of the court".[30] In the event where the *talaq* is pronounced outside the court and without the permission of the court, the husband should be liable to punishment under the law, but "the court will still take action" as Professor Ahmad Ibrahim added "to decide whether the *talaq* is valid according to Islamic law or not".[31] The latter part of this interpretation evidently read the *shari'a* separately from the provisions of the IFL 1984, as the possibility is envisaged that the court may still declare valid a *talaq* that is pronounced outside

---

[30] Ahmad Ibrahim, "Justice in the *shari'a* court", p. 101.
[31] *Ibid*.

the court. The IFL 1984 has not addressed the issue and has not actually declared that a *talaq* pronounced outside the court is invalid. It merely stipulated in section 124 that a man who divorces his wife by the pronouncement of *talaq* "outside the court and without the permission of the court commits an offence", which is punishable with fines or imprisonment. One would have thought that this legal text could equally be interpreted to the effect that *talaq* pronounced outside the court was invalid. This approach was, however, not attempted and evidently did not find favour with the subsequent amendment in 1994 of the earlier legislation. A new section 55A, introduced in 1994, provided for the court to approve the pronouncement of *talaq* by the husband "outside the Court and without permission of the Court . . . if the court is satisfied that the *talaq* that was pronounced is valid according to *Hukum Syara'*." The husband is under duty, however, to report the *talaq* so pronounced to the Court within "seven days of the pronouncement of *talaq*", and the court is under duty in turn to "ascertain whether the *talaq* that was pronounced is valid according to *Hukum Syara*". A valid *talaq* in *shari'a* can be pronounced by the husband who is in possession of his faculties and the words so uttered are indicative of his intention to divorce – and there is, of course, a subsisting marriage. When the court is satisfied as to the validity of the *talaq* pronouncement, then it shall make an order, subject to section 124 of the principal Act, to

(a)   approve the divorce by *talaq*;
(b)   record the divorce; and
(c)   send a copy of the record for registration to the appropriate Registrar or Chief Registrar.

Moreover, section 124 of the principal Act makes "a pronouncement of *talaq* in any form outside the court and without the permission of the court" a punishable offence liable to a fine of up to 1,000 ringgit or a maximum imprisonment of six months. The 1994 amendment has not changed this, and envisages therefore a situation whereby the court simply imposes the penalty even if it approves the *talaq* as being in accordance with the *hukum syarax*. The new amendment is thus not without complexity as it puts the judge in a difficult situation of (a) punishing a *talaq* pronounced outside the court and without the permission of the court; and (b) actually approving its validity under the *shari'a* and order its registration. Further complication is likely to arise in answer to the question whether the punishment is applicable only to a *talaq* that has not been reported within the seven days or even if it is reported within that time. What of the unreported cases of *talaq* pronounced out of court? Can the court also approve them as valid *talaq* in accordance with the *shari'a*? These questions would seem to call for further clarification. The general impression, however, is that the 1994 amendment has in effect overruled the reform measures that were introduced earlier. The substance of that reform was to prevent unilateral declaration of *talaq* by irresponsible husbands. "With these amendments, we are back where we started", wrote the National Council for Women's Organizations, Sisters in Islam, and the Association of Women Lawyers in a joint memorandum submitted to the government of Malaysia in March 1997. This letter also expressed the concern that the 1994 amendment will encourage "more men to divorce their wives outside the court and thus enable them to avoid their responsibilities toward their wives and children".[32] A 1996 survey conducted by the Women's Crisis Centre in Penang led to the finding that the number of men who pronounced the *talaq* outside the court and in contravention of the law is more than three times those who applied for divorce through the court.[33]

The signatories of the above mentioned memorandum proposed that the amended section 55 should be repealed and the original section 55 should be reinstated, which means that there should be no extra-judicial divorce outside the court, and that every *talaq* pronounced without the court permission should in all cases be liable to punishment as provided for under the IFL 1984. With regard to the quantum of punishment for violators, it was also suggested that the law should provide a minimum fine of RM1,000 and a mandatory custodial sentence of not less than four weeks. The maximum fine should be increased to RM5,000 and the maximum sentence should be extended from the present six months to one year.[34] It is thus stated that "Few other provisions in law are violated with such impunity and regularity as the divorce provisions under the Islamic Family Law Statutes."[35]

Two other aspects of divorce law in Malaysia which have given rise to frequent disputes before the *shari'a* courts are over the suspended divorce (*talaq ta'liq*) and gift of consolation (*mut'ah*). With regard to the first, the IFL enactments in many states entitle the prospective spouses to enter an agreement whereby the husband authorizes the wife to apply for a divorce in certain eventualities, such as his failure to maintain her for a period of four months, leaving or neglecting her, or causing hurt to her person. Under the IFL enactments that are currently in force in many states of Malaysia (except for Perlis which does not provide for a *ta'liq* agreement), the Registrar of Marriages makes available a form for this purpose which is completed at the time of registration. The form when duly completed is known as the *ta'liq* certificate and it becomes a part of the marriage contract. The IFL 1984 allows every married woman who is "entitled to a divorce in pursuance of the terms of a *ta'liq* certificate made upon a marriage" to apply to the *shari'a* court to declare that such divorce has taken place (section 50(1)). The court then examines the application and investigates the valid occurrence of the alleged *ta'liq* divorce and if satisfied that the divorce is valid according to *Hukum Syara'* confirms and records the divorce (section 50(2)).

The main problem encountered in *ta'liq* proceedings is the protracted court delays and difficulties over proof. Women groups and critics have expressed dissatisfaction over this and highlighted the case of *Mohd. Habibullah bin Mahmood v. Faridah bt. Dato Talib*,[36] which took six years before the plaintiff was finally granted a divorce after she applied for a *ta'liq* divorce in 1989 on the ground that her husband had abused her. The Selangor *shari'a* court rejected her application for divorce because of her husband's allegation that she was refractory (*nusyuz*) and neglected her marital obligations toward him. It took a declaration of apostasy, a failed

---

[32] National Council for Women's Organizations *et al.*, "Memorandum on reform of the Islamic family laws and the administration of justice in the *Syariah* system in Malaysia". Formulated and approved at the National Workshop on Reform of Islamic Family Laws and the Administration of Justice in the *Syariah* System in Malaysia on 4 January 1997, p. 4.

[33] *Ibid.*

[34] *Ibid.*, p. 5.

[35] *Ibid.*

[36] [1992] 2 MLJ 793.

attempt to have her case heard in the civil court, followed by intervention by the *shari'a* court of another jurisdiction before divorce was finally granted in 1995.

Women tend to be faced with difficulties in obtaining a *ta'liq* divorce, especially in cases when they claim ill-treatment and abuse against the husband. It was thus stated in a seminar paper prepared by women groups that "the court has often rejected medical and police reports of violence, demanding instead eye witness evidence". In cases of desertion, the court often goes to extraordinary lengths to trace the whereabouts of the husband instead of relying on the available evidence regarding the alleged desertion. The court is often reluctant to grant a divorce as provided for under section 50 of the IFL "even when the husband has failed to maintain the wife for years".[37]

Another point raised with regard to *ta'liq* proceedings is a certain lack of uniformity among the various state enactments. The current *ta'liq* agreement varies from state to state; Perlis does not even provide for a *ta'liq* agreement. It is consequently suggested that a standard *ta'liq* agreement should be adopted by all the states preferably on the following grounds:

(a) failure to maintain for four months;
(b) desertion for six months;
(c) any action that causes injury or, *darar shar'i* to the wife;
(d) any other grounds that the parties may agree to, including, for example, the husband's taking another wife. There is at present no provision for redress in cases where the husband contracts a polygamous marriage without the agreement of the existing wife.

And finally it is suggested that a new provision should be adopted to make it mandatory for the court to issue an order in default of appearance for the dissolution of the marriage, in the event, for instance, that the husband is absent for a maximum of three occasions within a maximum time frame of six months.[38]

With regard to *mut'ah*, the IFL 1984 provides, under section 56, that in addition to her right to apply for maintenance, a woman who has been divorced without just cause may apply to the court for *mut'ah* or consolatory gift, and the court may, upon being satisfied that the woman has been divorced without just cause, order the husband to pay "such sum as may be fair and just according to *Hukum Syara'*". Substantively similar provisions can also be found in the Islamic family law enactments of other states.[39] Critics have stated, however, that these provisions fail to provide detailed guidelines to assist the court in assessing the "fair and just" sum to be paid as *mut'ah*, and what is fair and just is therefore very much left to the discretion of individual judges.[40]

It is now generally understood in Malaysia that *mut'ah* is an obligatory compensation that must be paid to a divorced wife in all cases of divorce which was not caused by her. The main issue that is highlighted in many of the cases before the courts is over the quantum of *mut'ah* that should be paid to her. The difference

---

[37] "Memorandum on reform of Islamic family law", p. 8.
[38] *Ibid.*
[39] Cf. s. 44 of the IFL Enactment of Kelantan 1983.
[40] Cf. Nik Noriani, "Controversial areas", p. 149.

between the amount claimed by the wife and the offer made by the husband may be disproportionately large. The wife's right to *mut'ah* itself may be at issue when the wife herself has asked for a divorce. A perusal of the court cases on this subject shows that various factors are taken into account, including the wife's contribution to the family wealth, her negligence of marital obligations and *nushuz*, the duration of married life, the husband's income, the wife's own financial status etc., resulting in disparities in court decisions that have given rise to a demand for detailed legislative guidelines that should assist the court in the determination of the quantum of *mut'ah* that would hopefully be consistently applied by all the states.

Another feature of the IFL amendments on divorce is related to the court proceedings over ancillary reliefs. The 1994 amendments relaxed the strict requirements of the IFL 1984 on custody, maintenance and *mut'ah* which were to be determined first before the court issued an order of divorce. Section 55 of the principal Act thus disallowed registration of the divorce unless the Chief Registrar was satisfied that "The Court has made a final order or orders for the custody and maintenance of the dependent children, for the maintenance and accommodation of the divorced wife and for the payment of *mut'ah* to her." The amended version of this section removed all reference to custody, maintenance and *mut'ah* and simply provided that: "No pronouncement of *talaq* or order of divorce or annulment shall be registered unless the Chief Registrar is satisfied that the Court has made a final order relating to it."

All that the Chief Registrar is required as a result of this amendment is to ensure that the divorce itself has taken place without having to ascertain the custody and maintenance issues. The basic rationale for the new amendment, which was to avoid delays, was understandable, yet the uncertainties that are caused as a result are unjustified. A possible compromise has been suggested by the women's organizations of Malaysia in the form of setting a time frame for these additional orders. It is proposed that if no final order or orders have been made for the custody and maintenance of the dependent children, for the maintenance and accommodation of the divorced wife and for the payment of *mut'ah* to her after the lapse of three months from the date of divorce, the Chief Registrar shall register the divorce if he is satisfied that an interim order or orders have been made for the above ancillary reliefs. This, they said, would be in greater harmony with the *shari'a* and fairer to the divorced wife and children of the divorced marriage.[41]

Two other amendments that affect the right to maintenance of the divorced wife occur in sections 65 and 71. Section 65(1) of the principal Act has been amended to allow for the termination of the right of maintenance during the probation period (*'iddah*) if the divorced wife were charged with *nusyuz*. The amended version thus reads: "the right of a divorced wife to receive maintenance from her former husband under any order of Court shall cease on the expiry of *'iddah* or on the wife being *nusyuz*" (section 65).

The second amendment relates to the right to accommodation of the divorced wife during the period of *'iddah*. A new addition has been made in the 1994 Act (section 71(2)(d)) to provide that the right to accommodation during *'iddah* ceases "if the woman has been guilty of open lewdness (*fahisya*)". These amendments

41 "Memorandum on reform of Islamic family law", p. 4.

have given rise to unfair allegations of *nusyuz* being made against the women during their *'iddah* period. There were cases of wives who were accused of *nusyuz* even when they had left the marital home with their husbands' permission or because of fear of physical violence and abuse.

The new addition to section 71 is also likely to encourage false allegations of lewdness against the divorced women. Neither the original term *fahisya* nor in fact its English equivalent, "open lewdness" are precise enough to provide a reliable criterion on which to deprive a divorced wife of her right of maintenance. The law is also silent as to the kind of proof that might be necessary in order to prove the allegation of "open lewdness".

5 ENFORCING THE FATWAS

Section 9 of the *shari'a* Criminal Offences (Federal Territories) Act (SCOA) 1997, and many of its equivalent provisions in the various state enactments of Malaysia, granted fatwas issued by the state Mufti and the Islamic Religious Council the force of law outside the normal legislative processes. A fatwa, after approval by the State Executive Council and the Sultan, only needs to be gazetted to become law, without any requirement for it to be tabled for debate in Parliament or the state legislature. This is not altogether a new development as the state authorities had fatwa-making power under most of the state administrations of Islamic Law Enactments that have been in force in Malaysia in the latter half of the present century. The SCOA 1997, however, went a step further to declare it an offence for "any person who gives, propagates, or disseminates any opinion contrary to any fatwa" in force. Anyone who does so "shall be guilty of an offence and shall on conviction be liable to a fine not exceeding 3,000 ringgit or to imprisonment for a term not exceeding two years or both" (section 12). This provision also appears, with minimal change of words, in the Perak Administration of Islamic Law Enactment 1992 (section 21) and in many other state enactments.

Section 9 of the SCDA also makes "contempt of religious authority" a punishable offence which makes liable to fine and imprisonment of the same amount as in section 12 anyone who "defies, disobeys, or disputes the orders or directions of the Yang di-Pertuan Agong as the Head of the Religion of Islam, the *Majlis*, or the *Mufti*, expressed or given by way of fatwa . . ." The renewed emphasis in this enactment on conformity to fatwas represents a new development in Malaysia's legal history. The new measures have been criticized as having no precedent in other Muslim countries, reflecting rigidity and intolerance and therefore tantamount to imposing a "blanket ban on freedom of speech". The new measures are unconstitutional in so far as they do not relate to any of the eight restrictions on which freedom of speech could be curtailed under Article 10(2)(a) of the Federal Constitution. What is more is that over the past two years or so most states in Malaysia have adopted these same provisions in their respective *shari'a* criminal offences enactments.[42]

As a juristic concept, "fatwa" signifies an opinion, verdict, or response, of a learned scholar of *shari'a* over an issue in which a response has been solicited. The jurists

---

[42] Cf. Sisters in Islam's letter to the Prime Minister, p. 1.

have often used "fatwa" interchangeably with legal reasoning, or *ijtihad*, neither of which is, however, binding. The collection of fatwas that Muslim jurists and Muftis have compiled in their capacities as academic advisers to the judges, and writers, are basically issue oriented and provide feasible solutions to legal and religious issues. If one were to differentiate the fatwa from *ijtihad*, the former may simply consist of a response, however brief, to a question without necessarily elaborating its own justification and rationale, whereas the latter must specify its own evidential basis. A ruling of *ijtihad*, or of fatwa for that matter, can acquire the force of law either through general consensus (*ijma'*) or by the command of the lawful government (i.e. the *ulu al-amr*). A fatwa or *ijtihad* which is not supported by either of these is not binding. A distinctive genre of legal literature, known as *fatawa*, has developed over centuries consisting of a learned response to practical questions posed to the Mufti often by the disputing parties in a lawsuit. If a person was dissatisfied with the fatwa of one Mufti, he or she was free to consult another Mufti, or lawyer as in the current usage, for another opinion. It may readily be said even from these cursory remarks that if the authorities in the various states of Malaysia have decided, in their capacity as the *ulu al-amr* to give fatwas the automatic force of law they may be said to have exercised their legitimate authority. A simplistic answer of this kind may seem specious, yet it is basically correct from the perspective of *siyasah shar'iyyah* or a *shari'a*-oriented polity. I shall explore this question a little further as the discussion proceeds but it must be noted at this point that although the *shari'a* entitles the *ulu al-amr* to determine a certain procedure for fatwa, that procedure must in the meantime be in harmony with the dictate of a judiciary. As a doctrine of public law, *siyasah shar'iyyah* is inherently rational and consist mainly of Acts and policy decisions, be they within or outside the established *shari'a* , which facilitate efficiency and good government, provided that they do not violate the recognized goals and principles of *shari'a*. The issue before us is whether giving the fatwa the force of law outside normal constitutional procedures, and then creating a criminal offence on that basis is judicious and acceptable within the framework of *siyasah shar'iyyah*. If we envisage the Federal Constitution as a command of the *ulu al-amr par excellence* and then reach the conclusion that the fatwa procedure that is now devised is at odds with the Constitution, then the issue before us would be one of internal inconsistency and conflict within the general framework of *siyasah shar'iyyah*. For *siyasah shar'iyyah* advocates pursuit of the legitimate interests of the people and authorizes government leaders to take all necessary measures, including legislation, that facilitate efficient management of the community affairs.[43]

This analysis points to the conclusion that a certain ruling or decision may well be within the limits of a given jurisdiction but may still be at odds with the dictates of a sound policy, or *siyasah shar'iyyah*. With reference to fatwas, it may likewise be said that the government and the *ulu al-amr* may have the authority to give them the force of law and devise a procedure to that effect, but if that procedure is at odds with the Constitution, it could hardly be said to be in conformity with *siyasah shar'iyyah*.

In a constitutional government, if the state wishes to enforce the fatwa of a Mufti, it should open that fatwa to consultation and debate through normal procedures,

---

[43] For details on *siyasah shar'iyyah* see M.H. Kamali, "Siyasah Shar'iyyah or the policies of Islamic government", *The American Journal of Islamic Social Sciences*, 6, 1989, pp. 59–81.

before it can become law. The authority to make law rests with Parliament at the federal level and with Legislative Assemblies at the state level. The fatwa of a Mufti, or of a Council of Muftis, for that matter should in other words, be open to scrutiny and debate by the people's elected representatives. Otherwise, one runs the risk of marginalizing the representative assemblies in favour of non-elected and narrowly focused groups to make decisions that affect the basic rights of the people.

Furthermore, many of the state enactments in Malaysia grant to the Mufti alone the power to "amend, modify or revoke any fatwa that has been issued earlier by him or by any previous Mufti" and the modification or revocation of a fatwa "shall be deemed to be a fatwa" and may accordingly be gazetted (section 36, Administration of Islamic Law (Federal Territories Act) 1993). This is once again seen to be narrowly focused so much so as to approximate the idea of a theocratic dictatorship, and in disharmony therefore with the essence of consultation as envisaged in the Qur'an. In a thirteen-page letter that Sisters in Islam addressed to the Prime Minister Dr. Mahathir, it was noted that "We have in effect delegated total responsibility in the implementation and interpretation of Islam to a tiny minority whose views and values are often contrary to the vision of Islam held by federal leaders and the silent majority of Malaysians."[44] The letter also underscored a certain trend in recent years whereby laws which are "detrimental to public interest, and against the principles of justice and equality in Islam have been passed in silence . . . There is a need for those in religious authority to understand that they operate in a democratic multi-ethnic society where fundamental liberties are protected by the Federal Constitution."[45]

6 THE *HUDUD* BILL DEBATE

One of the major events of the 1990s that merits attention in discussing *shari'a*-related developments in Malaysia is the Kelantan *shari'a* Criminal Code (II) Bill, known as the *Hudud* Bill, which was passed in November 1993 by the State Legislative Assembly of Kelantan.[46] The Bill has, however, become controversial and remained in abeyance ever since for want of approval by the Federal Government. This is due to the fact that the Bill imposes a structure of punishments which exceed the jurisdictional limits of the *shari'a* courts under the constitutional specifications of the State List. The *shari'a* courts have limited jurisdiction in criminal matters under federal law and can only deal with offences punishable with imprisonment up to three years or a fine not exceeding RM5000 or caning up to six strokes. The Islamic Party of Malaysia, PAS, which is the ruling party of Kelantan, under the leadership of its enigmatic leader and Chief Minister, Nik Aziz, has protested over the delay in the enforcement of the *Hudud* Bill, which has to date been met with an equally resolute response from the Federal Government, especially the Prime Minister, Dr Mahathir Mohamad, who has taken the centre stage in the debate that became a familiar media topic in recent years. The issue over

---

[44] Sisters in Islam's Letter to the Prime Minister, p. 6.
[45] *Ibid.*, p. 7.
[46] Actual plans for the introduction of this Bill were announced by the state government earlier in 1991 and the debate over it also started at that time.

the *Hudud* Bill has remained unresolved as of this writing, but the debate has brought the wider subject of the applicability of *shari'a* in Malaysia into sharp relief. Many writers and public figures have spoken over the various aspects of the *Hudud* Bill and the prospects generally of the Islamization of law and government in Malaysia. This debate is unusually candid since the parties involved therein included not only the public and the media, but the state and federal governments whose leaders were called upon to clarify their positions often in response to particular developments.

The *Hudud* Bill itself consists of seventy-two clauses and five supplementary schedules, divided into six parts, namely *hudud* (prescribed) offences, *qisas* (just retaliation), evidence, implementation of punishments, general provisions, and (*shari'a*) court proceedings. The *hudud* offences in part one also appear under the six headings of theft, highway robbery (*hiraba*) unlawful carnal intercourse (*zina*), *qadhf*, that is, slanderous accusation of *zina* which is not proven by four witnesses, wine-drinking (*shurb*) and apostasy (*irtidad*). The structure of the punishments that the Bill has introduced and the detailed manner of their implementation read like a reproduction of the all too familiar textbooks of classical *fiqh* on the subject. Commentators have, in fact, stated that the *Hudud* Bill has adopted the renowned *Shafi'i* jurist Abul Hasan al-Mawardi's (d. 450 H) *Kitab al-Ahkam al-Sultaniyya*, and merely changed its style into a statute book format. Thus the Bill has incorporated punishments ranging from the mutilation of the hand for the capital offence of theft, lapidarian for a proven offence of *zina*, death punishment for *hiraba*, and flogging for wine-drinking (*shurb*) and slanderous accusation, or *qadhf*, without actually taking into account the realities of contemporary society in Malaysia. PAS has maintained the view that Muslims have no choice but to accept the proposed legislation: they cannot pick and choose what they consider reasonable and leave out the rest. Muslims who question the *hudud* were told that they were merely ill informed and influenced by the liberal secular West, which regards such laws as barbaric. Malaysians of other faiths should neither be fearful nor suspicious of the *hudud* because Malaysians are by and large law abiding, family loving and religious. Because of this, all Malaysians will eventually accept the *hudud* as they are meant to protect their lives and properties and enhance their peace of mind. To this, it is added that the prisons are over-crowded and financially burdensome. Enforcement of the *hudud* would drastically reduce these problems because once an individual has been tried, convicted and punished, he or she is released. The PAS government has moreover stated that under the *hudud* administration, reform and rehabilitation programmes will be made available for the convicts.[47] The Kelantan authorities have been active in some other areas too, introducing, for example, the *shari'a* law of evidence, and several municipal by-laws designed to facilitate a general enforcement of the *shari'a*.

PAS has evidently demanded a total implementation of the *shari'a*, a demand which, as one observer noted, is difficult to refuse "because it involves basic faith and has an emotional appeal which can grow out of hand".[48] This aspect of the *Hudud*

---

[47] Cf. Rose Isma'il (ed.), *Hudud in Malaysia: The Issues at Stake*, SIS Forum (Malaysia) Berhad, Kuala Lumpur, 1995, pp. 51–52.

[48] Razaleigh Hamzah, opening speech to the Semangat 46 Seminar of 17 October 1993, in *ibid.*, p. 57.

Bill scenario has been evident as from the outset and began on that note in so far as the proponents of the Bill saw their act as a religious duty and a dogmatic initiative rather than a response to the dictates of law and justice in society. In his initial announcement in November 1993 in which he informed the public of the ratification of the Bill by the State Assembly, the Chief Minister of Kelantan went on record to explain the Committee work and participation of the *ulema* in the drafting of the Bill and then added that the state government was "performing a duty required by Islam", and "failure to act in this regard would be a great sin".[49] As to the question whether the people had accepted the state government's plan to implement the *hudud* laws, the Deputy Chief Minister (Abdul Halim) made the remarkable announcement that "the question did not arise as Muslims in the State who rejected the laws would be considered *murtad* (apostate)".[50]

Razaleigh Hamzah criticized the dogmatic approach of the Kelantan government in saying that "the implementation of Islamic law must not be considered solely for its implementation aspect, but how the law can solve the problems of today's society".[51] Referring to the PAS totalitarian demand, Razaleigh Hamzah added that "there are many obstacles in complying with this demand", and then suggested that the implementation of Islamic law in Malaysia should be determined by democratic means. The Muslims of Malaysia should decide "as to who should have the mandate to implement the teachings of Islam". Can Islamic law be implemented and "function effectively in a country in which the system of government is not based on the philosophy and the teachings of Islam"?[52]

The general tenor of the critique that the federal government has advanced of the *Hudud* Bill is similar to that of Razaleigh Hamzah's and it is basically over the prospects of attaining justice. They have voiced the fear that in the event of the *hudud* being applied only in a part of Malaysia and as an isolated case from the rest of the *shari'a*, they may fail to achieve justice.

The Prime Minister, Dr Mahathir, stated the position of his government most explicitly when he said that "the government would not sit back and allow PAS to commit cruel acts against the people in Kelantan, including chopping off the hands of criminals". The Prime Minister added that "the Government would take action against the PAS-led Kelantan Government if it implemented the PAS-created *Hudud* laws". Dr Mahathir elaborated that the *Hudud* Bill amounted to discrimination against Muslims in cases, for example, when two people, a Muslim and non-Muslim, committed a crime, only the former was subjected to a heavy punishment but the latter is not. The PAS version of the *Hudud* law "punishes victims while actual criminals were often let off with minimum punishment; this is against the Islamic spirit of justice"; and therefore "against the true teachings of Islam".[53]

---

[49] Quoted in M.H. Kamali, *Punishment in Islamic Law: An Enquiry into the Hudud Bill of Kelantan*, Institute for Policy Research, Kuala Lumpur, 1995, p. 8. A summary of this book is due to appear in *Arab Law Quarterly* (London) (forthcoming).

[50] *Ibid.*, p. 8.

[51] Razaleigh Hamzah's speech quoted, in Ismail, *Hudud in Malaysia*, p. 59.

[52] *Ibid.*, p. 58.

[53] Dr Mahathir's Speech, "We will not allow PAS to commit cruel acts", *New Straits Times*, 10 September 1994, pp. 1–2.

In his 1996 publication, the *Asian Renaissance*, the then Deputy Prime Minister of Malaysia, Anwar Ibrahim, spoke explicitly on the *hudud* issue. In an attempt to read this issue in the general context of Southeast Asian Islam, Anwar Ibrahim wrote that "the proponents of the imposition of Muslim laws or the establishment of an Islamic state are confined to the periphery". Southeast Asian Muslims prefer to concentrate on economic growth and eradication of poverty "instead of amputating the limbs of thieves". They do not believe it would make one less of a Muslim to promote economic growth, to master the information revolution and ensure justice for women.[54] With reference again to the *hudud*, Anwar Ibrahim added that he is supportive of Yusuf al-Qaradawi's advocacy for *fiqh al-awlawiyyat*, the understanding of the priorities of Islamic law, and wrote that "the application of the *hudud* . . . is not necessarily among the top priorities of contemporary Muslim societies".[55] Many issues have been raised over the detailed provisions of the *Hudud* Bill, but space does not permit a wider coverage of the details.[56]

7 APOSTASY (*RIDDAH*)

Apostasy became a topical issue in Malaysia following the case of Nor Aishah Bokhari, a 26-year old Malay Muslim who became an apostate when she renounced Islam in October 1997. She did so in order to be able to marry Joseph Arnold Lee, 28, a Roman Catholic of Chinese-Indian parentage from Melaka. Lee worked as an Assistant Manager in a Citibank branch in Melaka where Nor Aishah also worked as a junior staff. In September 1997 they decided to get engaged. "The only difference for this couple", according to newspaper report, "was that this time, instead of the non-Muslim deciding to embrace Islam, the Muslim decided to leave the religion."[57]

On 22 October Nor Aishah renounced Islam in the presence of a Commissioner of Oaths. She then left her parental home to live with her fiancé's parents. Nor Aishah's own family and relatives were "saddened and shocked" by her renunciation of Islam, just as it angered certain quarters of the Muslim community to see what they considered to be a violation of the mores of Muslim society in Malaysia.

The Islamic party of Malaysia (PAS) printed and circulated some 100,000 posters bearing Nor Aishah's photo and urging her to return to Islam. Its official newspaper, *Harakah*, called on the government to consider arresting apostates under the Internal Security Act which allows for detention without trial. This is normally due mainly to the constitutional guarantee on freedom of religion. Article 11 of the Constitution thus declares that "every person has the right to profess and practice his religion and, subject to Clause (4) to propagate it". Clause 4 regulates the manner in which religious doctrines are propagated, by allowing legislation which may control or restrict the propagation of any religious doctrine among persons pro-

[54] Anwar Ibrahim, *The Asian Renaissance*, Time Books International, Singapore, 1996, p. 114.
[55] *Ibid.*, p. 119.
[56] For more details see Kamali, *Punishment in Islamic Law: An Enquiry into the Hudud Bill of Kelantan*.
[57] R. Mageswary, "Two young people from two different religions met and fell in love with tragic consequences", *Sun Magazine Special*, Kuala Lumpur, 16 April 1998, p. 6.

fessing Islam. Article 11 thus safeguards freedom of religion without any stipulation in favour of any particular group, but permits restrictions to be imposed on the manner in which religious doctrines are propagated.

In November 1997 Nor Aishah's family found her and brought her home. Her father, Bokhari Mohamed Tahir, subsequently told reporters that his daughter had regretted her actions and vowed to revert to Islam on 20 November. "I asked my daughter why she left Islam", Bokhari told reporters at his home in Pontian. "She said she is not sure but she has started reading the Qur'an and is more devout than ever." On 30 December 1997 she disappeared again.

"My daughter has been kidnapped", a tearful Bokhari told reporters this time. Two weeks after she disappeared, a letter was received by her lawyer which bore her signature, asking her lawyer to appeal to the High Court on her behalf for her right to choose her own religion. In this twenty-page long letter, dated 9 January 1998, Nor Aishah tells the High Court that she was kidnapped by her father, and brother (Nazaruddin) while waiting in front of the Amoda building in Kuala Lumpur on 20 November. But later in the evening, she called Lee who then waited for her in front of their house and they both went into hiding. In her affidavit, Nor Aishah urged the court to look into her case. She also asked her community and the media to leave her and Lee alone. A warrant of arrest has, in the meantime, been issued against Lee for kidnapping Nor Aishah, and her lawyer Leonard Teoh, was detained by police soon after his submission of the twenty-page letter and affidavit. Teoh apparently knew the whereabouts of the couple but refused to divulge it. The High Court in Johor Baru ruled that the solicitor–client privilege does not exist where there is an element of fraud, and said that the Nor Aishah case contained an element of fraud, and therefore Teoh must reveal whereabouts of the missing couple. It is now understood that the Bar Council is considering taking up the matter. Teoh spent fourteen days in remand but was released without being charged.[58]

Unconfirmed reports also had it that a draft Bill was being prepared by the Islamic Centre (*Pusat Islam*) at the Prime Minister's Department which contained punitive measures and provisions for a rehabilitation programme for prospective apostates. It was in response to such reports that the Minister of Religious Affairs at the Prime Minister's Department, Dr Abdul Hamid Othman, said that a law on apostasy was being drafted but it would focus on rehabilitative and preventive measures. "The law will not be punishment-oriented but would lay emphasis on how to prevent apostasy and handle reported cases."[59] The present writer's personal information suggested that an initial plan for a punitive approach was discussed at the Technical Committee at *Pusat Islam* but failed to find support and the Committee opted instead for a persuasive approach to the proposed legislation.

Apostasy is a serious offence under classical Islamic law and the leading schools of *fiqh* have adopted as standard law the ruling of the *hadith* which declares simply that "one who changes his religion shall be killed". But the issue of death punishment for apostasy is controversial, especially in view of the Qur'anic declaration that "there shall be no compulsion in religion" (2:256). It is evidently difficult to

---

58 *Ibid.*, p. 8.
59 Mazlan Nordin, "Things that people do in the name of religion", *New Straits Times*, Kuala Lumpur, 5 June 1998, p. 12.

uphold the normative Qur'anic principle on freedom of religion and the provision, at the same time, of the death punishment for apostasy. In an attempt to reconcile these positions, it has been suggested, and rightly so, that the *hadith* in question envisaged only a hostile renunciation of Islam which was, in the early days of Islam, equivalent to high treason. The punishment was, in other words, meant, not for apostasy that emanated from conviction and belief, but for blasphemy and rebellion against the community and its legitimate leadership.[60]

Notwithstanding the clear constitutional guarantee of freedom of religion, the pressure of public opinion strongly discourages apostasy among Muslims in Malaysia. The Islamic party of Malaysia, PAS, in its controversial *Hudud* Bill 1993, has included apostasy among the prescribed (*hudud*) offences and assigned the death punishment to it. As noted above, the *Hudud* Bill was passed by the State Legislature of Kelantan but the Federal Government refused to ratify it and it has consequently remained in abeyance.

It should be noted that the Supreme Court has, in a leading case, upheld the constitutional clause on religious freedom. In *Minister of Home Affairs v. Jamaluddin Othman*,[61] a Malay Muslim converted to Christianity and became a priest under a new name, Yeshua Jamaludddin, and proselytized Christianity among the Malays. It was alleged that he participated in a work camp and seminar for this purpose. He was detained under the Internal Security Act 1987 "for acting in a manner prejudicial to the security of Malaysia". But his plea for release on a *habeas corpus* application was eventually granted by the High Court of Kuala Lumpur. The trial judge, Justice Anuar, held that the Minister of Home Affairs had detained the defendant contrary to Article 11 of the Constitution, and ordered the defendant's release. The Minister appealed to the Supreme Court, which dismissed the appeal and stated the grounds of its decision as follows:

The sum total of the grounds for detention in this case was the supposed involvement of the respondent in a plan or programme for the dissemination of Christianity among the Malays . . . We do not think that mere participation, meetings and seminar can make a person a threat to the security of the country. As regards the alleged conversion of six Malays, even if it were true, it cannot by itself, in our opinion, be regarded as a threat to the security of the country.

While dismissing the appeal the Supreme Court also held that the guarantee provided by Article 11 of the Constitution concerning freedom of religion must be given effect unless the actions of a person go well beyond what can normally be regarded as professing or practising his or her faith.

8 THE BEAUTY PAGEANT ISSUE

A relatively minor issue which received a great deal of publicity in Malaysia during the second half of 1997 was the Miss Malaysia Petite 1997 pageant, held in Kuala

---

[60] For details see the chapter on blasphemy in M.H. Kamali, *Freedom of Expression in Islam*, The Islamic Texts Society, Cambridge, 1997, pp. 212–250.
[61] [1989] 1 MLJ 369, 418.

Lumpur in June 1997, in which three Muslim girls appeared and were arrested during the beauty contest by the Religious Affairs Department of Selangor (JAIS). Noni Mohamed, 19, of Penang, Fahyu Hanim Ahmad, 18, and Sharina Shari, 22, of Kedah participated in the Malaysia Petite contest in a hotel in Subang Jaya. They were arrested and charged for indecent exposure under the provisions of the Selangor *Shari'a* Criminal Enactment 1995, and also for having violated a fatwa that forbade them from taking part in beauty contests.[62] The Enactment penalizes indecent exposure with a fine of up to 1,000 ringgit or six months of imprisonment or both.

The media and the public spoke openly and critically for weeks of the JAIS action and the way its officials arrested the three girls for something which "countless other Malay/Muslim girls had done . . . in almost all states for as long as anyone can remember".[63] Critical remarks were also made over the lack of publicity and a relative obscurity of the fatwa by the Selangor religious authorities that forbade participation of Muslim women in beauty contests. The officers were said to have embarked on enforcing what was an "almost unknown law and fatwa". Instead of informing the three contestants about the laws they would be breaking, the "religious policemen" joined the audience of the beauty contest "waiting for the young women to appear on stage and then they pounced".[64] The religious authority clearly was not wishing for the law or modesty to be observed. "It wanted to arrest . . . and then convict. There is neither anything moral nor Islamic in that."[65] The explanation that they could not stop the girls from participating "because the complaint was made only hours before the show must have been the most absurd ever to come from people said to be so learned. They had the time to buy the tickets for the show . . ."[66]

Within two weeks of arrest, the three young women were charged, found guilty and fined for indecent dressing under section 31 of the Selangor *Shari'a* Criminal Enactment and for violating a fatwa under section 12(c) – a display of efficiency that the *shari'a* courts are hardly known for.

Anwar Ibrahim, the Deputy Prime Minister, commented concerning this incident that "no one should be over-zealous in implementing the law . . . we must use our wisdom and not simply pronounce the laws against anybody. We can inform the society by using a moderate and wise method which will not create fear or worry among the people."

Anwar Ibrahim added that in principle "we do not encourage Muslims to participate in beauty contests, but any action taken must be done carefully and wisely".[67] The Prime Minister Dr Mahathir Mohamad also warned those given "what little powers" they had to enforce religious matters not to abuse them, as this gave Islam a bad name. He also said that arrests and handcuffing religious offenders were not the way to promote Islam. Dr Mahathir added that there is lack of uniformity in the administration of Islamic laws in the states which is caused by the fact that the

---

[62] *The Sun*, Kuala Lumpur, 25 July 1997, p. 27.
[63] *Ibid.*
[64] *Sun*, Kuala Lumpur, 11 July 1997, p. 11. Report and comment by A. Ghani Ismail.
[65] *Ibid.*
[66] Aziz Hassan, "Syariah laws: forcing or enforcing?" *The Sun*, Kuala Lumpur, 25 July 1997, p. 20.
[67] *The Sun*, Kuala Lumpur, 6 July 1997, p. 5.

administration of Islamic law is controlled by the states. "I will try to talk to the rulers on this matter so that we can establish uniformity in our Islamic administration."[68] A commentator noted that "Islamic law should be implemented justly or not implemented at all . . ." The religious authorities should apprehend every Muslim and avoid scapegoating odd individuals, for "otherwise it will be terribly unfair to the three girls".[69] Will these measures be applied to athletes who appear in their sportswear, and to women at the beach and public swimming pools?

Commentators also noted that "any state laws and fatwas that affect the people's fundamental liberties must be consistent with the provisions of the Federal and State Constitutions". The fatwa is only issued by the religious authorities actually exercising powers that belong to Parliament. Moreover, the offence of indecency under the state *shari'a* Criminal Offences Enactments may be said to be "an unconstitutional trespass on federal powers". The public outcry over the beauty pageant issue shows that Malaysians are no longer willing to remain silent in the face of "injustice, extremism and overzealousness committed in the name of religion".[70]

The minister responsible for religious affairs at the Prime Minister's Department, Dr Abdul Hamid Othman, announced that he would call for a meeting of all heads of state religious departments to streamline guidelines and mode of enforcement on indecent dress and behaviour among Muslims. He added that the meeting would determine what constituted indecent dressing and behaviour before the law was generally enforced.[71] Dr Hamid Othman had, however, initially supported the action by JAIS. Although he did not repeat his stand, "he never retracted it".[72] The guidelines are still expected and it is not known whether Dr Othman has persuaded the state religious authorities to agree to a uniform set of guidelines.

9 CONCLUSION

This article enquired into a number of issues that are either caused or brought into focus by the recent amendments of the Islamic law enactments in the various states of Malaysia. It is a story generally of folding back of the reforms that were introduced and then revoked, as it seems, for no compelling reason that could relate to the realities of social and family life in Malaysia. We have not seen basic evidence to suggest that the initial reforms that were earlier introduced had given rise to new problems or had adverse effects on the health and stability of the family institution among Malaysian Muslims. One might speculate perhaps and say that the conservative backlash that we have seen was probably instigated by a somewhat belated effect in Malaysia of the general phenomenon of Islamic revivalism, and the prevailing Malaysian political climate, perhaps, during the 1990s and in particular the rise, perhaps, to power of the PAS Islamic party in Kelantan and the fresh

---

[68] *The Star*, Kuala Lumpur, 23 July 1997, p. 8.
[69] *The Star*, 22 July 1997, s. 2, p. 17.
[70] Sisters in Islam, "Modesty according to the Qur'an", *New Straits Times*, Kuala Lumpur, 9 August 1997, p. 11.
[71] *Ibid*.
[72] Abdul Aziz Bari, "Beauty contests and the *syariah* laws", *The Sun*, Kuala Lumpur, 27 July 1997, p. 12.

challenge it has presented to the Islamic credentials of the Federal Government in Kuala Lumpur.

Notwithstanding the conservative reaction to the initial IFL reforms, the basic tenor and egalitarian substance of those reforms and their proximity to the letter and spirit of Qur'anic teachings on polygamy and divorce have not been challenged. This is the substance, in fact, of many of the critical observations on these amendments that were examined in this article.

There are suggestions for change often consisting of a fresh demand to reinstate the original reforms and also a call for additional refinements which were discussed in appropriate places as the discussion proceeded and need not be repeated here. I propose, however, to end this article with some suggestions for consolidation in the administration of Islamic law in Malaysia, which is clearly fragmated. The general picture I have presented of the IFL in Malaysia is one of conflicting jurisdictions, disparity and divergence, which hardly ever fails to provide a cause for concern. Yet, for those who wish to see a positive side to this picture, it may be in the distinctive approaches that the various states of Malaysia have taken to the administration of Islamic law in their respective jurisdictions. Since Islam is an integral part of the Malay identity, the approaches taken toward the implementation of Islamic law are also seen as a part, perhaps, of that identity. There may be some persuasive force in this, but it seems that the course of events has been rather too strongly influenced by the forces of separation, and preservation of the political sovereignty of the Malay rulers. The view has thus prevailed that the people's interests are better served through diversity and separation. Colonial rule favoured this pattern and encouraged its recognition under the constitutional mandate which made Islamic law a state matter in Malaysia.

Justice and equality are the cherished values of both Islamic law and secular legislation and they are inherently holistic and unitarian. There is no inherent need for bifurcation and division of justice under the Islamic and statutory laws of Malaysia. For the Islamic perception of justice is no different from what it has meant in other great traditions. Malaysia may consider a reorganization of its judiciary along the lines that have been taken, perhaps, by Egypt and the Sudan by having a system of unified national courts that are committed to the same standards of efficiency and diligence in the service of justice, but may decide to have *shari'a* benches within the general structure of a unified judiciary. This would also necessitate substantive uniformity in the administration of Islamic law for the whole of Malaysia. This corporate merger, if I may use the expression, might even prove to be economically more cost-effective. Within a general plan for uniformity, the Malaysian judiciary could devise a structure that was best suited to the demographic realities of religious and cultural pluralism to which Malaysia is clearly committed. Islamic law and the *shari'a* system of adjudication could still apply only to the Muslims and the realities of a multi-religious society could still be acknowledged and sustained even if Malaysia took a unified approach to the administration of Islamic law throughout its territorial domain.

Islamic Law in Indonesia

Sebastiaan Pompe *

1 INTRODUCTION

Indonesia has the largest number of Muslims of any country in the world; they presently number approximately 185 million out of a total population of almost 205 million (87 per cent). Despite this overwhelming Muslim majority, Indonesia is not an Islamic state. A number of factors have contributed to this condition, and this introduction will briefly review them so as to provide a better understanding of the place and role of Islam within Indonesian state structures.[1]

1.1 Diversity within Islam

A first factor is that Indonesian Islam itself is very diverse. The Indonesian *'ummat* can be roughly divided into a devout and not so devout section, sometimes referred to as *Muslim Fanatik* and *Muslim Statistik* in Indonesian.[2] Each section itself is moreover subject to various nuances. The principal reason for this diversity lies in the way Islam came to the region. As with other countries in South and South-East Asia, Islam came to Indonesia by way of trade rather than by war of conquest. It arrived in the region in the fourteenth century by way of the traditional trade route along the Indian coast towards the Malacca Straits, and from there to the islands of Java, Kalimantan (Borneo), South Sulawesi (Celebes) and onwards towards the east.

---

* Senior Lecturer, Van Vollenhoven Institute, Faculty of Law, Leiden University, the Netherlands.
[1] Besides the sources cited hereafter see generally A. Ibrahim, S. Siddique and Y. Hussain, *Readings on Islam in Southeast Asia*, ISEAS, Singapore, 1985 and the sources cited therein; C. Geertz, *The Religion of Java*, The Free Press, Glencoe, 1960; D. S. Lev, *Islamic Courts in Indonesia: A Study in the Political Bases of Legal Institutions*, University of California Press, Berkeley, 1972.
[2] Geertz's classical study on Javanese Islam distinguishes between not two but three sections, being the devout *santri* (generally traders), the Hinduized *priyayi* (generally traditional elite), and the animistically oriented *abangan* (generally farmers): *The Religion of Java*. Later studies have qualified this classification in important ways, in part as a result of changes in the place and role of Islam in Javanese society itself.

This peaceful introduction of Islam means that rather than overwhelming and displacing, it settled in by a complex process of accommodation and adaptation. This may have been an important factor in creating a mellow form of religious expression, "a tolerant, syncretic creed that neither evangelizes nor excludes", as one journal put it recently.[3] It also promoted a condition where Islam is markedly stronger in some areas than in others. At the risk of oversimplification, it can be stated generally that Islam became particularly strong in coastal areas and rather less so in many inland states and communities where it arrived much later in history, or not at all, as with the Batak in Central Sumatra or the Dayak in Central Kalimantan (Borneo).

This development is also evident on the island of Java, which is traditionally regarded as the heartland of the archipelago, being one of the oldest centres of institutionalized political power with the largest and most influential ethnic minority group. As with the other islands, the Javanese coastal communities were exposed to Islam first. Their relatively quick and enthusiastic conversion was at least in part a reaction against the Hinduized inland states on the island, to whom they owed allegiance. By way of contrast, the process of subjection of the inland states and communities to Islam was much slower and more complex, since Islam had to compete, or be accommodated, with other belief systems that were strong and deeply rooted in society and state structures. Rather than overwhelming the inland states and communities on Java, Islam was accommodated to varying degrees and interpretations within existing societal structures. These structures were over time shaped by Islam in its turn. This condition, or rather ongoing process, of selective accommodation of different belief systems and reciprocal change is termed "syncretism" and has long been held to be the outstanding feature of central Javanese belief systems. The resulting situation on Java is that Islam on the coast has generally tended to be stronger, comprehensive, modernist and outward looking, whereas inland Islam is more inward looking and traditional, and is fused to varying degrees with Hindu or animist belief systems.

The resulting diversity within Indonesian Islam has been a prime factor in restricting its political influence. Resistance against a greater and more public role for Islam in Indonesia is at least partly rooted in sections of the Islamic community itself, particularly the section that retains a deep attachment to traditional or pre-Islamic belief systems.

1.2 Religious diversity

A second factor is that the majority portion of Islam does not deny an importance to other religions that outweighs their minority positions. Minority religions in Indonesia are important in two ways. The first is that in such a large population, small percentages still constitute significant absolute numbers. Thus, the 6 per cent Protestants number 12.3 million, the 3 per cent Catholics number 6.15 million, the 2 per cent Hindu number 4 million and the 1 per cent Buddhists number 2 million people. Minority religions, which typically tend to build coalitions when under pressure, therefore still account for almost 25 million people. This is a

---

[3] Indonesian survey, *The Economist*, 26 July 1997, p. 6.

significant political constituency. Of even greater importance is the fact that unlike Malaysia or Egypt, for instance, minority religions are in large part geographically concentrated in certain regions of the archipelago, such as the Protestant Batak on Sumatra, the largely Protestant Menadonese in Northern Sulawesi (Celebes), the Protestant Moluccans, the Catholic smaller Sunda islands and, of course, the Hindu Balinese.

The size and geographic distribution of minority religions in Indonesia are therefore compelling political arguments for restricting the political and legal role of Islam. A pronounced Islamization of the national constitutional or legal system would undoubtedly fuel centrifugal tendencies in regions where minority religions are concentrated. National unity therefore imposes a further significant constraint on the way Islam is handled by the central government. As former President Sukarno put it bluntly as early as 1953: "If we establish a state based on Islam, many areas whose population is not Islamic, such as the Moluccas, Bali, Flores, Timor, the Kai Islands and Sulawesi, will secede."[4]

In more recent times, this political aspect of the geographical concentration of certain minority religions has been illustrated in East Timor, where the political conflict has distinct religious undertones, most clearly illustrated by the role of Bishop Belo as mouthpiece and leader of community discontent.

1.3 Colonial reception theory

The complex condition of Indonesian Islam has long confused Dutch colonial authorities and scholars. Until well into the second half of the nineteenth century, they widely thought that Indonesians had subjected themselves to Islam in its entirety. As a result the view was held that Islamic religious prescripts should be applied to Indonesians under all circumstances. This view permeated colonial legislation relative to the subject in that period, such as the colonial Code on Religious Courts (section 1882-152 jo. 153) which was replaced only in 1989.

It was only at the turn of the century that awareness grew of the fused, syncretic condition of various norm and belief systems in the archipelago, notably the role of non-Islamic custom (*adat*).[5] Its identification, definition and record as "customary law" by Dutch scholars strengthened its position and gave it legal standing.[6] In fact, "*adat* law" was so extensively documented and generated such a sizeable body of scholarly publications, that some scholars have argued that its prominent place in the late colonial state and modern Indonesia is in essence a Dutch creation.[7] There can be no doubt that the distinctive position of *adat* within the colonial legal system supported conservative forces in the colony, concerned as they were about the politically unifying and mobilizing potential of Islam.

---

[4] B. J. Boland, *The Struggle of Islam in Modern Indonesia*, M. Nijhoff, The Hague, 1971, p. 47.
[5] C. Snouck Hurgronje, "Mr. L.W.C. van den Berg's beoefening van het Mohammedaansche recht", *De Indische Gids*, 1884, pp. 363, 737.
[6] C. van Vollenhoven, *De ontdekking van hetadatrecht*, Brill, Leiden, 1928.
[7] P. Burns, "The myth of *adat*", *Journal of Legal Pluralism*, 28, 1989, pp. 1–127. See also S. T. Alisjahbana, "Customary law and modernization in Indonesia", in D. C. Buxbaum (ed.), *Family Law and Customary Law in Asia: A Contemporary Legal Perspective*, M. Nijhoff, The Hague, 1968, p. 3.

As a result, colonial policy and legislation in the late nineteenth and twentieth centuries reflected the view that Islamic religious prescripts only applied to the extent that they had been accepted in Indonesian society through its customary law. This so-called "reception theory" eventually found its place in the colonial constitution. In the process, *adat* law and *adat* authorities were exaggerated, sometimes quite artificially,[8] resulting in a further marginalizing of Islamic religious prescripts. We will see below how this affected developments after independence, but suffice it to point out here that non-Islamic *adat* retains a very strong influence to the present day in the multicoloured normative patchwork, whether by colonial design, or by the piecemeal adoption of Islam by various Indonesian communities.

1.4 Basic developments after independence

The colonial system based on "reception" theory has been subject to criticism after independence, to the point of having been described as "satanic" by some Islamic scholars.[9] The prevailing view is that it was a deliberate instrument with which to contain Islam. In the past fifty years, debates on the reception of religious norms into state law are characterized by a confusion between religious (and political) ideals (the "ought" level) and social reality (the "is" level). As we have seen, Indonesian social reality is dictated by highly complex relationships and the interaction of various different normative systems. The overarching theme in political and legal discussions on Islam in Indonesia has been whether and how to bridge the gap between religious ideals and complex social realities.

This helps us to understand why the outspoken ideological condemnation of the colonial system was not matched by a fundamental change in state policies regarding Islam after independence. The complexity of Indonesian Islam and its relationship with deeply rooted competing normative systems have ensured that late colonial state policies have in essence been maintained in the modern Indonesian state.[10]

As in the colonial state, after independence religious prescripts were not constitutionally recognized as a source of law.[11] The history and debates on the constitu-

---

[8] Thus, as late as 1935 when social mobility was increasing and traditional structures were eroding rapidly and clearly for all to see, colonial judges were instructed to refer a case involving *adat* law to community *adat* law experts before proceeding (s. 1935-102). This reactionary measure reinforced *adat* institutions that were increasingly out of touch with social and political realities in the colony.

[9] Hazairin, *Tinjauan mengenai UU Perkawinan nr. 1/1974 dan lampiran UU nr. 1/1974*, Tirtamas, Jakarta, 1975; B. Siregar, "Pengembangan hukum Islam dan penerapannya dalam hukum nasional", *Varia Peradilan* 3 (36), 1988, p. 146.

[10] One difference from the colonial system is possibly the role of *adat* as a vehicle for Islamic religious prescripts. In colonial times, *adat* was accepted as a source of law within certain limits, but its place and role after independence are less clearly established. Moreover, the evident problems in bridging the gap between state law and policies and the community in recent years have led to a careful re-evaluation of *adat* by the Indonesian government.

[11] It has been argued that the 1974 Marriage Law makes Islamic religious prescripts relative to marriage a source of law in its own right: M. B. Hooker, *Islamic Law in South-East Asia*, Oxford University Press, Singapore, 1984, p. 273. However that may be, it is clear that from the state perspective at least, Islamic religious prescripts remain in a subsidiary position. Thus, Supreme Court judge Y. Harahap, who also was a prominent member of the Islamic Law Compilation Project discussed hereafter, protests that *fiqh*, *shari'a* and "Islamic law" are routinely viewed as

tional embodiment of Islam, or rather the lack of it, will be reviewed in the next section. Reflecting this condition of formal marginality, the influence of Islam on modern Indonesian state law and institutions is limited. As in society at large, Islam has been accommodated in certain select areas of state law, but does not reach beyond. The influence of Islamic law has still to cross the boundaries of marriage, divorce and, to a much lesser extent, inheritance law. This will be the subject of section 3. Special religious courts service the needs of the *'ummat*, but do not reach beyond the limited domain of substantive law. The place and role of the courts, and the related Compilation Project on Islamic Law in Indonesia, will be considered in section 4. Some concluding comments will be made in the final section.

2 ISLAM AND THE INDONESIAN CONSTITUTION

2.1 History and the Jakarta Charter

The constitutional framework of the modern Indonesian state took shape in the last months of the Second World War, when Indonesia was under Japanese control. Facing defeat, the Japanese installed a committee for the preparation of independence, including the drafting of a Constitution. In the discussions on the Constitution, the issue of the ideological foundation of the Indonesian state had to be addressed. The basic conflicting views were between the nationalist leaders who argued for a secular state, and religious leaders who favoured an Islamic state.[12] Initially both sides agreed on a basic document, later to be named the Jakarta Charter (*Piagam Jakarta*). This in effect amounted to a rough outline of the preamble to the Constitution and as such was the ideological basis of the new state that was being established. The Jakarta Charter included two key clauses, the first that the state be based upon the belief in God, and second that adherents of Islam be obliged to follow Islamic law. Islamic leaders later added some demands, such as the requirement that the President

---

cont.

identical in Indonesia, and that in fact these are wholly different concepts: Y. Harahap, "Informasi materi kompilasi hukum Islam", *Varia Peradilan*, 1993, p. 102. From this perspective, it is the state which in the end determines what religious prescripts should be enforceable as state law, and how this should be effected. Islamic religious prescripts are not a source of law *ipso facto*, but by "reception" by the Indonesian state. By implication, they may also be rejected as the state sees fit.

[12] See generally H. J. Benda, *The Crescent and the Rising Sun: Indonesian Islam under the Japanese Occupation 1942–1945*, W. van Hoeve, The Hague and Bandung, 1958; B. J. Boland, *The Struggle of Islam in Modern Indonesia*, Smits, Gravenhage, 1971, Chapter 1. Writings on Indonesian political and constitutional history generally refer to a "nationalist" and an "Islamic" dichotomy in the constitutional debates, in which they may have been inspired by Sukarno himself, who referred to such factions during the debates. It is important to remember that in line with the diverse nature of Indonesian Islam, Islamic leaders were divided among themselves, with respected Islamic leaders such as Haji Agus Salim and Hoesein Djajadiningrat opposing the demands for a state in which Muslims would be obliged to follow Islamic law, whereas others such as Sukiman agreed to those demands on the rather flimsy ground that "it would please the people and have no further consequences in fact": M. Yamin, *Naskah persiapan Undang-undang Dasar 1945*, Djakarta, 1959–1960, vol. I; Benda, *The Crescent and the Rising Sun*, p. 190 *passim*; Boland, *The Struggle of Islam*, p. 24 *passim*.

and Vice-President be a Muslim, and even the requirement that the obligation to follow Islamic law not be restricted to the Islamic community.

However, the debates in 1945 and after clearly focused on the two key clauses in the Jakarta Charter. Although the first clause played its part, it was the second clause, traditionally referred to as "the seven words", which constituted the focus of the political debates.[13] The wording of the second clause is extremely ambivalent. It does not specify the exact relationship between the state and Islam, as a result of which it can be read as a mere exhortation for Muslims to be pious, or as a requirement for the state to enforce Islamic law. This ambivalence allowed both sides to give the seven words the meaning they preferred, which considerably fuelled the debates both in 1945 and helped keep the issue alive in later years.

In the event, pressure to eliminate the specific Islamic *imprimatur* envisaged under the Jakarta Charter built up rapidly in the turbulent days after the Japanese surrender and before the arrival of the Allies. A broad coalition of nationalist leaders, representatives from minority religions and liberal Muslim leaders successfully advocated that the new state have a more neutral character. As the Japanese administration collapsed, more and more leaders from the outer islands where minority religions were concentrated came to Jakarta. This helped to shift the political balance, as it became clear that national unity would be endangered if the new state were to declare itself formally Islamic.[14] Thus, the Vice-President nominate M. Hatta, whose Islamic Sumatran background made him the natural focus of Islamic aspirations, repeatedly warned Islamic leaders that "they had to be mindful of the unity of the whole Indonesian population".[15]

As a result, and notwithstanding the initial concessions of President Sukarno to Islamic leaders, both key clauses of the Jakarta Charter were wholly or partly dropped in the definitive text of the 1945 Constitution. As we will see shortly, the first clause on the belief in God does reappear in the preamble of the 1945 Constitution, but in a much diluted form. It is in fact indicative of the political necessity to compromise that the wording of the clause was changed at the insistence of a Hindu representative from Bali. He proposed that the key word of "God" in the clause be changed from the Islamic *Allah* to the neutral Indonesian *Tuhan* (Lord). This proposal was accepted. It changed the entire thrust of the first clause from the specific Islamic God, and the adherence of the state to Islam which it implied, to a more general reference to a Supreme Being within Whose Existence all religions could be accommodated. In addition, the seven words of the second clause were summarily dropped. Similarly, the requirement that the President and Vice-President be Muslim, was not constitutionally enshrined.

2.2 Islam in the 1945 Constitution

References to religion in the 1945 Constitution are consequently worded in general neutral terms, and do not accord Islam a special privileged position. The preamble includes the state ideology *Pancasila* (five principles) which constitute the political

---

[13] See Boland, *The Struggle of Islam*, p. 27.
[14] The Japanese did not fail to point this out. See, for instance, M. C. Ricklefs, *A History of Modern Indonesia*, Macmillan, London, 1981, p. 201.
[15] Boland, *The Struggle of Islam*, p. 36.

foundation of the state. Couched in the most general terms, the first principle incorporates the diluted first principle of the Jakarta Charter by stating that the state must be based on the belief in a single almighty God. There is no requirement that the President be a Muslim. Finally, Article 29 secures religious freedom and equality, in that while emphasizing that the state is based on the belief in a single almighty God, the freedom of every citizen to adhere to his or her respective religion and perform his or her religious duties in conformity thereto is guaranteed.

From the text of the Constitution it would appear that religion, and Islam with it, has been pretty much excised from the formal state edifice. As one prominent author put it: Indonesia is not based on religion, nor is Islam the official religion of the Indonesian state.[16] Nevertheless, the first *Pancasila* principle referred to above requires careful treatment here, as in fact the Indonesian authorities have steadfastly denied that Indonesia is a secular state. In what some might view as a typical Javanese exercise to reconcile the irreconcilable and others as mere opportunistic political semantics, Indonesia is located in the grey area between the secular and religious:

... although Indonesia is not an Islamic state, it should not be a secular one either. Rather, Indonesia should have a religious state philosophy based on belief in God through which the ideals of every religious denomination could be realized.[17]

As will be apparent in the next paragraph, this reconciling of the secular with the religious may help to explain the prominence which religious institutions have achieved in the Indonesian state apparatus.

The 1945 events settled the debate on the role of Islam from a constitutional perspective which has not been fundamentally challenged since. This is not to say that the constitutionally restricted place and role of religion has commanded universal support within Indonesia. There is a persistent feeling in Muslim circles that the qualification and dumping of the key clauses of the Jakarta Charter in 1945 was a fraud, "an embezzlement against the Muslim stance".[18] At regular intervals in Indonesian history the Jakarta Charter has therefore re-emerged as a political issue.

This political pressure at times spills over in a way in which state institutions and officials have defined their role in the interpretation and application of Islam. As will become apparent in the next paragraphs, Islamic local government officials, civil servants religious judges test the constitutional boundaries with some frequency, and acting in their official capacity have tried to introduce Islamic religious prescripts into Indonesian law. Sometimes such interventions have been accommodated in the formal legal system, such as the moves to ban alcohol in Jakarta or forbid the screening of certain American movies for violating Islam or antagonizing the Islamic community.[19] Yet as we shall see in the next paragraphs, state

---

[16] Noer, *Administration of Islam in Indonesia*, Ithaca NY, Cornell Modern Indonesia Project, 1978, p. 8.
[17] A. Johns, "Indonesia: Islam and cultural pluralism", in J. Esposito (ed.), *Islam in Asia: Religion, Politics and Society*, OUP, New York, 1987, p. 210.
[18] A. Schwarz, *Indonesia: A Nation in Waiting*, Allen and Unwin, Sydney, 1994, p. 11.
[19] In 1994 the US movie *Schindler's List* was banned in Indonesia at the request of Islamic organizations for containing Zionist propaganda, and shortly afterwards in the same year, the movie *True Lies*, starring Arnold Schwarzenegger, was banned on the grounds that it insulted the Islamic community: *INIS Newsletter*, 12,1996, pp. 40–43. On a more constructive level,

officials or judges have also acted in open and unequivocal conflict with state law, as in the case of the refusal to record interreligious marriages in the Religious Registry or the application of Islamic contract law by the religious courts.

The Indonesian government consistently tries to contain these low-level rumblings within its own apparatus, and resists fundamental constitutional change. One of the principal methods which it has used has been to bolster the quasi-secular character of the Indonesian state by an ideological strengthening of the constitutional edifice. As a result Indonesia has witnessed a progressive sanctification of the 1945 Constitution at the hands of the Indonesian government, a policy which has grown stronger over the past ten or twenty years. Rather than as a highly authoritative legal text, the Constitution, most particularly the preamble, is presently viewed as an integral part of the Indonesian state ideology. Thus, all civil servants must follow ideological courses and pass exams on the 1945 Constitution, advancement is subject to their proven loyalty to it, all public organizations are required by law to have the preamble as their ultimate goal, and the constitutional procedures for amending the constitution have been drastically curtailed. The resulting situation is that issues that might be interpreted as challenging the 1945 Constitution have been placed beyond the boundaries of public debate. This assuredly includes calls to revive the Jakarta Charter or change the constitutional position of Islam.

This helps to explain why the Jakarta Charter remained a prominent issue on the political agenda of most Islamic parties until 1965, and then all but disappeared from public debate under the New Order Suharto government. This is not to say that it is dead, however, as on the contrary the heavy-handedness of the government on the matter may have fuelled public sympathies for Islam.

3 THE INSTITUTIONAL FRAMEWORK

Even though Islamic leaders failed to secure a privileged position for Islam within the Indonesian constitutional edifice at independence, in material terms the payoff for Islam was considerable. In what some view as a running "deal" in which the political ambitions of Islam were and remain restrained in return for a strong religious presence in state institutions, the fact is that the institutional basis of Islam in Indonesia has been strengthened on an unprecedented scale.[20] This section will consider two key central state institutions that emerged after independence, the Ministry of Religious Affairs and the Council of *'Ulama*. Religious institutions at lower levels, particularly the religious courts and the religious registry offices (*Kantor Urusan Agama*) will also be considered.

---

cont.
    the Indonesian government has pushed through a national mosque building programme and promoted the establishment of an Islamic bank.

[20] D. S. Lev, "Religious pluralism in an Islamic society: the politics of religious amity and conflict in Indonesia", *Conference on Pluralism and Religious Liberty*, Jerusalem, 1997. Noer views the institutional strengthening as a necessary "accommodation" at the time of independence and suggests that the institutional position of Islam is the subject of an ongoing power struggle: Noer, *Administration of Islam in Indonesia*.

3.1 The Ministry of Religious Affairs

The Ministry of Religious Affairs was established within a few months of the declaration of independence against strong opposition from nationalist circles. Clearly meant to serve the interests of the Islamic community, it was the first ministry of its kind in the Islamic world. The importance of the Ministry is difficult to underrate, as Lev describes:

> the formation of a Ministry of Religious Affairs made it possible to consolidate the entire administration of Islam into a single nationwide body controlled by Islamic groups. Ultimately the result was to be a degree of specialization, centralization, and autonomy for Islamic institutions unimaginable without the new ministry. It also lent Indonesian Islam institutional adaptability and bargaining power, on a national level, which it would otherwise not have had, and without which in other Islamic countries religious administrative institutions have atrophied under the pressure of "secular" state political and bureaucratic expansion.[21]

Technically, the ministry handles all religions on an equal basis, with separate Directorate Generals for Islamic, Catholic, Protestant and Hindu-Buddhist affairs. But the particular political origins of the ministry, the huge Islamic constituency in Indonesia and the specific Islamic institutions that require servicing, ensure that this is very much an Islamic institution.

The Islamic institutional basis has grown to phenomenal proportions, and bears little comparison in size and power with that of the other religions. The principal Islamic institutional components controlled by the ministry are the following:

(a)   the *Haj* administration: a huge operation, with Indonesia being allotted the largest contingent by the Saudi authorities;[22]
(b)   Islamic education at all levels, including 95 per cent of the IAIN religious universities which are the sole recruiting ground for religious preachers;
(c)   religious marriage offices at district level (*Kantor Urusan Agama*), which are competent in Islamic marriage affairs;
(d)   the religious courts, which handle Islamic cases both at district and provincial levels.

The latter two of these institutions have specific legal functions, and will be considered in greater detail below.

3.2 The Council of *'Ulama*

Besides the Ministry of Religious Affairs, one other important state institution services Islamic interests at central government level. This is the Council of *'Ulama* (*Majelis 'Ulama*). Originally councils of *'ulama* were established at a local level as

---

[21] Lev, *Islamic Courts in Indonesia*, pp. 44–45.
[22] The 1995 *Haj* quota for Indonesia was 197,000. The original quota was 195,000 but this number was later increased. There were 240,000 registrations for the *Haj* in Indonesia, and Bangladesh, which did not fulfil its quota, offered its surplus to Indonesia. *INIS Newsletter*, 14, 1997, pp. 31–32.

advisory institutions for local government. The function of these councils was to enable the participation and cooptation of local religious leaders to help bridge the gap between government administration and local communities, and thus assist in defusing potential friction and discontent.[23] In the early 1960s the structure was formalized, with the institution of a central Council of *Ulama* in Jakarta in 1962.

This central Council of *Ulama* has been increasingly influential in recent decades as a advisor on matters relating to Islam. It must be noted in the context of this contribution that the Council has no legislative powers that bind the religious community. It may issue fatwas that are highly influential indications on the way the religious authorities view certain matters.

The precise ambit of its mandate, as in fact the entire legitimacy of the Council itself, is an interesting topic of debate. As an organization, the Council is undeniably rooted in the modern state. By extension it is based on the idea that there is actually a section of life that lies outside its scope of control and hence, presumably, beyond the boundaries of the creed. What is more, the Council's existence and composition is evidently based on government intervention, and thus by implication subsidiary to the worldly authority of the state. Both points, as is generally known, are anathema to the all-encompassing way in which Islam and the central authority of the community is traditionally perceived.

The Council of *Ulama* therefore very much embodies the fundamental problematic of state primacy versus religious subsidiarity. This applies all the more as the Council has intervened on matters that by conventional constitutional thinking evidently reside in the secular state domain. To confuse matters even more, in so doing it has sometimes acted on the request of the government. Thus, in 1964 the Council issued a fatwa to the effect that the military confrontation with Malaysia constituted a *fardh 'ain* (a duty for individual Muslims).[24] Similarly, the Council stated during the 1997–8 economic crisis that hoarding foreign currency for speculative purposes amounted to usury (*riba*) and hence was prohibited.[25] As we shall see, the fundamental problematic easily spills over into the legal sphere, particularly in areas where emphatic Islamic rules clash with state policies and law, such as marriage law.

As with the Ministry of Religion, the Council has been influential both as an instrument by which the Islamic constituency can make its voice heard at central government levels, and as an instrument by which the Islamic constituency can be managed and controlled. It is telling in this context that the Council has been

[23] Noer, *Administration of Islam in Indonesia*, pp. 65–66.
[24] *Ibid.*, pp. 66–67.
[25] The fatwa reads as follows: "The hoarding of dollars or other foreign currencies for the purpose of trading constitutes usury (*riba*) and must be sanctioned as prohibited (*haram*)". The explanatory note runs in part as follows: "The Muslim community herewith has a legal right to confront (literally: fight) the disobedient (*fasiq*) who violate this fatwa of the Council of *Ulama*. This confrontation need not be by death, force or physical duress, but can be in the form of reporting the occurrence to the state apparatus. Only in case the state apparatus does not undertake any steps to resolve the issue, may the Muslim community take matters in their own hands and collectively sanction the disobedient who cause suffering to the community as a whole." Apakabar@clark.net; 21 January 1998 from HM Sodiq Sabilillah of the Council of *Ulama*.

an effective instrument by which religious leaders with a record of resistance and armed rebellion against the central government could be coopted.[26] In addition to the examples given above, the central Council of *Ulama* has a history of supporting the government on controversial issues which involved Islam. Thus, the Council denied that the profitable state-run lottery was gambling, it fought the rumour that Indonesian basic foodstuffs were produced with pork fat, etc. This is not to deny, however, that on other issues the Council refused to toe the government line, such as on the traditional participation of Muslims in school Christmas festivities or interreligious marriage between a Muslim girl and a non-Muslim boy (both of which it disallowed), and the wearing of a *jilbab* at school (which it supported).[27]

4 THE 1974 MARRIAGE LAW [28]

4.1 Government aims

Among the many issues which tested the place and role of Islam within the Indonesian legal system, none was more outstanding than the 1974 Marriage Law. The Indonesian government has been supportive of law reform in the field of family law for essentially two reasons. The first was a general drive to abolish the diverse and discriminatory colonial legal system and replace it with a unified set of rules to which all Indonesians would be subject, regardless of race or creed. This legal unification drive was, and indeed remains, an important element in Indonesian policies directed towards nation building. The second aim of the Marriage Law reform was to strengthen the legal position of women in marriage. The government, and some prominent champions of women's rights therein, felt that the Islamic institutions of unilateral divorce (*talak*) and polygamy in particular were not in accord with the aims and character of the modern state.

4.2 History and principal provisions

The original Bill tabled by the government as a result was a highly secular piece of work, in which marriage for all parties irrespective of creed would be conducted

---

[26] This includes T. Daud Beureuh, who at one time led a rebellion in Aceh, but was appointed honorary chairman of the central Council in 1967, as well as the present chairman H. Basri, who was previously a leader of the rebellious Darul Islam movement, which aimed at establishing an Islamic state in West Java.

[27] See for example D. Aqsa, D. van der Meij and J. H. Meuleman, *Islam in Indonesia*, INIS, Jakarta, 1995, pp. 197, 199; *Ensiklopedi Hukum Islam*, under *Perkawinan antaragama*, Ichtiar Baru van Hoeve, Jakarta, 1996.

[28] Aside from the publications cited hereafter, the following introductory works in English on the Indonesian marriage law can be referred to: J. Katz and R. Katz, "The New Indonesian Marriage Law: a mirror of Indonesia's political, cultural and legal systems", AJCL, 1975, p. 653; J. Katz and R. Katz, "Legislating social change in a developing country: the New Indonesian Marriage Law revisited", AJCL, 1978, p. 309; M. Cammack, "Islamic law in Indonesia's New Order", ICLQ, 1989, p. 53.

by the State Civil Registry, unilateral divorce and polygamy were disallowed, and divorce rights were not gender biased. The Islamic community strongly resisted the Bill. Islamic political parties staged a walk-out in Parliament and protests and riots erupted in the streets. As a result of this Islamic pressure, the Bill underwent a number of fundamental changes. In general terms, the principal change was that instead of excluding religion altogether, as originally proposed, the Bill which eventually became the Marriage Law included selected religious provisions as a part of substantive state law. Nevertheless, the law and its enacting regulations restricted the implementation of such religious provisions by way of a variety of procedural restrictions. The administration of Islam, and particularly the way its provisions were interpreted, as a result remained subject to state control.

The most fundamental section of the law is undoubtedly Article 2(2), which states that a marriage shall be concluded in accordance with the belief and religion of both parties. The precise meaning of the article has generated enormous debate, and in fact continues to do so to the present day, as will be briefly explained later. Its principal relevance for our purposes here is that it purports to give religion an important place in marriage. Nevertheless, as will be apparent from the key examples of polygamy and unilateral divorce, state law imposes clear and unequivocal restrictions on the way religious prescripts are actually realized within the context of state law.

The provisions regarding polygamy can be summarized as follows. The Marriage Law is based on the principle that marriage must be monogamous (Article 3(1) Marriage Law). Polygamy is allowed by way of exception, as defined in the law and its enacting regulations (Article 3(2) Marriage Law), and requires a specific procedure. The wording of the law makes it clear that only Muslim men can apply to conclude a polygamous marriage. As regards procedure, a request for concluding a polygamous marriage must be submitted to a religious court, without whose consent no polygamous marriage can be concluded (Article 4(1) Marriage Law; Article 40 Gov. Reg. 9/1975). A religious judge is not free to decide as he pleases, as the Marriage Law provides a limitative list of grounds on the basis of which a polygamous marriage may be concluded. The conditions can be distinguished into two groups. The first group relates to the physical condition of the wife to whom the applicant is married already. The first wife must fall into one of the following three categories: she cannot fulfil her obligations as a wife; she has a permanent physical handicap or suffers from an incurable illness; or she cannot bear any children. The second group relates to additional guarantees that presumably apply cumulatively, although this is not specified in the law. The first is that the first wife must give explicit agreement to the polygamous marriage, either in writing or by speaking out loud in court. The second is that the husband will be able to support all his wives financially, which must be proved by means of bank accounts and the like. The third and final condition is that he must promise to treat all his wives on equal terms.

Special conditions apply for civil and state servants, which includes ministers of state. The reasons for this special treatment is that according to the law "the civil servant has the duty to be an example to his subordinates and a model of a good citizen in society, which goes also for his family life". Polygamous marriages between civil servants are completely forbidden. If a civil servant wants to conclude a polygamous marriage with someone who is not a civil servant, approval must first be obtained from his hierarchical superior.

The courts appear to follow the law quite closely, though it would require more detailed field studies to fully determine present conditions in this respect. Well-known cases are an application for a polygamous marriage on the grounds of excessive sexual appetite (dismissed on the grounds that this was not a motivation listed in the law) and on the grounds of wanting children (dismissed when it was found that the applicant had nine children already).[29] A number of "hard" cases have been decided in which the courts opted quite unequivocally for state law rather then Islamic religious prescripts. Thus, in a case in which a polygamous marriage had been concluded in accordance with Islamic prescripts but in violation of the Marriage Law, the marriage was declared null and void and the *wali* who had concluded the marriage was incarcerated for twenty days for violating public order.[30]

Similarly, there are court decisions to the effect that a polygamous marriage in which no permission was given by the first wife is invalid, the parties being subject to imprisonment for violation of public order rules. Nevertheless, the law on the subject seems to be quite fluid. Thus, in a recent case the Supreme Court stated that only if a Muslim man married more than four wives could there be criminal sanction for bigamy. This would not be so if, without court approval, he concluded a polygamous marriage with a second, third or fourth wife. The decision implies that only in the former case can a marriage be voided. In the latter case the couple might be exposed to administrative sanction, but the marriage would not be invalidated.[31]

The principal provisions regarding divorce are the following. The Marriage Law provides that a marriage can only be dissolved by the death of one of the parties or by a court decision (Article 39(1) Marriage Law). The law does not allow for a divorce to be effected outside the control of a state court. The law and its enacting regulations emphatically state that a divorce by court decision may only be granted on certain grounds and following a specified procedure. A request for divorce must be submitted to a district court for non-Muslims and a religious court for Muslims. The Religious Courts Law 1989 requires that in a *talak* divorce the man present his claim before the court at the place of residence of his wife (Article 66(2) Rel. Ct. Law). It must be submitted in writing (Article 14 Gov. Reg. 5/1979), and properly reasoned with reference to the limited grounds for divorce which are listed in the Marriage Law and its enacting regulations. The grounds are the following: adultery, alcoholism, drug addition, compulsive gambling, absence without notice for two years or more, imprisonment for five years or more, incurable illness or permanent physical handicap which precludes the fulfilment of matrimonial duties, and finally, fundamental disaccord. These divorce grounds apply irrespective of gender or religion. If the husband is a civil servant, the law furthermore imposes the requirement that he obtain the permission of his superior before proceeding with the divorce.

Despite the general terms in which Indonesian divorce law is cast, there are some subtle procedural distinctions between divorce proceedings initiated by the

---

[29] Referred to in Katz and Katz, "Legislating social change in a developing country", p. 311.
[30] Supreme Court No. 435K/Kr/1979 dated 17 April 1980, *Yurisprudensi Indonesia*, vol. II, 1981, p. 28.
[31] Supreme Court No. 338K/Pid/1991 dated 7 September 1994, *Varia Peradilan*, 1997, p. 35.

Muslim husband, or those initiated by anyone else, either the Muslim wife or non-Muslim parties for that matter. These differences can be explained with reference to the divorce rights of the husband according to Islam, which the Indonesian legislator has tried to accommodate within the legal framework. According to Islam, and simplifying roughly here, a marriage is dissolved by the marriage parties themselves, without need for intervention by a third party, let alone the state. This particularly applies to a unilateral divorce effected by a man (*talak*), of course. The Indonesian legislator has been eager to ensure a role for the state in such unilateral divorce proceedings, so as to restrict spurious divorces, and better protect the rights of women in marriage.

In so doing, the legislator has tried to accommodate the role of the state with *talak* rules. This has been done in a number of ways. First, as regards procedure, the judge has been made the mandatory "witness" of divorce proceedings between Muslims, rather than a decisive actor. The judge verifies that procedures have been properly respected and witnesses the divorce declaration by the husband. A court decision following a *talak* divorce declaration for that reason is an affirmation of a situation which is already in existence, rather than creating a legal condition in its own right.[32] Divorce takes effect immediately, and its validity is not dependent upon registration requirements (a divorce between non-Muslims, by way of contrast, only takes effect upon registration with the Civil Registry).[33] Second, as regards substance, *taklik talak* practices prevailing in Islamic communities in Indonesia have been integrated in state marriage procedure. *Taklik talak* refers to an institution in many Indonesian Islamic communities in which upon marriage husbands issue a conditional divorce. This says that the wife could deem herself to be divorced upon the realization of certain conditions. It was a practice specifically designed to protect women in marriage, and strengthen their autonomous divorce standing. Under present Indonesian law, Muslims wanting to marry must agree to marriage conditions that reiterate the divorce grounds listed in the marriage law. The Marriage Law divorce grounds therefore can be viewed as the modern *taklik talak*, upon which the wife can sue for divorce on grounds identical to those of the husband. The only difference is one of procedure: whereas the husband requests a unilateral divorce before a court of law, the wife must issue a writ of summons.

Here again, there is a gap between the theory of the law and legal practice. On the one hand, court decisions are reported that fully accord with the law's intent. Thus, in one decision, a unilateral divorce outside a court of law was held to be

---

[32] The 1989 Religious Courts Act also states that a *talak* requires court sanction, although it is somewhat equivocal on the issue of whether an extra-judicial *talak* is valid by law. In 1990 the Supreme Court indicated that a *talak* divorce procedure was a contentious marriage action to be determined by way of a court decree (Circular Letter Supreme Court No. MA/KUMDIL/1973/IV/1990 dated 3 April 1990). The distinction between a decree (*penetapan*) and a decision (*putusan*) is important here, as the latter refers to the creation of a new legal situation, and the former affirms a condition which already exists. A. Manap, "Eksekusi ikrar talak menurut Undang-undang Nomor 7 tahun 1989 tentang Pengadilan Agama", *Varia Peradilan*, 1996, p. 134.

[33] A further point to be mentioned here is that in the Religious Courts Law 1989 Art. 70(2), a *talak* can only be pronounced after all legal remedies, including appeal, have been exhausted. This answers the problematic situation that a *talak* might be inviolated by a court decision on appeal, which is unacceptable from the Muslim perspective.

invalid, irrespective of the possibility of validity according to Islamic religious prescripts.[34] Also, unilateral divorce on grounds other than those listed in the law, such as the use of magic by the wife, have been declined.[35] Nevertheless, there are also cases which go in completely the opposite direction. Thus, in one case the legal validity of a divorce conducted outside a court of law has been upheld.[36] This points to considerable fluidity in the enforcement of the law.

4.3 Problems

The aim of the legislator to incorporate religious prescripts within a tight framework of state law was to a large extent frustrated by the equivocal wording of the key articles in the law. This ensured that they became the subject of debate and lasting political controversy. The law has been an important factor in creating rifts between religious communities, effectively frustrating the social unification which the Marriage Law was intended to bring about.

The controversy principally centres on the foundation and conclusion of marriage. To the outside observer, the two issues might appear to be of a different order, the first relating to ideology and public order and hence to substance, and the second to procedure. The problematic drafting of the key Article 2(2) ensured that they became confused. There are a number of troubling loose ends to the article, such as the difference between belief and religion, which is not specified, the fact that the Indonesian text does not clarify whether belief/religion must be read in the singular or plural, and the fact that the term "each party" is unspecific, so that it can be read either as the belief/religion that parties share, or the belief/religion of each individual party separately. While these matters have generated considerable debate and uncertainty, the more fundamental question to which Article 2 gives rise is whether it extends only to the marriage ceremony (to be conducted in accordance with etc.), or whether it means to incorporate religious prescripts *in toto*.

As might be expected, the official interpretation expressed notably by the Department of Religion and the Supreme Court, is the former, but many Islamic leaders and scholars have opted for the latter. In fact, some scholars have stretched the meaning of the article to the point that for all practical intents and purposes any state legislation pertaining to marriage or divorce is regarded as irrelevant: Article 2 declares religious prescripts applicable, and closes the door to state law.

The issue has come to a head in particular on the matter of interreligious marriages. This is a crucial point because the equal freedom of social interaction for all Indonesians, including the freedom to choose a marriage partner, is the whole point of the unification of legislation. Interestingly enough, the institutional and legal problems relating to the issue of interreligious marriages emerged more than a decade

---

[34] Supreme Court No. 09K/AG/83 dated 28 June 19893; No. 1335K/Pid/1985 dated 30 September 1987 (*Varia Peradilan* 1988 III/28), p. 54

[35] Supreme Court No. 024K/AG/1979 dated 22 October 1979, *Yurisprudensi Indonesia* (1980) I, p. 142.

[36] Supreme Court No. 1008K/Pid/1984 – see my comment on the case in S. Pompe, "De invloed van heatdatrecht bij de toepassing van het strafrecht in Indonesië", *Bijdragen tot de Taal-, Land- en Volkenkunde*, 143, 1987, pp. 499–506.

after the law was enacted. This suggests that perceptions on the role of Islam in society are changing. On the surface the problem is by what procedure such marriages are to be concluded, a matter on which the law is equivocal, as we have seen. From the early 1980s an increasing number of Religious Marriage Boards began to use this unclarity to deny marriage between couples of different religions. With highly formalistic reasoning, the Boards argued that as they were empowered to marry Muslims only, they could not marry a non-Muslim. Similarly, civil registries turned away mixed couples on the grounds that they were allowed to marry only non-Muslims. The fundamental problem is that many obviously feel that such marriages can only go through if permitted by substantive religious prescripts. Registrars feel justified in this view not just because this is their personal conviction, but often explicitly refer to Article 2 of the Marriage Law. In fact, court decisions instructing the registrars to register interreligious marriages often go unheeded.[37]

The problems surrounding Article 2(2) reveal the difficulties of the Indonesian government in holding the line of a residual position of Islamic normative prescripts to state law. The inclusion of references to religious prescripts in state legislation has incorporated religion into the legal edifice, giving it legal standing and making it harder to quite simply ignore, as some might wish. It has promoted a condition in which the state could not prevent getting embroiled in debates on religious issues, having to explain why certain religious prescripts have been included, and others have not, and why its particular interpretation of those prescripts should prevail. The failure of state institutions such as the Religious Marriage Boards and, incidentally, courts, to heed state policies, illustrates existing tensions between state law and religious prescripts.

These tensions are an important cause for more general problems of effectiveness that plague the Marriage Law. Despite earlier optimistic reports,[38] more recent field data supports the view that these problems are in fact much larger than the earlier reports suggested, or than generally thought. Thus, one publication convincingly demonstrates that the aim of the law to restrict child marriage has not succeeded at all.[39]

---

[37] I have argued elsewhere that despite official rhetoric the Marriage Law has in essence failed to create a uniform legal standard for the conclusion and dissolution of marriage. The reason is that it replaced the racial diversity underlying the colonial system with religious diversity. This religious diversity has proved itself no less hard to bridge than colonial racial diversity, not the least because the different groups are served by different institutions – as was the case in colonial times. This has problematized the sensitive issue of interreligious marriages, which shows that the Marriage Law, rather than promoting, has been an obstruction in the realization of the nation state, being the underlying goal of the unification drive. S. Pompe, "Mixed marriages in Indonesia: some comments on the law and the literature", BTLV, 144, 1988, p. 259; S. Pompe, "A short note on some recent developments with regard to mixed marriages in Indonesia", BTLV, vol. 147 (1991), p. 261; S. Pompe and J. M. Otto, "Some comments on recent developments in the Indonesian marriage law with particular respect to the rights of women", *Verfassung und Recht in Ubersee*, 4, 1990, p. 471.

[38] Thus, Katz and Katz, "Legislating social change", p. 310 report that according to official statistics declined by 70 per cent in 1978. The prevailing view now is that the overall picture presented by official statistics is unreliable. My own research, which concentrated on certain specific districts, indicates that official statistics show a high divorce figure throughout the years. See also note 39.

[39] M. Cammack, L. A. Young and T. Heaton, "Legislating social change in an Islamic society: Indonesia's Marriage Law", AJCL, 44, 1996, p. 45.

The article argues that "The roots of the statute's failure lie in the law itself and a fundamental disagreement over what it means" (p. 61). It would appear that this applies to polygamy and divorce rules as much as it does to child marriage. Thus, Campbell has argued that the law has driven polygamy and unilateral divorce underground. Both continue unabated but are merely not recorded in official statistics.[40] But even as far as official statistics go, I myself have tried to show that in some districts, official divorce statistics are so extraordinarily high (more than 200 divorces a week in the Indramayu district, for instance), that they suggest a high degree of ineffectiveness of the law, particularly its requirement that the judge try to reconcile parties and prevent a divorce, or that at least two hearings be conducted per divorce.[41]

5 THE 1989 RELIGIOUS COURTS LAW

Besides the 1974 Marriage Law, the other most important piece of state legislation regarding Muslims is the Law on Religious Courts of 1989.

5.1 History and principal provisions

Religious courts specifically serving the Islamic community had been established in colonial times.[42] The institutions were meant to serve as instruments which gave the Muslim community a certain autonomy in handling specific issues within the domain of the faith, including notably marriage, divorce and, within certain limits, inheritance. The enforcement of religious court orders depended on approval of the regular state civil courts. This rule was in part motivated by the fact that the courts were chaired by religious leaders who as often as not were poorly trained, but on a more general plane it deliberately affirmed state control over religious matters. It also made religious courts clearly subsidiary in importance to state courts.

In the early days of independence, the religious community pushed for their own religious courts with a standing equal to the regular state courts. Nationalist factions exerted strong pressure to abandon the religious courts altogether and bring their special jurisdiction under the civil courts. The issue remained unsettled until well into the 1980s, although admittedly the enactment of the 1974 Marriage Law made the tide flow in the favour of such courts. This underlying conflict may help explain why substantial legislation regarding religious courts was so long in coming, although the religious courts were mentioned as one of the special courts in general legislation regarding courts from the early days of independence. In effect, the 1882 colonial rule remained in force as the principal law regarding the organization and jurisdiction of the religious courts until the new 1989 law, and formally speaking religious court judges remained subject to the supervision of the regular state courts until that year.

---

[40] I. Campbell, *Family Law and Inheritance Law in West Java: Change and Continuity in the Period from 1900 to the Present Day* (unpublished MA thesis, University of Sydney, 1988).

[41] Pompe and Otto, *Verfassung und Recht in Übersee*, p. 431.

[42] The so-called *Priesterraden* s. 1882–152.

The enactment of the 1989 law effectively put an end to the debate on whether religious courts should be there at all. The law affirmed the institutional basis of the religious courts as special courts serving the Muslim community, and firmly rooted the courts in the state institutional framework. The law had a number of broadly defined goals, which included various institutional or procedural issues, but also had an impact on some matters of substantive law. This included a number of changes to the Marriage Law, which have been referred to in the previous section. This review limits itself to a brief outline of the structure and jurisdiction of the courts.

The law is divided into a number of sections, including general provisions, the structure and composition of the courts, its powers and procedure and various technical matters. The principal sections can be briefly summarized as follows.

The first sections provide for a uniform hierarchical court structure. The ground rule in organizational terms is religious courts of first instance in all districts and appeal courts in all provinces. Final appeal in cassation is open before the Supreme Court. It is to be expected that in areas dominated by minority religions, such as Bali, the Smaller Sunda Islands and the Moluccas, religious courts will be more thinly spread, as in fact the provinces of Bali and East Timor still do without a religious court of appeal. This means that presently there are about three hundred religious district courts and twenty-five religious appeal courts. Also, and in line with the French-based court system, the courts operate under departmental administrative management (in this case the Department of Religious Affairs) and under jurisdictional supervision of the Supreme Court. There are provisions for the recruitment of judges, who are civil servants, must hold proper academic qualifications and be Muslims.

The law broadens the powers of the religious courts in the field of family and inheritance law. As regards marriage law, the 1974 Marriage Law effectively restricted the powers of the court to questions relating to the validity of the marriage and divorce, with related issues such as child custody, alimony or financial support obligations, or the division of the marital estate to be handled by the civil courts. The 1989 Religious Courts Law establishes that henceforth such matters shall be handled by the religious courts as well. Nevertheless, it should be noted that such substantive powers only apply directly in relation to marriage or its dissolution. The law specifies that if in the course of a case serving before the religious courts, the proprietary rights to an object are contested in general terms, procedure before the religious courts must be suspended and the case must be referred to a normal civil court to determine the legal status of the said object (Article 50).[43]

With regard to inheritance, the 1989 law specifically includes the matter within the jurisdiction of the religious courts, thereby settling an issue which had been subject to some debate and confusion in the past. This power is subject to the qualification that parties can opt for state civil law and civil law courts for the division of the estate. If parties have opted for civil law rules, recourse to the religious courts is disallowed.[44] It may be noted here that Indonesian courts, particularly at higher

---

[43] This includes disputes regarding the ownership of property in family or inheritance cases. See S. Bahri, "Sengketa milik dan keperdataan lainnya dalam Undang-undang Nomor 7 Tahun 1989 tentang Peradilan Agama", *Varia Peradilan*, January 1997, p. 152.

[44] Supreme Court No. 97K/AG/1993 dated 30 March 1994, *Varia Peradilan*, May 1996, p. 51. In this case one of the parties sought recourse before the religious courts against an unfavourable civil court decision.

levels, are traditionally reluctant to fully apply Islamic gender-based inheritance rules. Over the years, the Indonesian Supreme Court has consistently pushed towards an equal position of heirs regardless of gender, including the traditionally underprivileged position of female heirs in Islam.

Thus, in a recent decision the court emphatically reiterated the point, saying that children had equal rights to the estate of the deceased irrespective of gender, and that relatives of the deceased were only permitted to claim the estate if no children existed.[45]

5.2 The Compilation Project[46]

The ongoing strengthening of the institutional basis, authority and powers of the religious courts over the years, has made consistent decision making increasingly important. Already in the late 1950s, the Department of Religion had tried to promote uniformity in decision making, when it instructed the religious courts that only specific texts from the Shafi'ite school could be referred to in deciding a case. By the 1980s pressures built to further tighten institutional discipline, and perhaps root religious courts more firmly within the state structures, by way of a compilation of Islamic religious rules to be applied in the courts.

As a result from 1985 onwards steps were taken to realize the Compilation by way of various means, including consultations with prominent religious leaders, a compilation of decisions of religious courts, a selection of arguments used in religious courts, a compilation of arguments of prominent scholars in various *mazhab en fiqh* sources and comparative studies of various other Islamic countries (Morocco, Turkey and Egypt). The broad focus of the research underlying the Compilation meant that not just sources from the *Shafi'ite mazhab* prevailing in Indonesia were used, but also from the Maliki, Hanbali and even Az-Zahiri *mazhab*.

As with the religious courts themselves, the Compilation Project was not without controversy. There were concerns that the compilation might lead to an Islamic Code, that would be fully binding on all Islamic citizens. This raised the spectre of the Jakarta Charter introduced through the back door of lower legislation. This undoubtedly was one of the factors explaining why the Compilation was never formally enacted as a state law. Instead, the government merely determined that the Compilation be distributed in the country.[47] Nevertheless, the Compilation com-

---

[45] Supreme Court No. 86K/AG/1994 dated 27 July 1995; see also M. G. Ja'far, "Masalah anak dan saudara dalam kewarisan Islam", *Varia Peradilan*, November 1996. The principle of gender equality in inheritance cases was first established by the Supreme Court not in relation to Islam, but in relation to traditional *adat* law, when the court disallowed the privileged position of Batak male heirs with regard to land. See D. S. Lev, "The Supreme Court and *adat* inheritance law in Indonesia", AJCL, 11, 1962, p. 205 and my own account in S. Pompe, *The Indonesian Supreme Court: Fifty Years of Judicial Development* (unpublished PhD thesis, Leiden University, 1996), pp. 379, 386.

[46] See generally *Varia Peradilan* (April 1993), p. 60; Y. Harahap, "Informasi matenri"; KH A. C. Muhammad, "Kedudukan kompilasi hukum Islam dalam sistem hukum nasional", *Varia Peradilan* (May 1996), p. 105.

[47] It has been argued that the compilation was given the force of law. See for instance Cammack, "Islamic law", p. 165 and *Ensikopledi Hukum Islam*, vol. 3, Ichtiar Baru Van Hoeve, Jakarta, 1996, p. 972.

mands considerable authority within the Islamic community and in the courts. The resulting Compilation totals 214 articles divided into three books: on marriage (and divorce), inheritance and charitable foundations. Book I on Marriage includes substantive and procedural rules on various subjects, including the basis of marriage, marriage obstacles, the marriage agreement, the frustration of marriage, the rights and duties of both spouses, the marital property, guardianship, divorce, the effects of divorce and reconciliation. Book II on Inheritance deals with a variety of issues, including a definition and order of precedence of heirs, the size of each estate, the testament (*wasiat*), bequests (*hibah*). Finally, Book III covers the functions, basis and conditions relating to charitable foundations, as well as the procedure by which these must be established and registration requirements of its properties. Substantive differences from state law are not very large, as in fact the Compilation explicitly refers to state law on several instances.

6 CONCLUSIONS

Indonesian Islam is of considerable complexity. This derives from the relatively strong position of minority religions, as well as the complex structure of Indonesian Islam itself, in which the multilayered belief structure generates slim support for an Islamic legal policy that is both more focused and embracing. This complexity imposes a condition of continuous debate on the religious community and its leaders, which brings them to mediate between different competing interests and factions and to constantly define and redefine theoretical and theological premises. It nurtures and strengthens Indonesian religious thinking, as in fact religious renewal may yet come from the supposed periphery rather than the perceived traditional heartland of Islam.

The complexity of Indonesian Islam helps explain why the religion has been institutionalized in Indonesian state structures and substantive law provisions. Islam has a strong institutional basis within Indonesian state structures, with a variety of

---

cont.

It should be remembered that the Encyclopaedia was heavily influenced on this point by the team which realized the Compilation in the first place, notably Busthanul Arifin. In reality the point its not so clear, however. As indicated by Muhammad, "Kedudukan kompilasi", pp. 118–119, for instance, the Compilation should have been enacted by Act of Parliament to be directly binding, but this could not be achieved. Instead, Presidential Instruction (*Instruksi Presiden*) No. 1/1991, without further comment, merely instructs the Minister of Religious Affairs to "distribute the Islamic Law Compilation". The wording of this instruction clearly did not mean the Compilation to be legally binding upon the general public, the general observations referring to the Compilation as a "guideline" (*pedoman*) only. Also, Presidential Instructions only serve internal matters relating to the Presidential Cabinet and internal government organization, as in fact this one does here. They are not instruments which are binding upon the general public. The form of "enactment" of the Compilation generated fierce debate between the compilers, headed by Supreme Court Judge Busthanul Arifin, and representatives of the State Secretariat, headed by Professor A. Hamid S. Attamimi. The compilers wanted to have the Compilation enacted by way of state law (preferably without submitting it to parliamentary scrutiny, exposing it to public debate and the probability that it might be changed), whereas the government wanted to restrict its impact and denied enactment.

institutions specifically established to administer the religion, including the Department of Religion and the religious courts.

The strong institutional basis of Islam is not reflected in the field of substantive law. Islam does play a role in some areas, notably in the field of marriage and divorce, as well as inheritance, but on the whole its application is closely controlled and restricted by state law. The approach that has been chosen is to more or less retain Islamic normative institutions, yet control their application through procedural requirements and state institutions. Thus, whereas the law does not disallow polygamy or unilateral divorce, it institutes procedural obstacles that limit their use, including the requirement to refer such cases to a court of law.

Official indicators suggest that the state has been successful in using these procedural and institutional restraints as instruments by which to limit the impact of Islamic substantive normative rules. Thus, state statistics show that cases of polygamy are declining and that unilateral divorce without court intervention is an incidental aberration from normal practice. Data are presently emerging, however, that qualify these official indicators in a number of ways, and there is a clear need for more field research on the subject to be conclusive on the actual impact on state law.

Finally, Islam is almost completely absent in areas of state law in which it traditionally makes its mark, such as criminal or banking law.

The Application of Islamic Law in Nigeria

*Mamman A. Lawan Yusufari**

1 INTRODUCTION

The Nigerian legal system, among other things, exemplifies Africa's triple heritage.[1] The historical antecedents of the country have necessitated the application of three distinct systems of law. Notwithstanding this, they make up a single but complex system. The customs of the various communities, Islamic law and the dominating English law are now the components of the Nigerian legal system.[2]

Although the first two are often grouped and given the appellation "native law and custom" or "customary law", generally, they are not nor have they ever been the same.[3]

The Nigerian court system clearly points to their disparity. Each of them has a separate court for application at the lower level but equally share the two apex courts for determination of appeals.[4]

Islamic law (in Arabic called *shari'a*) is a divine law that should regulate the entire life of a Muslim both as an individual and in association with others (i.e. in a state). It is neither an "imposed" nor an "internalized" system of law as it applies to persons of the Muslim faith only and acceptance of such faith is not compulsory.[5] The sources of the law are mainly the Qur'an and *hadith*. *Ijma* (consensus of jurists), *qiyas* (analogy) and *istihsan* (preference) and are also sources of the law.

---

* Lecturer in Islamic law at Bayero University, Kano. Currently a postgraduate student at the faculty of law, University of Lagos.
[1] Professor Ali Mazrui's documentary of the Africans reveals culture, religion and Western civilization as the three heritages.
[2] H. A. Olaniyan, "A critical appraisal of the application and enforcement of personal systems of law in Nigeria", A. O. Obilade (ed.), *A Blueprint for Nigerian Law*, University of Lagos, 1995, pp. 86–87.
[3] See *Muntiya Chiga v. Inuwa Umaru* (1986) 3 NWLR Part 29, p. 460.
[4] While Islamic law has area courts and the *Shari'a* Court of Appeal, customary law applies in customary courts and the Customary Court of Appeal. The two apex courts are the Court of Appeal and the Supreme Court.
[5] Qur'an 2:256 and 76:3.

Islamic law in Nigeria applies on territorial rather than on a personal basis. Its application is limited to the northern states only where the Hausa/Fulani are predominant. Although there are Muslims in the south (mostly the Yorubas), there has never been a court applying Islamic law. The reason given is that the majority of Muslims are content with the ritual aspect of Islam (i.e. *salat*, *zakat*, *saum* and Hajj) and so adhere to tribal customs in matters like marriage, divorce, inheritance, custody of children, etc.[6] Perhaps it is this contentment that led to their description as accommodating radicals and willing to respond to the wind of change and on the other hand caused a curse on the northerners for being conservative.[7]

Northern Muslims living in the south resort to informal settlement of disputes or, when the disputes involve a substantial question of law, travel home and submit themselves to the Islamic courts.

This being the case, application of Islamic law in Nigeria simply means its application in the northern states. This discourse is intended to look at the position before, during and after the British colonial rule. It also examines the law in the Nigerian constitutions and the extent to which it is allowed to apply.

2 APPLICATION OF ISLAMIC LAW BEFORE COLONIALISM

The Islamic religion came to the northern states through trading in the fourteenth century. It started with the Hausal of Kano and subsequently spread to the other parts. However, the religion was not deeply rooted as cases of its acceptance (by predecessors) and rejection (by successors) were found in the same ruling house.[8] But the frequent visits of Muslim scholars had influence in retaining it. Though retained, its mixing with traditionalism, feudalism, corruption and mass ignorance over the time led to the emergence of revivalist movement spearheaded by Sheikh Usman Ibn Fodio. Thus in 1804 the movement (which emanated from Sokoto) fought the system and established Islam with its legal system fully operational in all the territories. Already a similar movement had established Islamic law in the Borno empire under the leadership of Skeikh Muhammad El-amin El-Kanemi.[9] But having been based on the same principles of Islam, both Jihadist movements operated the same legal systems.

In each a government was established with the caliph or sultan as the head. He was assisted by officers such as the *Wazir* and *Amir*. A court system to settle disputes, suppress crime, protect the weak and all other areas based on the Qur'an, *hadith* and other sources was manned by the *aadis* (judges) who were learned, just and honest male persons. Officers like registrars, messengers etc. assisted in the dispensation of justice.[10] To do justice was not a mere state duty. It was (and still

[6] J. N. D. Anderson, *Islamic Law in Africa*, Frank Cass, 1970, p. 222. But there is a reported case that shows a court's upholding an Islamic marriage contracted by a Muslim Yoruba – *Asiata v. Guncallo* (1900) NLR 41.
[7] B.O. Nwabueze, *Constitutionalism in the Emergent States*, C. Hurst, London, 1973, pp. 84–85.
[8] A. I. Doi, *Islam in Nigeria*, Gaskiya Corporation Ltd, Zaria, 1984, pp. 19 *et seq*.
[9] *Ibid*., pp. 204 *et. seq*.
[10] See A. A. Gwandu, "Aspects of the administration of justice in the Sokoto caliphate and Skayhk Abdullah Ibn Fodio's contribution to it", in S. K. Rashid (ed.), *Islamic Law in Nigeria*, University of Sokoto Press, 1988, p. 16.

is) a religious one enjoined to be discharged even against oneself, one's parents or close relatives.[11] Such had been the position of Islamic law until the British conquest.

3 ISLAMIC LAW DURING COLONIAL RULE

The expansionist desire of the British led to conquest of Islamic lands and the consequent crack down on Islamic law.

As a matter of policy, the British allowed the machinery of government to continue subject to their control and supervision. That was the indirect rule system which could not apply in the east for want of central leadership. However, Islamic law and British rule were mutually exclusive. So the former being vanquished made a gradual exit with some areas left dependent on the new English law. This exit was necessary because of the claimed "inadequacy of . . . (the) law to cope with the bubbling commercial life of the new colony and the dynamics of the colonial life" coupled with "the belief and conviction of the colonial Masters that English law . . . (was) the fountain and cynosure of justice".[12]

Lord Lugard, the High Commissioner for the Protectorate of Northern Nigeria, reorganized the legal system through the Native Court Proclamation No. 5 of 1900. Thereunder, the jurisdiction of the Islamic courts in criminal matters was limited as neither death penalty or "inhuman" punishment would be inflicted and the practice and procedure of the courts were to be based on native law and custom (i.e. Islamic law) but subject to rules that were to be made by the High Commissioner. The effect of this provision was to phase out *hadd* (capital) punishments such as death, cutting off of hand and/or leg, caning, etc., which Islamic law provides for in cases like intentional murder,[13] adultery,[14] theft,[15] robbery,[16] fornication[17] and intoxication.[18]

The proclamation empowered the Resident (a British officer) to establish courts in his province; to enter and inspect the native courts; to transfer a matter from one court to another; to review the finding of courts; to approve appointment of judges made by the emir and where there was no emir, appoint the judges himself.

At the same time, the Protectorate Court Proclamation No. 4 of 1900 established the Supreme Court, the provincial courts and the cantonment courts with varying jurisdictions over non-natives, statutory offences and civil matters governed by English law.[19]

---

[11] Qur'an, 4:135.
[12] Quoted by M. Tabiu, "Application of English, Customary and Islamic Laws I", *New Nigerian Newspapers*, 22 January 1998.
[13] Qur'an, 2:178.
[14] Al-bukhari, *Kitab al-Hudud*.
[15] Qur'an, 5:41.
[16] *Ibid.*, 5:32.
[17] *Ibid.*, 4:16.
[18] See A. I. Doi, *Shar'ia: The Islamic Law*, Ta Ha Publishers, London, 1984, pp. 264–265 for the consensus of jurists.
[19] See T. O. Elias, *The Nigerian Legal System*, Routledge and Kegan Paul, 1962, pp. 113 *et seq.* and E. A. Keay and S. S. Richardson, *The Native and Customary Courts of Nigeria*, Sweet and Maxwell, 1966, pp. 19–27.

Later, in 1933, a High Court for the Protectorate of Nigeria (excluding Lagos colony) was established. With the exception of land and family matters over which Islamic law was allowed to apply, the court had a general jurisdiction.[20]

Even where Islamic law applied, it was subject to two tests or conditions – that it should not be repugnant to natural justice, equity and good conscience or incompatible either directly or by necessary implication with any law for the time being in force. These tests did not have a clear cut definition or a certain criterion for application. At best, they were tools for uprooting, as much as possible, Islamic law. Later, a third test was added. It was the public policy test[21] to which Islamic law had to conform to before getting a stamp of validity. It did not, however, have any practical influence.

It was based on the repugnancy test that a principle (wrongly ascribed to Islamic law) denying a person accused of highway robbery from calling witnesses in his defence was declared against natural justice, equity and good conscience.[22] But a proper understanding and application of the principle (that a party to a case is not a competent witness in the case under Islamic law) would not have led to a contrary decision as it appears not to square with the English natural justice principles of *audi alteram partem*.

Islamic law, squeezed and trampled by the English law, limped to the era of independence in 1960.

4 ISLAMIC LAW AFTER INDEPENDENCE

Nigeria's attainment of self-determination in 1960 did not alter the legal system created and nursed by the British. The extent of the application of Islamic law and the surveillance under which it faltered did not change. In fact, laws such as the Northern Nigerian Native Courts Law of 1956 (a re-enactment of the Protectorate Courts Ordinance of 1933) continued to apply up to 1968, when they were replaced with the Area Court Edict with drafting modifications. The Edict, which was originally for the north-eastern states of Nigeria, has now been adopted with little modifications by the northern states.

The area courts have civil jurisdiction in matrimonial causes (marriage and divorce), custody of children, civil actions (for debt, demand or damages), succession and administration of estates and ownership and possession or occupation of land.[23] The courts apply both substantive and procedural Islamic laws being "the native law and custom prevailing"[24] in the north. Therefore judges appointed are normally persons learned in Islamic law without necessarily having undergone a formal training.[25] Until 1979, legal practitioners were not allowed to appear in the courts.[26]

---

[20] S. Kumo, "Application of Islamic law in Northern Nigeria: problems and prospects", in S. K. Rashed (ed.), *Islamic Law in Nigeria*, Islamic Publishers Bureau, 1988, pp. 45 *et seq*.

[21] S. 14(3) Evidence Act Cap. 62 Laws of Nigeria 1958 (now Cap 112 LFN 1990).

[22] *Jalo Guri v. Hadejia*, NA (1959) 4 FSC 44.

[23] S. 18 of the Area Court Edict 1968.

[24] *Ibid.*, s. 20.

[25] The Edict does not require any academic qualification for appointment. But states such as Adamawa now insist that judges of upper area courts are legal practitioners.

[26] S. 28 prohibited it. But s. 33(6)(c) of the 1979 Constitution guarantees representation in any court as a fundamental right.

Although the courts try criminal matters, the applicable law is not the Islamic law. The Penal Code and the Criminal Procedure code apply.[27] These are British oriented laws having some minor Islamic elements in order to pacify the Muslims. Jurisdiction over offences and infliction of punishment are both restricted.[28] It has been said that today about 80 per cent of cases in the northern states are handled by the area courts.[29]

Despite the departure of the British, the twin tests of repugnancy and incompatibility still rear their ugly heads against the application of Islamic law. The Area Courts Edict has a provision for them.[30] The High Court laws of the northern states still contain this provision.[31] The application of these tests has further narrowed down or crippled the application of Islamic law even within the area. For instance, the Supreme Court in 1971 declared an Islamic law principle prohibiting a bequest in excess of one third of a testator's estate as incompatible with the Wills Act of 1837 (an imported English statute) which allows such a bequest.[32] The court opined that the testator, though a Muslim, having prepared a will not in accordance with Islamic law, clearly showed his option for the English law.

"The conduct of parties" and/or what they uttered in court became criteria for the application of Islamic law in appropriate cases. Thus in *Maryam v. Sadiky Ejo*,[33] a case over paternity of a child, the court held that by the conduct of the mother of the child in not observing *iddah* (waiting period) before contracting another marriage and from what both parties uttered in court, they preferred Igbira customary law to Islamic law. The court then sought to apply the customary law but did not for its "repugnancy to natural justice, equity and good conscience".

It is noteworthy, however, that the application of Islamic law is not a matter of choice. Once a person professes the religion of Islam the application of its laws in all aspects of his life becomes compulsory.[34] The fact that one was born in a community that has a system of customary law does not entitle one to choice of an applicable law. In fact, there is no law for a Muslim except Islamic law. Belonging to a tribe and/or custom does not enhance one's position in Islam. To be regulated by Islamic law is the only possibility open for a Muslim. Choice of another law is associating Islamic law with something else, which is tantamount to being an infidel.[35]

That has been the "life" of Islamic law in the trial courts exercising original jurisdictions. However, the upper area court, apart from its original jurisdiction, also exercises appellate jurisdiction (constituting two upper area courts judges) over decisions of the lower area courts.[36] The jurisdiction covers both civil and criminal

---

[27] S. 22 of the Edict.
[28] *Ibid.*, s. 17.
[29] *Justice Denied: The Area Courts System in the Nrothern States of Nigeria*, a report by the Civil Liberties Organization, 1992, p. 8.
[30] S. (20)(2) Area Court Edict.
[31] For instance, s. 34 (High Court) laws of Kano State, vol. 2, 1991.
[32] *Yunusa Rasaki v. Adesobukan* (1971) NNLR 77.
[33] (1961) NRNLR 31.
[34] Qur'an 33:36, 45:18.
[35] *Ibid.*, 45:23.
[36] S. 53 of the Edict.

matters.[37] The decision of the appellate court is appealable to the *Shari'a* Court of Appeal. Here, there is a limitation. Only matters of Islamic personal law go to the *Shari'a* Court.[38] Other cases, i.e. criminal cases or non-Islamic personal law matters, decided by the appellate upper area court go to the State High Court appellate division on appeal.[39]

The *Shari'a* Court of Appeal, created originally by the *Shari'a* Court of Appeal Law,[40] is only an appellate court having jurisdiction on the following matters defined as Islamic personal law:[41]

(a) marriage, divorce, or guardianship or care of an infant;
(b) *wakf*, gift, will or succession;
(c) issues relating to a Muslim infant, prodigal or person of unsound mind or maintenance or guardianship of a Muslim who is physically or mentally infirm; or
(d) any other matter where the parties (whether Muslims or not) request in writing, that the court of first instance apply Islamic law.

So other matters over which the area courts exercise jurisdiction (i.e. civil actions for debt, demand or damages, administration of estate, ownership, possession or occupation of land) are appealable only to the High Court. It was because of this mixture that the composition of Appellate High Court included a judge of the *Shari'a* Court judges.[42] However, a decided a case[43] based on the interpretation of section 238 of the 1979 Constitution and section 63(1) of the High Court law of northern Nigeria has now unseated the *Shari'a* Court judge[44] because the latter section is inconsistent with the former (providing for the Constitution of the Court in exercise of "any jurisdiction"). Presently, therefore, a High Court, in exercise of any jurisdiction (original or appellate) is duly constituted if it is constituted with one of its judges.[45]

To avoid the problem of an appeal against an area court decision (based on Islamic law) coming before the appellate High Court constituted by a judge not learned in Islamic law, a provision allowing the invitation of assessors to assist in hearing the appeal wholly or partially earlier contained in laws of northern Nigeria is now retained by the respective states.[46]

---

[37] S. 53 of the Edict does not make a distinction between civil and criminal matters. It uses "decision or order" of the lower courts and the inclusion of criminal matters is strengthened by s. 55 which says "an aggrieved party" in s. 53 includes a prosecutor in a criminal case. S. 53(a) and (b) of the Kano State Area Court Law is clearer by providing for an appeal to the upper area court "in all other cases" except Islamic personal law, which goes to the *Shari'a* Court of Appeal.

[38] *Ibid.*, s. 54(a).

[39] *Ibid.*, s. 54(b).

[40] Laws of Northern Nigeria 1963, Cap 122.

[41] *Ibid.*, ss. 10 and 11.

[42] *Ibid.*, s. 63.

[43] *Mallam Ado and Hajiya Rabi v. Hajiya Dije*, suit No. FCA/K/69/82 (unreported).

[44] Some states like Kano, Katsima and Niger have as a result deleted s. 63 from their High Court law.

[45] S. 238 1979 Constitution. But the practice now, sanctioned by the various High Court Civil Procedure Rules, is to have two High Court judges in the appellate court. The Court is not permanent. It is constituted as and when due.

[46] See for instance s. 64 High Court Laws of Kano State (Cap 57), 1991, High Court Niger State (Cap 53) and Katnina State (Cap 59) 1991.

5 ISLAMIC LAW UNDER THE NIGERIAN CONSTITUTIONS

Until 1979, Islamic law did not receive any serious recognition in Nigerian constitutions. For instance, the Republican Constitution of 1963 merely talked of the *Shari'a* Court of Appeal as one of the courts whose decision went to the Supreme Court on appeal.[47] The making of the 1979 Constitution (Preparatory to the Second Republic) was characterized by debates on the position and positioning of Islamic law. There were arguments for the creation of a Federal *shari'a* Court of Appeal so that appeals from the state *Shari'a* Court of Appeal could cease going to the Court of Appeal[48] (established in 1976). The move did not succeed. All that was done was to entrench the *Shari'a* Court of Appeal in the Constitution for states that desired to establish it.[49] Its jurisdiction was not altered.[50]

In short, the application of Islamic law did not make any progress. Another provision affecting the law was appointing judges learned in Islamic personal law in the composition of the Court of Appeal[51] and Supreme Court[52] for the purpose of hearing appeals relating to Islamic law.

The 1979 Constitution,[53] if anything, succeeded in further limiting the application of Islamic law. For instance, the Land Use Act of 1978,[54] which is part of the Constitution,[55] provided for the designation of land into urban and non-urban lands and divested the area courts of jurisdiction over the former. Any decision now by an area court on such land is a nullity for want of jurisdiction.[56]

Similarly, the Constitution has "dashed" the hope of regaining the application of Islamic criminal law by providing that nothing is an offence and punishable unless it is defined in written law and punishment therefore prescribed[57] (a written law excludes Islamic law).[58] What the colonial masters did through an ordinary law[59] has now been transferred (by us!) into the fundamental and supreme law of the land.[60]

In 1986, there was an attempt to delimit and expand the application of Islamic law. The Constitution (Suspension and Modification) (Amendment) Decree,[61] sought to extend the jurisdiction of the *Shari'a* Court of Appeal by providing for the deletion of the word "personal" wherever it occurs after the word "Islamic" in the

---

[47] S. 119(1) the Constitution contained in the laws of Nigeria 1963.
[48] See T. Muhammadu, *The Nigerian Constitution 1979, Framework for Democracy*, Fourth Dimension Publishers, 1982, pp. 29–31.
[49] S. 240(1) of the 1979 Constitution.
[50] *Ibid.*, s. 242.
[51] *Ibid.*, s. 217.
[52] *Ibid.*, s. 252.
[53] Now amended by Constitution (Suspension and Modification) Decree No. 107 of 1993.
[54] Ss. 39 and 41 thereof.
[55] S. 274(5), 1979 Constitution.
[56] *Sheh v. Salati* (1986) I NWLR Part 15, p. 158.
[57] S. 33(12) of the Constitution.
[58] *Ibid.*
[59] I.e. the Native Courts Proclamation No. 5 of 1900.
[60] S. 1(1) of the Constitution.
[61] No. 26 of 1986.

Constitution. In effect, "Islamic personal law" was intended to read "Islamic Law" so that the *Shari'a* Court of Appeal could have a jurisdiction as wide as that of the area courts. Unfortunately, the decree did not change the items contained in the enabling section of the Constitution. It was decided[62] that the failure could not allow the decree to serve its purpose.

A subsequent Constitution – the 1989 Constitution (which was overtaken by events following the annulment of the elections of 12 June 1993) and the 1995 Draft Constitution (now awaited in the fourth Republic) – did not make any substantial change to the position of Islamic law in Nigeria. The minor changes are all structural.[63]

Within the permitted areas, the courts have been busy applying Islamic law as it is. The judges are learned in the law and rely mainly on Arabic texts for their authorities. Cases emanate from the lowest grade of the area court and go as far as the Supreme Court running through the upper area court, the *Shari'a* or High Court of Appeal. For instance, the case of *Yibo Yari v. Alh. Ma'aruf Mikaila*[64] over the succession of house No. 285, Kafar Nassarawa, Kano and other properties commenced in an area court and reached the Court of Appeal.

The Court of Appeal has also adjudicated over a case[65] involving title over non-urban land heard originally by a village area court.

Similarly, the Supreme Court applied purely Islamic law in a question of whether or not a gift to a person who died before taking possession of the subject of the gift entitled his heirs to include the same in his estate for distribution. The Court in a leading judgment read by Wali JSC held such a gift to be valid under Islamic law.[66]

The courts were not confined to the areas spelt out in the laws in their decisions. By way of "judicial asides", they give opinions on issues that are strictly religious but not unconnected with the matter hand. Recently the Court of Appeal,[67] Per I. T. Muhammad J. C. A. preached thus:

Under Islamic law dispensation, *tatwa* (piety) or fear of Allah should be the Premier occupant of a Muslim mind. Therefore, a Muslim should not lay a vexatious claim in order to justify that which does not belong to him. Even if he takes such, a possession through his cleverness or prevarication, he is taking a portion of the hell-fire.[68]

This pronouncement, based on a saying of Prophet Muhammed (Peace be upon him) reaffirms the inseparability of Islamic law from Islam.

---

[62] In the case of *Alh. Hassan Abuja v. Lawan Gana Bizi* (1989) 5 NWLR Part 119, p. 120.
[63] See s. 260(3) of the 1989 Constitution and s. 280 of the Draft 1995 Constitution contained in the report of the 1994 Constitutional Conference, vol. 1.
[64] (1986) 5 NWLR Part 46 p. 1064.
[65] *Alh. Yusuf Saya-Saya v. Alh. Talla Saya-Saya* (1990) 7 NWLR Part 162, p. 652. This case went through the *Shari'a* Court of Appeal despite the fact that title over a property is not included in Islamic personal law in which the Court can exercise jurisdiction. But an earlier case, *Abuja v. Bizi* (see note 62) decided by the Court of Appeal had held that the *Shari'a* Court lacks jurisdiction on such a matter even if the parties agreed, in writing, at the lower court to the application of Islamic law.
[66] *Alh. Usman v. Alh. Salisu Kareem* (1995) 2 NWLR Part 379, p. 537.
[67] In *Mamuda Biri v. Tukur Mairuwa* (1996) 8 Part 467, p. 425.
[68] *Ibid.*, p. 435.

6 CONCLUSION

So far, Islamic law has been applied in almost the whole hierarchy of courts in Nigeria. But such application has been in part and under the guard of the English law. Of all the territories now forming Nigeria, the northern states were the most adversely affected by colonialism. This "killed" Islamic law and completed its "burial arrangements" to be performed after its departure. It caused Muslims a loss of their true religion and renewed their duty to live by it. To say that the application of Islamic law to "personal" matters is not enough is an understatement. The law is divinely meant to necessarily regulate the entire life of a Muslim. It does not impose itself on others.

It is Islam and Islam is it. So to allow part of it only to apply is a denial of religion which constitutions and international documents ironically but vociferously provide for as a human right.[69]

The growing abhorrence of its application is informed by ignorance of its and/or the plot to impose secular ideas in the name of unity in diversity and universality of concepts. Its subjects should realize the catastrophe that has befallen them and turn a deaf ear to the containment calls and disparagement now in vogue. And a point remains – the application of Islamic law (as it is) is not, and never has been, a matter of conference.

---

[69] See s. 35 1979 Constitution: The Universal Declaration of Human Rights (UDHR) of 1948 also provides for freedom of though, conscience and religion.

Social Security and Social Insurance Law: A Survey of Nine Arab States

Hyam Mallat

1 INTRODUCTION

Of the many issues in the Arab countries relating to development, social problems may be the most serious, since they involve providing social security and social insurance systems which are effective and fair, while remaining financially sound.

The financial cost of social welfare provision is now a major concern in contemporary societies where political economy has also become a financial issue, and where managers in both the private and public sectors must produce and distribute goods and services under competitive conditions, without excessively jeopardizing the financial capacity of the nation. This issue is at the forefront of the debate on social security systems in the developing world, given the great need in this sector to be prudent, while honouring the benefits of a social policy that has been operating for several decades.

In the light of the specific circumstances in each country, this study seeks to identify problems relating to social security and social insurance systems in general, and pensions in particular, in the context of current legislation and proposed reforms in nine Arab countries of the Asian Middle East.

Section 2 describes the current institutional and administrative structure of social security and social insurance systems in the countries concerned; Section 3 offers a brief overview of current benefits provided to workers and employees in the countries of the Middle East; Section 4 identifies current retirement pension schemes and lump sum payments, and Section 5 offers some conclusions which are intended to offer some guidelines for future action on social security and pension systems.

---

* Chairman of the Board of National Security Fund in Lebanon, Lawyer, Professor at Saint Joseph University, Beirut.

2 MANAGEMENT AND ADMINISTRATION OF SOCIAL SECURITY AND SOCIAL INSURANCE SYSTEMS

It is not enough to study and promulgate legislation and issue administrative provisions to ensure the success of social measures, especially in the field of social security and pensions. The administrative organization of services and activities must be effective so as to provide the necessary benefits as cheaply as possible. Of course, it is often difficult to control administration down to the last details and to achieve optimal costs, because a number of parameters relating to employment, geographical distribution of branches and offices and the physical location of the insured combine to prevent the ideal management/cost ratio. The fact remains that identification of the administrative and legal structure of institutions responsible for social insurance and social security can result in some broad recommendations for reform.

2.1 Saudi Arabia

Under the provisions of Royal Decree M/22 of 6.9.1389 (15 November 1969), the social insurance system in Saudi Arabia is administered by a body called the Organisation Générale de l'Assurance Sociale (OGAS) which has corporate legal status and financial and administrative autonomy.[1] This body, under the aegis of the Ministry of Labour and Social Affairs, is administered by a governor and an executive board composed of eleven members. Apart from the governor, four appointees represent the state, three the employers and the remaining three of the employees.

The social insurance scheme is administered by a mixture of centralization and decentralization. Policy development, including adaptation of regulations, rules and procedures, is the responsibility of the executive board and governor of OGAS, assisted by the competent services at the head office.

Implementation of the scheme and direct communication with employers and workers is the task of seventeen OGAS local offices in the main cities of the Kingdom. They are responsible for collecting contributions and paying benefits, using powerful computer systems, with highly advanced software and equipment. All the local offices are linked to the head office. They are equipped with terminals at which staff capture, process and extract data on employers and workers. They also use a microfilm network. Use of this technology has also allowed OGAS to automate its financial operations. The organization also cooperates with a number of large local of foreign banks to pay welfare benefits to beneficiaries in cash, at the place where they live.

2.2 Bahrain

The social insurance regime in Bahrain is administered by the Organisation Générale des Assurances Sociales (OGAS), whose head office is in Manama. It has corpo-

---

[1] For a good article on the subject, see "Social insurance regime in Saudi Arabia", *Revue Internationale de Sécurité Sociale*, 50(3), 1997, pp. 77 *et seq.*

rate legal status and financial and administrative autonomy. Given the small size of the country, contributions are collected and benefits paid in Manama. OGAS can set up regional offices wherever necessary by decision of the Minister of Labour and Social Affairs, on the recommendation of the executive board.

OGAS has an executive board under the chairmanship of the Minister of Labour and Social Affairs, and is composed of thirteen members of whom seven represent the government, namely:

- the Director of Labour at the Ministry of Labour and Social Affairs;
- the Director-General of the Bahrain Monetary Institution;
- the Director of the General Pension Fund;
- the Director of Litigation at the Finance and the National Economy;
- a director from the Ministry of Development and Industry;
- the Director of Health at the Ministry of Health.

In addition, there are three representatives of employers covered by social insurance provisions and three qualified employees' representatives. The employees and employers' representatives are appointed by decision of the Council of Ministers.

For the public sector, Article 47 of Law No. 13 of 28 June 1975 on civil services pensions for state employees of Bahraini nationality set up the Pension Fund, a public body with corporate status and an independent budget. The Fund is administered by an executive board and a director-general, and aims to meet the needs of pensioners through appropriate decentralization throughout the country.

2.3 Iraq

The administration of the Iraqi social security system is assigned by the Ministry of Labour and Social Affairs to the Pensions and Social Security Institution, which has corporate status and administrative and financial autonomy.

The Institution is directed by an executive board appointed by the President of the Republic on the recommendation of the Minister of Labour and Social Affairs. It has thirteen members, including the chairman of the executive board, a post occupied *ex officio* by the vice Minister of Labour and Social Affairs, who is the legal representative of the Institution and funds controller, with certain powers of delegation. Equal numbers of the members represent employers, the Federation of Industry and employee organizations such as the Federation of Trade Unions and certain ministries with an interest in the system. In total, the board consists of the chairman, the director-general (*rapporteur*), the president of the Workers' Institution for Employment, Training and Retraining, representatives of the Ministries of Health, Finance, Labour and Social Affairs and Planning, two employees' representatives nominated by the Federation of Trade Unions, one employers' representative and three people appointed by the President of the Republic.

The Institution is under the management of (a) the executive board, (b) a central directorate-general and (c) regional offices of the Institution in the regions (*muhafazats*).

2.4 Jordan

The social security system in Jordan is regulated by the Jordan Social Security Corporation under Law No. 30 of 1978. It is administered by an executive board made up of thirteen members, under the chairmanship of the Minister of Labour, who is president of the Institution *ex officio*, and the vice-chairman, who is director-general. The other members of the board are the Secretary-governor of the Central Bank, four representatives of the General Workers' Federation, two representatives of the Chamber of Industry and two representatives of the Union of Chambers of Commerce. The corporation enjoys corporate legal status and financial and administrative autonomy. Its head office is in Amman, and it has established five branches and eight liaison offices which provide regular information about insured employees to employers. The board is responsible for managing the affairs of the corporation and supervising its activities, as well as for carrying out general policy and planning investment of funds and resources. The corporation's budget and investments are not included in the general state budget and the accounts are audited by an external auditor.

A reform of the corporation's internal organization was carried out in 1995 to make benefits more effective and to implement a medium-term computerization plan in line with established priorities.

2.5 Kuwait

Social insurance in Kuwait is administered by the Public Social Security Institution. The Institution enjoys corporate legal status and administrative and financial autonomy. It is composed of an executive board under the chairmanship of the Ministry of Finance, the members being the director-general from the Ministry of Finance, and representatives from the Ministries of Labour and Social Affairs, Defence, the Interior, the Civil Service, the Kuwait Chamber of Commerce and Industry, the General Federation of Workers and Employees, and three members of acknowledged experience. The day-to-day management of the Institution is the responsibility of the director-general, with a single deputy director-general, who represents the institution *vis-à-vis* third parties and the judiciary. The state, having borne all the costs of setting up the social insurance system, the Institution, which has its own separate budget, is under the supervision of the Ministry of Finance.

2.6 Lebanon

The social security system in Lebanon is administered by the National Social Security Fund, an autonomous corporate institution, with legal personality and financial and administrative autonomy. It is supervised by the Ministry of Labour through a government commissioner, subject to prior approval by the Council of Ministers in respect of acquisition of assets and *a posteriori* control by the *Cour des Comptes*.

The organs of the Fund are the executive board, the technical committee and the secretariat headed by a director-general.

The executive board consists of twenty-six members, six of whom represent the state, ten the most representative employers' organizations and ten the most representative employees' organizations. At its first meeting, the executive board, which sits for a four-year term, must elect its bureau, consisting of the chairman, the vice-chairman, two secretaries and four members. The state must be represented in the Bureau by two delegates and the employees by two delegates. The executive board is the Fund's decision-making body, and for that purpose enjoys the prerogatives recognized in the current legislation and practice in this field. In addition, a finance committee responsible for investment has been set up in the Fund, and is appointed by decision of the Council of Ministers on the recommendation of the executive board.

The Fund's technical committee is responsible for internal audit and checks operations and accounts, recommending improvements to management systems and writing general and special reports including the annual report.

The director-general, who heads the Fund's secretariat, is responsible for implementing the decisions taken by the board and the management of the Fund's secretariat.

In 1993, following the troubled times experienced by Lebanon between 1975 and 1990, and the collapse of the administrative and financial position of the Fund, a special nine-member committee, a third each representing the state, employers' and employees' organizations was set up to restore the Fund. Since then, and with the success of the recapitalization phase, specific cooperation training and information programmes have been held in France to modernize the structure of the Fund, allow the integration of new categories of the population and improve benefits and services.

2.7 Oman

Established under Legislation Decree 91/72 of 2 July 1991, as amended, social insurance in Oman is administered by the General Authority for Social Insurance under the general supervision of the Ministry of Labour and Social Affairs, and consists of an executive board of eight members under the chairmanship of the Minister of Labour and Social Affairs.[2]

The general organizational structure of the Fund, as approved by the executive board in 1993 and modified by its Decision No. 95/49 is as follows :

– the chairman of the executive board;
– the director-general;
– staff sections: internal audit, experts and advises, information and public relations, legal service;
– five departments: (a) administration and finance, (b) computers and statistics, (c) investment, (d) benefits, and (e) registration and contributions;
– regional offices.

---

[2] See further ILO, *Report to the Government of Oman on the organization of the General Organization for Social Insurance with a view to its computerization*, 1997.

At the present time, in cooperation with the ILO, the Fund is planning to achieve specific targets by preparing a procedures manual, an accounts manual, a computerization plan and a training plan, as well as defining the methodology to be adopted in preparing an investment plan and a statistical plan.

2.8 Syria

Subject to the Civil Service Law No. 135 of 1 October 1945, Law 92/59 established the Social Insurance Institution of the Syrian Arab Republic, a public body with corporate legal status, operating under the general policies of the Council of Ministers.[3]

The Institution's executive board consists of ten members. Under the chairmanship of the Minister of Labour and Social Affairs, the Council is composed of the secretaries of the Ministers of Labour and Social Affairs (vice-chairman), the Economy, Health, the director-general of the Institution, two employers' representatives, two employees' representatives and a financial and economic expert. An alternate member is appointed to attend meetings in the absence of the member.

The director-general represents the institution *vis-à-vis* third parties and the executive board has the necessary powers to take decisions on the budget and expenditures, closure of accounts, principles for the investment of funds and staff rules.

In addition to the head office in Damascus, the institution has thirteen branches in the thirteen *mohafazats* (provinces) of the country, two liaison offices in Banias and Quneitra and a branch in Qameshli. Each branch deals with all pension matters in the *mohafazat*, except where the resident is registered in another *mohafazat*.

Finally, a special investment committee, composed of the director-general of the Institution, a representative of the central bank and an economic and financial expert appointed by the Minister of the Economy is responsible for proposing fund investment's plans.

2.9 Yemen

Under the provisions of Article 112 of law 26/1991 on social insurance, the "General Authority for Pension and Social Security" responsible for administration of social insurance activities, consists of an executive board made up of eight members, including the Minister for Social Affairs and Insurance, as chairman, the director-general, under-secretaries from the Ministry of Labour and Vocational Training and the Ministry of Industry, two members representing employers chosen by the Federation of Chambers of Commerce and Industry, and two members representing beneficiaries chosen by the Federation of Trade Unions. The Minister of Social Affairs and Insurance is required to form an investment committee composed of members of the board

---

[3] Art. 3 of Law 92/59.

and professional experts in the field to determine the basis of the investment pro-gramme for the Fund's resources in accordance with the instructions of the board.[4]

The Fund is administered by the director-general under the supervision of the Minister of Social Affairs and Insurance. The head office of the Fund is in Sana'a, with branches in Taiz, Aden and Hodeidah to reinforce the decentralization of ser-vices to the insured. Special internal and external training programmes have been prepared and implemented to improve the service to beneficiaries and to intro-duce computerization into the day-to-day operations of the Fund.

Since the administrative integration of benefits to the private and public sec-tors into a single authority called the General Pensions and Social Security Au-thority, and in the absence of a single piece of legislation, the executive board has been frozen and the body has been directed by a director-general, a deputy direc-tor-general and three directors appointed by the government under the supervision of the Minister of Social Insurance.

In conclusion to this section, it should be noted that, with the exception of Lebanon, all the bodies responsible for social security or social insurance are under the chairmanship of the minister responsible for social insurance, either directly or in-directly, as is the case in Kuwait where the Institution is under the chairmanship of the Minister of Finance. Day-to-day management is left to a director-general. Pub-lic authorities are therefore directly involved in the dialogue or any social tension merely by virtue of their presence at the head of the administrative bodies. Clearly, the speed of decision-making can facilitate solutions. But it should also be empha-sized that the dialogue may be subject to constraints the moment it is not engaged between equal forces fairly represented. The public authorities are actually not so much parties as guarantors of the process and means of dialogue and cooperation between the country's productive partners, the employers and the employees. For this reason, there is need for a case by case study in the field to determine the strengths and weaknesses new services and refine the role of the state as a moderator commit-ted to the success of social security and social insurance policies.

3 SOCIAL SECURITY AND SOCIAL INSURANCE SYSTEMS

The Arab countries of the Middle East have a long tradition of awareness of social and family solidarity as an integral part of the system of government. In recent decades, and apart from the fact that all these countries are members of the United Nations and the Arab League, the conventions and recommendations of the International Labour Office and the Arab Labour Organization have been benchmarks for the de-velopment of social security and social insurance systems. This especially applies to Con-vention 102 of 28 June 1952 by the International Labour Conference Convention on Minimum Standards of Social Security, and Arab Conventions No. 1 of 1966, No. 6 of 1976 (labour standards and need to promulgate specific laws on social insurance), No. 3 of 1971 (minimum standards of social insurance) and No. 24 of 1981 on the rights of Arab workers to social benefits when employed in other Arab countries.

---

[4]   ILO, *Report to the Government of Yemen on Social Security*, 1992.

The establishment of social security and social protection systems appears to be a main concern of Arab governments which, since the 1950s, have progressively promulgated and implemented systems and schemes for retirement, health insurance and work inquiries. The role and intervention of the state through appropriate legislation, often amended as necessary, is one of the key factors in an analysis of social security and social insurance systems.

However, while the role of governments is commendable, the fact remains that cooperation between the labour partners has always been encouraged. Thus, in the case of contributions, the legislator has applied the principle of financial partnership between employer and employee, with the state reserving the right to pay part of the contribution, cover the deficit or leave the partners to play their part without any financial involvement. The actual framework of social security systems is a public matter, derived directly from the prerogative to regulate social affairs and to involve the participation and cooperation of all those engaged in the field of employment, employers and employees. This view of the world was thus a rapid social and political change over the last thirty years from a family or social protection which, while probably not disappearing entirely, was seen as confined to covering cases of extreme need.

Thus, in less than a generation, responsibility for social security and benefits has become a public issue. This integration of social policy in the countries studied should be highlighted at the outset, for it is an essential element of any social policy that aims to make a qualitative leap programmed and coordinated between all the partners.

The very fact, therefore, that the state, in cooperation with its partners in the labour world (employers' associations and trade unions), is responsible for social protection is a major strategic plank which must be improved and brought to fruition.

Starting from this philosophy of a social security system based on the introduction of mechanisms for solidarity between all public and private partners, legislation has tried to meet social needs beyond the concept of social assistance itself. It is now a matter of right and, without generally covering workers' needs in all areas, the schemes in place are sufficiently ambitious to meet defined needs and to develop a sense of collective responsibility involving all the partners. A rapid systematic review of the current system of social security and social insurance in each of the nine countries under study will show the state of affairs and allow recommendations for desirable and possible reforms. It should be pointed out that the country case studies do not include Qatar and the United Arab Emirates, which do not at present have social insurance or social security systems comparable to the other countries studied.

3.1 Saudi Arabia

The Social Insurance Act published by Royal Decree No. M/22 of 6.9.1389 (15 November 1969) sets out the general framework for the different branches of social security in the Kingdom, or to be instituted subsequently by decision of the Council of Ministers. The two branches currently operating are employment risks (insurance against works injuries and work-related illness) and pensions (old age insurance, disability, surviving dependants).

Social insurance is a regime independently financed through employers' and employees' contributions, in addition to the yield on investment of reserves and the annual subsidy from the general budget of the state to cover any deficit and other types of income.

Workers in the private sector and all public sector employees not covered by the civil service or armed forces pension scheme are covered by the social insurance scheme, irrespective of their age or sex. Initially, the scheme covered foreign workers on the same footing as Saudi workers. In 1987, however, coverage of foreign workers under the scheme was terminated and only the professional risks benefit scheme was maintained.

The provisions of the Social Insurance Act will come into force progressively, as resources become available. The Ministry of Labour and Social Affairs determines the various stages of implementation of the pensions and professional risks branches, at the recommendation of the OGAS executive board. The coverage of the social insurance scheme now extends to all workers in enterprises with ten or more employees. The other branches of social security may be instituted by decision of the Council of Ministers.

Any agreement between any employer and his employees intended to reduce the benefits to which workers are entitled under the social insurance scheme is deemed to be null and void. In addition, social insurance benefits are neither transferable nor capable of any contractual amendment, except within the limits permitted by wage regulations.

The scheme for ARAMCO employees, who were covered by the pension scheme and employment risks schemes set up by their company prior to the introduction of the social insurance scheme continue in effect following the introduction of social insurance, so it has become, for ARAMCO workers, a supplementary scheme.

The following categories of the population are exempt from social insurance cover:

–   civil servants and members of the armed forces covered by their own sector's schemes;
–   foreign employees working in the international civil service, diplomatic or military missions;
–   employees in agriculture, forestry of livestock, or other similar sectors;
–   seamen including fishermen;
–   domestic servants other than drivers, caretakers, lift attendants and gardeners;
–   self-employed home workers;
–   members of the employer's family, including the spouse, sons and brothers under the age of 20, daughters and unmarried sisters and parents.

3.1.1 Employment risks benefits

This branch covers risks of work-related accidents and illnesses. Under the provisions of the Social Insurance Act, risks are deemed to be all accidents related to the exercise of a professional activity, road accidents and work-related illnesses contracted as a result of engaging in certain types of work or employment.

The following benefits are granted: full medical treatment, daily allowance, cost of transport and accommodation, permanent total disability benefit, permanent partial disability benefit, determination of scale of disability benefit by periodic examinations, allowance to the person responsible for caring for or arranging care of the victim, family allowances, lump sum payment, survivors' pension, orphan benefit, funeral grant, marriage benefit.

The pension's benefits, described further, cover old age, disability and death. The assured or his heirs in the event of death are entitled to a pension where the assured risk crystallizes, provided that the insured has fulfilled the minimum insurance period and satisfies the conditions laid down by law. However, when it transpires that the insured has not contributed for the minimum period required for a pension entitlement, only his contributions will be reimbursed to him or to his heirs.

3.2 Bahrain

The social insurance scheme in the state of Bahrain was introduced by Legislative Decree No. 34 of 1976, which covers all salaried workers of Bahraini or foreign nationality working under a contract of employment in the private sector, or in the mixed cooperative sector or in public institutions or bodies that are not covered by specific legislation.

Public sector employees of Bahraini nationality are governed by the provisions of Legislative Decree No. 13 of 1975 on pensions.

The entitlements of workers of foreign nationality who where covered by work accidents provisions under Legislative Decree No. 34 of 1976 on social insurance were transferred to the general Social Insurance Department (OGAS) under an amendment of Law No. 13 of 1975.

The social insurance scheme began to be mandatory from 1 October 1976, in several stages. In addition, from 1 November 1988, an optimal social insurance scheme was introduced for workers with five years service or more not covered by the compulsory scheme.

The social insurance scheme currently covers the following branches:

–   old age, disability and survivors;
–   work accidents;
–   temporary incapacity due to illness or maternity;
–   incapacity;
–   employees' self-insurance;
–   family allowances.

Only the first two branches are at present in effect. Until May 1977 they applied to all national and foreign workers. Since then, foreign workers have only been covered for work accidents.

The persons covered by social insurance are as follows.

3.2.1 Old age, disability and survivors

Employees in private companies employing ten or more workers are covered. Workers in companies employing less than ten people may contribute on a voluntary basis; domestic servants in private homes, certain categories of farm workers, casual workers, the self-employed and temporary foreign workers are excluded.

It should be noted that there is a special scheme for public sector employees. This branch is financed by employers' contributions (7 per cent of salary) and the insured person (5 per cent of salary). Voluntary contributors must pay 12 per cent of their income. The government makes no contribution to this branch.

3.2.2 Work accidents and professional risks

Employees in private companies employing ten or more workers are covered; domestic servants in private homes, casual workers, the worker's family, the self-employed and farm workers are excluded.

There is a special scheme for public sector employees. This branch is financed by a contribution of 3 per cent of the payroll paid by the employer. No contribution is paid by the insured person or the government.

3.3 Iraq

The first law on social security goes back to 1956. In 1971, Law No. 39 (The Labour and Social Security Code) was passed covering all employees from 1 April 1971, and the current insured benefits cover the following areas.

3.3.1 Old age, disability and survivors

This branch covers employers in companies employing five people or more. Farm workers, casual workers, domestic servants in private homes and the worker's family are excluded.

This branch is financed by the employee's contributions (5 per cent of salary) and the employer (12 per cent of salary), the latter being 25 per cent for oil companies. These contributions also cover sickness, maternity and industrial injury benefits. The government makes no contribution to this branch.

3.3.2 Sickness

The system covers employees in private sector companies with five employees or more. Farm workers, domestic servants, casual workers and the worker's family are excluded.

Like the pension scheme, this branch is financed by the insured person's contributions (5 per cent of salary) and the employer (12 per cent of salary), the latter being 25 per cent for oil companies. These contributions also cover sickness, maternity and industrial injury benefits. The government makes no contribution to this branch.

3.3.3 *Work accidents and professional risks*

The scheme covers the same people as the above, with the same exclusions, and has the same financing arrangements as for pensions and sickness-maternity benefit.

3.4 Jordan

There are three social security schemes in force in Jordan, covering government civil servants, members of the armed forces and private sector employees. The private sector personnel are governed by Social Security Law No. 30 of 1978, and administered by the Social Security Corporation. Law 30 1978 provides that the scope of social security provision covers the following:

– old age, disability and survivors;
– industrial accidents;
– sickness (temporary incapacity) and maternity;
– unemployment;
– family allowances;
– health insurance.

Of these, only the first two are in force with the following provisions.

3.4.1 *Old age, disability and survivors*

Employees aged 16 and over working in companies with five or more workers, state and public sector employees not covered by the law on civil and military pensions, university, local government and village council staff and Jordanians working in diplomatic missions and international organizations are covered.

Public sector employees covered by the laws on civil and military pensions, foreign employees in missions and international organizations, or diplomatic or military missions and employees engaged in casual work are excluded.

Other categories are also not covered by the scheme under a decision of the Council of Ministers on the recommendation of the Social Security Corporation. This applies to farm workers, seamen, fishermen, domestic servants, personal servants and the employer's family.

The scheme is financed by the insured, who pays 5 per cent of his salary and the employer who pays 8 per cent of the payroll. The state undertakes to cover any deficit in the scheme.

3.4.2 Work accidents and professional risks

The people covered by the industrial accidents branch are the same as those listed above under old age and disability.

However, although the same people are covered, the branch is financed in a different way, because the insured person does not pay any further contribution, and the employer pays 2 per cent of salary, which may be reduced to 1 per cent if the employer bears all costs of medical treatment and payment of the daily temporary incapacity benefit. In addition, no contribution is payable in respect of apprentices' wages.

3.5 Kuwait

The social insurance scheme in Kuwait was introduced by Law No. 61 of 1976, and took effect from 1 October 1977. The law, which has been amended on a number of occasions, provides for social protection for all Kuwaiti nationals employed in the public, private or oil sectors.

Two branches are currently in operation, the first old age, disability and survivors and the second maternity and sickness.

3.5.1 Old age, disability and survivors

Those covered by the social protection scheme are all employees working in Kuwait and all Kuwaitis working abroad. A special scheme was also set up for personal servants and military personnel on 1 March 1981.

The branch is financed by the employee, paying 5 per cent of salary, and the employer, paying 10 per cent of the payroll. The government pays an annual subsidy equivalent to 10 per cent of salaries.

3.5.2 Maternity and sickness

Free medical services are provided to all residents.

3.5.3 Work accidents and professional risks

Although the law on industrial accidents goes back to 1976, the programme has not yet been brought into operation.

3.6 Lebanon

The legislator had in mind to introduce social security provision at the end of the Second World War. Article 54 of the Labour Code, promulgated on 23 September 1946, announced the forthcoming drafting of the Social Security Code. However, it was only ten years later, in 1956, that an initial draft was prepared in cooperation with the International Labour Office, and Social Security in Lebanon was introduced on 23 September 1963 by Decree 13965. Four branches were envisaged, and brought into effect in three stages. Three of the four branches are now in effect: family allowances since 1 May 1965, retirement benefits since 1 November 1965 and sickness-maternity benefits since 1 February 1971. The fourth branch, work accidents and occupational diseases has not yet been implemented.

Under Article 9 of the Security Code, the following are entitled to social benefits: Lebanese permanent, casual, apprentice and student wage-earners (workers or employees), employees in a non-agricultural establishment on behalf of one of several employers of Lebanese or foreign nationality, and daily-paid or permanent state workers, or those in public bodies regardless of the form, nature and validity of the contract of employment, service, or apprenticeship, the amount and nature of their remuneration even if paid wholly or partly by third parties.

Foreigners in possession of a regular work permit and citizens with which Lebanon had a mutual recognition agreement in respect of social security are covered by the provisions of the Code.

It is further provided that "Lebanese employed in Lebanon by a company with its seat in Lebanon and working abroad are not subject to the provision of the Code if the State where they are working has not signed a reciprocal agreement with Lebanon."

The three branches currently in force are described below.

3.6.1 Retirement benefits

This is financed solely by the employer, with a contribution of 8.5 per cent of the total salary.

3.6.2 Family allowances

The employers' contributions are set at 15 per cent of the salary paid, up to three times the minimum salary ($US200 per month in 1998). The amount paid to the employee is a maximum of 75 per cent of the minimum salary, including spouse and up to five children.

3.6.3 Maternity and sickness

The fixed contributions of 15 per cent of salary with a ceiling of three times the minimum wage are paid 12 per cent by the employer and 3 per cent by the employee.

3.7 Oman

The social security scheme in the Sultanate of Oman was introduced in 1991 by Legislative Decree No. 91/72 of 2 July 1991 and subsequently amended by Legislative Decree No. 92-4 of 5 February 1992.

The social security scheme introduced under this legislation covers permanent salaried employees of Omani nationality in the private sector aged from 15 to 59. Foreigners are excluded from the social security scheme.

The current regime covers the following branches:

(a)   old age, disability and survivors;
(b)   insurance against industrial accidents and occupational diseases.

The total rate of contribution is set at 19 per cent, shared between the two branches as follows:

–   18 per cent for old age, disability and death, with 7 per cent paid by the employer, 5 per cent by the state and 5 per cent by the employee.
–   1 per cent for industrial accidents and occupational diseases, paid solely by the employer.

In addition to the contributions, the employer is required to pay a retirement premium which is paid to the employee for the period prior to the introduction of the scheme, 1 July 1992, as laid down in the contract between the two parties, under the current labour legislation in force in the country. Validation of these earlier periods is not, however, taken into consideration in determining the pension entitlements of the insured, which are based solely on periods of actual contributions.

The old age, disability and death branch came into operation on 1 July 1992, while it was intended to start the work accident and occupational diseases branch at the beginning of 1997.

3.7.1 Old age, disability and survivors

All national employees aged 15 to 59 employed in the private sector under a permanent contract of employment are covered.

All employees of foreign nationality, domestic servants and self-employed workers are excluded.

The scheme is financed through contributions, the employee paying 5 per cent of salary, the employer 8 per cent and 5 per cent of the total payroll by the government.

3.7.2 Work accidents and professional risks

National employees aged 15 to 59 employed in the private sector under a permanent contract of employment are covered, while all employees of foreign nationality, domestic servants and self-employed workers are excluded.

The scheme is financed through contribution of 1 per cent of salary paid only by the employer, with nothing paid by the employee or the state.

3.8 Syria

The social insurance scheme in Syria established by Law No. 92 of 2 April 1959 and amended by Legislative Decree of 11 October 1961 and Legislative Decree of 4 October 1976. It currently covers two branches; the first is work accidents and the second old age, disability and survivors.

Under the provisions of Article 2 of the law, all workers, employees and trainees are subject to the social security regulations. In the absence of specific provisions to the contrary, excluded are farm workers, casual workers such as those employed in the construction industry or seasonal workers, members of the employers' family and personal domestic servants or suchlike. However, under the provision or Article 19 of the above law, work accidents cover farm, workers working with machinery or exposed to occupational diseases and to casual workers and those working in construction companies, domestics being excluded from this branch too.

Social insurance is financed as follows:

(a)   For old age, disability and survivors, the contributions are fixed by Article 56 of the above law at 21 per cent of salaries, 14 per cent paid by the employer and 7 per cent by the employee.

(b)   For work accidents, Article 21 of the law set the contribution at 3 per cent of salary paid by the employer, with no payment by the employee or the state. Subsidies, aid and returns on investment could also be envisaged.

3.9 Yemen

With the reunification of Yemen in 1991, the Yemeni government passed two laws, one under number 25/1991 for public sector insurance and pensions, and the second, Law 26/1991, on social insurance covering the private sector. The schemes came into effect on 10 April 1991, and currently cover the following three sectors.

3.9.1 Old age, disability and survivors

All national and foreign employees working and Yemenis working abroad are covered.

Casual workers, farm workers, domestic servants, seafarers and fishermen are excluded from benefit. The branch is financed as follows:

Employee contribution	6 per cent of salary
Employer's contribution	9 per cent of salary
The state as employer	6 per cent of salary

3.9.2 Sickness and maternity

A special health insurance scheme has been introduced for public sector employees.

Table 1 Summary of contributions for pension and lump sum on retirement

Country	Employers' contribution (%)	Employees' contribution (%)	State contribution
Saudi Arabia	8	5	Annual subsidy to cover the deficit
Bahrain	7	5	None
Iraq	12 (20 in oil sector)	5	None
Jordan	8	5	Cover of deficit
Kuwait	10	5	Annual subsidy of 10% of salaries
Lebanon	(lump sum) 8.5	-	–
Oman	8	5	5% of remuneration
Syria	14	7	–
Yemen	9	6	6% as employer

3.9.3 Work accidents and professional risks

Government officials, public sector employees and those in the mixed ownership sector are covered by this branch.

It is financed through an employer contribution of 4 per cent of basic salary and 1 per cent by the state as employer.

In conclusion, one should note that social security or social insurance systems respond to determined situations of pensions and work accidents. They generally have the merit of recognizing partnership financing by employers and employees, but it is clear that an extension of benefits is a major aspect to take into account in the social policy field.

4 PENSION SCHEMES AND LUMP SUM PAYMENTS

With the exception of Qatar and the United Arab Emirates, all the Arab countries of the Asian Middle East have implemented pension and lump sum payment's schemes based on employer and employee participation. Lebanon is the only one to continue to apply terminal lump sums in the private sector.

4.1 The pension scheme in Saudi Arabia

4.1.1 Pension benefits

This branch covers old age, disability and death. The insured (or his heirs in the event of death) is entitled to a pension when the insured risk crystallizes, provided that the insured has fulfilled the minimum period of insurance and satisfied the conditions set out in the social insurance legislation. However, when it transpires that the insured has not contributed for the minimum period required for a pension entitlement, only his contributions will be reimbursed to him or to his heirs.

4.1.2 The old age pension and conditions for award

To receive an old age pension, the insured who ceases contributory employment must:

–   have reached the age of 60;
–   have paid a minimum of 180 months' contributions, or:
–   120 months of contributions, 36 of which were during the five years immediately preceding the date of retirement;
–   60 consecutive months of contributions immediately preceding the date of retirement.

However, an insured person who retires after the age of 60 during the five years following the date when his cover under the social insurance scheme started and who has not fulfilled the minimum period of 120 months of contributions is credited with the necessary amount on the basis of previous employment periods.

4.1.3 Non-occupational disability pension and conditions for award

The insured is entitled to this benefit when the competent medical board decides that disability is not the result of exercising his professional activity, and when he satisfies the following conditions:

–   he became disabled before reaching the age of 60.
–   his disability must prevent him from working or from earning at least one third of his former salary in his usual employment or in a comparable employment compatible with his capacities, age, physical and mental aptitudes and training.

It must be medically proved that the stare of disability is capable of lasting a minimum of six months.

The disability is established under the same procedure as for occupational risks. The disabled person must undergo periodic examinations until he reaches the age of 60, after which his disability pension is confirmed.

The insured must have contributed for a minimum of 120 months in total, or:

–   60 months, of which 24 were in the three years immediately preceding the date when his disability was admitted; or
–   30 consecutive months prior to the date when his disability was admitted.

4.1.4 Method of pension calculation

The old age or disability pension is equal to one-fifth of the average monthly pensionable salary for each year of insurance (contribution year). The formula used is as follows:

–   Amount of pension = number of contribution years × 1/50 × the mean monthly pensionable salary for the last two years.

Minimum amount of pension paid in the case of non-occupational disability pension
   This is equal to 40 per cent of the average monthly salary used to calculate the pension under the above formula.

4.1.5 *Allowance paid to person providing treatment and care of the insured*

The recipient of a disability pension who needs permanent assistance from another person in carrying out his daily functions receives an allowance for the person who looks after him, like in the occupational risks' scheme.

4.1.6 *Family allowances*

The recipient of an old age or disability pension receives family allowances for dependent members of his family, as in the occupational risks' scheme.

4.1.7 *Survivor's pension*

In the event of the death of an insured person who satisfies the conditions for award of a disability pension, or the recipient of an old age pension or a non-occupational disability pension, the dependent members of his family are entitled to a pension based on the same rules and conditions as those applied to the occupations risks' scheme. The orphan allowance mentioned above is added to that pension if the conditions for its payment are satisfied.

4.1.8 *Funeral grant*

When the recipient of an old age or disability pension dies, OGAS is required to pay a funeral grant to the person incurring those costs, without any other conditions. In the case of the death of an insured person, the grant is only payable if the deceased has contributed for at least six months out of the preceding twelve.

4.1.9 *Marriage grant*

The widow, daughter or sister who is getting married receives a marriage grant under the same conditions as the occupational risks' scheme.

4.1.10 *Entitlement of continuity of cover*

An insured person who has paid contributions for a least five years, who leaves his pensionable employment and who is unable to fulfil the contribution periods required for the payment of a pension, is entitled, under current legislation, to request continuity of cover under the scheme in exchange for payment of the employers' and his own contributions for the remaining months, in accordance with the rules and procedures set down by decision of the Council of Ministers.

4.1.11 Reimbursement of contributions

Any insured person who does not fulfil the conditions for award of a pension is entitled to reimbursement of his contributions in the following cases:

- if he is aged 60 or over and has been unemployed for at least six months; or
- if he suffers from a non-occupational disability; or
- if he dies (contributions reimbursed to the heirs).

In all cases, the insured must have paid at least twelve months' contributions.

4.1.12 Calculation of amount reimbursed

The amount is equal to the total contributions plus a premium of 5 per cent.

4.1.13 Entitled survivors

The contributions are reimbursed to the widow of the deceased insured or, if there is no widow, to the surviving heirs who satisfy the conditions for the grant of pension or the benefit as previously defined; the order of precedence is as follows:

- children (sons and daughters);
- parents, if there are no children;
- brothers, and sisters, if there are neither children and parents.

4.2 The pension scheme in Bahrain

Pension benefits cover the risks of old age, disability and survivors for all employers in the private and similar sectors. Public sector employees are covered under the provisions of Law 13 of 28 June 1975.

The old age, disability and survivor's scheme in the private sector. The insured, or his heirs in the event of his death are entitled to a pension when the insured risks crystallize in accordance with the following conditions:

4.2.1 Conditions for award of the old age pension

To receive an old age pension, the insured who has ceased pensionable employment must:

- have reached the age of 60 for men and 55 for women;

- have paid a minimum of 180 months' contributions; or
- 240 months of contributions prior to the age of 60; or
- 120 months of contributions after the age of 60, with at least thirty-five consecutive months of contributions during the five years preceding retirement. Reduced pensions in the case of early retirement are provided to persons who have already paid 240 months' contributions (for men) and 180 months for women.

It is not necessary to leave work to receive a pension.

The old age pension is calculated as follows:

- 2 per cent of the average salary for the last two years multiplied by the number of contribution years, with an additional credit of five years for those who retire aged sixty or before 30 September 1997. The minimum amount of pension is calculated as the lower of the insured's average salary for the last two years, or 155 dinars (about US$305).

4.2.2 *Reduced pension*

Pension reductions are envisaged in the following cases:

- 20 per cent on retirement before the age of 45;
- 15 per cent on retirement between 45 and 50;
- 10 per cent on retirement between 50 and 55.

4.2.3 *Supplement awarded to the insured and his dependants*

There is a provision for increasing the pension to 20 dinars a month for each member of the insured's family, provided that the total amount does not exceed the insured's average remuneration during the last two years.

4.2.4 *Retirement settlement*

In the case of ineligibility for a pension, a lump sum equal to 15 per cent of the insured's average remuneration during the last two years multiplied by twelve times the number of contribution years allocated to him 5 per cent interest from the date when cover ceased until payment of the final amount.

4.2.5 *Disability pension*

The conditions for award of a non-occupational disability pension are as follows:

- disability arising prior to the age of 60.
- contributions paid for six consecutive months prior to the disability (three consecutive months of the total contributions amount to twelve months) for men under the age of 60 and women under the age of 55.

The method of calculation of the disability pension is an amount equal to 2 per cent of the salary for the last year multiplied by the number of contribution years. The minimum pension is equivalent to 44 or 46 per cent of the average salary for the last contribution year, or 115 dinars, if his remuneration is higher, or the contributors' salary is lower than 115 dinars.

Additional family allowances are payable to the insured and his family, based on 20 dinars for each member of the family including the insured, provided that the total amount of family allowances does not exceed the average total remuneration during the last year.

Finally, on reaching retirement age, the specific old age pension provisions are applied to the insured.

In the event of death, it has to established whether the insured satisfies the conditions for an old-age pension, otherwise, he must have contributed for at least six consecutive months prior to his death (three months if the total contributions amount to twelve months).

The method of payment of the pension to survivors is as follows:

- for the widow: 37.5 per cent of the insured's pension;
- for the orphans: 50 per cent of the insured's pension shared between each heir under the age of 22 (26 if the children are studying at university). Orphans without a father or mother share the pension 100 per cent.

Other relatives or dependents of the insured: 12.5 per cent of the pension shared equally between them.

The minimum monthly amount is set at 20 dinars, the maximum being the average salary of the insured. Additional contribution years to allow the insured to earn the maximum pension give entitlement to a lump sum equal to 11 per cent of the total salary for each additional year.

4.2.6 Supplement for the insured and dependants

There is provision for a benefit of 20 dinars per month for the insured and each member of his family.

4.2.7 Survivor's allowance

The above mentioned provisions for settlement of the old age pension also apply in this case.

4.2.8 Death and funeral grant

Six months or pension, plus 300 dinars funeral expenses (400 dinars if the insured died abroad and is buried in Bahrain).

4.2.9 The public sector pension scheme

The provisions currently applied by the Civil Service Pension Fund under Law 13/1975 are as follows:

–   in the event of termination of service on grounds of disability or death by natural causes, the beneficiary or his heirs receive a pension equal to a least 40 per cent for the last salary, regardless of length of service;
–   in the event of retirement on reaching pensionable age, a pension is paid, calculated as 1/50 of the finals base salary subject to a maximum of 80 per cent of that salary and a minimum, of 80 dinars to the retiree;
–   a gratuity of 15 per cent of the final pensionable salary for each year of service over 40, with a ceiling of seven years;
–   a gratuity of 15 per cent of annual salary for each completed year of service, if ineligible for a pension;
–   gratuity of 2 per cent of final salary multiplied by 12 for each year of service counting towards retirement;
–   death benefit equal to six months salary or pension, as applicable;
–   funeral grant equal to three months salary or pension, as applicable;
–   gratuity of one month for any civil servant reaching pensionable age for each year of service before the age of 18;
–   interest on pension contributions;
–   credit for periods of service before 1 October 1975, the date of entry in force of Law 13/1975 for civil servants for whom contributions were not paid;
–   increase of gratuity by half in the case of abolition of a post or redundancy other than for disciplinary reason;
–   extension of the definition of permanent disability by adding illness without remission or mental illness;
–   in the event of disability, payment of all the insured's medical expenses until his recovery;
–   credit for period of disability and work stoppage during service years without payment of contribution;

In the event of 30 per cent disability or more, provision of a disability pension. Where the disability is less than 30 per cent, payment of a lump sum.

4.3 The pension scheme in Iraq

The following three situations can be distinguished with respect to pensions for old age, disability and death (survivors).

4.3.1 Old age pension

The conditions for the award of an old age pension are as follows:

–   men must have reached the age of 60 and women 55 and have paid contributions for twenty years, or

–   any age with thirty years of contributions for men and twenty years for women.
–   retirement from a regular employment.
–   the pension may be paid abroad in certain cases.
–   the pension is calculated on the basis of 2.5 per cent of the average salary for the last three years multiplied by the number of contribution months and divided by twelve. The minimum pension is set at 54 dinars a month and the maximum 140 dinars.

In the case of ineligibility for a pension, a lump sum equal to one month's salary for each year of contribution is paid to the insured.

4.3.2 Disability pension

This pensions is awarded in the case of the insured's permanent disability or loss of 35 per cent capacity.
    The pension is calculated on the basis of 2.5 per cent of the average salary for the last three years multiplied by the number of contribution months and divided by twelve. The minimum pension is set at 54 dinars a month and the maximum 140 dinars.
    In the case of partial disability, a percentage calculated on the full amount of disability and proportional to the degree of disability if awarded to the insured.

4.3.3 Death grant – survivors

This is awarded to any deceased person already enrolled in the scheme or anyone who meets the conditions required to receive an old age pension.
    The grant is awarded on the following basis:

–   60 per cent of the insured's pension is payable to the spouse, regardless of her age.
–   40 per cent of the insured's pension is payable to the orphans – or 60 per cent if they have lost both father and mother – payable to each child under the age of 17 (27 if a student), and each unmarried daughter up the age of 17. Dependants of the insured, father, mother, sisters and brothers then share the remaining 40 per cent of the pension.

The maximum amount of pension for survivors cannot exceed 100 per cent of the pension to which the insured was entitled.

4.4 The pension scheme in Jordan

The regime currently operating in Jordan covers three categories of risk.

4.4.1 Old age pension

The award of this pension requires the employee to:

–   have reached the age of 60 for men and 55 for women;
–   have contributed for 120 months (thirty-six consecutive months during the
     last five years), or a total cover of fifteen years.

Early retirement with a reduced pension is possible for those aged forty-six who have
contributed for fifteen years. In addition, those insured who have reached retirement
age and who need at least five more years of contributions to meet the conditions for
a pension may contribute up to the age of sixty-five to satisfy those conditions.

The pension calculation is based on 2 per cent of the average monthly salary for
the last two years multiplied by the number of years of contribution. The maximum pension payable must be equal to 75 per cent of the average monthly salary
for the last two years. An increase in pension of 10 per cent is provided for the first
dependent and 5 per cent for each of the second and third dependents.

In the case of early retirement, the pension is reduced as follows:

–   10 per cent of early retirement between 46 and 50.
–   5 per cent for retirement between 51 and 54.

In the case of ineligibility for an old age pension, a lump sum is granted to the insured, in the amount of 10 per cent of the average annual salary if the contribution
period is less than 60 months, 12 per cent if the contribution period is from 60 to
119 months, and 25 per cent if the contribution period is equal to or greater than
120 months.

4.4.2 Disability pension

The disability pension is awarded in the case of the insured's total or partial disability
provided that he has contributed from twelve consecutive months or twenty-four
months in total. In the case of permanent disability, a pension is awarded equal to
50 per cent of the average monthly salary in the insured's last year of contribution.

4.4.3 Survivor's pension

This pension is awarded provided that the insured has contributed for twelve consecutive months or twenty-four months in total.

The survivor's pension is calculated as 50 per cent of the insured's average monthly
salary during the last year of contribution, if the deceased was disable, 100 per cent
of the insured's pension. The pension is payable to the widow, children under age
of 18 (no limit if the child is handicapped), unmarried or divorced daughters, dependent parents, brothers, sisters and widowers, subject to termination on the
marriage of the widow, daughters and sisters. The pension may also be reduced
depending on the income of the survivors.

Finally, an allowance of 150 dinars for funeral expenses is paid to the deceased's
family.

The pension scheme for government employees was improved in 1994. The
calculation formula for the pension was reduced from 1/480 to 1/360, while the formula in the private sector is still 1/600. In addition, the retirement pension payable

to state employees rose from 71 dollars to 85 dollars, with the addition of early retirement without reduced pension after twenty years of service for men and fifteen for women, with regular adjustments of all pensions to reflect economic changes.[5]

In addition, employees of the state and the armed forces contribute to their pension by deduction from their salaries,

4.5 The pension scheme in Kuwait

The Kuwaiti pension scheme consists of an old age pension, a disability pension and a survivor's pension.

4.5.1 Old age pension

The award of this pension requires the employee to:

– have reached the age of 50 and have contributed for fifteen years;
– in the case of early retirement, to have reached a minimum age of 45 for men and 40 for women, having contributed for twenty years.
– it is anticipated that the minimum retirement age will rise progressively until 2020, when it will be 55 for men and 50 for women. In addition, early retirement for women with children is possible provided that they have paid contributions for a minimum of fifteen years.

To be entitled to an old age pension, the insured must take retirement and cease work, except in a few cases where the full pension is paid if the insured is aged 50 or over, and reduced by a quarter if he is under 50 where the salary and pension together exceed 1,250 dinars per month.

The pension calculation is based on 65 per cent of final salary plus 2 per cent of the final salary for each contribution year up to fifteen. The maximum pension payable must not exceed 95 per cent of the final monthly salary. Part of the pension may be paid as a lump sum at the request of an insured who becomes disable before the age of 65. Finally, transitional arrangements allow insured persons to enjoy a pension with less than fifteen years of contributions.

4.5.2 Disability pension

A disability pension may be granted in the case of total incapacity for work. The pension calculation is based on 65 per cent of final salary plus 2 per cent of the final salary for each contribution year up to fifteen. The maximum pension payable must not exceed 95 per cent of the final monthly salary.

---

[5] See Clive Bailey, *Coverage Under Social Security Pension Schemes,* ILO Report, 1995.

4.5.3 Survivor's pension

The condition for award of a survivor's pension is that the deceased meets the insurance conditions or that he was in receipt of a disability pension when he died.

The pension is calculated on the basis of 33 1/3 per cent up to 100 per cent for the deceased's salary depending on the number of widows, children, parents, brothers, sisters and grandchildren. The children must be aged under 26 (28 for students) and there is no age limit for unmarried daughters and handicapped boys.

A funeral grant equal to two months' salary or two months' pension of the insured is awarded to the family, with a minimum of 100 dinars.

4.6 The pension scheme in Lebanon

In Lebanon, a distinction needs to be made between public sector and private sector employees.

4.6.1 The public sector

Civil servants have the right to choose, between the ages of 64 for public employees and 68 for judges, between a retirement pension or an indemnity of retirement. For members of the armed forces, a mixed system of pension and lump sum indemnity is implemented.

If they choose a service termination payment, a lump sum is paid to retirees in the amount of one month's salary for each year of service for the first ten years, two months from ten to thirty years' service and three months for more than thirty years' service. After that, the retiree has no further financial relationship with the state, but he continues to enjoy medical benefits provided by the Civil Service Mutual Fund.

If they choose the retirement pension, this is calculated on the basis of 2.5 per cent of salary for each year of service. Thus for forty years' service, the retiree receives 100 per cent of salary, for thirty years, 75 per cent of salary and for twenty years, 50 per cent. Where the retiree's service is greater than forty years, he receives a pension in respect of the forty years and an additional lump sum of three months for each year of service over forty years.

In addition, where the retiree has been in service for less than twenty years, he is not entitled to a retirement pension and is eligible only for a termination payment.

4.6.2 The private sector

Although Article 49 of the Social Security Code 1963 laid down the transitional nature of the system of terminal payments, and despite studies carried out in cooperation with ILO to introduce a retirement pension scheme in the private sector, only the termination payment scheme is currently in operation in Lebanon.

The right to an end-of-service termination payment has been compulsory for all employees entering service after 1 May 1965, when the scheme came into effect, and any compulsory or voluntary contributor who satisfies the following conditions is eligible:

-   completion of a total of at least twenty years' employment, adding the period of contribution to the Fund to years spent in the employer's service prior to the date when this scheme came into effect;
-   disability of at least 50 per cent making him unable to keep his employment or carry out similar work, appropriate to his qualifications and training;
-   in the case of a female employee, marriage or leaving employment within the twelve months following the date of her marriage
-   having reached the age of 64.

In the event of an employee's death, the following heirs are entitled to his end-of-service indemnity:

-   the employee's father and mother, if aged over 60 or who, as result of physical or mental disability, are not able to earn a living;
-   the wife of the insured, or where more than one wife, the first wife;
-   the husband of the insured, if aged over 60 or who, as a result of physical or mental disability, is not able to earn a living;
-   the legitimate or adopted children of the insured up to the age of 16. The age limit may be extended up to a maximum of 25 for children who are unable to support themselves, either because they are in full time education, or as a result of physical or mental disability, provided that the disability is permanent or arose before the age of 16. Disabled children are supported by public welfare after the age of 25;
-   minor bothers and sisters of the insured who, at the date of his death, were his dependants.

4.6.3 Calculation of end-of-service indemnity

Article 51 of the Social Security Code determines the amount and method of calculation of the end-of-service indemnity. It is equal to one month preceding the date when he became eligible for the indemnity. In addition, if the salary is calculated wholly or partly on commission, it will be equal, for each year of service, to one-twelfth of the amounts actually paid to the person concerned for the twelve months preceding the date of crystallization of the indemnity.

In addition, for each year subsequent to the first twenty years, an insured who has reached the age of 60 (or 55 for a woman) is entitled to an additional indemnity equal to half a month due only in respect of the contributory period.

Finally, the employee is entitled only to a reduced indemnity in the following cases:

(a) if he voluntarily leaves the enterprise where he served his apprenticeship before the expiry of two years;
(b) if, as a voluntary member of the scheme, he voluntarily leaves his employment before the expiry of twelve months following the date of his admissions to the end-of-service indemnity scheme;

(c)   If he declares that he has permanently ceased his employment, the indemnity
       is equal to:
       –   50 per cent if he has contributed to the Fund for five years;
       –   65 per cent if he has contributed to the Fund for five to ten years;
       –   75 per cent if he has contributed to the Fund for ten to fifteen years;
       –   85 per cent if he has contributed to the Fund for fifteen but less than twenty
            years.

4.6.4 *Disability pension*

The disability pension, for which there is provision in the Social Security Code
and its amendments, is not yet in effect in Lebanon.

4.6.5 *Funeral grant*

Under Article 45 of the Social Security Code a grant for funeral expenses is currently
set at one and a half times the minimum salary, i.e. $300.

4.7 The pension scheme in Oman

The current scheme covers the old age pension, disability pension and survivor's pension for the private sector, under the provisions of Legislative Decree 91/71 of 2 July
1991 as amended by Legislative Decree 92-4 of 5 February 1992.

4.7.1 *Old age pension*

The award of the old pension is subject to the following conditions:

–   Reaching the age of 60 for men, with at least 180 months of paid contribu-
     tions, and fifty-five for women, with at least 120 months of contributions.
–   In the case of early retirement, the months of contributions must be 240
     months for men and 180 for women, with reduced rates of pension.
–   In the case of deferred retirement, 180 months of contribution are required,
     of which 36 at least during the final five years prior to retirement.

     The pension is calculated on the basis of 1/60 of the average salary for the final
two years of employment multiplied by the number of full years of contribution.

4.7.2 *Disability pension*

This pensions is awarded in the case of occupational disability with six months of
contributions prior to the onset of disability or twelve months' contribution, including the final three months immediately prior to disability. The pension is calculated on the basis of 1/60 of the average salary for the final two years of employ-

ment multiplied by the number of full years of contribution. The minimum guaranteed pension is 40 per cent of salary at the time when the insured became disabled.

4.7.3 Survivor's pension

This pension is awarded under the following conditions:

- the deceased's beneficiaries are unemployed;
- six months' contributed prior to death or twelve months' contributions, including the final three months immediately prior to decease.
- the pension calculation is based on three groups: orphans, widowers or widows and other eligible family members.
- orphans receive 50 per cent of the pension payable to children up to the age of 22 or up to 26 for students (no limit for handicapped children or unmarried daughters).
- the widower and the widow (provided she does not remarry) receive 25 per cent of the pension. If there is more than one widow, the pension is divided equally between them.
- the other dependent members of the family receive 25 per cent of the pension shared equally between the father, mother, brothers (up to the age of twenty-two) and unmarried sisters. If there are beneficiaries in any group, the share is distributed to one of the other groups where there are beneficiaries up to a maximum of 100 per cent.

In addition, a marriage allowance is granted to the daughter on her marriage based on a lump sum equal to fifteen times the insured's pension.

Finally, a funeral grant equal to three months' salary or pension of the insured is awarded as a lump sum.

4.7.4 Public sector pension scheme

By Decree of the Sultan No. 26-86, a pension scheme was introduced in Oman with effect from 1 January 1986 for government employees based on the following principles:

- fixing the age of retirement.
- creation of a Pension and Benefit Fund with corporate legal status, financially independent to manage and operate pension funds in accordance with best practice;
- employee participation to the extent of 5 per cent of basic salary, with a state contribution of 15 per cent paid to the fund;
- fixing a minimum and maximum pension;
- counting six months and over as a complete year if necessary to allow the employee to be eligible for an old age pension;
- entitlement to a pension in the event of death or disability regardless of the length of service;

- in addition to the principal pension beneficiaries, namely wife and children, inclusion of father, mother, brother and sister;
- equitable pension distribution to all those entitled, with reversion to the Fund only in the total absence of beneficiaries;
- payment of a death benefit to cover funeral expenses;
- in the case of death in service, or permanent disability, a lump sun is paid to the employee up to the equivalent of his annual salary with a minimum of 5,000 Omani rials. Other occupational accidents are eligible for indemnities in proportion to the accident.

4.8 The pension scheme in Syria

Under the provisions of Article 55 of Legislative Decree 92/59 as amended, the provisions under the social insurance law for the private sector apply to civil servants and government workers, employees of public committees and public bodies, and local government, except if, at the date of entry into force of this law in 1961, they enjoyed better provisions.

The three aspects of the Syrian pension scheme are as follows.

4.8.1 Old age pension

The award of the old age pension is subject to the following conditions:

- reaching the age of 60 for men, with 180 months of contributions, i.e. at least fifteen years of contributions; or
- reaching the age of 55 with twenty years' service and 240 months of contributions.

The pension may be reduced if the insured, on reaching the age of retirement, continues to work and receive a salary higher than his pension.

The method of calculation of the old age pension, under Article 58 of the Social Insurance Law 92/59 as amended by Legislative Decree 35/76, is based on 1/45 of the average final monthly salary for the last two years of contributions or the average monthly salary for the last five consecutive years of the final ten contribution years, provided that the old age pension does not exceed 75 per cent of the current monthly salary or 1127.5 Syrian pounds, set at 3450 Syrian pounds in 1996, with a minimum pension of 419 Syrian pounds.

In the case of ineligibility for a pension, an amount equal to 11 to 15 per cent of the total pensionable salary will be paid to the insured in full settlement.

4.8.2 Disability pension

The disability pension is payable in the event of loss of 80 per cent of the employee's ability to work provided that the insured has paid contributions for six consecutive months or twelve months intermittently (Article 63 of Law 92/59 as amended).

The pension is calculated to maximize the benefit to the insured, either based on 40 per cent of the average salary for the final two contribution years or for the contributory period or the contributory old age pension payable augmented by three years.

In addition, an additional lump sum equal to 50 per cent of salary during the final year in respect of contributions have been paid will be awarded to the disabled person in the following to cases: total disability and death. In cases of 35 per cent disability, half the additional lump sum will be paid.

A further lump sum indemnity equal to half the amount is awarded where the disability if due to an occupational accident.

4.8.3 Survivor's pension

This is payable if death occurs during the employment of the insured or within six months of termination of employment provided that death is not caused by an occupational accident and the deceased is not aged over 65 at the time of death.

The conditions for award are that contributions must have been paid by the insured for the six consecutive months or twelve months intermittently prior to death.

The pension is calculated to maximize the benefit to the insured, either based on 40 per cent of the average salary for the final two contribution years or for the contributory period or the contributory old age pension in respect of his service for which contributions have been paid augmented by three years.

Those entitled to the pension are the widow or widower, disabled person eligible for pension, widowed or divorced daughters and sisters of the insured, and the parents.

The maximum amount of pension is equal to 75 per cent of the disability pension with a monthly minimum of 400 Syrian pounds for the widow and 96 Syrian pounds for each of the other beneficiaries.

4.8.4 Death grant

A lump sum equal to 100 per cent of salary for the insured's final year of employment is paid to the survivors, with a supplement of 50 per cent if the death is due to an occupational accident.

4.8.5 Funeral grant

A lump sum equal to one month's salary and a maximum of 100 pounds is paid to survivors.

4.9 The pension scheme in Yemen

The three components of the pension scheme in the Republic of Yemen are the old age pension or end-of-service indemnity in the case of ineligibility for a pension, the disability pension and the survivors' pension.

4.9.1 Old age pension

Article 51 of law 26/1991 set out legal conditions for eligibility to an employment pension, namely:

–   reaching the age of 60 for men and 55 for women, provided that the contribution period is not less than 180 months, i.e. fifteen years' contributions;
–   reaching the age of 45 provided that the contributory period is not less that 240 months, i.e. twenty years' contributions, and the employee does not continue in employment, as defined in law 26/1991;
–   where the contribution period of a man who has reached the age of 50 is 300 months (twenty-five years) or 240 months (twenty years) for a woman aged 46;
–   the insured may continue to work until contributions amount to 180 months, provided that the extension of employment does not exceed five years, or contributions, for the purposes of being eligible for an old age pension. The insured may also make a single lump sum payment to top up his and the employers' missing contributions.

4.9.2 Calculation of the old age pension

Article 56 of Law 26/1991 specified that the amount of the old age pension should be calculated as 1/420 of the insured's average monthly pensionable salary for the final year, for each contribution month, provided that the total amount does not exceed 100 per cent of the average monthly pensionable salary and is not less than 50 per cent of that amount.

4.9.3 End-of-service indemnity

Where the employee is not eligible for an old age pension, on the grounds set out in Article 57 of law 26/1991, i.e. resignation of an insured woman, emigration of the Yemeni insured, definitive departure of a foreigner from the country, permanent total disability of the insured, reaching retirement age without having satisfied the conditions for eligibility for an old age pension, a lump sum is paid to the insured in the form of an end-of-service indemnity.

4.9.4 Calculation of the end-of-service indemnity

In the case of the resignation of an insured woman, emigration of the Yemeni insured, definitive departure of a foreigner from the country, the amount of the indemnity is set at 10 per cent of final average salary multiplied by the contribution period, or else the amount is calculated as 12/15 of the total amount of contributions paid if that is more beneficial.

In the case of permanent total disability of the insured, reaching retirement age without having satisfied the conditions for eligibility for an old age pension, the end-of-service indemnity is calculated as 12 per cent of final average annual salary multiplied by the number of contribution years.

4.9.5 Disability pension

In the case of total disability, and provided that the period of contributions is at least 60 months, a pension is granted equal to 50 per cent of the final average annual salary from employment or the amount of old age pension to which the insured is legally entitled, whichever is to the advantage of the insured.

4.9.6 Survivor's pension

This pension is granted to the heirs of the insured who dies during the period of his employment. In this case the same calculation is applied for the disability pension, except that the pension is divided equally between all the beneficiaries.

5 CONCLUSIONS

This systematic, albeit rapid evaluation of the current situation in some of the Arab countries allows us to set the markers for the programmed development of a social security policy. Of course, no magic solution can be provided for all the existing structures.

All the systems currently in force in the countries of the Middle East, with the exception of Lebanon and Iraq, cover only two branches pertaining to social security through a system of contributions paid by the employer and the employee, namely work injury and old age on the one hand, disability and survivors (death) on the other. The other services are either provided out of the state budget, without contributions by those involved – as in the case of maternity and sickness cover – or simply do not exist, as in the case of family allowances, unemployment benefits and others. This is why it is recommended to consider the implementation of a general social security system parallel to the promotion, upgrading or introduction of the pension system.

The pension or indemnity of retirement system is only one aspect of social security or social insurance. The need for a pension scheme is already recognized in all countries, with the exception of Lebanon, in the private sector. But it is necessary to know to what extent the benefits provided reflect the need of pensioners and whether they really cover the necessities of life and inflation. Are the minimum and maximum amounts adequate and are the contributions paid enough to justify an improvement in the systems?

The rapid change in the situation over the last thirty years has led to a marked change in mental and social attitudes to the concept of social protection, away from a purely individual or family matter. Social security has become a matter of national solidarity, recognized and supervised by the government. This public awareness is a major factor which deserves to be pushed further with a view to improving services and benefits. The elaboration and reinforcement of a statistical demographic, economic, social, financial and health base is of prime importance. No programme could be sustained without a source of reliable data stretching over long periods to justify policy.

The inclusion of social security and social insurance costs in the mechanisms of economic production is now an accepted fact. The effects of social costs are the subject of negotiations and discussions between the various partners in the world of work, and any discussion in this area deserves to be encouraged in order to achieve better comparative contribution costs, taking into account acquired rights and safeguarding benefit levels. The partnership between the parties (government, employers, employees) deserves to be developed to cover new branches. The introduction of a carefully prepared new systems is a way of making the participants in social policy even more responsible, moderate excessive claims and expenses, and authorize a good analysis of the relations between expenditures on social security and social insurance, and the competitiveness of national and regional economics. This will be necessary to reach agreements that do not impair workers' interests and permit investment within the confines of a well-understood social solidarity.

It will also be necessary to launch programmes of research and studies in order to identify the state and evolution of the established systems, the costs, management tensions, conflict of competence, exchange of experts and data, identification of handicaps and bottlenecks, and to generally evaluate the impact of any possible and/or desirable change.

BIBLIOGRAPHICAL ORIENTATION

The International Labour Office has, for several decades, carried out major research in Arab countries, some of which have served as benchmarks for the introduction of social legislation. The survey leading to the present Article had been originally commissioned under one of these scheme.

Some of the ILO studies are dated, but they remain useful for information and reflection on the trends to be developed in subsequent studies. In addition, various helpful studies have been carried out by a number of national and international institutions.

1. ILO series on operational framework for pension reform, Social Security Department, 1997
   C. Bailey, *Coverage under Social Security Pension Schemes; Governance Issues.*
   R. Beattie, *Reform and Development of pension systems in Asia and the Pacific.*
   C. Gillion, *Overview.*
   J. Gruat, *Adequacy and Social Security – Principles in Pension Reform.*
   D. Latulippe, *Comprehensive Quantitative Modeling for a Better Pension Strategy.*
   W. McGillivray, *Retirement system risks.*
   J. Turner and Sophie Kozczyk, *Design Issues for Defined Benefit and Defined Contribution Plans.*
   J. Turner, *Retirement Income Systems for Different Economic, Demographic and Political Environments.*
2. ILO – *Investment in Social Security Funds in Developing Countries – 1987.*
3. International Social Security Association (ISSA)
   P. Banna, *Old-age Protection System*, 1990.
   Social Security in the 1990s: the need for change, 1995
4. Arab Labour Organization (in Arabic)
   a. *The Arab Labour Organization and Social Insurance*, 1996
   b. *Towards an Arab Social Insurance Strategy*, 1996
   c. *Preliminary list of social insurance bodies*,1996
   d. *Report of the 8th seminar on social insurance*, 1996
5. United States Government, *Social Security Administration: Social Security Programs Throughout the World*, 1997.

Part II

Country Surveys

Egypt

Kosheri, Rashed and Riad*

1 CONSTITUTIONAL LAW CASES

The Supreme Constitutional Court pronounced a number of judgments in 1997 which demonstrated its very liberal interpretation of the Egyptian Constitution and the Muslim *shari'a*, with the obvious aim of safeguarding the rule of law in a modern liberal Islamic state.

We have selected four judgments in this respect which are translated below.

1.1 Judgment dated 1 February 1997 in Case No. 7 of the 16th judicial year: see *Mr Hamdy Goudah Badr v. the President of the Republic and the Prime Minister*

The Public Business Sector Law promulgated by Law No. 203 of 1991 provides in its Article 20 for the possibility of disposing of the shares of the public business sector companies, transfer of their ownership to the private sector and loss of public control over them.

This article was subject to a recourse for unconstitutionality on the basis of its contradiction to Article 30 of the Constitution which provides that:

Public ownership is the ownership of the people and it is confirmed by the continuous consolidation of the public sector. The public sector shall be the vanguard of progress in all fields and shall assume the main responsibility in the development plan.

The Supreme Constitutional Court stated in this case that the constitutional texts must not be interpreted as being the final and eternal solutions of economic situations that have been overtaken by the passage of time, and that those texts have to be interpreted in the light of higher values that aim at freeing the nation and the citizens politically and economically.

---

* Legal Consultants and Attorneys at Law, Cairo, Egypt.

The Court added that subjection of the constitutional texts to a specific philosophy is contrary to the need for their adaptation to the new horizons that the nation strives to reach and which may not be obstructed by the Constitution.

The Court then stressed that public and private investment are complementary, that public and private ownership support each other and that the two are subject to the supervision of the people.

In other words, public and private ownership form a close partnership and each of them plays the role better suited to it in development.

The Court also stated that it is not imperative for public investment to take the form of economic units created by the state and remaining so forever, if such units failed to achieve their goals and the money invested in them could be better spent in other ways.

Moreover, providing in Article 20 of the Public Business Sector Law that shares of the public business sector companies may be sold to the private sector does not negate the leading role of public investment, but in fact aims at preservation of resources, that should not be squandered, and also to ensure the continuity of development within the framework of cooperation between its partners.

The Supreme Constitutional Court in its judgment also stated that Article 59 of the 1971 Constitution provides that "Defence, consolidation and preservation of socialist gains is a national duty", and it reminded that this article did not define the content or the scope of those socialist gains; that the Constitution only protects the workers' rights mentioned in it and that the subsistence or abrogation of their rights as provided by law remains in the hands of the legislator within his discretionary authority.

The Court finally stressed that the Constitution is a progressive document that does not obstruct evolution and progress at a specific stage within the rules laid down in the Constitution.

The Supreme Constitutional Court judged the recourse unacceptable.

1.2 Judgment dated 3 May 1997 in Case No. 18 of the 14th judicial year: see *Mr El Sayed Mohamed Moustafa v. the President of the Republic, the Speaker of the People's Assembly and others*

The fifth paragraph of Article 1 of Law No. 24 of 1920 concerning alimony and some personal status matters, as amended by Law No. 100 of 1985, provides that the right of the wife to obtain an alimony is not foreclosed if she leaves the martial home – without her husband's permission – in the cases allowed for by *shari'a*, that are based upon a text, custom or necessity, or if she leaves for legal work, unless her use of this right entails an abuse of right, or is contrary to the interests of the family, and the husband asked her to refrain from it.

The Plaintiff in this recourse alleged that this paragraph was contrary to Article 2 of the Constitution which provides that Islamic *shari'a* is the main source of legislation and to Article 9 which provides that the family is the basis of society, founded on religion, and he added that his wife had no right to claim for an alimony from him as long as she refused to obey his request to refrain from work and to devote all her time to her husband and her children at home.

The Court in this case recalled its jurisprudence concerning the meaning of Article 2 of the Constitution, and reiterated that according to this article, a legislative Act may not be in contradiction to the Islamic *shari'a* principles that are definitive in certainty as to the source from which they derive and as to their meaning, because those principles alone are not subject to discretionary interpretation, because they represent the overall principles and the lasting bases of the Islamic *shari'a* that may not be interpreted or amended and because it is inconceivable that their meaning may be changed with the passing of time or change in place. They are perpetual, may not be transgressed and the competence of the Supreme Constitutional Court concerning them is merely to see that they are abided by and that they overrule all legal norms that contradict them, because Article 2 of the Constitution places the overall rules of Islamic *shari'a* above all other legal norms.

Those rules are the firm base which should always be respected in such a way as to deny approval of any legal norm that contradicts them, otherwise this would be construed as an encroachment upon religion.

The Court then added that in contrast to those principles are the considered rules in respect of which substantially divergent points of view have arisen, either with regard to their certainty and/or their meaning; and that these are the only ones that are subject to discretionary interpretation. Those last rules change with the passage of time and place in order to ensure flexibility and vitality, they cope with the different situations and organize the affairs of mankind in such a way as to secure their legitimate interests, although this discretionary interpretation has to be within the overall principles of Islamic *shari'a* without transgression, and the practical rules have to be drawn by reliance upon Islamic legal guidelines with a view to realizing the general aims of the Islamic *shari'a* which are the preservation of religion, body, mind, honour and property.

The Court also mentioned that the Islamic *shari'a* accepts flexibility in its subsidiary rules, which are subject to evolution, that the opinion of one canonist – concerning matters subject to difference in interpretation – is not sacred and may be amended or replaced, and that Islamic *shari'a* therefore is not rigid but is subject to evolution in its non-basic fundamentals.

The Court then stressed that woman is the partner of man in life, that denial of her right to work may cause her hardship and render her life difficult, that her work in a manner that advances society and is in accordance to the *shari'a* opens for her the doors of useful activity starting from learning to the penetration of new horizons.

Denial of a woman's right to work for fear of her going astray means that her religion is deemed incapable of preventing her from wrongdoing, and does not take into consideration her equality with man – except in the limited area where difference exists between them – nor does it take into consideration the identity in origin, obligations, reward and punishment which render women members of society eligible to work in all fields of activity that are suitable to their nature, are not contrary to women's responsibility as guardians of their homes, husbands and children, and that use their time in a balanced way between their duties, their families and their role, as productive elements of society.

The Court then mentioned that the husband does not shelter, protect and spend money on his wife in order to subjugate her will and to exercise an overwhelming authority over her, that the wife is, like the husband, invited to participate in the well-being of society and that women during the Prophet Muhammed's time used to go with men in wars, and participated in commercial and other activities outside their home and therefore their role outside their homes was not limited nor was it restricted to cases of necessity.

The court also referred to Article 11 of the Constitution which provides that the state shall guarantee coordination between the duty of the woman, her family and her work in society, and the Court stated that this implicitly shows that the right of women to work is guaranteed by the Constitution, because coordination between two matters presupposes their existence.

The Court added that Islamic *shari'a*, in its definitive principles in certainty as to source and meaning, does not contain a definitive rule concerning the alimony due to the working wife, that whether it is due or not is a discretionary matter which allows the legislator freedom of choice to decide on what is best for the society in this respect.

The legislator in the Court's opinion had achieved, in the paragraph of the article of the law subject of the recourse, a balance between the general obligation of the wife to obtain her husband's permission to leave her home, the primordial interests of the family and the specified right of the wife to work without abuse, and the Court ruled that paragraph 5 of Article 1 of Law No. 24 of 1920 as amended by Law No. 100 of 1985 was therefore not contrary to the Constitution and that the recourse was unacceptable.

1.3 Judgment dated 2 August 1997 in Case No. 35 of the 17th judicial year: see *The legal representative of Gulf Airline v. The President of the Republic, the Prime Minister and others*

The first paragraph of Article 35 of Law No. 119 of 1983 concerning civil aviation duties as amended by Law No. 209 of 1991 provides that:

> If the foreign state, of which depends an air transport Company or establishment, imposes as a condition for exercise by Egyptian Companies or establishments of their activities in it, the necessity for them to have a representative or guarantor in this state, those foreign Companies or establishments must have a representative or guarantor in Egypt, and the Egyptair Organization shall undertake the representation or the guarantee in this Case.

The imposition of the Egyptair Organization as the representative or guarantor of the foreign aviation companies in the above-mentioned case was subject to a recourse for unconstitutionality before the Egyptian Supreme Constitutional Court.

The Court first mentioned that the lawful state is the one that accords to those residing in its territory the basic rights and freedoms whose content concords with the standards regularly applied by democratic states in their societies and which regulate the actions of those states.

The Court added that the rights of states – on the international level – find their counterpart in a certain number of obligations which include preservation of human rights.

Although the independence of states and their equality in sovereignty allows them to regulate aliens' exercise of their activities within the national interests, their authority in this respect is limited by the commanding rules accepted by the community of states as a way of conduct, which form the international minimum standards for treatment of foreigners and which are subject to the control exercised by the Court from the angle of constitutional legality.

Those international standards may not be put aside by claiming that foreigners are not treated worse than the citizens of the state, because its protection of its citizens may be below those international standards and below those duties owed by all nations to their alien residents, as confirmed by the Decision of the United Nations General Assembly No. 40/144 dated 13 December 1985 concerning the declaration of the rights of aliens in the country in which they live.

The Court then stated that freedom to contract is a basic rule required by the Constitution for preservation of personal freedom.

On the other hand, freedom to contract is not absolute, but is a qualified right subject to restrictions that aim at reaching a balance between the excesses of this freedom and the justified need for its non-arbitrary regulation, therefore the Constitutionality of such regulatory measures depends upon whether or not this balance is achieved, and whether this freedom is merely regulated for motives related to justice and public interest or totally obliterated.

The present evolution of the basic rights of the human being makes them an integral part of the international standards adopted by civilized states as a basis for dealing with aliens residing in them, and unnecessary discrimination in exercise of those basic rights is considered a breach of their required protection.

The Court mentioned that freedom of the right of choice is – within objective criteria set by the legislator – part of the rights accorded by the international standards to aliens, and they include their right to freely manage certain affairs, among which is their right to choose the representatives and guarantors who are best able to protect their interests.

Finally the Court stated that the article subject of this recourse imposed on the plaintiff the obligation to exercise its activity in Egypt solely through the national company Egyptair even if the foreign country in which it operates does not impose a similar obligation.

And the Court decided that the part of the first paragraph of Article 35 of the above mentioned law relating to the representative and guarantor role of Egyptair, negated the principle of reciprocity mentioned in it, exceeded the logical limits within which free choice may operate, encroached on the right of the plaintiff to choose its own representative and guarantor from among those wishing to do so in Egypt and also excluded them from exercise of such an activity, and was therefore contrary to Articles 32 and 34 of the Constitution which safeguard private ownership, Article 40 which confirms equality before the law and in public rights and duties and Article 41 which confirms individual freedom.

1.4 Judgment dated 6 December 1997, in Case No. 86 of the 18th judicial year: see *Mr Osama Helmy Mohsen v. the President of the Republic, the Prime Minister and others*

Subsection 6 of the first paragraph of Article 14 of the Advocates Law promulgated by Law No. 17 of 1973 provides that a condition for inscription in the general Roll of Advocates, is the provision of proof of not being an active member in another professional syndicate.

An engineer inscribed in the rolls of active members of the engineers' syndicate obtained his licence of law and requested from the advocates' syndicate to be inscribed in the general roll of advocates, but his request was rejected because he was an active member in the engineers' syndicate.

The engineer brought a legal action before the Supreme Constitutional Court and claimed, *inter alia*, that subsection 6 of the first paragraph of Article 13 of the above mentioned Advocates Law was unconstitutional.

The Supreme Constitutional Court stated in this recourse that freedom to join an association or a group to defend its members' beliefs and opinions is an integral part of their personal freedoms, whether those beliefs are political, economic, religious, cultural or social, and that no authority may hinder their diffusion to others, because Articles 46, 47, 48, 49 and 63 of the Constitution guarantee freedom of belief, expression, opinion, the press, printing, publication and of the mass media, as well as the right of all individuals to address their grievances to the public authority without fear.

The Court added that there is a close nexus between the right to express one's opinions and the right of association, that the right to establish a political or syndical establishment is derived from the right of association, and a person may not be obliged to choose one of them or to abandon his membership in it; moreover, the validity of governmental regulations – in respect to the right of association – must be determined by assessing the degree of infringement of the right of association against the legitimacy, strength and the necessity of the government's interests, and the means of implementing these interests.

In other words, the establishment of a syndical organization – whether in the professional or labour fields – forms part of the liberty of association which may not be hindered by unjust bonds that do not form part of its organization but are an aggression against it, and the syndical freedom guaranteed by Article 56 of the Constitution takes the form of the right to choose the appropriate syndical organization, the right to join more than one syndicate if the person fulfils the conditions for joining them, and the right to refrain from joining any of them.

The Court also stressed that syndical freedom is necessary for the stability and improvement of the conditions of professionals and workers, and that syndical activity must be free and not imposed as provided in Article 56 of the Constitution which states that the creation of syndicates on a democratic basis is a right guaranteed by law.

The Court added that the right of each syndicate to organize itself on a democratic basis and to freely manage its own affairs does not entitle it to commit aggressions against the rights guaranteed by the Constitution, including the right of each citizen to join more than one syndicate if he fulfils the conditions necessary for joining each one of them, and the Court judged that subsection 6 of the first paragraphs of Article 13 of the Advocates Law was unconstitutional because it contravened the following articles of the Constitution: Article 13 which provides that work is a right, a duty and an honour guaranteed by the state; Article 47 which provides that freedom of opinion is guaranteed and that every human being has the right to express his opinion and to publicize it within the law; Article 54 which provides for citizens' right to private assembly; and Article 56 of the Constitution which provides that the creation of syndicates on a democratic basis is a right guaranteed by law.

2 LAW NO. 6 OF 1997 AMENDING SOME RULES RELATING TO NON-RESIDENTIAL PROPERTIES

The value and duration of rents of built properties in Egypt are subject to strict legislative constraints which have resulted in the near total rejection by landowners of building for "lease" and the prevailing tendency to build for "ownership" at sale prices which are beyond the financial means of most Egyptians.

This state of affairs has naturally resulted in an acute crisis, which led to the promulgation of Law No. 6 of 1997 with a view to improving the situation of built property owners, and encouraging them to "lease" rather than to sell, as well as to deal with the effects of a Supreme Constitutional Court decision which ruled that the perpetual extension of leases in non-residential properties (in accordance with Article 29 of Law No. 49 of 1977 regulating the relationship between landlords and lessees) was unconstitutional with retroactive effect.

Article 1 of this law amends the above-mentioned Article 29 of Law No. 49 of 1977 with retroactive effect and provides that the lease contract of non-residential properties is only extended in case of the decease of the lessee to his heirs up to the second degree who use the premises for the same purpose as that of the original lessee, whether by themselves or by their representatives.

Moreover, Law No. 6 of 1997 provides that such extension of the lease may only occur once as from the date of publication of this law.

Article 2 of Law No. 6 of 1997 aims at reducing the grave effects resulting from application of the first paragraph of its Article 1 with retroactive effect, in conformity with the Supreme Court's decision.

Finally, Article 3 of the law increases the rents of non-residential rented properties from 10 per cent (for properties built between 10 September 1977 and 31 January 1996) up to eight times the rent (for properties built before 1 January 1994).

Moreover, the law provides that those rents shall be increased by a yearly 10 per cent.

3 THE LAW ON INVESTMENT GUARANTEES AND INCENTIVES NO. 8 OF 1997[1]

Egypt is undergoing major changes in its economic policies for the purpose of encouraging foreign investment and accelerating development.

This new climate entailed a review of a number of laws, including the Investment Law No. 230 of 1989 which was replaced by the Law on Investment Guarantees and Incentives No. 8 of 1997.

This new law does not revolutionize the investment climate in the Arab Republic of Egypt, but is the result of experience gained in the execution of the previous investment law and of the necessity to amend a number of its rules that no longer reflect the prevailing liberalization of the Egyptian economy and in particular the freedom of dealings in foreign exchange.

---

[1] The law is fully set out in Part III, p. 517.

4 LAW NO. 3 OF 1998 AMENDING SOME RULES OF THE LAW CONCERNING JOINT STOCK COMPANIES, PARTNERSHIPS LIMITED BY SHARES AND LIMITED LIABILITY COMPANIES PROMULGATED BY LAW NO. 159 OF 1981[2]

The establishment of Egyptian joint stock companies, partnerships limited by shares and limited liability companies had first to be approved by an administrative committee formed and regulated in accordance with Law No. 159 of 1981.

This law also provided that the subscribers in joint stock companies had to pay, on subscription, a minimum of 25 per cent of the nominal value of the monetary shares and that the capital may not be increased, in general, except after full payment of the issued capital.

The new amendment of Law No. 159 of 1981 reflects the liberalization of the Egyptian economy and the present policy of limiting administrative interference in business relations. The new law allows the establishment of the above-mentioned companies without the need, in general, for administrative approvals, and also provides for less stringent rules regulating joint stock companies.

---

[2] The law is fully set out in Part III, p. 531.

Syria

*Jacques el-Hakim**

1 CIVIL PROCEDURE

1.1 Legalization of Powers of Attorney

Article 105, paragraph 1 of the Syrian Code on Procedure (1953) only authorized lawyers to represent parties before the courts if their mandate was evidenced by an authenticated deed. Paragraph 3 of the same article authorized the parties to appoint an attorney orally before the court, provided that appointment was recorded in the minutes of the hearing and signed by the respective party. However, the courts failed to enforce that provision to avoid collecting the fees and stamps due on powers of attorney. Therefore, the parties must execute a power of attorney before a notary public and have it legalized by the Syrian Foreign Ministry if it has been established outside Syria. The problem is that the Foreign Ministry fails to legalize the seal and signature of its embassies abroad before a security investigation has been conducted on the case, which requires several months or a year during which time all the proceedings regarding the power of attorney are stayed. Representatives of foreign companies or individuals executing a contract in Syria were therefore prevented from evidencing their capacity and carrying out their business. This is why, from the beginning of 1998, the Foreign Ministry started legalizing the powers of attorney established by a foreign party in favour of another foreign party. That measure did not, however, solve the problem of litigants residing abroad who must still wait several months before their attorney can protect their interests before the local courts or state agencies or organizations.

---

* Professor of Law, Damascus University.

1.2 Attachment of the public sector's entities

Under Legislative Decree No. 12 of 23 January 1972, properties of the public sector's entities can be attached if the three following conditions are fulfilled:

(a)   the entity has the status of a merchant;
(b)   the judgment is final; and
(c)   the judgment is rendered in a commercial matter.

The Central Bank of Syria has been created by legislative Decree No. 87 of 23 March 1953. Article 61, paragraph 2 provides that "it will be regarded as a merchant in its relationship with third parties". The Court of Appeal of Damascus has rendered a judgment (No. 309 of 9 May 1998) authorizing the attachment of the properties of the Central Bank to enforce a judgment ordering it to pay the difference in the rate of exchange of two transfers received by the bank and paid to the beneficiary at a lower rate.

2 LABOUR LAW

Under Legislative Decree No. 49 of 3 July 1962, an employer cannot dismiss an employee without the approval of a Commission of Dismissals held at the Labour Ministry in which only the President is a judge. This Commission rejects virtually all requests for dismissals and the Court of Appeal seldom annuls its judgments. Authorization is not needed when the employee has been employed for a determinate period which has never been renewed, or when the employee reaches the age of 60. As long as authorization has not been delivered, the Commission can order the employer to pay 80 per cent of the employee's salary until a final judgment is rendered in his case. On the other hand, the employer is forbidden to close down without being authorized to do so by the Labour Ministry, which usually requires the previous agreement or resignation of all his employees against a substantial compensation.

Even in the case of a criminal offence, the employee cannot be dismissed without the previous authorization of the Commission of Dismissals, which often grants him 80 per cent of his salary pending final decision in the criminal case, which may be delayed for several years. This has recently been confirmed by the Court of Cassation (Labour Chamber) in judgment No. 558 of 30 September 1997, in which it ruled that the employer (a private school) should pay one of its employees 80 per cent of his salary although he had hit one of the students and caused him minor injuries and has been condemned therefore by the Criminal Court of Appeal, pending confirmation of the judgment by the Court of Cassation.

3 COMMERCIAL LAW

3.1 Capital increase of a joint stock company

Article 222, paragraph 2(a) of the Commercial Code provides that the capital increase in a joint stock company (*société anonyme*) must be decided by an extraordinary shareholders' meeting and ratified by the Minister of Supply and Domestic Trade ("the

Minister") as any other amendment of the bylaws (Article 251, paragraph 1 of the Commercial Code). The Minister's decision can be challenged before the State Council in case of "abuse of authority" (*excès de pouvoir*) within fifty days of its publication in the Official Gazette. Before it is annulled, the enforcement of the shareholders' decision cannot be stayed by a court order (Article 223, paragraph 3 of the Commercial Code). A Syrian joint stock company decided on a capital increase, its decision was approved by the Minister and the decree of approval was duly published in the Official Gazette and in the Commerce Registry without being challenged by any shareholder. Some of the company shares had been seized by the state as per a legislative Decree (No. 23 of 25 January 1965) following the adoption of socialism in Syria, which transferred to the state (represented by the Directorate of Seized Assets at the Finance Ministry) the right to dispose of the seized assets. It is therefore the state representative who always exercised the seized shareholders' rights in the company from the date of that measure (1965) and voted at the shareholders' meeting which decided that capital increase. Nevertheless, some of those shareholders applied to the Civil Court asking that the capital increase be annulled (because they were still the legal owners of their shares although the state has the right to dispose of them) and that the enforcement of that increase be stayed pending final decision on their claim (which may last several years or decades). In a judgment dated 22 June 1998 (case No. 1823) the Damascus Court of Appeal decided to stay enforcement of the capital increase on the ground that the stay of execution was only a temporary measure which did not affect the merits of the case. That judgment will certainly be appealed before the Court of Cassation on the grounds that it violates Article 223 of the Commercial Code and Article 8 paragraph 6 of the Law organizing the State Council (Law No. 55 of 21 February 1959) which gives the Council exclusive jurisdiction in claims of annulment of final administrative decisions.

3.2 Time limitation for cheques

In Syrian law, obligations are time-barred after a period of fifteen years from the date they fall due (Article 372 of the Civil Code) and a period of ten years if they are commercial (Article 345 of the Commercial Code). The obligation arising from a cheque is formally commercial since it is subject to the provisions of the Commercial Code (Articles 514 to 567) but it is time-barred in a shorter period which is:

(a)   three years from the date the cheque is payable (between eight and ten days – Article 532 of the Commercial Code) in the relationship between the bearer and the drawer (Article 557, paragraph 1 of the Commercial Code).
(b)   six months in the bearer's relationship with the drawer, endorsers or other debtors (Article 557, paragraph 2 of the Commercial Code).

However, the ten-year period is only applicable if the drawer has failed to provide covering funds (provisions) or has withdrawn it or if the debtor has realized an unjust profit (Article 557, paragraph 4 of the Commercial Code).

A recent decision of the Court of Cassation (judgment of the commercial section No. 803 of 27 October 1997) has defined the statute of limitation for a cheque which did not contain all the statements necessary for its validity. In that case, the cheque did not mention the place where it was drawn (Article 514/c of the Commercial Code) and did not state the drawer's address, which is deemed to be the drawing place if it is not mentioned explicitly in the cheque (Article 515/c of the Commercial Code). Due to a dispute between the bearer and the drawer, the latter instructed the bank to block the amount and refuse payment. The bearer did not object for more than ten years, and then asked for payment of the amount. The drawer objected that the document was not legally a cheque since it did not mention the place where it was drawn from or the drawer's address.

The bearer replied that since the document was not a cheque, it nevertheless established an ordinary debt which was only time-barred after fifteen years from the date it fell due. The drawer contended that since the debt was originally commercial and since it was embodied in a cheque, it should be regarded as commercial and time-barred after ten years from the date it fell due. He also offered to give testimonial evidence on the nature of the debt. However, the Court of Cassation, adopting the grounds set in the judgment of the Court of Appeal:

(a)   did not authorize the drawer to prove the commercial nature of his debt;
(b)   ruled that the blocking of the cheque by the drawer was equivalent to the lack of funds and that the cheque would only be time-barred after fifteen years from the elapse of the payment period.

3.3 Interest on a deposit account

Due the laws restricting transfer of foreign currency abroad, many foreign firms deposit their local returns in a local bank (usually the Central Bank of Syria (CBS) which is state-owned and has a monopoly over commercial bank operations) pending their hypothetical transfer abroad when the Central Bank provides the necessary foreign currency – which virtually never occurs. A foreign airlines company had opened with CBS a deposit (cheque) account at 4 per cent interest and has continuously received, over several years, account statements recording the interest paid for the last period. All of a sudden, CBS informed the company that its management had decided unilaterally to cancel the interest and to withdraw from its account the interest already paid for the pervious periods, on the contention that the deposit of funds was provisional and did not yield interest since it was supposed to be transferred within a short period. The company objected that such an interpretation was contrary to the facts since the amounts deposited had been with the bank for several years and that the bank could not unilaterally violate the stipulations of its agreement with the company. Furthermore, even in the absence of such an agreement, Article 402, paragraph 3 of the Commercial Code expressly provided for the payment of interest in all deposit accounts "from the day following each deposit" and CBS could not avoid the enforcement of that provision particularly since it was the only bank authorized to receive deposits in commercial matters. In judgment No. 419 of 7 October 1997, the First Degree Civil Court of Damascus confirmed those submissions and ordered CBS to pay interest on the company's deposits. CBS has appealed the judgment.

4 INTELLECTUAL PROPERTY: TRADEMARKS

Syria has ratified the Paris Convention on Industrial Property of 20 March 1883 (Legislative Decree Nos. 14 for 1931 and 153 for 1939) and has issued a law (Legislative Decree No. 47 of 10 October 1946) governing matters which do not fall under the international provisions. Under these provisions, the legitimate owner of a trademark which has been deposited in someone else's name has two means to object thereto:

(a)   to file a claim before the State Council (Court of Administrative Disputes) asking that the decree of the Minister of Supply and Domestic Trade authorizing the deposit of the mark be annulled for "abuse of authority" (*excès de pouvoir*) within sixty days from its publication in the Official Gazette;
(b)   to file a claim before the First Degree Civil Court within five years from the deposit, asking for its cancellation due to the plaintiff's previous use of the mark. Such a claim can be presented to the First Degree Civil Court even after the elapse of the five years if the plaintiff establishes in writing that the depositor did not ignore his rights on the mark when he deposited it in his own name.

In addition, the owner of a mark duly deposited in Syria can complain about the undue use, registration or imitation of his mark by a third party, before either the criminal courts or the civil courts.

In a recent case, the owner of a mark called "Cruz di Malta" applied to a *yerba mate* tea asked the State Council (Court of Administrative Disputes) to cancel the deposit of another mark called "Kharita" by a third party several years after its deposit.

The defendant challenged that claim because:

(a)   the State Council did not have jurisdiction over disputes between individuals or private entities;
(b)   assuming that the claim was directed against the Minister's Decree authorizing the deposit of the mark, it had not been presented within sixty days from the publication of that decree; and
(c)   the "Malta Cross" used by the plaintiff as a trade mark represented the official emblem of a public international entity (the Sovereign and Military Order of the Knights of Malta) which cannot be used and is protected as a trademark.

On 25 September 1997, the Court of Administrative Disputes rendered a judgment under No. 31, staying execution of the decree authorizing the deposit of the mark for alleged imitation of the plaintiff's mark and the Higher Administrative Court in a judgment of 1 December 1997 rejected the appeal filed against that decision. That judgment constitutes a dangerous innovation in the law on trademarks because it obviously violates the law on the jurisdiction of the State Council and authorizes the stay of a mark deposit several years after the maximum period set for objecting thereto.

Iraq

Sabah Al-Mukhtar*

1 CONSTITUTIONAL AND ADMINISTRATIVE LAW

1.1 National Emblem

In accordance with Article 3 of the Emblem of the Republic of Iraq, Law No. 85 of 1965 new Statutory Regulations No. 3 of 1997 were gazetted on 17 November 1997. The Regulations specify the occasions, places and documents on which the emblem must be used.

1.2 Local People's Council

Law No. 25 of 1995[1] (page 190 of 1996 Yearbook) was amended by Law No. 14 of 1997. The law gave the Council of Ministers to issue the rules and procedures governing the work of the local people's councils. Before the amendment these were decided by each council, which issued its own rules and procedures.

The central government rules and procedures were issued by means of Statutory Regulation No. 3 of 1998. They detail the frequency of meetings, order of precedence, seating arrangements, quorums, recording and minute taking. It also detail how and when the agendas are prepared and deviates from rules on debates, speeches, interruptions, suggestion and voting. They set out the immunities for the members and the circumstances in which they may be removed. They list the committee that are to be set up and the procedures for their deliberations and workings.

---

* Member of the Iraqi Bar and Arab Lawyers Federation; Legal Consultant in Iraqi, Arab and Islamic Law; Founding Member and Partner of Arab Lawyers Network, London; Chairman, Arab Lawyers Association, London.
[1] See the *Yearbook*, vol. 3 (1996), p. 190.

1.3 National census

Iraq carries out a national census every ten years as recommended by the UN. The first was that of 1937 and sixth was in 1997. For this purpose RCC Resolution No. 13 of 1997 set up the Higher Census Committee headed by the deputy Chairman of the RCC, with the Deputy Prime Minister, Ministers of the Interior and of Information, chairmen of the legislative council of the Autonomous Regions and representatives from other departments being members. A budget of 1.5 billion Iraqi dinars was allocated for this purpose. The necessary powers and authorities were vested in the committee to ensure that the census take place of time.

Presidential Decree 225 of 1997 declared 16 October a national holiday for the purpose of carrying out the census and a curfew was imposed on that day.

The census was carried out by almost 160,000 government employees. The official census form contained eighty questions relating to personal, family, ethnicity, education, income, housing and employment matters.

Subsequently it was officially announced that the population of Iraq was 22,170,764 excluding the areas of the north which are outside the control of the central government. FAO's census shows there are some 3.1 million people in that region. These figures show an increase in the population of Iraq of about 5 million since the 1987 census thereby giving about a 3 per cent annual increase in the population.

1.4 Cabinet reshuffle

The first cabinet reshuffle took place when the Minister of Labour and Social Services, Mr Latif N. Jassim, was replaced by Mr M. Abdul Hameed Al-Saigg as of 1 January 1997.

The second cabinet reshuffle was carried out in August 1997. By means of five RCC Resolutions (187–191) Mr Hamid Hammadi, who was Minister of Culture and Information, became "Advisor to the President". Dr Humam Abdul Ghafour, who was Minister of Scientific Research and Higher Education, became Minister of Culture and Information. The Minister of Education, Dr Abdul Jabar Mohammed, who was the Education Minister, became the Minister of Scientific Research and Higher Education. Dr Fahad Al-Shaghaa was appointed Minister of Education.

1.5 National service

Law No. 32 of 1996 which came into effect on 6 January 1997 provides that members of the Iraqi Air Forces who serve in the fighting militia called the "Saddam Commandos"[2] will be deemed to be in continuous military service in the armed forces.

Revolutionary Command Council ("RCC") Resolution No. 86 of 1997 granted young men born in 1979 in the Autonomous Regions the right to apply for the

---

[2] See the *Yearbook*, vol. 3 (1996), p. 194.

postponement of national service rather than serving now or risking being considered "deserters". All Iraqi 18-year-olds must do their national service at that age or as soon as completing their education if they were still students.

Young men who are outside Iraq who are ineligible to do their national service may pay money in lieu of conscription. RCC Resolution No. 16 of 1998 has increased the amount from previous levels to the equivalent of $1,000 (almost 1.5 million dinars).

1.6 Think tank

Two RCC Resolutions (72 and 99 of 1997) established two new departments attached to the presidential office which are believed to be presidential think tanks. Further Statutory Instructions were gazetted detailing the composition of the two departments. The first is called "Civil Service Reserve Department" and the second "Reserve Service Department". The first is made up of senior civil servants of the grade of director general and higher who have served in that capacity for at least seven years and who either wish to retire or are otherwise unable to continue in full time work. The Resolution includes all persons who fulfil these conditions starting with the beginning of Gulf war against Iraq on 17 January 1991.

The Reserve Service Department is made up of those who were ministers or had special "grades" and also senior military officers of the rank of major general and higher. Members of these departments have a number of privileges and prerogatives. If any of them had not completed the length of service necessary to secure a full pension he may do so by adding this service to his earlier one. When members reach the age of retirement they may continue to receive the full salary they were receiving when they were in active service. After leaving these departments they will receive 80 per cent of their salary for the duration of their natural lives.

1.7 Savings linked to the price of gold

RCC Resolution No. 71 of 1997 provides that the Ministry of Finance is to establish a number of special saving accounts in which the Ministry deposits monthly Iraqi dinars that are equal to 50 per cent of the total salary of all state employees. On the day of deposit the said amounts will be evaluated to the price of gold on the free market. One year later, or when the sanctions are lifted, whichever is the earlier, these gold linked amounts shall be revalued according to the then prevailing price of gold on the market and the resulting number of dinars will be paid out to each of these employees.

This seems to be a promise to give a 50 per cent increase in salaries after September 1998 but taking into consideration the value of the Iraqi currency in relation to the price of gold. This resolution also applies to the President, the ministers and members of the Baa'th party politburo.

The Minister of Finance issued instructions No. 9 of 1997 to facilitate the implementation of the RCC Resolution. They provide that the deposits will attract a 10 per cent interest. They also direct government departments to set up accounting procedures to ensure that each state employee is informed of the amount being deposited on his behalf.

1.8 The Ministry of Industry and Minerals

The Ministry was reorganized by Law No. 8 of 1997 to deal with the present day needs of Iraq. The last time the Ministry was reorganized was in 1988 (RCC Resolution 333). Since then Iraqi industry has been almost obliterated by the Gulf war in 1991, the systematic destruction by the special UN Commission UNSCOM which has over the last seven years not only destroyed the military industry of Iraq but also the rest of the industry unless UNSCOM was satisfied that the industry was absolutely and totally for civilian purposes and that it was not capable of being converted or considered a dual use industry. The destruction included most of the mineral extraction industries, including oil, sulphur, phosphate, glass and others.

The new law is aimed at putting the industrial policy for the nation and regulating state-owned industry as well as private and mixed sector industry. The law sets out the Ministry's obligations, authorities and duties. The organization includes the Ministry's head office and almost sixty state-owned entities. The sectors of industry include: clothing, carpets, milk products, vegetable oil, cigarettes and tobacco, sugar, pharmaceuticals, tyres, phosphate, sulphur, fertilizers, petrochemicals, paper, steel mills, electrical, mechanical, cement, glass and the like. Many of the infrastructure industries are given public utility status with statutory rights such as legal powers of right of passage and compulsory purchase rights.

1.9 Working abroad

RCC Resolution No. 15 of 1998 established a Commission attached to the Minister of Foreign Affairs to regulate the work of Iraqis outside Iraq. In addition to five members who are senior civil servant from the Ministry of Foreign Affairs, the Commission has representatives from various ministries. The Commission is charged with establishing the rules under which senior civil and military personnel are seconded to regional and international organizations or to permit their employment by such organizations. It is also charged with considering the working conditions of Iraqi expatriates working outside Iraq and granting them permission to do so against a fee which needs to be renewed biannually. The Commission is also charged with considering the means of strengthening the links between Iraqis abroad and the motherland by passing changes to the existing legislation. The Commission has a wider mandate than it predecessor, the committee on "work and scholarships".

1.10 Automatic naturalization of Arabs

Iraqi naturalization of Arabs No. 5 of 1975 was amended by Law No. 12 of 1997 to speed up the process of granting of Iraqi nationality to foreigners of Arab origin. It provides that:

Any Arab, except Palestinians may apply for naturalisation provided that he has attained 18 years of age, born to parents who both Arabs and still lives in the Arab homeland. The minister of interior is obliged to grant such a person Iraqi nationality within three months. Should the Minister have reasons that warrant not granting nationality then he must refer the matter and his reason to the office of the President of the Republic.

1.11 The environment

The *raison d'être* of Law No. 3 of 1997 provides:

To give the environment the necessary protection and to protect nature and in particular water resources from contamination which will have beneficial effect on the health, wealth and development on the nation and to increase awareness via specialised agencies with necessary powers and authorities to active those aims.

The Environment Protection and Improvement Law No. 3 of 1997 repealed the earlier Law No. 76 of 1986. The law established a national Environment Protection and Improvement ("EPI") Council which is attached directly to the Council of Ministers and is headed by the Minister of Health. It has a high ranking civil servants representing the main ministries (agriculture, industry, interior, education, oil foreign affairs, information, etc.). It also has independent persons who are specialists in environmental issues.

The law further provides for the establishment of local government EPI Council in each of the eighteen governorates of Iraq. The National EPI Council has duties and powers set out in detail along with its objectives, which include making national policy for protecting the environment which is then implemented by the relevant ministries and local government EPI Council.

The law contains wide definitions of pollution and pollutants. It obliges all government and private entities to provide all necessary information to the Council and to implement its instructions. The law also provides for penalties which include fines and prison sentences as well as the recovery of cost of cleaning up operations.

Statutory Regulations No. 1 of 1998 was passed by the Council of Ministers detailing the organization and structure and the EPI Council. The Regulations established a number of centres for the protection of natural resources, centres for studies, and environmental laboratories. The Nuclear Protection Centre was therefore established to deal with the serious problem that Iraq is facing because of contamination by and presence of radioactive material in the Iraqi soil and water, air and vegetation resulting from the use of depleted uranium by the US and British forces during the Gulf war against Iraq in 1991.

Statutory Instructions No. 4 of 1997 (17 November 1997) established local government EPI Councils in each of the Iraqi governorates. This was followed by Ministerial Instructions of the Minister of Health No. 1 of 1998 (9 March 1998) setting out the functions of the local government EPI Councils.

2 JUDICIARY AND JUDICIAL SYSTEM

2.1 Judiciary under siege

The judicial system in Iraq has in fact passed the point of breakdown. It suffers from dilapidated buildings, shortage of equipment, furniture, law books and even paper and stationery and every conceivable requirement of a court. The most serious problem is the shortage of manpower. There are no judges, lawyers, administrators or supporting staff to man the system.

2.2 Salary for life

To enable the senior members of the judiciary to cope with the effect of the current hyperinflation and collapse of the currency, and their effect on the standard of living, RCC Resolution No. 120 of 1997 was gazetted on 1 September 1997. The Resolutions provide that the president and members of the Court of Cassation and all other senior judges (Grade A), shall continue to receive the same salary, even if they retire because of old age.

2.3 Court delay

RCC Resolution No. 18 of 1997 was gazetted on 24 March 1997 to empower the courts to deal aggressively with delays in proceedings. It provides that "in the case where one party to a suit applies repeatedly for adjournments, the court may infer that such a party has a weak case and take such inference into consideration when giving judgment".

The courts are also empowered by this Resolution to impose a financial penalty on in-house counsel who has the conduct of a case involving his department if he is found to be causing the delay by his negligence.

The courts are obliged by RCC Resolution No. 669 of 1987 to adhere to the ceiling determined by the rules and practices of the courts, issued from time to time, except where the delay is attributable to the parties.

2.4 Abolishing of fines

The Penal Code of Iraq No. 111 of 1969 was amended by RCC Resolution No. 5 of 1998, which provides "Wherever a fine is prescribed as a penalty in the Penal Code No. 111 of 1969, it shall be replaced by a prison sentence as a penalty provided that the prison term shall not exceed three days in the case of minor offences" (*Mukhalafa*).

2.5 Lawyers' fees

The Iraqi Bar Association No. 173 of 1965 was amended by Law No. 15 of 1997. This is the fourteenth amendement to the law. The amendment has two aims: the first is to enable for the first time in-house counsel in government departments and public sector entities to represent their departments in court cases and determine the fees payable to them. Prior to this amendement such lawyers had to pass the litigation to independent counsel to plead and defend. This was on the basis that should an independent counsel have a more objective view of a court case than an in-house counsel and also that he could not be influenced by internal management considerations.

The second aim is to increase the statutory ceiling of legal fees charged by and paid to independent counsel, to meet the present economic hardships resulting from the blockade of Iraq.

Subsequently (15 December 1997) the Ministry of Finance issued Statutory Instructions No. 10 of 1997 to facilitate the implementation of the law which provides for such instructions to be issued. The instructions set out the scale of fees, ceilings, interim and progressive payment charges of counsel before or during the trial, final payment, appeals, etc.

2.6 National Audit Bureau code of conduct

A code of conduct for members of the Bureau was gazetted on 10 March 1997. It detailed the professional rules to be followed through out the stages of audit (planning, management, follow up, reporting, note taking, etc.) It imposed the obligation to follow the instructions of the board and President of the Bureau. It called on the auditors to continue to update their knowledge and professional abilities. It stressed the independence and impartiality of the auditors, prohibited undertaking any other work or accepting any gifts or presence. It called for absolute discretion and for the work to be carried out with utmost secrecy. The members of the board are to have exemplary behaviour and maintain the highest standard in their personal conduct. They must reduce their social associations and must not have any with those under audit. The code sets out the objectivity expected from the auditors which must also be seen to be so. It lists the manner and procedures with which auditing must be carried out. The code sets out the acts which will not be excused; these, *inter alia*, include failure to report violations, take initiatives, follow up violations, investigate the individuals concerned, report accounting and calculation mistakes and breach of trust. The code also sets out a system of penalties which begins with administrative reprimand and escalates into fines, delay of promotion, or being discharged from service. This is notwithstanding the application of the relevant provisions of the criminal code and other legislation.

2.7 Planning and building licences

RCC Resolution No. 53 of 1997 extended the validity of RCC Resolution No. 37 of 1987 (which was valid for a period of ten years) for a further five years. Under this legislation a heavy fine is imposed on the owner, the contractor and the architect of any building work which is carried out without the necessary licence or if it violates town planning regulations. Such a violation will also have to be removed. These decisions are imposed by the municipality of Baghdad and although subject to administrative appeal to the municipality itself, the ordinary courts are barred from hearing such cases.

3 COMMERCIAL LAW

3.1 New Companies Law

At the end of September 1997 a new Companies Law No. 21 of 1997 was gazetted. The new law is in fact very similar to its predecessor. It was promulgated to give the private sector a "better opportunity to take a more effective role in the national economic development programme and the economic activities within the national plan" according to the *raison d'être* of the law. The new law is, *inter alia*, aimed at dealing with the "defects that became apparent from the implementation of the 1983 law". Another aim of the law is to regulate "investment companies", to which the 1983 law made no reference.

It is to be noted that the tone of the law shows a shift from the "socialist" one of its predecessor. Further, instead of amending the proceeding law, which was possible, considering the limited changes, the government chose to publish a whole new law that is more readily available.

The new law has 221 articles and came into effect on 28 December 1997. It is divided into eight parts that are divided into chapters and many are further divided into sections. The first three articles of the law state the objective and its application as "this law shall apply to private and mixed sector companies". Article 4 defines the company as: "A contract between two or more persons to participate in an economic enterprise where each contributes assets of work to divide the profit or loss resulting there of." However, a natural person may exceptionally establish a "sole trading enterprise". The law confers on companies independent juridical personality as of there incorporation. There are principally four types of companies:

(a)   public company;
(b)   private limited liability company;
(c)   partnership company;
(d)   sole trading company.

Public companies and private limited companies may be owned by the private sector or are "mixed sector" companies where the state may own no less than 25 per cent of its share capital.[3]

The law deals with the various sectors of the Iraqi economy by giving special prominence to "financial investment companies". They are defined as the "intermediary financial entities" referred to in the Law of the Central Bank of Iraq No. 6 of 1976. Their

---

[3]   Public sector companies (fully owned by the state) are now the subject of a new Public Sector Companies Law No. 22 of 1997 which came into effect on 1 September 1997.

aim is limited "to direct savings towards investment in commercial instruments, stocks, shares, debentures and fixed assets". The law provides that banks, insurance and investment companies must take the form of public companies.

Membership of companies remains confined and limited to Iraqi nationals (however the need to be resident in Iraq has been removed); nationals of Arab states are treated as Iraqis.

All companies have to have a Constitution in the form of a memorandum and articles of association that are signed and deposited with the Registrar of Companies. The Registrar after approval will issue a certificate of incorporation that is also published in the *Companies Bulletin* as well as in a daily newspaper.

The third part of the law deals with the capital of the company and related matters. The capital must be specified in Iraqi dinars (no less than 50,000) paid or reserved solely for the fulfilment of the company's obligations. Debts and loans may not exceed three times the capital. The capital must be divided into equal shares of one dinar each. Public companies may after incorporation offer their shares at the Baghdad Stock Exchange. No one person may own more than 20 per cent of the capital of a company (5 per cent in investment companies). A shareholder's liability is limited to the value of the shares he owns in a public company or private limited company but it is unlimited in a partnership company and a sole trading company.

Public companies must offer to the public the remaining shares after the promoters have subscribed to 30–55 per cent in mixed sector companies and 20–51 per cent in private sector companies. Promoters are joint and severally liable for misrepresentations or failure to disclose relevant information in the prospectus.

If the subscribed shares do not reach at least 75 per cent of the nominal capital then the capital must be reduced to that subscribed unless the floatation is abandoned and in such instance the promoters bear the cost. Over-subscribed shares will be distributed proportionally among the subscribers. The commercial courts has the jurisdiction to deal with all matters arising from the flotation.

Articles 48–53 (Chapter 4) deal with payment of the capital of the company. At least 25 per cent of it must be paid on incorporation and at least 25 per cent must be subscribed to by the public. The remainder could be paid in interest bearing instalments within four years. Shares will otherwise be sold through the Baghdad Stock Exchange upon notice. In the case of private limited liability companies, partnership and sole trading companies the full capital must be paid before the certificate of incorporation is issued.

The capital which is fully paid up may be increased by a resolution of the general meeting of the company and new shares issued and paid for by the subscribers or from the reserves. New shares of a public company must be offered to the public within thirty days of the Registrar's approval and in the case of the other companies paid within thirty days.

The capital may also be reduced in cases of loss and other circumstances described in the law which details the procedures of so doing in Articles 58–63.

The shares of the promoters may be sold no earlier than the lapsed of two or the distribution of profit with certain restrictions. Priority for the purchase of shares in a private limited company is given to the other share holders. The shares are passed to the heirs in the event of the death of the owner and the sale and transfer of shares are all registered in the company's register of shares.

Sole trading companies and partnership companies are subject to more restrictive rules in respect of the sale and transfer of their shares (Article 70 and 71).

Shares of public companies and private limited companies may also be mortgaged. Liens may be created in cases where the shareholder is in debt and the court or the appropriate authority ask the company to mark its register of shares accordingly.

Before distributing profits, companies must set aside 5 per cent as reserve. Fifty per cent of the loss may be paid out from the reserves; however, should the losses reach 50 per cent of the capital, the Registrar of Companies must be warned and steps taken to remedy the situation. If the loss reaches 75 per cent of the company's capital then it must be liquidated or its capital reduced (Article 76). The company may issue bearer or registered debenture to borrow from the public.

The company has a general meeting of shareholders which is the supreme authority that must meet annually. The law details the rules regarding the call for such meeting, powers, notices, quorum, voting and proxy and the like (Articles 85–102). Minority shareholders rights are provided for in Article 100. The company is managed by a board of directors appointed by the general meeting. The law also provides for the allocation of certain management seats for the employees and the trade unions on the board of directors. The must have regular meetings and the rules, procedures, powers and duties are set out in Articles 103–120 of the law.

Companies are managed under Iraqi law by a chief executive who is appointed by the general meeting as "president" (usually referred to as the "manager") whose duties and powers are principally set out in Articles 121–124.

Companies are subject to statutory management auditing by the competent authority within the economic sector in which it operates (banking, agriculture, industry, tourism, etc.) (Articles 125–131). They are also subject to statutory external financial auditing that is carried out by the National Audit Office in the case of mixed sector companies or by a registered chartered accountant appointed by the general meetings (Articles 133–139). Finally, companies are subject to strict supervision by the Registrar of Companies through his wise statutory powers under Articles 140–164 (headed "Inspection").

Companies are wound up and struck off the register if they:

(a)   do not commence to trade within a year from incorporation or cease to do so for a year;
(b)   their objectives are fulfilled or become impossible;
(c)   are amalgamated or converted into a different type;
(d)   lose more than 75 per cent of their capital;
(e)   are placed in voluntary liquidation.

Amalgamation and conversion are defined and the procedures to be followed to as well as the rights and obligations of the company, its members and third parties are dealt with in Articles 148–157.

Liquidation including the powers and duties of liquidators, questions of liability and the disposal of the company's assets are detailed in Articles 158–180.

The law has general provisions relating to the registered office, company seal amending the constitution, vacancy of directors, etc. It also has a chapter containing "transitional provisions" which, *inter alia*, deals with branches of foreign companies. Finally there is an inevitable chapter dealing with penalties for violation of the provisions of the law.

The law provides in the last two articles that law No. 36 of 1083 is repealed and that the present law becomes effective ninety days after publication in the Official Gazette.

At the same time another important but details law was gazetted, namely, Law of Public Sector Companies No. 22 of 1997. This law provides that such companies are established with the approval of the Council of Ministers, their constitution is published, they are registered with the registrar of companies and their capital is paid by the Treasury. The law provides for the distribution of profit and deals with losses. It empowers these companies to issue bonds and stocks both within Iraq and outside. It details the management of such companies and the voting rights within its Board of Directors. It provides for auditing, amalgamation and conversion of such companies. Liquidation of these companies can only by achieved by a decision of the Council of Ministers of the Republic of Iraq.

3.2 Commercial Agency Law

Commercial Agency Law No. 26 of 1994 was amended by Law No. 18 of 1997. The amendment is aimed at granting an agency licence only to those who have experience and already have at least one agency. The amendment confines the licence to trading in one commodity, thereby ensuring a degree of specialization. Finally it confines the agent to having no more than five agencies at any given time.

3.3 Foreign currency bank accounts

Foreign companies have been permitted to bring into Iraq any amount of foreign currency. They are entitled to open current accounts in Iraqi banks in foreign currency. The balance on these accounts may be repatriated at any time without restrictions. This Ministry of Trade announcement was published in the Official Gazette No. 3690 dated 6 October 1997.

3.4 Baghdad Stock Exchange

Article 26 of the Baghdad Stock Exchange Law No. 24 of 1991 ("BSE") provided for Internal Regulations to be approved by the Ministry of Finance. The Regulations were approved and published on 29 March 1992. They have now been replaced by new Regulations that were approved and gazetted on 13 January 1997.

The Regulations set out the rules relating to listing and acceptance of financial instruments. These includes treasury bonds and other such instruments guaranteed by the treasury. Foreign instruments may be listed with the approval of the government and the board of BSE. Stocks and shares of Iraqi public companies may be listed with the approval of the board. To apply for listing companies must submit incorporation documents, resolutions, detailed reports about the activities of the company and its future plans. They must also submit their audited and certified accounts with auditor's reports that are approved by the general meeting of the company.

Before listing the company must give detailed undertakings which include compliance with BSE rules, prompt discharge of all financial obligations, provide the BSE with all notices to meetings, timely and full disclosure of annual accounts, reports, budgets, all minutes of annual meetings, changes to the board of directors, give prior notice of all major decisions affecting the financial standing of the company, etc. After approval the shares of the company may be traded on the floor after a period of fifteen days.

Companies, brokers and other intermediaries pay a registration fee and annual membership fees. The annual fees are in the range of 0.1 per cent of the capital of the company or broker's fees. Brokerage is determined by the board of the BSE and is about 1 per cent of the value of the shares and 0.4 per cent of the value of traded stocks.

The BSE is managed by a board that meets at least once a month. It has the power to establish the rules, specify financial obligations, determine policy, and control the trading floor. The chairman and members of the board are assisted by the director-general and executive departments. The regulations sets out the qualifications, rights and obligations of brokers including disciplinary measures and complaints.

Trading on the floor is limited to the listed instruments, by admitted traders within the opening hours only. The regulations classify the sale and purchase order as ordinary, not ordinary, special and reciprocal. The BSE issues a daily bulletin showing the operations undertaken in the previous day. The BSE has a centralized clearing office with representatives of member companies. All concerned have to sign annually a full disclosure of their financial status. The regulations contain general provisions dealing with such matters as setting up committees, confidentiality requirements, prohibitions and discipline.

3.5 Customs and Excise

The Economic Committee of the Councils of Ministers issued a new tariff (No. 16) for importing goods (Official Gazette 3661 of 17 April 1997). The tariff ranges between 10 per cent for books and children clothes and 200 per cent on fresh fruits and soft drinks. Some of these tariffs were increased on 14 July 1997. All goods of Arab origin are subject to 10 per cent lower tariffs (Official Gazette of 2 March 1998).

The Minister of Finance announced (Official Gazette No. 3663 of 31 March 1997) that to prevent smuggling a border zone of 70 km wide along the desert border with Syria, Jordan and Saudi Arabia which is called a "customs controlled area". The width of the zone is reduced to 30 km on the border with Kuwait and to 20 km on the Iranian and Turkish side.

3.6 Tax

The exemption from income tax which was granted to doctors and dentists practising privately was abrogated (Official Gazette No. 3663) as of the 1997 financial year.

Sales tax of 10 per cent has been imposed by RCC Resolution No. 36 of 1997. The tax applies to all services provided by first class hotels. Statutory Instruments

No. 7 of 1977 were gazetted (4 August 1997) by the Ministry of Finance to facilitate the implementation of the Resolution.

4 LABOUR LAW

4.1 Water charges

Water charges have been increased, especially for commercial and industrial consumers. The amounts so collected are to be distributed to the employees of the Water
and Sewerage Department (RCC Resolution No. 9 of 1997). The distribution is
carried out in accordance with Statutory Instructions No. 8 of 1997 (Official Gazette
3673). These SI are just one of a number of such instruments dealing with distribution of income generated by the state departments to supplement the salary of government employees. These Statutory Instructions are referred to as "Incentive Instructions". Among these instruments are those related to employees of the banking
sector (SI 6 of 1997 OG 3678), Ministry of Culture and Information (SI 1 of
1997 (amendment) OG 3683), Ministry of Justice (SI 2 of 1997 (amendment) OG
3695). The Ministry of Minerals and Industry had similar incentive instructions but
they took the form of an RCC Resolution No. 51 of 1997.

In other instances to encourage inventors, innovators and to promote initiatives, lump sum amounts are being offered and paid to state employees who display such qualities. One such instance is that the Ministry of Communications offered payment to the employees in the telephone and communication establishment
when they managed to in keep the communications working in the absence of spare
parts and new equipment (RCC No. 8 of 1997).

4.2 Exit visas

The exit visa fee which is payable by Iraqi nationals leaving the country (amounting to ID 400,000) may be waived by the Presidential Office (RCC 7 of 1997).

At the same time Iraqi Passport Regulations No. 61 of 1959 where amended
to reflect the issuance of a new edition of Iraqi passports (which are now printed
within Iraq instead of overseas printing) (Official Gazette 3660 of 10 March 1997).

5 LAW OF PROPERTY

5.1 Palestinians to own land

Two years after the end of the Gulf war by RCC Resolution No. 23 of 1994
(14.3.1994), Iraq suspended all legislation which permits non-Iraqis to own immovable assets, invest in Iraqi companies or any other form of ownership and investment. This obviously applies to the Palestinians who hold travel documents
whether issued by Iraq or other Arab states. RCC Resolution No. 133 of 13 September 1997 exempted the Palestinians who are resident permanently in Iraq and

their children who are resident with them and who are 18-years-old from the provisions of the 1994 Resolution. The present resolution permits such Palestinians to own land upon which a house may be built.

5.2 Ownership of property by foreigners

RCC Resolution No. 33 of 1997 amended the earlier resolution No. 23 of 1994 which prohibited foreigners from owning immovable assets or investing in Iraq. The amendment provides for the imprisonment of those who violate these provisions in addition to confiscating the assets concerned. This is thought to have become necessary to deal with the wave of such violations.

5.3 Pavement and rubbish collection

Owners of properties are obliged by RCC Resolution No. 184 of 1997 to pay the cost of maintaining and repairing pavements in front of their properties. The municipality may require the owners on the other hand to undertake the repairs, maintenance and improvement according to the specifications its sets out.

All non-domestic properties (factories, garages, restaurants, hotels, offices, workshops, stores, shops, etc.) are required to pay to the municipality monthly amounts ranging ID 500–8,000 for rubbish collection according to the notice published in the Official Gazette No. 3628. This is another example of raising income to pay for the employees of the state and local authorities.

6 CRIMINAL LAW

6.1 No bail for car thieves

RCC Resolution No. 157 of 1997 was gazetted to deal with the car theft epidemic. The Resolution prohibits the release on bail until the end of their trial, of those accused of car theft or in possession of stolen cars. The price of all cars (since none can any longer be imported) has soared to such an extent that the price of a used ordinary car is higher than that of a reasonable sized house with garden.

6.2 Amnesty

Kurdish members of the armed forces who had deserted and who are resident in the Kurdish area are given amnesty from prosecution if they return to the "national fold". Legal measures against them will be terminated in respect of all crimes except murder, rape and theft of public property. The amnesty is also offered to those whose present circumstances do not permit them to immediately benefit from such amnesty. This amnesty, which is one in a series offered to the Kurds, is thought to be directed at those who were recruited by the US Central Intelligence Agency.

6.3 Smuggling

To keep goods and assets from being sold outside Iraq, the government since the blockade of 1990, has prohibited the export or the taking out of the country all goods other than limited personal effects of those able to travel.

However, because of the collapse of the Iraqi currency, all goods of whatever nature are being smuggled and sold outside Iraq. Whatever price they are sold for in other countries actually represents a wealth in Iraqi currency. Smuggling includes every conceivable asset: machinery, livestock, food, books, consumer goods, pieces of art work, antiques, medicine, etc. Stringent measures, some of which are quite draconian, have been imposed over the years. In 1997 RCC Resolution No. 10 provides that the property movable and immovable of intermediaries who help in smuggling gold or hard currency through transfering such goods to others with a view of smuggling them outside Iraq are to be confiscated. However, if such a person informs the authorities within 180 days of the transfer of possession, he will be immune from prosecution and be entitled to keep the value of the gold and currency involved. Failure to do so on the other hand makes him, in addition to the confiscation, liable to a fine that equals half the value of the smuggled goods.

The Resolution provides for rewards to be paid to third parties discovering or informing about such activities.

Three months later (16 June 1997) the Ministry of Finance issued Statutory Instrument No. 5 of 1997 to facilitate the implementation of the Resolution.

Another Resolution No. 11 of 1997 granted the governors of the 18th governorate of Iraq the power to confiscate a herd of sheep intended to be driven out of Iraq. They are empowered to impose financial penalties which are not subject to judicial review by the ordinary courts.

RCC Resolution No. 39 of 1997 granted the armed services, security and police forces the right to confiscate oil products and the means of their transport if the products were transported to the northern part of Iraq which is controlled by the Kurdish rebels.

6.3.1 Tribal claim for compensation

Iraq had been encouraging tribal allegiance among its citizens to resist the American plots to overthrow the regime. However, this has given rise to the problem of individuals coming to the aid of or making claims for compensation when a fellow tribesmen is apprehended, detained or otherwise penalized by members of the law enforcement agencies. To remedy this problem RCC Resolution No. 29 of 1997 was gazetted on 7 April 1997. It provides: "Any person making a tribal claim against another who was acting in compliance with the law or orders given to him by a competent authority will be sentenced to no less than 3 years imprisonment."

Another RCC Resolution No. 169 of 1997 was promulgated to ban the tribal custom of firing shots in the air when there are occasion to celebrate (weddings, births, etc.) The penalty is a fine not exceeding one million dinars and the confiscation of the firearm. However, half the fine may be paid to the law enforcement agents who apprehend the culprit.

7 INTERNATIONAL LAW

7.1 Relations with the UN

In twelve months (June 1997–1998) the Security Council of the United Nations have issued ten resolutions.[4] They are:

UNSCR 1111	4 June 1996
UNSCR 1115	21 June 1996
UNSCR 1129	21 September 1996
UNSCR 1134	23 October 1996
UNSCR 1137	12 November 1996
UNSCR 1143	4 July 1996
UNSCR 1153	20 February 1997
UNSCR 1154	2 March 1997
UNSCR 1158	25 March 1997
UNSCR 1175	19 June 1997

The problem between Iraq and the UN seems to be insurmountable. Iraq accuses the Security Council and its instruments – the weapons inspectors, otherwise referred to as UNSCOM, headed by Ambassador Richard Butler and the sanctions committee (661 Committee) – of being instruments to implement US foreign policy. This policy is backed only by the UK government. These UN agencies accuses Iraq of "failure to comply with UN Resolutions" without specific reference to specific provisions of UN Resolutions. They accuse Iraq of withholding information and hiding weapons of mass destruction thereby threatening world peace. Apart from the non-specific and so far unsubstantiated assertions made by American and British politicians and the media, no weapons have been identified or discovered for at least the last two years. The inspectors have carried out almost ten thousand inspections and have almost five hundred surveillance cameras operating in important sites inside Iraq.

Iraq and the UN on behalf of the USA have a single item agenda but it is approached from exactly the opposite side. The USA, through the UN, is determined to keep the blockade of Iraq indefinitely at any price and regardless of what Iraq does of fails to do. Iraq, on the other hand, desperately wants (but is unable to achieve) an immediate end to the blockade, at any price and regardless of what Iraq does or fails to do.[5] In the meantime Iraq has lost almost 1.5 million people according to UN agencies (UNICEF, WHO, FAO) and NGOs, as a direct result of the blockade that is no less than a Middle Ages siege.

The situation (similar to two trains heading towards each other on the same track) manifests itself in repeated accusations that Iraq is not complying; the USA threatens to bomb it and then Iraq complies. October 1996 and February 1997 were vivid examples.

---

[4] The text of the eleven Resolutions are fully set out in Part III, p. 465.
[5] There is a catalogue of US official statements to the effect that sanctions will not be lifted as long as the present regime in Baghdad (usually referred to as Saddam Hussain) remains. Among them is the pronouncement of President Clinton in his speech on 15 November 1997.

Iraq's case is that under UNSCR 687 (Ceasefire Resolution of 3 November 1991),[6] it had three distinct disarmament obligations:

(a)   to destroy the weapons of mass destruction it possesses;
(b)   to disclose the history of its armament programme;
(c)   to be subject to a strict and indefinite monitoring system.

The blockade is linked solely to the first obligation, namely that once the weapons of mass destruction that Iraq posses have been destroyed then paragraph 22 of the Resolution must be implemented. That paragraph provides:

Decides upon the approval by the Council of the programme called for in paragraph 19 above and upon Council agreement that Iraq has completed all actions contemplated in paragraphs 8, 9, 10, 11, 12 and 13 above, the prohibitions contained in Resolution 661 (1990) shall have no further force or effect.

In fact it is not even possible to link the sanctions to the other two obligations as these two obligations are not time linked and they could stay in effect for a very long time while the blockade, which is killing people, must have a time limit and be removed as soon as possible.

UNSCOM, on the other hand, has for more than three years now been refusing to confirm to the Security Council that there are no weapons left to be destroyed. The President of UNSCOM argues that since he is not "certain" that there are no weapons left, he is not in a position to confirm this to the Council. It is to be noted that over the last eight years every report which was submitted to the Security Council stated what has not been done without making any reference whatsoever to what has been achieved. Iraq for the last three years has been expected to "prove it is innocent". Additionally it is already being "punished" because Ambassador Butler still suspects Iraq is not innocent.

UNSCOM inspectors have over the years moved from being experts charged with disarming Iraq and monitoring its weapons production capability, to conducting more of a police homicide investigation. There is video footage which shows the inspectors examined private letters, personal files, waste paper baskets, women's handbags, books in university libraries and inspecting prisons, hospitals, chemistry laboratories in primary schools, convents and kindergartens. They have been described by those who came across them in Iraq as behaving like an occupation army.

Demands have been made by UNSCOM by way provocation to inspect the Iraqi Security Service, intelligence agencies, elite forces, offices of the President, ministers and presidential palaces. Iraq in many instances was forced into complying with these demands to avoid being hit by US Cruise and Tomahawk missiles if it did not yield. February 1998 saw one such incident where the US government formally announced that President Saddam Hussain has palaces in which he was hiding weapons of mass destruction including VX gas.[7] It announced that there are "sixty -three such palaces – some are larger than Washington.[8] UK Foreign Secretary Robin Cook on a visit to Hong Kong said on 22 January 1998 that: "Saddam is produc-

---

6   Text of UNSCR 687 is set out in full in this *Yearbook* vol. 1 (1994), p. 523.
7   US Secretary of Defence William Cohen 26 November 1997.
8   US Secretary of Defence William Cohen 23 November 1997.

ing sufficient anthrax to fill two war heads every week." The US at that time was poised to use its armada in the Gulf and was about to do so had it not been for the UN Secretary General's intervention. Iraq not surprisingly had to yield and agreed to the inspection.[8]

It is to be noted that

(a)   there are eight palaces throughout Iraq (not sixty-three);
(b)   the total area of all the palaces is less that 6 per cent of the area of Washington;
(c)   no anthrax or VX was found anywere or indeed could be produced in the palaces or anywhere else in Iraq.

The other aspect of the relationship between to Iraq and the UN related to UNSCR 986 (oil for food Resolution 14 April 1995). Although the blockade of Iraq in theory does not apply to food or medicine, Iraq's assets are frozen worldwide and many countries refuse to unfreeze any even for barter with food or medicine. Iraq is also prohibited from exporting oil, and thus earns no income to purchase the food or medicine it needs. The effect of these UN measures, is contrary to Article 54 of Protocol No. 1, addition to the Geneva Conventions, 1977, which states that: "Starvation of civilians as a method of warfare is prohibited". For this reason UN Security Council Resolution No. 986 permitted the export of oil from Iraq as "a temporary measure" to buy food and medicine. The Council was "concerned by the serious malnutrition and health situation of the Iraqi people, and by the risk of further deterioration in this situation". However, the Resolution has in fact granted to some UN bureaucrats, the sanctions committee (representatives of the twelve states on the Security Council) and some few hundred UN observers the right to be the new authority that has "mandate" over Iraq. They decide to whom Iraq can sell oil, at what price, to receive the money on its behalf, and deduct almost 40 per cent to pay itself and the UN Compensation Fund. From the remaining amount they decide what Iraq needs, buys, from whom, at what price, and then permit the supply to Iraq when they decide.

Aside from giving those bureaucrats an impossible task (a few hundred people to run by remote control from New York and Geneva the life of 22 million Iraqis), many are acting on behalf of the US and British governments who have the right to veto any matter by withholding approval.

Iraq views this situation as contrary to its right of sovereignty under the UN Charter, the Geneva Convention, the Convention on Genocide and many other rules of international law. Therefore conflict continues between Iraq and the UN in this area as well, due to the UN's failure to agree, approve, supply or release the food and medicine desperately needed for the civilians' survival.

Iraq, which had its capabilities and infrastructure severely destroyed in the name of UN (90 per cent of the electricity, 60 per cent of the oil industry, 80 per cent of the other industries, 80 per cent of the agriculture, 80 per cent of the telecommunications, 60 per cent of the health) eight years on is still not allowed to import the supplies needed for rebuilding, repair or rehabilitation of any of these vital areas.

---

[9]   Text of the Memorandum of Understanding between Iraq and UN is set out in full in Part III, p. 484.

This Resolution has now been extended for the fourth term (renewed every six months) while Iraq continues to complain that the "temporary measure" is becoming permanent to keep Iraq as a "mandate territory" of the USA through UN action.

7.2 Countries of the south

Iraqi ratified the Treaty Establishing the Centre of the South which was concluding on 1 September 1994. This was done by promulgating the Enabling Act Law No. 4 of 1997. The *raison d'être* states that Iraq has ratified the treaty in support of the work of the countries of the south and the non-aligned movement.

7.3 Arab Civil Aviation Authority

Iraq ratified the Treaty Establishing the Arab Civil Aviation Authority which is the regional body that was created and approved by the Council of the League of Arab States on 15 September 1994.

7.4 Bilateral treaty with the Russian Federation

Iraqi ratified the Treaty on Educational and Scientific Cooperation with the Government of the Russian Federation. The treaty was signed in Baghdad on 20 March 1997. It is aimed at expanding the relationship between the two countries and the field of science and education.

7.5 Montreal Treaty

Iraq has ratified the protocol amending the International Civil Aviation Convention signed in Montreal on 10 May 1984 by enabling Act No. 23 of 1997. Also Law No. 24 of 1997 ratified the other protocol signed in Montreal on 26 October 1990.

8 EDUCATION

8.1 Central education fund

A fund is established to supplement teachers pay and stabilize the profession, provide social and health support, assist and encourage research, writing and publishing of writings in the field of education. The fund, which was established by statutory instrument No. 4 of 1996 (gazetted 6 January 1997), is attached to the Ministry of Education but is run by an elected board of directors. The revenues of the fund is generated by school fees, charges for sports, social, scout and other extra curriculum activities in school. The revenues are distributed on the basis of 50 per cent is paid to the teachers and 20 per cent to play and primary schools.

Further, funds were subsequently created in each university for similar purposes of that of the education fund. This was done by Statutory Instructions 111 of 1997 issued by the Ministry of Higher Education and Scientific Research. However, the income of such funds are principally derived from allocating 85 per cent of the "college fees" payable in accordance with RCC Resolution No. 148 of 1996.

8.2 No free education

Iraq, which prided itself on universal free education from infancy to postgraduate university studies, can no longer afford even primary education without charging the pupils. For this reason, the provisions of the series of RCC Resolution promulgated in December 1996,[10] were expanded by a number of Statutory Instruments by the Ministries of Education and Higher Education and Scientific Research.[11] Further RCC Resolutions (77–82) of 1997 were promulgated for similar objectives.

The effect of these legislation may be summarized as follows:

(a) Any five Iraqis, at least one of whom must be an experienced teacher, may apply for a licence to establish a private school for languages or vocational training or to give private tuition. The number of applicants is reduced to three in the case of licensed playschool. Professional bodies, trade unions, charitable organizations, and recognized cultural and social societies may also be granted licenses. The buildings must meet certain health and safety requirements and the teaching and administrative staff be approved by the Ministry. Such schools may not accept foreign donations or aid without ministerial approval.
(b) All schools and other educational institutions were empowered by RCC Resolution 69 of 1996 to charge pupils and students school fees and to take other measures to generate revenues. The Ministry of Education issued statutory instruments which were gazetted on 16 June 1997 to facilitate the implementation of the Resolution. They give guidance of the activities which may be undertaken for profit. They also establish the rules of managing and expending the revenues earned.
(c) Further instructions (23 June 1997) set out guidelines for the fees to be charged for extra-curricular activities which the school may provide for its pupils.
(d) Acceptance of donations and aid by educational institutions must be unconditional and from recognized sources within Iraq. Foreign donations are subject to approval. These are the main provisions of a second Statutory Instructions published in the Official Gazette No. 3675 of 23 June 1996.

8.3 Consultancy bureaux in universities

Law No. 64 of 1979 (regulated University Research and Consultancy Bureaux), was replaced by new Law No. 7 of 1997. The earlier law established and regulated

---

[10] See the *Yearbook*, vol. 3 (1996), p. 205.
[11] Official Gazette 3674 and 3675.

principally engineering bureaux. The present law expanded the scope to include all the disciplines that are taught in all universities. This policy is directed at getting university teaching staff to be involved in more "applied" work in their field of specialization. It is also aimed at achieving total self-reliance to which Iraq is forced as a result of the UN Resolutions prohibiting the provision of consultancy or advisory work to Iraq in any fields of human knowledge. Law No. 7 of 1997 empowers and encourages all universities, colleges, institutes and other centres of learning to set up research, consultancy and advisory bureaux, either specialized or multi-disciplinary. Such bureaux are granted independent financial, administrative and juridical personality. They empowered to render their services to state-owned entities, private companies and individuals at commercial rates. They are run by managers who are chosen from members of the teaching staff, who hold professorial status in their own field, under the supervision of board of directors. Seventy-five per cent of the profit realized by these bureaux is distributed, tax free, to the academic staff. This in fact is the third objective of the policy of setting up these bureaux, namely to secure further income to the teaching profession at the university level. The law has come into force on experimental basis for a two-year period from publication. The promulgation of this law has in effect amended the Statutory Instrument of the Ministry of Higher Education and Scientific Research No. 104, 106 and 107 of 1997 (Official Gazette 3655, 3658 and 363 respectively).

8.4 National Computer Centre

Law No. 6 of 1997 amended Law No. 100 of 1972. The Centre which was originally attached to the Ministry of Planning, was in 1994 attached instead to the Ministry of Higher Education and Scientific Research. The amending law is aimed at redefining the objectives of the centre by putting more emphases on training and re-education. For almost a decade now, computers have been banned from being supplied to Iraq for any purpose whatsoever.

8.5 Saddam College for Religious Preachers

Law No. 19 of 1997 establishing a new college to teach and graduate Iraqis who wish to become religious preachers, imams and other religious orders.

8.6 National Students Union and Federation of Youth

Two laws, Nos. 26 and 27 of 1997, were gazetted and came into effect on 6 October 1997. The first organizes and regulates the activities of the national students unions. The second, Law No. 40 of 1986, the General Federation of Iraqi Youth, amalgamated the two bodies in 1986 to form the National Federation of Students' Union and Youth and was abrogated by the present legislation. Both bodies have independent juridical personality aimed principally at mobilizing the younger generation of the society. Membership is open to all Iraqis whose age qualifies them to become members (and are students for NSU membership). The objectives are to instill patriotic and nationalistic ideas, promote ethical and cultural values, improve education and social standards and promote contact with youth and students organizations outside Iraq. Each has a general council made up of all members which elects an executive bureau and has a general secretariat. The main source of finance is membership fees, government grants and revenues from activities.

8.7 Iraq satellite television

Not to be left behind by other Arab states, Iraq, despite the sanctions, decided to launch its own satellite television station. RCC Resolution No. 154 was gazetted on 23 December 1996 established Baghdad International Television. A year later Statutory Instrument No. 6 of 1997 were published on 1 December 1997 to facilitate the implementation of the Resolution. Experimental transmission is due to begin on the National Day (30 July 1998).

9 HEALTH

9.1 Cost of medical care

Iraqis for many years have enjoyed a health service of a very high quality by Middle East standards. It was generally advanced and was available totally free to all Iraqis and residents of Iraq and was repeatedly praised by World Health Organization. After almost eight years of blockade, the health service in Iraq has all but collapsed for lack of medicine, equipment staff and infrastructure. At present a health care of a sort is available in many private hospitals which are rapidly being established.

This seems to be encouraged as part of campaign that seems to be "privatization" programme which the government is pursuing. RCC Resolution No. 124 of 1997 empowered the Ministry of Health to convert state-owned hospitals to the equivalent of health trusts to become fund holding hospitals that are self-financing entities. Such hospitals are granted independent juridical personality, are run by a board of directors and have their own budgets. The income is derived from fees and charges levied for services, sale of medicine, revenue from rent of property, gift and loans. The profit of such a hospital is divided as follows:

–   50 per cent for developing the hospital;
–   25 per cent to the staff (income tax exempted);
–   20 per cent to other hospitals that are non-fund holders;
–   5 per cent to the Ministry's staff.

In addition to the above a percentage of the fees charged by the hospital is distributed tax free to the surgeons, doctors and nursing staff. Such distribution is treated as "cost" before calculating the profit of the hospital. These percentages are treated as "incentives"[12] and they range from 25 per cent of the fees charged for laboratory and X-ray services to 60 per cent of the fees are paid to operating surgeons and even to 70 per cent in the cases of care for premature babies.

---

[12] See Labour above.

For the overwhelming majority of the population, the state-owned and run hospitals remain the only source of medical care available. To be able to render such service all medical care in Iraq has now to be paid for by those who need it. For this purpose the Ministry of Health regularly issues price lists for operations, treatment, laboratories and X-ray services in-patient stays, fees for doctors, nurses and other staff and services.

There are four tariffs:

(i) for the general public in major general hospitals and these has the lowest tariff (OG 3688 of 11 August 1997);
(ii) for the general public in smaller hospitals and clinics outside cities (OG 3709 of 16 February 1998);
(iii) many of the major hospitals have began to treat people as "private patients" at much higher tariffs, thereby creating a two-tier healthcare system (OG 3653 of 20 January 1997);
(iv) non-Iraqis have to pay in foreign currency which is a still higher tariff (OG 3655 of 3 February 1997).

The income generated in non-fund holding hospitals, is also divided between the hospital (45 per cent) and the staff (45 per cent) according to the "incentive instructions".[13]

9.2 Saddam Cosmetic Surgery Centre

Statutory Instruments No. 1 of 1997 issued by the Minister of Health established this Centre in Wasitee Teaching Hospital in Baghdad. The Centre is aimed at providing an retraining Iraqi surgeons, physicians to deal with modern techniques and advancement in surgery relating to plastic and cosmetic surgery. The establishment of the Centre has become necessary to deal with two serious problems. The first is the huge number of defective births which are being encountered and which is thought to be linked to the use of depleted uranium by the British and American forces during Desert Storm campaign.

The second problem is the UN imposed prohibition on the supply of medical knowledge to Iraqi doctors. The medical knowledge is Iraq is frozen at the 1980s level, since even medical books, journals, conference attendance and other sources of knowledge are banned from being made available to the doctors of Iraq.

9.3 Alternative medicine

Because of the shortage of medicine due to the UN blockade, Iraqis have been forced to go back to traditional herbal medicine. That form of medicine had given way to modern chemical medicine since the 1950s and herbal medicine has all but disappeared.

Statutory Instructions No. 1 of 1997 issued by the Ministry of Health in accordance with Public Health Law No. 89 of 1981 are aimed at regulating the produc-

---

[13] See Labour above.

tion and sale of herbal medicine. They establish a licensing system for herbalists who meet the legal requirements and qualifications. They specify the rules for storage, packing and displaying in the shops. The instructions set out the rules relating to herbs in respect of contents, conditions, ingredients, hygiene, labelling and the like.

9.4 Eye transplants

To enable hospitals to remove the eyes of the dead for the purpose of transplant, the Eye Bank Law No. 113 of 1970 was amended by Law No. 11 of 1997. The amendment is aimed at permitting the removal of the eyes of those Iraqi nationals whose death sentence has actually been carried out. It also permits the removal of the eyes of mentally ill people who die in hospital when no one claims their remains.

9.5 Iraq Cancer Council

Law No. 25 of 1997 was gazetted to amend Law No. 63 of 1985 to expand the Council membership to include further medical disciplines. This has become necessary due to the 600 per cent increase in the cases of cancer in Iraq since the Gulf War. These cases have become a major health problem. The problem was further compounded by the UN prohibition on the supply of all chemotherapy drugs and equipment to Iraq on the grounds that such drugs and equipment could be used to produce nuclear weapons.

9.6 Epidemic and contagious diseases

Due to the precarious health conditions prevailing in Iraq because of the eight years of blockade, fear of the spread of epidemics is heightened. Therefore, new Health Statutory Instructions No. 3 of 1997 were gazetted (10 November 1997) listing those diseases for which reporting of their occurrence is mandatory. In accordance with the Public Health No. 89 of 1981 thirty-three diseases are classified into three categories for which reporting must be immediate within twenty-four hours or within seven days.

Jordan

Hamzeh Haddad

1 JUDICIAL AND LEGAL SYSTEM

No legislative changes or developments of interest have occurred under this title.

2 CONSTITUTIONAL AND ADMINISTRATIVE LAW

2.1 Regulation of Civil Service No. 1 of 1998

A decision reported under the heading "Commercial and Economic Law" (5.7) below is of relevance.

3 CIVIL LAW

4 CIVIL PROCEDURE AND EVIDENCE

No legislative changes or developments of interest have occurred under these titles.

---

* Professor of and attorney at law, Law and Arbitration Centre (LAC). The contributor acknowledges the assistance of his colleagues Dr Ziadat, Dr Amosh and Ms Khleifat of the LAC.

5 COMMERCIAL AND ECONOMIC LAW

5.1 Companies Law No. 22 of 1997

The need to promote investment in Jordan has rendered necessary the updating of the Companies Law by enacting the Companies Law No. 22/97 abolishing the Companies Law No. 1/1989.

In order to meet this need, new provisions have been introduced in the new law relating to the procedures of establishing companies, abolishing the 15 per cent capital tax imposed on the capitalization of the voluntary reserve, adopting the single member company in respect of private limited companies, amending the directors' power to bind the company. According to the new law, power given to the directors to bind the company is not limited to its memorandum or articles of association as long as the third party dealing with the company is acting in good faith.

5.2 The Securities Law (Provisional Law) No. 23/97[1]

This law aims to regulate the trading in securities in the stock market. It has established a commission called the "Securities Commission" which has a separate legal entity. The task of the Commission is to achieve sound dealing in securities, to regulate, develop and monitor the securities market and the capital market in Jordan and protect securities holders, investors and the public from fraud and deceit.

To achieve these objectives, the Commission has to regulate and/or monitor the following:

(a) the issuance of and dealing in securities;
(b) business operations of the entities that fall under its supervision;
(c) the disclosure of information concerning securities and issuers and dealing of insiders, major holders and investors;
(d) short sale of securities;
(e) public tenders to purchase shares in public shareholding companies.

A securities market called the Amman Bourse has been established by the law. The Amman Bourse is the only agency authorized to operate as a formal market for trading in securities in Jordan. The law has also established the Securities Deposit Centre for the deposit and transfer of ownership of securities traded in Amman Bourse and for the settlement of price of such securities among stockbrokers. In addition, the law contains several provisions regulating financial services, investment funds, investment companies and disclosure. Article 73/2 of the law authorized the Board of Commissioners of the Securities Commission to issue the necessary instructions to execute its provisions. After the execution of the provisions of the Securities Law in full, the Amman Financial Market Law No. 1/90 and its amendments thereto will be repealed (Article 77/a).

---

[1] Editors' note: see also the article in Part I by Lu'ayy Minwer Al-Rimawi entitled "Jordan's Financial Laws", p. 73.

5.3 Law No. 5 of 1997 amending the Law of Banking No. 24 of 1971

This amendment relates to Articles 2 and 11 of the original law. The definition of authorized banks in Article 2 is amended to include banks that conducted their operations in accordance with *shari'a* (Islamic law). A new paragraph is added to Article 11 by virtue of which the Council may decide not to apply Article 11 to Islamic banks.

5.4 Regulation No. 39 of 1997 on Promoting Investments of Non-Jordanians

The above-mentioned regulations have been issued according to the Investment Law No. 16 of 1995. Under these regulations, foreign investors may own 100 per cent of the project unless the investment falls within one of the following areas, in which foreign ownership may not exceed 50 per cent: (a) construction contracting; (b) commercial services and trade; and (c) mining. The regulations also fix a foreign investor's equity holding in any project at a minimum of JD50,000 (approximately US$71,400). However, investment in public shareholding companies is not subject to the above restriction.

5.5 Regulation No. 50 of 1997 on Companies and its amendment by Regulation No. 21 of 1998

Fees payable on the registration of a public shareholding company are as follows: (a) a percentage of 0.003 (3 per 1,000) of the declared capital of the company if such capital does not exceed JD10 million; (b) a percentage of 0.0002 (2 per 10,000) of the declared capital if it exceeds JD10 million up to JD50 million and (c) no registration fees may be paid on any sum of the capital exceeding JD50 million. The same rules apply to private limited companies and companies limited by guarantees with the exception that, in respect of the first ten million of the registered capital, a percentage of 0.002 (2 per 1,000) shall be paid instead of 0.003.

5.6 Court of Cassation (Civil Division) No. 1522/96, BAJ, 1997, p. 3513

An ordinary performance bond differs from an on-demand performance bond. In the former, the obligation of the guarantor is a secondary one; he is not bound to pay the sum of the guarantee unless the original debt has been proven and the guarantor may raise all defences available to the debtor against the creditor. The latter is an unconditional undertaking by the bank made upon the request of its customer to pay a stipulated sum of money to the beneficiary on demand if the demand is made on or before the stipulated expiry date.

The obligation of the bank issuing an ordinary performance bond is a primary obligation, and a relationship between the bank and the beneficiary is independent from the relationship between the customer and the bank on the one hand, and the relationship between the customer and the beneficiary on the other. Ordinary performance bonds are also subject to the provisions of Civil Law, whereas on demand performance bonds are subject to banking customs.

Whether an instrument is an ordinary performance bond or an on demand performance bond depends on the wording of the instrument. For instance, there was an instrument before the Court containing that:

The bank guarantees . . . in the amount of . . . until . . . for the good performance of the project of . . . The bank undertakes to pay the full or part of the value of the guarantee when demand is made. The bank is not responsible after the expiry date of the guarantee.

The Court concludes that an undertaking in this from and in this wording is not an on demand performance bond, but rather an ordinary bank guarantee subject to the rules that generally govern the guarantees in Civil Law.

5.7 Court of Cassation (Civil Decision), No. 825/96, BAJ, 1998, p. 1428

The damage sustained by public administration due to the contractor's delay in providing the materials and goods that he was bound to supply according to an administrative contract, is a presumed damage, and a party concerned, i.e. the other contracting party, may not prove otherwise. This is due to the fact that a public entity, by being a party to a contract, reflects and at the same time seeks public interest of the country.

5.8 Court of Cassation (Civil Decision), No. 118/97, BAJ, 1998 p. 1444

Damage resulting from the fall of the exchange rate of the Jordanian dinar against the US dollar is not recoverable. Under Article 162 of the Jordanian Civil Code, if the subject matter of the obligation is money, the amount must be stated and the fluctuation of its exchange rate at the time of payment has no effect on the obligation of the parties.

5.9 Court of Cassation (Civil Decision), No. 2273/97, BAJ, 1998, p. 1399

Under Article 4 of the Ottoman Morabaha Regulation (OMR), the amount of accumulated interest may not exceed the amount of the loan. This provision is mandatory to the extent that the contracting parties may not violate or derogate from. Furthermore, the argument that instructions of the Central Bank allow banks to charge compound interest even if it exceeds the original amount of the loan does not operate; for such instructions issued by the Central Bank may not contradict the provision of the OMR.

6 LABOUR LAW

Regulation No. 8 of 1998 on Conditions and Procedures of Strikes and Lockouts was passed.

7 PROPERTY LAW

8 INTELLECTUAL PROPERTY

9 FAMILY LAW AND SUCCESSION

10 CRIMINAL LAW AND PROCEDURE

No legislative changes or developments of interest have occurred under these titles.

11 PUBLIC INTERNATIONAL LAW

The following are some of the most important conventions and bilateral agreements to which the Hashemite Kingdom of Jordan has acceded:

(a) Chemical Weapons Convention (CWC);
(b) Agreement between the Government of the Hashemite Kingdom of Jordan and the UNCHR;
(c) Agreement between the Government of the Hashemite Kingdom of Jordan and the USA on Mutual Promotion and Protection of Investment.
(d) Jordan's Association Agreement with the European Union.[2]

12 PRIVATE INTERNATIONAL LAW

No legislative changes or developments of interest have occurred under this title.

13 ENVIRONMENTAL LAW

Statutory instruments for Limitation and Prevention of Noise have been issued according to Article 27 of the Environmental Protection Law No. 12 of 1995.

---

[2] See Comment by Lu'ayy Minwer al-Rimawi on this, Part III, p. 486.

Palestine

Anis Al-Qasem*

1 CONSTITUTIONAL LAW

1.1 Struggle for accountability

The years 1997–98 have been characterized by a struggle between the Legislative Council and the executive in search for the limits of authority for each and the accountability of the executive to the Legislative Council. The Council has been trying to assert its authority as the elected parliament to which the executive is accountable, particularly concerning allocation and disposal of public funds. The second front relates to the right of the Council and its members to initiate legislation. This struggle has erupted mainly because the Basic Law has remained without promulgation by President Arafat.

The crisis was brewing for some time, and came to a head with the publication of the first Report of the Monitoring Commission which referred to alleged financial corruption in the administration. The Council, in May 1997, formed a special committee to study the Report. In its report of 27 July 1997, the committee submitted its report and recommendations. The Council, on 31 July 1997, called on the President to restructure the Council of Ministers, abide by the guidelines of the general budget and observe the rule of law. The call was not heeded, although sixteen ministers submitted their resignation. The crisis continued, particularly with the delay by the President of the promulgation of the Basic Law and other legislation. In a resolution adopted on 17 February 1998, the Council called on the executive authority to respond immediately to issues that continue to be barriers to the work of the Council, and in particular to correct the internal problems and the endorsement of the laws and resolutions passed by the Council and to work positively towards the principles of accountability, transparency and the rule of law.[1]

---

* Barrister, Consultant on the Laws of the Middle East (London), Chairman of the Legal Committee of the Palestine National Council (PNC).
[1] *PLC Report*, Palestinian Legislative Council, Information Department, No. 2, 1988, p. 5.

In October 1997, a joint committee of the Council and the executive was established to study the resolutions of the Council which were still awaiting implementation. However, the efforts of this committee came to nothing.

In addition to the charges of corruption, there was the problem of promulgation of legislation passed by the Council and referred to the President. Among these laws was the Basic Law which was finally enacted by the Council. The President did not promulgate the Basic Law and delayed the promulgation of other legislation, which included the Civil Service Law.

Another source of conflict between the legislative and executive authorities has been the mounting criticism of the executive's record in the field of human rights. In its anxiety to meet security pressure by Israel and the United States, the executive exposed itself to violations of human rights. The Council and Palestinian and international human rights organizations attacked the violations, and in the end the Attorney General was forced to "resign". A new Attorney General, a respected lawyer, Fayez Abu Rahma, was appointed. However, the violations continued and, not being able to curb them, he submitted his resignation. No new Attorney General was appointed.

The confrontation has led ultimately, in June 1998, to the acceptance of the resignation of the government and the promulgation of some laws, but not the Basic Law. The confrontation is not over yet. Meanwhile, the Council was able to assert its right and the right of its members to initiate legislation and to reject draft legislation submitted by the government. The Council even rejected the budget and forced the government to re-submit it.

The struggle between the Council, as a legislative body, and the executive is a lively aspect of the relationship between the two authorities. The Council is fighting to establish a rule of effective accountability and transparency, while the executive is resisting such attempts. This struggle is, of course, not new in constitutional history. However, in the present case the Council is waging this struggle while, at the same time, it has to remain supportive of the government in its struggle against Israeli occupation. This explains, in part, the patience and compromises to diffuse the confrontation.

1.2 The Basic Law

On 2 October 1997, the Legislative Council passed a Basic Law, which retained many of the features of the first draft, and referred it to the President on 4 October 1997 for promulgation. At the time of writing, the President has not yet promulgated it.

In the course of the conflict between the President and the Council, the question was raised as to the promulgation of the Basic Law as a number of separate laws. The reasoning behind the suggestion was not clear and, after consultations, the idea seems to have been rejected.

2 LEGISLATION

Between 1997 and June 1998, the following laws were passed by the Legislative Council and promulgated by the President:

(a) Election of Palestinian Local Councils Law – passed and promulgated (December 1996);
(b) Palestinian Local Councils Law;
(c) the 1997 General Budget;
(d) Monetary Authority Law;
(e) Encouragement of Investment Law;
(f) Firearms and Ammunitions Law;
(g) Civil Service Law;
(h) Tax and Stamp of Precious Metals Law;
(i) Civil Defence Law;
(j) Rehabilitation and Qualification Centres (Prison) Law.

The following bills have been passed by the Council, referred to but not promulgated by the President:

(a) the Basic Law – referred on 4 October 1997;
(b) Foreign Ownership of Land in Palestine Bill – referred on 4 October 1997;
(c) Palestinian General Petroleum and Natural Resources Council Bill – referred on 7 December 1997;
(d) Livestock Bill – referred on 9 March 1998;
(e) Regulation of General Budget and Fiscal Affairs Bill – referred on 20 April 1998.

Had the Basic Law been promulgated and put into effect, these Bills would have become law by force of the Basic Law thirty days after their submission to the President, unless he returned them to the Council for reconsideration.

About twenty more Bills are under consideration by the Council ranging from the Judicature Authority Bill to the Protection of the Environment.

Draft laws have been submitted by the Council of Ministers, the Minister of Justice, committees of the Legislative Council such as the Legal Committee, and members of the Council. Private members' Bills are treated in the same way as government Bills.

3 WOMEN AND THE LAW

One development of significance, which, I think, is the first of its kind in a Muslim country, is the publicly organized initiative taken by Palestinian women to eliminate discriminatory legislation from which women suffer. The campaign for equality in rights is pioneered by the Women's Centre for Legal Aid and Counselling (WCLAC), which has been offering advice and assistance to women in the West Bank regarding their rights. In 1997, the Centre published a book in Arabic entitled *Towards Equality: Law and the Palestinian Woman*. The book, which is mainly written by men, surveys the place of women in current legislation as a basis for the understanding of the legal factual situation as a springboard for reform. Workshops were created to study the various aspects of discrimination.

During the first week of April 1998, the Centre organized a "model" parliament on women and legislation which was broadcast on the Palestinian Al-Watan TV channel. The focus of the discussion was personal status legislation. The Centre was campaigning for radical departures from existing legislation which is mainly based on the *shari'a*. As would be expected, the challenge to them came from Islamic groups who were opposed to change. Although the "parliament" left the question to the Legislative Council, one should not underestimate the value of the initiative or the determination of the Centre in 1994 in the course of its consultations on the Basic Law. I was impressed with their organizational and campaigning skills and sincerity of purpose. My feeling is that their success will depend to a good extent on ridding themselves of some extremist feminist views. It was wise to raise the issues and engage in a public debate, and that by itself stands to their credit.

4 THE JUDICIARY

Having reached retirement age, the Chief Justice, Qusai Al-Abadlah, was retired through a letter addressed to him from the head of the civil service department. No new Chief Justice has been appointed.

The judicature is still not unified under one judicature Act; the courts in the West Bank remain governed by inherited Jordanian legislation, and are, in the main, subject to some old Palestinian legislation from the times of the British mandate.

The problems are not limited to absence of unification of the judicial authority. More serious problems have persisted: lack of sufficient adequately qualified judges and administrative personnel, limitations and restrictions on the competence of regular courts through the continued existence of Israeli military courts which still exercise jurisdiction in certain areas, the creation of security courts, failure to enforce court decisions by the executive, lack of security for judicial appointments, interference by security forces in the administration of justice. A healthy development was the restoration to the Court of Appeal in the West Bank of its jurisdiction as a High Court with the power of review. The two High Courts in Gaza and Ramallah have been able to provide some protection against administrative arbitrariness. However, in a number of cases, their decisions were not enforced by the administration. Much needs to be done to ensure the existence of a strong, efficient and independent judiciary.[2]

5 HUMAN RIGHTS

The Palestinian Independent Commission for Citizens' Rights published its third annual report covering the period from 1 January to 31 December 1997. The report dealt with violations of human rights committed by Israel, the occupying power, and the Palestine National Authority. While the Commission was able to intervene in the latter case, it was powerless as regards Israeli violations.

The Oslo Declaration for Principles, the report reminded the reader, did not change the legal status of the Palestinian territories: they remained under occupation with Israel as the occupying power, and, in that capacity, were still bound by

---

[2] For a review of the judicial system its achievement s and shortcomings, see the third annual report (January – December 1997) of the Palestinian Independent Commission for Citizens' Rights, pp. 67–92.

the Fourth Geneva Convention and international human rights law. Nevertheless, Israel has continued in its violation of both.

Israeli violations reported by the Commission have included violation of the right of life. The report documents the killing of twenty-nine Palestinians: seventeen were killed by Israeli soldiers and Israeli settlers, four in Israeli jails because of medical negligence or torture or beating and four were killed in obscure circumstances or at the hands of special Israeli forces. Administrative detention, lasting sometimes for years, has continued without charge or trial. Torture of prisoners to extract confessions has continued with judicial authorization. Demolition of Palestinians' homes, expropriation of land and creation of settlements have continued. According to the report, 53 per cent of the total area of the West Bank and the Gaza Strip has been expropriated by Israel.

The Israelization of Jerusalem has also continued through annexation of further Palestinian villages to the city, the withdrawal of identity cards from Palestinian residents, the demolition of houses and settlement of Israelis. Israeli violations in Hebron, where only a handful of Israeli settlers have been allowed to remain, were intensified.

The report detailed the Commission's intervention with the Palestinian National Authority in pursuance of complaints by citizens or at the initiative of the Commission. During 1997, the Commission intervened in respect of 450 cases, and solved 390. The Commission reports that 1997, compare with previous years, has witnessed improvement in Palestinian citizen's rights, and greater response from Palestinian administrative bodies and institutions to the Commission's monitoring of cases. However, the situation remains far from reaching a proper stage. Violations, some of which are very grave, continue to occur.[3]

The report of the Commission is submitted to the President, the Legislative Council and the Executive. It is also a published document available to the public. Thus after a period of ups and downs, the Commission is gradually, but firmly, discharging the role for which it has been created. To a citizen whose human right have been violated by the administration, the Commission seems a much shorter cut to regaining his right than judicial proceedings.

6 RULE OF LAW SECTOR AND LEGAL DEVELOPMENT

Despite the above shortcomings, the Ministry of Justice of the PNA has launched, with the World Bank, a most ambitious Legal Development Project, defined and reflected in the Ministry of Justice's "Rule of Law: Strategic Development Plan (August 1996)".[4] Donors include the World Bank, USAID, Norway, the UK, Australia, Canada, the Netherlands, the European Union, Denmark, Sweden, Switzerland, Spain and others. Various implementing organizations and consultants are already involved and the work is being coordinated by the United Nations Special Coordination in the Occupied Territories (UNSCO). Primary objectives in the legal

---

[3] *Op. cit.*, p. XVI.
[4] The Strategic Development Plan and details of the Legal Development Project are fully set out in Part III, pp. 536 and 543.

sector are the promotion of good government and the rule of law, a unified legal and judicial system through laws which encourage and provide economic development.

7 UPGRADE OF PALESTINE'S STATUS IN THE UNITED NATIONS

On 7 July 1998, the status of Palestine within the UN system was upgraded from observer status to a status more akin to a full member. The UN General Assembly voted, 124 in favour and only 4 against (the USA, Micronesia, the Marshall Islands and Israel), to upgrade Palestine's role at the UN so that it can have a delegation with six seats like member states (instead of the two granted to an observer organization), so that its representatives can speak in debates and co-sponsor resolutions in the Middle East. It will, however, have no right to vote or to field candidates in UN elections.

The Palestinian representative to the UN hoped that this would be the first step towards the admission of Palestine as a full member when it is planned to declare UDA at the end of the transitional period of the Oslo peace process next May.

Lebanon

*Chibli Mallat**

There have been unusually few legislative developments in Lebanon since last year's survey, and the length of this short contribution is a reflection of the reduced legislation. This does not mean that the debate was any less heated in the legislative field, for the political scene was filled with discussions on legislative proposals in key areas. This was particularly true for two legislative initiatives which the President started, but which were stopped dead in their tracks by a mixture of opposition and diffidence.

The two proposals concerned a Bill for what came to be known as the "optional civil marriage", and the suggestion to carry out a constitutional amendment for the direct popular election of the President. In the first case, the idea was that, considering the strictness of the religious-confessional system, under which it is not possible for spouses from different sects to marry outside a given sectarian denomination within Lebanon, the least that should be offered was the option for them to carry out a civil marriage. In other words, if a Sunni man wants to marry a Christian Maronite woman, the current law allows them to perform the marriage following Sunni law and before the Sunni courts (or before a Maronite priest). They cannot, however, go to a civil judge to do so, for there is no civil official competent in the matter. They could, if they wanted, travel abroad – the nearest country being Cyprus – and marry under Cypriot civil law, thereafter returning to Lebanon and registering marriage with the civil Lebanese authorities. The result is bizarre: Lebanese citizens can carry out a civil marriage abroad, which is recognized by Lebanese law, but Lebanese law does not allow them to marry before the civil authorities in Lebanon. Hence the suggestion, coming at the initiative of the President, to establish the "option" of a civil marriage within Lebanon. The system is optional in the sense that the current arrangements would remain in place, but that civil marriage would be possible if the spouses so wished.

It is hard to imagine why anyone would stand against such a proposal, but it was soundly defeated. The reasons behind the freezing of the proposal are eminently

---

* Attorney-at-Law, Beirut, Professor of Law, University of St Joseph, Beirut.

political, and there is no point in going into the details of the opposition to the presidential motion. More interesting from a constitutional point of view is the curious manoeuvring of the Prime Minister, who did not like the idea and/or did not want to resist religious pressures from his own Sunni community (and, by another curious twist in international law, did not try to resist a strident intervention in matters Lebanese by the Saudi Mufti Ibn Baz, who declared any such scheme anathema to Lebanese Muslims). The Prime Minister simply prevented the Council of Ministers from relaying the legislative proposal adopted by the Council to Parliament. The precedent therein established will be interesting to follow.

The other presidential proposal was no less important, and no less difficult to oppose on purely legal grounds. It concerned the election of the President of the republic by direct universal suffrage, a change which requires a constitutional amendment to the present system. Under the present constitutional arrangements, Members of Parliament are vested with the task of electing the President, and 1998 is important since it should normally bring to an end the incumbent's President prolonged nine-year mandate. (Under the constitution, a President can stay in power for six years, and the term is not renewable. In October 1995, a constitutional amendment modified the system to allow President Hrawi a three-year extension.)[1]

However, the proposal of the President was not presented formally, and there is no point in dwelling too long on a hypothetical matter; except to note that in such an important electoral year as the current one, a proposal to amend the constitution in such a radical manner was bound both to capture the imagination and to be a non-starter politically.

Indeed, both proposals required a fresh governmental team which a President in power for nine years, whose mandate was to come to a constitutional end on 23 November 1998, could hardly put together. At the time of writing, the whole process surrounding the elections of a new President is shrouded in mystery, and all options remained open a few days before the formal opening of the Presidential elections.

The *fin-de-règne* atmosphere also accounts for the dearth of meaningful legislation, and it is curious to see the quality of judgments also go down in the last two years of the mandate. This explains this much shorter chapter than usual. We will present constitutional review developments, then rapidly cover the various legislative and judicial developments.

1 CONSTITUTIONAL REVIEW

Three decisions were rendered by the Constitutional Council over the period. The two first decisions closely mirror each other, as they came in the wake of a new law on the municipalities and on the mayors which had sought to extend, yet again, the councils and mayors in place since 1963.[2] Fourteen deputies (four more than the ten required) petitioned the Council, which decided by a majority of seven to three that the laws were unconstitutional. The decisions were somewhat verbose,[3]

---

[1] See this *Yearbook*, vol. 2 (1995), p. 164.

[2] OJ 37, 31 July 1997, Laws 654 and 655, both at 2926.

[3] OJ 44, 30 October 1997, Decisions 1/97 and 2/97 both dated 12 September 1997, at 3203 and 3207 respectively.

explaining in detail basic constitutional norms about the right to vote and the regularity of elections, together with a history of the successive extension of these councils and mayoralties with a tinge of drama: Parliament was "surprised" (*fuji'a*) by the government reversal, and the Council noted "the rise of popular and parliamentary demand" for elections, and exposed the inconsistency of the statements of the Minister of the Interior.[4] More worrying than such unnecessary expatiation was the fact that three out of the five judges appointed to the Council last year, including the new President of the court, opposed the judgment, and would therefore have allowed the extension to stand. Also odd was the concluding reasoning of the majority, which ultimately invalidated the law because the legislative and governmental motivations behind the law "did not justify the extension of the councils' mandates for the unreasonable duration stipulated in the law, which leads us to say that there is clear lack of correspondence between the extension of the councils and the prevention of the citizen from exercising his constitutional right to cast his vote with regularity".[5] Presumably, under this reasoning, if the extension had been reasonable (i.e. less than the two years stipulated by the challenged law), the Constitutional Council might find that the citizen could be prevented from exercising his or her constitutional voting rights. Fortunately, the law as amended in the wake of its invalidation allowed the elections to go forward.[6] The government could, however, not resist postponing the elections in some cases for reasons which were not all too clear, as in the city of Baabda.

The third decision by the Constitutional Council was made on 25 February 1998, formally rejecting the petition of three deputies (ten are needed, as just mentioned) who had asked the Council to invalidate the budget law.[7]

2 OTHER DEVELOPMENTS

A decree established a thirteenth chamber in the Court of Appeal,[8] while conflicts continued between various courts over competence, as illustrated in a poor decision of the administrative Council of State in which that Court ruled that, for all intents and purposes, a magistrate being investigated by the highest civil jurisdiction in the country (*Majlis al-qada' al-a'la*) would still be able to bring proceedings against such a decision before the Council. The decision argues that the *Majlis'* competence does not prevent the magistrate who was found guilty by the *Majlis*, from questioning that finding on grounds of an administrative nature, which fall within the competence of the Council of State.[9] Coming on the heels of an attempt to meddle in matters relating to the Constitutional Council during the constitutional crisis which arose upon the abrupt resignation of its former President, Wajdi Mallat,[10] that decision further emphasized the frustration of judges and the increasingly

---

[4] Quotes at 3204, repeated verbatim at 3209.
[5] At 3207, repeated at 3212.
[6] OJ 59, 30 December 1997, 4165-74.
[7] Decision 1/98, OJ 11, 5 March 1998, 529.
[8] OJ 55, 64 December 1997, 3855.
[9] Council of State, decision dated 9/10/1997, *al-'Adl*, 1997; 3–4, Case-law section 1-8.
[10] See this *Yearbook*, vol. 3 (1996), pp. 221–227.

fissiparous character of the court system.[11] A less serious sign of the confusion of court competence arose in a case decided by the Court of Cassation meeting en banc (*hay'a 'amma*). In that decision, the Court declined competence in a conflict which involved a Christian petitioner who was arguing that she was prevented from receiving her share under the civil law of inheritance by a decision of the Sunni court before which the case was originally argued. The Court, by a majority of four to one, declined competence because of what it considered the mootness of the case. A strong dissent of Juge Mitri emphasized the distress caused by the impairment of the right of the woman petitioner to oppose the decision of a religious court which did not share her affiliation.[12]

The Court of Cassation also ruled *en banc* that disputes over attorney's fees were rightly handled by the Court of Appeal, which is normally competent in such cases, even if the dispute arose between the attorney and his client bank. The competence of the special first instance court which handles civil and commercial disputes involving the banking sector was not relevant in disputes over attorneys' fees.[13]

In criminal law, a heavily criticized statute pardoned drug offenders for crimes committed before 31 December 1995, "of whatever nature".[14] Coming seven years after the return to peace in the country, and six years after a general pardon law which was much more balanced, the new law had no purpose other than the release of some political figures who had been jailed for drug trafficking. The law created an understandable stir in judicial circles, especially after the prosecutor general brought a case for professional incompetence against two Court of Cassation judges who had ordered the release of two convicts, in a split decision in which the President of the court dissented. Both the judgment releasing the convicts and the decision of the prosecutor were subject to intense controversy.

In family law, the personal status law of the Oriental Assyrian Orthodox community was published and approved by the Council of Ministers, thus adding another marriage, divorce and custody code (186 articles) to the plethora of such legislative enactments in the Lebanese mosaic of religious communities.[15]

In public international law, Law 664 of 23 October 1997[16] ratified the 1979 New York treaty on hostage-taking. A number of other conventions were also ratified, notably treaties encouraging investment between Syrian and Lebanese entrepreneurs,[17] treaties against double taxation and tax evasion between the two countries,[18] and a 1979 international convention on the transportation of goods.[19]

Other similarly insignificant changes were also inspired by the sense of *fin-de-règne*, including an extension of the laws on the merger of banks, an important fea-

---

[11] See my brief evaluation in "The Lebanese Legal System", 2, *The Lebanon Report*, Beirut, 1997, pp. 29–36, with a "bibliographical essay" at pp. 42–45.

[12] Court of Cassation, *hay'a 'amma*, decision dated 15 April 1997, *Ijtihadat Hatem*, 214, 719–23, dissent at pp. 721–23.

[13] Court of Cassation, *hay'a 'amma*, decision dated 7 April 1997, *Ijtihadat Hatem*, 214, 758–60.

[14] Art.1, Law 666, 29 December 1997, OJ 59, 30 December 1997, 4175.

[15] OJ 43, 11 September 1997, 3175.

[16] OJ 50, 30 October 1997, 3587.

[17] OJ 37, 31 July 1997, 2927.

[18] OJ 37, 31 July 1997, 2930.

[19] OJ 37, 31 July 1997, 2891.

ture of the country's attempt to strengthen its strategic banking sector; a law extending the deadline for correcting contraventions in buildings, and various other laws of an administrative rather than a strictly legislative nature.[20]

3 NEW PUBLICATIONS

This year has seen the resumed publication of both *al-Huquq al-Lubnaniyya wal-'Arabiyya* (with four issues in 1997 and 1998) and of *Ijtihadat Hatem*, which was momentarily stopped during its editor's chairmanship of the Beirut bar. Two issues of *La Revue Libanaise de l'Arbitrage Arabe et International*, edited by Professor Ibrahim Najjar, were also published.

There were few strictly legal books outside the continued compilation of case laws in various fields. A collective volume was published under the editorship of Fares Abi Saab on *Al-Intikhabat al-Niyabiyya 1996 wa azmat al-dimuqratiyya fi Lubnan* (The 1996 parliamentary elections and the crisis of democracy in Lebanon). In a similar, not strictly legal vein, see also my little book *Al-Ri'asa al-Lubnaniyya bayn al-Ams wal-Ghad*, published at Dar al-Nahar in September 1998, with versions in French and in English (*Presidential Choices 1998*; see further www.mallat.com, a website which also includes various material on Lebanese and Middle Eastern laws). Talal al-Huseini published a strong criticism of the judiciary, *Raddan 'ala wazir al-'adl* (response to the Minister of Justice), Beirut, 1997. The full works of the late Antoine Qazan (1927–1973), lawyer and man of letters, were published in six volumes in 1998. Volume 5 includes his legal studies (*Abhath Qanuniyya*).

One should perhaps note the publication in Lebanon of a new journal informed by Shi'i law, *al-Minhaj*, with nine issues over the past two years. The editor of *al-Minhaj*, Khaled al-'Atiyya, has also completed a major six-volume compendium of Shi'i law, *Mu'jam fiqh al-jawahir*. The book is an extremely useful alphabetical restatement of the fifty-volume nineteenth-century treatise on Shi'i law by al-Muhaqqiq al-Najafi (d. 1266 AH), *Jawahir al-Kalam fi Shar' Shara'e' al-Islam*. Also in the Islamic law field, *al-Ijtihad*, which is edited in Beirut by Professor Ridwan al-Sayyed, is now well established with some forty thematic issues over a decade.

---

[20] Fifteen laws, including those just mentioned, to be found in OJ 14, 26 March 1998, 975–1085.

Libya

Mustafa El-Alem*

1 THE PEOPLE'S COURT

The People's Court is a court of special jurisdiction which was established in 1988 to hear certain political, criminal and economical cases and crimes. Act No. 5 of 1988 establishing the People's Court has been amended in 1991. A second amendment has been made in 1997 by virtue of Act No. 7/1426. A third amendment has been made in 1998 by virtue of Act No. 3/1427.

The most important results of these two latest amendments are the following:

(a) the jurisdiction of the People's Court has been slightly modified;
(b) the judges of the People's Court must have graduated in law;
(c) the judgments of the People's Court rendered by the appeal circuit may not be challenged before the Supreme Court with the exception of the death sentence;
(d) as an exception to the principles of the Libyan criminal law, crimes which fall within the jurisdiction of the People's Court shall not be extinguished by the elapse of time;[1]
(e) according to Article 13, as amended by Act No. 7/1426, pleading and advocacy before the People's Court is limited to the lawyers employed by the Popular Advocacy Department.[2] The accused has the right to choose a lawyer from

---

* Attorney at Law before the Libyan Supreme Court.
[1] See 2.1, Extinction of Crimes.
[2] Act No. 4 of 1981 established the Popular Advocacy Department (PAD), and limited the pleading and representation before the courts to the lawyers employed by the state and working within the said department. In 1990 an Act was passed to reorganize the profession of advocacy. This Act allowed the free practice of this profession. Accordingly, an accused or a party to a civil action may seek the judicial assistance of PAD, or appoint – at his own expense – an independent lawyer. It should be noted here that PAD offers its assistance to Libyan citizens free of charge.

this department to defend him. Failing such a choice, the court would ask
the said department to assign a lawyer to this mission.

(f)   Article 13 has been amended again by Act No. 3/1427 which came into force
on 21 February 1998. Accordingly, pleading and advocacy is no longer limited to the Popular Advocacy Department. The accused and the parties to a
civil case have the choice either to seek the assistance of this department, or
to appoint an independent lawyer to defend them.

2 CRIMINAL LAW

2.1 Extinction of crimes

According to the general principles of the Libyan criminal law, felonies are extinguished by the elapse of ten years, and misdemeanours are extinguished by the elapse
of three years as from the date of the crime.

Act No. 11/1427 which came into force on 21 February 1998 abolished this rule
and provided that crimes and criminal cases shall not be extinguished by the elapse
of time.

2.2 Rules of talion and criminal compensation

Act No. 4/1423 on the rules of talion (*qisas*) and criminal compensation (*diyya*)
was issued on 29 January 1994.[3]

Article 1 of this Act used to read as follows: "Is punished by death whoever kills
a person with intent, if the blood relatives [of the victim] request it. *Qisas* is not
applied if pardon is granted, in which case the penalty is the *diyya*." Article 1 has been
amended by virtue of Act No. 4/1427 which came into force on 21 February 1998
to read as follows: "Is punished by death whoever kills a person with intent. *Qisas*
is not applied if pardon is granted, in which case the penalty is the *diyya*."

2.3 Amendment of Article 195 of the Penal Code

Article 195 of the Penal Code has been amended by virtue of Act No. 8/1427 which
came into force on 21 February 1998 to read as follows:

Without prejudice to any severer penalty punished by imprisonment[4] whoever commits
what may be detrimental to the Great Al-Fateh Revolution or to its leader.

Some penalty shall be applied to whoever insults the People's Authority, any of the
judicial, defence or security institutions, and the like, or publicly insults the Libyan Arab
People, the symbol of State or its flag.

---

[3] This Act was published in full in this *Yearbook*, vol. 1 (1994), p. 543.
[4] Imprisonment under Libyan law ranges between three and fifteen years.

3 TRADE LAW

3.1 Partnership Act

Act No. 9 of 1985 authorized the establishment of a special form of commercial partnership known as *Tasharukia*, which is based on the personal efforts of the partners without employment of workers. Article 4/1 of the said act requires the partners to be fully devoted to the activities of the *Tasharukia*.

As an exception to this rule, Article 4/2 allows a partner not to be fully devoted to the activities of the *Tasharukia* if his other activities do not interfere with his original job. In addition, the employees of the public companies and administrative units must obtain the consent of their employees therefor.

This exceptional rule decided by Article 4/2 of Act No. 9/1985 has been abolished by the coming into force of Act No. 3/1426 on 29 May 1997 which contained only one article repealing the said Article 4/2.

3.2 Import and distribution of commodities

Act No. 4/1426 of 1997 regulating the import and distribution of commodities came into force on 28 June 1997. According to the provision of this Act, importation of commodities and goods shall be carried out by the public companies "i.e. companies owned by the State", joint stock companies and merchants. Such importation is to be made by way of bank transfers through the financial institutions operating in the country, and according to the exchange rates in force at the time of transfer.

Imported goods and commodities are subject to the specifications and prices to be defined by the General People's Committee for Economy and Trade.

Distribution is to be carried out by consumer's cooperative societies, individual distributors and merchants as follows:

(a)   Consumers' cooperative societies shall sell directly to their members, the food product and other commodities to be prescribed by the General People's Committee for Economy and Trade.
(b)   Individual distributors shall distribute the commodities ready for consumption for the account of those who produce such commodities, against salesmen's commission rates.
(c)   Merchants shall import and distribute commodities directly to the consumers, to the licensed distribution channels or to the individual distributors.

The General People's Committee shall issue the Executive Regulations of this Act. The Regulations shall contain the following:

(a)   the bases and rules regulating import, distribution and the relative licensing systems;
(b)   the procedures to be followed in order to guarantee that the consumer obtains the commodities he needs at reasonable prices, and to prevent the illegitimate distribution of commodities;

(c)   the bases on which the salesmen's commission rates (due to individual dis-
      tributors) are to be defined.

4 TAX LAW

According to Article 27 of the Income Tax Law (No. 64 of 1973) the right of the
state to claim payments by virtue of this law is to be extinguished by the elapse of
five years. This article has been amended by Act No. 23 of 1996 to extend the prescription period to ten years.[5]

Another amendment has been made to the text of Article 27 by virtue of Act
No. 2/1426 (1997) to read as follows: "The right of the state to claim payments
by virtue of this law shall not be extinguished by the elapse of time."

5 FOREIGN CAPITAL INVESTMENT ACT

Act No. 5/1426 (1997) on Encouragement of Foreign Capital Investment has come
into force as from the date of its publication in the Official Gazette (29 May 1997).
It has repealed Act No. 37 of 1968 on Foreign Capital Investment.

According to its Article 1, this Act aims at the encouragement of foreign capital
investment for the purpose of carrying out investment projects within the state's general policy, the objectives of the economic and social development plans, and in
particular:

(a)   transfer of modern technology;
(b)   construction of Libyan technical elements;
(c)   variation of income resources;
(d)   participation in developing the local products to help them enter the interna-
      tional markets.

Article 5 provides for the establishment of the Investment Encouragement Organization. It is an independent body supervised by the Secretariat of Trade and Economy. It is charged with the study and suggestion of the foreign capital investment
plans, granting foreign investment licences and all other matters relating to such
investment according to the provisions of this Act.

According to Article 7, the investment project must realize all or some of the
following:

(a)   production of commodities for export, participation in increasing their export,
      the total or partial avoidance of import of commodities;
(b)   provision of jobs and technical training for Libyan workers;
(c)   employment of modern technology, trademark or technical expertise;
(d)   offering a service required by the national economy or the participation in
      improvement of such service;
(e)   decreasing the production cost;

---

[5] Act No. 23 of 1996 was surveyed in this *Yearbook*, vol. 3 (1996), p. 249.

(f)   participation in providing materials and operation requirements for pending economic projects;
(g)   exploitation of local raw materials;
(h)   participation in developing of the remote and least developed areas.

Investment is allowed, according to Article 8, in the fields of industry, health, tourism, services, agriculture, and any other field to be prescribed by the General People's Committee.

The projects carried out within the frame of this Act shall enjoy the following prerogatives:

(a)   equipment and machinery required for carrying out the project are to be exempted from all taxes and customs duties;
(b)   mobilizers, spare parts and primary materials required for operation of the project are to be exempted from all customs duties imposed on imports for a period of five years;
(c)   the project is to be exempted from income tax for a period of five years from the date of production or commencement of the work pursuant to the nature of the project. This period may be extended to an additional period of three years;
(d)   exported commodities shall be exempted from production taxes and export taxes and duties;
(e)   the project shall be exempted from revenue stamp duties.

According to Article 12 the investor shall have the following rights:

(a)   re-exportation of his invested capital in the following cases:
    (i)   expiry of the project's period;
    (ii)   liquidation of the project;
    (iii)   total or partial sale of the project;
    (iv)   elapse of a period not less than five years since the issuance of the investment licence;
(b)   re-transfer of the foreign capital in the same form it was brought to the country after six months if circumstances or difficulties beyond the investor's control would impede its investment;
(c)   net profits realized by the project are transferable abroad every year;
(d)   the investor is allowed to employ foreigners if Libyans are not available. Foreign workers shall be allowed to transfer abroad certain percentages from their salaries.

As an exception to the legislation, the investor shall have the right to benefit from lands, to own them or lease them for the purpose of carrying out or operating the project in accordance with the situations and conditions to be defined by the Executive Regulations of the Act.

The investor shall have the right, as per Article 13, to open for his project a bank transferable account in one of the commercial banks.

The project may not, according to Article 23, be nationalized or confiscated except by virtue of law or court judgment providing a fair and immediate compensation.

Article 24 allows the settlement of any dispute that may arise between the foreign investor and the state by way of arbitration. The provision of the Act shall not be applicable to the foreign capital invested in oil projects in accordance with the provisions of Act No. 25 of 1955.

6 PUBLIC INTERNATIONAL LAW

On 27 February 1998, the International Court of Justice delivered its judgment[6] on the preliminary objectives in the case concerning questions of interpretation and application of the 1971 Montreal Convention arising from the aerial incident at Lockerbie (*Libyan Arab Jamahiriya v. USA*). The preliminary objectives of the USA as to jurisdiction and admissibility were rejected by the Court.

---

[6] The judgment is reproduced in full in Part IV, p. 583.

Sudan

*John Wuol Makec**

1 PERMANENT CONSTITUTION

The date of **30 June 1998** witnessed the birth of a new permanent and Islamic constitution in the Sudan. The fourteen constitutional decrees which had provided the framework of the salvation government since 1989 automatically ceased to exist upon the promulgation of this constitution.

The constitutional document is divided into eight parts. Part I deals with the state and the guiding principles, for example, the nature of the state; decentralization of the state; the language, governance and sovereignty in the state; the national unity; defence of the *Umma*, and so on. Part II on the other hand provides for fundamental human rights which include the sanctity of nationality and *huriah of tawaly* (freedom of association). Furthermore, Parts III, IV and V deal with the three main organs of the constitution, namely the executive, the legislative power and the judicial system respectively. Part VI contains provisions for a federal system, while Part VII provides the subordinate organs of the executive and those of (a) the People's Armed Forces, (b) the Police Forces, (c) the Security Forces, and (d) the Popular Forces. These, of course, are paramilitary forces which consist of *mujahidin* (the holy warriors), *dufa el Shabby* (the People's defence forces) and the militias. Finally, Part VIII embodies provision for state of emergency and declaration of war.

1.1 The state and the guiding principles

The first article of the constitution describes the Sudan as a country where a variety of ethnic communities and cultures "harmonize". It describes Islam as a religion of the majority while Christianity and other beliefs are followed by a considerable majority. Arabic is the official language (Article 3). Article 4 is fundamental in the establishment of an Islamic state in the Sudan. It bestows the *Hikimia* or the

---

* LLB; LLM: Justice of the Supreme Court of the Sudan.

governance of the *Umma* in Allah (God) the Creator of mankind while sovereignty in the *Umma* (homeland) is for the successor people of the Sudan. Sovereignty is exercised by the faithful or the worshippers of Allah. In fact, the people act as trustees when they exercise sovereignty.

From the vesting of *Hikimia* of the *Umma* in Allah, it follows that the defence of the *Umma* becomes an honour while the call for *Jihad* (holy war) and national service are duties imposed on the citizens (Articles 7 and 35). On the other hand, the state has a duty to (a) care for the defenders of the *Umma*, the injured (in holy war) and the families of *mujahidin* (martyrs); (b) purify the society of evils such as corruption, crime, drinking of alcohol by Muslims; (c) promote noble traditions, righteous manners, association and fraternity in adherence other faith in Allah (Article 16). These ideals are to be enforced on people or society through laws and guiding policies. Furthermore, it is a noble duty imposed on the state employees and those in public life to devote their efforts to the worship of Allah. Muslims (Article 18) are bound to adhere to the Book and the Sunna (Traditions of the Prophet). Religious spirit must be reflected in public life by the people, for example when they make state plans, laws, policies and in discharge of their official work in political, economic, social and cultural fields.

1.2 Constitutional organs

Constitutional organs comprise of three main institutions, namely the executive power, the legislative power and the judicial system.

1.2.1 *The executive organ*

The executive power under the Constitution consists of three main institutions or bodies, namely the Presidency of the Republic, the Central Council of Ministers and the state executives, which comprise the state's governors (*Walla*) and the state's Council of Ministers. Apart from these three, there are subordinate institutions of the Executive which hold the public service, armed forces and police forces.

1.2.1.1 The Presidency of the Republic

The Constitution establishes the executive presidency, where the President of the Republic must be directly elected by the people to serve a tenure of five years in office, from the date he takes the oath. The qualifications of a candidate for presidency are simple and they convey the impression that any person who fulfils them may be elected. However, a subtle impediment lies in store elsewhere, against certain candidates. When the expressed qualifications are read together with the text of the oath, under Article 40, which an elected President must take before the assumption of his office, the impression that anyone who fulfils them may be elected easily gives way. The text of the oath represents the fundamental qualification that the candidate who is to be elected to the office of the President of the Republic must be a Muslim. The President is assisted by two vice-presidents and assistants whom he appoints. They take the same oath under Article 40. It is of course, implicit that the person appointed as the first vice-president must be a Muslim because he acts for the President in the latter's absence. As the situation was prior to the promulgation of the Constitution, the second vice-president and the assistants were not necessarily required to be Muslims. Now under the Constitution the text of the oath is the same for the President and his deputies and assistants. It is not yet clear if the third deputy and assistants will all be Muslims as the oath indicates. The powers conferred on the President are very wide and are substantively the same as those which were previously provided for him under the Constitutional Decree No. 13 of 1996.[1]

The power of the President falls vacant where, *inter alia*, his resignation has been accepted by a vote of two thirds majority of members of the National Assembly or where he has been removed by the same vote of members of the National Assembly if he had been convicted for commission of treason or other offences involving honour. Any aggrieved citizen may impeach the President before the Constitutional Court in a matter related to violation of a Constitutional right.

1.2.1.2 The Council of Ministers

The Constitution provides for the establishment of a Council of Ministers from the number of ministers who are appointed by the President of the Republic (Article 471). The Constitution, however, is silent about the post of Prime Minister. The constitutional silence implies that the situation remains as it had been under the Constitutional Decree No. 13 of 1996 where the President of the Republic (and in his absence, the first Vice President) had been presiding over the meetings of the Council. The Council "shall have the higher federal executive power in the state". Its decisions are made by consultation and unanimity (or by a majority).

The functions of the Council are provided under Article 49, while the ministers' functions are under Article 50. The Minister is responsible for the work of his Ministry to the President of the Republic, the Council of Ministers and the National Assembly. The text of the oath taken by a minister is in substance the same as that of the President except in relation to the state responsibilities assigned to each person.

1.2.1.3 The state executive power

Sudan is divided into regional governments, known as "states". Each of the states has a governor or *Wali* at the top of the executive and a Council of Ministers who are appointed by the governor in consultation with the President of the Republic. The governor is directly elected by the people but after a primary procedure has already been undertaken. The election of the governor begins with the nomination of six persons among the candidates by an electoral college consisting of members of the National Assembly representing the state in question; members of the State

Assembly and Chairmen of local councils. The list of six nominees is submitted to the President of the Republic to nominate three persons who are thereafter referred to the people to elect one as the governor for a period of four years. The governor presides over the meetings of the State Council of Ministers.

The text of the oath taken by the governor and his ministers is substantively the same as the one the President of the Republic takes. The governor and his ministers are responsible to the President of the Republic (Articles 62 and 64(4)).

The state executive power is rested in the state Council of Ministers. The Council of Ministers takes decisions by consultation or unanimity or by majority. The State Council has powers which correspond with those of the Central Council of Ministers. Furthermore, the functions of the state minister (Article 64) correspond with those of his counterpart in the central government.

1.2.2 The legislative power

The legislative power for the whole country is vested in the National Assembly, which is presided over by the Chairman who is elected by the Assembly members among themselves. The Assembly also elects its leadership comprising of Deputy Chairman and Chairman of (Specialized) Committees and heads of other functions. Seventy-five per cent of the members are directly elected in geographical constituencies by the people while 20 per cent are brought in through special or indirect elections and these members represent women, intellectual and professional organizations and the state or national electoral colleges.

The sources of legislation by the National Assembly are Islamic *shari'a*; the consensus of the *umma* through referendum and the Constitution and custom. No legislation must exceed these sources. However, the legislation (apart from these sources) shall be guided by the public opinion of the *umma*, the *ijtihad* of the *ullama* (Islamic jurists), the thinkers and the decisions of the *Walla* (rulers).

Referenda referred to above may be carried out by the people on the initiative of the President of the Republic or by a resolution of the National Assembly supported, by at least half the number of its members. The subject of referendum must be of great importance or national demand or public interest, and must be conducted by the National Election Commission. The matter for referendum is deemed to represent the will of the people where it is supported by half of the number of votes cast by the registered voters (Article 66) and can only be reversed by another referendum.

The National Assembly has power (Article 73) to pass the country's general budget, Bills, constitutional amendments, provisional decrees, state plans, policies and ratifying treaties and international agreements. The term of the National Assembly is four years starting from the date of its first session. Members of the National Assembly enjoy immunity against criminal proceedings and arrest, unless such immunity has been lifted by the Chairman of the Assembly. The Assembly is called into session by the President of the Republic.

Article 73(2) seems to suggest that the National Assembly has power of control over the executive since it may recommend to the President of the Republic the removal of a federal minister, if in the minds of half the number of members, the said minister has lost the confidence of the Assembly. But the question is, what happens if the President refuses to remove the minster? After all, the minister is not necessarily an elected member of the National Assembly. Furthermore, the President is not elected to his post by the National Assembly but directly by the will of the people. The Constitution is silent about what follows the President's refusal to remove the minister. Probably resort may be had to the *shura* (advisory opinion) in order to arrive at any solution.

1.2.3 *The judicial system*

The judicial system under the new constitution consists of three bodies, namely the judiciary, the Constitutional Court, the legal advisors and Attorney General. The legal advisors and Attorney General in fact constitute one body.

1.2.3.1 The judiciary

Article 99 declares that the administration of justice is vested in an independent judiciary which is responsible to the President of the Republic. Article 101(1) restricts the independent of judges to the performance of their duties only. The organs of the judiciary are the same as had existed before the Constitution. The President of the Republic appoints and removes the Chief Justice, deputy Chief Justices and all other judges. Conditions of service and immunities of judges are determined by law (Article 104).

1.2.3.2 The Constitutional Court

For the first time in the Sudan, the Constitutional Court has been created as a separate organ from the judiciary. Its president and members are appointed by the President of the Republic with the approval of the National Assembly. Its members need not be professional lawyers. The jurisdiction of this Court includes:

(a)   the interpretation of the Constitution, laws presented by the President, the National Assembly or half the number of governors of half of the number of the states assemblies;

(b)   cases of aggrieved persons which are related to the protection of freedoms or constitutional rights; and

(c)   cases of conflict of jurisdiction between the central organs and states units.

This Court is the custodian of the Constitution (Article 195).

1.2.3.3 Legal advisors and the Attorney General

This institution consists of legal counsels and attorneys who represent the government in legal disputes. They serve as government legal advisors and there is a special unit which deals with prosecution of persons who are accused of crimes.

1.3 The federal system

Sudan, as stated earlier, has been divided into twenty-six regional governments or states and there is a central government for the whole country (Article 108). Article 2 describes the Sudan as

a decentralized republic governed at the upper level of power on the basis of a federal system as prescribed by the Constitution nationally centralized and regionally divided into states . . . It shall be ruled at the base by local governments.

The formulation of this provision, which fuses varying concepts together, tends to make it difficult to comprehend exactly whether the system of government in the Sudan is a federation or central state, with devolution of some powers to the regional governments. The draftsmanship of the contents of this article is a clear manifestation of a logical expression of the intention to accommodate the conflicting views of two groups of Sudanese citizens. One group of citizens desires the maintenance of a complete centralized system of government and national unity, while the other view comes from the advocates of unity in diversity, which ranges from federation to confederation.

However, the Constitution provides that the system in the Sudan is a federation, for example, the title of Part VI is "the Federal System". But strictly speaking, the analysis of the established system does not show that it is a federation,[2] but a centralized government with devolution of some executive powers. In the permanent Constitution, the government of the centre is not limited. For example, the appointment of the governor involves the power to select three people of his own choice out of the list of six candidates nominated by the electoral college. He also consults with the General Election Commission about the eligibility of the three candidates to hold the office. The Election Commission, of course, consists of the appointees of the President of the Republic. The governor is responsible, *inter alia*, to the President of the Republic. This means that he falls under the control of the President of the Republic. This further means that the governor and all his ministers are under the control of the President, who is practically not only the head of the executive in the central government but in the whole country. Further, the governor must consult with the President of the Republic when he is appointing state ministers. The ministers (Articles 64(4) and 50) are also responsible to the President of the Republic. On the other hand the central legislature (National Assembly) legislates for the whole country. Although the state assemblies (Article 90) apparently have the power to legislate, it is inconceivable that they should enact substantive laws such as criminal laws, law of evidence, land law and so on. There is no apparent limitation of the power of the National Assembly to legislate for the

---

[2] Of course in a true federal Constitution "the powers of the government are divided between a government for the whole Country and government for parts of the Council in such a way that each government is legally independent within its own sphere. The government for the whole Country has its own area of powers and it exercises them without any control from the governments of the constituent parts of the Country, and these latter in their turn exercise their powers without being controlled by the Central Government. In particular the legislature of the whole Country has limited powers and the legislatures of the states . . . have limited powers. Neither is subordinate to the other, both are coordinate": K. C. Where, *Modern Constitutions*, Oxford University Press, Oxford, at p. 19.

whole country. Under Article 120, both the National Assembly and state assembly may request each other to postpone the passing of a Bill (before it) until each gives its opinion on the Bill, if it has a national effect or special effect on the state. It is not shown whether the giving of such an opinion in the Bill may ultimately result in preventing that Bill from being passed, if the National Assembly thinks that it has a national effect. This provision is likely to be used to curtail or limit the legislative power of the state assemblies by the National Assembly and in fact there is no distinct margin between what has "national effect" and what has not. Further, under Article III(i), the powers of both the state executive and the state assembly are limited to hose matters which conform with federal laws. In other words neither the state executive nor the state assembly has any power to act or legislate contrary to the federal laws which are enacted by the National Assembly. This provision enshrines the subordination of the state assembly to the National Assembly.

The other organ of the Constitution, namely the judiciary, is a completely centralized institution. There is no state judiciary. Hence both the Supreme and Constitutional Courts have an unlimited jurisdiction over all of the Sudan.

Finally, the system of government in the Sudan is not therefore a federation, but a centralized government with devolved powers to the regional government.

1.4 Declaration of state of emergency

Where an imminent or serious danger, such as war, invasion, blockade, catastrophe or epidemic occurs or threatens the country or the safety or the economy of the land, the President of the Republic may declare a state of emergency in all or part of the country. The declaration of emergency shall be presented to the National Assembly within fifteen days from the date of its issue for approval. An extraordinary session shall be called if the National Assembly is not in session.

During the emergency period, the President of the Republic has extensive and extraordinary powers. He may suspend the operation of fundamental human rights except those which are related to freedom from slavery, torture, right of faith, litigation, defence and indiscrimination on basis of sex or religion.

The President may dissolve or suspend any of the state organs or suspend the constitutional powers conferred on the state. He shall personally exercise the function so of the dissolved or suspended organs. The National Assembly may agree to extend the period of emergency. Any exceptional decisions taken by the President during the emergency shall be presented to the National Assembly for approval or amendment or repeal.

2 LAW OF EVIDENCE

2.1 Introduction

Law of evidence is one of the laws which experienced rapid changes in recent years as a result of the new policies aimed at "going back to the roots" (i.e. of *shari'a* law). Prior to 1983, Sudanese courts applied the English law of evidence as adapted by the Indian Evidence Act 1872. The policy of returning to the roots largely gained ground in September 1983 when the Evidence Act 1983, which reflected the principles of *shari'a* law, was enacted. However, in 1993 the Evidence Act 1983 was repealed when the current Evidence Act (Act 1993) was promulgated. Although some of the rules under this Act appear to be secular in nature, they must be interpreted by courts in the light of the general principles and the spirit of Islamic *shari'a*.

2.2 Fundamental principles: general presumptions

Section 5 of the Evidence Act 1993 lays down fundamental or basic principles which are supposed to serve as guides to judges or courts when they are handling cases. Most of these fundamental principles are, in fact, rebuttable general presumptions. Of course, some of these principles existed in the Sudanese law prior to the introduction of the *shari'a* law. The section provides as follows:

(a) Freedom from liability is the basic presumption in transactions, but he who asserts the contrary has a duty to adduce evidence to prove it.

(b) An accused person is presumed to be innocent until proved guilty beyond reasonable doubt.

   In contrast with a standard of proof in civil matters, which is attained by a preponderance of evidence, the standard of proof in criminal matters is very high. There must not be any slightest doubt as to whether an accused person is guilty or not. The benefit of doubt goes in favour of the accused. Of course, this is not a new rule of evidence in the Sudan. It has always been the guiding principle in the Sudanese courts. It is a reminder of the traces of the general principles of English law which were applicable in the Sudan.

(c) A person is presumed to be qualified to be able to dispose of his personal matters and where any other person asserts the contrary or the existence of temporary incapacity or that a guardian has been appointed to manage his affairs (i.e. as a result of incapacity or some inability) he is bound to prove this.

   This principle is a replica of the rule that things which are known to exist are normally presumed to continue to exist till the contrary is proved (see section 5(d)). Life would be very onerous if every person were required to live out of fear or suspicion, though on the contrary what is always known to be true must be proved by a person who asserts it.

(d) The legislative, executive and judicial matters are presumed to be in conformity with the law and where a person asserts their non-conformity with the law, he is under duty to prove it.

   The judges or the courts are required to take judicial notice of the conformity of these matters with the law. In other words, a court of law or a judge will not require a person who claims that these matters conform with the law to prove it by adducing evidence. Again this is not a new concept in Sudan.

(e) No specific statement may be attributed to a person who remains silent; such silence in circumstances which require an answer may lead a court to draw a reasonable inference from it.

   In circumstances as stated above, silence may be equated with admission by conduct. No fact could be deemed to have been established by proof if a person who had done an act by his own hands were to be allowed to deny that he had done it. This is similar to a situation where a person has been caught red-handed in the commission of an act or offence.

2.3 Objectionable (or rebounding) evidence

Section 9 of the Evidence Act prescribes the circumstances or conditions in which a judge or court of law is entitled to refuse to admit evidence adduced by a party or his witness. Evidence is rejected on the following grounds:

(a)   Where it contravenes the general principles of Islamic *shari'a*, or law or justice or public order.
       A court of law, for example, is entitled to reject the evidence of one, two or three men who claim that they had witnessed the commission of the act of adultery. *Shari'a* law requires the evidence of four just male persons (Section 62(b)). A further example of evidence which contravenes Islamic *shari'a* is that which has been adduced by a woman or women for proof of the commission of the act of adultery. Women are in fact incompetent witnesses in cases of adultery and so their testimony must be rejected.
       Under this clause, the word "law" means law or rule of law other than *shari'a* law. It may be a piece of legislation or a judicial precedent. But some recent judicial interpretations of law in Sudan contend that what contravenes or is contrary to the ordinary law or justice or public order is equally contrary to or contravenes *shari'a* law even where there is no direct violation of a specific *shari'a* law rule.

(b)   Where the evidence is based on the judges' personal knowledge, it must be rejected.
       However, it may be submitted that if evidence known to the judge personally is also adduced by an independent witness or witnesses, it must be admitted on this ground. This rule cannot be construed to mean that evidence produced by independent witnesses ought to be rejected merely because it is also within the knowledge of the judge trying the case.

(c)   Where the evidence comes from a non-expert. The rule must not, however, be construed to mean that evidence adduced by persons who have special technical or professional skills. However, under section 10 of the Evidence Act 1991, a piece of evidence is not necessarily objectionable or inadmissible merely on the grounds that it was obtained through improper procedure where the court believes or is satisfied that it was independently obtained and is worth of admission. This is somewhat of a divergence from the previous legal position in the Sudan. Previously any evidence obtained through improper means, such as a search conducted without a warrant signed by a magistrate or judge or through coercion was absolutely inadmissible as a matter of policy. The objective for inadmissibility of this type of evidence was to ensure more effective protection of accused persons. It was enough for the rejection of evidence by court that it had been wrongly obtained. The value and the weight of that evidence were immaterial in such circumstances.
       It is only in criminal matters, now under section 20(2) of the Evidence Act, 1991 where an admission lacks credit if it is a result of torture or coercion.

The section is still silent as to whether an admission obtained through torture or coercion is inadmissible or not if the court believes in its truth. Clause 3 of the same section goes on to state that:

Without prejudice to the provisions of clause 2, coercion (or torture) has no effect as to the truth or correctness of the admission of the commission of the act or transaction (complained of).

The query posed in relation to clause 2 can also be applied in relation to clause 3. If an accused person, through coercion, admits the commission of the act subject of the charge against him and the court believes that he had committed the act, can it admit the evidence so obtained? Further, the Act provides that a mistake in the admission or rejection of evidence does not itself constitute a reason for ordering a retrial or remission of judgment by the appellate court, in any case where it appears to the appellate court that the judgment subject of appeal or objection, is already supported by sufficient evidence, and that even if the evidence mistakenly admitted is rejected or if the evidence mistakenly rejected is re-admitted, the judgment will not be affected or altered (section 12).

2.4 Judicial notice

Matters of common knowledge or those which are presumed to be so notorious need no proof in courts. Under section 14 of the Act, public matters or institutions are judicially noticed. A court of law does not require a litigant or witness before it to prove these matters by production of evidence. These matters include:

(a) the Constitution, statutory provisions, judicial precedents and declarations which have a force of law;
(b) the general particulars related to the structure or organization or institutions of the legislature, the executive, the judiciary and their units;
(c) every state recognized by the government of the Sudan and in general all matters of state and policies connected with Sudan foreign relations;
(d) division of time (i.e. hours, days of the week, month, year), geographical divisions, weights and measures;
(e) public and national holidays;
(f) Sudanese general customs which are recognized by courts;
(g) the general meanings of words; and
(h) ordinary laws and their normal operation.

In all the matters by which a court takes a judicial notice, it may investigate or consult with a concerned official or make any suitable reference or revise any documents for the purpose of taking such judicial notice.

2.5 Proof of specific offences

There are specific offences known as *hudud* in *shari'a* law, which require a special type of proof. These offences are adultery, false accusation of unchastity, theft, *haraba* (armed robbery) and drinking of alcohol. The offence of adultery, apart from the rest of *hudud* offences, has a separate procedure or way of proving its commission. There are two distinct procedures. In the first place, a husband may accuse his wife of adultery and there may be no way of proving his case. In such circumstances, the procedure to be followed by the court is provided under section 60 of the Act. It is technically known as "*liaan* oath".

This procedure requires the husband to swear before the court that his wife has committed adultery or that her pregnancy was not caused by him. He must take the oath four times in the name of God that he is telling the truth. He must then swear for a fifth time by saying that the curse of God shall be upon him if he is one of the liars.

When the husband has taken the oath, it is the turn of the wife to take he oath four times in the name of God that her husband is one of the liars and in the fifth time, she swears that the wrath of God shall be upon her if she is not sincere.

The result of the oath taking by both spouses is that the court will declare the termination of the marital relationship between them. The question as to who stated the truth is left to God's judgment.

However, where the husband takes the oath while the wife refuses, she will be punished by the court for the commission of the offence of adultery. Her refusal to take the oath shall be construed as an admission.

The second procedure is followed by the court where adultery may be proved by testimony of eye witnesses or wife's admission.

2.5.1 Proof of adultery by evidence

Adultery may be proved in one of the following ways:

(a)   clear admission by wife before the court, provided that this admission has not been retracted before the execution of the sentence;

(b)   testimony of four just male men.

It is not shown by section 62 whether or not the court will have to follow a procedure of investigating the character of the witnesses in order to ascertain whether they are just or not. Further the section does not show whether the court is entitled to reject the testimony of the four witnesses if it thinks that they are not just.

The section is silent about the testimony of just "women". This is because women, in *shari'a* law, are incompetent witnesses in the case of adultery;

(c)   where the woman's pregnancy has been well established beyond doubt that it was not caused by her husband;

(d)   where the wife refuses to take the oath after her husband has taken *liaan* oath that she has committed adultery.

2.5.2 Proof of the commission of other hudud offences

The commission of a *hudud* offence other than adultery may be proved in any one of the following (see section 63):

(a)   express admission (even once) before the court of law;
(b)   the testimony of two men or one man and two women or of four women.

Of course, under the *shari'a* law, the testimony of one man equals that of two women.

2.5.3 Proof for the offence of drinking liquor or alcohol

Despite the general proof for the commission of the *hudud* offences, as prescribed under section 63 of the Act, it is enough (under Section 64) to prove the drinking of alcohol by mere smell of it. The commission of the offence is established if two just persons testify that the smell is that of alcohol or by the report of a concerned expert that the smell is that of alcohol.

2.5.4 Remission of the hudud offence

The offence of *hudud* is remitted (Section 65) in three specific instances, namely:

(a)   where there is specific reasonable doubt as to the commission of a *hudud* offence;
(b)   where witnesses retract their testimonies or where such testimonies contradict each other or where a witness retracts his admission.
(c)   where the wife takes the oath that she has not committed the offence of adultery.

3 LAND LAW AND PLANNING

3.1 Development Planning and Disposal of Lands Act 1994

Land in the Sudan is indisputably the most important asset. For this reason, the previous Land Acts had been reviewed, updated and amalgamated (except for the Land Settlement and Registration Act of 1925) to effectively regulate land development and disposal to meet the more complex needs of the people, for example in the fields of economy, agriculture, human settlements, housing schemes for humanitarian purposes, towns and village planning and re-planning, services rendered by bodies such as municipalities, rural councils and health and educational institutions.

While land settlement and registration and the settlement of legal disputes between proprietors or owners of registered lands remain under the Land Settlement and Registration Act 1925, the new Act bears the title Development Planning and Disposal of Lands Act 1994, and deals with the problems of land planning, development and its disposal.

The new Act repealed the previous Land Acts, namely the Development Planning Act 1986, the Disposal of Lands Act 1986 and the Town Planning and Re-planning Act 1950.

The new Act has been divided into six distinct parts. The first part from sections 1 to 3 deals with preliminary issues such as the title of the Act, repeal of previous

Acts and definitions of legal terminologies. The second part, (sections 4 to 7) deals with the creation of the Federal Council of Development Planning and its supervisory role in the implementation of the provisions of the Act.

The third part of the Act (sections 8 to 18) deals with problems of land development planning, while the fourth part (sections 19 to 39) deals with land re-planning. The fifth part (sections 40 to 62) deals with land disposal. Part six deals with regulations for the implementation of the Act.

3.1.1 *The creation of the Federal Council for Development*

Under this Act, the three most important institutions are namely the Federal Council for Development and Planning, the State Development Planning Committee and the Re-planning Committee. The Federal Council for Development and Planning is appointed by the Council of Ministers while its Chairman is appointed by the President of the Republic with a recommendation from the Council of Ministers. The Council's membership includes among others: (a) the Minister of Housing in every state; (b) the Director General of the Survey Department; and (c) the first Under-secretaries of certain services ministries, including the Ministry of Finance.

3.2 Jurisdiction and Council's powers (section 8)

The Council has been vested with wide general powers of land development and planning. These include the power to:

(a) lay down strategies for national development planning for land use. These strategies must conform with the balanced and comprehensive national development plans provided that there has to be balanced development planning between various states and also between the urban and rural areas in relation to services renders by institutions such as municipalities. These strategies for national planning must be approved by the Council of Ministers;

(b) conduct studies and researches in cooperation with states' development institutions in the fields of development planning, especially in the field of land use for the purpose of housing transport and services rendered in the municipalities and rural areas;

(c) revise planned schemes for development which had already been prepared by the states' institutions. After the completion of the revision, the planned schemes are forwarded to the Council of Ministers for approval;

(d) grant approvals for development structure and the establishment of fuel depots or fuel storage centres and housing complexes for humanitarian projects;

(e) grant approvals for alteration of land use according to the plans passed by the Council of Ministers. However, open spaces and public squares are exempted from such alteration of land use;

(f) supervise the conduct of states' planning institutions and to follow up the execution of national development plans;

(g)   prepare legal bills which are intended to regulate the execution of special policies for development planning.

3.3 The powers of the minister (section 9)

The minister in this context means the Minister of Housing in each state. The minister is very instrumental in the development, planning or in the execution of the
provisions of the Act. He has been vested with wide powers, which include:

(a)   the issuing of directives to the state land authorities to prepare land development plans in conformity with the national development planning and the
national economic and social development plans which had already been passed
by the Council of Ministers;
(b)   the laying down of plans for housing projects in the state in conformity with
national land development planning and in relation to the national, social
and economic development plan. The minister's plans must receive the approval of the Council of Ministers before they are executed;
(c)   supervision of the executive bodies in their execution of policies which are
related to the housing and development planning in the states;
(d)   the declaration upon the recommendation made to him by the State Development Committee, of the boundaries of any town or village and the alteration of such boundaries from time to time;
(e)   the making of recommendations to the Council of Ministers to give approvals
to change, when necessary, the use of open spaces and public squares for different purposes;
(f)   the disposal of appeals submitted to him against the decisions of the State
Development Committee.

Where the minister intends to exercise the powers of planning which are vested in
him by the Act, he must publish a prior and detailed notice in the Official Gazette
that he intends to exercise his powers in a specific area (section 12).

3.4 State Development Planning Committee (section 11)

This Committee is very important for land development planning in each state. It
prepares general policies for development planning, housing, bases of or condition
for allotment of and land uses in the state. It lays down these plans in conformity
with national economic and social development planning. The Committee is responsible for making plans, projects for land development, drawing maps and structural plans for towns and rural development in accordance with the standard already
laid down in the state. It grants approvals for detailed plans leading to the use of
vacant and developed lands. The Committee also approves the plans for the establishment of fuel depots and building complexes which are related to major humanitarian development in the state. The Committee has the power to alter the use of
open spaces and public squares for other objectives whenever it deems it necessary.
It approves project structures for re-planning and environmental improvement in
developed areas. It grants permits for development and fixes areas for storey buildings

and decides the number of flats in each building. The powers conferred on the above institutions overlap in many areas.

3.5 Government power over undeveloped lands (section 14)

Owing to the importance of land to the state and people, once it has been allotted to a person or body, it must be developed according to the stipulated conditions in the lease. Where it remains undeveloped after its allotment for a specified period, the presumption is that the proprietor does not need it and so it may be reclaimed and allotted to a person who will develop it.

The procedure is that where the land after its classification remains in the hand of the proprietor undeveloped, whether before or after the enactment of this Act, the Committee may request the settlement of its ownership according to the provisions of the Land Ownership Settlement Act 1930. The proprietor must be notified for a period of one year. This period is calculated to give him a chance to develop the land. But if the period passes without any development, the settlement proceedings begin. Section 14(3) of the Act regulates the procedure for the payment of compensation of the settlement of land ownership.

3.6 Penalties

There are penalties for any person who develops land without prior permission from the government. He may be imprisoned for a period which does not exceed one year or fined or both sentences may be passed (section 18). Of course, the registration of any land or permission to develop it cannot be made or given unless it has been shown that all sums lawfully due as difference of improvement (of land) have been paid.

3.7 Re-planning of towns and villages (sections 19 to 39)

The objectives for the re-planning of towns and villages are many. They are aimed at the improvement of the layout of towns and villages to match the modern standards of living. The original town (or village) planning might have been carried out when the economic standard of the people was very low and thus led to the building of poor houses, or when the population was too small and traffic was very light and the roads were narrower and fewer. Services could have been designed to suit the small size of the population at that time.

With the increase of the population, traffic and a rise in the economic standard of the people, a serious need arises for better and more houses, more and wider roads and the establishment of more and efficient services, institutions (such as municipal and rural councils), schools, hospitals, dispensaries, fuel depots, play or sports grounds and so on. The increase of these factors demands, on the part of the government, the adoption of the policy for the re-planning of towns and villages.

Hence under the Act, when it appears to the state governor, on the recommendation submitted to him by the Minister of Housing, that the re-planning of any town or village is a requisite in the interest either of the public health or amenities or development, he shall cause notice to be published in the Official Gazette or in any other appropriate manner (section 19).

After this official notice has been published, no person is allowed to erect any new building or boundary wall or make any structural repairs to any existing building unless he has obtained a written notice from the Minister of Housing. The procedure for the re-planning begins after the official publication of the notice. The governor starts to issue orders fro the framing of a draft of general plan of the new layout of the area in which the classification of the land is altered. The draft plan is submitted to the State Development Planning Committee for approval before its execution is ordered by the minister. The re-planning programme is executed by a Committee (Section 27) known as the Re-planning Committee which is heading by a re-planning officer who is appointed by the state governor upon a recommendation made by the Minister of Housing (section 26). The Committee follows the procedure prescribed under sections 30 and 31 of the Act. Its powers which include the opening of new roads etc. are provided under section 33 of the Act. It is the duty of the Committee to assess the losses incurred by persons who are affected by the re-planning orders under section 33. The Re-planning Committee is required under section 35 to request the hovernment to pay compensation as it has been assessed under section 34, to persons who are adversely affected by the re-planning orders issued by them under section 33. Orders issued by the Committee under sections 33, 34 and 35 of the Act bind both the government and the persons affected (section 36). All of the Committee's orders must be registered and they affect the land ownership acquired under the provisions of Land Settlement and Registration Act 1925.

Where a person, who has been ordered by the Committee to remove his building within a fixed period, fails to do so, the governor is entitled to demolish it (section 36).

Any person who is adversely affected by any assessment of loss made by the Committee according to the provisions of section 34 or who is injured by order issued by the Committee under section 35 is entitled to appeal to the province judge (section 38). The law provides penalties for persons who violate its provisions. A penalty of imprisonment for a period which is not less than two years or a fine or both may be imposed by the court (section 39).

3.8 Disposal of lands (sections 40 to 62)

Provisions of this part of the Act apply to all government lands and they regulate the disposal of such lands through sale, lease, allotment, *wakf*, mortgage, gift and so on. These provisions also regulate lands where licences for mining of petroleum are granted as well as lands allotted under the Encouragement of Investment Act 1990.

The implementation of these provisions is carried out by the Federal Council for Development Planning, the Minister of Housing and the Director General of Lands. Each of these bodies is vested with wide powers (sections 42 and 43).

In the allotment of lands to applicants the minister follows the following priorities:

(a)   central and states' government ministries' units, government corporations;
(b)   education and health institutions;
(c)   religious institutions according to recommendations of concerned authority;
(d)   sports, social, cultural, cinema, etc.;
(e)   fuel depots and storage; and
(f)   compensations (with lands) for those affected by the re-planning.

The Act prohibits the disposal of government land unless certain specific procedural requirements are taken. For example, it must be shown prior to the disposal that the land, whether it is registered or not, is free from encumbrances. There must be an approval for its development from the land development authorities. Furthermore, its survey and demarcation must have been completed (section 45).

Before the disposal of any government land, the Minister or Director General must ascertain first whether or not the land in question has been correctly registered in the name of the government (section 46). Disposal of government land may be concluded by means of a binding lease contract. The government is represented, in the lease contract, by the Director General or his delegate as the first party.

The tenant or the usufructuary (or the leasee) is bound by the conditions of the lease contract. He cannot invest on land for different purposes other than those stipulated in the lease unless he has obtained approval from land authorities. The tenant or the leasee must make development on the land leased to him within a stated period. However, where he fails to make development within the stated period or within the extended period without stating any reasonable grounds to justify such failure, the concerned land authorities may abrogate the lease contract and recover the land from him.

The Act imposes penalties, consisting of imprisonment for a period which does not exceed two years or a fine or both, on persons who violate its provisions (section 62).

4 LABOUR LAW

4.1 Labour Act 1997: Repealed Acts and Exemptions

This Act was enacted and came into force on 22 June 1997. It repealed the following Acts:

(a)   Manpower (Labour Force) Act 1974;
(b)   Industrial Relations Act 1976;
(c)   Industrial Security Act 1976; and
(d)   Labour Relations Act 1981.

The Act exempts from its operation the state officials or employees who are governed by special laws. These included judges, legal counsellors from the Attorney-General's chambers, members of the organized forces, (namely the army, police, prison warders and state security personnel) and other employees of government or public corporations and companies of the public sector who are governed by the terms of their employments. House servants (as defined by the House Servants Act 1955), agricultural workers, workers (of the government) who repair machines or who deal in mechanical work, factory workers, ginning factories and laboratory workers and member of the family of the owner of the business are exempted (section 3).

4.2 Conditions of work

Chapter 3 of the Act enacts provisions for organizational structure and procedure, while chapter 4 lays down conditions of work. For example, women are not employed to do dangerous work or work which requires much physical ability. They must not remain at the place of work between 10 pm and 6 am. A prior medical examination must be carried out before a person is employed.

Contracts of labour are provided under chapter 5. It is prescribed that any contract of a period exceeding three months must be written. Any contract which conflicts with the provisions of this Act is null and void (section 31). The owner of the business is prohibited from assigning his employee to discharge a work for which he was not employed to do under the contract.

Provisions which regulate the period of work and annual leave fall under chapter 7. The normal period of work is forty-eight hours a week (section 42(1)). However, the employer is entitled, after consultation with the concerned minister (of manpower) or governor, to amend the hours of work daily or weekly. A worker is entitled to an annual leave (section 44(1)) with full wages after completing a period of one year form the date of his employment. A woman (Muslim) whose husband has died is entitled to observe an *idda* period of four months and ten days with full salary.

4.3 Termination of contract with or without notice

Conditions or circumstances which regulate the termination of the contract of labour after the giving of notice, either by employer or employee are provided for under chapter 8. However, the party objecting to the termination of contract is entitled to appeal to the minister (of manpower) or the governor within two weeks from the date of receiving notice. The minister or governor on his part is required to respond within fourteen days from the date he received the appeal. The employer is bound to pay to the employee all the rights due to him where the minister or the governor has accepted the termination of the contract of labour. However, where the minister or governor rejects the termination of the contract, the employee must be returned to his job (section 52) while he is entitled to receive all his entitlements for the period of his suspension from work.

Although such a contracting party is entitled to notify the other for the termination of contract, there are exceptional circumstances where such prior notice is not required. For example, where a person has been employed through the inducement cause by the forgery he had committed or where the employee has made a mistake resulting from his negligence which causes a substantial economic loss to the employer, the latter is entitled to terminate the contract of labour without giving prior notice to the employee. Likewise, the employee is entitled to terminate the

contract of labour where, for example, the employer or his representatives had in-
duced him by means of deceit to accept the contract (section 54(a)).

4.4 Closure of business and deceased's family rights

The employer (section 56) is entitled to reduce his work force or close his business, after he has sought and obtained the approval or consent of the minister concerned or the governor on the grounds of economic deterioration. Further, the
employer is entitled to terminate the labour contract when the business for which
the contract was concluded has been completed. In this case, the employer is required to issue certificates of work to the employees.

Chapter 10 provides general principles. Among these are the principles of rules
which entitle the members of the family of a deceased employee the right to receive wages, gratuities and other amounts of money to which the deceased was entitled to receive when he was alive (section 68).

4.5 Safety measures and certain workers' rights

The Act embodies provisions which ensure the safety of employees against hazardous
works. For the purpose of ensuring adequate security against dangers, the labour office authorities, or anyone else authorized by the minister or governor, is entitled
to inspect the place of work, whether by day or night, to ascertain the safety conditions (section 69). Sections 37 to 98 provide rules to ensure safety of industrial workers. Further, the Act provides favourable conditions regarding certain rights of employees. For example (in cases of insolvency of the employer), monetary entitlements
of employees have a priority to be discharged before other debts of the employers
are ordered to be paid by the courts (section 71). Further suits for claims of rights
by workers against employers at any judicial state are exempted from payment of
court fees.[3] Again, the right of action by a worker against his employer is not affected
by the limitation of time (section 73).

The Act does not embody any express provision for the reference of legal disputes
between the employers and employees to the Labour Court (as the repealed Act did)
although sections 100, 1010 and 103 give the impression that labour disputes go
to the courts.

4.6 Settlement of labour disputes

Where a legal dispute arises, the employer and employee (or employees) enter into
negotiations, with a view to settle it within fourteen days (section 105(1)). The minister concerned or the governor may attend the negotiations although he is not en-

---

[3] This provision gives the impression that cases arising out of contract of labour are litigated in
civil courts. However, s. 103 of the Act prohibits the raising of a civil suit before a civil court
against employer or employee for doing any act in expectation of labour dispute or its
continuation. No suit must be raised on the grounds of breach of labour contract.

titled to contribute. His presence at the negotiations, in fact, puts pressure on the parties to reach a settlement. The minister's or governor's attendance also provides him with full knowledge of the extent of the legal dispute.

If the parties fail to reach a settlement during their negotiations, each of them is entitled to petition to the minister concerned or the governor to intervene (section 106). Each party is entitled to choose three representatives to appear before the minister or governor concerned for the settlement of the dispute. However, if the minister or the governor fails to bring about the settlement of the dispute he will have to refer it to arbitration (section 113). Advocates, representing the parties, are entitled to appear before the arbitration. The arbitrators are required to make their decision by majority and where there is a dissenting opinion it has to be written. Decisions made by arbitration are final and cannot be questioned in any way prescribed for raising objections. It is not yet clear whether the stated finality of the decisions of the Arbitration Board precludes the power of judicial review. In many similar instances where the laws make decisions of certain executive authorities final, the Sudanese courts have often held that such "finality" only affects or curtails the appellate right but it does not preclude the inherent power of judicial review which is aimed at protecting the laws themselves. It provides courts with the power to correct mistakes of law or violations of the laws by bodies who are entitled to make decisions.

5 LAW OF TORTS

5.1 Liability in tort: compensation awards in criminal courts

Upon the enactment of criminal laws in 1983 and 1991 (whose rules are largely based on the general principles of *shari'a* law), the volume of civil cases involving liability in tort noticeably diminished before the courts. Prior to the enactment of these criminal laws, litigation in tortious liability was carried out in accordance with the general principles or concepts of the English common law. General damages were determined on concepts such as loss of pecuniary benefits or income, loss of amenities and so on. These general concepts of English common law have now become obsolete.

Today, people who have suffered physical injuries caused by acts done by others may be compensated under the specific provision of the Criminal Procedure Law. The criminal court may, after the conviction of an accused, impose a sentence of a fine on him and thereafter order that a specific sum, out of the fine money, shall be paid to the injured party (or the complainant) as compensation (see section 198 of the Criminal Procedure Act 1991). Under this section, the criminal court may order the compensation of the complainant directly. Very few injured persons who believe in the inadequacy of compensation in criminal courts may struggle to claim more damages before Civil Courts thereafter.

In cases where the injured person dies, his relatives are entitled to a liquidated sum of money which is reviewed and fixed from time to time (to meet the rate of inflation) by the Chief Justice by means of a judicial circular in exercise of his powers under section 212 of the Criminal Procedure Act 1991. Compensation in traffic cases is dealt with under the Traffic Act and a judicial circular promulgated by the Chief Justice.

Despite the shifting of much volume of litigation in the area of claims of compensation or damages to the Criminal Courts, there are still legal provisions (see chapters 1, 2 and 3 of the Civil Transaction Act 1984) which regulate liability of defendants in specific types of liability.

5.2 Liability for personal acts

It is provided under section 138 of the Civil Transactions Act 1984 (CTA 1984), that for every act which causes harm to another, the perpetrator shall be obliged to pay compensation to the victim. The act of a minor also causes liability. Acts include omissions. The law not only imposes a duty to protect the lives (or bodies) of other people, but the safety of others' property and reputation (section 139).

5.3 Exceptions to liability for personal acts (section 40)

There are exceptions to liability for personal acts and these include cases where:

(a) it can be proved that the harm was due to extraneous cause such as *force majeure* (act of God), or where the defendant was not negligent, or where the act was done by a third person;
(b) the defendant acted out of necessity, or acting in exercise of his right of private defence of his life, reputation or property;
(c) the defendant was obliged in the prevailing circumstances to choose the lesser of the two evils; or
(d) the defendant is a public servant who acted at the time in accordance with the orders of his superiors, provided he was (legally) bound to obey such orders, or he believed himself to be bound, and that his belief was based on reasonable grounds and that he acted with due care and diligence (section 144).

5.4 Liability for acts of others

Chapter 2 provides rules which regulate the liability for acts of others. In this field, a guardian is liable for tortious acts done by his/her ward. The ward may be a person who is suffering from mental deficiency or some physical condition. However, the liability is not absolute as the guardian may be exonerated from liability where he/she proves that he/she had performed his/her duty as a guardian with due care and attention.

The second example is the liability of a master for the acts of his servant. However, his liability attaches where it has been proved that the servant was acting during the course of his employment when he caused the harm (section 146). The third example is the liability of the principal for the act of his agent who caused the harm during the course of his employment or when he acted under ostensible (apparent) authority.

5.5 Liability for harm caused by things under control

Chapter 3 deals with liability for things under one's personal control. A person is liable for the injury caused by a thing under his personal control, but it is not clear whether the liability of the keeper of the thing attaches only where the thing caused the harm complained of after it had escaped from the keeper's control, or whether the keeper is liable even if the thing did not escape from the control. Further, it is not clear if the keeper of the thing is liable for harm caused to trespassers on his land. The law provides:

Whoever is guarding (keeping) something shall be liable for any harm caused by that thing to another person, whether such thing is an animal or matter, moveable or immovable.

Kuwait: Setting up and Marketing Investment Funds*

*Fadi B. Nader***

Law No. 31/1990, as amended by a series of directives and most recently by Ministerial Decree 52/1996, regulates "the trading of securities and the incorporation of investment funds" in the state of Kuwait. Under Article 1 of the said legislation, "it is not permitted to offer any shares or bonds of Kuwaiti or non-Kuwaiti joint stock companies or any other securities through a public offering in the state of Kuwait without obtaining a prior permission issued by the Minister of Commerce and Industry". Moreover, Article 3 of this Law prohibits any individual or entity from "engaging in the activity of buying and selling non-Kuwaiti securities or shares of foreign investment funds for the account of third parties without obtaining a licence issued by the Minister of Commerce and Industry". The same article compels any foreign company wishing to engage in such activity, to appoint a Kuwaiti agent, who will be considered in this respect as a guarantor of all the foreign institution's obligations while carrying out its activities in Kuwait.

Under the most recent amendment, the Kuwaiti authorities introduced a clear distinction between marketing shares of a foreign investment fund through a "public offering" and offering such shares through a "private placement". Accordingly, an authorized Kuwaiti financial company or a Kuwaiti agent seeking to sell shares of companies or investment funds in Kuwait should comply with the following:

(a) qualify as a joint stock company who is permitted to act as a fiduciary manager of third parties' assets;
(b) undertake to guarantee all the liabilities of the fund manager *vis-à-vis* any investor acquiring the fund's shares in Kuwait;

---

*   Reprinted from the April 1997 issue of the *Arab Regional Forum Newsletter* published by the International Bar Association.
** Legal Counsel, The International Investor KCSC, Kuwait.

(c)   submit the relevant documentation mainly, a certified copy of the placement agent agreement and certified copies of the fund's organizational documents and prospectus;

(d)   all the fund's bookkeeping as well as a register evidencing the shares purchased in Kuwait should be handled by the Kuwaiti entity;

(e)   obtain the approval of the Ministry of Commerce and Industry who shall determine the period of the offering;

(f)   if the Kuwaiti agent is under the supervision of the Central Bank, an approval from the latter should be obtained.

However, offering shares in foreign investment funds could be conducted through a private placement subject to fulfilling the above mentioned conditions and the satisfaction of the following:

(a)   The minimum value of the subscription should be equal to KD 50,000 which is a prerequisite condition to consider the offering as a private placement.

(b)   The offering should not be advertised in any media or via any public forum.

(c)   The Kuwaiti agent should complete and submit a special application form to the Ministry of Commerce enclosing an Arabic translation of all the fund's organizational documents and offering memorandum.

Under the new regulation, the Kuwaiti legislator clearly distinguishes between an "ordinary" and a "sophisticated" investor. While treating the offering of shares of foreign investment funds through a public offering on the same basis as offering shares in domestic investment funds, the recent amendment reserves a different treatment for companies wishing to target a special segment of the market by offering its shares to well informed and high net worth investors.

As a matter of fact, a licence to effect the private placement could be obtained within two to three weeks and does not require the regulatory authorities to approve the investment strategy, the fee structure, the risk allocation or the redemption mechanism of the fund, as is imperative in the case of a public offering.

The party wishing to conduct a private placement should complete the relevant official application form and submit the same together with the supporting documents to the Ministry of Commerce and Industry who will in its turn refer the application to the Central Bank for its final approval.

However, the placement agent could incur a penalty and could risk the suspension of his licence if he breaches his undertaking to maintain the minimum investment at the equivalent of KD 50,000. On the other hand, any offering of shares below KD 50,000 or its equivalent is treated as a public offering and should in this respect comply with all the requirements imposed by the Kuwaiti regulatory authorities on the listing and offering of domestic shares, mainly the conditions which require the founder of the company or found to subscribe in no less than 10 per cent of the capital of such company or fund. Moreover, the fund or company seeking to offer its shares to the public or to the ordinary investors, should ascertain that there is no restriction imposed on the investors/shareholders to dispose of their shares in the fund, and the fund's/company's Articles of Association and offering Memorandum do not contain any provision which might contradict or violate the "public policy" and the "ethics" of the state of Kuwait.

In summary, a public offering of shares in Kuwait is submitted to a thorough and scrutinized process, while the private placement is a more flexible and practical route for companies and investment managers wishing to tap the Kuwaiti market for funding.

The introduction of the new law is a first step towards regulating a complex area in the financial services industry and in providing a minimum level of protection to individual investors. This legislation puts Kuwait ahead of many Arab countries in attempting to "regularize" a rather "illegitimate" activity which became a common practice among investors and financial institutions alike.

Saudi Arabia

*Michael Dark and Vernon Handley**

A variety of important legal developments have taken place since 1996.

1 FRAMEWORK FOR LOCAL ACCESS TO THE INTERNET ESTABLISHED

Local access to the Internet in Saudi Arabia is currently not generally available. Council of Ministers Resolution No. 163 dated 24/10/1417 AH (corresponding to 3 March 1997) charges the King Abdul Aziz City for Science and Technology (the "KAACST"), in cooperation with the Ministry of Post, Telegraphs and Telecommunications, with general responsibility for establishing an Internet local access network.

Resolution No. 163 anticipates that the KAACST will oversee a bidding process between qualified national firms for the provision of local Internet services on a regional basis within Saudi Arabia. It is understood that qualification requirements will be explained more fully at the beginning of May 1998.

Resolution No. 163 provides that companies offering local Internet access services, as well as parties using the Internet, must:

(a) not reach, or attempt to reach, any of the computer systems connected to the Internet system, to obtain special information or sources of information, without having obtained the approval of the owners of those enjoying (holding) the copyrights, the said system, information or sources;
(b) not use the Internet for unlawful purposes, such as, without limitation, debauchery (seduction and gambling), or practising activities to the prejudice of the social, cultural, political, economic and religious values of Saudi Arabia;
(c) not violate intellectual property rights;

---

* Both of the law firm of Salah Al-Hejailan, Riyadh, Saudi Arabia. The survey covers developments from 1996 to May 1998.

(d)   not use the network in a way that will cause disturbance, threats or rumours to any person;
(e)   not send or receive coded information, without having first obtained a licence;
(f)   not access third party accounts or attempt to use the network without having first obtained a licence;
(g)   not permit a third party to use any access code;
(h)   show respect to the internal systems of the national and international network when accessing them;
(i)   not endanger the security of the local network;
(j)   not use the Internet intensively, preventing third parties from being able to effectively use the Internet; and
(l)   abide by such guidelines and policies regarding the use of the Internet that are issued by the "Internet Service Unit" established by the KAACST.

Resolution No. 163 also establishes a standing committee consisting of various governmental entities and chaired by the Ministry of the Interior, with a brief, amongst other things, to control information on the Internet which may be "prejudicial to any rights, religion and [Saudi Arabian] laws".

2 FOREIGN CAPITAL INVESTMENT: POWER PROJECTS TO CONSTITUTE "DEVELOPMENT ENTERPRISES"

In Saudi Arabia, foreign equity investment is generally prohibited unless the foreign investor first obtains a licence issued by the Ministry of Industry and Electricity upon the recommendation of the Foreign Capital Investment Committee (a "Foreign Capital Investment Licence"). In order to obtain a Foreign Capital Investment Licence pursuant to Royal Decree No. M/4 of 2/2/1399 AH (corresponding to 31 December 1978) the foreign investor must demonstrate that it will invest its capital in a "development project". Ministerial Order No. 11/W/D of 17/7/1410 AH (corresponding to 12 February 1990) defined "development projects" to include the development of (a) manufacturing industry, (b) agricultural production, (c) health services, (d) the provision of services and (e) contracting.

Ministerial Order No. 7/Q/D dated 1/3/1418 AH (corresponding to 5 July 1997) (the "Order") specifically permits foreign capital investment in electric power generation facilities to qualify as a "development project" for the purposes of obtaining a foreign capital investment licence. It is anticipated that the order will provide the legislative basis to enable foreign investors to participate in the construction and operation of power generation facilities in Saudi Arabia (as the applicable legislation prior to the order appeared to suggest that a foreign capital investment licence might be available for the construction of power generation plants, but not for the operation of power generation plants).

Foreign investors in industrial projects are generally entitled to a ten-year tax holiday and the Saudi investment vehicle may be able to obtain low cost financing from the Saudi Industrial Development Fund and will be entitled to certain exemptions from customs duties. Despite the order and the aforementioned benefits, it is thought that foreign investment in power generation projects may continue to be hindered in Saudi Arabia by commercial and practical factors, such as the current low level of electricity prices.

It is widely anticipated that the rules relating to foreign capital investment will generally be amended shortly with a view to making capital investment in Saudi Arabia more attractive to foreign investors. Such changes could include permitting the carrying forward of losses incurred during any tax holiday period (which is not currently permitted).

3 AGREEMENT FOR THE ENFORCEMENT OF JUDGMENTS, DELEGATIONS AND JUDICIAL SUMMONSES IN THE GCC

Royal Decree No. M/3 dated 28/4/1417 AH (corresponding to 11 September 1996) implemented the Agreement for the Enforcement of Judgments, Delegations and Judicial Summons in the States of the Cooperative Council of the Arab States of the Gulf (the "Agreement").

The Agreement provides that judgments rendered in a state that is a member of the Gulf Cooperation Council (the "GCC") will be enforced in another member state unless:

(a) the judgment is contrary to the provisions of *shari'a* law or to the constitution of the state in which the judgment is to be enforced;
(b) the judgment to be enforced was rendered against a person who was not present at the court proceedings and was not properly notified of the court proceedings;
(c) the courts in the jurisdiction where enforcement is sought have previously issued a contrary judgment or have previously considered the subject matter of the dispute giving rise to the judgment;
(d) the judgment was rendered against the government of the state in which enforcement is sought, or against any employee of such government in his capacity as such; or
(e) such enforcement would cause the state in which enforcement is sought to breach the terms of any international agreement to which it is party.

Article 7 of the Agreement provides that the courts before which enforcement proceedings are sought in respect of judgment falling within the ambit of the Agreement will not reconsider the merits of the case in question (other than for the purposes of determining that the restrictions on enforcement of judgments set forth above are not applicable).

The Agreement also permits certain activities connected with legal proceedings required in one jurisdiction to be carried out in another jurisdiction (such as the hearing of witnesses), specifies the means of serving documents relating to legal proceeding in one member state upon persons resident in other member states and seeks to determine when the courts of a member state have jurisdiction to hear a particular case.

The current members of the GCC are Saudi Arabia, Qatar, Kuwait, Bahrain, Oman and the United Arab Emirates.

4 JOINT STOCK COMPANIES

Business entities in Saudi Arabia are governed by Royal Decree M/6 of 22/3/1385 AH (corresponding to 20 July 1965) (the "Companies Regulations"). The principal forms of Saudi Arabian business entities as governed by the Companies Regulations are limited liability company, joint stock company and general partnership. Public joint stock companies are the only type of Saudi companies whose shares can be offered for subscription to the general public.

Shares in Saudi companies cannot generally be owned by non-Saudis in the absence of a foreign capital investment licence (see our comments on foreign capital investment above). As an exception to this general rule, Circular No. 1667 dated 6/9/1418 AH (corresponding to 4 January 1998), implementing Council of Minister Resolution No. 16 dated 20/1/1418 AH (corresponding to 2 May 1997), provides that non-Saudi GCC nationals (that is nationals of Bahrain, Kuwait, United Arab Emirates, Oman and Qatar) may own up to 25 per cent of the shares of a joint stock company, except joint stock companies which are banks, exchange companies and insurance companies.

The Companies Regulations anticipate that business entities established thereunder may convert from one permitted form to another, subject to certain restrictions. Ministerial Order No. 495 dated 25/03/1418 AH (corresponding to 29 July 1997) introduced a number of restrictions on the ability of business entities to convert into public joint stock companies. It is thought that these restrictions were imposed so as to prevent unsound companies from offering their shares for public subscription. These restrictions include requirements that the relevant business entity must:

(a)   have achieved "significant" turnover and profitability in the financial year preceding the date of this conversion application;
(b)   have net assets of not less than SR75,000,000 (approximately US$20 million);
(c)   have had an annual rate of return on equity in each of the financial years preceding the date of the conversion application of not less than 10 per cent;
(d)   be projected (according to a feasibility study required to be submitted by the applicant) to achieve an annual rate of return on equity in each of the financial years succeeding the date of the conversion application of not less than 10 per cent;
(e)   have been established for not less than ten years; and
(f)   be able to demonstrate that it has the management and internal controls appropriate for a joint stock company.

5 WITHHOLDINGS ON THE VALUE OF CONTRACTS

Government departments have for sometime been required to make withholdings from payments to contractors until evidence is presented by the contractor that it has discharged its Saudi tax liabilities.

Resolution 1205 (the "Resolution") dated 28/5/1418 AH (corresponding to 29 September 1997) issued by the Ministry of Finance and National Economy extended this withholding requirement to private sector bodies.

The Resolution provides that:

all companies, establishments, contractors and individuals (Saudis and non-Saudis) who make contracts with any private sector bodies, whether companies, establishments or individuals (Saudis or non-Saudis) are obliged to provide the Department of Zakat and Income Tax with copies of such contracts and to retain 10 per cent of the amount of each contract or the implemented works until submitting a valid certificate from the Department to enable the Department of Zakat and Income Tax to perform its assigned duties to pursue and collect the Zakat dues[1] or the tax payable to the State Treasury within the official specified times.

The amount withheld is not paid to the Department of Zakat and Income Tax, but is retained by the payer pending presentation of the Department of Zakat and Income Tax certificate. Although not expressly set out in the Resolution, the requirement of the Resolution would only seem to be applicable where the payments under the relevant contract are subject to Saudi tax.

---

[1] Zakat is a religious tax on income and property levied on nationals of states belonging to, and companies incorporated in, countries of the Gulf Cooperation Council.

Legal Developments in Saudi Arabia

*Salah Al-Hejailan**

I would like to direct this article at legal developments in my country in five broad areas:

(a)   jurisprudence;
(b)   legislation and treaties;
(c)   the role of the Saudi sponsor and foreign investment generally;
(d)   the philosophy behind the government's new relationship with the private sec-
       tor; and
(e)   the criminal defence process.

PRELIMINARY OBSERVATIONS

I must clarify at the outset that whatever I say about recent reforms in the legal
system in my country, or about what ought to be done in the future, should not
from an analytical perspective be deemed to be inventions or remarkable additions,
because each development is derived from Islam and from *shari'a* law and has at
one point or another historically been put forward in the instructions and rules
and outstanding researches made by Islamic scholars. What we will be talking about
in effect is the written announcement in a modern phraseology or by a promulgation of law of some of those rules that are deeply rooted in *shari'a* law.

Let me give you an example.

A Royal Decree was issued in 1992 by King Fahd announcing the Basic System
of Rules of the country, called in the West a new Constitution. This powerful announcement contains the characterization and confirmation of basic elements that
needed to be codified or announced in a modern style.

* Text of a lecture given at SOAS on 18 June 1998 entitled "Legal Developments in Saudi Arabia".
   (*Editors' note*: although this is included in the country survey, it deals with changes other than
   those covered in 1997–1998.)

These include Article 9, which states that the nucleus of Saudi Arabian society is the family, the members of which shall be brought up according to Islamic belief, with requisite loyalty and obedience to God; Article 10, which states that the state shall strive to strengthen family ties and the safekeeping of Arab and Islamic values; as well as other clauses pertaining among other topics to the working basis of society, the objects of education, and economic principles concerning the wealth of the land, exploitation of resources, public property, seizure of property, taxes and dues and *zakat*.

These are all deemed to be the basic foundation for the structure of our society and all these articles in the Royal Decree contain definitions and statements that are now very useful to have codified and announced as law, so that they can be used in people's presentations and dialogue and in their exchange of views. Again, and this would perhaps be important for our audience to know, there are several articles in the law explaining the rights and obligations of the people and declaring the protection of human rights.

It is mentioned in Article 27 that the state guarantees the rights of the citizen and his family in the event of emergency, sickness, incapacity and old age and supports the Social Security Law. And in Article 28 the state shall create employment for anyone who is capable to work and shall enact laws for the protection of both employee and employer.

Article 29 sets forth that the state shall sponsor science, morality and culture and, in other articles, public education, public health, the environment, defence and so forth. The well-known principles are stated that the penalty is personal, that no offence will be found or penalty imposed except in accordance with the principles of *shari'a* law or legislation; and that no person's liberty may be restricted nor may he be arrested or imprisoned except in accordance with the process of law. The Basic System of Rules addresses means of information, publication and expression, as well as means of communication.

I have noticed in my practice as a lawyer the impact of such legal announcements and such laws containing basic rules that are known beforehand to everyone and are well emphasized in our religion; but the significance of announcing these in the form of a Royal Decree has changed the pattern of presentation in the legal practice and in the judicial system. It is true that reference to these rules has been made in the past, but it has been a heavy burden for whoever was presenting a point to deal with such fundamental concepts. Previously he needed to engage in elaborate analysis and justification from Islamic sources before he asked for anything. Now he makes reference to the relevant articles in the Basic System of Rules and does so in language whose meaning and impact is self-explanatory.

Let us turn now to examination of recent legal developments in certain areas.

1 JURISPRUDENCE

There is a growing tendency towards resuming publication of the decisions of the Board of Grievances, which generally speaking has jurisdiction over disputes with the government and over commercial disputes. Systematic publication was most active in the 1980s and was discontinued several years ago. There was actually no official notice that publication was being interrupted, or explanation, and it may well be that publication was only slowed down due to a review of the approach being taken. In the interim, there has been sporadic reporting of decisions, or exchange of decisions among lawyers or within law firms.

The absence of systematic reporting of cases stems largely from the absence of the doctrine of precedence in Islamic jurisprudence, but without seeking to challenge that concept itself, there is a growing awareness that public review of a judge's decisions leads to an improvement in the quality of his decisions and to better effort on the judge's part to produce reasoned decisions with at least some recognition given, if only implicitly, to decisions or legal thinking in similar cases. None the less, there remains concern among some that over-attention to the formal correctness and consistency of decisions might tend to undermine justice in particular cases and to impinge on the exercise of a judge's wisdom and insight with respect to the actual parties and the dispute before him.

This sort of ongoing fundamental analysis of what from a Western, particularly common law, perspective is taken for granted – the self-evident benefit from publication of judicial decisions – demonstrates not only the still wide divide between the Western and the Arab worlds in some respects, but also the still formative period through which we are moving in parts of the Arab world at this time.

A related development is the codification by the Minister of Justice in a multi-volume set of all circulars relating to the *shari'a* courts. Although this refers to the authoritative instructions to the *shari'a* judges, not to the judicial decisions themselves, none the less allowing concerned parties to have access to these materials and therefore to use the same in making arguments before the *shari'a* courts will lead to greater consistency in the decisions and therefore higher predictability and also towards a better quality of legal reasoning of both advocates and judges.

I might also mention the very up-to-date library at the Institute of Public Administration in Riyadh which contains a codified collection of government resolutions, regulations and administrative rulings. Similarly useful is the monthly *Legal Bulletin* issued by the headquarters in Riyadh of the Gulf Cooperation Council.

You may ask what would I like to see in the future in the legal development of our judicial system, and in that respect I have specific ideas which I am sure the authorities in the Kingdom at the appropriate time will review, and perhaps some similar promulgation will be issued:

(a) We should improve the infrastructure and ambience of the courtroom to make it consistent with the judicial principle that all presentations are public and that there can be suitable publicity.

(b) Judgments of the *shari'a* court are technically not subject to appeal, but are only subject to objection by either party who is not convinced. If that happens, the case will go to the Court of Cassation just to make sure that the judge has paid sufficient attention to the point of objection. There is virtually no re-argument, nor re-trial, nor re-examination of files, nor review of witness statements, except in certain cases. The deed of the judgment contains only the facts and restatements sometimes of the parties' submissions but does not contain the rationale of the judgment. This rationale is available in the internal court file and can be given by the judge only to the Court of Cassation, but not to the parties. Here again, some improvement must be observed.

(c) Generally, there is only a single judge presiding and that may not be adequate for the complexity of some of today's cases. Therefore, we should encourage the practice of a panel of three judges. As matters develop, I am sure this improvement will be considered.

(d) The jurisdiction of the commercial courts in Saudi Arabia is not yet well defined. Sometimes commercial cases are presented to the Board of Grievances in a rather narrow application of the term "commercial", and sometimes to the *shari'a* court, which has very broad jurisdiction. In the Board of Grievances, there is the concept of a panel of more than one judge, which is usually not the same in the *shari'a* court. It is now anticipated, with the complexity of commercial language and the sophistication of agreements, as well as with the development of the infrastructure, that a more specialized body would be placed in charge of commercial disputes more broadly considered. The government is aware of this and a review in this direction is underway.

2 LEGISLATION AND TREATIES

I will direct my remarks to developments in the areas of intellectual property, arbitration and bankruptcy.

A number of significant developments in intellectual property law have occurred recently in Saudi Arabia. Although Saudi Arabia remains on the "priority watch list" maintained by the United States Trade Representative because of lax enforcement of intellectual property rights, the Kingdom's accession to the Universal Copyright Convention and recent cases and administrative actions enforcing trademark laws are positive developments for foreign owners of intellectual property.

Protection of foreign-owned copyrights in Saudi Arabia has been changed substantially by the Kingdom's decision to accede to the Universal Copyright Convention with effect from 1994. Saudi Arabia has had a Copyright Law since 1989, but according to its terms that law does not offer protection for foreign-owned copyrights unless they are first published in Saudi Arabia. Nevertheless, Saudi authorities consider that this limitation has been changed by the Kingdom's accession to the Convention and, in practice, the authorities have begun applying the Copyright Law to foreign-owned copyrights as well.

As regards resolution of intellectual property disputes, a recent development of note is the establishment of the World Intellectual Property Organization (WIPO) Arbitration Centre in Geneva, Switzerland with effect from 1 October 1994. WIPO is a specialized agency within the United Nations, and Saudi Arabia is a party to the Convention Establishing the World Intellectual Property Organization.

The WIPO Arbitration Centre administers four dispute settlement procedures including mediation, arbitration, expedited arbitration and a combination approach.

Of relevance to Saudi Arabia (and the Gulf) is representation on the distinguished WIPO Arbitration Consultative Commission by three Arab members, including one Saudi, who offer opinions and advice to the Centre as requested on non-routine issues.

With the advent of this specialized arbitration system for intellectual property disputes, as well as the stimulus which its activities will give to existing arbitration institutions, further advances with respect to the clarification and enforcement of intellectual property rights in Saudi Arabia are expected.

Until recently, Saudi Arabia was not a party to any convention relating to the recognition or enforcement of foreign judgments or arbitral awards delivered outside the Arab world. Saudi Arabia was a party to the 1952 Convention of the Arab League Concerning the Enforcement of Judgments and the 1995 Agreement for Enforcement of Legal Judgments of the Arab Gulf States Cooperation Council.

This situation has now been modified by the accession of Saudi Arabia to the New York Convention on the Recognition and Enforcement of Foreign Arbitral Awards which entered into force for Saudi Arabia in 1994. The Royal Decree approving accession provided that recognition and enforcement of foreign arbitral awards shall be limited to those made in the territory of states which have also acceded to the New York Convention. It should, however, be stated that, in addition to this requirement, the contents of the awards must neither contravene *shari'a* law nor general public policy prevailing in the Kingdom. There has not as yet been experience with any attempt to enforce a foreign arbitral award by invoking the Kingdom's accession to the New York Convention.

The new Anti-Bankruptcy Regulations of 1996 (with official Explanatory Memorandum) are designed to deal with the situation where a trader who is a debtor is unable to achieve an amicable settlement by unanimity with all of his creditors. The Regulations give the debtor the right to file a settlement petition before the Board of Grievances, which if accepted will cause the Board of Grievances to appoint one of its members and a controller to supervise protective settlement proceedings. The Board may appoint one or more experts to report on the debtor's financial position.

The Board of Grievances is authorized to issue orders taking necessary measures so as to preserve the debtor's property, such as claiming on a negotiable instrument before expiry of the prescribed time limit, provisional attachment, seizure of the debtor's property held by a third party, confiscation of a letter of guarantee before expiry of its term, depositing amounts collected from the debtor's business in a bank, the appointment or dismissal of employees, and so forth.

Solutions are both traditional (debt rescheduling and forgiveness) as well as novel (changes in management and expert assistance).

The protective settlement differs from bankruptcy in that the protective settlement does not aim to liquidate the debtor's property, but rather to provide the debtor acting in good faith with the means to continue his business activities under the controller's supervision.

After completing satisfaction of the conditions of the protective settlement, the Board of Grievances shall upon petition close the proceedings, whereupon the debtor shall practise his business as before he filed for the protective settlement.

3 THE ROLE OF THE SAUDI SPONSOR AND FOREIGN INVESTMENT GENERALLY

The current trend is towards playing down the role of the Saudi sponsor of foreign companies and individuals. This is best seen in the relaxed procedure for foreigners to obtain business visas to visit Saudi Arabia, thereby reducing the importance of the Saudi sponsor as compared to the previously more complicated procedure. Moreover, even for foreigners' resident visas in Saudi Arabia, it has become easier to obtain multiple entry visas, thereby further reducing dependence on the Saudi sponsor.

One historically problematic aspect of the Saudi sponsor has been the ease with which the Saudi sponsor has been able to detain expatriate managers and staff of the foreign company being sponsored, in the event an ordinary commercial dispute arises between the Saudi sponsor and the company, particularly in the context of termination of the relationship. I refer to the travel ban. The travel ban has also been used by a Saudi who is not the sponsor of the targeted company, and who could for various reasons act without interference on the part of the foreign company's sponsor.

This should be distinguished from the legitimate detention by government authorities of persons who are suspected of illegal activities or who are material witnesses. Moreover, the government has in the past been sensitive to excesses connected with the travel ban. One celebrated case comes to mind, in which my law firm represented a British businessman who, after being subjected to a travel ban for a great many years, was in the end compensated by the Saudi government at the rate of one million Saudi riyals for each year he was forced to remain in the country against his will.

Until recently it was too easy for any Saudi sponsor, and to a lesser extent any Saudi claimant, not only to physically hold or even confiscate or have confiscated a foreigner's passport, but more importantly to intervene effectively with the immigration authorities at the borders (sometimes through the intermediation of the Principality or Governorate) in order to indefinitely prevent a foreigner under the Saudi's sponsorship from leaving the country. There were some notorious abuses of this privilege, the starkness of which was thought to be softened simply by institution of ordinary commercial litigation with respect to the dispute. In some cases, the foreigner being detained might have had a personal role in the business activity under dispute. More commonly, he was merely an available employee of the company which was at odds with the Saudi.

Starting in the mid-1980s, largely as a result of arguments put forward by my law firm, the pertinent authorities have begun to regulate the practice of the travel ban.

In effect the right of the Saudi sponsor *vis-à-vis* a foreigner has been made consistent with the right set forth in the Personal Rights Claims Procedure Regulations of 1406H (and also in the Commercial Court Regulations) whereby any creditor can apply for a restraining order against any debtor, Saudi or foreign, preventing him from leaving the country. Such an order, however, is intended to be temporary and provisional and is only to be obtained after a court hearing and judgment. The primary rule is not to ban travel but rather to require that the defendant, while travelling, appoint an attorney to pursue his defence and that the defendant provide the claimant with a suitable guarantee, if requested and appropriate, in the form of either a bank, corporate or personal guarantee.

I am pleased to report that the practice has begun to conform to these legal requirements, and abuses of the legal process are more and more being curtailed.

The role of the Saudi sponsor is also changing in the context of his being a partner together with a foreign partner, especially in a joint venture limited liability company established under the laws of Saudi Arabia. The Saudi authorities have recently reiterated that a foreign company need not, as a legal matter, have a Saudi partner in order to establish a permanent presence in Saudi Arabia, that is in order to obtain a foreign capital investment licence.

This not only applies to the formation of a limited liability company, but it is also increasingly easy for a foreign company to establish a permanent presence in Saudi Arabia by forming a branch of the foreign company without any Saudi participation.

It remains true as a practical matter, however, that there are still considerable advantages or incentives which attach according to the degree of Saudi participation in the company, in terms of tax holiday, preference in government tenders, preference for national products, and benefits as an industrial project under the Foreign Capital Investment Regulations, including customs exemption, tariff protection, access to industrial estates, financing and land holding.

Another sign of the times is the relaxation at government offices dealing with foreigners of the requirement that business be conducted solely in Arabic. Foreigners are no longer harassed about talking or writing in English, which has lessened the serious bottleneck arising from the need for Arabic–English translation. Of course, Arabic is still the required language for all court proceedings.

Finally, in the context of Saudi Arabia's application to join the World Trade Organization, there must begin to be a radical rethinking as to how the WTO requirement of "national treatment" of foreign businesses can be made consistent over time with the way Saudis have historically been favoured in the conduct of business in their country.

The benefit to the Saudis of accession to WTO, in terms primarily of better access to world markets at lower tariffs for their petrochemical products, can only be gained by moving towards a more level playing field for foreign and national businesses in the domestic Saudi economy. It is not easy for us to square WTO's free trade principle with the Saudi requirement that only Saudis be allowed in engage in trading and importation, *and* with the prevalence of commercial agency and distributorship as a legal and commercial requirement, *and* with the concessions referred to above encouraging Saudi participation in foreign investment within the country, *and* with the protectionist Saudi mind-set generally, and so forth.

Much of this discussion is now only going on in the rarefied diplomatic confines of the WTO negotiating sessions, not as a matter of either public debate within Saudi Arabia or debate within influential circles. Moreover, the reforms needed are still being considered on a very conceptual level, far removed from legislation and implementation, which is still decades away.

None the less, we can expect to see in the coming years a growing trend towards reducing the differences between Saudi and foreigner in our national economy. These changes will for better or worse also extend to the professions, including law firms.

Coincidentally, this development will be taking place alongside the parallel and not necessarily complementary trends towards development of the Saudi private sector, including privatization, and towards increased Saudization of the work force.

4 THE PHILOSOPHY BEHIND THE GOVERNMENT'S NEW RELATIONSHIP WITH THE PRIVATE SECTOR

The government has always supported the Saudi private sector, which was fundamentally a product of the government's various policies and programmes. That relationship has now reached a stage where the private sector has grown so large and important that the government in preparing to give away some of its own traditional tasks to the private sector.

As regards the trend towards privatization, already evident in the ports authority and telecommunications and in plans for power supply and airlines, it is not my wish to discuss in this forum the wisdom or details of individual cases, but rather to comment upon the new philosophy with which the government is now dealing with the private sector, including carrying out these privatization schemes.

In short, the Saudi government now deals with the private sector with more recognition and respect. There is a new sharing of information and a new dialogue.

In the "old days", as recently as seven or eight years ago, that is before the Gulf war, the general theme was to be secretive. Confidentiality was linked with wisdom; secrecy was considered a stylish way of behaving. After the Gulf war, disclosure became the dominant theme in everything. Confidentiality was seen as a sign of weakness, and of having something to hide. Much of this change was the inevitable result of advances in technology, especially satellite reception of unfiltered and instant news reportage symbolized by CNN and the BBC.

The government now has more respect for its audience and actually cares about tomorrow's judgment. There is a better quality of drafting in official documents, which have become less ambiguous and a more skilful means of communicating needed information in a public and objective manner.

This greater openness is not only a matter of having easier access to more informative public documents, but rather has consequences for society at large. Not everybody is minding his own business. The criticism or indeed condemnation of one family member affects them all, because the structure of Saudi society is still very tribal. But out of this, when added to the new openness, comes an increased sense of responsibility, which translates positively into good behaviour.

In a related development, the government has been encouraging large family companies to become joint stock or public companies. The focus has been on those family companies which are productive and industrious, as distinct from those traditionally holding valuable agencies for the distribution of foreign products in Saudi Arabia. More and more, these traditional family companies represent a transitional stage in the economic development of the country.

There are many problems lurking in these large family companies. In fact, if these companies are well run and profitable, there is little incentive for them to convert. The pie is so large, that the partners are not too concerned about how the pie is divided, or even whether it could be larger.

Still, increasingly, there are disputes among heirs, sometimes over differences of policy and philosophy, more often for subjective reasons. It takes a very troublesome dispute, however, for the partners to have sufficient incentive to unify or rationalize their operations. Some partners want very much to leave the embrace of the family company, but they do not want to go out naked. A natural selection process may be at work with respect to certain of these traditional family companies which, if they were pushed out of business, would face many hungry people who would immediately take over. The moral of course for foreign companies, as this drama is played out, is not to be overly influenced by the old traditional names.

5 CRIMINAL DEFENCE PROCESS

You are all no doubt fairly familiar with the case of the two British nurses accused of the murder of an Australian nurse, which well into its second year has recently been concluded with the freeing of the nurses and their return to the UK. That outcome has been very gratifying in many respects, although I have reservations as discussed below. Without delving into the particulars of the case, there are several aspects of the case which deserve comment as reflecting important developments on the Saudi legal scene.

(a)   First, it was unprecedented that a Saudi lawyer was allowed to represent the accused in a criminal case and to appear before the *shari'a* court.

(b)   Second, there is now public debate over the proper weight to be given to a written confession in a criminal case.

The nurses case sparked an open discussion of the subject, including comments by the President of the Public Prosecution Department, the Public Prosecutor, whose extensive remarks had been published prior to the nurses case and were brought to light when the nurses case arose. The Public Prosecutor has taken a position at variance with the common practice until now in Saudi *shari'a* courts of affording near total conclusory weight to written confessions affirmed before a *shari'a* judge, regardless of the conditions in the detention and police custody leading up to the confessions.

The President of the Public Prosecution Department has stated that a written confession is not alone adequate, if the confession is recanted in a timely manner and if there is an indication that the confession was obtained under duress or by trickery.

It should be noted in the nurses case that, besides the confessions, the only other evidence before the court relevant to the guilt or innocence of the two nurses was evidence submitted by the defence. This evidence consisted of written reports from leading experts provided by Scottish counsel that the confessions were unlikely to have been made voluntarily and also evidence as to the unreliability of convictions based on confessions alone. In addition, the defence lawyers in Saudi Arabia filed a number of detailed legal submissions (as published in full in the *Yearbook of Islamic and Middle Eastern Law*, 1996, Volume 3, pp. 491–505) arguing that under *shari'a* law no conviction can be based solely on the evidence of a confession if subsequently withdrawn, and requesting the court to disclose any other evidence in the case, whether it tended to incriminate the two nurses or not.

(c)   Third, other aspects of the Saudi criminal court system may not be well appreciated in the West. Even in the case of the nurses, which received wide media attention, the government did not see fit to reveal any forensic or other evidence against the accused and then to withstand examination of same.

This attitude on the part of the government arose in my view from several factors:

(i)   the degree of anxiety shown by the British Foreign Office and the nurses' families in an effort to buy the consent of the victim's family over blood money, and to do so speedily;

(ii) the very high figure demanded by the Australian brother of the victim; and

(iii) the rootedness of the traditional concept that hand-written confessions, as confirmed in front of judges, are deemed to be conclusive, however physically exhausted or confused or misled the accused might be, these conditions being only considered as irrational interference with a well-established rule. Stated otherwise, there is the feeling that the exploration of justice has to stop somewhere. This holds true in oriental countries generally, not only in the Arab world.

Whether or not such other evidence existed, it was left as a matter to be considered in private by the competent authorities, or worse to be dealt with on the level of rumour. Indeed, bundles of papers, presumably evidence, sat unexplained before the judges on the bench, but played no role in the court sessions. This was certainly not a case of the accused being found at the scene of the crime.

One might conclude that the matter had reached a rather inconclusive end on the judicial level, and moved into the realm of executive and diplomatic action, largely behind the scenes.

One might even say that the British Foreign Office found it politically convenient from the start to deal with the issue of the nurses (not the nurses as individual persons) on the assumption that they could as well be considered guilty, and thereby to focus efforts on moving offshore to Australia the issue of clemency to be sought from the victim's brother. The early overture to the victim's brother in Australia, as orchestrated by the Foreign Office, as well as the manifest anxiety on the part of the families of the accused, created a sense of guilt. A premature monetary settlement with the victim's brother only further highlighted the impression that these nurses, despite their eloquent protests to the contrary, were admitting guilt.

In the end, this strategy did succeed in freeing the nurses, with minimum damage to Saudi–British relations; but at what cost to the nurses' reputation and mental states?

As this was in the final analysis and on balance to the benefit of my clients, I am hesitant to make much comment, although from a Western perspective there might appear to be an unaccustomed blurring of these separate realms and an abdication of responsibility to determine, and to declare openly and in public, within of course the limitations of human imperfection, what happened on that fateful night in December 1996. One might say that the nurses have yet to clear their names. But then, on the larger canvas of national interests and social stability and other such broad concerns, it may not really be most important to reach definitive findings of guilt or innocence, if the negative consequences to my clients in this saga were minimized or contained.

(d) Fourth, on the role of *kisas* and *diyah* in Islam, that is the right of the victim's family, including to demand the death penalty (for which see the submissions as cited above), I will note that in a Saudi capital case the willingness of the victim's family to be merciful and forgiving has a dramatic influence on the nature and course of the proceedings against the accused. I cannot, however, emphasize too strongly that the discussion about *diyah* is not premised on an admission of guilt, whereas the actual payment of blood money may be so viewed by the public.

Indeed, much of the time in court in the case of the nurses was taken up clarifying the authority and intentions of the victim's family. That saga was still until very recently being played out in Australia, where the brother of the victim, or rather his lawyers, remained in court there demanding payment in full in compliance with what they viewed as a hard commercial bargain, regardless of whether one or both of the nurses were actually found guilty of murder.

In the absence of such foundation, the demand of the victim's brother to be paid "blood money", which he wrongly terms "compensation", should properly be seen as the abuse of an element in another culture, by one who not only misunderstands the other culture but is acting at sharp variance to the finer and more progressive elements of his own culture. It should be noted that, after the two British nurses had withdrawn their defective confessions, immediately upon the end of the nurses' seclusion, and had effectively pleaded not guilty to having been involved in the murder, and before any evidence was presented to the court, the lawyers for the victim's brother vehemently demanded that the death penalty be imposed on these two nurses and continued to do so until some months later a financial agreement was reached.

(e) Putting together therefore the above remarks, I wish to leave you with this overview of the serious reservations, in my mind at least, at the way this case has been concluded. The British Foreign Office and the nurses' families have prematurely speeded up communication with the victim's brother. An unusual pressure has also been displayed by the British High Commissioner in Australia. Moreover, at the same time as the two nurses were trying to justify retracting their confessions and were otherwise seeking to demonstrate their innocence, they were confronted with the phenomenon of their own government and families asking for clemency and also of their Saudi lawyer producing the Rationale for Early Waiver of Death Penalty. I did this in response to the concerted efforts of the Foreign Office and the families of the two nurses.

If you read the Rationale for Early Waiver of Death Penalty, you would see the careful emphasis given therein that the document should not be taken as an admission of guilt. But no matter what I said, the Rationale was perceived differently by some. On the other hand, Frank Gilford, after procrastinating over the procedural matter of his power of attorney, realized soon that this was essentially a commercial deal and he asked for an amount thirty-five times as much as he would have been paid as *diyah* in Islam, and moreover he called the payment not blood money but rather compensation, a concept not recognized in our system. It is either blood money, or not.

Now that the two nurses are free due to the merciful act of the Saudi authorities, I do not agree with their current approach of proclaiming their innocence on the basis of supposedly cruel treatment at the hands of the Saudi police. The British Embassy in Riyadh and a member of my law firm have given statements that they have seen no evidence of torture or abuse of the nurses, nor did the doctor who examined the nurses. Of course, the severe mental anguish, the deprivation of legal and consular assistance for many days, the allegations of sexual threats and other factors on which the nurses retracted their confessions are another matter altogether.

I think therefore that the nurses should instead argue, as they have the legitimate right to do, that their Foreign Office and British High Commissioner in Australia, and perhaps their own families too, maintained too great an insistence on desperately seeking clemency starting only a few weeks after they were accused. That attempt to seek clemency could have always taken place after the trial and after the examination of evidence, and the negotiation over money could have taken place during or after the trial.

There is no question that the act of clemency was deemed to be the most convenient outcome for all concerned. We can all see that quite clearly here on the English side by the collection of such a large sum within forty-eight hours of the demand and the payment of such a large sum to the Australian only forty-eight hours after the nurses' release. From the Australian side, the insistence on putting the money in trust and ensuring that the two nurses themselves sign the Deed of Settlement was a very neat package indeed.

I cannot conceal the fact that people in our part of the world do not appreciate the sensational media coverage of a matter which has been brought before the national court system, especially when, to make it worse, the tragedy has been converted into a windfall of money and financial incentives to the two nurses, who are not in the business of dealing with the media but would perhaps be led to make statements that would satisfy the requirements of the media. We can understand someone writing a book or memoir upon reflection about an unfortunate experience in life, but for those who are not possessed of writing talent to be paid so much almost immediately upon their release from prison is deemed to be conduct that would negatively reflect on the objectivity of the media as a powerful source of protection for society or as the spokesman of public opinion.

Arabs would neither agree with this behaviour of the nurses' making money nor with the behaviour of Mr Gilford, whom as I understand had not seen his sister for many years and was virtually excluded from her will and who, unlike his sister, has never been in Saudi Arabia and does not belong to the religion of Islam or have Arab nationality or ancestry, and yet took full advantage of a religious concept, that is the blood money or *diyah*, which is meant to be the final act in a conciliatory process towards healing the wounds, not part of the media circus which Mr Gilford created.

I think in all fairness the attention of the Australian side should have been concentrated on who Yvonne Gilford was and, when they saw that the two accused nurses came from the same culture and background and were insisting that they had not committed the crime, the Australians should indeed have joined us in demanding that the evidence be produced and only then, if they were satisfied as to guilt based on what they would have been provided, only then should they have asked for blood money or the death penalty. This never happened.

The behaviour of the Australian brother was a commercial one to a great extent and based upon arrogant indifference and upon overlooking what had been said in the extensive Rationale sent to him. If the two nurses are genuinely interested in clearing their names, they should put as their top priority directing questions to the Foreign Office and their own family members and also their British lawyers over this untimely panic and anxiety in running after the

Australian for clemency and forgiveness when the two nurses were saying that they were innocent.

How could the two accused, who were locked up in jail thousands of miles away from home, properly have defended themselves, even with effective local legal counsel, when they saw people supposedly on their side going down on their knees seeking forgiveness from an Australian who acted very arrogantly and viciously, including his wife saying in public that she would like to shoot darts through the nurses' organs, while I and anyone with sense knew all along this was just an act to raise the price of blood money? The Australian family were not satisfied with the Saudi riyal equivalent of US$30,000 which is the standard figure. How, they wondered, could they raise the ante as high as possible? The only way was to play tough and ask for the death penalty whatever the evidence (or absence of the same) and at the same time to engage in a vicious campaign against the two nurses, using for example a photograph of Yvonne Gilford as an angel in the nursing industry. Nobody asked about the evidence or why the confessions were not allowed to be retracted. Nobody asked why the authorities did not probe similarities with the other recent murder of another nurse in the same compound. Nobody cared to examine reports about the character of the victim. It was all along clemency, clemency, forgiveness, forgiveness, money, money.

In the final analysis, it becomes important to remove the sensational aspects of the nurses case, and such political considerations as defence contractors' supposedly contributing money for the settlement sum to be paid to the victim's brother, and the headline grabbing of some of the participants, and personal animosities and petty ambitions, and after removing all these extraneous factors to try to determine what of more lasting value has been gained through all the terror, confusion and effort attached to this case.

I think I can say in the end that the criminal defence lawyer will become an *occasional* feature in criminal prosecutions in Saudi Arabia. That judges will examine the circumstances connected with confessions more closely. Above all, I hope that Western onlookers of the Saudi scene will have gained a more balanced view of the Saudi approach to seeking justice and a heightened appreciation of the relative openness, although it is still guarded and tentative, of Arabs to having their actions examined in the overly harsh light of Western scrutiny.

United Arab Emirates (UAE)

*Richard Price**

1 SOURCES OF LAW: JUDICIAL AND LEGAL SYSTEM

There have been no significant statutory or case developments in the relevant period. There has, however, been an interesting announcement in relation to the capacity of the Dubai Court to hear urgent applications.

1.1 Extension of working hours of court

The Dubai Court announced on 11 October 1997 that in order to deal with urgent matters outside of the Court's normal working hours (which at present are from 8 am to 2 pm, Saturdays to Thursdays), it would henceforth also be open from 5 pm to 8 pm, Saturdays to Wednesdays. During these times a judge will sit with supporting staff and deal with urgent applications in the normal fashion. Once a decision has been reached it can be immediately served on the relevant department or authority concerned (provided, of course, that the department/authority itself is open). The Court has been liaising with a number of such departments/authorities within Dubai in order to ensure the effectiveness of the procedure.

Such a procedure will only apply to urgent matters such as the grant or release of attachment or arrest orders. The Court has made it clear that the procedure will not apply to matters which are not considered to be urgent (and for this purpose, the Court will take into account the risk of dissipation of the assets belonging to the party against whom an order is sought).

2 CONSTITUTIONAL AND ADMINISTRATIVE LAW

There have been no significant developments in the relevant period.

---

* Gulf Resident Partner, Clifford Chance, Dubai, UAE.

351

3 CIVIL LAW

There have been no significant developments in the relevant period.

4 COMMERCIAL LAW

There have been no significant statutory developments in the relevant period. There have, however, been a number of Dubai Court of Cassation judgments on various issues of interest and these are as follows.

4.1 A guarantor to a bank facility will not be liable to repay the overdraft if the bank granted a facility beyond the limit

The Dubai Court of Cassation[1] has held in a recent case that a bank could not claim the payment of an outstanding debt from a guarantor where the bank has granted a facility to a company in excess of the limit of the guarantee.

In this particular case, the plaintiff bank brought an action against the first defendant, a debtor company and the second, third and fourth defendants, the company's guarantors, in relation to a facility granted by the plaintiff to the first defendant for payment of an amount representing the balance outstanding to the plaintiff which the first defendant had not paid.

In this particular case, the first defendant had applied to the plaintiff for banking facilities up to a specified limit. In accordance with the facility, the first defendant signed a pledge assigning its rights in respect of a factory and its contents in favour of the plaintiff as security for the facility. Similarly, the second, third and fourth defendants guaranteed to settle on behalf of the first defendant any amounts which fell due from it and the guarantee mentioned the specific liability limit. Subsequently, the plaintiff granted the first defendant a facility by which it could have withdrawn a greater amount than that specified in the limit. The defendant proceeded to withdraw further amounts on this understanding until it reached the amount of the claim.

The Dubai Court of First Instance dismissed the action against the second, third and fourth defendants and ordered the first defendant to pay the plaintiff the amount of the claim. The plaintiff appealed against the decision to the Dubai Court of Appeal. The Court of Appeal however, dismissed the appeal and upheld the judgment of the lower Court.

The plaintiff argued before the Dubai Court of Cassation that the lower courts had based their decision upon insufficient reasons and had misconstrued a banking facility to be limited to a specific finance deal. The plaintiff considered this reasoning to be incorrect since it failed to differentiate between loan and bank facilities in accordance with Article 409 of the Commercial Transactions Law. Article 409 defines a bank loan as a contract whereby the bank provides the borrower with a sum of money as a loan by entering it to the credit side of his account at the

---

[1] Case No. 87/97.

bank on the agreed terms and conditions. The plaintiff considered that banking facilities were distinguishable from such a loan as, in the latter case, the bank does not hand over to the client an amount of money nor deposits this amount in his account (it only allows the client to carry out certain procedures without paying the value). Therefore the client is entitled to make use of banking facilities several times while, in the case of a loan, it can only be utilized once for its specific purpose. The plaintiff concluded that, taking into account the characteristics of banking facilities described above, the obligations of guarantors continued and the guarantee would be valid for the full amount of the outstandings.

The Court of Cassation rejected this argument, stating that the intention of the parties must be taken into consideration and that a guarantee in relation to a loan for a specific amount is therefore to be considered as exactly that and does not imply any other meaning.

The Court based its judgment on the following grounds. The second, third and fourth defendants were parties to a contract stating a maximum amount of credit and consequently the guarantee was restricted to this limit of credit and therefore could not include any other amount granted to the plaintiff under any other facility.

Furthermore, by providing the additional facility, the plaintiff had provided the defendant with an amount in excess of the specified amount in the guarantee and this is deemed to be an implied approval for a new and independent credit facility which is not covered by the guarantee (except with the second, third and fourth defendants' agreement and the rights of any other relevant party being taken into consideration).

4.2 Guarantee given in favour of a bank will not be affected by a statutory time bar where parties agree that the guarantee will be extended until such time as the debt is repaid in full

The Court of Cassation[2] has held that strict adherence to the six month time bar provisions contained in Article 1092 of the UAE Civil Code is not required as a matter of public policy and it is open to parties to agree to other arrangements.

In this particular case, the plaintiff, an international bank, brought an action against three defendants, requesting that the Court order the defendants, jointly and severally, to pay an amount plus interest and legal costs. The plaintiff claimed that the first defendant had obtained a loan from it which was guaranteed by the second and third defendants up to a certain amount. The first defendant has failed to repay the loan and the plaintiff brought the action to recover the loan plus interest and costs. The second and third defendants argued that the guarantee which they had given to the bank was time barred as the action was brought after six months from the date on which the debt became due. They argued that the plaintiff could not call on a guarantee which had been time barred according to Article 1092.

The Court of Cassation held that strict adherence to the time bar provisions contained in Article 1092 is not required as a matter of public policy as it is meant to protect personal interests as opposed to society's interests. The Court also held

---

[2] Case No. 65/97.

that parties are free to contract outside of the operation of Article 1092 and the effectiveness of a guarantee may be extended beyond six months.

On the facts of the case, it was evident from the guarantee that the second and third defendants had agreed to pay the total indebtedness that was incurred by the first defendant, plus interest, and that this indebtedness would continue until the debt was paid in full. The wording of the guarantee made it clear that the second and third defendants had agreed to extend the validity of their guarantee. Accordingly, the Court held that it was not open to them to argue that the guarantee had been time barred. The Court also held that as the evidence before it showed that the guarantee covered the principal amount plus interest at a rate agreed between the parties, judgment against the defendants should be for the principal amount plus interest at the agreed rate.

4.3 Parties to a commercial contract are free to stipulate any interest rate for the late payment of a debt

The Dubai Court of Cassation[3] has held that parties to a commercial contract are free to determine among themselves the interest to be calculated on the late payment of a debt. The Court will intervene to alter this determination only if the amount stipulated contravenes public policy.

In this particular case, the plaintiff, a Dubai trading company, brought an action against the defendants, an interior decoration firm based in Dubai and the proprietor of the company, requesting that the Court order the defendants, joint and severally, to pay an amount plus legal costs and interest at the rate of 15 per cent from the date on which the action was filed until final payment. The plaintiff also requested that the Court uphold an attachment order previously ordered by the Dubai Court against the defendants' assets.

The Court held that it was evident from the agreement between the parties that the goods were delivered as stated in the invoice, that payment should be within thirty days and that interest should be calculated at the rate of 15 per cent as agreed between the parties.

The Court held that it is established law that, in a commercial transaction, a party may agree to and be awarded interest for late payment where the opposite party defaults in its obligation to pay within a specified time. The Court had no power to amend or minimize the rate contained in an agreement to this effect unless the agreement was contrary to UAE public policy.

4.4 A carrier's liability for goods damaged in transit will be presumed even if the bill of lading is marked "shipper's stow and count"

The Dubai Court of Cassation[4] in a recent case held that a maritime carrier will be responsible for the condition of goods within a container from the time the container

---

[3] Case No. 261/96.
[4] Case No. 275/96.

is delivered to it at the port of shipment to the port of discharge unless the carrier is able to prove that the damages could be attributed to one of the conditions listed under Article 275 of the UAE Maritime Code. The burden of proof rests with the carrier even if the bill of lading was marked with the words "shipper's stow and count".

In this particular case the plaintiff, an insurance company, claimed an amount against the defendant, the owners of a vessel, for damage to and loss of goods which were shipped from Istanbul to Dubai. The applicable bill of lading was endorsed "shipper's stow and count".

The Court of Cassation held that according to Article 275 of the UAE Maritime Code, the carrier is responsible for damage to goods occurring during the period from the time the container is delivered to the carrier at the port of shipment to the time the container is delivered to the consignee at the port of discharge. There is a presumption of liability on the carrier's part and the burden of proof is on the carrier to prove that the damage took place for any of the reasons listed under Article 275.

The Court held that it was of no use to the defendant to argue that the bill of lading was marked with the reservation "shipper's stow and count" as the goods in the container had been short landed and damaged and, unless he can prove to the contrary, this will be attributed to the defendant.

4.5 An innocent third party may claim against a company for transactions carried out by an employee "apparently" authorized to act on the company's behalf

In Case 249/96, the Dubai Court of Cassation held that it is enough for a person to be "apparently" authorized to act on behalf of a company for an innocent third party to claim against the company for any transactions which were carried out by this individual on behalf of the company.

The Court explained that whenever a principal, through positive or negative conduct leads the public, or an innocent third party, to believe that one person has the authority to act or deal on behalf of the principal, the innocent third party who relies on the apparent act or omission may claim from the principal in respect of any transactions carried out by the person who apparently represented the principal. However, if the principal has evidence to show that the innocent third party was aware of the identity of the person and that he did not represent the principal, or if such third party acted in bad faith, this will absolve the principal of his liability in this matter.

The Court stated that in order to rebut this presumption of apparent authority, evidence must be provided to show that the third party was aware of the identity of the person and the lack of his authority.

5 EMPLOYMENT AND LABOUR LAW

There have been no significant statutory developments in the relevant period. There has, however, been a recent Dubai Court of Cassation[5] judgment of interest.

---

[5] Case No. 9/97.

5.1 To enforce a non-competition clause an employer must prove that he has suffered actual damage consequent on a breach of the clause

In Case 9/97 the Dubai Court of Cassation held that where an employer cannot show that he has suffered any damages or loss as a result of his employee's competition with a subsequent employer after the termination of the contract of employment, the original employer cannot claim for damages or for the restraint of trade of his former employees with new employers, competitive or otherwise.

The Court held that this is so, notwithstanding the existence in this particular case of an express agreement in the relevant contracts precluding the employees from working in competing businesses after the termination of their contracts. The Court further held that the original employer was not entitled to claim damages from the subsequent employer as there was no evidence pointing towards the latter's knowledge of the nature of the contracts entered into between the original employer and the two ex-employees.

6 PROPERTY LAW

There have been no significant developments in the relevant period.

7 INTELLECTUAL PROPERTY (TRADEMARKS)

There have been no significant statutory developments in the relevant period but the following Dubai Court of Cassation judgment[6] is of interest.

7.1 Famous trademarks will be protected even if they are not used in the UAE

The Dubai Court of Cassation has held that trademarks which are famous worldwide will be protected in the UAE, even if not used there.

In this particular case the plaintiff, a local paint company, filed an action against the defendants, the international owner of the trademark "Canon". The plaintiff claimed that the registration of "Canon" under Class 2, the "International Trademark Class" of the UAE Trademark Register, for the protection of paint and paint products by the defendant was inappropriate as the defendant did not deal in paint products. The plaintiff requested that the Court order the trademark be removed from the Register.

The plaintiff also claimed that whereas it had been manufacturing and selling paints under the trademark name "Canon" since 1977 the defendant had, as of the date of the action, never sold any paint products in the UAE using the disputed trademark. Furthermore the plaintiff argued that the protection of foreign trademarks should not be an absolute right for foreign companies. Protection, it argued, should be accorded to local trademarks which are used in the UAE, with an exception

---

[6] Case No. 251/96.

granted to international trademarks which are registered according to the terms and conditions of the Paris Convention to which the UAE adhered by virtue of Decree No. 20 of 1996. This latter exception, the plaintiff claimed, should only be granted to those trademarks which were used locally and where there was a chance that the international trademark may be confused with similar products bearing the same mark.

The Court of Cassation held that Article 4 of the UAE Trademarks Law No. 37 of 1992 which states that internationally renowned trademarks may not be registered except upon application of the original owner is clear and unambiguous and leaves little room for misinterpretation. The Court further held that this Article is an exception to the general principle that trademarks are usually protected if used in the UAE. The exception provides that international trademarks must have exceeded the boundary of the country where they were originally registered. In such cases, the Court held that such famous trademarks cannot be registered by any party other than the proprietor of the mark.

Whether or not a trademark becomes famous or not is a matter of fact which can be assessed by the Court based on the evidence and facts before it. In this case, the trademark "Canon" which had been registered in Japan, the country of origin since 1936, and in many other countries including the UAE, had an international reputation and name and some of the products produced by its proprietor were registered under Class 2. The Court held that, as the plaintiff had no licence to use the trademark, they therefore had no corresponding right to challenge the defendant's right to register the trademark under the UAE Trademarks Law, or to use the trademark "Canon" in the UAE.

8 FAMILY LAW AND SUCCESSION

There have been no significant statutory developments in the relevant period but the following Dubai Court of Cassation judgment is of interest.

8.1 A parent's custodial rights may be relinquished by agreement

The Dubai Court of Cassation[7] has held that each person who has a right of custody over children is entitled to relinquish that right by agreement, provided that such an agreement will not harm the children involved and that the terms of the agreement do not conflict with UAE public policy on the subject.

In this particular case the plaintiff, a local individual, brought an action against the defendant, his ex-wife, requesting that the Court order the defendant to relinquish custody of their two children. The plaintiff claimed that as the defendant had remarried, he did not want his children to be raised with their new stepfather. According to Islamic principles of *shari'a* (which is the principal source of UAE law) a mother would lose her custody rights to children if she were to re-marry a stranger unless the father were aware of the re-marriage and has consented to it.

---

[7] Case No. 8/97.

The Court held that each person who has a right of custody over children may relinquish that right by agreement with another, if no harm results to the children. The competing interests of the parents and the children must be addressed in the event of conflict and the interests of the children would supersede those of either parent.

On the facts of the particular case, the Court held that it was evident from the written declaration given by the plaintiff that he had relinquished his custodial rights and had no objection to the defendant's remarriage. Furthermore, as nothing in the agreement appeared to run contrary to UAE public policy the plaintiff could have no objection to the defendant retaining custody of the children.

9   CIVIL PROCEDURE AND EVIDENCE (ENFORCEMENT OF FOREIGN JUDGMENTS)

There have been no significant statutory developments in the relevant period. There has, however been a number of Abu Dhabi and Dubai Court of Cassation cases of interest.

9.1 Arbitrators need not follow strict procedural rules while conducting arbitrations and delivering awards

In Case 433/17 the Abu Dhabi Court of Cassation held that in an arbitration the parties and arbitrators are not obliged to follow strict procedural rules regarding the production of evidence, witnesses and documents relevant to the matter under dispute. There is nothing in public policy or law which prohibits an arbitrator from establishing his own procedural rules and reviewing matters according thereto unhampered by the procedural guidelines applicable to Court cases.

In this particular case one of the parties argued that the arbitrator had violated the UAE Law of Evidence and the terms and conditions of the contract between the parties since he had awarded a consultant's fee in respect of the time that the work was not in progress and the project was, in fact, suspended.

The Court of Cassation held that according to Articles 212 and 216 of the UAE Law of Civil Procedure, arbitration is usually based on the parties' mutual agreement to refer a matter to arbitration. Therefore, arbitrators are generally under no obligation to follow the same procedural rules that are applicable to Court cases heard before judicial authorities. An arbitrator may follow his own procedure in conducting the arbitration, subject to matters of public policy.

The Court of Cassation further held that the UAE Law of Civil Procedure set out the conditions under which a party may request the invalidation of an arbitration award. None of these conditions were argued in this case. The appointed arbitrator had the right to assess the facts and to formulate procedure and there was nothing in his assessment or award, as put before the Court, which would serve to invalidate this.

9.2 Interest on a debt will be payable from the date on which the debt becomes due and not from a subsequent judgment date

In Case 52/97 the Dubai Court of Cassation held that the time bar provisions contained in Article 1092 of the UAE Civil Code will not apply to transactions which were carried out before this legislation was enacted. Article 1092 of the Civil Code provides, where relevant, that where a debt is due, the creditor must claim it within six months from the date on which it fell due. The Court further held that interest on a quantified amount will be payable on the date from which the debt became due even if the debtor challenged liability to payment of interest on the debt.

The Court reasoned that according to Article 112 of the UAE Constitution, a law will normally apply to transactions carried out only after its enactment and not before. Article 1092 does not deal with a matter of public policy and, therefore, will apply only to those transactions which were carried out after its enactment. As the Civil Code was not applicable until 29 March 1986, Article 1092 will not apply to any transactions completed or entered into before this date, even if an action regarding the transaction was filed at a later date.

Regarding the commencement date for interest, the Court held that whenever the amount of a claim is quantifiable at the time when an action is filed and the debtor has failed to pay the same, the debtor will be liable for payment of interest by way of damages for late payment, commencing from the date upon which the debt became due, regardless of whether or not the debtor sought to challenge liability for the same. In this particular case, the defendants failed to pay their debt and therefore they were liable to pay interest for the late payment from the due date of the debt as judged by the Court.

9.3 Publication in a newspaper is a valid alternate means of effecting service when the defendant cannot be located

The Dubai Court of Cassation[8] has held in a recent case that effecting service on a defendant by publication in the newspaper will be a valid alternative where the plaintiff has previously followed all legal means to effect service without result. The defendant argued before the Court of Cassation that the judgment of a lower Court should be declared null and void as the summons to appear, which had allegedly been served on it, had been effected by publication in the local newspaper. It was the responsibility of the plaintiff, the defendant claimed, to have investigated the actual whereabouts of the defendant before resorting to this means of service.

The Court of Cassation, in its decision, referred to sections 4 and 5 of Article 8 of the UAE Law of Civil Procedure and held that these two sections read together established that if a bailiff, having responsibility to serve a summons, was unable to personally serve the party who is supposed to be served, the summons may be given to any person who may be able to receive it on behalf of the defendant who is the intended original recipient. If the latter refuses to receive the summons or if the person receiving the summons is not fit to do so, the bailiff must put this matter to a

---

[8] Case No. 250/96.

Judge or Chief Justice for an order allowing service either by announcing it on a public notice board kept for this purpose at the Court or by posting up the summons at the defendant's place of residence, or alternatively, by publication in a widely read UAE newspaper. If the service is effected by such means it will be held valid and effective.

On the facts of this particular case, the Court found that an attempt was made to serve the summons at the defendant's last known address. The watchman at this location advised the bailiff that the defendant had vacated the premises to an unknown location. The Court held that the plaintiff had followed the means to effect service provided by the law and the defendant's argument that the plaintiff should have done more to locate his whereabouts was insufficient to overturn the validity of the service and the subsequent judgments.

9.4 Foreign jurisdiction clause is contrary to public policy

A recent decision of the Abu Dhabi Court of Cassation[9] has held that a foreign jurisdiction clause will not be upheld as the subject of jurisdiction is a matter of both public policy and sovereignty and parties to a contract are not at liberty to agree otherwise.

In this particular case the plaintiff shipowner brought an action before the Fujairah Court requesting that it order the defendant, a towing company, to pay the plaintiff a sum which represented the value of the plaintiff's vessel. The vessel had been lost at sea while being towed in an allegedly negligent manner by the defendant. In an addendum to the towage contract the parties had agreed to give jurisdiction to the English Court in the event that a dispute arose under the contract. The Fujairah Court of First Instance dismissed the plaintiff's action on the ground that the Court lacked jurisdiction. The Fujairah Court of Appeal reversed this judgment and held that the Court did have jurisdiction to hear the matter.

The Court of Cassation held that it was evident on the facts that the Fujairah Court had jurisdiction to hear this matter. Even if the parties had agreed to foreign jurisdiction, the Court will not uphold such a clause as the issue of jurisdiction is a matter of public policy and sovereignty. Accordingly the foreign jurisdiction clause is superseded by these principles. The Court further held that in accordance with Article 21(3) of the UAE law of Civil Procedure, a UAE Court will have jurisdiction to hear any action filed against a foreign party who has no place of domicile in the UAE where the contract was executed, signed or intended to be executed in the country or if the contract was authenticated in the UAE.

This decision may clarify the position arising from a recent decision of the Abu Dhabi Court in which a foreign arbitration clause was upheld (see 1996 entry).

---

[9] Case No. 487/18.

9.5 UAE courts will have jurisdiction to hear the merits of a maritime case if the vessel was arrested within UAE territorial waters

The Dubai Court of Cassation[10] has held that when a vessel is arrested within UAE territorial waters pursuant to a maritime debt, the local Court will have jurisdiction to hear the matter. The Court further held that even if the parties to the dispute had earlier agreed upon a foreign jurisdiction clause, such an agreement was contrary to UAE public policy and will be ignored by the Court.

In this particular case the plaintiff, an American oil company which specialized in supplying bunkers to ships around the world, applied for the arrest of a vessel berthed in Rashid Port in Dubai. Following the arrest of the vessel, the plaintiff filed a civil case and requested that the Court order the defendants, the owners and operators of the vessels, to pay it an amount plus legal costs and interest for the bunkers which had been supplied to the defendants and to uphold the arrest order.

The defendants argued that the local Dubai Court had lacked jurisdiction as the relevant sales agreement between the parties gave jurisdiction to a United States Court over any disputes that arose. The Court of Cassation, referring in its decision to Article 151 of the UAE Law of Civil Procedure, held that a party may appeal against a judgment to the Court of Cassation in cases relating to an attachment order or matters relating to the jurisdiction of the local Court.

Finally, the Court held that the Dubai Court had jurisdiction to hear the dispute notwithstanding the fact that the parties had agreed to give jurisdiction to a US Court. Article 24 of the Law of Civil Procedure states that jurisdiction is a matter of public policy and that parties may not agree otherwise.

10 CRIMINAL LAW AND PROCEDURE

There have been no significant developments in the relevant period.

11 PUBLIC INTERNATIONAL LAW

There have been no significant developments in the relevant period.

12 PRIVATE INTERNATIONAL LAW

There have been no significant developments in the relevant period.

---

[10] Case No. 83/96.

13 ENVIRONMENTAL LAW

There have been no cse developments in the relevant period. There has, however, been a significant statutory development in relation to federal environmental law.

13.1 Federal Environmental Law

A draft federal environmental law regarding protection and development of the environment has been drafted by the Federal Environmental Agency together with various institutions. It includes issues such as the maritime environment in the UAE, water pollution, environmental disaster, dangerous substances, harmful substances, maritime resources, means of transportation of oil and both governmental and military vessels.

Bahrain

Husain M. Al-Baharna*

There was little activity in the field of substantive legislation during 1997 and the current year 1998.

The following titles of legislation are cited below in the order of their issuance.

1 LOCAL LAWS AND DECREES

1.1 Law by Decree No. 2 for 1997 Concerning Offices Providing Educational Services

This law, which was issued on 26 January 1997, concerns the regulation of offices established in Bahrain for the purpose of offering educational services to Bahraini nationals who apply for studying or continuing their education in universities abroad. The law comprises twenty-seven articles distributed over five chapters:

Chapter 1   deals with general definitions.
Chapter 2   deals with the office licence and its conditions. Thus Article 2 provides that no natural or a legal person shall perform any of the activities or services specified in this law except through a licensed office, in accordance with the provisions of this law.
Chapter 3   deals with the conditions, requirements and organization of the educational offices services.
Chapter 4   deals with disciplinary and penal punishments that may be imposed on the educational services office, the owner or the director of which contravenes the conditions under which the licence was issued. In ac-

---

* PhD in International Law (Cambridge); Barrister-at-Law of Lincoln's Inn; Council Member of ICCA; Member of the UN International Law Commission (ILC); Attorney and Legal Consultant, Bahrain; Former Minister for Legal Affairs, Bahrain.

cordance with Articles 20 and 22 the punishments may involve the cancellation of the office licence, in addition to imposing a penal punishment under the Penal Code, on the owner or the director of the office who contravenes the conditions of the licence.

Chapter 5   deals with the final provisions of the law which provides, under Article 23, that all licensed offices under this law are subject to supervision and monitoring procedures by the authorized employees of the Ministry of Education who are officially designated as supervisors under this law.

1.2 Law by Decree No. 18 for 1997 Concerning the Profession of Pharmacy

This law concerns the organization of the profession of pharmacy and pharmaceutical centres.

This law comprises 109 articles, distributed over thirteen chapters. The titles of the chapters are as follows:

Chapter 1   concerns the qualifications required for issuing a licence for practising the profession of pharmacy.

Chapter 2   concerns the duties of pharmacists and the acts that they are prohibited from practising.

Chapter 3   concerns the conditions under which pharmaceutical centres are established. This chapter deals with specific conditions required for opening pharmaceutical centres which could take the form of either public pharmacies or private pharmacies. Each of these two kinds of centres functions under different and specific conditions.

Chapter 4   concerns the conditions under which medicines and pharmaceutical products are imported and exported.

Chapter 5   deals with requirements for the registration of medicines and pharmaceutical products.

Chapter 6   deals with the conditions of promotion and advertisement of medicines.

Chapter 7   deals with the conditions under which prescriptions are issued.

Chapter 8   deals with the conditions for the pricing of medicines and pharmaceutical products.

Chapter 9   concerns the conditions under which licensed pharmacies may open commercial sections for the sale of simple medicines which do not need prescriptions, and some other healthy foods.

Chapter 10   deals with supervision of pharmaceutical centres by health authorities.

Chapter 11   concerns punishments imposed on pharmacists and pharmacies' staff for offences and other contraventions under the law.

Chapter 12   concerns disciplinary measures applicable under the law to pharmacists and pharmacies' staff.

Chapter 13   deals with the final provisoin of the law. Under this chapter, it is provided, *inter alia*, that the present law supersedes Law by Decree No. 26 for 1975 and its amendments concerning the organization of the profession of pharmacy.

1.3 Amiri Order No. 1 for 1997 Establishing the National Guard

The Amiri Order of 1997 provides for the establishment of an independent military force called the "National Guard".

The Amiri Order comprises nine articles. According to Article 3, the National Guard is regarded as a complementary military force to the Bahrain Defence Force. It acts in support of the latter force. According to Article 4, the National Guard performs its functions under the direction and supervision of its head who is appointed by an Amiri Order.

2 LAWS AND DECREES INCORPORATING OR RATIFYING INTERNATIONAL CONVENTIONS

2.1 Law by Decree No. 6 for 1997 Concerning Chemical Weapons

By this law, the state of Bahrain ratified on 28 April 1997 the Convention on the Prohibition of the Development, Production, Stockpiling and Use of Chemical Weapons and on their Destruction. The Convention was signed in Paris on 13 January 1992. Bahrain was a signatory to the Convention.

Under the general obligations of this Convention, Article 1 provides as follows:

1. Each state party to this Convention undertakes never under any circumstances:
   (a) to develop, produce, otherwise acquire, stockpile or retain chemical weapons, or transfer, directly or indirectly, chemical weapons to anyone;
   (b) to use chemical weapons;
   (c) to assist, encourage or induce, in any way, anyone to engage in any activity prohibited to a state party under this Convention.
2. Each state party undertakes to destroy chemical weapons it owns or possesses, or that are located in any place under its jurisdiction or control.
3. Each state party undertakes to destroy all chemical weapons it abandoned on the territory of another state party.
4. Each state party undertakes to destroy any chemical weapons, production facilities it owns or possesses, or that are located in any place under its jurisdiction or control.
5. Each state party undertakes not to use riot control agents as a method of warfare.

According to Article 16, the Convention has an unlimited period of operationn. And according to Article 22, the provisions of the Convention are not subject to any reservations by the states parties to it.

2.2 Decree No. 22 for 1997 Concerning the International Labour Organization

By this decree, issued on 22 October 1997, the state of Bahrain aproved its accesion to the Instrument of Amendment of the Constitution of the International Labour Organization, adopted on 19 June 1997.

2.3 Law by Decree No. 1 for 1998 Concerning Accession to the Warsaw Convention

By this law, the state of Bahrain acceded on 3 January 1998, to the Warsaw Convention concerning the Unification of Certain Rules of International Civil Aviation of 1929 and the Hague Protocol of 1955 and the 1961 Complementary Agreement to the Warsaw Convention applicable to a person other than the civil aviation contractor.

2.4 Law by Decree No. 4 for 1998 Concerning Accession to the Convention Against Torture

This law, issued on 18 February 1998, provides for the accession of the state of Bahrain to the Convention against Torture and other Cruel Inhuman or Degrading Treatment or Punishment. The said Convention was adopted by the UN General Assembly on 10 December 1984.

Ths Bahraini law, however, makes two reservations to the provisions of this Convention. Article 1 of the law states:

1. The Government of the state of Bahrain does not recognize the competence of the Committee contained in paragraphs 1, 2, 3, 4 and 5 of Article 20 of the Convention. The provisions of this Article deal specificaly with the monitoring role of the said Committee with respect to conducting investigations about allegations regarding the systematic practice of torture in the territory of a state party.
2. The Government of the state of Bahrain does not recognize the compulsory jurisdiction of the International Court of Justice, as provided in paragraph 1 of Article 30 of the Convention.

Under Articles 28 and 30 of the Convention, a state party is entitled to make such reservations.

The Convention against Torture is divided into three main parts. Part I deals with the definition of torture and sets out the basic obligations of states. Part II establishes an international machinery to monitor the implementation of the Convention. Part III contains the final and general clauses.

The Convention provides, under the title "The Basic Obligations of States", that states parties must not only refrain from practising torture, but are also obliged to prevent it by all appropriate means and, in particular, by legislative, administrative, judicial and educational measures.

Unfortunately, the application of the Convention against Torture will be very much weakened in the territories of those states parties which have conditioned their ratification or accession to the Convention by entering reservations to Article 20 of the Convention. Article 20 of the Convention deals with the establishment of an effective system of investigation to be conducted by the monitoring Committee, formed under the Convention.

2.5 Law by Decree No. 15 for 1998, Concerning Terrorism

By this law, the state of Bahrain ratified the Arab Agreement for Combating Terrorsim, signed in Cairo on 22 April 1998 by the Arab Ministers of the Interior. The Arab Agreement for Combating Terrorism which was adopted by the League of Arab States, comprises forty-two articles distributed over four chapters:

Chapter 1 deals with definitions.
Chapter 2 deals with the basis of Arab cooperation in the field of combating terrorism. This chapter deals with combating terrorism in two sections: (a) in the sphere of national security and (b) in the judicial sphere.
Chapter 3 deals with the machinery for the implementation of the law. Under this chapter, the procedures of extradition between states parties are discussed.
Chapter 4 deals with final clauses of the Agreement. These include a provision in Article 31, which prohibits states parties from making reservations to the Agreement which contravene, whether expressly or impliedly, the provisions or purposes of the Agreement.

2.6 Decree No. 6 for 1998, Concerning Accession to an Arab Labour Agreement

By Decree No. 6 for 1998, issued on 18 April 1998, the state of Bahrain acceded to the Arab Agreement No. 18 for 1996 concerning the Employment of Young Workers. This Agreement, which was adopted by the Arab Labour Organization on 24 March 1996, concerns the conditions required for the employment in the territories of the Arab states parties, of child workers, whether male or female, who are above 13 but less than 18 years old. The Agreement comprises twenty-nine articles distributed over six chapters. The provisions of this Agreement are directed towards providing better healthy, educational, economic and soical conditions for young workers who are under eighteen years of age. These conditions apply to young workers whether employed in factories or in any other economic and commercial enterprises.

2.7 Decree No. 7 for 1998, Concerning Accession to the Forced Labour Agreement

With Decree No. 7 for 1998, issued on 18 April 1998, the state of Bahrain formally acceded to the International Agreement No. 105 for 1957 on Forced Labour, adopted by the Intenraitonal Labour Organization on 25 June 1957. This Agreement, comprising ten articles, is entitled "Forced LabourTermination Agreement". According to Article 1, each state member of the International Labour Organization that ratified this Agreement is thereby prohibited from practising any kind of forced labour or imposing compulsory work on persons, or resorting to such acts. Moreover, forced labour must not be resorted to as a means of coercion or political direction or as a punishment against the adoption or belief in political views or ideas which are contrary to the political, economic or social dogma upon which the existing political regime is established.

Article 2 states that each state member of the International Labour Organization wihch ratified this Agreement undertakes to take effective measures that will guarantee the immediate and complete termination of forced labour or compulsory work of the kind specified in Article 1 of this Agreement.

Qatar

*Najeeb Al-Nauimi**

1 JUDICIAL AND LEGAL SYSTEM

1.1 Advocacy

1.1.1 Law No. 4 for the year 1998 amending some of the provisions of the Law No. 10 for the year 1996 promulgating the law of advocacy

This amendment deals with the issue of the non-Qatari advocates where the law has given them the right to practice advocacy according to the registration in the temporary register schedule under Article 3 of the Law No. 10 of 1996.[1]

This amendment consists of only two articles – Article 1 changes the provision of Article 3 of the Law No. 10 of 1996 to be read as follows:

(a) The registration in the temporary schedule shall be closed from the validity date of this law, and no new advocate shall be registered.
(b) The register of the advocates in that schedule shall be cancelled after two years from the date of this law's validity. This period may be extended by the Council of Ministers decision only once upon the justification shown by the Minister of Justice, then the schedule will be finally cancelled.
(c) The advocates registered in the temporary schedule will practise all advocates' work until the date of their register cancellation.
(d) The registered advocate before the cancellation of the schedule within a reasonable time shall authorize one or more of the practising advocates to assume any suits done by him until the date of the schedule cancellation. This should be conditioned by the client's consent, and in case of non-agreement to the

---

* LLB; PhD; Former Minister of Justice, State of Qatar, Professor of Public International Law, University of Qatar; National President of World Jurists Association in Qatar; Ex-President Asian African Legal Consultative Committee 1995–96.
[1] See Qatar survey in this *Yearbook*, vol. 3 (1996), pp. 297–300.

new advocate's fees, it shall be decided in accordance with the provisions of Article 36 of the annexed law.

Article 2 provides for the validity of this law which is crucial as to the date of the temporary schedule cancellation which shall be two years from 8 July 1996.

2 CONSTITUTIONAL LAW: RULER AND SUCCESSION TO THE EMIRATE

2.1 Emir of the Qatar States Decision No. 3 of 1995 amending some of the provisions of the Provisional Amended Basic Law concerning the ruling of the state

This decision regulates and changes the rule of governing the state of Qatar. The decision consists of only two articles.

Article 1 provides for the alteration of Article 21 of the Provisional Amended Basic Law of 1995 and reads as follows:

The rule in the state of Qatar is inherited in the family of Al-Thani. The rule shall be succeeded from the father to one of his sons, if not the heir apparent will be chosen by the Emir from Al-Thanis family.
The Emir will nominate the heir apparent through an Emiri order after consulting "the wise men in the country" and having their unanimous consent to the nomination.
All provisions concerning the inheritance of the rule in the state shall be organized by Emiri order to be issued specially for the purpose.

2.2 Emir of the Qatar States Decision No. 4 of 1995 concerning the rules regulating the succession of the rule in the state

This decision lays down succession of the rule in Qatar.

This rule consists of four articles, which are made with reference to Article 21 of the Provisional Amended Basic Law of the year 1995.

Article 1 is the core of this decision and although it is the same as Article 21 mentioned above of the Emir Decision No. 3 of 1995 – but it added a provision concerning the heir apparent as titled in the decision (HH the heir apparent).

Article 2 stipulates the two conditions to be satisfied by the heir apparent, i.e. to be

(1)   sane;
(2)   adult.

Article 3 lays down the procedure of succession according to the provisions of Article 12 of the law of 1995, viz. that the heir apparent will only be changed if:

(a)   he ceases to fulfil one of the above conditions mentioned in Article 2;
(b)   he becomes unfit to deal with his authorities;
(c)   the high public interest of the state so requires.

3 COMMERCIAL LAWS

3.1 Customs

3.1.1 Law 25 of 1994 Amending Some of the Provisions of Qatar Customs Law No. 5 of 1988.

This amending law deals with many provisions but we shall tackle the important amendments that reflect the improvement and progress in customs in Qatar that run parallel with the significant role played by the customs in ways of economic, international trade and supervision of goods and products to the benefit of the citizen and interest of the state. Article 1 alters the two phrases:

(a)　Minister of Finance and Petroleum;
(b)　Ministry of Finance and Petroleum;

to

(a)　Minister of Finance, Economy and Trade;
(b)　Ministry of Finance, Economy and Trade.

Article 2 consists of many amendments in different articles of the law but the most striking ones are:

(a)　Article 2 section 1: marine customs scope includes the area which extends from the customs line to a distance of 12 sea miles starting from the outer limit of territorial waters.
(b)　Article 12: no new or additional customs duties may be imposed, or any amendment or abolishing of a custom tariff in force effected, without a decree issued upon a proposal by the customs Tariff Council. A cabinet decision will be issued upon a proposal from the Minister of Finance Economy and trade to formulate the council.
(c)　Article 154: the new amendment raised the fine to be imposed by customs director to 3,000 Qatari riyals in place of 1,000 Qatari riyals for each contravention, and made it compulsory to confiscate the smuggled goods.
(d)　Articles 189, 193 and 198 are amended in a way to raise the maximum fine to be imposed in cases of customs contamination up to 3,000 Qatari riyals.
(e)　Articles 156–160 contains the alteration of the phrase "public prosecution" to the phrase "criminal prosecution".

3.2 Stock Exchange

3.2.1 Minister of Finance, Economy and Commerce Decision No. 8 of 1997 issuing the internal Regulation for Doha Stock Exchange

To face other challenges in economic and commerce, Qatar has started to establish a good basis for trade and commerce by issuing Law No. 14 of 1995 for the formation of the Doha Stock Exchange. These Regulations are issued by the Minster in pursuance of that law.

The most important section in chapter 1 is section 3 which lays down in Article 5 the objectives of the stock exchange as follows:

(1) opening opportunities for savings and money investment in the stock exchange for the good and interest of the Qatari national economy;
(2) working for the progress of financial marketing in a way that serves economic development so as to help in achieving the objects of the state's economic policy;
(3) progressing and refining the means and procedures for the good process and smooth dealings in the stock exchange so as to protect the dealers;
(4) progressing and organizing the issuance of the stocks in the primary market and fixing the requirements that should be satisfied by the issuance publication when calling for subscription to stocks;
(5) registration of the new stocks in the market, and the facilitation and speed in the liquidation of invested monies with granting the process of the (supply and demand) for determining the prices of these stocks and the protection of the junior investors through the right basis for dealing;
(6) the collection of information and statistics about the running stocks for the purpose of reporting on condition that the reports must provide correct information;
(7) giving studies on the financial status of the companies that help the investors and the financial executors when buying the stocks;
(8) making of studies for giving recommendations and proposals to the respective official bodies about the valid laws and necessary amendments in accordance with development required by the market;
(9) communicating with stock exchanges abroad for the access and exchange of information and experience to achieve progress in the means of dealing in those markets and help the quick progress of the Qatar Stock Exchange and also to join international and Arab organizations and unions of the same nature;
(10) organizing and making easier the procedure of stock transfer and conveyance;
(11) deepening the professional behaviour, self-supervision and the discipline between mediation companies and their agents and other dealers in the stock exchange;
(12) making available mediation companies and qualified brokers in the market and also re-qualifying new companies and brokers and other professionals in the stock exchange for upgrading their practical and scientific qualifications;
(13) granting the completion of selling and buying transactions of the stocks in an impartial and honest atmosphere by following the expressed policy about the trading in stocks and publishing all information available about joint stock companies and making it accessible to the dealers.

Chapter 2 deals with the registration and acceptance of the stocks and the duties of joint stock companies.

Chapter 3 deals with the mediation companies, their work, the condition for licensing, responsibilities, duties, rights and other provisions concerning mediation and brokers dealings.

Chapters 4 to 9 deal with the regulation of dealing in stocks, the administration of the stock exchange, the censorship role of the stock exchange, the resource of the market, the arbitration and disciplinary, the crimes and punishments.

4 PUBLIC HEALTH: TRANSPLANT OF HUMAN ORGANS

This is a new area of law dealt with by only a very few countries in the developed world. The issues involved in this law are of essence to human life safety and cover a wide range of discussion and controversy between lawyers and law-makers all over the world – the religious and ethical sides of the subject are still controversial.

This law has only fourteen articles; the most important ones are:

Article 2   provides that specialist doctors may carry out surgery to ablate human limbs from a living person's body or a corpse and transplant in another living person body to sustain his life or to achieve probable curative effect.

Article 3   prohibits the transplant of genital organs which carry hereditary characteristics from a living person's body or a corpse to another living person's body.

Article 4   provides permission for a legally competent person to donate or make a will that a limb or more of his body will be donated, by a written consent testified by two mature witnesses.

Article 5   provides that it is not allowed to transplant a limb from a living person's body, even if consented to, if the ablation of that limb will:
(1)   lead to his death or
(2)   disablement to fulfil his duty or
(3)   the doctors think it improbable that the surgery will be a success.

Article 6   deals with the duty to give notice to the donor of all medical and health results in a written statement so the donor may consider withdrawing his donation.

Article 7   provides for the transplant from a corpse and lays down the conditions:
(1)   to ensure the death on a definitive basis by a written medical report from a consulting committee;
(2)   that no written or testified objection was made by the deceased during his life to this ablation.

Article 8   provides for the transplant of limbs from the corpses of dead unidentified persons through the consent of the *shari'a* court on two conditions:
(1)   only if it is in the interest of the patient, and.
(2)   if it is of high necessity to save the patient's life.

Article 9   prohibits the sale or buying of human limbs by any means.

Article 10   provides that the surgeries for human limb ablation and transplant shall be performed only in government hospitals according to the conditions and procedures issued by the Minister of Public Health.

Article 11   provides for the conditions and requirements to be satisfied in the places specially made for saving the limbs.

Articles 12–14   provide for the contravention and punishments, the authority of the Minister of Public Health to make decisions executing this law.

Oman

*David Wilson and Richie Alder**

1 SOURCES OF LAW, JUDICIAL AND LEGAL SYSTEM

After the extensive legislative changes which were implemented during 1996, particularly those relating to easing of restrictions on foreign investment, government policy has been directed to strengthening the role of the private sector in the Omani economy. His Majesty the Sultan Qaboos bin Said has continued this policy by designating 1998 as the Year of the Private Sector. The policy of liberalization which was evident during 1997 played a part in the marked development of the capital markets in Oman, with the Muscat Securities Market being one of the best performing markets in the world, although it has fallen back to more realistic levels during the second quarter of 1998.

Promulgation of legislation anticipated by the Basic Law has continued with the establishment of the Council of Oman and the Defence Council. In relation to the court system, Royal Decree 30/97 marks a major development by reconstituting the Authority for the Settlement of Commercial Disputes as a formal court of law, under the title Commercial Court of Oman. The Authority developed from a quasi-arbitral committee overseen by the Ministry of Commerce and Industry and has now developed into the Commercial Court of Oman, with exclusive jurisdiction in relation to all commercial matters, including taxation appeals. The change in status of the Commercial Court has been further recognized by the transfer of responsibility for appointment of judges from the Ministry of Commerce and Industry to the Ministry of Justice.

The settlement of disputes in Oman has also been affected by promulgation of a new arbitration law, which is modelled closely on the UNCITRAL model law as promulgated in Egypt.

Promulgation of the new Arbitration Law and reconstitution of the Authority as the Commercial Court are consistent with the programme of legislation which

---

* Solicitors, Trowers & Hamlins, Sultanate of Oman.

is anticipated by the Basic Law which is set out and discussed in volume 3 of the *Yearbook*.

2 CONSTITUTIONAL AND ADMINISTRATIVE LAW

Royal Decrees promulgated during December 1997 have effected a number of significant Constitutional changes within the Sultanate of Oman.

2.1 Defence Council

Royal Decree 105/96 established the Defence Council, a body which was anticipated by the Basic Law of the State which was promulgated in 1996 and is set out as an appendix in the 1996 *Yearbook*.

2.2 New ministries

Royal Decree 84/97 changes the name of the Ministry of Petroleum and Minerals to the Ministry of Oil and Gas. The responsibility for minerals (together with all staff and allocations) has been transferred to the Ministry of Commerce and Industry. By the same Royal Decree, the Ministry of Justice, *Awqaf* and Islamic Affairs has been renamed the Ministry of Justice. A new Ministry of *Awqaf* and Religious Affairs has been created. It is interesting to note that the new Ministry specifically refers to religious affairs as opposed to Islamic Affairs which may indicate a wider remit for this Ministry in future. Royal Decree 84/97 also abolishes the Ministry of Development and transfers its staff and allocations to the Ministry of National Economy.

2.3 Vocational training

The Vocational Training Authority has been abolished with staff and allocations being transferred to the newly named Ministry of Social Affairs, Labour and Vocational Training.

2.4 Council of Ministers

Royal Decree 85/97 has reformed the Council of Ministers and has been used for the purpose of appointing new ministers. Key new positions include the appointment of HE Mohammed Al Rumhi as Minister of Oil and Gas, replacing HE Said Al Shanfari (who had been a Minister in His Majesty's Government since the early 1970s and who has now retired). The other new ministerial appointments include the Minister of Social Affairs, Labour and Vocational Training, the Minister of Agriculture and Fisheries, the Minister of Justice and the Minister for Environment and Regional Municipalities. Although some of the new ministerial appointments arises as a result of a reshuffle of existing ministers, new appointees appear to have come from outside the established civil service hierarchy.

2.5 Council of Oman

Royal Decrees 86, 87 and 89/97 all deal with the establishment of the Council of Oman (*Majlis Adwala*). The Council of Oman's role in the constitution arises out of the reference to this new body in the Basic Statute of the State introduced by Royal Decree 101/96. The ex-Minister of Justice has been appointed as the first President of the *Majlis Adwala*.

2.6 Omanization Committee

Royal Decree 95/97 creates a new Committee within the Diwan of the Royal Court, whose role will be to monitor and follow up Omanization policy. While Omanization remains the responsibility of the Ministry of Social Affairs, Labour and Vocational Training, the introduction of this new Committee, under the Chairmanship of Abdul Alim Al bin Musthail Rakhyout is expected to provide additional impetus to the Omanization programme introduced and implemented by the new Minister of Social Affairs, Labour and Vocational Training.

2.7 Establishment of the Commercial Court

Royal Decree 13/97 amends the structure and powers of the Authority for the Settlement of Commercial Disputes, which is renamed the Commercial Court. Its operation is to be overseen by the Minister of Justice.

One important innovation is the introduction of a Summary Court of Jurisdiction in various regions in Oman, to settle claims up to RO15,000. The formation and functions of each of these summary courts is to be defined by a decision of the Minister of Justice. Appeals against such decisions are to be made to the Primary Court, but only where the amount claimed exceeds RO5,000.

Cases involving sums in excess of RO15,000 will be dealt with by a Court of First Instance, but the previous threshold of RO10,000 below which an appeal could not be pursued has been increased to RO25,000.

The importance of the legislation, however, lies in two specific areas. The first is that the reference in the previous legislation governing the Small Fee Court that government bodies "may accept the jurisdiction of the courts" has been removed in its entirety, which, in conjunction with the wording of the new legislation which provides that the Commercial Court shall specialize in trying cases and examining arbitration petitions in commercial disputes arising between parties of the private sector, government departments, or authorities or general establishments, suggests that government bodies may no longer decline to be sued.

The second relates to the enforcement of foreign judgments or arbitration awards. Express reciprocal enforcement provisions have been introduced, which may be applied by the Commercial Court upon application to it, subject to a number of conditions being fulfilled, including that both parties (or their representatives) must appear before the Commercial Court, the judgment must not be contrary to Omani law, and must have been obtained in a jurisdiction in which Omani judgments or arbitration awards are themselves enforceable. While this latter provision relating to reciprocity limits the scope for enforcement of foreign judgments or arbitration awards, the potential for formal recognition of a foreign judgment or arbitration award is of considerable importance.

2.8 The Law of Arbitration in Civil and Commercial Disputes

Royal Decree 48/97 introduces, for the first time, a law relating to and governing arbitration.[1] It applies to any arbitration conducted in Oman, or abroad, if it is expressly agreed that the arbitration will be so governed. The law is based on the UNCITRAL model law. It preserves the right of the parties to agree upon a procedure for the resolution of disputes between them, and the Commercial Court will not intervene or interfere save for the purposes of enforcing the terms of the arbitration agreement. In particular, the Commercial Court is vested with the authority to elect arbitrators in circumstances where the parties cannot agree or refuse to proceed, and it may also intervene if the arbitrator fails to properly discharge his duties under the arbitration agreement. In addition, the Commercial Court is expressly entitled to take temporary measures for or during the arbitration process. The Commercial Court has the power to fine any witness who refuses to cooperate, and to comply with any request for legal assistance.

The new law aims to preserve the rights of the parties to agree upon any procedural matters, but in the absence of agreement imposes certain rules. Proceedings must be taken in Arabic. A timetable is imposed in the absence of any timetable agreed between the parties requiring a judgment to be given within twelve months from the beginning of the arbitration, which may however be extended by a six-month period. The judgment must be made available to the parties within thirty days of its issue; clarifications may be sought within a further thirty-day period thereafter. The parties are entitled to ask for a further judgment on any issue or aspect that has been ignored, which must be given within sixty days of the application.

The law expressly provides that arbitration judgments shall not be capable of appeal, but sets out specific grounds upon which an application can be made to the Commercial Court to nullify judgments, such as a breach of the rules agreed upon between the parties. Furthermore, there is a provision that the court, when examining the validity of the judgment, shall "automatically consider it invalid if it contains anything contrary to public order in the Sultanate of Oman". It remains to be seen how this article will be interpreted, particularly in view of the express provision that the parties are entitled to choose the law governing the dispute. The Commercial Court is vested with the power to enforce any arbitration judgment, and any application for nullification will not necessarily delay such enforcement, although an execution order cannot be made until the period in which the application to apply for a nullity, being ninety days from the declaration of the judgment, has expired.

---

[1] For free text of the law, see Part III, p. 550 and the comments of Dr Hamid Al-Ahdab, p. 556.

It is to be presumed that in cases of a genuine argument as to the legality of the judgment, the court will delay execution.

2.9 Arbitration: New York Convention 1958

Furthermore, Royal Decree 36/98 approves Oman becoming a signatory to the New York Convention on the Recognition and Enforcement of Foreign Arbitral Awards, and that the competent authorities are to take the necessary steps to join the Agreement.

2.10 Lawyers' Law

Implementation of the Lawyers' Law promulgated by Royal Decree 108/96[2] has continued with establishment of the Lawyers' Committee in accordance with Ministry of Justice, Ministerial Decision 52/97. The Lawyers' Committee has responsibility for admissions to the register of lawyers to be maintained by the Ministry of Justice.

3 CIVIL LAW (CONTRACT AND OBLIGATIONS)

The Personal Status Law is discussed in more detail at 9 below.

4 CIVIL PROCEDURE AND EVIDENCE

Changes relevant under this heading arise in terms of Royal Decree 13/97, which is discussed at 2.7 above.

5 COMMERCIAL LAW

5.1 Insurance

Royal Decree 5/98 amends certain provisions of the existing legislation relating to vehicle insurance. The new Decree states that vehicle insurance must now extend to covering medical costs of passengers, that compulsory vehicle insurance must be in place as long as the vehicle is validly registered with the Royal Oman Police and that, if the compulsory insurance expires, the owner of the vehicle shall be solely responsible for any claims resulting from any accident which occurs while there is no valid insurance cover.

---

[2] See this *Yearbook*, vol. 3 (1996), p. 310.

5.2 Companies

Royal Decree 66/97 introduced certain changes in the procedure for nominating government directors and managers of companies with a government shareholding. More importantly, Royal Decree 39/98, which was published in the Official Gazette on 1 July 1998, made a number of amendments to the Commercial Companies Law (CCL) including:

(a) Article 58 of the CCL is amended such that the minimum capital for a closed joint stock company is RO500,000 and for an open joint stock company is RO2,000,000. Previously the minimum capital for both open and closed joint stock companies was RO150,000.

(b) An additional provision has been added to Article 65 of the CCL such that in the event of an undersubscription the promoters may allow banks and brokerage companies which work in the field of securities to cover such remaining shares and to have the right to re-offer them to the public in accordance with the terms and conditions specified by a Decision of the Minister of Commerce and Industry. The CCL did not previously made adequate provision for underwriting arrangements.

(c) An additional paragraph has been added to Article 67 of the CCL such that the constitutive general meeting of a joint stock company may amend its articles of association, although such an amendment is subject to the approval of the Directorate General of Commerce. Previously, it was thought possible to amend the articles of a joint stock company at its constitutive general meeting, however, this amendment makes such a right explicit.

(d) The Amending Decree adds a provision to Article 77 of the CCL. The existing Article 77 includes a provision that the founder members of a joint stock company may not deal with or dispose of their shares until the accounts of two financial years have been published. The new decree adds a provision to Article 77 such that the above prohibition may be extended by a further year by decision of the Minister of Commerce and Industry upon the request of the MSM.

(e) An amendment to Article 82 makes provision for establishment of employee share schemes.

(f) Article 85 has been amended so as to allow a company to purchase its own shares provided the shares so purchased do not exceed 10 per cent of its issued share capital and the approval of the Muscat Securities Market is obtained.

5.3 Banking and finance

Ministerial Decision 79/97 issued under Article 80 of the Commercial Code has maintained the maximum rate of interest chargeable in relation to commercial obligations at 10 per cent. This Ministerial Decision does not apply to bank lending.

Central Bank of Oman Regulation BM/40/96 introduces certain restrictions on share ownership in banks by related parties. The regulation took effect on 1 March 1997 and places certain restrictions on the number of voting shares in a bank which may be held by any one family or by bodies acting in concert.

5.4 Muscat Securities Market (MSM)

As mentioned in the introduction, the MSM was one of the best performing markets in the world during 1997, and continued to advance into the first quarter of 1998, but has since fallen back during the second quarter of 1998. There have been no legislative changes in relation to the MSM. More comprehensive regulations relating to prospectus requirements, financial intermediaries and mutual investment funds are being developed. The regulations are expected during the second half of 1998 and will be an interim measure pending a more comprehensive review of the MSM Law itself.

5.5 Construction

There have been no major developments in this area.

5.6 Taxation and customs

5.6.1 *Withholding Tax Regulations*

In November 1996, the tax laws in force in Oman were amended by the introduction of a withholding tax on certain payments made by businesses in Oman to foreign companies which do not have a permanent establishment in Oman; otherwise the existing rule that a business must have a permanent establishment before a tax liability arises continues to apply.

The withholding tax was introduced by Royal Decree 87/96 by means of an amendment to the Law of Income Tax on Companies (RD 47/81). The 1996 Decree was published in the Official Gazette on 2 November 1996 and has now been implemented by means of Ministerial Decision 70/97 which was published on 1 July 1997.

The new legislation gives rise to some uncertainty. Omani businesses are responsible for making withholdings but will not necessarily know whether the recipient has a permanent establishment in Oman; if so, it might reasonably be expected that the foreign company would receive a tax credit in respect of any deductions. This is not expressly stated in the legislation but would seem to follow from the fact that the withholding tax is imposed in terms of the Law of Income Tax on Companies and not as an entirely separate tax. The usual procedures apply as to (a) enforcement measures available to the Tax Department (save that these would be directed against the Omani business responsible for making withholdings) and (b) the ability of taxpayers to appeal against assessments.

5.6.2 *Ministerial Decision 78/97: tax exemptions*

This Ministerial Decision specifies the regulations and procedures to be followed in order to qualify for exemptions from income tax in the case of commercial companies, and exemptions from profit tax in the case of commercial and industrial establishments. It also sets out the procedures for renewing those exemptions. The company or establishment can only enjoy the benefit of one tax exemption, in the case of there being more than one exemption applicable to that company or establishment. The exemption will be for a period of five years, and can be renewed for a further period of five years. For an industrial company or establishment to seek renewal, it will have to show that it has achieved an increase in development according to the industrial strategy criteria set out by the Ministry of Commerce and Industry.

5.6.3 *Ministerial Decision 79/97: renewal of customs duty exemptions*

This Ministerial Decision sets out the regulations and procedures for the renewal of an exemption from customs duty in respect of imports of raw materials, and semi-manufactured products which are needed by industrial establishments. The Decision provides that the renewed exemption, in the case of strategic and semi-strategic enterprises, will be for five years at 100 per cent of customs duties for the first renewal of exemption, and for a further five years at 75 per cent of customs duties in the case of a subsequent renewal. For non-strategic enterprises, the first period of exemption will be for five years at 75 per cent of customs duties, and any subsequent renewal for a period of five years at 50 per cent of customs duties.

5.6.4 *Ministerial Decision 80/97: tax and customs duty exceptions for foreign investment projects*

This Ministerial Decision sets out further regulations and procedures for obtaining exemptions for certain classes of foreign investment projects from tax and customs duties.

5.6.5 *Double taxation treaties*

Oman has ratified a number of comprehensive double taxation treaties with India, Tunisia, the United Kingdom of Great Britain and Northern Ireland and Mauritius (Royal Decrees 29/97, 10/98, 18/98 and 28/98 respectively).

5.6.6 *Tax law amendments*

Royal Decree 57/97 amends the Second Schedule annexed to the Income Tax Law of 1981, in order to remove two specific anomalies. Joint investment accounts (investment funds), government bodies, and pension funds are now to be treated as Omani owners for the purposes of calculating whether or not a public joint stock company is 51 per cent or more Omani held (such companies enjoy the beneficial tax rates available to wholly Omani owned companies). In addition, public joint stock companies established before the implementation of Royal Decree 13/89 will not be required to demonstrate that 40 per cent of their shares have been offered to the public in order to avail themselves of the lower tax rates applicable to public joint stock companies.

5.6.7 *Tax appeals*

Royal Decree 100/97 provides that tax appeals shall now be referred to the Commercial Court's Court of First Instance and goes on to set out procedural rules in relation to such appeals. Tax appeals were previously dealt with within the Ministry of Finance.

5.7 Commercial Agencies Law

Following the recent amendments to the Commercial Agencies Law, which removed the exclusivity previously enjoyed by an agent, and which sought to clarify the provisions relating to the registration of agency agreements at the Ministry of Commerce and Industry, Ministerial Decision 112/97 has amended the regulations relating to registration and deregistration of commercial agency agreements.

The registration of an agreement is to be cancelled at the request of the principal after its expiry. Previously, an aggrieved agent would be able to delay the cancellation of the registration by lodging a claim at the Commercial Court, but this provision relating to cancellation appears to be applicable regardless of whether a claim has been lodged or not. However, it does not extend to the cancellation of registration upon termination, as opposed to expiry, and it remains the case that in such circumstances the agent alone can require the deletion of the registration prior to the exhaustion of any claim lodged with the Commercial Court.

However, this ought not, in reality, to present a problem to a principal, who is now entitled to appoint more than one agent, and register such agreement, in any event. While the Minister of Commerce and Industry retains a residual jurisdiction to prohibit the import of goods which are subject to an agency which has been cancelled "without an acceptable reason", we have no knowledge of this power having been exercised since the removal of exclusivity.

6 EMPLOYMENT AND LABOUR LAW

There have been various developments in relation to the Government's Omanization programme (the programme whereby Omani nationals are employed in preference to expatriates). Ministerial Decision 127/94 sets out various requirements, mainly as to the percentage of Omani nationals who must be employed by different classes of commercial establishments. The deadline for compliance with those requirements was originally the end of 1996 but Ministerial Decision 19/97 extended that deadline for one more year to 31 December 1997. Ministerial Decision 41/98 has specifically required that at least 50 per cent of employees at filling stations around the country must be Omani. Implementation of the Omanization programme has been supported by Ministerial Decision 8/98 of the Diwan of Royal

Court, which names the members of the committee which is responsible for following up Omanization (see 2.6 above).

Royal Decree 30/98 has amended certain provisions of the Labour Law in relation to employers' contributions to vocational training schemes (this has now been set at 7 per cent of the annual salary for each non-Omani employee). Certain additional contributions are required in relation to different classes of employees by Ministerial Decision 83/98 of the Ministry of Social Affairs, Labour and Vocational Training.

7 PROPERTY AND LAND LAW

Royal Decree 2/98 has issued new regulations in relation to the Register of Real Estate maintained by the Ministry of Housing. The main purpose of the regulations is to control land ownership rights and to ensure the stability of those rights and any dealings in relation thereto. The regulations are valuable as they are clearer than the previous regulations in terms of the kind of interests which may be recorded and the extent to which registered owners may deal with in those interests. In particular, Article 10 of the new regulations details the various interests in land which exist under Omani law, which now clearly includes such things as servitudes. Article 11 details particular security interests which are available, including mortgage, pledge and lien, although the precise nature of these rights, in relation to land, is not detailed. In general terms, the regulations support and reinforce the approach whereby interests in land exist in terms of the interests which are registered with the Ministry of Housing, i.e. land ownership in Oman is very much a system of registered title.

Ministerial Decision 43/98 of the Ministry of Housing provides that companies which are 100 per cent Omani owned may register interests in land but that they must purchase this land from individuals or other companies which are already registered as holding that interest. In relation to public joint stock companies (listed companies) the required proportion of Omani ownership is reduced to 51 per cent. All companies are subject to the restriction that corporate owners may only own land for the purpose of carrying out their commercial objectives and may not do so purely for investment purposes.

8 INTELLECTUAL PROPERTY

It is almost two years since Oman's first Copyright Law, Royal Decree 47/96, was introduced, which was seen as a positive step towards answering the criticism that had been levelled at the intellectual property regime in Oman by those such as the United States Trade Representative, and necessary in view of Oman's decision to join the World Intellectual Property Organization.

Ministerial Decision No. 43/98 sets out the regulations for depositing literary artistic and scientific works. In a statement by the Commerce and Industry Undersecretary, it was acknowledged that the problem of copyright violation occurred most commonly with respect to audio and video tapes, and computer programmes. The delay in putting in place the means of implementing copyright protection was to allow those businesses which had previously dealt in material which would now be subject to the law to be wound down.

Whilst the Ministerial Decision states that it will come into force with effect from the date of publication, it also states that anyone who possesses non-original work which enjoys protection abroad should dispose of such items by 31 December 1998. It is not clear, therefore, whether the law will actually be enforced by the government before then.

The Ministerial Decision provides for a special register, the Register of Literary, Artistic and Scientific Works, in which will be recorded details of the work to be protected. An official number will be allocated to each work and notification of registration will appear in the Official Gazette.

As a practical measure, it is understood that import permits are now only issued by the Ministry of National Heritage and Culture for original video tapes, which should prevent pirate tapes from being imported in the future.

9 FAMILY LAW AND SUCCESSION

Royal Decree 32/97 promulgates extensive rules in relation to institution of marriage and deals with various related areas such as guardianship of children and succession. The legislation details in detail with the nature of the marriage bond, the issue dowry and consanguinity and affinity. The matters of separation and divorce are dealt with in detail and the decree sets out various substantive rules as to grounds upon which divorce is available as well setting out certain procedural rules.

In relation to matters of succession, the Personal Status Law makes provision for testamentary disposition, broadly within the limitations available under the *shari'a*. The law deals in detail with entitlement of heirs to the estate of the deceased and represents a substantial codification of the *shari'a* as interpreted and applied in Oman. To the extent that a particular point is not covered by the terms of the Personal Status Law, reference is to be made to the *shari'a*, subject to the requirement that it be interpreted in a manner which is consistent with the Personal Status Law. The Personal Status Law does not apply to non-Muslims unless chosen by them.

10 CRIMINAL LAW AND PROCEDURES

There have been no developments under this title.

11 PUBLIC INTERNATIONAL LAW

See 2 (above) in relation to Oman's accession to the New York Convention of 1958 in relation to enforcement of arbitral awards.

12 PRIVATE INTERNATIONAL LAW (CONFLICTS)

There have been no developments under this title.

Yemen

*Nageeb Shamiri**

1 CONSTITUTIONAL LAW

1.1 New Supreme Elections Commission

A new Supreme Elections Commission had been appointed in October 1997, according to the provisions of the Elections Law of 1996, for a term of four years. It is this Commission which will supervise the first local council elections (in the provinces and districts), which are expected to take place in the second half of 1998 at the latest, as well as the presidential elections due to take place in October 1999, which will be through direct election by the people for the first time in the history of Yemen, and the next general (or parliamentary) elections, due to take place (according to the Constitution and the Elections Law of 1996) in April 2001. It is worth mentioning, however, that the main responsibilities of the Commission are as follows.

(a) administration, preparation, supervision, control of the stages of the general elections and public referendum;
(b) dividing up the electoral constituencies in the Republic, on the basis of equality among the population, and taking into consideration geographical and social factors;
(c) setting up supervisory committees for preparation of voter lists, administration of the voting and distribution thereof among the ballot stations, and appointments of the chairmen of the said committees;
(d) making available the forms, voter lists, documents, voting cards, ballot boxes and ballot papers;
(e) preparation of a guide book for the election process, for the assistance of the various committees;

---

* LLD and member of the Supreme Judicial Council of Yemen.

(f) defining the rules regarding the election campaigns by the candidates, and for making use of the official media (television, radio and newspapers), taking into consideration that it is not permissible, according to law, to use mosques, university colleges, institutes, schools, government departments, army camps, sports clubs and stadia for the purpose;

(g) taking whatever steps are necessary to encourage women to exercise their rights in this respect, and forming women's committees with responsibility to register women voters.

On 15 April 1998, by-elections were held in four different provinces; the first since the General Elections of 27 April 1997:

(a) in the Province of Ibb;
(b) in the Province of Dhamar;
(c) in the Province of Sana'a; and
(d) in the Province of Hajjah.

The results were announced on 17 April 1998, with the success of the ruling party (the Popular General Congress).

1.2 Issuing the Standing Orders of Parliament

Law No. 43 of 1997 has been promulgated, in connection with the Standing Orders of the House of Representatives (the Yemeni Parliament) to replace those issued immediately after re-unification in May 1990 by Law No. 5 of 1990. There are 288 Standing Orders in total. They deal with, and regulate, the following matters:

(a) general principles, which are articles from the Constitution, related to Parliament, e.g. that the House of Representatives is the Legislative Branch of State power; the House consists of 301 members; the election of the House is for a term of four years; the House meets in the capital (Sana'a), except under extraordinary circumstances; that the sittings of the House are public and there is media coverage of its sittings;

(b) the organs of the House: the Speaker and his deputies (three in number), together constituting the Presidium of the House; the Standing Committees (nineteen in number) and the General Secretariat;

(c) the election of the Presidium of the House:
   (i) the Speaker;
   (ii) First Deputy-Speaker for organizational and technical affairs;
   (iii) Second Deputy-Speaker for legislative and supervisory affairs; and
   (iv) Third Deputy-Speaker for parliamentary affairs and forging relations;

(d) the responsibilities of the Presidium of the House;

(e) the responsibilities of the Speaker of the House;

(f) the formation of the Standing Committees and responsibilities thereof.
   there are nineteen Standing Committees, each consisting of eleven members (minimum) and fifteen members (maximum), as follows:

   (i)   constitutional and legal affairs;
   (ii) development, oil and mineral resources;
  (iii) trade and industry;
  (iv) financial affairs (responsible, *inter alia*, for the budget);
   (v) education;
  (vi) higher education, youth and sports;
 (vii) information, culture and tourism;
(viii) electricity, water, construction and urban planning;
  (ix) environment and public health;
   (x) telecommunications and transport;
  (xi) agriculture, fisheries and water resources;
 (xii) work force and welfare;
(xiii) foreign affairs and immigrants;
(xiv) justice and religious endowments (Islamic *awkaf*);
 (xv) Islamic *shari'a* principles codification;
(xvi) defence and security;
(xvii) local administration;
(xviii) petitions and complaints; and
 (xix) public freedoms and human rights.

The House may form new Standing Committees, or amalgamate two or more Standing Committees, and specifying the responsibilities thereof, provided that that does not contradict the articles of the Constitution and provisions of these Standing Orders;

(g)   the formation of the General Secretariat and responsibilities;
(h)   the sittings of the House:
   (i)   keeping order in the House;
  (ii)   the order of work in the sittings;
 (iii)   closing discussions/guillotine procedure;
 (iv)   voting/division; and
  (v)   minutes of the sittings.

The House convenes two sessions every year:

(i)   The first session commences on 1 February and ends on 30 June (July is a vacation);

(ii)   The second session commences on 1 August and ends on 31 December, provided the House should have approved the budget (January is a vacation).

The fasting month of Ramadan is an official vacation for the House, and in case it coincides with a month in which the House ought to be in session, the House reconvenes in the month succeeding Ramadan.

The House may be summoned, in case of urgency, to an extraordinary session, by a Resolution of the President of the Republic, or of the Presidium of the House, or on the written application of one-third of the members.

(i) Work of the House:
   (i)   legislative affairs:
      – Bills;
      – laws issued;

- laws issued by Resolutions (by the President under the Constitution) when the House in recess;
- treaties and agreements.
 (ii) supervisory affairs:
- questions and general debates;
- resolutions, directives, requests for discussions and inquiries;
- discussion on the government's programme or on statements as regards government policies;
- petitions and complaints.
 (iii) financial affairs:
- budget and audit reports;
- budget and accounts of the House.
(j) membership:
 (i) formation (by the members) of Parliamentary "groups";
 (ii) determining the validity/legality of membership;
 (iii) declaring membership null and void;
 (iv) resignations.
(k) vacant seats:
 (i) resignation; declarations of memberships null and void; deaths. Within sixty days, with effect from declaration of the seat vacant, a by-election should be held, provided it is not the last year of the term of the House;
 (ii) regulations of absentees.
(l) members' immunity.
(m) rights and privileges of members.
(n) procedure as regards nominations for Presidential Elections.
(o) procedure as regards amending the Constitution.

1.3 Appointing a Consultative Council to the President

A Consultative Council to the President of the Republic, the first since the amended Constitution came into force on 1 October 1994, has been appointed, headed by the ex-Prime Minister.

 Article 125 of the Constitution describes the Consultative Council, and states as follows:

A Resolution by the President of the Republic shall form a Consultative Council from experienced and qualified specialists in order to expand the base of participation through consultation, and to make use of national expertise and qualifications available in different areas of Yemen. The law shall clarify the special rules that concern the Council.

That law is the Consultative Council Law No. 14 of 1994. According to the law, it has fifty-nine members. The main functions of the Council are as follows:

(a) local administration; and
(b) all/any other matters referred to them by the President.

2 JUDICIAL SYSTEM AND COURTS

2.1 Judicial Reform Programme

On 12 October 1997, the Cabinet approved an ambitious and comprehensive judicial reform programme, submitted by the Minister of Justice, in accordance with the government programme on the basis of which the government won the confidence of Parliament. At a later stage, in January 1998, the Supreme Judicial Council approved the said programme and started its gradual implementation.

The question of reforming the judiciary has become a pressing issue, given the general consensus throughout the country and the admission by the constitutional establishments that the judiciary is suffering from great shortcomings and irregularities which have reflected negatively on the various governmental plans in the fields of development, security, investment and administrative reforms. These shortcomings have left their evidence in the failure to bring about peace and stability in society. For this reason, reforming the judiciary has became a great national cause, receiving special attention from the state and stressing the following points:

(a)   reformation of the independence of the judiciary so that judges submit to no other authority except that of legislation;
(b)   no interference with the judiciary and judicial bodies to adhere to the policy of rejecting any interference in any case until a judgment has been given;
(c)   enhancing the reputation of the judiciary and respecting its judgments.

The programme aims to enhance the independence of the judiciary, to ensure the equitable administration of justice, and solve the failings of the judiciary, by providing effective court administration, case management and continuing education for judges. It represents a milestone in Yemen's progress towards strengthening the rule of law and institutionalizing democracy. It concentrates on the following areas for reform and restructuring, which are as follows:

(a)   The framework reform of the judiciary and the correction of concepts and practices, which involve two questions:
  (i)   What sort of judicial system do we need to establish?
  (ii)   What is the definition of independence of the judiciary?
  The Arab and international experiments (unity and plurality in the judiciary; separation of powers) are considered.
     The Constitution of the Republic of Yemen has made clear that a unified judiciary is the form to be adopted, in the sense that all jurisdictions are concentrated in one institution: the Supreme Court of the Republic.
(b)   Reforming the bodies responsible for judicial reforms:
  (i)   the Supreme Judicial Council, which works on the application of the guarantees granted to judges on issues of appointment, promotion, transfers, discipline, dismissal and retirement, in addition to studying and approving the budget of the judiciary;
  (ii)   the Supreme Court of the Republic, which is the highest judicial organ through which errors in judgments can be corrected, which means that

the Supreme Court is a court of law and therefore, any provisions in the laws in force which contradict this principle ought to be abolished or amended, in order to bring to an end any illegal practices;

(iii) the Ministry of Justice, which is the administrative and executive apparatus that serves the judiciary and improves its performance, in addition to being entrusted with providing all courts and judges with all preparation and services (technical, financial and administrative);

(iv) the Judicial Inspection Commission, which examines the judges' understanding of the procedures and principles in the laws in force, as well as their ability to adjudicate properly, and evaluates the judges' conduct as regards their duties and obligations.

(c) Protection of the judiciary's autonomy is a subject of great importance in reforming the judiciary, and depends on the following foundations:

(i) clear understanding of the concept of judicial autonomy and its administrative and financial independence;

(ii) presence of clearly defined and binding legal codes and texts upon which judges can depend in case adjudications and which cannot be compromised by authoritative litigants;

(iii) self-protection, through which judges can feel security which comes as an outcome of the presence of a strong and autonomous judiciary;

(iv) constitutional protection which is effected by establishing the principles of judicial autonomy and by guaranteeing such autonomy in constitutional provisions;

(v) penal protection, which means constitutional provision(s) stipulating that interference with claims or court affairs would be treated as crimes (there are penal provisions in the Penal Code in force);

(vi) popular protection, which means that the independence of the judiciary should be an essential part of the concern of the people and be deeply embedded in their conscience, which means adopting an informative policy and an integrated education programme to create public awareness of the importance of protecting the independence of the judiciary.

The steps required to achieve protection for judiciary independence are:

– enactment of the Judiciary Independence Protection Law;
– commitment to abolish all forms of control over court procedures;
– providing security to judges, for instance any incident that involves a breach as regards the security of a judge's life should be dealt with promptly and with resolution and firmness at the highest level;
– highlighting the state's concern towards any offence through the use of the mass media;
– adherence, by all authorities, not to accept or allow any requests or intervention dealing with the appointment of judges in certain provinces, or their transfer; and
– ending all connections between the judiciary and the executive branch in all provinces.

(d) Judges are the focal point on which reforms in the judiciary revolve. Such reforms should focus on the following:

(i) ensuring the proper selection for those appointed as judges in accordance with high criteria of moral and scholarly qualities, especially when they are admitted to study at the High Judicial Institute, in addition to enhancing judicial stability by adhering strictly to a well establishing system of appointments, promotions, transfers, etc.

(ii) subjecting the graduates of the Institute to ongoing scrutiny and supervision;

(iii) training for a certain period before a graduate is finally appointed to a full judge;

(iv) upgrading and improving judicial syllabuses and instructor qualities at the High Judicial Institute;

(v) organizing workshops on judicial education and special educational tours for judges to Arabic, Islamic and foreign countries to benefit from their expertise;

(vi) initiating a programme for enhancing judges' skills in different specialisms, especially those who have witnessed changes in technology and the problems associated with them;

(vii) publishing judges' benchbooks for the reference of judges on correct judiciary practices;

(viii) issuing regular judicial publications to provide awareness on judicial procedures;

(ix) improving salaries and allowances paid to members of the judiciary, as an essential procedure to prevent corruption and the temptation to receive bribes;

(x) increasing the number of judges to make justice available to the public and to meet the increasing needs of society, which should enable the establishment of Divisional Courts within the First Instance Courts, for petty offences and small claims.

(e) Public prosecution is a judicial organ entrusted with responsibilities to defend society and supervise criminal investigations as well as following up judicial cases, in addition to the enforcement of sentences, and the inspection of prisons. Reforms in this sphere involve improving performance to ensure the accurate handling of cases for the general protection of public interest; clearly defining the principles guiding the relations between judges and prosecutors; adherence of public prosecutors to the rules and ethics of the profession and developing prosecutors' skills and specialization.

(f) Regulating and organizing relations between the judiciary and the judiciary control apparatus (such as the security forces).

(g) Courthouses: reforms include, but are not restricted to, better organization; good staffing; necessary records and judicial documents and forms; organizing the administrative as well as the written work in the courts, with a view to establishing certain standardized methods of keeping records; paying special attention to judicial statistics by improving the facilities thereof, with a view to using them during judicial, financial and administrative inspection as well as in the distribution of judicial functions, and the preparation of a special budgetary plan with a view to assigning budgets for courts at the provincial level (otherwise known as decentralization in the financial matters), in addition to issuing the Executive Regulations of the Court Fees Law.

(h) The legal profession reforms are designed to improve the legal profession and ensure efficiency, which will lead to greater impact on the performance of the judiciary and realization of justice, in addition to better cooperation with the Lawyers Union (in England: the Law Society) for, in the Yemen, there is no division of the legal profession into barristers and solicitors. Moreover, the absence of the legal profession of law since reunification has meant that the profession has suffered many set backs and, henceforth, consideration of the Legal Profession Bill, with the cooperation of the Lawyers Union, is one of the priorities in the judicial reform programme.

(i) Authentication of documents and land register, issuing the Executive Regulations of the Authentication of Documents Law, and the establishment of a Real Estate Declaration Procedure for the Land Register Authority has not achieved the objective under consideration, namely the establishment of a proper legal system as regards land registration.

(j) Experts before the courts: a survey of the different provinces of the country is to be carried out, to collect information about the experts in, for example, real estate and the proper price estimation thereof; accountancy; foreign legislation; translators, etc. so as to put that survey, and the technical advice needed, under the service of the courts.

(k) Forensic medicine: there is urgent importance to establish this service and put it to use for the service of justice.

(l) Reforming conditions inside prisons and preventive detention centres: this is the responsibility of the government in order to ensure better treatment of those under detention, whether on short term, or those serving longer terms; prisons, generally speaking, should receive attention so that prisoners become productive individuals in society.

The programme's three main goals are:

(a) to ensure the independence of the judiciary by protecting judges from outside interference;
(b) to standardize court procedure and judicial administration;
(c) to enhance training and infrastructure.

The most noteworthy elements of the programme include:

(a) criminalizing all forms of interference in the judiciary;
(b) systematizing judicial appointments;
(c) developing standards for judicial conduct and performance;
(d) strengthening the capacity of the Judicial Inspection Commission to investigate abuses and enforce standards.

The first step in this direction took place on 23 January 1998, when the Supreme Judicial Council resolved to reconstitute the Judicial Inspection Commission, of thirty-six members, the majority of whom are judges from the Supreme Court of the Republic (the highest court in the land), the Courts of Appeal in the Provinces and some magistrates in the trial courts, in addition to some prosecutors and private lawyers. For the first time in the history of the Yemen, lawyers from the private profession have been recruited to join the Commission: a step which may soon lead to having private lawyers recruited as judges for the Commercial Courts. During the period 7 March to 2 April 1998, seven groups of judicial inspectors travelled all over the country, and accomplished their assignments as regards all the Courts of Appeal, in addition to all the trial courts in the capital (Sana'a) and the provinces of (Sana'a, Aden, Ta'iz, Hadhramawt and Al-Hudaidah).

The principal items of legislation needed to carry out the reform programme are as follows:

(a) the Judicature Bill;
(b) the Supreme Judicial Council Rules;
(c) the Supreme Court Rules;
(d) the Ministry of Justice Regulations;
(e) the Judicial Inspection Regulations;
(f) the Financial Regulations of the Judiciary Budget;
(g) the Judiciary Fund Regulations;
(h) the Higher Judicial Institute Bill;
(i) the Regulatory Rules of the Relations Between the Judiciary and the Judicial Control Apparatus;
(j) the Court's Rules;
(k) the Executive Regulations of the Court Fees Law;
(l) the Executive Regulations of the Authentication Law;
(m) the Legal Profession Bill;
(n) the Executive Regulations of the Real Estate Law;
(o) the Experts' Regulations Bill;
(p) the Forensic Medicine Bill; and
(q) review (and amendments) regarding substantive and procedural laws.

2.2 Setting up Dar Al-Ifta' Ash-Shr'iyyah Al-Yemeniah

A Resolution of the President of the Republic (No. 17 of 1997) has been issued regarding setting up a new religious/legal institution, called the Yemen Fatwa Organization, under the auspices of the Presidential Office, in the capital (Sana'a) with branches, if needed, in the provinces (*Dar Al-Ifta' Ash-Shr'iyyah Al-Yemeniah*).

The main functions of the new institution are as follows:

(a) giving opinions regarding the beliefs, prayers, transactions, morals, personal status matters such as marriage, divorce, succession, probates, etc. based on the well-known Islamic *shari'a* principles;
(b) stating the religious principle regarding a matter whether that matter comes within the ambit of permissible, undesirable, obligatory or prohibited;
(c) stating the *shari'a* principle regarding a matter in accordance with Islamic *shari'a* and on the basis of the prima facie facts revealed by the matter in issue.

The governing body of the new institution is the Supreme Commission, consisting of the Chairman (Mufti Ad-Dayar Al-Yemeniah) and four members, all appointed by Presidential Resolution. The main responsibilities of the Commission are the following:

(a) giving replies to the questions raised by the public;

(b) investigating the commencement of the Hijra (Arabic) months, with the collaboration of the organs concerned. In this connection, the new institution shall set up subcommittees for the purpose, in Hudaidah, Aden and Hadhramat, as well as in other coastal areas;

(c) publishing the *shari'a* fatawa (opinions) given by the new institution, and distribution thereof to the law courts, the educational institutions and the individuals or public at large.

The members of the institution should fulfil the following qualifications and conditions:

(a) be Yemeni nationals, of honesty and integrity;
(b) be at least 40 years old;
(c) be versed in the Holy Qur'an and *Hadith*, and interpretation as well as explanation thereof;
(d) be well-versed in the Arabic language; and
(e) with judicial experience.

2.3 The court structure

2.3.1 *Juveniles' care*

Explanatory note: in 1992, a law, called the Juveniles' Care Law No. 24 of 1992 was issued, providing for the establishment, in the capital (Sana'a) and the centres of the Provinces, of "Juvenile Courts" (equivalent to Youth, or Young Offenders Courts in England and Wales), each consisting of:

(a) a judge, as president, and;
(b) two social experts, as assessors, one of whom should be female.

The first juvenile court was set up in the province of Aden in 1995. More juvenile courts are to be set up in other provinces during 1998.

The amended Juveniles Care Law No. 26 of 1997 was promulgated, with the following main amendments:

(a) A juvenile is someone below the age of 15 according to the Gregorian calendar, at the date of the commission of the crime (previously, according to the *Hijra* calendar).
(b) The age of the juvenile at the date of the commission of the crime is of the essence for determining whether the juvenile should be brought before a juvenile court or an ordinary First Instance Court.
(c) A juvenile whose age does not exceed 12 years should not be kept at a police station, but should be handed over to his guardian, failing which should be kept at an approved juveniles' rehabilitation institution for twenty-four hours, in case it is not expedient to release him, for fear of danger to him or third parties, after which period the juvenile should be referred to the public prosecution.

(d) A juvenile whose age exceeds 12 years may be kept at a police station for twenty-four hours, provided that juvenile is kept at a place separate from that specified for adults.

(e) An attorney/advocate should be provided to defend a juvenile (accused) of any crime, whether serious or otherwise, and the prosecution or the court should ensure that this is done in accordance with the provisions of the Criminal Procedure Law.

(f) The enforcement of sentences of confinement of freedom (or imprisonment), should take place in separate places within the penal institutions; it is the responsibility of the said institutions to train and rehabilitate the juveniles, professionally and socially, in accordance with the principles and criteria specified in the Executive Regulations of this law.

(g) Apart from confiscation and closure of a place, no punishment under the Penal Code shall be inflicted as regards a juvenile whose age has not yet exceeded 10 years. Irrespective of the crime/offence the commission of which he has been charged, the following alternative punishments may be passed against him:

   (i) reprimand;
   (ii) handing the juvenile over to the care of one of his parents, or guardian, failing which to someone who can take good care of him;
   (iii) attachment to a vocational training institution, either a factory or commercial place, for a period not exceeding three years;
   (iv) social/community work, for a minimum period of six months and maximum period of three years;
   (v) to be under a judicial court's supervision for a maximum period of three years;
   (vi) remand in an approved school/juveniles' social care home, under the supervision of the Ministry of Welfare and Social Insurance, provided the period of reprimand does not exceed ten years for serious crimes, three years for other crimes and one year for offences, and on condition that the remand home or approved school submits a social/character report regarding the juvenile to the juvenile court concerned at least once every six months; or
   (vii) remand in a specialized hospital, under the supervision of the juvenile court concerned, for a maximum period of one year.

(h) "Subject to the principles of Islamic *shari'a*". This proviso has been added to the new amendments, which may not be be in the interests of the juvenile, in the sense that age may not be of the essence if the juvenile has already reached the age of puberty prior to the age limit fixed by the law:

   (i) a juvenile who is 10 years of age, but has not yet reached the age of 15, and has committed a crime the punishment of which is death, should be sentenced to a term of imprisonment the minimum of which is three years and the maximum seven years (previously, a minimum of ten years);
   (ii) with regards to the rest of the crimes, the punishment should not exceed one-quarter of the maximum sentence for the particular crime/offence (previously, one-third);

(iii) if the juvenile has committed two or more crimes, he should be sentenced to one appropriate/suitable punishment, irrespective of whether he has previous convictions, etc.

2.3.2 Authentication of Documents

During 1992 the Authentication of Documents Law No. 29 of 1992 was promulgated, the first since re-unification. According to the Law, a General Department for Authentication was set up in the Ministry of Justice, with offices for the purpose established in the district courts throughout the country. The Law also regulated the work of registrars of Muslim marriages and divorces, as well as powers of attorney and contracts of sale of real property, together with the work of notaries public, usually magistrates and their assistants, performing their functions in the district courts, under the supervision of the Presidents of the said Courts.

The amended Authentication Law No. 34 of 1997 was promulgated, introducing the following amendments to the Law of 1992:

(a) A General Department for Authentication of Documents is to be set up in the Ministry of Justice, with responsibility for the supervision of the work done in this respect by the offices for Authentication at the District Courts and the Courts of Appeal.

(b) Offices for Authentication of Documents are to be set up in the Courts of Appeal in the provinces (governorates), to supervise the work of the Authentication offices in the district courts within the Province.

(c) Registrars (called *Umanaa*, singular, *Amin*), who are usually private citizens, perform their duties, such as marriages, divorces, powers of attorney, etc. according to the Islamic *shari'a* principles, under the supervision of the district court concerned, and are licensed by the district court. The licences are valid for, and renewable every three years; the heirs of a deceased registrar should deliver all the documents in their possession in this respect to the court concerned.

(d) The notary public, who is usually a magistrate, performs such duties as executor and registers the documents which, under the laws in force or at the request of the parties concerned, should be registered, in addition to verification of commercial registers.

(e) notaries public and registrars are under an obligation to keep records and registers, which should be kept at the courts, and should under no circumstances be removed or transferred therefrom.

(f) There are prescribed fees.

2.3.3 Arbitration (Domestic)

Arbitration Law No. 22 was issued in 1992; it applies to any arbitration taking place within the country, as well as outside the country if the parties thereto agree that its provisions shall apply to their arbitration. Modern trends in commercial arbitration have been taken into consideration, following the government's economic, financial and administrative reform programme.

The amended Arbitration Law No. 32 of 1997 was promulgated to have the following effects:

(a) A party to an arbitration, knowing that any of the provisions of the law or the terms of the Arbitration Agreement have been contravened, and which carries on with the arbitration proceedings without raising any objection promptly or immediately thereafter, shall be (stopped) from raising any objection at a later stage, provided the contravention does not contravene a *shari'a* principle.

(b) The parties to an arbitration shall bear all the expenses of the arbitration, including the remunerations for the arbitrators, in accordance with the agreement to this effect between the parties and the arbitrators, and in case of dispute, the matter should be referred to the competent court for settlement.

(c) The arbitration agreement should be executed in writing, and should specify the dispute/subject of the arbitration, before or after the dispute has arisen, and even if the parties have filed a case before a court of law, otherwise the arbitration agreement shall be null and void.

(d) The arbitration committee is under an obligation to give its award in accordance with the legal principles/laws agreed upon by the parties if the parties have agreed to apply laws other than those in force in the Yemen. The committee has discretion to resort to international law principles as well as principles of justice and equity if the parties have so agreed. However, under all circumstances the arbitration committee should give its award in accordance with the laws in force in Yemen or the terms and conditions of the agreement between the parties, and should take into consideration the usage and social customs, as well as the usage and commercial/trade customs in this respect, provided that such usage and customs are not inconsistent with Islamic *shari'a* principles.

(e) If the parties during the arbitration proceedings agree to settle the dispute amicably, the arbitration committee should record the consent–agreement as an award settling the dispute and end the proceedings.

(f) The arbitration committee/panel should give its award with the reasons (unless the parties have agreed otherwise) in writing, signed by all the arbitrators, if the award has been reached unanimously; if the award has been reached by majority, it should be signed by those in favour and the dissenting arbitrator may not sign and may give his reasons for so doing.

The award should state the following particulars:
(i) the names of the parties to the arbitration, addresses and nationalities thereof;
(ii) summary of the claims and defences of the parties, their statements/documents in support;
(iii) the decisions and reasons thereof; and
(iv) the date and place where the award has been given.

The award is final and enforceable:
(i) should the parties agree;
(ii) if the arbitration has been concluded by settlement; and
(iii) in the event the award is so regarded by law.

The arbitration tribunal should send copies of the award, duly signed by the arbitrators, to the parties to the arbitration.

Choice of the arbitrators: it is within the rights of the parties to agree the number of arbitrators, and failing which the number should be three. If there is only one arbitrator and no agreement between the parties, the court, upon application by one of the parties, will nominate. If there are two, each party appoints one. If there are three, each party appoints one, and the two choose a third within the thirty days following their appointment; failing which the court nominates the third upon an application by one of the parties, and the third arbitrator shall be the chairman of the arbitration tribunal.

2.3.4 *Military courts and prosecution offices*

According to Republican Resolutions Nos. 189–192, under the Judicature and Military Criminal Procedure Laws, and after the approval of the Supreme Judicial Council, five first instance military courts have been established as follows:

(a) First Instance Military Court in the Eastern Region;
(b) First Instance Military Court in the Middle Region;
(c) First Instance Military Court in the North-Western Region;
(d) First Instance Military Court in the Western Region; and
(e) First Instance Military Court in the Central Region.

In addition, the Military Appeal Court has been established.

At the same time, five military prosecution offices have been established in the same regions. It is worthwhile mentioning however, that the Military Division of the Supreme Court of the Republic is the highest law court in the land, as regards the ordinary courts as well as the military courts in the Republic of Yemen.

2.4 Judicial and legal training

A refresher judicial course for thirty judges and prosecutors from the capital (Sana'a) took place (17–30 November 1997) at the Higher Judicial Council, Sana'a, sponsored by the British Embassy and the British Council in the Republic of Yemen. The course was held under the title, "Judges' Legal Refresher Training – Priority Objectives Addressed: Good Government". The training took the form of practical task-based workshops, where the judges and prosecutors discussed the problems of the topics as experienced by lawyers. The topics covered were:

(a) Islamic jurisprudence;
(b) judicial ethics (a code of judicial conduct);
(c) the theory of evidence;
(d) the theory of nullity;
(e) commercial arbitration;
(f) court procedure: practical issues;

(g)   contractual and tortious liability;
(h)   the role, duties and powers of the Public Prosecution;
(i)   drafting of judgments (and in general, legal drafting);
(j)   court management (and in general, judicial administration).

The goal of the course was:

to contribute to good government and the success of the government's administrative
reform programme by providing training to support the administrative abilities of the
judges, assistant judges (and public prosecutors) in Sana'a courts: for efficiency and
competence at these courts are crucial for the success of the government's attempts to
implement its reform programme. This will allow courts to play effective roles in human
rights protection activities. By helping to upgrade management skills in the courts, the
course will make a direct contribution to development of better government in the
Republic of Yemen.

The course was followed by a three day Workshop on Judicial Reform in the Republic of Yemen, attended by more than one hundred judges, public prosecutors,
legal advisors, university professors, instructors of the Higher Judicial Institute
and lawyers from all the provinces of the Republic. Officials from the Ministry of
Justice and Ministry of Legal and Parliamentary Affairs, as well as the Judicial Inspection Commission, participated. The British Embassy and British Council in
the Republic of Yemen, and the World Bank, sponsored and financed the event.

The workshop was an important opportunity for the judiciary to learn about
the outlines of judicial reform that were approved by the Council of Ministers on
12 October 1997. The participants were also asked to rank their priorities for judicial reform.

The Minister of Justice and Minister of Legal and Parliamentary Affairs, the Chairman of the Judicial Inspection Commission in the Republic of Yemen, Supreme
Court Judges, the British Ambassador to Yemen (Mr Victor Henderson), the Head
of the Legal Department of the World Bank (Mr Hans Jürgen Gruss) and some of
his personnel and the Director of the Commonwealth Institute for Judicial Education in Halifax (Nova Scotia, Canada) participated in the workshop – the first of
its kind in the Republic of Yemen.

The main lectures and topics were as follows:

(a)   a lecture entitled "Forward to the millennium – judicial reform in the Republic
       of Yemen", by the Minister of Justice, Mr Isma'il Al-Wazir;
(b)   a lecture entitled "Application of international experience to judicial reform
       in the Republic of Yemen", by the Chairman of the Judicial Inspection Com-
       mission, Justice Nageeb Shamiri;
(c)   a lecture on "Pathway to judicial reform" by the Minister of Legal and Parlia-
       mentary Affairs, Mr Abdulla Ahmed Ghanem;
(d)   a lecture on "Comparative initiatives in judicial reform – the international ex-
       perience", by the Hon. Judge Sandra E. Oxner, President of the Common-
       wealth Judicial Education Institute, and another lecture by Judge Sandra Oxner
       on "Judicial Education";
(e)   a lecture on "Judicial reform in Egypt", by Counsellor Mohamed Ibrahim
       Sharif, Egypt;

(f)   a lecture on "Delay reduction", by Dr Richard Woolfson, UK.

The objectives of the above lectures were as follows:

(a)   to review Yemen's judicial reform objectives;
(b)   to canvas international experience in similar reforms;
(c)   to determine the role of the judiciary in achieving effective judicial reform;
(d)   to explore practical ways for the judiciary to give leadership and support to judicial reform;
(e)   discussion groups on the following topics:
     (i)   an independent judiciary;
     (ii)   an accountable judiciary;
     (iii) judicial education;
     (iv)   a code of judicial ethics;
     (v)   the judicial role in achieving effective judicial reform;
     (vi)   potential model courts: location, objectives and required support; and
     (vii) other judicial leadership issues.

3   COMMERCIAL LAW

3.1   Customs tariffs

Law No. 37 of 1997, in connection with customs tariffs, has replaced Law No. 15 of 1990 and any amendments thereof, on the same subject. Customs duties shall be determined in the tariffs prescribed in accordance with the coordinated regulations. Furthermore, the explanatory notes of the said regulations, issued by the International Customs Organization (in English) as well as the Unified Explanatory Notes of the said regulations (for the Arab League States), translated from the English Notes, shall be regarded as legal reference for the enforcement of the provisions of the customs tariffs.

3.2   Auctions and government stores

Law No. 3 of 1997, replacing Law No. 49 of 1991 in connection with auctions and government stores, consists of sixty sections, covering the following subjects:

(a)   the main objectives of the law, which are:

     (i)   laying down a general system for state auctions, purchases, sales and stores, and simplifying the procedures connected therewith;
     (ii)   working in accordance with the financial and administrative regulations in the sphere of organizing, regulating and preparing the contracts of contractors, and implementation thereof; and
     (iii) laying down supervision and control regulations in the sphere of state auctions, purchases, sales and stores, with a view to protect the public interest and property;

(b)   the law applies to the ministries, corporations, authorities and other bodies,
      and their branches (in the provinces and districts), which come within the state
      budget (with the exception of the Ministry of Defence), in addition to the pub-
      lic sector bodies; the responsibilities of which are mainly dealing with services,
      and those bodies having independent budgets; in addition to the administra-
      tive bodies and the local councils in the capital (Sana'a) and the provinces;
(c)   the bids and procedure thereof;
(d)   the committees and responsibilities thereof;
(e)   the auctions and procedure thereof;
(f)   government stores;
(g)   general provisions governing the committees.

3.3 Public corporations, authorities and companies

Law No. 7 of 1997, amending Law No. 35 of 1991 in connection with public
corporations, authorities and companies, provides as follows:

(a)   Under the amended law, definitions regarding public bodies have been stan-
      dardized as follows:

      (i)   corporation, or public corporation, means every service unit, owned
             wholly by the state;
      (ii)   authority, or public authority means every economic unit engaged in
             productive activities, or service activities connected with production and
             owned wholly by the state;
      (iii) public holding authority means every public authority which performs
             its activities through economic units under its umbrella;
      (iv)   public company means every public company owned by two or more
             of the public personalities;
      (v)   mixed company means every company the shareholders of which are
             one or more public personalities, together with the private sector; and
      (vi)   board means the board administering the public corporation, author-
             ity or company, or board of directors.
(b)   Public corporations: a board of directors administers the corporation, and
      the Republican Resolution establishing the corporation specifies:
      (i)   how the board of directors is to be set up;
      (ii)   the method of selection of the said board;
      (iii) the provisions as regards their salaries and remunerations. In addition,
             the law confers upon the corporation the right to resort to the law courts
             regarding attachment procedures, with a view to protect its interests.
(c)   Public authorities are established by Republican Resolutions, after the consent
      of the Cabinet has been given, with the following particulars:
      (i)   the name of the authority and its principal office;
      (ii)   the minister supervising the authority;
      (iii) the objects for which the authority has been established, as well as the
             scope of activities;
      (iv)   the capital of the authority and components thereof;
      (v)   the powers conferred upon the authority in order to realize its objects.

The Authority may be reorganized or wound up as follows:
- the realization of the objective thereof;
- the merger with another authority, or split into a number of authorities;
- the perishing of the whole, or the larger part, of the capital/assets of the authority, in such as way as to make it impossible to invest the remaining part, unless the Cabinet decides otherwise as of necessity and for public interest;
- the losses of the authority amounts to half its capital;
- the transfer of the authority to a mixed or private enterprise.

(d) Public companies: the board of directors prepares the articles of association of the company, in order to organize and regulate its work, management, accounts system and financial affairs, which ensure better performance as well as supervision. The company, under all circumstances, is not empowered to grant loans to the chairman, or any member, of the board of directors, or to stand guarantor as regards any loan transaction executed by (them) with third parties for their personal benefit: all such actions are considered null and void.
The company is wound up/dissolved in the following events:
  (i) the expiry of its term;
  (ii) the realization of its objectives;
  (iii) the perishing of the whole or the larger part of the capital/assets, in such a way that it is impossible to invest the remaining part;
  (iv) the merger/amalgamation;
  (v) the transfer to mixed or private enterprise;
  (vi) losses incurred for three consecutive years, or losses which amount to half the capital.
The winding up/dissolution is subject to the approval of the Cabinet.

(e) Public holding authorities: the board of directors of the authority should include "technical secretariat", having among its members a limited number of specialists/advisors and employees.
The secretariat has the following duties:
  (i) to assist the board in the performance of its responsibilities;
  (ii) to notify the bodies concerned of the resolutions and recommendations of the board;
  (iii) to furnish the minister concerned, as well as the state bodies concerned, with all the data and particulars, required by them, regarding the economic companies and units which come under the umbrella of the authority.
The holding authority performs the following duties:
- establishing shareholding companies or cooperative societies, alone or in partnership with others;
- owning shares in the said companies, either by subscription or by purchase;
- granting loans to the economic units under its umbrella, or standing as guarantor as regards the loans' transactions executed by the said economic units.

(f) Arbitration: according to the state cases system, or Government Arbitration System, undertaken by the Ministry of Legal Affairs.

3.4 Commercial Companies (Law No. 22 of 1997)

This law is considerd to be part of the Commercial Law No. 32 of 1991. Its provisions apply to all commercial companies incorporated in the Republic, and come within the types provided for in this law, or those commercial companies having their main offices in the Republic.

A commercial company is a contract in which two or more persons undertake to participate in the financial enterprises of the commercial company, by contributing money or services, and dividing the profits or losses resulting from the enterprises. Furthermore, the interpretation of any provision in the memorandum or articles of association according to the text, supplemented by reference to the provisions of this law, the commercial law and commercial custom, provided that it does not expressly contradict the provisions of this law.

The commercial companies which are permitted under the law are the following:

(a)   Partnerships:

    (i)   general partnership (*sharikat al-tadhamun*);
    (ii)   limited partnership (*sharikat al-tawsiyyah*);
    (iii) joint venture (*sharikat al-muhassah*).

(b)   Companies:

    (i)   joint stock company (*sharikat al-mosahemah*);
    (ii)   company limited by shares (*sharikat tawsiyah bel-as-hum*);
    (iii) limited liability company (*sharikat that massouliyyah mahdudah*).

All the companies permitted under the law, with the exception of joint ventures, enjoy independent legal personality.

All companies, with the exception of joint ventures, must have their memoranda of association and any amendments thereto in writing, which should be published by registering two copies with the Director of Commercial Registry, at the Ministry of Trade and Supply, within one month following the formation, and which should include the following particulars:

(a)   date and location of the contract;
(b)   names, addresses and nationalities of the parties;
(c)   name of the company;
(d)   principal office of the company;
(e)   form of the company;
(f)   object/purpose of the company;
(g)   the capital of the company and the shares of each partner (if the contract does not specify the shares of each partner, all partners are deemed to have equal shares, unless there is an agreement to the contrary or custom dictates otherwise);
(h)   names of associations or partners who are delegated to manage the company and sign in its name;
(i)   the duration of the company;
(j)   other provisions regulating the rights and obligations of the partners.

Request for registration should include the following particulars:

(a) date of the request;
(b) name of the company;
(c) form of the company;
(d) object/purpose of the company;
(e) capital of the company;
(f) names of the partners/organizations and their respective shares of the capital;
(g) main office of the company and address;
(h) delegated matters;
(i) duration of the company.

Commercial companies come to an end upon the occurrence of any of the following events:

(a) expiration of the specified period of existence;
(b) attainment of the objects/purposes of which the company was established;
(c) the objective for which the company was formed ceases to exist;
(d) unanimous decision of the partners/shareholders, provided that all outstanding obligations are satisfied;
(e) court order regarding liquidation for just cause(s) on the request of one or more associates.

In addition to any other provisions in certain types of commercial companies, e.g. partnerships, where a partnership comes to an end:

(a) if one of the partners dies and the memorandum so provides;
(b) due to insolvency of one of the partners;
(c) for the withdrawal of one of the partners;
(d) due to insanity or otherwise of one of the partners;
(e) for occurrence of an event which renders continuation of the company, or the partners, illegal.

As regards joint stock companies, where the company comes to an end:

(a) if a merger takes place with another commercial company;
(b) by a resolution of an extraordinary meeting of the general society of the company.

After reunification on 22 May 1990, a law was promulgated in connection with commercial companies – Law No. 34 of 1991. The new law takes into consideration the government's economic, financial and administrative reform programme, which is supported by the World Bank, the International Monetary Fund, the European Union, the United States of America, etc.

3.5 Organization of Agencies and Affiliates of Foreign Companies (Law No. 23 of 1997)

This law governs and regulates the activities in the Republic of Yemen of foreign companies, which must receive permission to trade from the Minister of Trade and Supply. Such activities should be done through a branch or an agency. Foreign companies should register with the Director of Commercial Registry, have autonomous budgets, profit and loss accounts and at least one Yemeni auditor.

Foreign companies may engage, in the Republic, in the following activities:

(a)   banking;
(b)   technical and consultancy services;
(c)   private construction, as well as that related to roads, ports, airports, public util-
      ities and housing estates;
(d)   tourism and hotels activities;
(e)   investment in industrial activities;
(f)   investment in oil and minerals; or
(g)   investment in agricultural, animal and fishing activities.

The courts of the Republic alone have jurisdiction to hear and settle disputes arising from the commercial agency contracts. However, in the event of any dispute
arising as a result of the agreement between the local representative and the foreign company, the Department concerned at the Ministry has no power to accept
another representative at the request of the foreign company, until after the dispute has been settled, whether amicably, or by court decision.

   The foreign companies are wound up, and struck off the Register, in accordance
with the provisions applying to the commercial companies incorporated within
the Republic.

4 LABOUR LAW

4.1 Labour (Law No. 25 of 1997, amending Law No. 5 of 1995

According to the 1997 law:

(a)   A non-Yemeni worker's rights include being granted a worker's permit; non-
      payment of fees for the worker's permit on the basis of reciprocity; obliga-
      tion of the new employer, if the term of employment is still valid, to carry
      out all the terms and conditions.
(b)   Collective employment contracts should be in writing according to the spec-
      imen prepared by the Ministry of Labour, containing the main terms and con-
      ditions regarding working means/tools (*wasa'il al-'amal*); obligations regard-
      ing payment of wages and method of payment thereof; working hours;
      holidays; bonuses; safety protection; the specification of the job; any other
      terms and conditions agreed upon between the employer and the trade union
      committee or workers' representatives, according to the laws in force in this
      respect; no individual employment contract should be executed in contra-
      vention with the collective employment contract; any proposals by the em-
      ployer regarding amendments or additions should be submitted to the work-
      ers at a general meeting by the trade union committee or the representatives
      of the workers; any term or condition in the collective employment contract
      against the laws in force, public order or morality or security or the economic
      interests of the state, shall be null and void; employers and trade unions com-
      mittees not parties to a collective employment contract are entitled to join
      the contract, independently, by agreement between the employers and the

trade union committees, without the need to have the consent of the original contractors, and the application to join has to be submitted to the branch of the Ministry, but the agreement is not enforceable until after it has been reviewed and registered by the Ministry's branch; any party to a collective employment contract is entitled to terminate it, on condition that it notifies the other party in writing of that intention in one of the following events:

(i) contravention by one of the parties of the contract's terms or the labour laws in force;

(ii) permanent, partial or total completion of work;

(iii) redundancy due to technical or economic reasons;

(iv) absence of the worker without cause for more than thirty days during the same year or fifteen continuos days, provided a notice should have been sent prior to termination;

(v) attainment, by the worker, of the retirement age under the labour laws in force;

(vi) unfitness by the worker, for health reasons, to carry on working, certified by a report of the medical committee concerned.

5 INTELLECTUAL PROPERTY

A national seminar regarding the protection of intellectual property (*al-haq al-fikry*) was held in Sana'a, during the period 7–9 October 1997. Officials attended from the Ministries of Trade and Supply, Legal and Parliamentary Affairs, Justice, Culture and Tourism, Industry, Chambers of Commerce and Industry of Yemen, in addition to Supreme Court judges and international experts from the World Intellectual Property Organization (WIPO).

The seminar discussed the following topics:

(a) international protection as regards copyrights and related rights;

(b) treaties which are administered through WIPO and the agreements as regards the components related to commerce in the sphere of intellectual property rights;

(c) international protection as regards industrial rights;

(d) which are administered through WIPO, etc.;

(e) copyrights, as regards inventions as a source of technological database;

(f) law and practices of trademarks, general principles, criteria, extent of protection accorded to trademarks (patents);

(g) the administration and protection of the rights of the authors/writers: the Jordanian experiment;

(h) the struggle against violations of copyrights;

(i) the reaction against, and solutions of, the violations and forgery of trademarks;

(j) WIPO and its development cooperative programme for the Arab states;

(k) the impact of the establishment of the appropriate infrastructure for the implementation of intellectual property rights in the Arab states, as provided for in the international treaties;

(l) the effects of the international treaties on the Arab states;

(m) the Intellectual Property Law in the Republic of Yemen:

(i)   the rights of the authors/writers;
(ii)   the Intellectual Property Law (industrial property); and
(iii) the intellectual property in the Intellectual Property Law.

It is worthwhile remembering, however, that in this respect, there are the following legislation in the Republic of Yemen:

(a)   Intellectual Property Law No. 19 of 1994; and
(b)   Control of Artistic Publications Decree No. 6 of 1994.

6 SOCIAL, COMMUNITY CARE, EDUCATIONAL AND SPORTS LAWS

6.1 Establishment of Social Fund for Development (Law No. 10 of 1997)

A Fund, called the Social Fund for Development, shall be established. The Fund shall enjoy legal personality and have financial independence. It shall have powers to own, rent, hire and dispose of property, *in rem* or *in personam*; as well as power to execute contracts or agreements, file legal suits in courts of law and according to the laws in force.

The main office of the Fund is in Sana'a, and it may establish branches and offices in the provinces.

The main objectives of the Fund are to participate actively in the achievement of the state as planned in the social economic spheres, with a view to enabling the individuals, families, small enterprises, poor communities or those with low incomes, to work and start production, through rendering/giving services, facilities and loans, in order to set up productive and service projects, leading to the reduction of poverty (*al-batallah*) and the side effects of the economic reform programme.

The principal responsibilities of the Fund are as follows:

(a)   financing the projects in the productive or service spheres for the individuals, families, small enterprises, subject to easy terms;
(b)   financing the social development activities, such as health, education, environment, etc. which come within the ambit of the objectives of the Fund;
(c)   assisting the local enterprises with a view to enhancing their capabilities and to raise their efficiency in order to deliver better services;
(d)   creating new jobs through establishment of private enterprises, or supporting productive enterprises, in order to improve the living standards, as well as to raise the income, of the poor in the rural and urban areas;
(e)   implementation of projects involving many workers, including improvement of roads, water and sewerage projects, maintenance of the public installations, directly from the Fund;
(f)   supporting the training centres in the professions which come within the ambit of the activities of the Fund.

The Fund is administered by a Board as follows:

(a)   the Prime Minister: Chairman;
(b)   the Minister of Insurance and Social Welfare: Vice Chairman.

The following are members:

(a) the Minister of Planning and Development;
(b) the Minister of Finance;
(c) the Minister of Labour;
(d) the Minister of Local Administration;
(e) the Minister of Education;
(f) two representatives from each of the following bodies:
  (i)   the NGOs;
  (ii) private sector; and
  (iii) two experts.
(g) a representative of the financial and banking sector; and
(h) the executive director, who is the secretary of the Board.

The membership is for three years, subject to the possibility of renewal.
  The financial resources of the Fund are as follows:

(a) the annual grant from the government;
(b) loans and facilities; and
(c) grants, donations, etc. from the governments, individuals, organizations (local and foreign), subject to the consent of the Prime Minister (Chairman).

The items, commodities and projects of the Fund are exempted from all customs and taxes.

6.2 Law No. 33 of 1997 (amending Law No. 4 of 1996) in Connection with the Establishment of the Higher Institute for Physical Training Law No. 4 of 1996

According to the Law, a Higher Institute for Physical Training is to be established, as body corporate, in the capital (Sana'a) and branches may be set up in the other provinces. The Institute may make use of the services of foreign teachers. Graduates of the Institute are to be awarded a BA in Physical and Sports Training Sciences. The objectives of the Institute, *inter alia*, are:

(a) to contribute to the development of the sports activities in the country;
(b) to train Yemeni teachers for physical and sports training subjects in all schools, as well as qualified instructors for the national teams in the various sports and games;
(c) to provide sports clubs, colleges and institutions with qualified instructors;
(d) to prepare and publish studies and research in the fields of physical training and sports.

The Institute is to have a Supreme Council, consisting of the Minister of Youth and Sports (as Chairman), principal, vice-principal and fifteen representatives of the Universities, Ministries of Youth and Sports (1997 Amendment), Education and Health, in addition to three well-known public figures.
  The financial resources of the Institute come, principally, from the grants in the State budget, fees by the students for registration, activities and examinations, donations and any other sources agreed to by the Supreme Council.

A disciplinary council shall be constituted, with responsibility for taking action against those instructors who are charged with contraventions, as follows:

(a)   a member of the Supreme Council as Chairman;
(b)   a lecturer from the law faculty of one of the Yemeni universities;
(c)   a member of the teaching body of the Institute, chosen by the accused.

6.3 Law No. 27 of 1997, amending Vocational and Technological Training Fund Law No. 15 of 1995

The executive regulations prescribe the ratio of the support to be granted to the training centres and institutes, which are under the supervision of the Public Corporation of Vocational Training, provided the support starts with half the revenues of the Fund, and that priority be given to the following:

(a)   maintenance of the equipment, workshops' installations and making available spare parts;
(b)   purchase of the consumer items utilized during training;
(c)   retraining and raising/improving the efficiency of the trainers and instructors;
(d)   improving the curriculum; and
(e)   contracting with specialized instructors, from those working, in order to benefit the trainees at the centre for short terms.

The Fund will finance the centres and institutions, on the basis of the actual expenditure regarding each of them, with a maximum of 10 million riyals for maintenance, the actual amounts needed for improving the curriculum, retraining and improving the efficiency of the instructors and teachers by a maximum of 15 per cent from the total number of the staff of the centre or institute concerned, and the actual amounts needed for the specialized teachers/instructors with contracts for short terms. Sixty per cent of the financial grants for in-service training should be spent on trainees and 30 per cent on the supervisors. The financial resources of the Fund consist of the following:

(a)   the monthly contribution of the employers is 1 per cent of the monthly total of the wages, allowances, etc. received by all the workers, without exception;
(b)   5,000 riyals to be paid by the employer as regards each work permit for non-Yemenis, and similar amount to be paid when that permit is renewed each year;
(c)   the grants and donations approved by the Council;
(d)   the financial support (grant) by the government for the Fund.

The board of directors of the Fund is composed as follows:

(a)   the Chairman of the board of directors of the Public Corporation of Vocational and Technological Training;
(b)   the Deputy Ministers of Social Security, Labour, Finance and Planning;
(c)   five persons representing the employers from the public and private sectors;
(d)   one representing the General Workers Union; and
(e)   the General Manager of the Fund.

The chairman of the board of directors of the Fund shall be elected from among the representatives of the employers, for a term of three years, and the vice-chairman from among the members of the board of the Fund, for a term of three years.

6.4 The Public Holidays Law No. 8 of 1997 Amending Law No. 8 of 1996 on the same subject

According to which the following days have been declared public holidays:

(a) *Idd al-Fitr*, with effect from the 28th of Ramadan up to the 4th of *Shawwal* (6 or 7 days depending on whether Ramadan is 29 or 30 days);
(b) *Idd al-Adha*, with effect from the 8th of *Dhi-al-Hijjah* up to the 13th of the same month (6 days);
(c) Islamic New Year Day (First *Muharram*) (1 day);
(d) the Prophet's Birthday (12th day of the 4th month in the Islamic Year: *Rabi' al-Awwal*) (1 day);
(e) the Declaration of the Republic of Yemen (or National Day) 22 May (1 day);
(f) 26 September Revolution Anniversary (1 day);
(g) 14 October Revolution Anniversary (1 day); and
(h) 30 November (Independence Anniversary (1 day).

7 INTERNATIONAL LAW AND HUMAN RIGHTS

7.1 International Arbitration: Yemen and Eritrea regarding the Greater Hanish Red Sea Islands[1]

On 31 August 1997, the two parties submitted the "First Memorial" to the Registrar of the Tribunal. On 30 November 1997, the two Parties submitted the "Counter Memorials". The oral arguments/pleadings took place between 26 January and 6 February 1998 in the Foreign and Commonwealth Office, London. The Tribunal was expected to issue its award with regard to the First Stage, the questions of the scope of dispute and sovereignty during the second half of 1998. It was issued and communicated to the parties on 9 October 1998.[2]

7.2 International Commercial Arbitration[3]

The Centre for Legal Research and Studies (under the Minister of Legal Affairs) held a number of workshops/seminars, to discuss the question of the Republic of Yemen becoming a Party to the New York Convention on the Recognition and Enforce-

---

[1] See *Yearbook*, vol. 3 (1996), p. 334 and pp. 497–459.
[2] For details of the award see the postscript on p. 416. The full award will appear in next year's volume.
[3] See *Yearbook*, vol. 3 (1996), p. 328 and pp. 555–559.

ment of Arbitral Awards. However, the Cabinet, in a meeting held on 7 December 1997, approved – in principle – the question of the Republic of Yemen becoming a Party to the Centre of Settlement of Investment Disputes Agreement (known as the Washington Agreement 1967).

7.3 Human Rights

7.3.1 The Supreme National Commission for Human Rights

A Supreme National Commission for Human Rights has been established in the Republic of Yemen, by a Republican Resolution (No. 20 of 1998) on the recommendation of the Council of Ministers in its weekly meeting dated 30 December 1997 as follows:

(a)   Deputy Prime Minister and Minster of Foreign Affairs: Chairman;
(b)   Head of the Presidential Office: Vice-Chairman;
(c)   Head of Legal and Parliamentary Affairs: member;
(d)   Minister of Justice: member;
(e)   Minster of Welfare and Social Security: member;
(f)   Minister of Interior: member;
(g)   Attorney-General: member;
(h)   Chairman of Judicial Inspection Authority: member;
(i)   Head of Political Security: member.

The aims and objectives are as follows:

(a)   formulation of the policies, plans and programmes with a view to guaranteeing the procession of human rights in the Republic of Yemen, as well as strengthening the role of the bodies concerned with the solution of human rights and, generally, protection thereof, according to the Constitution, the laws in force, the international agreements and conventions regarding which our country is signatory;
(b)   coordination, and keeping contacts, with the United Nations Human Rights Centre, as well as the international organizations concerned with human rights, with a view to creating cooperation relation as regards the solution of any human rights matter concerning our country;
(c)   supervision of the appropriate and good implementation of the international human rights conventions, covenants, treaties and instruments by the organs concerned in the Republic of Yemen;
(d)   supervision of the preparation of the regular reports to be submitted to the international organizations, as regards the level of implementation of the international human rights instruments to which our country is signatory;
(e)   consideration of the reports of the international human rights organizations and commenting thereon;
(f)   giving support and aid to the non-governmental human rights organizations in our country;
(g)   drawing and implementing plans and programmes regarding propagating public awareness, in the media, in the field of human rights, and convening of specialized symposia and discussion groups: for those working in the judiciary,

prosecution, security, the functions and activities of which are connected with human rights matters, and inviting experts from the international organizations to give lectures in this respect;

(h)   supervision of the preparations as well as implementation of the activities representing the participation of our country on occasions and anniversaries commemorating the achievements of the international community in the field of human rights.

There is a secretariat for the Commission, the main functions of which are the following:

(a)   collection of the main international human rights instruments, covenants, conventions, protocols, etc. to which the Republic of Yemen is signatory, as well as the correspondence and other material in connection with the fields and activities of human rights;

(b)   preparation of the necessary studies, reports and analysis regarding human rights matters, and giving recommendations as regards the appropriate solutions in this respect;

(c)   receiving the letters, memos and notifications/statements sent by the various international personalities, organizations and bodies concerned with human rights, studying thereof and replying thereto promptly, in accordance with the regulations and procedure laid down by the Supreme National Commission for Human Rights;

(d)   addressing the various bodies concerned, gathering of the information and data regarding each matter connected with alleged violation of human rights, and making use of such information and data in the replies to the queries of the international organizations and bodies;

(e)   consideration of the reports and maters connected with the level of implementation of the international human rights agreements and instruments by the concerned bodies, and giving remarks and suggestions thereon to the Supreme National Commission;

(f)   preparation for the meetings/sessions of the Supreme National Commission, recording the minutes thereof, implementation of the resolutions/decisions thereof as well as the following up of such implementation by the bodies concerned;

(g)   following up the bodies concerned as regards submission of their regular reports on the level of implementation of the respective international human rights agreements and instruments within the specified time;

(h)   stating the remarks and opinions regarding the laws, agreements, conventions and reports related to human rights;

(i)   submission of regular reports as regards execution of its functions and responsibilities;

(j)   carrying out any other functions at the request of the Supreme National Commission.

The Republic of Yemen is signatory to the majority of the international human rights covenants, conventions and instruments (fifteen in number), the most important of which are the following:

(a)   International Convention on the Elimination of All Forms of Racial Discrimination (1972);

(b) International Convention on the Suppression and Punishment of the Crime of Apartheid (1974, 1986 and 1987);
(c) Convention relating to the Status of Refugees (1980);
(d) Protocol relating to the Status of Refugees (1980);
(e) Convention on the Elimination of All Forms of Discrimination Against Women (1984);
(f) International Covenant on Civil and Political Rights (1987);
(g) International Covenant on Economic, Social and Cultural Rights (1987);
(h) Convention on the Prevention and Punishment of the Crime of Genocide (1987);
(i) Slavery Convention (1987);
(j) Convention on the Political Rights of Women (1987);
(k) Convention on Consent to Marriage, Minimum Age for Marriage and Registration of Marriage (1987);
(l) Convention on the Rights of the Child (1991);
(m) Convention Against Torture and Other Forms of Cruel, Inhuman or Degrading Treatment or Punishment (1992).

(NB A National Committee Against Torture (NGO) has been set up on 16 April 1998.)

7.3.2 United Nations High Commission for Human Rights and the Human Rights Situation in Yemen

The United Nations High Commissioner for Human Rights and the Human Rights Situation in Yemen:

Pursuant to Decision 5 (XXXIV) of the Commission on Human Rights, the United Nations had conveyed an invitation from the Commission to be represented at a closed meeting(s) of its current fifty-forth Session at Geneva, during consideration of the [Human Rights Situation in Yemen], under item 10(b) of its agenda, within the framework of the confidential procedure governed by Economic and Social Council Resolution 1503 (XLVIII).

The representative(s) of the Government would be expected to address the Commission on the issues which it had before it and to answer any questions which might be raised by the Commission's members. There was a recommendation, pursuant to the Commission's Decision 14 (XXXV), relating to Yemen adopted by the Working Group on Situations (established by Resolution (1990/41) of the Economic and Social Council) at its recently concluded session: which recommendation reads as follows:

The Working Group on Situations submits to the fifty-forth Session on the Commission on Human Rights the following recommendation:

Yemen

The Commission on Human Rights,
Having examined the material relating to the human rights situation in Yemen brought before it under Economic and Social Council Resolution [1503] (XLVIII),

Welcoming the detailed observations received from the Government of Yemen,
Noting with satisfaction the establishment on 15 January [1998] the National High
Commission for Human Rights by the Government of Yemen,

(1) Decides to discontinue consideration of the human rights situation in Yemen under
    Council Resolution [1503] (XLVIII);
(2) Encourages the Government of Yemen to continue to develop human rights institu-
    tions and cooperate with the Office of the High Commissioner for Human Rights;
(3) Requests the Secretary-General to communicate this Decision to the Government of
    Yemen.

The Commission met with the representatives of the Government of Yemen on 8
April 1998, for consideration of the Human Rights Situation in Yemen and, unanimously, resolved to accept the recommendation of the Working Group.

7.3.3 National Seminar Regarding the Rights of the Accused

The first national seminar regarding the rights of the accused – under the title "The
Accused is Innocent until Proven Guilty, By Fair Trial, where Rights of Defence
are Guaranteed" – was convened in the High Judicial Institute in the capital (Sana'a)
during the period 9–11 May 1998. The seminar was sponsored by:

(a) the Red Crescent Society;
(b) the United States Information Service (USIS) in the Republic of Yemen;
    and
(c) a number of human rights organizations (NGOs).

The Ministries of Justice, Legal and Parliamentary Affairs and Interior, the Attorney General's office, the Judicial Inspection Commission, the Bar Association, the
Supreme National Human Rights Commission, the Human Rights Standing Committees in the House of Representatives and the Consultative Council were also in
attendance.
    The main topics were as follows:

(a) the rights of the accused under Islamic *shari'a* principles and under Yemeni leg-
    islation;
(b) the rights of the accused under international law;
(c) the main organs concerned with the protection of the rights of the accused;
(d) the role of the state in protecting individual freedoms;
(e) the consequences of the violations of the rights of the accused.

The main objectives of the seminar were, *inter alia*:

(a) consolidation of the golden principle of innocence in criminal law;
(b) spreading public awareness as regards the rights of the accused;
(c) ensuring adherence to the principles of criminal procedure;
(d) realization of coordination and cooperation among the official organs and
    the non-governmental organizations in the field of protection of the rights of
    the accused.

POSTSCRIPT – YEMEN AND ERITREA

The award of the Arbitral Tribunal in the matter of the arbitration between Eritrea and Yemen on territorial sovereignty regarding the Great Hanish Red Sea Islands was in the following terms:

"The Tribunal . . . unanimously finds in the present case that:

i. the islands, islet, rocks, and low-tide elevations forming the Mohabbakah islands, including but not limited to Sayal Islet, Harbi Islet, Flat Islet and High Islet are subject to the territorial sovereignty of Eritrea;

ii. the islands, islet, rocks, and low-tide elevations forming the Haycock Islands, including, but not limited to, North East Haycock, Middle Haycock, and South West Haycock, are subject to the territorial sovereignty of Eritrea;

iii. The South West Rocks are subject to the territorial sovereignty of Eritrea;

iv. the islands, islet, rocks, and low-tide elevations of the Zuqar-Hanish group, including, but not limited to, Three Foot Rock, Parkin Rock, Rocky Islets, Pin Rock, Suyul Hanish, Mid Islet, Double Peak Island, Round Island, North Round Island, Quoin Island (13°43'N, 42°48'E), Chor Rock, Greater Hanish, Peaky Islet, Mushajirah, Addar Ail Islets, Haycock Island (13°47'N, 42°47'E); not to be confused with the Haycock Islands to the southwest of Greater Hanish), Low Island (13°52'N, 42°49'E) incl uding the unnamed islets and rocks close north, east and south, Lesser Hanish including the unnamed islets and rocks close north east, Tongue Island and the unnamed islet close south, Near Island and the unnamed islet close south east, Shark Island, Jabal Zuquar Island, High Island, and the Abu Ali Islands (including Quoin Island (14°05'N, 42°49'E) and Pile Island) are subject to the territorial sovereignty of Yemen;

v. the island of Jabal al-Tayr, and the islands, islets, rocks and low-tide elevations forming the Zubayr group, including, but not limited to, Quoin Island (15°12'N, 42°03'E), Haycock Island (15°10'N, 42°07'E; not to be confused with the Haycock Islands to the southwest of Greater Hanish), Rugged Island, Table Peak Island, Saddle Island and the unnamed islet close north west, Low Island (15°06'N, 42°06'E) and the unnamed rock close east, Middle Reef, Saba Island, Connected Island, East Rocks, Shoe Rock, Jabal Zubayr Island, and Centre Peak Island are subject to the territorial sovereignty of Yemen; and

vi. the sovereignty found to lie with Yemen entails the perpetuation of the traditional fishing regime in the region, including free access and enjoyment for the fishermen of both Eritrea and Yemen.

14. Further, whereas Article 12.1(b) of the Arbitration Agreement provides that the Awards shall include the time period for their execution, the Tribunal directs that this Award should be executed within ninety days from the date hereunder.

Done at London this 9th day of October, 1998

The President of the Tribunal

/s/Professor Sir Robert Y. Jennings

The Registrar

/s/P. J. H. Jonkman"

Algeria

*Yamina Kebir**

1 ADMINISTRATIVE AND CONSTITUTIONAL LAWS

Further to the cancellation of the first ballot of the elections of 1991, the executive and legislative powers were reorganized for a transitional period of three years pending the setting up of new institutions through elections, in line with the Platform on National Consensus under Presidential Decree No. 94-40 of 29 January 1994.[1]

The process set up by the Platform on National Consensus of 1994 is being progressively implemented; the President was elected in November 1995, the referendum on the amendment of the Constitution took place on 28 November 1996 and the elections for a multiparty assembly and for regional and local representatives are scheduled for 1997.

The initial aim of the amendment of the Constitution was in fact to prohibit political parties from being established on a religious or regional basis. What, in fact, was at stake is the ban of the exploitation of political parties for religious ends. But the scope of the amendment was widened so as to bring changes in the respective powers of the executive and the legislature and in the machinery of legislation. The result being a reinforcement of the President's powers.

Apart from the definition of the role and duties of political parties, the other significant amendment consists in the composition of the Parliament which now comprises, in addition to the National People's Assembly a second House, the Council of the Nation.

The proposed amendments were adopted by 10,785,919 votes in favour out of 13,111,514 and introduced in the text of the Constitution in force which was adopted in 1989.

The following amendments were incorporated in the Constitution:

---

* Attorney-at-Law, Algiers Bar admitted to appear before the Supreme Court of Algiers. This survey covers 1996; the years 1997 and 1998 will be covered in the 1998–1999 volume.
[1] See *Yearbook of Islamic and Middle Eastern Law*, vol. 1 (1994) p. 397.

(a)   the right to set up political parties (the wording which was previously used referred to "political associations") is guaranteed under the Constitution but this right may by no means be used to hurt the national values, the security of the national territory and the democratic and republican character of the state.

No political party will be allowed to be set up on a religious, linguistic, racial or gender basis. Political parties may not refer in their platforms or propaganda to any of the aforementioned elements. Political parties are also strictly forbidden to have recourse to violence or to constraint. Their obedience to foreign political parties or interests, whatever their form, is prohibited (Article 42). The right to set up associations is likewise guaranteed.

(b)   The Parliament is henceforward composed of two Houses: the National People's Assembly and the Council of the Nation. The National People's Assembly is composed of members who are the elected representatives of the nation. Voting is by direct, universal and secret ballot.

The Council of the Nation is composed of members elected, for two-thirds by and from among the regional and local representatives by indirect and secret ballot. The remaining third of the members are appointed by the President of the Republic from among the prominent personalities in the scientific, cultural, professional, economic and social spheres.

The number of members of the Council of the Nation is equal to half the members of the National People's Assembly. The mandate of the Council of the Nation is of six years and its members are renewed by a third every three years. The President of the Council of the Nation is elected after each partial renewal of its members.

In a situation of illness, inability or death of the President, it is the President of the council of the Nation who becomes the Head of the State for a period not exceeding sixty days.

The relations between the two Houses are to be determined by a special organic law.

The proceedings of the Parliament are public (entirely televised) and are held twice a year for a minimum period of four months.

The Parliament may also be summoned for an extraordinary session at the request of the President of the Republic; it may also be convened by the President of the Republic, the Head of Government or of two-thirds of the members of the National People's Assembly.

In order to become law, a Bill must be successively discussed by both Houses, Bills may be introduced by the Head of Government and by the deputies, in such case by at least twenty deputies.

The Bills are set forth at the Ministers' Council after the Council of State (*Conseil d'Etat*) has delivered its opinion. A Bill that has passed the National People's Assembly is debated by the Council of the Nation which adopts it at a three-quarter majority.

In the case of dissenting votes by the two Houses, a committee consisting of members from both House proposes a new text on the provisions that were disagreed upon, at the Prime Minister's request. In the case of persistent disagreement, the Bill is withdrawn.

The most significant laws, called "organic laws", require specific procedures for their passing. Apart from the domain of such laws as stated by the Constitution (relations between the Houses of Parliament, adoption of the state of emergency), the following laws may be passed only as organic law:

– the organization and functioning of public powers;
– the ballot act;
– the law relating to political parties;
– the law relating to information;
– the regulations relating to the judiciary and the judicial organization;
– money bills;
– the law relating to national security; and
– the proclamation of the state of emergency.

Organic laws are adopted at the absolute majority of the deputies and at the three-quarter majority of the Council of the Nation. Prior to their passing, these laws are submitted to conformity control by the Constitutional Council, such control being mandatory.

The organization of the voting for the amendment of the Constitution has also been modified; when decided by the President of the Republic, the amendment of the Constitution is voted on in identical terms by the National People's Assembly and the Council of the Nation like any other law.

An amendment of the Constitution may also be proposed by three-quarters of all the members of the two Houses of Parliament to the President of the Republic who may decide to submit it to a referendum. An amendment of the Constitution may not affect the fundamentals of the state, namely its republican character, the democratic order based on a multiparty system, Islam as the state religion, Arabic as the national and official language, basic liberties and human rights, the unity and integrity of the national territory.

The President of the Republic retains a legislative power; he is entitled to pass laws by way of ordinances in the case of vacancy of the National People's Assembly or in the inter session periods of the Parliament. Such ordinances are submitted to the approval of each of the Houses of Parliament. Ordinances that are not adopted by the Parliament become null and void. The President may also take ordinances in a situation of state of emergency.

The role of the National People's Assembly to control the government has not been fundamentally modified; the powers of the Assembly to adopt the government's programme remain unchanged and a government which is outvoted on its programme by the National People's Assembly must resign. The Council of the State does not have a real say in the government's activity as the latter is only required to set forth its programme but not to seek its approval.

The composition of the Constitutional Council has been modified in order to reflect the representation of new institutions such as the Council of the Nation and the Council of the State and it now comprises nine members, three of them being appointed by the President, two members elected by the National People's Assembly, two by the Council of the Nation, one by the Supreme Court and one by the Council of the State.

The role of the Constitutional Council and its functioning remain unchanged, except for its mandatory control of the organic laws.

1.1 Creation of the Function of Commissioner for the Republic

Presidential Decree No. 96-113 of 23 March 1996 creates the post of "Ombudsman". The function of the Commissioner is to monitor and follow up the relations between Administration and the public. The Commissioner is appointed by the President of the Republic.

His function is mainly to investigate complaints by members of the public who have sustained injustice in consequence of actions of public authorities. The Commissioner is invested with all powers to carry out its investigations; when the investigation is completed, the Commissioner must report to the President of the Republic and when appropriate, proposes all actions and measures to be taken against the authorities and/or their employees. He also reports to the public authorities concerned and proposes or recommends to correct the injustice that has been committed or measures that they should take in order to improve their functioning and their relations with the public.

The public authorities who are subject to investigation by the Commissioner must respond to his enquiries within a reasonable delay; when the Commissioner is not satisfied with their response, he reports to the President of the Republic.

The Commissioner's function being purely investigatory, he has no executive powers. The areas to be investigated are circumscribed and exclude domains relating to the security of the state, to national defence and to foreign policy. In addition, the Commissioner is not empowered to investigate conflicts between the Administration and its employees, nor to interfere in legal proceedings or question a Court decision.

2 CIVIL LAW

No legislative changes or developments have occurred in 1996 under this title.

3 CIVIL PROCEDURE AND EVIDENCE

No legislative changes or developments have occurred in 1996 under this title.

4 COMMERCIAL LAW

The passing of an economic legislation in conformity with a market oriented economy is still begin carried out.[2]

In this field, important developments have occurred this year (1996) also. In line with the privatization programme of the Government, a series of Executive Decrees were enacted for the implementation of Ordinance No. 95-22 of 26 August 1995 relating to privatization of publicly owned enterprises.[3]

---

[2] See this *Yearbook*, vol. 1 (1994), p. 397 and vol. 2 (1995) p. 260.
[3] See this *Yearbook*, vol. 2 (1995), p. 261.

The aim of Executive Decrees Nos. 96–104, 96-105 and 96-106 of 11 March 1996 is to define the bodies in charge of privatization, to determine their field of competence and functioning and the appointment and status of their members. These bodies are the Privatization Committee, the Control Committee of Privatization, invested with the power to investigate on the actions of privatization and to report on these actions to the Delegate in charge of privatization whose role and status are determined by Executive Decree No. 96-106 of 11 March 1996.

The conditions and procedures for the detention by the state of a *golden share* which were provided for by Ordinance No. 95-22 are determined by Executive Decree No. 96-133 of 13 April 1996.

The state may retain a share in the capital of privatized enterprises in order to have a say in the conduct of its activities for reasons of national interest. In particular, the golden share enables the state to oppose a change in the purpose of the company or in its activities, its winding up and its closing down.

It also enables the state to have representatives on the board of directors of the company; these representatives attend its meetings but with no voting right. The state may retain a golden share for a duration not exceeding five years.

4.1 Amendment of the Code of Commerce by Ordinance No. 96-27 of 9 December 1996

This Ordinance provides in particular, that a SARL can be made up of one shareholder. Such a company is called the *Entreprise Unipersonnelle à Responsibilité Limitée* (EURL). It is an SARL with one shareholder, and the rules governing the EURL are the same with certain exceptions. These exceptions take into account the fact that there is only one shareholder who may be an individual or an entity. In particular, the sole shareholder will exert all the powers which normally are those of the meeting of shareholders. The EURL may have a manager who would be distinct from the shareholder. In such a case, the accounts and records kept by the manager must be approved by the shareholder following a report drawn by the auditor.

The main justification for this form of company is the fact that the liability of the shareholder for the debts of the company is limited to his contribution to the share capital. And should the shareholder decease, his heirs would not be liable for his debts.

4.2 Ordinance No. 96-09 of 10 January 1996

This relates to leasing sets up this form of credit which is new is Algeria. The leasing may be applied to real estate and to stock in trade. The Ordinance sets out the rights and obligations of the parties to a leasing contract.

4.3 Insurance: Ordinance No. 96-06 of 10 January 1996 relating to Export Credit Guarantee

The Export Credit Guarantee may be subscribed by any individual or legal entity residing in Algeria and provides insurance cover for export credit. Exports of hydrocarbons are excluded from the scope of this Ordinance.

The Ordinance determines the risks covered: commercial, political, failure of transfer and catastrophe risks. The implementation Decree for this Ordinance is Executive Decree No. 96-235 of 2 July 1996.

The decree determines the conditions and procedures for the Credit Company called "CAGEX" under the form of a joint stock company to guarantee the risks covered, under the control the state.

The Export Insurance Committee is also set up with the function to study and make a decision upon requests for guarantee by exporters, to decide upon all matters relating to export insurance and make proposals to the Minister of Finance. The Committee is composed of representatives of the Ministry of Finance (three) and of various ministries, of foreign affairs, of external trade of agriculture, of industry and one representative of the Bank of Algeria.

4.4 Foreign exchange regulations

In line with the policy of developing a market driven economy, a series of regulations were issued aiming at a relaxation of the very strict foreign exchange control rules. But a discrepancy remained between the new eased rules and the provisions of the Criminal Code of 1975 which set out the determination of such offences and the penalties. In order to bridge the gap and to adjust criminal penalties to the new regulations, Ordinance 96-22 of 9 July 1996 was enacted.

The Ordinance determines offences against foreign exchange control regulations and which are false declaration of currency, failure to comply with the requirement to repatriate capital, failure to comply with the required proceedings and formalities, failure to provide required authorizations. Penalties range from three months to five years' imprisonment and a fine equal to twice the amount of the *corpus delicti*.

Any purchase, sale, import, export of gold, gold coins or precious stones or metal which do not comply with the laws in force are also considered offences against foreign exchange control regulations.

In addition to the aforementioned penalties, the person convicted of such offences may be deprived of his capacity to act in foreign trade transactions or as an intermediary in such transactions for a period not exceeding five years from the date of the final judgment rendered by the court of jurisdiction.

When these offences are committed by legal entities, the penalties are aggravated with the fine being equal to give time the value of the *corpus delicti* and the confiscation of same; in addition these entities are excluded from procurement and prohibited from carrying out transactions in foreign trade.

Offences against foreign exchange control regulations may be prosecuted only at the request of the Ministry of Finance or its authorized representatives.

5 EMPLOYMENT AND LABOUR LAWS

In the context of an alarmingly high rate of unemployment, especially among young people, and in order to reduce the painful effects of layoffs which will inevitably be the result of privatization of publicly owned enterprises, the laws on retirement have been amended.

Normally, the employee is entitled to retirement at the age of 60 for men and 55 for women. But in the case where the employee is likely to lose his employment due to economic lay off, he may be admitted to the benefit of early retirement at the age of 50 for men and 45 for women and under the condition that they have been working for a continuous period of twenty years. The employer is then under the obligation to contribute with the salary for thirteen months.

When the employer does not meet these requirements, he is entitled to an unemployment benefit. This benefit is paid by the National Social Insurance Fund. Since 1 July 1994, contributions to the Insurance Fund have been made by the employer, who contributes 2.5 per cent on each paid salary and the employee with 1.5 per cent of his salary.

At the same time, labour laws have been amended and complemented with the aim of clarifying certain provisions of Law No. 90-11 of 21 April 1990; amendments of the provisions relating to hiring and dismissing employees also aim at ensuring a better protection of employees. Thus, Ordinance No. 96-21 of 9 July 1996 modifying and complementing Law No. 90-11 relating to Labour Relations provides that the labour inspector is invested with the powers to verify that fixed term labour contracts are concluded for one of the reasons set forth by Law No. 90-11 and that the duration stipulated in the contract corresponds to the duration of the activity.

Dismissal procedures are slightly amended in the sense that when a court decides that dismissal was effected in violation of the rules prescribed by the law, the dismissal is cancelled and the employer must initiate new procedures. If the court holds that the dismissal is unfair, the employer is obliged, either to reintegrate the laid off employee and if either party refuses the reintegration, compensation is due to the employee.

6 PROPERTY LAW

No legislative changes or developments have occurred in 1996 under this heading.

7 INTELLECTUAL PROPERTY

7.1 Copyright

Ordinance No. 96-16 of 2 July 1996 relating to registration of copyright states that this registration is a compulsory procedure imposed on any individual or legal entity being the author of an intellectual or artistic work intended to be available to the public.

Copies of the work are registered, free of charge, with the institution in charge of the copyright. The registration of copyright must be effected before any diffusion of the work by whatever means, either sale, rental or transfer.

The works submitted to the requirement of registration of copyright are the following: any printed, visual works, pictures, photographs, sound recordings as well as all sorts of software or data.

The following institutions are in charge of copyright registrations: the National Library of Algeria and the Algerian Centre for the Cinema.

8 ENVIRONMENT

8.1 Ordinance No. 96-13 of 15 June 1996 Amending and Complementing Law No. 83-17 of 16 July 1983 Governing the Water Supply

In a country where the water supply is a major problem and after several years of severe drought, the law relating to water supply had to be amended in order to provide for the implementation of the national policy relating to the water supply and its compatibility with the requirements of regional development and the protection of the environment.

9 PUBLIC INTERNATIONAL LAW

The following agreements and treaties signed by the Government of Algeria were ratified:

(a) Order No. 96-03, dated 19 Shaban 1416 corresponding to 10 January 1996, giving conditional approval to the Convention of the United Nations of 1979 concerning the elimination of all forms of discrimination against women;

(b) Order No. 96-04, dated 19 Shaban 1416 corresponding to 10 January 1996, ratifying the Convention of the United Nations on the war on desertification in countries severely affected by drought and/or the process of turning into desert, especially in Africa, adopted at Paris on 17 June 1994;

(c) Order No. 96-05, dated 19 Shaban 1416 corresponding to 10 January 1996, ratifying the Convention of the United Nations on Maritime Law;

(d) Presidential Decree No. 96-51, dated 2 Ramadan 1416, corresponding to 22 January 1996, setting out the conditional accession of the Democratic and Popular Republic of Algeria to the Convention of the United Nations of 1979 concerning the elimination of all forms of discrimination against women;

(e) Presidential Decree No. 96-52, dated 2 Ramadan 1416, corresponding to 22 January 1996, ratifying the Convention of he United Nations on the war on desertification in countries severely affected by drought and/or the process of turning into desert especially in Africa, adopted at Paris on 17 June 1994;

(f) Presidential Decree No. 96-53, dated 2 Ramadan 1416, corresponding to 22 January 1996, ratifying the UN Agreement on Maritime Law;

(g) Presidential Decree No. 96-78, dated 16 Ramadan 1416, corresponding to 5 February 1996, ratifying the agreement between the Government of the DPRA and the Consultative Council of the Maghreb Arab Union on the site of its headquarters, signed at Algiers on 9 June 1994;

(h) Presidential Decree No. 96-79, dated 16 Ramadan 1416, corresponding to 5 February 1996, ratifying the agreement between the Government of the DPRA and the Government of Namidia creating a Joint Algerian–Namibian Commission for Cooperation, signed at Addis Abeba on 24 June 1996;

(i) Presidential Decree No. 96-80, dated 21 Ramadan 1416, corresponding to 2 February 1996, ratifying conditionally the Constitution and Convention of the International Telecommunication Union, signed at Geneva on 22 December 1996;

(j) Presidential Decree No. 96-81, dated 21 Ramadan 1416, corresponding to 2 February 1996 ratifying the Agreement between the Governments of the Democratic and Popular Republic of Algeria and the Republic of Tunisia on cooperation in the fields of tourism and crafts, signed at Tunis on 5 April 1993.

(k) Presidential Decree No. 96-90, dated 14 Shawwâl 1416, corresponding to 3 March 1996, ratifying conditionally the Convention on the marking of plastic and sheet explosives for detection purposes, signed at Montreal on 3 March 1991;

(l) Presidential Decree No. 96-144, dated 5 Dhu l-Hijja, corresponding to 23 April 1996, setting out the ratification by Algeria of the Agreement creating the Islamic Investment and Export Credit Guarantee Co.;

(m) Presidential Decree No. 96-145, dated 5 Dhu l-Hijja, corresponding to 23 April 1996, setting out the conditional accession of the Democratic and Popular Republic of Algeria to the international Agreement against the taking of hostages, adopted by the UN General Assembly on 17 December 1979;

(n) Presidential Decree No. 96-153, dated 16 Dhu l-Hijja, corresponding to 4 May 1996, ratifying the protocol of cooperation between the Governments of the DPRA and the Republic of France concerning the issuing of consular passes, signed at Algiers on 28 September 1994;

(o) Presidential Decree no. 96-161, dated 20 Dhu l-Hijja, corresponding to 8 May 1996, ratifying the Convention on reciprocal collaboration at administrative level, aimed at preventing, investigating and suppressing Customs offences between the Member States of the Maghreb Arab Union, signed at Tunis on 2 April 1994;

(p) Presidential Decree No. 96-162, dated 20 Dhu l-Hijja, corresponding to 8 May 1996, ratifying the Agreement between the Governments of the Democratic and Popular Republic of Algeria and the Arab Republic of Egypt on cooperation in the fields of tourism and crafts, signed at Tunis on 10 April 1995;

(q) Presidential Decree No. 96-174, dated Muharram 1417, corresponding to 20 May 1996, ratifying the Agreement between the Government of the DPRA and the Socialist People's Libyan Arab Jamahiriyah on reciprocal recognition of scientific diplomas, degrees and qualifications;

(r) Presidential Decree No. 96-224, dated 6 Safar 1417, corresponding to 22 June 1996, ratifying the protocol relating to the Certificate of Origin between the member countries of the Maghreb Arab Union, signed at Tunis on 2 April 1994;

(s) Presidential Decree No. 96-225, dated 8 Safar 1417, corresponding to 24 June 1996, approving loan agreement No. 4005 AL, signed at Washington DC on 3 May 1996 approval to the loan agreement between the DPRA and the International Bank for Reconstruction and Development, to participate in the financing of the programme of structural adjustment;

(t) Presidential Decree No. 96-289, dated 18 Rabia II 1417, corresponding to 2 September 1996, setting out the conditional accession of the DPRA to the Convention relating to the prevention and suppression of offences against persons enjoying international protection, including diplomatic personnel, signed at New York on 14 December 1973;

(u) Presidential Decree No. 96-294, dated 24 Rabia II 1417, corresponding to 8 September 1996, ratifying the agreement between the Government of the DPRA and the Arab Iron and Steel Union on the site of its headquarters, signed at Algiers on 8 April 1996;

(v)   Presidential Decree No. 96-342, dated 29 Jumada II 1417, corresponding
      to 12 October 1996, setting out the adherence of the DPRA to the agree-
      ment on an international programme for a satellite search and rescue system
      (COSPAS/SARSAT), signed at Paris on 1 July 1988;
(w)   Presidential Decree No. 96-435, dated Rajab 1417, corresponding to 1 De-
      cember 1996, ratifying the Agreement between the DPRA and the Interna-
      tional Atomic Energy Agency relating to the application of a guarantee within
      the framework of the Treaty of non-proliferation of nuclear weapons signed
      at Algiers on 30 March 1996.

Morocco

Michèle Zirari-Devif*

1 ORGANISATION JUDICIAIRE

L'organisation judiciaire du Maroc est héritée du Protectorat français. En 1912, avait été mise en place, parallèlement aux juridictions traditionnelles, une organisation calquée sur celle de la France mais simplifiée pour diverses raisons, essentiellement le faible nombre des justiciables, puisque les tribunaux mis en place par le dahir sur l'organisation judiciaire du 12 août 1913 n'étaient compétents, sauf exceptions, que pour juger les Français et les étrangers ressortissants des Etats ayant renoncé aux privilèges des Capitulations. Il existait donc une seule catégorie de juridictions, compétente en tous domaines, civil, commercial, pénal et administratif. C'est cette organisation qui a été conservée après l'indépendance.

Au fil des années, avec l'évolution économique et sociale du Maroc et l'augmentation du nombre des justiciables, le besoin s'est fait sentir d'améliorer l'organisation judiciaire et de créer des tribunaux spécialisés. C'est ainsi qu'ont été créés, en 1991, les tribunaux administratifs, compétents essentiellement pour connaître des recours en annulation pour excès de pouvoir formés contre les décisions des autorités administratives, des litiges relatifs aux contrats administratifs et des actions en réparation des dommages causés par les actes et les activités des personnes publiques. La création des tribunaux de commerce s'inscrit dans cette évolution. Ces tribunaux, ainsi que les récents tribunaux administratifs sont, en outre, appelés à servir de moteur à l'opération de modernisation et d'assainissement de la justice entreprise depuis quelques mois. Cette création était également indispensable pour sécuriser les investisseurs en particulier les investisseurs étrangers que le fonctionnement de la justice inquiétait quelque peu jusque là. Elle s'inscrit dans l'ensemble de la réforme du droit commercial entamée en 1996 avec la promulgation d'un nouveau code de commerce et d'une loi sur les sociétés anonymes.[1]

---

* Professeur à la faculté des sciences juridiques, économiques et sociales de Rabat-Agdal.
[1] Voir *Yearbook*, vol. 3 (1996), pp. 357–358.

La création de juridictions de commerce, projetée depuis plusieurs années, est réalisée par la loi n° 53-95 instituant des juridictions de commerce, publiée en mai 1997.[2]

La loi comprend 25 articles répartis en 8 titres:

(a)   dispositions générales;
(b)   composition et organisation des tribunaux de commerce et des cours d'appel de commerce;
(c)   compétence des tribunaux de commerce;
(d)   procédure devant les tribunaux de commerce;
(e)   procédure devant les cours d'appel de commerce;
(f)   attributions du président du tribunal de commerce;
(g)   exécution des jugements et des ordonnances;
(h)   dispositions diverses et transitoires.

Sont donc créés des tribunaux de commerce et des cours d'appel de commerce. Les audiences de ces juridictions sont tenues et leur jugements rendus par trois magistrats dont un président, assisté d'un greffier.

Ces tribunaux sont compétents pour connaître:

(a)   des actions relatives aux contrats commerciaux;
(b)   des actions entre commerçants et à l'occasion de leurs activités commerciales;
(i)   des actions relatives aux effets de commerce;
(ii) des différends entre associés d'une société commerciale;
(iii) des différends à raison de fonds de commerce.

Sont exclues de la compétence des tribunaux de commerce, les affaires relatives aux accidents de la circulation.

En outre, le commerçant peut convenir avec le non commerçant d'attribuer compétence aux tribunaux de commerce pour connaître des litiges pouvant les opposer à l'occasion de l'exercice de l'une des activités du commerçant.

Les parties peuvent convenir que les différends relevant de la compétence des tribunaux de commerce seront soumis à l'arbitrage dans les conditions prévues au code de procédure civile.

Les tribunaux sont compétents en premier et dernier ressort pour les demandes dont la valeur n'excède pas 9000 dirhams, à charge d'appel pour toute demande supérieure à ce montant.

Le nombre, le siège et le ressort des tribunaux de commerce sont fixés par décret n° 2-97-771 du 28 octobre 1997.[3] Ce décret fixe à 6 le nombre de tribunaux de commerce (Rabat, Casablanca, Fès, Tanger, Marrakech et Agadir) et à 3 le nombre de cours d'appel (Casablanca, Fès et Marrakech).

Ces juridictions ont commencé à fonctionner le 4 mai 1998.

---

[2]   Bulletin officiel n° 4482 du 15 mai 1997, p. 520.
[3]   Bulletin officiel n° 4532 du 6 novembre 1997, p. 953.

2 DROIT CONSTITUTIONNEL

Plusieurs textes importants ont été publiés en 1997, dans le domaine du droit constitutionnel. C'est la suite logique de la réforme constitutionnelle de 1996 modifiant la composition du Parlement.[4] Après cette réforme, et pour permettre l'organisation rapide des élections, plusieurs lois sont intervenues. On relève la promulgation et la publication d'un code électoral et de deux lois organiques relatives aux chambres composant le nouveau parlement.

La loi n° 9-97 formant code électoral a été promulguée par dahir n° 1-97-83 du 2 avril 1997.[5] Cette loi révise et regroupe en un code unique des dispositions jusque là éparses dans des textes divers: organisation des référendums, établissement des listes électorales, élections aux assemblées préfectorales et provinciales, aux conseils communaux et aux chambres professionnelles; ce code prévoit également les élections aux conseils régionaux créés par la loi n° 47-96 relative à l'organisation de la région, promulguée par dahir n° 1-97-84 du 2 avril 1997 (voir infra).

La première partie de la loi est consacrée à l'établissement et à la révision des listes électorales. Elle prévoit, dans son article 4, que tous les citoyens marocains des deux sexes âgés de 20 années grégoriennes révolues à la date d'établissement ou de révision des listes électorales doivent se faire inscrire sur la liste de la commune où ils résident effectivement depuis trois mois au moins à la date de leur demande. L'inscription sur les listes électorales devient donc obligatoire, mais aucune sanction n'étant prévue, cette obligation reste tout à fait théorique.

Ne sont privées du droit d'être électeur et éligible que les personnes frappées d'incapacité électorale. Les articles 5 et 6 du code électoral énumèrent limitativement ces incapacités. Il résulte de ces articles que ne sont pas électeurs:

(a) les militaires de tous grades en activité de service, les agents de la force publique (gendarmerie, police, forces auxiliaires, ainsi que toutes personnes qui, sous une dénomination et dans une mesure quelconque, sont investies d'une fonction ou d'un mandat même temporaire, rémunérés ou gratuits et concourent à ce titre au service de l'Etat, des administrations publiques, des municipalités, des établissements publics ou à un service d'intérêt public et auxquelles le droit de porter une arme dans l'exercice de leurs fonctions a été conféré;

(b) les naturalisés marocains pendant les cinq ans qui suivent l'obtention de leur nationalité;

(c) les personnes condamnées irrévocablement à une peine criminelle;

(d) celles condamnées irrévocablement à certaines peines délictuelles limitativement énumérées, pendant un délai de cinq ans ou dix ans suivants les scrutins à compter de la date où la peine a été purgée ou prescrite;

(e) Les personnes privées du droit de vote par décision de justice pendant le délai fixé par cette décision;

(f) les individus en état de contumace;

(g) les interdits judiciaires;

(h) les personnes ayant fait l'objet d'une liquidation judiciaire;

---

[4] Voir *Yearbook*, vol. 3 (1996), p. 354.
[5] Bulletin officiel n° 4470 du 3 avril 1997, p. 306.

(i)   les personnes condamnées à la peine de la dégradation nationale jusqu'à l'ex-
        piration de la période pour laquelle la condamnation a été prononcée.

La deuxième partie du code électoral prévoit les dispositions communes à l'organisation des référendums et à l'élection des conseillers régionaux, des membres des assemblées préfectorales et provinciales, des conseillers communaux et des membres
des chambres professionnelles: dépôt des candidatures, durée des mandats, opérations de vote, contentieux électoral, infractions commises à occasion des élections.
    La troisième partie prévoit les dispositions spéciales à chacune de ces élections.
On notera, en ce qui concerne les élections aux assemblées des collectivités locales,
que seuls les conseillers communaux sont élus au suffrage universel direct, au scrutin
uninominal à la majorité relative à un tour. Les membres des conseils régionaux sont
élus au suffrage indirect par les membres des conseils communaux, les membres
des assemblées préfectorales et provinciales, les représentants des chambres professionnelles et des représentants des salariés. Les membres des assemblées préfectorales
et provinciales sont élus par et parmi un collège électoral formé des membres des
conseils communaux de la préfecture ou de la province.
    La quatrième partie traite du financement et de l'utilisation des moyens audio-
visuels publics lors des campagnes électorales menées à l'occasion des élections
générales, communales et législatives. Elle prévoit la participation de l'Etat au financement des campagnes électorales, le respect par les candidats d'un plafonnement
des dépenses fixé par décret et le contrôle du respect de ce plafonnement avec la création d'une commission ad hoc.
    Deux lois organiques interviennent organisant les Chambres du Parlement: la loi
organique n° 31-97 relative à la Chambre des Représentants, promulguée par dahir
n° 1-97-185 du 4 septembre 1997 et la loi organique n° 32-97 relative à la Chambre des Conseillers, promulguée par dahir n° 1-97-186 du 4 septembre 1997.[6]
    Jusqu'à la modification constitutionnelle approuvée par référendum du 13 sep-
tembre 1996, le Parlement était composé d'une seule chambre, la Chambre des
Représentants, élus pour six ans. Cette Chambre comprenait dans la proportion
des deux tiers, des membres élus au suffrage universel direct, et dans la proportion
d'un tiers, des membres élus par un collège électoral composé de conseillers communaux et de représentants des chambres professionnelles et des salariés.
    Depuis la révision constitutionnelle de 1996, le Parlement est composé de deux
chambres. La Chambre des Représentants, élus pour cinq ans au suffrage universel
direct et la Chambre des Conseillers. Cette dernière comprend, dans la proportion
des $^{3}/_{5}$ des membres élus dans chaque région par un collège électoral composé de
représentants des collectivités locales, et dans la proportion des $^{2}/_{5}$ des membres élus
dans chaque région par des représentants des chambres professionnelles et à l'échelon national par des représentants des salariés. Les membres de la Chambre des Conseillers sont élus pour 9 ans. La Chambre est renouvelable par tiers tous les trois ans.
    La loi organique n° 31-97 relative à la chambre des Représentants comprend onze
chapitres. Le premier prévoit qu'elle se compose de 325 membres élus au suffrage
universel direct au scrutin uninominal à la majorité relative à un tour et que les cir-
conscriptions électorales sont fixées par décret.

---

[6]   Bulletin officiel n° 4518 du 18 septembre 1997, pp. 847 et 856.

Le deuxième chapitre est consacré à l'électorat et aux conditions d'éligibilité. Sont électeurs les Marocains des deux sexes inscrits sur les listes électorales. Pour être éligible à la Chambre des représentants, il faut être électeur et âgé de vingt-trois années grégoriennes à la date du scrutin.

Sont inéligibles, les personnes frappées d'incapacité électorale, ainsi que celles exerçant effectivement ou ayant cessé d'exercer depuis moins de six mois à la date fixée pour le scrutin les fonctions suivantes:

(a) magistrats;
(b) magistrats de la cour des comptes et des cours régionales de comptes;
(c) gouverneurs, secrétaires généraux des préfectures ou province, premiers khalifas des gouverneurs, pachas, chefs de cabinets de gouverneur, chefs de districts, chefs de cercle et caïds ainsi que leurs khalifas, les khalifas d'arrondissement et les chioukhs et moqadddemine;
(d) les chefs des régions militaires;
(e) les chefs des services provinciaux de la direction générale de la sûreté nationale et les commissaires de police.

La loi prévoit au chapitre 3 les incompatibilités: Le mandat de membre de la Chambre des Représentants est incompatible avec celui membre de la Chambre des Conseillers ou de membre du Conseil constitutionnel ou du Conseil économique et social. Il est également incompatible avec l'exercice de plus de deux présidences de collectivité locale, communauté urbaine ou chambre professionnelle, ainsi qu'avec l'exercice de toutes fonctions publiques non électives, à l'exception des fonctions gouvernementales, dans les services de l'Etat, des collectivités locales ou des établissements publics. Sont également incompatibles avec le mandat de membre de la chambre des Représentants les fonctions de président du conseil d'administration, d'administrateur délégué ainsi que celles de directeur général ou de directeur, et le cas échéant, celles de membre de directoire ou de membre de conseil de surveillance, exercées dans les sociétés anonymes dont le capital appartient directement ou indirectement pour plus de 30 pour cent à l'Etat. Enfin, l'exercice de fonctions rémunérées par un Etat étranger ou une organisation internationale est également incompatible avec le mandat de Représentant.

Les chapitres 4 et 5 sont consacrés à la procédure de dépôt des candidatures et au déroulement des campagnes électorales. Le chapitre 6 concerne les infractions commises à l'occasion des élections, le 7ème prévoit le déroulement des opérations électorales (bulletin de vote et carte d'électeur, opérations de vote, dépouillement et recensement des votes, proclamation des résultats). Le chapitre 8 organise le recensement des votes et la proclamation des résultats. Les trois derniers sont consacrés au contentieux électoral, aux élections partielles et à des dispositions diverses.

La loi n° 32-97 relative à la chambre des conseillers est composée de neuf chapitres. Le premier intitulé "dispositions générales" fixe le nombre des conseillers à 270 dont:

(a) 162 élus dans chaque région, par un collège électoral composé des membres élus des conseils communaux, des assemblées préfectorales et provinciales et des conseils régionaux;
(b) 81 membres élus, dans chaque région, par des collèges électoraux composés des membres élus par chacune des chambres professionnelles suivantes existant

    dans la région: chambre d'agriculture, chambre de commerce, d'industrie et
    de service, chambre d'artisanat et chambre des pêches maritimes;

(c)   27 membres élus à l'échelon national, par un collège électoral composé de
    l'ensemble:

     (i)   des délégués des personnels des entreprises;

    (ii)   des représentants du personnel aux commissions du statut et de person-
         nel des entreprises minières;

   (iii)   des représentants du personnel au sein des commissions administratives
         paritaires prévues par le statut général de la fonction publique et les statuts
         particuliers du personnel communal et des personnels des établissements
         publics.

Le même chapitre prévoit la répartition des sièges entre les régions et le déroulement
du tirage au sort en vue des premier et deuxième renouvellement (les Conseillers
sont élus pour neuf ans, la chambre étant renouvelable par tiers tous les trois ans).

    Le chapitre 2 prévoit l'électorat et les conditions d'éligibilité. Sont électeurs les
membres composant les collèges électoraux prévus au chapitre 1er. Sont éligibles les
candidats âgés d'au moins trente ans. Le candidat doit être membre du collège dans
lequel il se présente. Les autres conditions d'éligibilité sont identiques à celles prévues
pour les Représentants, de même que les incompatibilités prévues au chapitre 3.

    Les chapitres suivants sont consacrés aux déclarations de candidature, aux opéra-
tions électorales, au recensement des votes et à la proclamation des résultats au
contentieux électoral et aux élections partielles.

3 DROIT ADMINISTRATIF

Le texte le plus important de l'année est sans aucun doute la loi n° 47-96 relative à
l'organisation de la région, promulguée par dahir n° 1-97-84 du 2 avril 1997.[7]

    Les régions avaient été créées en 1971 par un dahir[8] qui les définissaient comme
"un ensemble de provinces qui sur les plans tant géographique qu'économique et
social, entretiennent ou sont susceptibles d'entretenir des relations de nature à sti-
muler leur développement et, de ce fait, justifient un aménagement d'ensemble".
L'assemblée régionale n'avait qu'un rôle consultatif dans le domaine des programmes
de développement économique et social et d'aménagement du territoire intéres-
sant la région.

    La constitution de 1992 fait pour la première fois figurer les régions dans
l'énumération des collectivités locales (article 94) et la révision constitutionnelle de
1996 prévoit l'existence des régions et d'assemblées "provinciales, préfectorales et
régionales" dans les conditions fixées par la loi".

    La loi n° 47-96 est donc l'acte de naissance des nouvelles collectivités locales
que sont les régions. Elle comporte 8 titres. Le premier (article 1 à 5) pose les
principes généraux. Les régions sont des collectivités locales dotées de la personnalité
morale et de l'autonomie financière. Leurs affaires sont gérées par un conseil régional

---

[7]   Bulletin officiel n° 4470 du 3 avril 1997, p. 292.

[8]   Dahir n° 1-71-77 du 16 juin 1971 portant création des régions, Bulletin officiel n° 3060 du 26
    juin 1971, p. 685.

élu pour une durée de six ans. L'exécution des décisions de ce conseil est assurée par le gouverneur du chef lieu de la région. Le conseil ne peut délibérer sur des questions à caractère politique ou étrangères aux intérêts de la région.

Le titre II porte sur les attributions du conseil régional qui exerce:

(a)   des compétences propres (vote du budget, élaboration des plans de développement de la région, élaboration du schéma régional d'aménagement du territoire, assiette, tarif et règles de perception des taxes, actions de promotion des investissements privés, de promotion de l'emploi, de protection de l'environnement...).

(b)   des compétences transférées par l'Etat avec les moyens financiers nécessaires, notamment en matière de réalisation et d'entretien d'hôpitaux, lycées, établissements universitaires, formation des agents et cadres des collectivités locales et équipements d'intérêt régional.

(c)   enfin le conseil régional peut proposer, suggérer ou émettre des avis sur la politique de l'Etat dans la région, en matière d'investissements de l'Etat, d'aménagement du territoire et de planification.

Le titre III est consacré à l'organisation et au fonctionnement du conseil régional. Il prévoit l'élection d'un bureau, d'un président et de vice-présidents, les modalités de dissolution du conseil régional (décret motivé publié au Bulletin officiel) ou de suspension (arrêté motivé du ministre de l'intérieur publié au Bulletin officiel) et enfin les règles de fonctionnement du conseil. Le conseil se réunit trois fois par an en session ordinaire de quinze jours. Des sessions extraordinaires sont possibles lorsque les circonstances l'exigent. Le conseil doit constituer des commissions permanentes (au nombre de 7) traitant des questions financières, de planification et d'aménagement, des questions économiques et sociales, de l'agriculture et du développement rural, de santé et d'hygiène, d'urbanisme et d'environnement, de culture, enseignement et formation professionnelle.

Le titre IV traite de la tutelle qui est exercée par le ministre de l'intérieur pour les décisions les plus importantes (énumérées à l'article 41) et par le gouverneur du chef lieu de la région pour les autres. En cas de refus d'approbation par l'autorité de tutelle, le tribunal administratif peut être saisi.

Le titre V précise les compétences respectives du président du Conseil régional et du gouverneur du chef lieu de la région. Le conseil régional est représenté par son président au sein des établissements publics à caractère régional; il peut faire appel aux services de l'Etat dans la région par l'intermédiaire du gouverneur du chef lieu de la région. Le gouverneur du chef lieu de la région exécute les délibérations du conseil; il prend les mesures nécessaires à cet effet après avoir recueilli l'avis du président; les mesures ne sont exécutoires que si les actes sont revêtus du contreseing du président.

Le titre VI est consacré à la coopération inter-régionale. Celle-ci se fait par des comités inter-régionaux de coopération qui sont des établissements publics dotés de la personnalité morale et de l'autonomie financière.

Le titre VII traite des finances de la région qui dispose de moyens diversifiés de financement: impôts et taxes perçus par les collectivités locales, taxes additionnelles à certaines taxes (taxes d'édilité, taxes sur les contrats d'assurances et sur les carrières), taxe sur les exploitations minières et les service portuaires, ainsi que des produits des impôts ou des parts d'impôt d'Etat.

Enfin le titre VIII et dernier prévoit les dispositions finales et transitoires.

Cette loi sur les régions est complétée par un décret n° 2-97-246 du 17 août 1997 fixant le nombre des régions, leur nom, leur chef lieu, leur ressort territorial et le nombre de conseillers à élire dans chaque région ainsi que la répartition des sièges entre les divers collèges électoraux et la répartition entre les préfectures et provinces du nombre des sièges revenant aux collectivités locales.[9] Ce texte fixe le nombre des régions à seize.

4 DROIT DES AFFAIRES

En droit des affaires, deux textes importants interviennent en 1997: Une loi sur les sociétés en nom collectif, en commandite simple, en commandite par action et à responsabilité limitée qui achève la réforme des sociétés commencée en 1996 et une loi instituant des juridictions de commerce. Cette dernière loi est présentée sous le titre 1: Organisation judiciaire.

Après la loi sur les sociétés anonymes promulguée et publiée en 1996,[10] la loi n° 5-96 sur la société en nom collectif, la société en commandite simple, la société en commandite par actions, la société à responsabilité limitée et la société en participation, promulguée par dahir n° 1-97-49 du 13 février 1997,[11] complète le code des sociétés annoncé depuis plusieurs années.

Cette loi regroupe l'ensemble des dispositions applicables aux sociétés commerciales (à l'exception des sociétés anonymes qui ont fait l'objet d'une loi particulière en 1996), dispositions jusque là éparpillées dans le code de commerce et dans des textes divers.

On constate dans cette loi une revalorisation du rôle du juge. Auparavant, lorsqu'il s'agissait de réguler les relations des associés entre eux ou avec les gérants, la loi était muette ou prévoyait des dispositions dont la mise en oeuvre était laissée à l'initiative des associés, le juge n'étant saisi qu'en cas de conflit. La nouvelle loi lui donne un rôle plus étendu et lui confie des pouvoirs élargis lui permettant de contrôler la bonne gouvernance de la société.

On peut également souligner l'introduction de dispositions pénales importantes, renforçant la responsabilité pénale des gestionnaires, en particulier dans la société à responsabilité limitée.

La loi contient neuf titres: dispositions générales; de la société en nom collectif; de la société en commandite; de la société à responsabilité limitée; de la société en participation; de la publicité; des infractions et des sanctions pénales; dispositions diverses et transitoires.

Le titre premier présente les dispositions générales communes à tous les types de sociétés, dispositions posées par renvoi à certaines des règles figurant dans la loi de 1996 sur les sociétés anonymes.

La société en nom collectif est définie comme "une société dont tous les associés ont la qualité de commerçant et répondent indéfiniment et solidairement des dettes sociales". Il n'y a pas d'innovation particulière en ce qui la concerne. Le légis-

---

[9] Bulletin officiel n° 4510 du 21 août 1997, p. 781.
[10] Voir la présentation de ce texte en *Yearbook*, vol. 3 (1996), p. 358.
[11] Bulletin officiel n° 4478 du 1er mai 1997, p. 482.

lateur a repris les dispositions anciennes tout en renforçant les possibilités dont disposent les associés pour suivre la vie de la société.

La société en commandite n'était auparavant réglementée que par quelques articles du code de commerce. La loi lui consacre ses articles 19 à 43 et distingue la société en commandite simple et la société en commandite par action.

La société en commandite simple est constituée d'associés commandités qui ont le statut des associés en nom collectif, et d'associés commanditaires qui répondent des dettes sociales à concurrence du montant de leur apport. Les commanditaires apportent les capitaux et les commandités leur industrie.

Dans la société en commandite par actions, les commanditaires sont assimilés à des actionnaires et le statut d'associé de société anonyme leur est applicable. Pour renforcer la transparence, le législateur a introduit un conseil de surveillance qui assume le contrôle permanent de la gestion de la société et qui dispose des mêmes pouvoirs que les commissaires aux comptes.

En ce qui concerne les sociétés à responsabilité limitée, la nouvelle loi apporte plusieurs innovations. La plus important est sans aucun doute la SARL à associé unique. Le législateur n'institue pas une société unipersonnelle, il permet simplement la continuité de la société en cas de réunion en une seule main de toutes les parts d'une SARL. A partir de là, il prévoit le statut juridique de cette société, mais il est impossible de créer une société à associé unique.

Le capital de fondation est fixé à 10.000 dirhams. Il est divisé en parts sociales égales dont le montant ne peut être inférieur à cent dirhams.

Le nombre des associés ne peut être supérieur à 50. S'il dépasse ce nombre, la société doit se transformer en société anonyme. Cette règle est nouvelle, auparavant il existait seulement une obligation d'instituer un conseil de surveillance quand le nombre d'associés dépassait 20.

On constate également, comme pour les autres formes de sociétés, un renforcement des règles destinées à assurer la transparence: obligations pour les gérants d'informer les associés, moyens donnés aux associés de contrôler la gestion.

La société en participation n'était jusque là ni définie, ni réglementée; elle se fondait sur les dispositions générales du dahir formant code des obligations et contrats. Lorsque ce type de société se révélait, on lui appliquait le statut de la société en nom collectif.

La nouvelle loi la définit et pose quelques règles la concernant. La société en participation n'existe que dans les rapports entre associés et n'est pas destinée à être connue des tiers; elle n'a pas la personnalité morale; elle n'est soumise ni à l'immatriculation ni à aucune forme de publicité et son existence peut être prouvée par tous les moyens; elle peut être créée de fait. Sauf stipulation contraire, si la société a un caractère commercial, les rapports entre associés sont régis par les dispositions applicables aux sociétés en nom collectif.

5 DROIT DE L'EAU

La loi sur l'eau n° 10-95 publiée le 20 septembre 1995 a opéré une refonte de la législation relative à l'eau.[12] La plupart des dispositions de cette loi nécessitent,

---

[12] Voir *Yearbook*, vol. 2 (1995), pp. 97–111.

pour entrer réellement en vigueur, à la publication de textes d'application. Cette publication, commencée à la fin de 1996, s'est poursuivie en 1997.

Fin 1996, un décret fixe la composition et le fonctionnement du Conseil Supérieur de l'eau et du climat, chargé par la loi de "formuler les orientations générales de la politique nationale en matière d'eau et de climat". A la même date est créée la première agence de Bassin, celle du bassin hydraulique de l'Oum-Er-Rbia, dont le siège est fixé à Beni-Mellal.[13]

En 1997, trois décrets sont publiés.

5.1 Décret n° 2-97-178 du 24 octobre 1997 fixant la procédure de déclaration pour la tenue à jour de l'inventaire des ressources en eau[14]

L'article 92 de la loi sur l'eau prévoit, pour la mise à jour de l'inventaire des ressources en eau que l'exploitant ou le cas échéant le propriétaire d'un cours d'eau, source, puits ou forage est tenu de déclarer auprès de l'agence de bassin les installations de dérivation, captage, puisage et d'en permettre l'accès à ses agents à effet d'obtenir tous renseignements sur les débits prélevés et les conditions de ce prélèvement.
Le décret n° 2-98-168 fixe la forme et les modalités de cette déclaration qui doit être faite dans un délai de douze mois à compter de sa publication.

5.2 Décret n° 2-97-223 du 24 octobre 1997 relatif à la procédure d'élaboration et de révision des plans directeurs d'aménagement intégré des ressources en eau et du plan national de l'eau.[15]

Ces plans sont prévus par les articles 15 à 19 de la loi sur l'eau. Les plans directeurs d'aménagement intégré des ressources en eau ont pour objectif principal , selon l'article 16 de la loi, la gestion des ressources en eau du bassin, eaux d'estuaire comprises, en vue d'assurer quantitativement et qualitativement, les besoins en eau présents et futurs, des divers usagers en eau du bassin. Le décret prévoit qu'ils sont établis pour chaque bassin ou ensemble de bassins par l'agence de bassin. Ils sont soumis à l'avis des départements ministériels concernés (intérieur, finances, agriculture, santé, énergie et mines, commerce, industrie et artisanat, environnement et population), puis à l'avis du Conseil supérieur de l'eau et du climat. Ils sont ensuite approuvés par décret et publiés au Bulletin officiel.

Le plan national de l'eau est établi sur la base des plans directeurs d'aménagement; il doit définir les priorités nationales, les programmes hydrauliques et les articulations entre les différents plans directeurs d'aménagement. Le décret prévoit que ce plan est établi par le ministère de l'équipement, soumis pour avis aux départements

---

[13] Décret n° 2-96-158 du 20 novembre 1996 relatif à la composition et au fonctionnement du Conseil supérieur de l'eau, Décret n° 2-96-536 du 20 novembre 1996 relatif à l'Agence du bassin hydraulique de l'Oum-Er-Rbia, Bulletin officiel du 5 décembre 1996, respectivement p. 788 et p. 791.
[14] Bulletin officiel n° 4532 du 6 novembre 1997, p. 971.
[15] Bulletin officiel n° 4532 du 6 novembre 1997, p. 971.

ministériels concernés et au Conseil supérieur de l'eau et du climat, approuvé par décret et publié au Bulletin officiel.

5.3 Décret n° 2-97-224 du 24 octobre 1997 fixant les conditions d'accumulation artificielle des eaux[16]

L'article 25 de la loi sur l'eau prévoit que les conditions d'accumulation artificielle des eaux sur les propriétés privées sont fixées par voie réglementaire. Le décret n° 2-97-224 fixe ces conditions. Les ouvrages d'accumulation artificielle d'un volume inférieur à 2000 mètres cubes sont soumis à une simple déclaration. Les autres sont soumises à une autorisation. La demande doit préciser notamment le régime des eaux à accumuler, le type d'ouvrage d'accumulation, le volume d'eau, les besoins et l'usage prévus, l'étendue et la profondeur d'eau accumulée. Elle doit être accompagnée d'une étude technique ou d'une étude d'impact, selon l'importance des travaux envisagés. La demande est déposée à l'agence de bassin qui dispose d'un délai de deux mois pour accorder ou refuser l'autorisation.

L'accumulation des eaux usées brutes n'est autorisée que si elle fait partie d'un système d'épuration de ces eaux, agréé par l'agence de bassin concernée.

6 DROIT DE L'ENVIRONNEMENT

Dans le domaine de l'environnement on signalera une loi relative au commerce des produits pesticides à usage agricole et deux décrets d'application de la loi du 12 octobre 1971 relative à la protection des rayonnements ionisants.

En mai 1998 est publiée la loi n° 42-95 relative au contrôle et à l'organisation du commerce des produits pesticides à usage agricole.[17]

Dans son titre premier, la loi définit ce qu'il faut entendre par pesticide à usage agricole, interdit tout commerce de pesticides n'ayant pas fait l'objet d'une homologation ou à défaut d'une autorisation de vente, prévoit l'étiquetage, l'emballage et diverses mesures de précaution.

Le titre II est consacré aux activités d'importation, de fabrication, et de commerce des pesticides à usage agricole et le titre III aux dispositions pénales applicables aux éventuels contrevenants. Les sanctions sont des peines d'amende mais l'emprisonnement est possible en cas de récidive.

Deux décrets du 28 octobre 1997, pris pour l'application de la loi n° 005-71 du 12 octobre 1971 relative à la protection contre les rayonnements ionisants[18] sont publiés en décembre 1997.

---

[16] Bulletin officiel n° 4532 du 6 novembre 1997, p. 972.
[17] Promulguée par dahir n° 1-97-01 du 21 janvier 1997, Bulletin officiel n° 4482 du 15 mai 1997, p. 533.
[18] Décret n°-97-30 du 28 octobre 1997 pris pour l'application de la loi n° 005-71 du 12 octobre 1971 relative à la protection contre les rayonnements ionisants et Décret n° 2-97-132 du 28 octobre 1997 relatif à l'utilisation des rayonnements ionisants à les fins médicales ou dentaires, Bulletin officiel n° 4540 du 4 décembre 1997, p. 1013 et 1025.

Le premier décret n° 2-97-30 fixe les principes généraux de protection contre les dangers pouvant résulter de l'utilisation des rayonnements ionisants et les conditions auxquelles est soumise toute activité impliquant une exposition aux rayonnements ionisants. C'est un texte de 69 articles comportant dix titres: le premier intitulé "champ d'application et définitions" classe les établissements en deux catégories et définit ce qu'il faut entendre par rayonnement ionisant, nucléide, radioactivité, radionucléide (radioélément) et activité (radioactive).

Les titres suivants sont consacrés aux:

(a)   dispositions générales (conditions de radioexposition et du système de limitation de doses).
(b)   limites de doses équivalentes annuelles pour des radioexpositions contrôlables;
(c)   radioexposition accidentelle ou due aux situations d'urgence;
(d)   principes fondamentaux de la surveillance de la santé des travailleurs;
(e)   principes fondamentaux de la surveillance de la santé publique;
(f)   irradiation médicale;
(g)   autorisation et déclaration;
(h)   contrôle et inspection;
(i)   commission nationale de protection radiologique;
(j)   dispositions finales.

Le titre IX est consacré aux dispositions finales; il prévoit que dans un délai de six mois à compter de la publication du texte au Bulletin officiel, tout détenteur de substances radioactives ou sources de rayonnements ionisants doit en faire la déclaration au ministre de la santé publique et éventuellement obtenir une des autorisations prévues au titre VIII.

Le deuxième décret n°-97-132 du 28 octobre 1997 est relatif à l'utilisation des rayonnements ionisants à les fins médicales ou dentaires. Il prévoit l'homologation par le ministère de la santé publique des appareils ou sources de rayonnements ionisants utilisés à des fins médicales ou dentaires. L'utilisation de ces appareils est réservée à un personnel qualifié et dans des locaux spécialement aménagés à cet effet. Une annexe du décret prévoit les conditions d'aménagement des locaux où sont installées et utilisées des sources de rayonnements ionisants à des fins médicales ou dentaires, et les procédés d'évacuation et de stockage des effluents et déchets radioactifs.

On signalera enfin, toujours dans le domaine de l'environnement, la publication au Bulletin officiel de la convention des Nations Unies sur la lutte contre la désertification dans les pays gravement touchés par la sécheresse ou par la désertification en particulier en Afrique, faite à Paris le 17 juin 1994, ratifiée par le Maroc le 7 novembre 1996.[19]

---

[19] Bulletin officiel n° 4515 du 4 septembre 1997, p. 799.

Tunisia

*Afif Gaigi**

L'année 1997 n'a pas connu de réformes législatives marquantes introduisant des modifications notables dans la législation en cours. Nous ne retiendrons dans cette étude que les textes qui méritent l'attention et qui ont paru au cours de la session législative de 1997 pour l'assemblée parlemantaire ou ceux adoptés par l'organe exécutif au cours de la même année.

1 DROIT CONSTITUTIONNEL ET ADMINISTRATIF

La loi 97-48 du 21 juillet 1997 (Journal officiel No. 59 du 25 juillet 1997) a concerné le financement public des partis politiques. Désormais les partis politiques sont financés sur le budget de l'état sous forme de primes à la condition qu'il existe à la chambre des députés un ou plusieurs députés adhérant au parti financé. La prime cesse si le parti ne présente pas ses comptes à la cour des comptes conformément à la législation en vigueur.

La loi constitutionelle 97-65 du 27 octobre 1997 modifiant et complétant certains articles de la constitution (Journal officiel No. 87 page 1967) a fixé l'âge pour être électeur à vingt ans et avoir la nationalité tunisienne depuis cinq ans et pour être éligible à vingt-trois ans et être né de père et mère tunisiens. L'article 32 nouveau a affirmé la supériorité des traités internationaux ratifiés sur la loi interne mais sous réserve de leur application par l'autre partie.

L'article 34 a redéfini le domaine de la loi de manière limitative et l'article 35 rèserve au pouvoir réglementaire général les matières autres que celles consacrées à la loi. Le Président de la République peut rejeter tout projet de loi relatif au domaine du pouvoir réglementaire général mais il doit soumettre la question au Conseil Constitutionnel qui statue dans un délai maximum de dix jours. Il peut également soumettre au référendum les projets de loi d'importance nationale ou touchant à l'intérêt supérieur du pays sans être contraire à la Constitution.

L'article 76 modifié par la nouvelle loi autorise le Président de la République à soumettre au référendum les projets de révision de la Constitution.

---

* Avocat à la Court de Cassation, enseignant universitaire.

L'article 77 tel qu'il est modifié par la nouvelle loi régit l'adoption des projets de loi soumis au référendum. Le Président de la République soumet le projet de révision de la constitutoin au peuple après son adoption par la chambre des députés à la majorité absolue de ses membres au cours d'une seule lecture.

La nouvelle loi a d'autre part ajouté aux articles 8 et 52 de la constitution de nouvelles dispositions importantes.

Les nouvelles dispositions complétant l'article 8 sont relatives aux partis politiques. Elles en définissent notamment les objectifs et les buts et soulignent surtout que les partis politiques doivent bannir toute forme de violence de fanatisme, de racisme et toute forme de discrimination. Les partis politiques ne peuvent s'appuyer fondamentalement dans leurs principes, objectifs au programmes sur une religion, une langue, une race, un sexe ou une région. Il leur est interdit d'avoir des liens de dépendance vis à vis des parties ou d'intérêts étrangers.

L'article 52 tel qu'il est modifié indique quels sont les pouvoirs du président de la république pour renvoyer un project de loi ou certains de ses articles après modification à la chambre des députés pour une nouvelle délibération. Après adoption de modifications par la chambre des députés à la majorité de ses membres, le président de la république promulgue la loi et en assure la publication dans un délai maximum de quinze jours.

En matière de droit administratif la loi No. 97-83 a modifié la loi du 12 décembre 1983. Portant statut général des personnels de l'état, des collectivités locales et des établissements publics à caractère administratif (Journal officiel No. 103 page 2404). Ces modifications adoptées par la nouvelle loi sont relatives au recrutement par concours ou par nomination directe, à la promotion, au congé, au pouvoir disciplinaire, à la mise en disponibilité, à l'honorariat, à la situation des agents temporaires et à la gratification exceptionnelle accordée aux fonctionnaires qui se sont distingués par un esprit inventif dans leur travail ou ont évité à l'administration des pertes. Cette gratification est accordée par le Président de la République sous forme d'avancement ou de prime. Ce pouvoir est accordé aussi à l'autorité de nomination mais après l'avis d'une commission et sur le base d'un rapport circonstancié.

La loi No. 97-80 du 1 décembre 1998 porte promulgation du code des décorations. Ce code classe les médailles en ordres nationaux, médailles du travail et médailles particulières. La nouvelle loi interdit à tout tunisien d'accepter ou de porter une décoration étrangère ou son insigne sans autorisation du ministère des affaires étrangères. La loi rappelle également que toute personne qui porte une décoration sans y avoir droit encourt les peines prévues par l'article 159 du code pénal.

2 DROIT INTERNATIONAL PUBLIC

La loi No. 97-13 du 3 mars 1997 a porté ratification de la convention sur l'interdiction de la mise au point, de la fabrication, du stockage et de l'emploi des armes chimiques et sur leur destruction (J. ORT. No. 19 du 7 mars 1997).

La loi No. 97-14 du 3 mars 1997 a autorisé l'adhésion de la Tunisie à la convention internationale contre la prise d'otages. Le décret 97-1811 du 3 septembre 1997 a ordonné ensuite la publication au Journal Officiel de la dite convention (J.ORT. No. 75 du 19 septembre 1997).

La loi No. 97-81 du 15 décembre 1997 a autorisé quant à elle l'adhésion de la République Tunisienne à la convention pour la répression d'actes illicites contre la sécurité de la navigation maritime.

La loi No. 97-82 du 15 décembre 1997 a autorisé de son côté l'adhésion de la république Tunisienne au protocole pour la répression d'actes illicites contre la sécurité des plates-formes fixes situées sur le plateau continental. (J.ORT No. 75 du 19 septembre 1997.

3 DROIT CIVIL

La loi No. 97-68 du 27 octobre 1997 (J. ORT No. 87 du 31 octobre 1997) a modifié certains articles du Code des droit réels.

Les articles 85, 89, 90, 91, 92, 97, 99 et 102 du code des droits réels modifiés par la dite loi sont relatifs aux immeubles construits appartenant à plusieurs personnes et comportant plusieurs étages ou appartements ou locaux commerciaux ou professionnels appartenant privativement à une ou plusieurs personnes. La loi a redéfini les parties communes. La loi impose désormais la constitution de syndicat de propriétaires doté de la personnalité civile, d'un président mandataire légal. Un règlement de copropriété doit être adopté. La loi organise le fonctionnement du syndicat, la réunion des assemblées des propriétaires et la prise des décisions, la désignation du président du syndicat et son remplacement.

La loi indique aussi que lorsque deux appartements au moins appartiennent à deux ou plusieurs personnes on doit extraire du titre foncier initial autant de titres fonciers dérivés que de parties privatives le titre foncier intial demeure uniquement aux parties communes indivises.

La nouvelle loi a également modifié l'article 380, 381 384 et 394 du code des droits réels relatifs aux registres qui doivent être tenus par la conservation de la propriété foncière.

L'article 388 du même code a été également modifié. Cet article concerne les pouvoirs du conservateur quant à l'acceptation d'une inscription sur le registre foncier, sa radiation, sa réduction, sa rectification.

Le conservateur ne peut refuser ou retarder une inscription régulière ni retarder ou refuser la délivrance d'un certificat de propriété à toute personne qui y a droit sauf cas d'empêchement légal.

La décision de refuser ou de déférer du conservateur peut faire l'objet d'un recours devant le président du tribunal immobilier dans le mois qui suit la notification de cette décision. Le requérant peut obtenir la prenotation de ce recours sur le titre.

4 DROIT DU TRAVAIL ET DE LA SECURITE SOCIALE

Le décret No. 97-291 du 3 février 1997 (J. ORT No. 13 du 14 février 1997) a modifié le régime de vieillesse d'invalidité et de survivants dans le secteur non agricole en donnant ouverture à d'avantage de droits au conjoint suvivant d'un bénéficiaire de pension même décédé avant l'age de la mise à la retraite.

L'arrête du ministre des affaires sociales du 4 février 1997 a porté agrément de la convention collective des cliniques privées publié au J. ORT No. 14 du 18 février 1997.

L'arrêté du même ministre du 13 février 1997 a porté agrément de l'avenant No. 4 à la convention collective nationale de l'enseignement privé (J. ORT No. 15 du 21 février 1997. L'arrêté du même ministre du 15 mai 1997 a porté agrément de la convention collective nationale des agences de voyages (J. ORT No. 41, p. 912).

Les lois 57, 58, 59, 60 et 61 du 28 juillet 1997 (J. ORT No. 61 du août 1997) ont modifié ou amendé le régime de retraite des députés, l'organisation des régimes de sécurité sociale, le régime des pensions civiles et militaires de retraites et des survivants pour le secteur public, le régime de prévoyance sociale des fonctionnaires et le régime de sécurité sociale dans le secteur agricole.

Toutes ces lois ont ouvert le droit à plus d'avantages sociaux aux bénéficiaires en prolongeant notamment le droit aux soins accordés aux enfants ou aux orphelins jusqu'à un âge plus avancé.

Le décret No. 97-1925 du 29 septembre 1997 (J. ORT No. 80 du 7 octobre 1997) est relatif aux interventions sociales en faveur des travailleurs.

Ce texte a créé auprès de la caisse nationale de sécurité social une dotation annuelle destinée à financer les interventions et les actions sociales en faveur des travailleurs ayant perdu à titre temporaire leur emploi pour raisons économiques ou technologique indépendant de leur volonté.

L'aide accordé est plafonnée à trois mensualités du salaire d'activité perçu et dans la limite du salaire minimum interprofessionnel garantie. Le texte pose les conditions d'octroi de cette aide et les modalités de leur versement.

Le décret No. 97-1926 du 29 septembre 1997 paru dans le même numéro du J. ORT a déterminé les conditions et les modalités de la prise en charge des indemnités dues à ces travailleurs par la caisse nationale de sécurité sociale lorsqu'il s'avère que l'enterprise qui les emploie est en état de cessation de paiement pour faillite, fermeture définitive ou liquidation judiciaire. Le présent décret ne concerne pas le secteur des entreprises publiques dont les salariés bénéficent d'un fond spécial. La prise en charge couvre les salaires impayés les congés payés, non réglés et les préavis de licenciement, et qui ont fait l'objet d'une décision de justice devenue définitive ou d'un procès verbal de l'accord établi par l'inspection du travail ou de la réunion de la commisssion du contrôle de licenciement. L'impossibilité de recouvrement doit être établi. La caisse après vérification des conditoins d'octroi verse les montants dus aux salariés bénéficiaires déduction faite de l'aide perçu éventuellement au titre du décret No. 97-1925 ci-dessus mentionné.

Le décret No. 97-1927 du 29 septembre 1997 a amendé le décret du 27 avril 1974 relatif au régime de vieillesse d'invalidité et des survivants dans le secteur non agricole et ce en élargissant les conditions d'octroi des pensions temporaires dues aux orphelins et ce en prorogeant la durée du droit à la pension.

5 DROIT BANCAIRE ET LEGISLATION EN MATIERE DE CHANGE ET DE COMMERCE EXTERIEUR

Décret No. 97-385 du 14 avril 1997 modifiant le décret No. 77-608 du 27 juillet 1977 fixant les conditions d'application de la loi No. 76-18 du 21 janvier 1976 portant refonte et codification de la législation des changes et du commerce extérieur régissant les relations entre la Tunisie et les pays étrangers tel que modifiée par la loi du 3 mai 1997 apparu au J. ORT No. 15 du 21 février 1997. Ce décret a fixé le taux de participation étrangère dans le capital des sociétés visées par le texte à 50 pour cent du capital de la société ou plus.

Un deuxième décret datant du 3 septembre 1997 (J. ORT No. 73 du 12 septembre 1997) a apporté de nouvelles modifications au décret du 27 juillet 1977 sus indiqué. Ce décret a défini les opérations encore soumises à autorisation de la banque centrale et celles qui ne sont plus soumises à une telle autorisation. Le texte nouveau a redéfini les conditions soumettant l'acquisition de valeurs mobilières Tunisiennes qui confèrent un droit de vote ou de parts sociales de sociétés établies en Tunisie à l'approbation de la commission supérieure d'investissement crée par la loi du 27 décembre 1993.

6 DROIT DE TRANSPORT ET L'ENVIRONNEMENT

La loi 97-56 du 28 juillet 1997 parue au J. ORT No. 61 du 1 août 1997 a organisé le transport routier des marchandises en fixant les règles d'exercice de cet activité conformément à la législation et à la réglementation en vigueur relative à la sécurité de la circulation et à la protection de l'environnement. La loi distingue entre le transport de marchandise pour son propre compte et celui pour le compte d'autrui lequel nécessite l'inscription du transporteur à un registre spécial. Le transport de marchandises pour le compte d'autrui comprend deux catégories, le transport intérieur et le transport international. Seules les sociétés dont l'objet social se limite au transport international peuvent exercer cet activité. La loi traite ensuite de la location de véhicules de transport de marchandises et des conditions de l'inscription des personnes physiques ou morales au registre prévu à cet effet. La loi prévoit également ment des sanctions pénales en cas d'infraction.

Loi No. 97-37 du 2 juin 1997 (J. ORT No. 45 p. 1020) est relative au transport par route de matières dangereuses.

7 DIVERS

Loi du 23 mars 1997 (J. ORT No. 24 p. 491 du 25 mars 1997) relative à l'enregistrement des jugements et arrêt au droit minimum au profit des parties non condamnées aux dépens.

Loi No. 97-33 du 26 mai 1997 modifiant la loi du 22 septembre 1969 relative à la réforme des structures agricoles (J. ORT No. 44 p. 1008).

Loi No. 97-34 du 26 mai 1997 relative à l'exercise de la pêche (J. ORT No. 44 p. 1008).

Loi No. 97-41 du 9 juin 1997 modifiant le décret loi du 23 octobre 1992 créant l'ordre des ingénieurs.

Loi No. 97-46 du 14 juillet 1997 sur l'hébergement touristique à temps partagée (J. ORT No. 57 du 18 juillet 1997 p. 1262).

Loi No. 97-47 du 14 juillet 1997 organisant la profession de médecin vétérinaire (J. ORT No. 57 p. 1264).

Avis du premier ministre portant à obligation de la certification des équipements informatiques pour le passage à l'an deux mille (J. ORT No. 72 p. 1700).

Loi No. 97-69 du 27 octobre 1997 modifiant la loi 95-33 du 14 avril 1995 portant organisation des professsion de la marine marchande (J. ORT No. 87 du 31 octobre 1997 p. 1970).

Loi No. 97-71 du 11 novembre 1997 relative aux liquidateurs, mandataires de justice, syndics et administrateurs judiciaires (J. ORT No. 91 p. 2047).

Pakistan

*Martin Lau**

1 INTRODUCTION

Pakistan is in turmoil. Fifty-one years after independence from British colonial rule the country is facing its so far gravest economic crisis ever. At the time of the writing of this year's survey Pakistan is about to default on its international debts, the Rupee is in free fall, the value of the Karachi stock exchange has fallen by half between May and July 1998, petrol prices have increased by 25 per cent and restrictions have been placed on withdrawals from foreign currency bank accounts. The economic crisis is accompanied by civil unrest in Sindh, the suicide of the Bishop of Faisalabad in protest against the continued persecution of Pakistan's Christian community under the blasphemy laws, the testing of five nuclear bombs in the hills of Baluchistan, the declaration of emergency accompanied by the suspension of all fundamental rights, the resignation of Pakistan's President and the removal of the Chief Justice, and, most recently, an attempt by Prime Minister Nawaz Sharif to amend the Constitution of Pakistan in order to make Islamic law the supreme law of the land. This year's survey will therefore not be restricted to the purely legal developments of the period under review. In fact, it is likely that the legal aftermath of this year's events will take some time to manifest itself. Suffice to say that the social, economic and political crisis of Pakistan has also engulfed the legal system.

2 THE SUPREME COURT UNDER SIEGE

Nawaz Sharif's return to power on 3 February 1997 as a Prime Minister with a solid two-third majority in the National Assembly and a simple majority in the Senate should have heralded a time of political stability, economic recovery and social development. This hope was underpinned by Sharif's successful removal of Article 58 2(b) from the Constitution which had hitherto enabled the President to dissolve

---

* Barrister, Lecturer in Law and Director of CIMEL, SOAS.

the National Assembly and to dismiss the Prime Minister. However, last year's survey closed on a cautious note pointing out the dangers of a concentration of power in the hands of the Prime Minister and the fact that the Supreme Court of Pakistan was the only institution which could now impose any checks on the government. Unfortunately, the concerns expressed last year could have come straight from Cassandra herself: in December 1997 both the President and the Chief Justice of Pakistan were forced to resign as a result of an extraordinary power struggle between the Prime Minister and the President – a struggle which involved the denunciation of Pakistan's Supreme Court judges by the members of the National Assembly and the storming of the Supreme Court itself by supporters of Nawaz Sharif. Tensions between the Prime Minister and the Sajjad Ali Shah, Chief Justice of the Supreme Court (as he then was), had been rising over the issue of appointment of judges – in spite of two judgments on this issue Nawaz Sharif had refused to appoint judges proposed by the Chief Justice.[1]

However, Sharif's desire to consolidate his power can be identified as the root cause of the constitutional crises which engulfed Pakistan at the end of 1997. The government's solid majority was not guaranteed to last forever since members of the National Assembly could always change their party-political allegiances during the five-year duration of the parliament. This practice, known in Pakistan as "floor crossing", could potentially have weakened the majority enjoyed by the ruling party, the Muslim League. The solution to the danger of being threatened by the defection of members of his own party appeared to be a simple one: another amendment to Pakistan's Constitution would solve the problem. Sharif had successfully removed Article 58 2(b) from the Constitution and had thereby pre-empted any attempt by the President to unseat him. The Fourteenth Amendment to the Constitution would make the practice of "floor crossing" a thing of the past. A new Article 63 A would disqualify members of the National Assembly who changed their party allegiance. The new Article provides *inter alia* that

63A. (1) If a member of a Parliamentary Party defects, he may by means of a notice addressed to him by the Head of the Political Party or such other person as may be authorised in this behalf by the Head of the Political Party, be called upon to show cause, within no more than seven days of such notice, as to why a declaration under clause (2) should not be made against him. If a notice is issued under this clause, the Presiding Officer of the House shall be informed accordingly.

Explanation: A member of a House shall be deemed to defect from a political party if he, having been elected as such, as a candidate or nominee of a political party [....]
(a) commits a breach of party discipline which means a violation of the party constitution, code of conduct and declared policies, or
(b) votes contrary to any direction issued by the Parliamentary Party to which he belongs, or
(c) abstains from voting in the House against policy in relation to any Bill. [....][2]

The disciplinary committee of the political party can eventually decide whether or not the member is deemed to have defected. There is a right to an appeal to the

---

[1] See *Al-Jehad v. The Federation of Pakistan* PLD 1997 SC 84 and PLD 1996 SC 324.
[2] See the Constitution (Fourteenth Amendment) Act, 1997.

chairman of the party, but once this is exhausted, the Chief Election Commissioner can declare the seat vacant which would lead to a by-election. The new law applies to both the National Assembly and the four Provincial Assemblies.

There was little doubt that Nawaz Sharif's government would secure the two-thirds majority necessary for an amendment of the Constitution but there was nevertheless disquiet both in the opposition and in judicial circles about the effects of the proposed amendment on the constitutional order of Pakistan. The amendment would *de facto* make it impossible to challenge Nawaz Sharif's power during the duration of the National Assembly. The President had already lost his power to dissolve Parliament and under the proposed amendment even the National Assembly itself would find it very difficult to unseat Nawaz Sharif's government. Nevertheless, Nawaz Sharif succeeded in amending the Constitution.[3]

The Supreme Court of Pakistan was the only check on Sharif's inexorable rise to absolute power and, perhaps somewhat predictably, the constitutionality of the new Article 63 A was challenged in a writ petition. Even before a substantial hearing could take place, Chief Justice Sajjad Ali Shah (as he then was) suspended the operation of the Fourteenth Amendment Act. Nawaz Sharif reacted promptly by denouncing the Supreme Court's interim order. Other members of the National Assembly, as well as several newspapers, followed the Prime Minister's example and launched an at times vitriolic attack on the Supreme Court. Former Chief Justice Sajjad Ali Shah reacted swiftly by invoking Article 204 of the Constitution, which provides that the Supreme Court shall have the power to punish any person who "scandalizes the Court or otherwise does anything which tends to bring the Court or a Judge of the Court into hatred, ridicule or contempt". Seven parliamentarians, three newspapers, Pakistan State Television (PTV) and the Prime Minister himself were the target of the Supreme Court's retaliatory strike. According to press reports Nawaz Sharif's had publicly stated, in reaction to the suspension of the "floor crossing" amendment, that "the filth in the form of floor crossing which was cleansed by the parliament has been restored by the Chief Justice"[4] and that the interim order passed by the Supreme Court was of no consequence.

This development constituted a grave threat to Nawaz Sharif: a conviction for contempt of court by the apex court would have spelt the end of his tenure as Prime Minister since he could not have appealed against the conviction. Any conviction would therefore have resulted in a *de facto* "judicial impeachment" of Nawaz Sharif. The first hearing against Nawaz Sharif in Islamabad ended in chaos with supporters of the Muslim League storming the building of the Supreme Court and forcing an early end to the proceedings. Nawaz Sharif also tried to prevent "judicial impeachment" by amending the Contempt of Court Act, 1976 to allow an appeal to a larger bench of the Supreme Court in case he was convicted in the first instance. However, despite being passed by both the National Assembly and the Senate without any delay, President Farooq Leghari refused to sign the bill, thereby clearly siding with the Chief Justice.

---

[3] See the Constitution (Fourteenth Amendment) Act, 1997. The Act received the assent of the President on 3 July 1997.
[4] See Tahir Akram, "Nawaz Sharif charged with contempt", 19 November 1998, Reuters.

3 THE APEX COURT DIVIDED

The closing days of November 1997 witnessed the peak of Pakistan's constitutional crisis. The contempt of court hearings against Nawaz Sharif were severely disrupted by angry crowds and with no compromise solution in sight a constitutional melt-down seemed imminent. In fact, there were rumours that the army itself might be tempted to get involved in the dispute between the Supreme Court and the President on the one hand and the Prime Minister on the other. However, nobody could have predicted the unprecedented chain of events which were about to unfold within the Supreme Court of Pakistan itself.

On 26 November 1997 the Quetta Bench of the Supreme Court of Pakistan admitted a writ-petition which challenged the appointment of Sajjad Ali Shah as Chief Justice in 1994. According to the writ petition Sajjad Ali Shah was at that time not the most senior judge of the Supreme Court and his elevation to the position of a Chief Justice was therefore unconstitutional. The two Supreme Court judges hearing the petition, Irshad Hassan Khan and Khalil-ur-Rehman, took the somewhat unusual step of passing an interim order immediately suspending the operation of the notification, dated 5 June 1994, appointing Sajjad Ali Shah as the Chief Justice of Pakistan. The effect of the order amounted to an internal mutiny – two judges of the Supreme Court had broken ranks with the Chief Justice and had challenged his position. Until then nobody had appeared unduly troubled about the fact that Mr Sajjad Ali Shah had not been the most senior judge of the Supreme Court at the time of his appointment.

Sajjad Ali Shah reacted the very same day by issuing an administrative order directing the writ petition to be placed before himself arguing that under Order XXV of the Supreme Court Rules, 1980 a petition under Article 184(3)[5] on the original side of the Supreme Court has to be filed only at the principal registry in Islamabad and not at any other registry of the Supreme Court. Further, Shah's administrative order declared that the two judges had acted without lawful authority. Shah's order reached the two judges and, by what appears to be an extraordinary coincidence, also Mr Asad Ali, who had filed the original writ petition earlier in the day, at the Judges Rest House in Quetta in the late evening. Khalil-ur-Rehman, Irshad Hassan Khan and a third judge, Nasir Aslam Zahid, proceeded to hear the petitioner's counsel at their rest house and issued another interim order declaring that

We deem it fit and proper to declare that the impugned executive order of the Hon'ble Chief Justice (under suspension) is nullity and is to be ignored. The order passed by two Hon'ble Judges of this Court at Quetta today in C.P. No. 248-Q of 1997 still holds the field and is hereby reiterated and confirmed.[6]

---

[5] Article 184(3) provides for the admission of writ petitions for the enforcement of the constitutionally guaranteed fundamental rights.
[6] See *Asad Ali v. Federation of Pakistan* PLD 1998 SC 161 at p. 198, an earlier shorter judgment is reported as *Asad Ali v. Federation of Pakistan* PLD 1998 SC 33.

The stand-off continued the next day with Sajjad Ali Shah, joined by four other judges of the Supreme Court who happened to be in Islamabad, issuing an Order by a majority of four to one to the effect that "the orders passed by the Bench of the Court at Quetta are not to be given effect to as the matter would be heard at the Principal Seat as directed earlier". The Chief Justice seemed to have managed to muster some support among the judges but the tide of insurrection had not been stemmed completely. While Sajjad Ali Shah issued the Order in Islamabad another bench of the Supreme Court, this time in Peshawar, consisting of Judges Saiduzzaman Siddiqui and Fazal Ilahi Khan, admitted a second writ-petition challenging the 1994 appointment of Sajjad Ali Shah as Chief Justice. Their interim order, which was passed on the same day, went along the lines of the Quetta order: Sajjad Ali Shah has been restrained from passing any judicial or administrative order in his capacity as Chief Justice of Pakistan.

The battle continued with another order from the Quetta branch of the Supreme Court followed by another order issued by the Peshawar branch. The latter had in the meantime received a order in support issued by the senior judge Ajmal Mian, who was sitting at the Karachi branch of the Supreme Court. The Peshawar branch of the Supreme Court issued yet another order this time including an appeal to all state functionaries not to support the purportedly suspended Chief Justice:

In these circumstances, in order to save the situation from taking a disastrous turn, we call upon all state functionaries, to fulfil their constitutional obligations and acting in aid of the Supreme Court in accordance with Article 190 of the Constitution of the Islamic Republic of Pakistan to ensure that the order passed by us yesterday is complied with in letter and spirit and necessary arrangements are made for holding of the Full Court Session at the Principal Seat at Islamabad, for hearing of the above and all other, similar constitutional matters.[7]

Accordingly an order was issued for the constitution of a Full Court to hear the constitutional petitions which had been filed in Peshawar and Quetta. All judges were requested to be in Islamabad on 1 December 1997 to hear the petitions and to decide upon the fate of Chief Justice Sajjad Ali Shah (under restraint) (as he then was).

4 CONSTITUTIONAL MELTDOWN

The events which were to follow can be regarded as the darkest hours of the Supreme Court of Pakistan. The stand-off between the Chief Justice and the renegade judges, by now assembled in their official rest houses in Islamabad, continued with another order by the Chief Justice cancelling the full court hearing which had been scheduled by the renegade judges for the next day. Instead the Chief Justice constituted three benches, one consisting of the dissenters to hear the petitions against him, and two more benches, one of which was to be presided over by himself, to hear other constitutional matters. As it turned out, ten judges out of a total of fifteen judges joined the bench which was to hear the writ-petitions against the ap-

---

[7] See *Asad Ali v. Federation of Pakistan* PLD 1998 SC 161 at p. 202.

pointment of the Chief Justice, whereas the remaining five judges spread over the other two benches. When the three hearings commenced in separate court rooms of the Supreme Court, Chief Justice Sajjad Ali Shah was about to play his final card: in the middle of the hearing he admitted a writ-petition filed in open court by a politician praying for the suspension of the Thirteenth Amendment of the Constitution.[8] The petition was immediately admitted by the Chief Justice, and without hearing any counsel an interim order reviving Article 58 2 (b) was issued, which was rushed to the Presidency straightaway.

However, before the President could act on the newly given powers by dismissing Nawaz Sharif's government, the bench hearing the petitions against the appointment of the Chief Justice was informed of the developments which had taken place in the very same building. The ten judges hastily drafted what turned out to be the final victorious order which completed the judicial *coup d'état* against Chief Justice Sajjad Ali Shah:

[...][we] direct the Federal Government as well as the President of Pakistan to make an immediate order under Article 180 of the Constitution appointing Mr Justice Ajmal Mian, the senior most Judge of this Court as Acting Chief Justice.[...][9]

The government compiled with this order immediately and issued an appointment order which was presented to President Leghari for signature. Predictably, the President refused to sign the order and resigned on the same day. Nawaz Sharif hailed the resignation of the President and the suspension of Justice Shah as "a victory for the Pakistani people".[10] Justice Ajmal Mian was appointed Acting Chief Justice on 4th December 1997.

The outcome of the Mr Asad Ali's original writ-petition is not entirely surprising: in a reported judgment which covers close to three hundred pages in the law report the nine judges confirm that Sajjad Ali Shah's appointment as Chief Justice had been unconstitutional. The judgment does not break any new judicial ground nor does it explain the extraordinary action of the judges sitting in Quetta who had initiated the judicial "coup" by passing an interim order suspending their own Chief Justice. The judgment also fails to mention the legal and political developments which formed the backdrop of the case – the reader will search in vain for any mention of the resignation of the President or the contempt of court case against Nawaz Sharif.

The battle between Nawaz Sharif and the Supreme Court of Pakistan and the President of Pakistan has seen the Prime Minister emerge as the winner. The new President, Rafiq Tarar, appears to be more supportive of the Nawaz Sharif than his predecessor. Somewhat predictably, Nawaz Sharif was also able to mount a successful defence against the contempt of court charges.[11]

---

[8] The Thirteenth Amendment to the Constitution had removed Article 58 2 (b) from the Constitution. A revival of the article would have allowed President Leghari to dismiss Nawaz Sharif's government.

[9] See *Asad Ali v. Federation of Pakistan* PLD 1998 SC 161 at p. 208.

[10] See "Nawaz Sharif completes 'coup' as Acting Chief Justice takes oath", *The Asian Age*, 4 December 1997.

[11] The decision has not as yet been reported but according to Mr Makhdoom Ali Khan, one of the lawyers involved in the case, the judgment does not appear to break any new ground in the law of contempt of court.

It is to early for a full assessment of the constitutional crisis and its effect on the powers of the Supreme Court of Pakistan. Ostensibly, the Supreme Court sided with Nawaz Sharif but it is far from clear whether this trend will continue for ever. A sign of judicial independence was the Supreme Court's reaction to the legal aftermath of Pakistan's nuclear tests between 28 and 30 May 1998. After the tests President Rafiq Tarar declared a state of emergency and suspended all fundamental rights. This order was declared to be unconstitutional by the Supreme Court in a recent decision and the fundamental rights have been restored.[12] Nevertheless, public confidence in the Supreme Court has been shaken and it will take time for the Court to restore its image as an impartial and independent institution.

5 OTHER DEVELOPMENTS

5.1 Blasphemy law

The suicide of the Bishop of Faisalabad on 6 May 1998 in protest against the death sentence imposed on a young Christian man has highlighted the seriousness of the continued persecution of Pakistan's religious minorities under the blasphemy laws.[13] Bishop Dr John Joseph shot himself in front of the courthouse of Judge Abdul Khan, the sessions judge who had sentenced Ayub Masih to death under section 295-C of the Pakistan Penal Code, 1860. Section 295-C makes it a criminal offence to blaspheme Islam punishable by life imprisonment or death penalty. The Federal Shariat Court decided in 1990 that only the death penalty would be appropriate for blasphemy and since then anybody convicted for blasphemy faces the death penalty. So far, nobody has actually been executed under this law but as of January 1996 658 cases were pending against 2,467 individuals.[14] Bishop Dr John Joseph had been campaigning against the blasphemy laws for a long time declaring during a procession on the day of his suicide that "The Christians in Pakistan are being held in a "death sentence" blackmail by the blasphemy law, under which their small businesses are being taken over, their property is being seized, and the situation is such that their women are not safe."[15] However, the government through Religious Affairs Minister Raja Zafarul Haq has ruled out any changes to the blasphemy laws. The fate of Ayub Masih is uncertain: he was sentenced to death on 27 April 1998 and his sentence has been suspended by the Multan bench of the Lahore High Court pending an appeal.

5.2 Anti-corruption

Nawaz Sharif's promise to eradicate corruption has found a visible expression in the passing of the Ehtesab Act, 1997. The Act was passed for "the eradication of cor-

---

[12] The decision has not as yet been reported.
[13] For an accessible account see Maggie O'Kane, "Two faiths, one bullet", *The Guardian Weekend*, 27 June 1998, pp. 37–41.
[14] See Amit Baruah, "An extreme step", *Frontline*, 5 June 1998.
[15] *Ibid.*

ruption and corrupt practices from the public offices and to provide for effective measures for prosecution and speedy disposal of cases involving corruption and corrupt practices . . .". The Act establishes an Ehtesab Cell to investigate corruption. The definition of corruption is wide and includes a presumption of corruption in cases where the accused possess property or pecuniary resources disproportionate to the accused's known sources of income which he cannot reasonably account for. As soon as the presumption of corruption has been established the burden of proof to show that the monies or properties were obtained through corruption shifts to the accused. The Court has stringent powers of enforcement including the freezing of assets. It is no secret that the Ehtesab Act 1997 also provides a powerful weapon against any re-election of Benazir Bhutto: section 9 of the Act provides that "where a holder of a public office is convicted for an offence of corruption or corrupt practices and sentenced to a term of imprisonment of no less than two years, he shall stand disqualified from being elected or chosen as and from being a member of the *Majlies-e-Shoora* (Parliament), or the Provincial Assembly, as the case may be, for a period of five years reckoned from the date when he is released." Benazir Bhutto was charged under the Ehtesab Act, 1997 earlier this year.

5.3 Legislation

Nawaz Sharif's government has utilized its solid majority to pass several legislative measures which had been under a consideration for some time. A new Environmental Protection Act, 1998 was passed as was a Consumer Protection Act, 1997. However, the latter is for the same being confined in its application to the Islamabad Capital Territory. An interesting piece of social reform legislation is the Marriages (Prohibition of Wasteful) Expenses Act, 1997. The Act seeks to restrict the practice of lavish wedding receptions which often stretch over several days and involve vast expenditure. Section 3 of the Act prohibits the decoration of the wedding venue with lights or illumination and the exploding of fire crackers including the firing of fire-arms whereas section 4 makes it a criminal offence to serve any edibles to the guests of wedding receptions held at a restaurant, club or other public space with the exception of hot and cold soft drinks. Ehtesab Committees are supposed to be constituted for each administrative sub-division to implement the Act.

Another remarkable step is the passing of the Criminal Law (Amendment) Act, 1997. The Act amends the Pakistan Penal Code (PPC) by introducing the Islamic concepts of *qisas* and *diyat* into Pakistan's criminal law. The gestation period of the Act has been very long and commenced as soon as courts were given the power to examine and strike down certain laws which were judged not to be in accordance with the injunctions of Islam.[16] The first case challenging the validity of certain parts of the Pakistan Penal Code came before a Shariat court in 1979, when Gul Hassan, convicted and sentenced to death for murder under section 302 PPC, filed a Shariat Petition seeking a declaration that the provisions of section 302 PPC, certain sections of the Criminal Procedure Code with regard to section 302 PPC and

---

[16] See Martin Lau, "The legal mechanism of Islamization: the new Islamic criminal law of Pakistan", *Journal of Law and Society*, 18, 1992, pp. 43–58.

the laws relating to mercy were repugnant to the injunctions of Islam.[17] The Shariat Bench of the Peshawar High Court declared after having looked extensively at the Quranic provisions relating to *qisas* and *diyat* that

1. The penalties prescribed in the chapter XVI of the Pakistan Penal Court with respect to offenses against the human body particularly section 302 are in not accordance with the injunctions of Islam inasmuch such offenses can be condoned by pardon or on payment of *Diyat* and particularly a non-pubert can not be subjected to *Qisas*.
2. Neither a Provincial Government nor the Federal Government can remit, reduce or commute any sentence – such powers can only be exercised by a Court in accordance with the injunctions of Islam.
3. There is not going to be any violation of the Injunctions of Islam if law provides *Tazir* (e.g. Imprisonment or death) in case of a recidivist including the one accused of theft or of a murder other than accidental even if there is pardon by the heirs of the dceased or payment of blood money.[18]

The case was taken up again by the newly constituted Federal Shariat Court in its first judgment. The court agreed with the Shariat Bench of the Peshawar High Court and held that section 302 PPC was repugnant to the injunctions of Islam since[19] "No exemption of death sentence has been provided for an offender who is insane at the time of the execution; and b. a parent killing his/her son." Section 304 and 304A were held to repugnant because they do not provide for compensation and payment of *diyat*. All sections relating to hurt in the Pakistan Penal Code were struck down as well since they were not compoundable nor did they make provision for the payment of *diyat*.

The provisions of the Pakistan Penal Code 1860 relating to murder and personal injury were challenged in ten more petitions to the Federal Shariat Court. The government of Pakistan, however, filed appeals against the decision and it was only in 1989 that the original Shariat Appeal No. 1 of 1980 was heard by the Shariat Bench of the Supreme Court.[20] The Shariat Bench declared that provisions of sections 299 to 338 PPC which deal with offences against the human body and several other provisions relating to murder and injury were repugnant to Islam. The judgment was to take effect on 23 March 1990, but the government of Pakistan managed in a further review petition to get an extension of this deadline which was now to be 5 September 1990.[21] The government stated in its petition that it had drafted an ordinance relating to *qisas* and *diyat* and was in the process of "final scrutiny". The Supreme Court accepted the application but stated that "even if the required law was not enacted and/or enforced by 12 Rabi-ul-Awwal 1411 AH, the said provisions would nevertheless ceased to have effect on 12 of Rabi-ul-Awwal 1411 AH". It held that "in such stage of vacuum, *vis-à-vis* the statute law on the subject, the common Islamic law the Injunctions of Islam as contained in the Quran and Sunnah relating to the offence of Qatl and Jurh (hurt) shall be deemed to be the law on the subject." The court was well aware that an Ordinance would lapse

[17] Gul Hassan Khan PLD 1980 PLD 1
[18] *Ibid.*, p. 20.
[19] PLD 1981 FSC 1
[20] *Federation of Pakistan v. Gul Hasan Khan* PLD 1989 SC 633.
[21] *Federation of Pakistan v. N.-W.F.P.Government* PLD 1990 SC 1172

after four months if it had not met the approval of Parliament and explained that the court may decide murder and hurt cases on the basis of such an Ordinance "if it, having once been enforced had lapsed or otherwise had become unenforceable".[22]

Ever since the Ordinance had been re-promulgated every four month in identical form so as to comply with the judgment of the Federal Shariat Court. However, successive governments had considered it imprudent to attempt to pass an Act to replace the Ordinance. Nawaz Sharif has finally committed the law relating to *qisas* and *diyat* to the statute book. It remains to be seen whether these laws will now become better known – in spite of strenuous efforts by the Lahore High Court to promote knowledge of the *qisas* and *diyat* laws there is virtually no mention of it in any of the reported case law.

5.4 The Fifteenth Constitutional Amendment Bill

The grave economic crisis of Pakistan, which was aggravated by the country's complete isolation from the Western donor community following the nuclear tests of May 1998 has put enormous pressure on the government of Nawaz Sharif. The Fifteenth Constitutional Amendment Bill can be regarded as the government's policy to cope with this pressure: the bill introduces a new Article 2 B into the Constitution of Pakistan, which not only elevates the *shari'a* to the highest law of the land but also facilitates the amendment of the Constitution so as to bring it into line with the injunctions of Islam. The Bill, if enacted, would allow Parliament to amend the constitution by simple majority in order to "provide for the removal of any impediment in the enforcement of any matter relating to *shari'a* and the implementation of the Injunctions of Islam".[23] Nawaz Sharif when introducing the bill to the National Assembly on 28 August 1998 stated that

Through this constitutional amendment, we have begun to build a society where there is rule of law, where there is an atmosphere of brotherhood and love; where police and courts are always willing and ready to help the poor and helpless people; where the rich and poor are equal; where all people receive honour in an equitable manner; where the oppressed become powerful because the power of the law is with them; where the oppressor remains weak because the long arm of the law has risen against him; where every person's right to national resources and wealth is acknowledged; and where corruption, bribery and maladministration are eliminated.[24]

An analysis of the fate and effects of the bill, provided it is enacted, have to be reserved for next year's survey. However, it should be mentioned that the Bill received a rather critical reception by the Pakistani English language press. [25]

---

[22] *Federation of Pakistan* PLD 1990 SC 1172 [Shariat Appellate Bench], at p. 1173.
[23] See Section 3 of the Constitution (Fifteenth Amendment) Bill, 1998.
[24] See "Premier's speech announces plan to create Islamic state", SWB, Part 3, FE/3319 A/5.
[25] The Indian press has expressed grave concerns about a rise of Islamic fundamentalism in Pakistan, see Zahid Hussain, "Holy mess", *India Today International*, 14 September 1998.

6 CONCLUSION

The year under review can only be described as the *annus horribilis* of Pakistan's Supreme Court. The only redeeming feature and the only saving grace of the crisis is that a complete constitutional breakdown has been avoided. Further hope can be derived from the fact that the Supreme Court was able to return to normality after the turmoil of November and December 1997. Nevertheless, a bitter taste remains after the open division of the country's apex court, the barely hidden politicization of judges and the successful "judicial *coup d'état*" which led to the restraining of the Chief Justice. Judicial independence will come under further pressure if the Constitution (Fifteenth Amendment) Bill, 1998 becomes law. The government will be able to remove or change constitutional provisions more easily thereby making it more difficult for the Supreme Court to declare any action of the government to be *ultra vires*.

The country's return to Islamization as a way to muster popular support in a time of economic crisis has been attempted before. Experience has shown that there is no guarantee of success. However, inevitably the measure introduced during these waves of rapid and thoughtless Islamization, notably the ones introduced by Zulfiqar Bhutto and Zia-ul Haq, have never been removed from the country's legal system. The prime witnesses to this fact are the members of Pakistan religious minorities who tend to end up as the real victims of these measures. So much is therefore certain: the legal position of Pakistan's religious minorities is unlikely to improve in the foreseeable future.

Turkey

Sibel Inceoglu *

Several legislative and constitutional developments took place in 1996 and 1997. In this survey, only important developments in five fields (constitutional law, international law, administrative law, criminal law and civil law) will be examined.

1 CONSTITUTIONAL LAW

1.1 Constitutional amendments

The 1982 Constitution has so far been amended three times. The first amendment took place on 17 May 1987. Four articles were changed; the most important of these was the change in the constitutional amendment procedure itself (Article 175). The second amendment dated 8 July 1993 repealed the state monopoly on radio and television broadcasting (Article 133). Finally, the amendments dated 23 July 1995 were the most extensive amendments ever realized in Turkey by civil authority. The most important amendments were:

(a) recognition of the right to establish trade unions (but not the right to strike or the right of concluding collective agreements) for civil servants (Article 53/3);
(b) the repeal of the ban on political activities of scholars and students in the institutions of higher education (Article 68/7);
(c) the repeal of the bans on political activities of associations (Article 33/4), trade unions (Article 52), foundations (Article 69/2), cooperatives (Article 171/2) and public professional organizations (Article 135/3) to allow political cooperations between political parties and such civil groups;
(d) the regularization of effective judicial control on the suspension from activity of associations and public professional organizations by administrative authority.

Before the 1995 amendments, the article regulating suspension from activity of associations (Article 33/6) had been as follows:

---

* Associate Professor at the Law Faculty of Marmara University, Istanbul.

Associations may be dissolved by the decision of the judge in cases prescribed by law. They may be suspended from activity by the competent authority designated by law pending a court decision in cases where delay endangers the indivisible integrity of the state with its territory and nation, national security or sovereignty, public order, the protection of the rights and freedoms of others, or the prevention of crime.

Today, the fourth paragraph of Article 33 of the Constitution states that:

Associations may be dissolved or suspended from activity by the decision of a judge in cases prescribed by law. In cases where delay endangers national security or public order and in cases where it is necessary to prevent the perpetration or the continuation of a crime or to arrest, an authority designated by law may be vested with power to suspend the association from activity. The decision of this authority shall be submitted for approval to the competent judge within twenty-four hours. Unless the judge declares a decision within forty-eight hours, this administrative decision shall be annulled automatically.

A similar amendment had also been made for public professional organizations (Article 135/7); in cases similar to those mentioned above, suspension from activity decisions given by administrative authority for public professional organizations shall be submitted for approval to the competent judge within twenty-four hours and controlled by him/her within forty-eight hours, otherwise the administrative decision shall be annulled automatically.

In 1997, the Turkish Grand National Assembly promulgated several statutes to be in conformity with the constitutional amendments. Thus, non-conformity between Constitution and statutes was ended.

The Article 1 of the Statute on Amendments Civil Servants Statute states that: "In accordance with provisions prescribed by constitution and law, civil servants may establish trade unions and may be the member of them."

Article 1 of the Statute on Amendment of Higher Education Statute's Article 59,[1] allowed the scholars and students in the institutions of higher education to become members of political parties. Article 1 states that:

Scholars in the institutions of higher education may be the members of the political parties; if they submit their status within a month to their institutions, scholars may undertake duties in the central organs and their research and counselling branches of political parties, unless they neglect their duties in the institutions of higher education. However, the scholars in this situation cannot be the member of Higher Education Council and Higher Education Control Council, rector, dean, director of a institute or academy and director of a department, and cannot be elected as an assistant to them.

Students in the institutions of higher education may be the members of the political parties.

Students and scholars who are the members of the political parties, cannot engage in political activities and propagate for the party in the institution of higher education.

---

[1] Statute No. 4278, dated 2 July 1997, OG (Official Gazette) No. 23040, dated 5 July 1997.

The Statute on Amendments of Some Articles of the Statutes Relating Public Professional Organizations[2] repealed the ban on political activities of the public professional organizations such as Chambers of Veterinarians and their Association (Article 1), Bars (Article 3), Bars' Association (Article 5), Chambers of Engineers and Architects and their Association (Article 6,7), Chambers of Physicians and their Association (Article 9), Chambers of Agriculture and their Association (Article 11,13), Chambers of Dentists and their Association (Article 14,15), Chambers of Chemists and their Association (Article 17), Chambers of Commerce, Chambers of Industry, Chambers of Naval Commerce and their Association (Article 19). The same statute regularized the effective judicial control on the suspension from activities of these organizations by administrative authority[3] as guaranteed by the amendment of the Constitution (Constitutional Article 135/7).

Article 2 of the Statute on Amendments of Trade Unions Statute[4] and Article 1 of the Statute on Amendments of Cooperatives Statute[5] repealed the ban on political activities of trade unions and cooperatives. The Statute on Amendments of Associations Statute[6] allowed the associations to engage in political activities (Article 6) and brought effective judicial control on the decisions of suspension from activity given by administrative authority (Article 3), as guaranteed by the amendment of Constitution (Constitutional Article 33(6)). Promulgation of these two statutes was a significant change realized in Turkey. Although amendments to the Associations Statutes and Trade Unions Statute are similar to the amendments realized for public professional organizations, their functions are extremely important.

In the Turkish legal system, there are many statutes which are immune from constitutional challenge. According to paragraph 3 of the Provisional Article 15 of the Constitution: "No allegation of unconstitutionality shall be made in respect of decisions or measures taken under laws or decrees having force of law enacted during this period or under Act No. 2324 of the Constitutional Order." The period mentioned in the above paragraph began from the date of the *coup d'etat* on 12 September 1980 and ended with the formation of the Turkish Grand National Assembly on 6 December 1983.[7]

The Associations Statute was enacted on 6 September 1983, the Trade Unions Statute was enacted on 5 May 1983; therefore, they are statutes which are immune from constitutional challenge, in other words it is impossible to bring the provisions of these statutes, which are unconstitutional, before the Constitutional Court in order to invalidate them. As a matter of fact, before the amendments on these statutes, just after the constitutional amendments, Giresun Criminal Court, referred the Article 5/11 of the Associations Statute, which forbade the political activity of associations, to the Constitutional Court. The Constitutional Court dismissed the case, because of the provisional Article 15/3 of the Constitution.[8] Therefore, in spite

---

[2] Statute No. 4276, dated 18 June 1997, OG No: 23025, dated 20 June 1997.
[3] Statute No. 4276, Articles 2, 4, 8, 10, 12, 16, 18, 19, 21, 23, 27
[4] Statute No. 4277, dated 26 June 1997, OG No. 23033, dated 28 June 1997.
[5] Statute No. 4274, dated 12 June 1997, OG No. 23022, dated 17 June 1997.
[6] Statute No. 4279, dated 3 July 1997, OG No. 23043, dated 8 July 1997.
[7] See Osman Dogru, in this *Yearbook*, vol. 2 (1995), p. 79.
[8] The Decision of Constitutional Court, E. 1996/6, K. 1996/6, 14 February 1996, OG No. 22695, dated 13 July 1996.

of constitutional amendments passed in 1995, associations and trade unions had
to wait for the statutory change to engage in political activities till 1997.

1.2 Constitutional Court decisions relating to political parties

In 1996 and 1997, two political parties – the Democracy and Variation Party and
the Revival Party – were dissolved by the Constitutional Court.

On 5 June 1995, Principal Public Prosecutor at the Court of Cassation applied
to the Constitutional Court for an order dissolving the Democracy and Variation
Party. He accused the party of having carried on activities likely to undermine the
territorial integrity of the state and the unity of the nation (Articles 2, 3, 14, 69 of
the Constitution and Article 78 of Political Parties Statute No. 2820), having pursued the aim to change the principle of unity of the State (Article 80 of Statute
No. 2820) and to create minorities (Article 81 of Statute No. 2820).

The Constitutional Court, having examined the programme and constitution
of the party, found no violation of Article 80 of the Statute No. 2820, but held
that the Democracy and Variation Party's constitution and programme contained
statements likely to undermine the territorial integrity of the state and to create
minorities. The Constitutional Court relied on some passages from the Party's programme, those passages states that:

The founders of Republic, neglected to create a political and administrative structure
which is in conformity with the ethnic reality and the structure which has multi culture
and language; they aimed to force the other ethnic groups to become Turk; these pressures
caused the rebellion of Kurts; ending the pressure policy, it is necessary to give their rights
and to constitute the political, administrative cultural structures on the basis of equality;
will be adopted the regulations which are necessary for the usage of the Kurdish language
freely in the social life and in official procedures.[9]

The Constitutional Court dissolved the Democracy and Variation Party. The Revival Party, unlike the Democracy and Variation Party, was dissolved for procedural
reasons. The Article 105 of the Political Party Statute states that any party which has
not participated in elections twice without interruption from the date of its establishment, shall be dissolved by the Constitutional Court. The Revival Party, after
its establishment date, did not participate in the elections, therefore it was dissolved by the Constitutional Court.

2 PUBLIC INTERNATIONAL LAW

Turkey ratified three protocols in 1997. The first is the Protocol No. 11 to the
Convention for the Protection of Human Rights and Fundamental Freedoms, Restructuring the Control Machinery Established thereby. The ratification of this Protocol adopted by Turkish Grand National Assembly by a statute approving the

---

[9] The Decision of the Constitutional Court, E. 1995/1, K. 1996/1, 19 March 1996, OG No.
    23149, dated 23 October 1997, p. 173.

ratification and this statute published in the Official Gazette on 22 May 1997[10] and it was ratified on 20 June 1997.[11]

The second and third Protocols which were ratified by Turkey are Protocol Nos. 1 and 2 to the European Convention for the Prevention of Torture and Inhuman or Degrading Treatment and Punishment. They were published in the Official Gazette on 23 June 1997.[12]

3 ADMINISTRATIVE LAW

The judgment of the Constitutional Court, dated 21 September 1995 and published on 27 December 1997 in the Official Gazette, is the most significant development which took place in the administrative law field.

The 1982 Constitution in Article 125/1 laid down the rule that "all acts and actions of the Administration shall be subject to judicial review". This rule guarantees the effective judicial control which is not only a matter of distribution of justice, but it is a matter of supremacy of law, constitutional government, legality of the Administration and sound protection of rights and freedoms of the people.

Therefore the Article 2 of the Administrative Courts Procedure Statute (No. 2577) had recognized the right to bring an action for annulment by a complainant whose "interests" had been infringed by an administrative act. Article 2 was amended on 10 June 1994; according to the new version of the article, the complainant whose "personal rights" were infringed by an administrative act could not bring an action for annulment. This amendment meant that a great part of the complainants whose interests were infringed but personal rights not, could not sue the administration.

Istanbul Fourth Administrative Court referred the case about the amendment on Article 2 of the Administrative Courts Statute, which limits the capacity to bring an action, to the Constitutional Court. The Constitutional Court decided that the amendment is against the Constitutional Article 125/1 (mentioned above) and Articles 2 and 5 which state that "The Republic of Turkey is a State governed by the rule of law." Therefore the Constitutional Court determined that the amendment is unconstitutional and invalidated it.[13]

When a law is invalidated by the Constitutional Court, it becomes ineffective as of the date of publication of the Court's decision in the Official Gazette, but if the Court deems it necessary, it may set some later date which cannot be more than one year from the date of publication of the original decision, as the effective date. In this case, as a matter of fact, the Constitutional Court, taking into consideration the legal gap and the negative effect to the public interest which the decision would cause, decided to give the time to the legislation and declared that the judgment would come into force three month later. However, the Turkish Grand National Assembly has not yet enacted a law which regulates the capacity to bring action against administrative acts. In order to fill the legal gap, the Turkish Council of State

---

[10] Statute No. 4255, dated 14 May 1997, OG No. 22996, dated 22 May 1997
[11] No. 97/9506, OG No. 23025, dated 20 June 1997.
[12] No. 97/9455, OG No. 23028, dated 23 June 1997.
[13] The Decision of Constitutional Court, E. 1995/27, K. 1995/47, 21 September 1995, OG No. 22607, dated 10 April 1996.

developed a jurisprudence which gives the possibility to bring an action for the person whose interests are infringed by an administrative act.[14]

4 CRIMINAL LAW

Adultery is a crime in Turkish criminal law. Two different forms of adultery were prescribed by the Criminal Code; the first one was adultery of by a woman (Article 440), the second one was adultery by the man (Article 441).

When a married woman engaged in a sexual relationship with a man other than her husband, this action formed the crime of adultery by a woman. However, the crime of adultery by a man was committed, when a married man lived with a woman other than his wife as a married couple in a residence. In other words, there was an inequality between man and woman. When a married woman engaged even only in one sexual relationship with another man, this action was a crime, but the same action was not a crime for a man. He committed a crime of adultery when he lived with another woman as a married couple in a residence.

Sabonözü Criminal Court applied to the Constitutional Court for a decision invalidating the Article 441 of the Criminal Code. The Constitutional Court took into consideration the principle of equality which is prescribed by the Article 10 of the Constitution. Article 10 states that "all individuals are equal without any discrimination before the law, irrespective of language, race, colour, sex, political opinion, philosophical belief, religion and sect, or any such considerations". The Court decided that Article 441 is against the principle of equality and invalidated it.[15]

The Constitutional Court, in order to give the time to the legislation, declared that the judgment would come into force one year later, the time given by the Court ended on 27 December 1997, but the new law has still not been enacted. Therefore, the result of the Constitutional Court judgment created a situation which is more unequal than the situation which existed before the judgment. Now, the crime of adultery for woman still exists, but the crime of adultery for man is invalidated; an application to the Constitutional Court for an judgment invalidating Article 440 of the Criminal Code will be a solution.

Another significant development in criminal law is the change of the detention periods in police custody. The Statute No. 4229 on Amendments of the Criminal Judgment Procedure Statute and the Statute on the State Security Courts' Establishment and Judgment Procedures changed the periods of detention in police custody.[16]

As a rule, a person who is detained shall be brought before a judge within twenty-four hours, excluding the time necessary to send the individual to the court nearest to the place of arrest, but if the investigation shall not end within this period (twenty four hours), the period can be extended up to seven days with the request of the Public Prosecutor and the decision of the judge (Article 128/2 of the Criminal Judg-

---

[14] The Decision of Council of State, E. 1995/4416, K. 1996/1911, 17 May 1996, Danistay Der., 1997, No. 92, pp. 451–459.
[15] The Decision of the Constitutional Court, E. 1996/15, K. 1996/34, 23 September 1996, OG No. 22860, dated 27 December 1996.
[16] Statute No. 4229, dated 6 March 1997, OG No. 22931, dated 12 March 1997.

ment Procedure Statute). The extended period was eight days; Statute No. 4229 shortened this period to seven days (Article 1).

The periods of detention in police custody are different when the person is detained because of a crime which is within the state Security Courts' ground of judgment, e.g. crimes against state security. As a rule, the person who is detained because of a crime against state security shall be brought before a judge within forty-eight hours, excluding the time necessary to send the individual to the court nearest to the place of arrest, but in the case of offences committed collectively this period could be extended up to fifteen days (Article 16 of the Statute on the State Security Courts' Establishment and Judgment Procedures). The Article 3 of the Statute No. 4229 shortened this extended period. According to Article 3, in the case of offences committed collectively, Public Prosecutor can give a written order to extend this period (forty-eight hours) up to four days and if the investigation shall not end within this period (four days), the period can be extended up to seven days with the request of the Public Prosecutor and the decision of the judge. This periods could be extended up to thirty days in during a state emergency, Article 3 of the Statute No. 4229 also shortened this period. The detention period can be extended up to ten days in during a state of emergency.

Article 3 accepted the right to meet any time his/her advocate for the person under arrest because of a crime against the state security. The person whose the detention period extended by the decision of a judge also has the same right.

5 CIVIL LAW

Article 153 of the Turkish Civil Code was amended on 22 May 1997. According to Article 153, a woman who was married had the surname of her husband. The Article 1 of the Statute No. 4248[17] amended this article; a woman who is married shall have the surname of her husband, but may also have her former surname before the surname of her husband with an application to the officer of marriage or to the Bureau of the Census later.

---

[17] Statute No. 4248, dated 14 May 1997, OG No. 22996, dated 22 May 1997.

Part III

Selected Documents and Legislation

Resolutions and International Agreements

United Nations–Iraq
Resolutions

Security Council
S/RES/1111 (1997)

RESOLUTION 1111 (1997)

ADOPTED BY THE SECURITY COUNCIL AT ITS 3786TH MEETING,
4 JUNE 1997

The Security Council,

Recalling its previous resolutions and in particular its resolution 986 (1995) of 14 April 1995,

Convinced of the need as a temporary measure to continue to provide for the humanitarian needs of the Iraqi people until the fulfilment by Iraq of the relevant Security Council resolutions, including notably resolution 687 (1991) of 3 April 1991, allows the Council to take further action with regard to the prohibitions referred to in resolution 661 (1990) of 6 August 1990, in accordance with the provisions of those resolutions,

Determined to avoid any further deterioration of the current humanitarian situation,

Convinced also of the need for equitable distribution of humanitarian relief to all segments of the Iraqi population throughout the country,

Welcoming the report submitted by the Secretary-General in accordance with paragraph 11 of resolution 986 (1995) (S/1997/419), as well as the report submitted in accordance with paragraph 12 of resolution 986 (1995) (S/1997/417) by the Committee established by resolution 661 (1990) of 6 August 1990,

Reaffirming the commitment of all Member States to the sovereignty and territorial integrity of Iraq,

Acting under Chapter VII of the Charter of the United Nations,

465

1.   *Decides that* the provisions of resolution 986 (1995), except those contained in paragraphs 4, 11 and 12, shall remain in force for another period of 180 days beginning at 00.01 hours, Eastern Daylight Time, on 8 June 1997;

2.   *Further decides* to conduct a thorough review of all aspects of the implementation of this resolution 90 days after the entry into force of paragraph 1 above and again prior to the end of the 180 day period, on receipt of the reports referred to in paragraphs 3 and 4 below, and expresses its intention, prior to the end of the 180 day period, to consider favourably renewal of the provisions of this resolution, provided that the reports referred to in paragraphs 3 and 4 below indicate that those provisions are being satisfactorily implemented;

3.   *Requests* the Secretary-General to report to the Council 90 days after the date of entry into force of paragraph 1 above, and again prior to the end of the 180 day period, on the basis of observation by United Nations personnel in Iraq, and on the basis of consultations with the Government of Iraq, on whether Iraq has ensured the equitable distribution of medicine, health supplies, foodstuffs, and materials and supplies for essential civilian needs, financed in accordance with paragraph 8 (a) of resolution 986 (1995), including in his reports any observations he may have on the adequacy of the revenues to meet Iraq's humanitarian needs, and on Iraq's capacity to export sufficient quantities of petroleum and petroleum products to produce the sum referred to in paragraph 1 of resolution 986 (1995);

4.   *Requests* the Committee established by resolution 661 (1990), in close coordination with the Secretary-General, to report to the Council 90 days after the date of entry into force of paragraph 1 above and again prior to the end of the 180 day period on the implementation of the arrangements in paragraphs 1, 2, 6, 8, 9 and 10 of resolution 986 (1995);

5.   *Directs* the Committee established by resolution 661 (1990) of 6 August 1990 to process expeditiously contract applications submitted under the present resolution as soon as the Secretary-General has approved the new Plan submitted by the Government of Iraq, guaranteeing equitable distribution and including a description of the goods to be purchased with the revenues of the sale of petroleum and petroleum products authorized by the present resolution;

6.   *Decides* to remain seized of the matter.

Security Council
S/RES/1115 (1997)

RESOLUTION 1115 (1997)

ADOPTED BY THE SECURITY COUNCIL AT ITS 3792ND MEETING,
21 JUNE 1997

The Security Council,
   Recalling all its previous relevant resolutions, and in particular its resolutions 687 (1991) of 3 April 1991, 707 (1991) of 15 August 1991, 715 (1991) of 11 October 1991 and 1060 (1996) of 12 June 1996,

Recalling also the letter from the Executive Chairman of the Special Commission to the President of the Security Council of 12 June 1997 (S/1997/474), which reported to the Council the incidents on 10 and 12 June 1997 when access by a Special Commission inspection team to sites in Iraq designated for inspection by the Commission was excluded by the Iraqi authorities,

Determined to ensure full compliance by Iraq with its obligations under all previous resolutions, in particular resolutions 687 (1991), 707 (1991), 715 (1991) and 1060 (1996) to permit immediate, unconditional and unrestricted access to the Special Commission to any site which the Commission wishes to inspect,

Stressing the unacceptability of any attempts by Iraq to deny access to any such site,

Reiterating the commitment of all Member States to the sovereignty, territorial integrity and political independence of Kuwait and Iraq,

Acting under Chapter VII of the Charter of the United Nations,

1. *Condemns* the repeated refusal of the Iraqi authorities to allow access to sites designated by the Special Commission, which constitutes a clear and flagrant violation of the provisions of Security Council resolutions 687 (1991), 707 (1991), 715 (1991) and 1060 (1996);

2. *Demands* that Iraq cooperate fully with the Special Commission in accordance with the relevant resolutions; and that the Government of Iraq allow the Special Commission inspection teams immediate, unconditional and unrestricted access to any and all areas, facilities, equipment, records and means of transportation which they wish to inspect in accordance with the mandate of the Special Commission;

3. *Demands* further that the Government of Iraq give immediate, unconditional and unrestricted access to officials and other persons under the authority of the Iraqi Government whom the Special Commission wishes to interview, so that the Special Commission may fully discharge its mandate;

4. *Requests* the Chairman of the Special Commission to include in his consolidated progress reports under resolution 1051 (1996) an annex evaluating Iraq's compliance with paragraphs 2 and 3 of this resolution;

5. *Decides* not to conduct the reviews provided for in paragraphs 21 and 28 of resolution 687 (1991) until after the next consolidated progress report of the Special Commission, due on 11 October 1997, after which time those reviews will resume in accordance with resolution 687 (1991);

6. *Expresses* the firm intention, unless the Special Commission advises the Council in the report referred to in paragraphs 4 and 5 that Iraq is in substantial compliance with paragraphs 2 and 3 of this resolution, to impose additional measures on those categories of Iraqi officials responsible for the non-compliance;

7. *Reaffirms* its full support to the Special Commission in its efforts to ensure the implementation of its mandate under the relevant resolutions of the Council;

8. *Decides* to remain seized of the matter.

Security Council
S/RES/1129 (1997)

RESOLUTION 1129 (1997)

ADOPTED BY THE SECURITY COUNCIL AT ITS 3817TH MEETING,
12 SEPTEMBER 1997

The Security Council,

Recalling its previous resolutions and, in particular, its resolutions 986 (1995) of 14 April 1995 and 1111 (1997) of 4 June 1997,

Reaffirming that the implementation period of resolution 1111 (1997) began at 00.01, Eastern Daylight Time, on 8 June 1997, and that the export of petroleum and petroleum products by Iraq pursuant to resolution 1111 (1997) did not require the approval by the Secretary-General of the distribution plan mentioned in paragraph 8 (a) (ii) of resolution 986 (1995),

Taking note of the decision by the Government of Iraq not to export petroleum and petroleum products permitted pursuant to resolution 1111 (1997) during the period 8 June to 13 August 1997,

Deeply concerned about the resulting humanitarian consequences for the Iraqi people, since the shortfall in the revenue from the sale of petroleum and petroleum products will delay the provision of humanitarian relief and create hardship for the Iraqi people,

Noting that, as set out in the report of the Committee established by resolution 661 (1990) (S/1997/692), Iraq will not be able to export petroleum and petroleum products worth two billion United States dollars by the end of the period set by resolution 1111 (1997) while complying with the requirement not to produce a sum exceeding one billion United States dollars every 90 days set out in paragraph 1 of resolution 986 (1995) and renewed in resolution 1111 (1997),

Acknowledging the situation with regard to the delivery of humanitarian goods to Iraq as described in the report of the Secretary General (S/1997/685) and encouraging the continuing efforts to improve this situation,

Stressing the importance of an equitable distribution of humanitarian goods as called for by paragraph 8 (a) (ii) of resolution 986 (1995),

Determined to avoid any further deterioration of the current humanitarian situation,

Reaffirming the commitment of all Member States to the sovereignty and territorial integrity of Iraq,

Acting under Chapter VII of the Charter of the United Nations,

1. Decides that the provisions of resolution 1111 (1997) shall remain in force, except that States are authorized to permit the import of petroleum and petroleum products originating in Iraq, including financial and other essential transactions directly relating thereto, sufficient to produce a sum not exceeding a total of one billion United States dollars within a period of 120 days from 00.01, Eastern Daylight Time, on 8 June 1997 and, thereafter, a sum not exceeding a total of one billion United States dollars within a period of 60 days from 00.01, Eastern Daylight Time, on 4 October 1997;

2. Decides further that the provisions of paragraph 1 above shall apply only to the period of implementation of resolution 1111 (1997), and expresses its firm intention that under any future resolutions authorizing States to permit the import of petroleum and petroleum products originating in Iraq, the time limits within which imports may be permitted established in such resolutions shall be strictly enforced;

3.   Expresses its full support for the intention of the Secretary General, stated in his report to the Security Council (S/1997/685), to follow up his observations concerning the needs of vulnerable groups in Iraq by monitoring the actions of the Government of Iraq in respect of these groups;

4.   Stresses that contracts for the purchase of humanitarian supplies submitted in accordance with resolution 1111 (1997) must be limited to items which appear on the list of supplies annexed to the second distribution plan prepared by the Government of Iraq and approved by the Secretary General pursuant to paragraph 8 (a) (ii) of resolution 986 (1995), or appropriate amendments to the plan must be requested prior to purchasing items not on the annexed list;

5.   Decides to remain seized of the matter.

Security Council
S/RES/1134 (1997)

RESOLUTION 1134 (1997)

ADOPTED BY THE SECURITY COUNCIL AT ITS 3826TH MEETING,
23 OCTOBER 1997

The Security Council,

Recalling all its previous relevant resolutions, and in particular its resolutions 687 (1991) of 3 April 1991, 707 (1991) of 15 August 1991, 715 (1991) of 11 October 1991, 1060 (1996) of 12 June 1996, and 1115 (1997) of 21 June 1997,

Having considered the report of the Executive Chairman of the Special Commission dated 6 October 1997 (S/1997/774),

Expressing grave concern at the report of additional incidents since the adoption of resolution 1115 (1997) in which access by the Special Commission inspection teams to sites in Iraq designated for inspection by the Commission was again denied by the Iraqi authorities,

Stressing the unacceptability of any attempts by Iraq to deny access to such sites,

Taking note of the progress nevertheless achieved by the Special Commission, as set out in the report of the Executive Chairman, towards the elimination of Iraq's programme of weapons of mass destruction,

Reaffirming its determination to ensure full compliance by Iraq with all its obligations under all previous relevant resolutions and reiterating its demand that Iraq allow immediate, unconditional and unrestricted access to the Special Commission to any site which the Commission wishes to inspect, and in particular allow the Special Commission and its inspection teams to conduct both fixed wing and helicopter flights throughout Iraq for all relevant purposes including inspection, surveillance, aerial surveys, transportation and logistics without interference of any kind and upon such terms and conditions as may be determined by the Special Commission, and to make use of their own aircraft and such airfields in Iraq as they may determine are most appropriate for the work of the Commission,

Recalling that resolution 1115 (1997) expresses the Council's firm intention, unless the Special Commission has advised the Council that Iraq is in substantial compliance with paragraphs 2 and 3 of that resolution, to impose additional measures on those categories of Iraqi officials responsible for the non-compliance,

Reiterating the commitment of all Member States to the sovereignty, territorial integrity and political independence of Kuwait and Iraq,

Acting under Chapter VII of the Charter of the United Nations,

1. *Condemns* the repeated refusal of the Iraqi authorities, as detailed in the report of the Executive Chairman of the Special Commission, to allow access to sites designated by the Special Commission, and especially Iraqi actions endangering the safety of Special Commission personnel, the removal and destruction of documents of interest to the Special Commission and interference with the freedom of movement of Special Commission personnel;

2. *Decides* that such refusals to cooperate constitute a flagrant violation of Security Council resolutions 687 (1991), 707 (1991), 715 (1991) and 1060 (1996), and notes that the Special Commission in the report of the Executive Chairman was unable to advise that Iraq was in substantial compliance with paragraphs 2 and 3 of resolution 1115 (1997);

3. *Demands* that Iraq cooperate fully with the Special Commission in accordance with the relevant resolutions, which constitute the governing standard of Iraqi compliance;

4. *Demands in particular* that Iraq without delay allow the Special Commission inspection teams immediate, unconditional and unrestricted access to any and all areas, facilities, equipment, records and means of transportation which they wish to inspect in accordance with the mandate of the Special Commission, as well as to officials and other persons under the authority of the Iraqi Government whom the Special Commission wishes to interview so that the Special Commission may fully discharge its mandate;

5. *Requests* the Chairman of the Special Commission to include in all future consolidated progress reports prepared under resolution 1051 (1996) an annex evaluating Iraq's compliance with paragraphs 2 and 3 of resolution 1115 (1997);

6. *Expresses* the firm intention – if the Special Commission reports that Iraq is not in compliance with paragraphs 2 and 3 of resolution 1115 (1997) or if the Special Commission does not advise the Council in the report of the Executive Chairman due on 11 April 1998 that Iraq is in compliance with paragraphs 2 and 3 of resolution 1115 (1997) – to adopt measures which would oblige all States to prevent without delay the entry into or transit through their territories of all Iraqi officials and members of the Iraqi armed forces who are responsible for or participate in instances of non-compliance with paragraphs 2 and 3 of resolution 1115 (1997), provided that the entry of a person into a particular State on a specified date may be authorized by the Committee established by resolution 661 (1990), and provided that nothing in this paragraph shall oblige a State to refuse entry into its own territory to its own nationals or persons carrying out bona fide diplomatic assignments or missions;

7. *Decides further,* on the basis of all incidents related to the implementation of paragraphs 2 and 3 of resolution 1115 (1997), to begin to designate, in consultation with the Special Commission, individuals whose entry or transit would be prevented upon implementation of the measures set out in paragraph 6 above;

8. *Decides* not to conduct the reviews provided for in paragraphs 21 and 28 of resolution 687 (1991) until after the next consolidated progress report of the Special Commission, due on 11 April 1998, after which those reviews will resume in accordance with resolution 687 (1991), beginning on 26 April 1998;

9.   *Reaffirms* its full support for the authority of the Special Commission under its Executive Chairman to ensure the implementation of its mandate under the relevant resolutions of the Council;

10.   *Decides* to remain seized of the matter.

Security Council
S/RES/1137 (1997)

RESOLUTION 1137 (1997)

ADOPTED BY THE SECURITY COUNCIL AT ITS 3831ST MEETING,
12 NOVEMBER 1997

The Security Council,
    Recalling all its previous relevant resolutions, and in particular its resolutions 687 (1991) of 3 April 1991, 707 (1991) of 15 August 1991, 715 (1991) of 11 October 1991, 1060 (1996) of 12 June 1996, 1115 (1997) of 21 June 1997, and 1134 (1997) of 23 October 1997,
    Taking note with grave concern of the letter of 29 October 1997 from the Deputy Prime Minister of Iraq to the President of the Security Council (S/1997/829) conveying the unacceptable decision of the Government of Iraq to seek to impose conditions on its cooperation with the Special Commission, of the letter of 2 November 1997 from the Permanent Representative of Iraq to the United Nations to the Executive Chairman of the Special Commission (S/1997/837, annex) which reiterated the unacceptable demand that the reconnaissance aircraft operating on behalf of the Special Commission be withdrawn from use and which implicitly threatened the safety of such aircraft, and of the letter of 6 November 1997 from the Minister of Foreign Affairs of Iraq to the President of the Security Council (S/1997/855) admitting that Iraq has moved dual-capable equipment which is subject to monitoring by the Special Commission,
    Also taking note with grave concern of the letters of 30 October 1997 (S/1997/830) and 2 November 1997 (S/1997/836) from the Executive Chairman of the Special Commission to the President of the Security Council advising that the Government of Iraq had denied entry to Iraq to two Special Commission officials on 30 October 1997 and 2 November 1997 on the grounds of their nationality, and of the letters of 3 November 1997 (S/1997/837), 4 November 1997 (S/1997/843), 5 November 1997 (S/1997/851) and 7 November 1997 (S/1997/864) from the Executive Chairman of the Special Commission to the President of the Security Council advising that the Government of Iraq had denied entry to sites designated for inspection by the Special Commission on 3, 4, 5, 6 and 7 November 1997 to Special Commission inspectors on the grounds of their nationality, and of the additional information in the Executive Chairman's letter of 5 November 1997 to the President of the Security Council (S/1997/851) that the Government of Iraq has moved significant pieces of dual-capable equipment subject to monitoring by the Special Commission, and that monitoring cameras appear to have been tampered with or covered,
    Welcoming the diplomatic initiatives, including that of the high-level mission of the Secretary General, which have taken place in an effort to ensure that Iraq complies unconditionally with its obligations under the relevant resolutions,

Deeply concerned at the report of the high-level mission of the Secretary General on the results of its meetings with the highest levels of the Government of Iraq,

Recalling that its resolution 1115 (1997) expressed its firm intention, unless the Special Commission advised the Council that Iraq is in substantial compliance with paragraphs 2 and 3 of that resolution, to impose additional measures on those categories of Iraqi officials responsible for the non-compliance,

Recalling also that its resolution 1134 (1997) reaffirmed its firm intention, if inter alia the Special Commission reports that Iraq is not in compliance with paragraphs 2 and 3 of resolution 1115 (1997), to adopt measures which would oblige States to refuse the entry into or transit through their territories of all Iraqi officials and members of the Iraqi armed forces who are responsible for or participate in instances of non-compliance with paragraphs 2 and 3 of resolution 1115 (1997),

Recalling further the Statement of its President of 29 October 1997 (S/PRST/1997/49) in which the Council condemned the decision of the Government of Iraq to try to dictate the terms of its compliance with its obligation to cooperate with the Special Commission, and warned of the serious consequences of Iraq's failure to comply immediately and fully and without conditions or restrictions with its obligations under the relevant resolutions,

Reiterating the commitment of all Member States to the sovereignty, territorial integrity and political independence of Kuwait and Iraq,

Determined to ensure immediate and full compliance without conditions or restrictions by Iraq with its obligations under the relevant resolutions,

Determining that this situation continues to constitute a threat to international peace and security,

Acting under Chapter VII of the Charter,

1. *Condemns* the continued violations by Iraq of its obligations under the relevant resolutions to cooperate fully and unconditionally with the Special Commission in the fulfilment of its mandate, including its unacceptable decision of 29 October 1997 to seek to impose conditions on cooperation with the Special Commission, its refusal on 30 October 1997 and 2 November 1997 to allow entry to Iraq to two Special Commission officials on the grounds of their nationality, its denial of entry on 3, 4, 5, 6 and 7 November 1997 to sites designated by the Special Commission for inspection to Special Commission inspectors on the grounds of their nationality, its implicit threat to the safety of the reconnaissance aircraft operating on behalf of the Special Commission, its removal of significant pieces of dual-use equipment from their previous sites, and its tampering with monitoring cameras of the Special Commission;

2. *Demands* that the Government of Iraq rescind immediately its decision of 29 October 1997;

3. *Demands also* that Iraq cooperate fully and immediately and without conditions or restrictions with the Special Commission in accordance with the relevant resolutions, which constitute the governing standard of Iraqi compliance;

4. *Decides,* in accordance with paragraph 6 of resolution 1134 (1997), that States shall without delay prevent the entry into or transit through their territories of all Iraqi officials and members of the Iraqi armed forces who were responsible for or participated in the instances of non-compliance detailed in paragraph 1 above, provided that the entry of a person into a particular State on a specified date may be authorized by the Committee established by resolution 661 (1990) of 6 August 1990, and provided that nothing in this paragraph shall oblige a State to refuse entry into its own territory to its own nationals, or to persons carrying out bona fide diplomatic assignments, or missions approved by the Committee established by resolution 661 (1990);

5.   *Decides also,* in accordance with paragraph 7 of resolution 1134 (1997), to designate in consultation with the Special Commission a list of individuals whose entry or transit will be prevented under the provisions of paragraph 4 above, and requests the Committee established by resolution 661 (1990) to develop guidelines and procedures as appropriate for the implementation of the measures set out in paragraph 4 above, and to transmit copies of these guidelines and procedures, as well as a list of the individuals designated, to all Member States;

6.   *Decides* that the provisions of paragraphs 4 and 5 above shall terminate one day after the Executive Chairman of the Special Commission reports to the Council that Iraq is allowing the Special Commission inspection teams immediate, unconditional and unrestricted access to any and all areas, facilities, equipment, records and means of transportation which they wish to inspect in accordance with the mandate of the Special Commission, as well as to officials and other persons under the authority of the Iraqi Government whom the Special Commission wishes to interview so that the Special Commission may fully discharge its mandate;

7.   *Decides* that the reviews provided for in paragraphs 21 and 28 of resolution 687 (1991) shall resume in April 1998 in accordance with paragraph 8 of resolution 1134 (1997), provided that the Government of Iraq shall have complied with paragraph 2 above;

8.   *Expresses* the firm intention to take further measures as may be required for the implementation of this resolution;

9.   *Reaffirms* the responsibility of the Government of Iraq under the relevant resolutions to ensure the safety and security of the personnel and equipment of the Special Commission and its inspection teams;

10. *Reaffirms also* its full support for the authority of the Special Commission under its Executive Chairman to ensure the implementation of its mandate under the relevant resolutions of the Council;

11. Decides to remain seized of the matter.

Security Council
S/RES/1143 (1997)

RESOLUTION 1143 (1997)

ADOPTED BY THE SECURITY COUNCIL AT ITS 3840TH MEETING,
4 DECEMBER 1997

The Security Council,

Recalling its previous resolutions and in particular its resolutions 986 (1995) of 14 April 1995, 1111 (1997) of 4 June 1997 and 1129 (1997) of 12 September 1997,

Convinced of the need as a temporary measure to continue to provide for the humanitarian needs of the Iraqi people until the fulfilment by Iraq of the relevant resolutions, including notably resolution 687 (1991) of 3 April 1991, allows the Council to take further action with regard to the prohibitions referred to in resolution 661 (1990) of 6 August 1990, in accordance with the provisions of those resolutions,

Convinced also of the need for equitable distribution of humanitarian relief to all segments of the Iraqi population throughout the country,

Welcoming the report submitted by the Secretary General in accordance with paragraph 3 of resolution 1111 (1997) (S/1997/935) and his intention to submit a supplementary report, as well as the report submitted in accordance with paragraph 4 of resolution 1111 (1997) by the Committee established by resolution 661 (1990) of 6 August 1990 (S/1997/942),

Noting with concern that, despite the ongoing implementation of resolutions 986 (1995) and 1111 (1997), the population of Iraq continues to face a serious nutritional and health situation,

Determined to avoid any further deterioration of the current humanitarian situation,

Noting with appreciation the recommendation of the Secretary General that the Council re-examine the adequacy of the revenues provided by resolution 986 (1995) and consider how best to meet the priority humanitarian requirements of the Iraqi people, including the possibility of increasing those revenues,

Noting also with appreciation the Secretary General's intention to include in his supplementary report recommendations on ways to improve the processing and supply of humanitarian goods under resolution 986 (1995),

Welcoming the efforts made by the Committee established by resolution 661 (1990) to refine and clarify its working procedures and encouraging the Committee to go further in that direction in order to expedite the approval process,

Reaffirming the commitment of all Member States to the sovereignty and territorial integrity of Iraq,

Acting under Chapter VII of the Charter of the United Nations,

1. *Decides* that the provisions of resolution 986 (1995), except those contained in paragraphs 4, 11 and 12, shall remain in force for another period of 180 days beginning at 00.01 hours, Eastern Standard Time, on 5 December 1997;

2. *Further* decides that the provisions of the distribution plan in respect of goods purchased in accordance with resolution 1111 (1997) shall continue to apply to foodstuffs, medicine and health supplies purchased in accordance with this resolution pending the Secretary General's approval of a new distribution plan, to be submitted by the Government of Iraq before 5 January 1998;

3. *Further* decides to conduct a thorough review of all aspects of the implementation of this resolution 90 days after the entry into force of paragraph 1 above and again prior to the end of the 180-day period, on receipt of the reports referred to in paragraphs 4 and 5 below, and expresses its intention, prior to the end of the 180-day period, to consider favourably renewal of the provisions of this resolution, provided that the reports referred to in paragraphs 4 and 5 below indicate that those provisions are being satisfactorily implemented;

4. *Requests* the Secretary General to report to the Council 90 days after the date of entry into force of paragraph 1 above, and again prior to the end of the 180-day period, on the basis of observation by United Nations personnel in Iraq, and on the basis of consultations with the Government of Iraq, on whether Iraq has ensured the equitable distribution of medicine, health supplies, foodstuffs, and materials and supplies for essential civilian needs, financed in accordance with paragraph 8 (a) of resolution 986 (1995), including in his reports any observations he may have on the adequacy of the revenues to meet Iraq's humanitarian needs, and on Iraq's capacity to export sufficient quantities of petroleum and petroleum products to produce the sum referred to in paragraph 1 of resolution 986 (1995);

5.   *Requests* the Committee established by resolution 661 (1990), in close coordination with the Secretary General, to report to the Council 90 days after the date of entry into force of paragraph 1 above and again prior to the end of the 180-day period on the implementation of the arrangements in paragraphs 1, 2, 6, 8, 9 and 10 of resolution 986 (1995);

6.   *Welcomes* the intention of the Secretary General to submit a supplementary report, and expresses its willingness, in the light of his recommendations, to find ways of improving the implementation of the humanitarian programme and to take such action over additional resources as needed to meet priority humanitarian requirements of the Iraqi people, as well as to consider an extension of the time-frame for the implementation of this resolution;

7.   *Requests* the Secretary General to submit his supplementary report to the Council no later than 30 January 1998;

8.   *Stresses* the need to ensure respect for the security and safety of all persons appointed by the Secretary General for the implementation of this resolution in Iraq;

9.   *Requests* the Committee established by resolution 661 (1990) to continue, in close coordination with the Secretary General, to refine and clarify working procedures in order to expedite the approval process and to report to the Council no later than 30 January 1998;

10. *Decides* to remain seized of the matter.

Security Council
S/RES/1153 (1998)

RESOLUTION 1153 (1998)

ADOPTED BY THE SECURITY COUNCIL AT ITS 3855TH MEETING,
20 FEBRUARY 1998

The Security Council,
   Recalling its previous relevant resolutions and in particular its resolutions 986 (1995) of 14 April 1995, 1111 (1997) of 4 June 1997, 1129 (1997) of 12 September 1997 and 1143 (1997) of 4 December 1997,
   Convinced of the need as a temporary measure to continue to provide for the humanitarian needs of the Iraqi people until the fulfilment by Iraq of the relevant resolutions, including notably resolution 687 (1991) of 3 April 1991, allows the Council to take further action with regard to the prohibitions referred to in resolution 661 (1990) of 6 August 1990, in accordance with the provisions of those resolutions, and emphasizing the temporary nature of the distribution plan envisaged by this resolution,
   Convinced also of the need for equitable distribution of humanitarian supplies to all segments of the Iraqi population throughout the country,
   Welcoming the report submitted on 1 February 1998 by the Secretary General in accordance with paragraph 7 of resolution 1143 (1997) (S/1998/90) and his recommendations, as well as the report submitted on 30 January 1998 in accordance with paragraph 9 of resolution 1143 (1997) by the Committee established by resolution 661 (1990) of 6 August 1990 (S/1998/92),

Noting that the Government of Iraq did not cooperate fully in the preparation of the report of the Secretary General,

Noting with concern that, despite the ongoing implementation of resolutions 986 (1995), 1111 (1997) and 1143 (1997), the population of Iraq continues to face a very serious nutritional and health situation,

Determined to avoid any further deterioration of the current humanitarian situation,

Reaffirming the commitment of all Member States to the sovereignty and territorial integrity of Iraq,

Acting under Chapter VII of the Charter of the United Nations,

1. *Decides that* the provisions of resolution 986 (1995), except those contained in paragraphs 4, 11 and 12, shall remain in force for a new period of 180 days beginning at 00.01 hours, Eastern Standard Time, on the day after the President of the Council has informed the members of the Council that he has received the report of the Secretary General requested in paragraph 5 below, on which date the provisions of resolution 1143 (1997), if still in force, shall terminate, except as regards sums already produced pursuant to that resolution prior to that date;

2. *Decides further that* the authorization given to States by paragraph 1 of resolution 986 (1995) shall permit the import of petroleum and petroleum products originating in Iraq, including financial and other essential transactions directly relating thereto, sufficient to produce a sum, in the 180-day period referred to in paragraph 1 above, not exceeding a total of 5.256 billion United States dollars, of which the amounts recommended by the Secretary General for the food/nutrition and health sectors should be allocated on a priority basis, and of which between 682 million United States dollars and 788 million United States dollars shall be used for the purpose referred to in paragraph 8 (b) of resolution 986 (1995), except that if less than 5.256 billion United States dollars worth of petroleum or petroleum products is sold during the 180-day period, particular attention will be paid to meeting the urgent humanitarian needs in the food/nutrition and health sectors and the Secretary General may provide a proportionately smaller amount for the purpose referred to in paragraph 8 (b) of resolution 986 (1995);

3. *Directs* the Committee established by resolution 661 (1990) to authorize, on the basis of specific requests, reasonable expenses related to the Hajj pilgrimage, to be met by funds in the escrow account;

4. *Requests* the Secretary General to take the actions necessary to ensure the effective and efficient implementation of this resolution, and in particular to enhance the United Nations observation process in Iraq in such a way as to provide the required assurance to the Council of the equitable distribution of the goods produced in accordance with this resolution and that all supplies authorized for procurement, including dual-usage items and spare parts, are utilized for the purpose for which they have been authorized;

5. *Requests* the Secretary General to report to the Council when he has entered into any necessary arrangements or agreements, and approved a distribution plan, submitted by the Government of Iraq, which includes a description of the goods to be purchased and effectively guarantees their equitable distribution, in accordance with his recommendations that the plan should be ongoing and should reflect the relative priorities of humanitarian supplies as well as their interrelationships within the context

of projects or activities, required delivery dates, preferred points of entry, and targeted objectives to be achieved;

6. *Urges* all States, and in particular the Government of Iraq, to provide their full cooperation in the effective implementation of this resolution;

7. *Appeals* to all States to cooperate in the timely submission of applications and the expeditious issue of export licences, facilitating the transit of humanitarian supplies authorized by the Committee established by resolution 661 (1990), and taking all other appropriate measures within their competence in order to ensure that urgently required humanitarian supplies reach the Iraqi people as rapidly as possible;

8. *Stresses* the need to ensure respect for the security and safety of all persons directly involved in the implementation of this resolution in Iraq;

9. *Decides* to conduct an interim review of the implementation of this resolution 90 days after the entry into force of paragraph 1 above and a thorough review of all aspects of its implementation prior to the end of the 180-day period, on receipt of the reports referred to in paragraphs 10 and 14 below, and expresses its intention, prior to the end of the 180-day period, to consider favourably the renewal of the provisions of this resolution as appropriate, provided that the reports referred to in paragraphs 10 and 14 below indicate that those provisions are being satisfactorily implemented;

10. *Requests* the Secretary General to make an interim report to the Council 90 days after the entry into force of paragraph 1 above, and to make a full report prior to the end of the 180-day period, on the basis of observation by United Nations personnel in Iraq, and on the basis of consultations with the Government of Iraq, on whether Iraq has ensured the equitable distribution of medicine, health supplies, foodstuffs and materials and supplies for essential civilian needs, financed in accordance with paragraph 8 (a) of resolution 986 (1995), including in his reports any observations he may have on the adequacy of the revenues to meet Iraq's humanitarian needs, and on Iraq's capacity to export sufficient quantities of petroleum and petroleum products to produce the sum referred to in paragraph 2 above;

11. *Takes note* of the Secretary General's observation that the situation in the electricity sector is extremely grave, and of his intention to return to the Council with proposals for appropriate funding, requests him to submit urgently a report for this purpose prepared in consultation with the Government of Iraq to the Council, and further requests him to submit to the Council other studies, drawing upon United Nations agencies as appropriate and in consultation with the Government of Iraq, on essential humanitarian needs in Iraq including necessary improvements to infrastructure;

12. *Requests* the Secretary General to establish a group of experts to determine in consultation with the Government of Iraq whether Iraq is able to export petroleum or petroleum products sufficient to produce the total sum referred to in paragraph 2 above and to prepare an independent report on Iraqi production and transportation capacity and necessary monitoring, also requests him in the light of that report to make early and appropriate recommendations and expresses its readiness to take a decision, on the basis of these recommendations and the humanitarian objectives of this resolution, notwithstanding paragraph 3 of resolution 661 (1990), regarding authorization of the export of the necessary equipment to enable Iraq to increase the export of petroleum

or petroleum products and to give the appropriate directions to the Committee established by resolution 661 (1990);

13. *Requests* the Secretary General to report to the Council, if Iraq is unable to export petroleum or petroleum products sufficient to produce the total sum referred to in paragraph 2 above, and following consultations with relevant United Nations agencies and the Iraqi authorities, making recommendations for the expenditure of the sum expected to be available, consistent with the distribution plan referred to in paragraph 5 above;

14. *Requests* the Committee established by resolution 661 (1990), in coordination with the Secretary General, to report to the Council 90 days after the entry into force of paragraph 1 above and again prior to the end of the 180-day period on the implementation of the arrangements in paragraphs 1, 2, 6, 8, 9 and 10 of resolution 986 (1995);

15. *Requests further* the Committee established by resolution 661 (1990) to implement the measures and take action on the steps referred to in its report of 30 January 1998, with regard to the refining and clarifying of its working procedures, to consider the relevant observations and recommendations referred to in the report of the Secretary General of 1 February 1998 in particular with a view to reducing to the extent possible the delay between the export of petroleum and petroleum products from Iraq and the supply of goods to Iraq in accordance with this resolution, to report to the Council by 31 March 1998 and thereafter to continue to review its procedures whenever necessary;

16. *Decides* to remain seized of the matter.

Security Council
S/RES/1154 (1998)

RESOLUTION 1154 (1998)

ADOPTED BY THE SECURITY COUNCIL AT ITS 3858TH MEETING,
2 MARCH 1998

The Security Council,
  Recalling all its previous relevant resolutions, which constitute the governing standard of Iraqi compliance,
  Determined to ensure immediate and full compliance by Iraq without conditions or restrictions with its obligations under resolution 687 (1991) and the other relevant resolutions,
  Reaffirming the commitment of all Member States to the sovereignty, territorial integrity and political independence of Iraq, Kuwait and the neighbouring States,
  Acting under Chapter VII of the Charter of the United Nations,

1. *Commends* the initiative by the Secretary General to secure commitments from the Government of Iraq on compliance with its obligations under the relevant resolutions, and in this regard endorses the memorandum of understanding signed by the Deputy Prime Minister of Iraq and the Secretary General on 23 February 1998 (S/1998/166) and looks forward to its early and full implementation;

2.   *Requests* the Secretary General to report to the Council as soon as possible with regard to the finalization of procedures for Presidential sites in consultation with the Executive Chairman of the United Nations Special Commission and the Director General of the International Atomic Energy Agency (IAEA);

3.   *Stresses* that compliance by the Government of Iraq with its obligations, repeated again in the memorandum of understanding, to accord immediate, unconditional and unrestricted access to the Special Commission and the IAEA in conformity with the relevant resolutions is necessary for the implementation of resolution 687 (1991), but that any violation would have severest consequences for Iraq;

4.   *Reaffirms* its intention to act in accordance with the relevant provisions of resolution 687 (1991) on the duration of the prohibitions referred to in that resolution and notes that by its failure so far to comply with its relevant obligations Iraq has delayed the moment when the Council can do so;

5.   *Decides,* in accordance with its responsibility under the Charter, to remain actively seized of the matter, in order to ensure implementation of this resolution, and to secure peace and security in the area.

Security Council
S/RES/1158 (1998)

RESOLUTION 1158 (1998)

ADOPTED BY THE SECURITY COUNCIL AT ITS 3865TH MEETING,
25 MARCH 1998

The Security Council,
   Recalling its previous resolutions and, in particular, its resolutions 986 (1995) of 14 April 1995, 1111 (1997) of 4 June 1997, 1129 (1997) of 12 September 1997, 1143 (1997) of 4 December 1997 and 1153 (1998) of 20 February 1998,
   Welcoming the report submitted on 4 March 1998 (S/1998/194 and Corr.1) by the Secretary General in accordance with paragraph 4 of resolution 1143 (1997) and noting with appreciation, as mentioned in this report, the commitment expressed by the Iraqi Government to cooperate with the Secretary General in the implementation of resolution 1153 (1998),
   Concerned about the resulting humanitarian consequences for the Iraqi people of the shortfall in the revenue from the sale of petroleum and petroleum products during the first 90-day period of implementation of resolution 1143 (1997), due to the delayed resumption in the sale of petroleum by Iraq and a serious price drop since the adoption of resolution 1143 (1997),
   Determined to avoid any further deterioration of the current humanitarian situation,
   Reaffirming the commitment of all Member States to the sovereignty and territorial integrity of Iraq,
   Acting under Chapter VII of the Charter of the United Nations,

   1. *Decides* that the provisions of resolution 1143 (1997) shall remain in force, subject to the provisions of resolution 1153 (1998), except that States are authorized to permit the import of petroleum and petroleum products originating in Iraq, including financial and other essential transactions directly relating thereto, sufficient to produce a sum not exceed-

ing a total of 1.4 billion United States dollars within the period of 90 days from 00.01, Eastern Standard Time, on 5 March 1998;

2. *Decides* to remain seized of the matter.

Security Council
S/RES/1175 (1998)

RESOLUTION 1175 (1998)

ADOPTED BY THE SECURITY COUNCIL AT ITS 3893RD MEETING,
19 JUNE 1998

The Security Council,

Recalling its previous relevant resolutions and in particular its resolutions 986 (1995) of 14 April 1995, 1111 (1997) of 4 June 1997, 1129 (1997) of 12 September 1997, 1143 (1997) of 4 December 1997, 1153 (1998) of 20 February 1998 and 1158 (1998) of 25 March 1998,

Welcoming the letter of the Secretary General of 15 April 1998 (S/1998/330) annexing the summary of the report of the group of experts established pursuant to paragraph 12 of resolution 1153 (1998) and noting the assessment that under existing circumstances Iraq is unable to export petroleum or petroleum products sufficient to produce the total sum of 5.256 billion United States dollars referred to in resolution 1153 (1998),

Welcoming the letter of the Secretary General of 29 May 1998 (S/1998/446) expressing his approval of the distribution plan submitted by the Government of Iraq,

Convinced of the need to continue the programme authorized by resolution 1153 (1998) as a temporary measure to provide for the humanitarian needs of the Iraqi people until fulfilment by the Government of Iraq of the relevant resolutions, including notably resolution 687 (1991) of 3 April 1991, allows the Council to take further action with regard to the prohibitions referred to in resolution 661 (1990) of 6 August 1990 in accordance with the provisions of those resolutions,

Reaffirming its endorsement, in paragraph 5 of resolution 1153 (1998), of the recommendations of the Secretary General in his report of 1 February 1998 (S/1998/90) concerning an improved, ongoing and project-based distribution plan,

Reaffirming also the commitment of all Member States to the sovereignty and territorial integrity of Iraq,

Acting under Chapter VII of the Charter of the United Nations,

1.   *Authorizes* States, subject to the provisions of paragraph 2 below, to permit, notwithstanding the provisions of paragraph 3 (c) of resolution 661 (1990), the export to Iraq of the necessary parts and equipment to enable Iraq to increase the export of petroleum and petroleum products, in quantities sufficient to produce the sum established in paragraph 2 of resolution 1153 (1998);

2.   *Requests* the Committee established by resolution 661 (1990), or a panel of experts appointed by that Committee for this purpose, to approve contracts for the parts and equipment referred to in paragraph 1 above according to lists of parts and equipment approved by that Committee for each individual project;

3. *Decides* that the funds in the escrow account produced pursuant to resolution 1153 (1998) up to a total of 300 million United States dollars may be used to meet any reasonable expenses, other than expenses payable in Iraq, which follow directly from contracts approved in accordance with paragraph 2 above;

4. *Decides also* that the expenses directly related to such exports may, until the necessary funds are paid into the escrow account, and following approval of each contract, be financed by letters of credit drawn against future oil sales, the proceeds of which are to be deposited in the escrow account;

5. *Notes that* the distribution plan approved by the Secretary General on 29 May 1998, or any new distribution plan agreed by the Government of Iraq and the Secretary General, will remain in effect, as required, for each subsequent periodic renewal of the temporary humanitarian arrangements for Iraq and that, for this purpose, the plan will be kept under constant review and amended as necessary through the agreement of the Secretary General and the Government of Iraq and in a manner consistent with resolution 1153 (1998);

6. *Expresses* its gratitude to the Secretary General for making available to the Committee established by resolution 661 (1990) a comprehensive review, with comments by the group of experts established pursuant to paragraph 12 of resolution 1153 (1998), of the list of parts and equipment presented by the Government of Iraq, and requests the Secretary General, in accordance with the intention expressed in his letter of 15 April 1998, to provide for the monitoring of the parts and equipment inside Iraq;

7. *Decides* to remain seized of the matter.

Security Council
S/RES/1194 (1998)

RESOLUTION 1194 (1998)

ADOPTED BY THE SECURITY COUNCIL AT ITS 3924TH MEETING,
9 SEPTEMBER 1998

The Security Council,

Recalling all its previous relevant resolutions, and in particular its resolutions 687 (1991) of 3 April 1991, 707 (1991) of 15 August 1991, 715 (1991) of 11 October 1991, 1060 (1996) of 12 June 1996, 1115 (1997) of 21 June 1997 and 1154 (1998) of 2 March 1998,

Noting the announcement by Iraq on 5 August 1998 that it had decided to suspend cooperation with the United Nations Special Commission and the International Atomic Energy Agency (IAEA) on all disarmament activities and restrict ongoing monitoring and verification activities at declared sites, and/ or actions implementing the above decision,

Stressing that the necessary conditions do not exist for the modification of the measures referred to in section F of resolution 687 (1991),

Recalling the letter from the Executive Chairman of the Special Commission to the President of the Security Council of 12 August 1998 (S/1998/767), which reported to the Council that Iraq had halted all disarmament activities of the Special Commission and placed limitations on the rights of the Commission to conduct its monitoring operations,

Recalling also the letter from the Director General of the IAEA to the President of the Security Council of 11 August 1998 (S/1998/766) which reported the refusal by Iraq to cooperate in any activity involving investigation of its clandestine nuclear programme and other restrictions of access placed by Iraq on the ongoing monitoring and verification programme of the IAEA,

Noting the letters of 18 August 1998 from the President of the Security Council to the Executive Chairman of the Special Commission and the Director General of the IAEA (S/1998/769, S/1998/768), which expressed the full support of the Security Council for those organizations in the implementation of the full range of their mandated activities, including inspections,

Recalling the Memorandum of Understanding signed by the Deputy Prime Minister of Iraq and the Secretary-General on 23 February 1998 (S/1998/166), in which Iraq reiterated its undertaking to cooperate fully with the Special Commission and the IAEA,

Noting that the announcement by Iraq of 5 August 1998 followed a period of increased cooperation and some tangible progress achieved since the signing of the Memorandum of Understanding,

Reiterating its intention to respond favourably to future progress made in the disarmament process and reaffirming its commitment to comprehensive implementation of its resolutions, in particular resolution 687 (1991),

Determined to ensure full compliance by Iraq with its obligations under all previous resolutions, in particular resolutions 687 (1991), 707 (1991), 715 (1991), 1060 (1996), 1115 (1997) and 1154 (1998), to permit immediate, unconditional and unrestricted access to the Special Commission and the IAEA to all sites which they wish to inspect, and to provide the Special Commission and the IAEA with all the cooperation necessary for them to fulfil their mandates under those resolutions,

Stressing the unacceptability of any attempts by Iraq to deny access to any sites or to refuse to provide the necessary cooperation,

Expressing its readiness to consider, in a comprehensive review, Iraq's compliance with its obligations under all relevant resolutions once Iraq has rescinded its above-mentioned decision and demonstrated that it is prepared to fulfil all its obligations, including, in particular on disarmament issues, by resuming full cooperation with the Special Commission and the IAEA consistent with the Memorandum of Understanding, as endorsed by the Council in resolution 1154 (1998), and to that end welcoming the proposal of the Secretary-General for such a comprehensive review and inviting the Secretary-General to provide his views in that regard,

Reiterating the commitment of all Member States to the sovereignty, territorial integrity and political independence of Kuwait and Iraq,

Acting under Chapter VII of the Charter of the United Nations,

1.   Condemns the decision by Iraq of 5 August 1998 to suspend cooperation with the Special Commission and the IAEA, which constitutes a totally unacceptable contravention of its obligations under resolutions 687 (1991), 707 (1991), 715 (1991), 1060 (1996), 1115 (1997) and 1154 (1998), and the Memorandum of Understanding signed by the Deputy Prime Minister of Iraq and the Secretary-General on 23 February 1998;

2.   Demands that Iraq rescind its above-mentioned decision and cooperate fully with the Special Commission and the IAEA in accordance with its obligations under the relevant resolutions and the Memorandum of Understanding as well as resume dialogue with the Special Commission and the IAEA immediately;

3. Decides not to conduct the review scheduled for October 1998 provided for in paragraphs 21 and 28 of resolution 687 (1991), and not to conduct any further such reviews until Iraq rescinds its above-mentioned decision of 5 August 1998 and the Special Commission and the IAEA report to the Council that they are satisfied that they have been able to exercise the full range of activities provided for in their mandates, including inspections;

4. Reaffirms its full support for the Special Commission and the IAEA in their efforts to ensure the implementation of their mandates under the relevant resolutions of the Council;

5. Reaffirms its full support for the Secretary-General in his efforts to urge Iraq to rescind its above-mentioned decision;

6. Reaffirms its intention to act in accordance with the relevant provisions of resolution 687 (1991) on the duration of the prohibitions referred to in that resolution and notes that by its failure so far to comply with its relevant obligations Iraq has delayed the moment when the Council can do so;

7. Decides to remain seized of the matter.

United Nations–Iraq
Memorandum of Understanding

Text of the agreement signed by Iraqi Deputy Prime Minister Tariq Aziz and UN Secretary General Kofi Annan

Memorandum of Understanding between the United Nations and the Republic of Iraq

1. The Government of Iraq reconfirms its acceptance of all relevant resolutions of the Security Council, including resolutions 687 (1991) and 715 (1991). The Government of Iraq further reiterates its undertaking to cooperate fully with the United Nations Special Commission (UNSCOM) and the International Atomic Energy Agency (IAEA).
2. The United Nations reiterates the commitment of all Member States to respect the sovereignty and territorial integrity of Iraq.
3. The Government of Iraq undertakes to accord to UNSCOM and IAEA immediate, unconditional and unrestricted access in conformity with the resolutions referred to in paragraph 1. In the performance of its mandate under the Security Council resolutions, UNSCOM undertakes to respect the legitimate concerns of Iraq relating to national security, sovereignty and dignity.
4. The United Nations and the Government of Iraq agree that the following special procedures shall apply to the initial and subsequent entries for the performance of the tasks mandated at the eight Presidential Sites in Iraq as defined in the annex to the present Memorandum:

    (a) A Special Group shall be established for this purpose by the Secretary General in consultation with the Executive Chairman of UNSCOM and the Director General of IAEA. This Group shall comprise senior diplomats appointed by the Secretary General and experts drawn from UNSCOM and IAEA. The Group shall be headed by a Commissioner appointed by the Secretary General.
    (b) In carrying out its work, the Special Group shall operate under the established procedures of UNSCOM and IAEA, and specific detailed procedures which will be developed given the special nature of the Presidential Sites, in accordance with the relevant resolutions of the Security Council.

(c) The report of the Special Group on its activities and finding shall be submitted by the Executive Chairman of UNSCOM to the Security Council through the Secretary General.

5. The United Nations and the Government of Iraq further agree that all other areas, facilities, equipment, records and means of transportation shall be subject to UNSCOM procedures hitherto established.

6. Noting the progress achieved by UNSCOM in various disarmament areas, and the need to intensify efforts in order to complete its mandate, the United Nations and the Government of Iraq agree to improve cooperation, and efficiency, effectiveness and transparency of work, so as to enable UNSCOM to report to the Council expeditiously under paragraph 22 of resolution 687 (1991). To achieve this goal, the Government of Iraq and UNSCOM will implement the recommendations directed at them as contained in the report of the emergency session of UNSCOM held on 21 November 1997.

7. The lifting of sanctions is obviously of paramount importance to the people and Government of Iraq and the Secretary General undertook to bring this matter to the full attention of the members of the Security Council.

Signed this 23rd day of February 1998 in Baghdad in two originals in English.

For the United Nations
Kofi A. Annan
Secretary General

For the Republic of Iraq
Tariq Aziz
Deputy Prime Minister

Annex to the Memorandum of Understanding between the United Nations and the Republic of Iraq of 23 February 1998

The eight Presidential Sites subject to the regime agreed upon in the present Memorandum of Understanding are the following:

1. The Republican Palace Presidential Site (Baghdad).
2. Radwaniyah Presidential Site (Baghdad).
3. Sijood Presidential Site (Baghdad).
4. Tikrit Presidential Site.
5. Tharthar Presidential Site.
6. Jabal Makhul Presidential Site.
7. Mosul Presidential Site.
8. Basrah Presidential Site.

The perimeter of the area of each site is recorded in the survey of the "Presidential sites" in Iraq implemented by the United Nations Technical Mission designated by the Secretary General, as attached to the letter dated 21 February 1998 addressed by the Secretary General to the Deputy Prime Minister of Iraq.

European Union–Jordan

Jordan's Association Agreement with the European Union: Comment

*Lu'ayy Minwer Al-Rimawi**

Before proceeding to discuss the Jordanian–EU Association Agreement, it is worth point-ing out that Jordan today enjoys stable macroeconomic conditions following its successful 1989 IMF adjustment programme. The Jordan dinar exchange rate has now stabilized with no major fluctuations recorded in recent years. A consistently tight fiscal policy (though ad-mittedly high interest rates) has resulted in reducing external indebtedness (and the burden of debt service) both in absolute and relative terms. A more efficient tax system is now in place. In addition, domestic public expenditure has been steadily decreasing as a result of lifting government subsidies on many formerly subsidized items. For its part, the Central Bank of Jordan's foreign currency reserves have been appreciating steadily at an assuring rate. Jordan also achieved a growth rate of 5.2 per cent in 1997.[1]

However, the European Union has so far signed Association Agreements with a number of Arab countries including Egypt, Tunisia and Morocco. Such partnerships between the EU and these Arab countries are expected to lead to the establishment of a free trade zone by the year 2010. The implementation of the Jordanian–EU Association Agreement is due to take place in 1999. Yet, from the previous experience of Morocco, it has been observed that such Association Agreements with the EU do not necessarily bring immediate substantive bene-fits to Arab countries. Morocco was able marginally to increase its quotas for exporting agri-cultural products to the EU, though the Association Agreement changed little for exporting local manufactured products to the EU, with which Morocco maintains two-thirds of its trade. Yet, despite this, some domestic sources in Morocco have remained sanguine, seeing the benefits in forcing Moroccan industrial firms to streamline their internal structure in order to remain competitive. This "paradoxical optimism" is supported by the observation that fol-lowing the Tunisian Association Agreement with the EU, 30 per cent of local firms had to

---

* LLB (Jordan University), LLM (Cambridge University), Msc (LSE). Part-time lecturer in public international law and researcher in financial regulation at the London School of Economics and Political Science, University of London.

[1] Though the IMF division of the Middle Eastern Department visiting Jordan to review its economic performance said in mid-February 1998 that Jordan had reacted "favourably" to controversial mar-ket reforms which were introduced ten years ago and that developments in the Jordanian economy were "very positive" and moving in the right direction.

undergo rigorous internal restructuring.[2] However, in respect to its Association Agreement with the EU, Morocoo has agreed that from the year 2000 it will be reducing its tariffs on manufactured goods by 10 per cent per year for ten years. In exchange for this, the EU has agreed to provide a subsidy totalling US$1.2 billion paid in five years.[3]

Jordan's Assocation Agreement with the EU has provoked similar fears in Jordan, mainly concerning refugee, agricultural, pharmaceutical and intellectual property matters.[4] These four contentious matters can be outlined as in the following brief account. The intellectual property complications have arisen from the EU's demands that Jordan should sign the Treaty of Intellectual Property Rights within five years of signing the partnership agreement. Most Jordanian commentators deem this period as "unrealistic", as it does not provide ample time to make the necessary legal, cultural and procedural adjustments.

The refugee dispute has resulted form the EU's desire to deport back from Europe into Jordan non-Jordanians who were first granted visas to enter Europe by European embassies in Amman but later refused entry.

While Jordan has requested the EU to allow it to expand the number of items in order to benefit its agricultrual sector, some EU members have rejected this, arguing that it would threaten their own agricultural interests. One bone of contention was over Jordan's quota to export tomato paste. Under the initial Association Agreement, Jordan can export up to 3,000 tonnes of tomato paste. However, Spain saw this as a threat to its own products and had initially vetoed Jordan's partnership agreementwith the EU as protest against the "large" size of Jordan's tomato paste quota. Spain had also demanded a revision of a clause in the treaty, which allowed Jordan and the EU to revise Jordanian export volumes. Spain's view was that such a revision clause could provide a precedent for other southern Mediterranean coutnries to demand higher quotas. However, this serious problem was resolved in the end. A trade off between Jordan and Spain took place. Jordan dropped this contentious clause as a *quid pro quo* for Spain's support for Jordan's request to an increase in the EU's financial contributions by US$60 million to a proposed EU financial fund.[5]

With regard to pharmaceutical products, it was domestically reported that withdrawing price preferential treatment granted to Jordanian companies would cause the local pharmaceutical industry to lose by a margin of 15 per cent. In addition, there have also been complications arising from matters relating to patent rights over the manufacturing process and end product.[6] Concerns have also been voiced pointing out that the three-year grace period is too short to prepare the local pharmaceutical industry to absorb these changes. This is especially significant given the fact that the local pharmaceutical industry is a leading export-oriented sector of the national economy, earning Jordan 10 per cent of its total exports or US$140 million in 1996.[7]

---

[2] However, it is also estimated that almost 30 per cent of Tunisian firms have failed due to their inability to compete with EU firms.

[3] See *Euromoney*, June 1996.

[4] For an intitial discussion on the early ramifications of the Jordanian–EU Association Agreement, see article by Lu'ayy Minwer Al-Rimawi, "Middle Eastern review: regulation in the Jordanian and Palestinian securities markets", in *European Financial Services Law*, 4, 1997, pp. 158–161. See also the author's articles, "Jordan's recent association with the EU and the latest reforms in Arab company and financial laws", in *European Business Law Review*, 9, 1998, pp. 30–37, and "Middle East: recent reforms in Arab company regulations and an outline of Jordan's recent Association Agreement with the European Union", *The Company Lawyer*, 9, 1998, pp. 89–91.

[5] The EU financial fund was proposed in line with the Middle East Stability Fund, which was announced earlier by the USA in 1997.

[6] The degree of protection of patents over pharmaceuticals demanded by the Jordanian–EU Association Agreement is akin to the WTO's standards applied in the Trade Related Aspects of Intellectual Property Rights.

[7] See the *Jordan Times*, 26 November 1997.

However, other Jordanian industries have also raised similar concerns. Many local industrialists and economists have contended that Jordanian industries will not be able to be strong enough to stand on their own within the twelve years grace period. Proponents of these views have even defended the continuation of Jordanian protectionist policies, pointing to the mushrooming technological gap between Egypt and Europe. While Egypt in the 1950s lagged by ten years, it is now fifty years behind Europe. Other disadvantages have been seen through the loss to the treasury of future tax and excise revenues on imported goods, especially as European subsidies are not expected to match such loss. In addition, defining "Jordanian products" for the purposes of EU tax exemptions has not been straightforward and has caused some anxieties among Jordanian industries.

However, in late January 1998, the European Commission Delegation in Amman stated that Jordan and the EU would sign the framework convention governing the implementation of financial and technical cooperation under the MEDA Programme. This Programme is the EU's main financial instrument for the implementation of the Euro–Mediterranean partnership, which was established in 1996 following the Barcelona conference of November 1995. The Programme also aims at encouraging more accelerated economic and structural reforms of the EU's Mediterranean partners in preparation for the creation of the world's largest free zone area by 2010. In the past two years, a total of 100 million ECUs (US$110 million) was provided for structural adjustment support, 7 million ECUs for the establishment of risk capital in support of small and medium-sized enterprises from the European Investment Bank. However, the European Commission and Jordan are currently working out a programme for financial and technical cooperation covering 1997–1999.[8]

In addition, Jordan has in the past few months signed an investment accord with the US which aims at allowing free access to investors from both countries. The accord is expected to stimulate the flow of private capital and "encourage recent Jordanian market-orientated domestic policies".[9] In addition, the accord grants both countries most favoured nation status. In recent months, Jordan has also undergone negotiations to join the WTO. However, Arab countries, which have already joined the WTO, are Kuwait, Qatar, Egypt, Morocco, Tunisia, the United Arab Emirates, Djibouti and Bahrain. Arab countries, which in recent months have been negotiating to join the WTO, include Algeria, Oman, Saudi Arabia and Sudan. Jordan is also currently examining the possibility of joining EFTA.[10]

---

[8] See the *Jordan Times*, 1 February 1998.

[9] As stated by the American ambassador in Jordan following the signing of the accord in Amman.

[10] In late February 1998, an EFTA delegation presented a tentative outline for a draft agreement to Jordan. However, a joint committee will be formed to examine all relevant matters and is expected to hold a meeting by the middle of 1998.

United States–Iraq

Resolutions

NOVEMBER 13, 1997: US HOUSE OF REPRESENTATIVES PASSES
RESOLUTION CALLING FOR AN INDICTMENT OF THE IRAQI
LEADERSHIP

Expressing the sense of the House of Representatives concerning the urgent need for an international criminal tribunal to try members of the Iraqi regime for crimes against humanity.

HCON 137 EH
105th CONGRESS 1st Session
H. CON. RES. 137

CONCURRENT RESOLUTION

Whereas the regime of Saddam Hussein has perpetrated a litany of human rights abuses against the citizens of Iraq and other peoples of the region, including summary and arbitrary executions, torture, cruel and inhumane treatment, arbitrary arrest and imprisonment, disappearances and the repression of freedom of speech, thought, expression, assembly and association;

Whereas Saddam Hussein and his associates have systematically attempted to destroy the Kurdish population in Iraq through the use of chemical weapons against civilian Kurds, the Anfal campaigns of 1987–1988 that resulted in the disappearance of more than 182,000 persons and the destruction of more than 4,000 villages, the placement of more than ten million landmines in Iraqi Kurdistan, and the continued ethnic cleansing of the city of Kirkuk;

Whereas the Iraqi Government, under Saddam Hussein's leadership, has repressed the Sunni tribes in western Iraq, destroyed Assyro-Chaldean churches and villages, deported and executed Turkomen, massacred Shi-ites, and destroyed the ancient Marsh Arab civilization through a massive act of genocide;

Whereas the status of more than six hundred Kuwaitis who were taken prisoner during the Gulf War remain unknown and the whereabouts of these persons are unaccounted for by the Iraqi Government, Kuwait continues to be plagued by unexploded landmines six years after the end of the Gulf War, and the destruction of Kuwait by departing Iraqi troops has yet to be redressed by the Iraqi Government;

Whereas the Republic of Iraq is a signatory to the Universal Declaration on Human Rights, the International Covenant on Civil and Political Rights, the Convention on the Prevention and Punishment of the Crime of Genocide and other human rights instruments, and the Geneva Convention on the Treatment of Prisoners of War of August 12, 1949, and is obligated to comply with these international agreements;

Whereas Saddam Hussein and his regime have created an environment of terror and fear within Iraq and throughout the region through a concerted policy of violations of international customary and conventional law; and

Whereas the Congress is deeply disturbed by the continuing gross violations of human rights by the Iraqi Government under the direction and control of Saddam Hussein: Now, therefore, be it Resolved by the House of Representatives (the Senate concurring),

That it is the sense of the House of Representatives that—

(1) the Congress—
(A)   deplores the Iraqi Government's pattern of gross violation of human rights which has resulted in a pervasive system of repression, sustained by the widespread use of terror and intimidation;
(B)   condemns the Iraqi Government's repeated use of force and weapons of mass destruction against its own citizens, as well as neighboring states;
(C)   denounces the refusal of the Iraqi Government to comply with international human rights instruments to which it is a party and cooperate with international monitoring bodies and compliance mechanisms, including accounting of missing Kuwaiti prisoners; and

(2)   the President and the Secretary of State should—
(A)   endorse the formation of an international criminal tribunal for the purpose of prosecuting Saddam Hussein and all other Iraqi officials who are responsible for crimes against humanity, including unlawful use of force, crimes against the peace, crimes committed in contravention of the Geneva Convention on POW's and the crime of genocide; and
(B)   work actively and urgently within the international community for the adoption of a United Nations Security Council resolution establishing an International Criminal Court for Iraq.

Passed the House of Representatives November 13, 1997.

26 February 1998: US SENATE

RESOLUTION 179 RELATING TO THE INDICTMENT AND PROSECUTION OF SADDAM HUSSEIN FOR WAR CRIMES AND OTHER CRIMES AGAINST HUMANITY

Mr. SPECTER submitted the following resolutions; which was referred to the Committee on Foreign Relations: S. Res. 179 Whereas, the International Military Tribunal at Nuremberg was convened to try individuals for crimes against international law during World War II;

Whereas, the Nuremberg tribunal provision which held that "crimes against international law are committed by men, not by abstract entities, and only by punishing individuals who commit such crimes can the provisions of international law be enforced" is as valid today as it was in 1946;

Whereas, on August 2, 1990 and without provocation, Iraq initiated a war of aggression against the sovereign state of Kuwait;

Whereas, the Charter of the United Nations imposes on its members the obligations to "refrain in their international relations from the threat or use of force against the territorial integrity or political independence of any state";

Whereas, the leaders of the Government of Iraq, a country which is a member of the United Nations, did violate this provision of the United Nations Charter;

Whereas, the Geneva Convention Relative to the Protection of Civilian Persons in Times of War (the Fourth Geneva Convention) imposes certain obligations upon a belligerent State, occupying another country by force of arms, in order to protect the civilian population of the occupied territory from some of the ravages of the conflict;

Whereas, both Iraq and Kuwait are parties to the Fourth Geneva Convention;

Whereas, the public testimony of witnesses and victims has indicated that Iraqi officials violated Article 27 of the Fourth Geneva Convention by their inhumane treatment and acts of violence against the Kuwaiti civilian population;

Whereas, the public testimony of witnesses and victims has indicated that Iraqi officials violated Articles 31 and 32 of the Fourth Geneva Convention by subjecting Kuwaiti civilians to physical coercion, suffering and extermination in order to obtain information;

Whereas, in violation of the Fourth Geneva Convention, from January 18, 1991 to February 25, 1991, Iraq did fire 39 missiles on Israel in 18 separate attacks with the intent of making it a party to war and with the intent of killing or injuring innocent civilians, killing two persons directly, killing 12 people indirectly (through heart attacks, improper use of gas masks, choking), and injuring more than 200 persons;

Whereas, Article 146 of the Fourth Geneva Convention states that persons committing "grave breaches" are to be apprehended and subjected to trial;

Whereas, on several occasions, the United Nations Security Council has found Iraq's treatment of Kuwaiti civilians to be in violation of international law;

Whereas, in Resolution 665, adopted on August 25, 1990, the United Nations Security Council deplored "the loss of innocent life stemming from the Iraq invasion of Kuwait";

Whereas, in Resolution 670, adopted by the United Nations Security Council on September 25, 1990, it condemned further "the treatment by Iraqi forces on Kuwait nationals and reaffirmed that the Fourth Geneva Convention applied to Kuwait";

Whereas, in Resolution 674, the United Nations Security Council demanded that Iraq cease mistreating and oppressing Kuwaiti nationals in violation of the Convention and reminded Iraq that it would be liable for any damage or injury suffered by Kuwaiti nationals due to Iraq's invasion and illegal occupation;

Whereas, Iraq is a party to the Prisoners of War Convention and there is evidence and testimony that during the Persian Gulf War, Iraq violated articles of the Convention by its physical and psychological abuse of military and civilian POW's including members of the international press;

Whereas, Iraq has committed deliberate and calculated crimes of environmental terrorism, inflicting grave risk to the health and well-being of innocent civilians in the region by its willful ignition of 732 Kuwaiti oil wells in January and February, 1991;

Whereas, President Clinton found "compelling evidence" that the Iraqi Intelligence Service directed and pursued an operation to assassinate former President George Bush in April 1993 when he visited Kuwait;

Whereas, Saddam Hussein and other Iraqi officials have systematically attempted to destroy the Kurdish population in Iraq through the use of chemical weapons against civilian Kurds, campaigns in 1987–88 which resulted in the disappearance of more than 182,000 persons and the destruction of more than 4,000 villages, the placement of more than 10 million landmines in Iraqi Kurdistan, and ethnic cleansing in the city of Kirkuk;

Whereas, the Republic of Iraq is a signatory to international agreements including the Universal Declaration on Human Rights, the International Covenant on Civil and Political Rights, the Convention on the Prevention and Punishment of the Crime of Genocide, and the POW Convention, and is obligated to comply with these international agreements;

Whereas, Section 8 of Resolution 687 of the United Nations Security Council, adopted on April 3, 1991, requires Iraq to "unconditionally accept the destruction, removal, or rendering harmless, under international supervision of all chemical and biological weapons and all stocks of agents and all related subsystems and components and all research, development, support, and manufacturing facilities";

Whereas, Saddam Hussein and the Republic of Iraq have persistently and flagrantly violated the terms of Resolution 687 with respect to elimination of weapons of mass destruction and inspections by international supervisors;

Whereas, there is good reason to believe that Iraq continues to have stockpiles of chemical and biological munitions, missiles capable of transporting such agents, and the capacity to produce such weapons of mass destruction, putting the international community at risk;

Whereas, on February 22, 1993, the United Nations Security Council adopted Resolution 808 establishing an international tribunal to try individuals accused of violations of international law in the former Yugoslavia;

Whereas, on November 8, 1994, the United Nations Security Council adopted Resolution 955 establishing an international tribunal to try individuals accused of the commission of violations of international law in Rwanda;

Whereas, more than 70 individuals have faced indictments handed down by the International Criminal Tribunal for the Former Yugoslavia in the Hague for war crimes and crimes against humanity in the former Yugoslavia, leading in the first trial to the sentencing of a Serb jailer to 20 years in prison;

Whereas, the International Criminal Tribunal for Rwanda has indicted 31 individuals, with three trials occurring at present and 27 individuals in custody;

Whereas, a failure to try and punish leaders and other persons for crimes against international law establishes a dangerous precedent and negatively impacts the value of deterrence to future illegal acts;

Whereas, on February 17, 1998, the President of the United States outlined his policy on engaging in a military action against Iraq and stated that his purpose is "to seriously diminish the threat posed by Iraq's weapons of mass destruction program" and further stated that if a United States military operation does not prevent Saddam Hussein from rebuilding his weapons of mass destruction, future military strikes will be necessary;

Whereas, current plans are grossly inadequate because it is insufficient to "seriously diminish" the threat posed by Saddam Hussein to the international community through the use of weapons of mass destruction;

Whereas, there is a need for a long-term approach to removing Saddam Hussein from his position as President of Iraq; Now, therefore, be it Resolved, That the President should—

(1) call for the creation of a commission under the auspices of the United Nations to establish an international record of the criminal culpability of Saddam Hussein and other Iraqi officials; and
(2) call for the United Nations to form an international criminal tribunal for the purpose of indicting, prosecuting, and imprisoning Saddam Hussein and other Iraqi officials who are responsible for crimes against humanity, genocide, and other violations of international law; and
(3) devise a long-term plan, in consultation with allies of the United States, for the removal of Saddam Hussein from his position as President of Iraq, so that he can be prosecuted fully for war crimes and other violations of international law.

HJ 125 IH
105th CONGRESS
2nd Session
H.J. RES. 125

Finding the Government of Iraq in material and unacceptable breach of its international obligations.

IN THE HOUSE OF REPRESENTATIVES
June 25, 1998

Mr. GINGRICH (for himself and Mr. GILMAN) introduced the following joint resolution; which was referred to the Committee on International Relations

JOINT RESOLUTION

Finding the Government of Iraq in material and unacceptable breach of its international obligations.

Whereas hostilities in Operation Desert Storm ended on February 28, 1991, and the conditions governing the cease-fire were specified in United Nations Security Council Resolutions 686 (March 2, 1991) and 687 (April 3, 1991);

Whereas United Nations Security Council Resolution 687 requires that international economic sanctions remain in place until Iraq discloses and destroys its weapons of mass destruction programs and capabilities and undertakes unconditionally never to resume such activities;

Whereas Resolution 687 established the United Nations Special Commission on Iraq (UNSCOM) to uncover all aspects of Iraq's weapons of mass destruction programs and tasked the Director-General of the International Atomic Energy Agency to locate and remove or destroy all nuclear weapons systems, subsystems or material from Iraq;

Whereas United Nations Security Council Resolution 715, adopted on October 11, 1991, empowered UNSCOM to maintain a long-term monitoring program to ensure Iraq's weapons of mass destruction programs are dismantled and not restarted;

Whereas Iraq has consistently fought to hide the full extent of its weapons programs, and has systematically made false declarations to the Security Council and to UNSCOM regarding those programs, and has systematically obstructed weapons inspections for seven years;

Whereas in June 1991, Iraqi forces fired on International Atomic Energy Agency inspectors and otherwise obstructed and misled UNSCOM inspectors, resulting in UN Security Council Resolution 707 which found Iraq to be in 'material breach' of its obligations under United Nations Security Council Resolution 687 for failing to allow UNSCOM inspectors access to a site storing nuclear equipment;

Whereas in January and February of 1992, Iraq rejected plans to install long-term monitoring equipment and cameras called for in UN resolutions, resulting in a Security Council Presidential Statement of February 19, 1992, which declared that Iraq was in 'continuing material breach' of its obligations;

Whereas in February of 1992, Iraq continued to obstruct the installation of monitoring equipment, and failed to comply with UNSCOM orders to allow destruction of missiles and other prescribed weapons, resulting in the Security Council Presidential Statement of February 28, 1992, which reiterated that Iraq was in 'continuing material breach' and noted a "further material breach' on account of Iraq's failure to allow destruction of ballistic missile equipment;

Whereas on July 5, 1992, Iraq denied UNSCOM inspectors access to the Iraqi Ministry of Agriculture, resulting in a Security Council Presidential Statement of July 6, 1992, which declared that Iraq was in 'material and unacceptable breach' of its obligations under UN resolutions;

Whereas in December of 1992 and January of 1993, Iraq violated the southern no-fly zone, moved surface to air missiles into the no-fly zone, raided a weapons depot in internationally recognized Kuwaiti territory, and denied landing rights to a plane carrying UN weapons inspectors, resulting in a Security Council Presidential Statement of January 8, 1993, which declared that Iraq was in an 'unacceptable and material breach' of its obligations under UN resolutions;

Whereas in response to continued Iraqi defiance, a Security Council Presidential Statement of January 11, 1993, reaffirmed the previous finding of material breach, followed on January 13 and 18 by allied air raids, and on January 17 with an allied missile attack on Iraqi targets;

Whereas on June 10, 1993, Iraq prevented UNSCOM's installation of cameras and monitoring equipment, resulting in a Security Council Presidential Statement of June 18, 1993, declaring Iraq's refusal to comply to be a 'material and unacceptable breach';

Whereas on October 6, 1994, Iraq threatened to end cooperation with weapons inspectors if sanctions were not ended, and one day later, massed 10,000 troops within 30 miles of the Kuwaiti border, resulting in United Nations Security Council Resolution 949 demanding Iraq's withdrawal from the Kuwaiti border area and renewal of compliance with UNSCOM;

Whereas on April 10, 1995, UNSCOM reported to the Security Council that Iraq had concealed its biological weapons program, and had failed to account for 17 tons of biological weapons material resulting in the Security Council's renewal of sanctions against Iraq;

Whereas on July 1, 1995, Iraq admitted to a full scale biological weapons program, but denied weaponization of biological agents, and subsequently threatened to end cooperation with UNSCOM resulting in the Security Council's renewal of sanctions against Iraq;

Whereas on March 8, 11, 14, and 15, 1996, Iraq again barred UNSCOM inspectors from sites containing documents and weapons, in response to which the Security Council issued a Presidential Statement condemning 'clear violations by Iraq of previous Resolutions 687, 707 and 715';

Whereas from June 1115, 1996, Iraq repeatedly barred weapons inspectors from military sites, in response to which the Security Council adopted United Nations Security Council Resolution 1060, noting the 'clear violation on United Nations Security Council Resolutions 687, 707 and 715' and in response to Iraq's continued violations, issued a Presidential statement detailing Iraq's 'gross violation of obligations';

Whereas in August of 1996, Iraqi troops overran Irbil, in Iraqi Kurdistan, employing more than 30,000 troops and Republican Guards to suppress the Patriotic Union of Kurdistan, in response to which the Security Council briefly suspended implementation on United Nations Security Council Resolution 986, the UN oil for food plan;

Whereas in December of 1996, Iraq prevented UNSCOM from removing 130 Scud missile engines from Iraq for analysis, resulting in a Security Council presidential statement which 'deplore[d]' Iraq's refusal to cooperate with UNSCOM;

Whereas on April 9, 1997, Iraq violated the no-fly zone in southern Iraq and United Nations Security Council Resolution 670, banning international flights, resulting in a Security Council statement regretting Iraq's lack of 'specific consultation' with the Council;

Whereas on June 4 and 5, 1997, Iraqi officials on board UNSCOM aircraft interfered with the controls and inspections, endangering inspectors and obstructing the UNSCOM mission, resulting in a UN Security Council presidential statement demanding Iraq end its interference and on June 21, 1997, United Nations Security Council Resolution 1115 threatened sanctions on Iraqi officials responsible for these interferences;

Whereas on September 13, 1997, during an inspection mission, an Iraqi official attacked UNSCOM officials engaged in photographing illegal Iraqi activities, resulting in the October

23, 1997 adoption of United Nations Security Council Resolution 1134 which threatened a travel ban on Iraqi officials responsible for non-compliance with UN resolutions;

Whereas on October 29, 1997, Iraq announced that it would no longer allow American inspectors working with UNSCOM to conduct inspections in Iraq, blocking UNSCOM teams containing Americans to conduct inspections and threatening to shoot down U.S. U-2 surveillance flights in support of UNSCOM, resulting in a United Nations Security Council Resolution 1137 on November 12, 1997, which imposed the travel ban on Iraqi officials and threatened unspecified 'further measures';

Whereas on November 13, 1997, Iraq expelled U.S. inspectors from Iraq, leading to UNSCOM's decision to pull out its remaining inspectors and resulting in a United Nations Security Council presidential statement demanding Iraq revoke the expulsion;

Whereas on January 15, 1998, an UNSCOM team led by American Scott Ritter was withdrawn from Iraq after being barred for three days by Iraq from conducting inspections, resulting in the adoption of a United Nations Security Council presidential statement deploring Iraq's decision to bar the team as a clear violation of all applicable resolutions;

Whereas despite clear agreement on the part of Iraqi President Saddam Hussein with United Nations Secretary General Kofi Annan to grant access to all sites, and fully cooperate with UNSCOM, and the adoption on March 2, 1998, of United Nations Security Council Resolution 1154, warning that any violation of the agreement with Annan would have the 'severest consequences' for Iraq, Iraq has continued to actively conceal weapons and weapons programs, provide misinformation and otherwise deny UNSCOM inspectors access;

Whereas on June 24, 1998, UNSCOM Director Richard Butler presented information to the UN Security Council indicating clearly that Iraq, in direct contradiction to information provided to UNSCOM, weaponized the nerve agent VX;

Whereas Iraq's continuing weapons of mass destruction programs threaten vital United States interest and international peace and security; and

Whereas the United States has existing authority to defend United States interests in the Persian Gulf region:

Now, therefore, be it Resolved by the Senate and House of Representatives of the United States of America in Congress assembled, That the Government of Iraq is in material and unacceptable breach of its international obligations, and therefore, the President of the United States is urged to act accordingly.

UNITED STATES SENATE
105th Congress, 2nd Session
S. 2334
1 September 1998

Purpose: To support the Iraqi democratic opposition. Making appropriations for foreign operations, export financing, and related programs for the fiscal year ending September 30, 1999, and for other purposes.

AMENDMENT intended to be proposed by Mr. Loft (for himself), Mr. Kyl, Mr. Brownback. At the appropriate place in the bill insert the following. "Notwithstanding any other provision of law, of the amounts made available under Title II of this Act, not less than $10,000,000 shall be made available only for assistance to the Iraqi democratic opposition for such activities as organization, training, communication and dissemination of information, and developing and implementing agreements among opposition groups;

Provided, that any agreement reached regarding the obligation of funds under the previous provision shall include provisions to ensure appropriate monitoring on the use of such funds;

Provided further that of this amount not less than $3,000,000 shall be made available as a grant to Iraqi National Congress, to be administered by its Executive Committee for the benefit of all constituent groups of the Iraqi National Congress;

Provided further that of the amounts previously appropriated under section 10008 of Public Law 105-174 not less than $2,000,000 shall be made available as a grant to INDICT, the International Campaign to Indict Iraqi War Criminals, for the purpose of compiling information to support the indictment of Iraqi officials for war crimes;

Provided further that of the amounts made available under this section, not less than $1,000,000 shall be made available as a grant to INDICT,[1] the International Campaign to Indict Iraqi War Criminals, for the purpose of compiling information to support the indictment of Iraqi officials for war crimes;

Provided further that of the amounts made available under this section, not less than $3,000,000 shall be made available only for the conduct of activities by the Iraqi democratic opposition inside Iraq;

Provided further that within 30 days of enactment of this Act the Secretary of State shall submit a detailed report to the appropriate committees of Congress on implementation of this section.

---

[1] INDICT is an effort by various Iraqi opposition groups and non-governmental organizations to document Iraqi war crimes and other violations of international humanitarian law. The ultimate aim is to ensure that Saddam Hussein is brought to justice before an international tribunal. This movement is also supported by the British House of Commons.

Legislation and Documents

Rules of Conciliation, Arbitration and Expertise of the Euro–Arab Arbitration System

Adopted by the General Board of the Company during its meeting of 17 December 1997*

PREAMBLE

The Euro–Arab Arbitration System (hereinafter referred to as the System, and previously called the System of Conciliation, Arbitration and Expertise of the Euro–Arab Chambers of Commerce) is intended to offer any European or Arab party, whether a natural or juristic person, as well as other users insofar as they are directly involved with any of the Arab countries, the availability of the procedures for conciliation, arbitration and expertise set out in the Rules of the System (the Rules) whenever commercial disputes with an international characteristic arise out of their dealings. This may be achieved either by including in contracts the appropriate conciliation, arbitration and expertise clauses or by recourse to the provisions embodied in these Rules whether or not the appropriate clauses have been included in such contracts.

The aim of the System is to be available to all those users who require the most convenient arbitration procedure in accordance with the most recent developments in the resolution of international disputes which by definition have mixed characteristics. The System offers the parties guarantees which take into consideration the specificity of the relations of the two groups, namely the European states and the Arab states, by establishing bodies which operate under conditions of strict parity, thus providing the parties with a better and more reliable approach to arbitration.

The System further provides for better control of actual arbitration procedure by bodies that are autonomous but well acquainted with the specific characteristics of both such groups. All these factors assist in creating a great likelihood of decisions being implemented voluntarily, independently of the good offices provided by the System.

---

* A one-day conference on the re-launching of the Euro–Arab Arbitration System entitled "Conciliation and Arbitration at the Junctions of Two Worlds" was held on 16 June 1998 in London supported by CIMEL and the Centre of Construction Law and Management at King's College London. The Secretariat of the System has moved from Paris to London and the new Secretary-General is Mr Nabil Saleh.

The Euro–Arab Chambers of Commerce, in the light of the ever-increasing contribution made by conciliation and arbitration in international, industrial and commercial relations and the desirability of introducing an expertise procedure to reduce the frequency and extent of potential disputes, adopted the principle of these Rules through their appointed Chairmen and Secretaries-General at their conference in Tunis on 11th June 1981. The text of the Rules was settled by the Conference of Chairmen and Secretaries-General at their meeting in Paris on 1st June 1982. The Rules were modified on 28th November 1990 and were substantially amended by the General Meeting of Chairmen and Secretaries-General held in Agadir on 18th December 1994.

On 8th May 1997 the Euro–Arab Arbitration System Company (the Company) was incorporated in England. On 14th May 1997 the Company formally adopted the Rules of the System of Conciliation, Arbitration and Expertise of the Euro–Arab Chambers of Commerce, took over the powers and duties of the Conference of Chairmen and Secretaries-General in relation to the Rules and chose the abbreviated name "Euro–Arab Arbitration System" for the arbitration system which it was set up to manage and promote.

The Rules in their present form were adopted by the General Board of the Company during its meeting held in Damascus on 17 December 1997.

Notes

1. The words "conciliator", "arbitrator" and "expert" which appear in the following Articles may apply to one or more conciliators, arbitrators and experts, as the case may be.
2. In the following Articles the masculine gender may refer to the feminine gender with regard to any appointment or nomination.

RECOMMENDED CLAUSES

1. Arbitration Clause

Any and all disputes arising out of or in connection with this contract shall be finally settled in accordance with the arbitration provisions of the Rules of Conciliation, Arbitration and Expertise of the Euro–Arab Arbitration System by one or more arbitrators appointed in accordance with the said Rules which are said by the parties to be known and accepted by them.

2. Conciliation Clause

Any and all disputes arising out of or in connection with this contract shall be submitted to conciliation conducted by one or more conciliators appointed and acting pursuant to the conciliation provisions of the Rules of Conciliation, Arbitration and Expertise of the Euro–Arab Arbitration System which are said by the parties to be known and accepted by them.

3. Conciliation and Arbitration Clause

Any and all disputes arising out of or in connection with this contract shall be finally settled in accordance with the conciliation and arbitration provisions of the Rules of Conciliation,

Arbitration and Expertise of the Euro–Arab Arbitration System which are said by the parties to be known and accepted by them.

If attempts at conciliation prove unsuccessful, the dispute shall be finally settled by one or more arbitrators appointed in accordance with the said Rules.

4. Conciliation, Arbitration and Expertise Clause

Any and all disputes arising out of or in connection with this contract shall be finally settled in accordance with the Rules of Conciliation, Arbitration and Expertise of the Euro–Arab Arbitration System which are said by the parties to be known and accepted by them.

If attempts at conciliation prove unsuccessful, the dispute shall be finally settled by one or more arbitrators appointed in accordance with the said Rules.

Moreover, the parties state their acceptance of Article 27 of the said Rules providing for expertise.

Note to parties

– With regard to arbitration, it is desirable for the contracting parties to stipulate the law governing their contract, the number of arbitrators, and the place and language of the arbitration.

Part I
Organization of the Euro–Arab Arbitration System
SECTION ONE
THE BODIES

Article 1

The Bodies of the Euro–Arab Arbitration System are

– The Arbitration Board
– The Arbitration Committees of the Arab and Joint Chambers of Commerce
– The Plenary Assembly
– The Secretary–General and the Secretariat-Registry.

Article 2

Formation of the Arbitration Board

2.1 The Arbitration Board (the Board) shall be composed of no less than ten and no more than twenty members comprising an equal number of Arab and non-Arab members, appointed by the Company on account of their professional experience, legal competence and impartiality.

The Board shall not include two members of the same nationality.

2.2 The Company shall determine the total number of the members of the Board and shall appoint them.

2.3 Members of the Arbitration Board shall be appointed for a term of three years. One third of the members shall retire by rotation every year. Retiring members shall be eligible for re-appointment.

2.4 The Company may, provided that parity is maintained, nominate substitute members of the Board who may replace members of the Board who are unable to act. The conditions governing substitution are laid down in the internal procedure referred to in Article 3.5 below.

2.5 In the event of a vacancy caused by death, resignation, disqualification or incapacity of a member or for any other reason, the Arbitration Board shall, if it considers it necessary, call upon a substitute member to act until such time as a new member is designated in accordance with the provisions of 2.1 to 2.4 above.

Article 3

Functioning of the Arbitration Board

3.1 Members of the Board shall be totally independent and shall undertake to remain totally impartial.

3.2 The Board shall elect among its members and by a majority vote, a Bureau comprising a President and an odd number of Vice-Presidents. The functions of the Bureau shall be distributed on the basis of parity between Arab members and non-Arab members.

3.3 The quorum for Board meetings requires the attendance of half its members and the participation of both Arab and non-Arab members. An absent member may give a proxy to another member, provided parity is maintained. A member may not hold more than two proxies.

3.4 Decisions shall be taken by consensus. Should any of the members present dissent, the Board's decision shall be valid if taken by a simple majority on condition that half the Arab members and half the non-Arab members are either present or represented.

3.5 Subject to the provisions of this Article, the Board shall establish its own internal procedure and determine the frequency of its meetings.

3.6 The internal procedure shall determine the powers of the Bureau, which may be authorized in case of urgency and subject to ratification by the Board, to exercise any powers of the Board.

3.7 Ordinary meetings of the Board shall be held at the offices of the Secretariat-Registry. Extraordinary meetings may be held at any other place which the Board designates.

Article 4

Arbitration Committees

4.1 An Arbitration Committee (the Committee) may be established with each Arab Chamber of Commerce, Federation of Chambers of Commerce in an Arab country, and each Euro–Arab Chamber of Commerce subscribing to the present Rules.

4.2 A Committee may be set up either on the initiative of the Company, the relevant Chamber or Federation of Chambers referred to in Article 4.1 above.

4.3 A Committee shall be composed of Arab and non-Arab members residing or active in the territory covered by the relevant Chamber or Federation of Chambers. Its members shall be selected on account of their experience, professional and juridical competence and their knowledge of arbitration matters.

4.4 The composition and the selection of members of each Committee shall be determined by the competent authority of the relevant Chamber or Federation of Chambers.

4.5 Each Committee shall determine its own internal procedure.

Article 5

Plenary Assembly

5.1 The Plenary Assembly shall consist of the full and substitute members of the Arbitration Board and of delegates from the Arbitration Committees.

5.2 The Board shall determine the number of delegates from each Committee and the manner of their selection.

5.3 The Assembly shall meet at the initiative of the Company after consultation with the Arbitration Board.

Article 6

The Secretary-General/The Secretariat-Registry

6.1 The Secretary-General shall be responsible for the administration of the System. He shall be appointed by the Company for a period of three years and may be re-appointed.

6.2 A Registrar shall be appointed by the Company and shall be responsible for the Secretariat-Registry under the authority of the Secretary-General.

6.3 The office of the Secretariat-Registry is in London, United Kingdom. The office may be moved by a decision of the Company.

SECTION TWO
POWERS AND JURISDICTION

Article 7

The Arbitration Board

7.1 The Arbitration Board shall exercise all powers conferred upon it by the present Rules.

7.2 In particular, the Board shall have power to determine *prima facie* whether or not a dispute referred to it is governed by these Rules.

7.3 The Board shall draw up and keep up to date the list of arbitrators, conciliators and experts. It shall register new names in accordance with the procedure laid down by the Company for that purpose.

7.4 The Board shall by all appropriate means publicize these Rules and bring them to the attention of the public authorities and potential users in the countries concerned.

Article 8
The Arbitration Committees

8.1 The Arbitration Committees shall co-operate with the Board and shall themselves take all appropriate steps to publicize and bring these Rules to the attention of the authorities and potential users in their respective countries.

8.2 The Committees may be consulted by the Arbitration Board on the updating of the list of arbitrators, conciliators and experts and on the registration of new names.

8.3 The Committees shall have no jurisdiction in respect of the procedures laid down in these Rules. They may, however, be consulted by the Arbitration Board, or by the arbitral tribunal, on matters pertaining to legislation, rules and procedure in the country where they are located.

Article 9
The Plenary Assembly

The Plenary Assembly shall be responsible for monitoring the operation of these Rules and for suggesting to the relevant bodies any advisable changes or additions thereto.

Article 10
The Secretary-General/The Secretariat-Registry

10.1 The Secretary-General shall be responsible for the administration of the System and shall exercise the duties and powers contained in these Rules.

10.2 The Secretary-General shall attend the General Meeting of the Company, the Meetings of the General Board of the Company and the Meetings of the Executive Committee of the General Board of the Company, with no right to vote.

10.3 Under the authority and responsibility of the Secretary-General, the Registrar shall be responsible for the organisation of the Secretariat-Registry for the System. He shall provide secretarial services for the meetings of the Arbitration Board. The Secretary-General shall attend the Meetings of the Arbitration Board and of the Bureau with no right to vote.

10.4 Any requests for the implementation of the provisions of the Rules shall be referred to the Secretariat-Registry which shall forthwith notify the Secretary-General of the same.

10.5 The Registrar is authorized to receive money in respect of the costs and fees payable in connection with the conciliation, arbitration and expertise procedures.

10.6 The Registrar shall safe-keep all minutes.

Part II
The Procedures

SECTION ONE
CONCILIATION

Article 11

Choice of Conciliation

11.1 Parties wishing to have recourse to conciliation have the choice of bringing the proceedings in the Joint Chamber of Commerce in the country in which the non-Arab party is situated (the local Chamber), or in the Secretariat-Registry of the Euro–Arab Arbitration System.

11.2 In the case of conciliation proceedings before the local Chamber, references in the following Articles to the Secretary-General, the Registrar or the Secretariat-Registry shall mean the Secretary-General of the local Chamber.

Article 12

Request for Conciliation

12.1 The party wishing to have recourse to conciliation proceedings shall send a written Request to the Secretariat-Registry comprising a summary of the dispute, its full name and address and the full name and address of the other party involved in that dispute. The Registrar shall determine the required number of copies of the Request.

12.2 The Registrar shall write to the other party involved in the dispute, providing a copy of the Request, and asking for written confirmation within fifteen days that the procedure for conciliation as laid down in the Rules is accepted for the purpose of settling that dispute.

12.3 If all the parties concerned have accepted the procedure for conciliation, the Registrar shall request them to pay in equal shares a deposit on account of the administrative charges, costs and fees for the conciliation. The deposit shall be fixed by the Secretary-General.

Article 13

Appointment of Conciliator

13.1 After reviewing the Request for conciliation, the Secretary-General shall appoint a conciliator.

13.2 If the parties so agree and request, more than one conciliator may be appointed.

Article 14

Duties of Conciliator

14.1 The conciliator shall carry out his mission in full accordance with the principles of impartiality, equity and justice.

14.2 Unless all the parties agree otherwise, a conciliator who has accepted his appointment shall not act in any proceedings, including arbitration proceedings, which relate to the dispute which has been the subject of conciliation, whether as an arbitrator, expert witness, witness, representative or counsel of a party to the conciliation process.

Article 15

Conciliation Process

15.1 Written statements and documents may be presented to the conciliator by each side of the dispute. Anything in writing shall be communicated to the other side before the open session.

15.2 The conciliator shall fix an open session during which each side, accompanied at its choice by legal adviser(s), will be given the chance to inform the conciliator and the other side as to the nature of their dispute and the remedies sought.

15.3 After the open session, each side will go to separate rooms and the conciliator will visit each in turn. The conciliator shall not reveal to the other side what he has been told during the private sessions, unless he is given permission to do so.

Article 16

Drafting Minutes of Agreement

16.1 When agreement is reached, the conciliator will bring all the parties together again and draw up minutes of agreement to be signed by all concerned.

16.2 The said minutes will be held by the conciliator until full payment of fees and costs.

Article 17

Ending the Conciliation

The conciliator or the either of the parties may end the conciliation at any time without giving reason.

Article 18

Confidentiality

18.1 With the exception of the minutes of written agreement, any information, whether written or spoken during the conciliation, may be used for the purpose of conciliation only and may not be referred to in any other proceedings.

18.2 All documents, discussions and negotiations during the conciliation shall be privileged and deemed to be "without prejudice" unless such privilege is waived by the parties by agreement either generally or in relation to any specific aspect.

18.3 The parties to a conciliation are deemed to have agreed that they will not seek to call the conciliator as a witness in any court action or other proceedings.

SECTION TWO
ARBITRATION

Article 19

Request for Arbitration

19.1 Any party wishing to have recourse to the arbitration procedure of the Euro–Arab Arbitration System shall submit to the Secretariat-Registry a written Request stating:

(a) the applicant's full name, capacity and address;
(b) the full name, capacity and address of the other party;
(c) a summary of the nature, circumstances and extent of the dispute;
(d) if appropriate, the applicant's proposal for a single arbitrator or the full name and address of the arbitrator appointed under the provisions of Article 21 below.

19.2 True copies of the contract forming the basis of the dispute or the agreement between the parties to submit their dispute to the arbitration of the Euro–Arab Arbitration System, as the case may be, shall be appended to the Request. Correspondence or other relevant documents may also be appended.

19.3 Three copies of the Request and the accompanying documents, if any, must be sent to the Secretariat-Registry with one copy for each arbitrator. The Secretariat-Registry may request additional copies whenever needed.

Article 20

Transmission of the Request–Reply–Counter–Claim

20.1 Upon receipt of the Request, in accordance with Article 19 above, the Registrar shall acknowledge receipt thereof to the applicant, and transmit a copy of the Request and any annexes to the other party.

20.2 If it does not appear that the parties have made an arbitration agreement, the Registrar shall invite the respondent to tell whether he accepts the application of these Rules to the dispute referred to him.

20.3 If the parties have not already upon the constitution of the arbitral tribunal, the Registrar shall draw to their attention Article 21 below and request them to inform him within thirty days whether they wish the tribunal to consist of one or three arbitrators and, within the same period, to make their respective appointments or, as the case may be, signify their position with regard to any proposed appointment.

20.4 The applicant shall within thirty days from the filing date of the Request, deliver to the Secretariat-Registry a full statement of the case with all supporting documents. The Registrar shall forthwith deliver a copy to the respondent.

20.5 The respondent shall, within thirty days from receipt of the full statement of the claimant's case, submit its response, accompanied by any relevant documents and counter-claim, if any.

20.6 In the event of a counter-claim, the claimant shall, within thirty days from the date of receipt, submit its response in reply.

20.7 The periods mentioned in this Article may be extended by the Secretary-General.

Article 21
Structure of the Arbitral Tribunal

21.1 The arbitral tribunal shall consist of a sole arbitrator if either the arbitration clause so provides or the parties inform the Secretariat-Registry that they have so agreed within thirty days of the Request being transmitted to the respondent according to Article 20.1 above.

21.2 Otherwise the tribunal shall consist of three arbitrators. Each party shall notify the Secretariat-Registry of the name of its chosen arbitrator within thirty days, from the date the Respondent was notified of the Request. A third arbitrator shall be designated by agreement of the parties or by agreement of the appointed arbitrators and his name notified to the Secretariat-Registry within a further period of fifteen days, from the date of the appointment of both arbitrators. The third arbitrator shall be the chairman of the tribunal.

21.3 If the parties fail to agree on the name of the sole arbitrator or if either party fails to appoint an arbitrator, as required, or if the parties or the two appointed arbitrators fail to designate the third arbitrator, the Arbitration Board shall proceed to make the necessary appointment(s).

21.4 If any party contests the validity or the operation of the arbitration clause, the arbitral tribunal shall nonetheless be constituted in accordance with these Rules and will, as soon as formed, determine the validity of its appointment and any other questions relating to its jurisdiction or powers.

Article 22
Challenge to Arbitrator

22.1 Every appointed arbitrator must be and remain independent of the parties involved in the arbitration.

22.2 Either party may challenge the arbitrator initially appointed by the other party without giving reasons. In the event of such a challenge, this must take place and be notified without delay to the Secretariat-Registry. The other party shall appoint another arbitrator within fifteen days of being notified of the challenge.

22.3 A further challenge to any arbitrator, including the third arbitrator once the proceedings are in progress, must state the grounds of challenge. The challenge must be filed with the Arbitration Board through the Secretariat-Registry within a period of fifteen days from the date of discovering the facts which form the grounds of challenge, otherwise the challenge will not be heard.

22.4 The Board shall deliberate in private on such a challenge, after giving the challenged arbitrator and the parties the opportunity to comment in writing within a suitable period of time. If the Board upholds a challenge, the arbitrator shall be replaced after giving the party which appointed him, the opportunity to make a further appointment. The appointment of a new third arbitrator will follow the same procedure as for the arbitrator being replaced.

22.5 The Board alone, and at all times, shall have jurisdiction to deal with any challenges and with any dispute arising from such challenges.

Article 23

Arbitration Proceedings

23.1 The rules applicable to the arbitration proceedings are those embodied in these Rules. If these Rules are silent on any matter, the proceedings shall be governed by the rules covering such matters that the parties have expressly elected. If no such election is made, the rules adopted shall be those that the arbitrator considers most likely to achieve a swift, economical and conclusive solution to the dispute.

23.2 The parties expressly agree to renounce any plea or appeal to any courts or tribunals in connection with any question of law arising out of or raised in the course of the proceedings.

23.3 The arbitration venue shall be agreed between the parties or, failing such an agreement, shall be determined by the Bureau of the Arbitration Board. The consequence of the choice of venue shall be the application of the mandatory provisions of the procedural laws of the place chosen.

23.4 The arbitrator shall act on the basis of good faith and equity (amiable compositeur) if that is the express desire of the parties and provided that the applicable procedural law so permits.

23.5 No Request for arbitration shall be submitted to the arbitrator before the payment of a deposit on account of administrative charges, costs and fees, as determined in accordance with Article 29.

23.6 The Registrar shall send the arbitration file to the arbitrator not later than the expiry of the periods allowed to the claimant or respondent to file their written statements subject, however, to payment of the deposit on account of the charges, costs and fees.

The Secretary-General may nonetheless, in appropriate circumstances, extend the periods fixed by these Rules before the matter is under the arbitrator's jurisdiction.

23.7 Subject to any rules of procedure which may be binding upon him, the arbitrator shall have full power and authority to direct the proceedings. He may refer to the Bureau of the Arbitration Board or the Secretary-General if he considers appropriate.

23.8 After receiving the file, the arbitrator may draw up a document defining his terms of reference either on the basis of the file before him or in the presence of the parties, stating in particular:

(a)   the full names, capacities and addresses of the parties and, if possible, the addresses to which all notices or communications may validly be sent during the course of the arbitration;
(b)   a summary of the facts and circumstances of the case;
(c)   a summary of the claims made by each party;
(d)   a list of the issues in dispute that have been submitted to the arbitrator for determination;

(e)   the full name, capacity and address of the arbitrator;
(f)   the arbitration venue;
(g)   the legal rules applicable to the merits of the case, if the parties have not already agreed on them; and
(h)   any other matter either suggested by the Arbitration Board and accepted by the arbitrator or which may be required so as to give the arbitral award full local effect.

23.9 This document shall be submitted by the arbitrator to the Arbitration Board, then signed by the members of the arbitral tribunal and finally submitted for signature to each of the parties to the dispute.

23.10 The fact that one party refuses to co-operate in the preparation of the document which defines the arbitrator's terms of reference, or to sign such a document, shall not preclude from pursuing the arbitration procedure or giving an award, as set out below in Article 24.

23.11 In the absence of terms of reference, the arbitrator will investigate and determine the legal rules applicable to the merits of the dispute if the parties have not previously agreed upon them.

23.12 The arbitrator may fix an oral hearing for the parties. However, he must do so at the request of either of them.

23.13 If one of the parties defaults and does not, within a reasonable time, give any acceptable explanation for defaulting, the arbitration proceedings may nonetheless proceed as if in the presence of that party. The parties may either appear in person or be accompanied or represented by legal counsels.

23.14 If one of the parties or the parties request(s) the appointment of an expert for finding facts, other than those in documents, and/or opinion, the arbitrator shall decide whether or not to grant the request after hearing the parties.

23.15 The arbitrator shall not be bound by rules of evidence; he may admit and take into account any element which may in his opinion be relevant.

23.16 The period within which the arbitrator must give his award is one hundred and twenty days from the date that he was given the arbitration papers as stipulated in Article 23.6 above. The Secretary-General may, however, extend this period, at the request of the arbitrator, or by his own initiative if deemed necessary.

Article 24

Arbitration Award

24.1 If the parties reach an agreement during the course of the arbitration, the arbitral tribunal shall, as soon as requested, make an award confirming the agreement between the parties.

24.2 If no such agreement is reached, the award shall be made by the arbitral tribunal. Where the arbitral tribunal is formed of three arbitrators, the award shall be made by a majority decision. If there is no majority, the chairman of the tribunal shall draw up the award on his own and render it on behalf of the entire arbitral tribunal.

24.3 The award shall be written with sufficient precision to show that the rights of the defence have been respected. It must necessarily incorporate decisions on the merits of the issues which have been submitted to arbitration.

24.4 After drawing up the award, but before signing it, the arbitrator shall submit the award in draft to the Board.

24.5 Without affecting the role of the arbitrator or intervening in the arbitration proceedings, but with a view of giving full effect to the award to be rendered, the Board may draw to the arbitrator's attention any matter of form and/or merit that appear relevant.

24.6 Following such examination, the arbitrator shall sign and date the arbitration award as when signing. Should one or more arbitrators refuse to sign the award, such refusal shall be expressly noted in the award.

Article 25

Notification and Enforcement

25.1 The arbitral award, bearing the signature of the arbitrator, shall be filed with the Secretariat-Registry in at least as many copies as are required by the law of the country where the award is to be enforced, plus two copies for the Secretariat-Registry's file. The Registrar alone shall be empowered to notify the text of the award to the parties after the arbitration charges, costs and fees have been settled in full, either by both parties or by one of them.

25.2 Any award made under these Rules shall be final and may not be the subject of any form of appeal. By submitting their dispute to the arbitration of the Euro–Arab Arbitration System, the parties shall be deemed to have undertaken to comply with the resulting award without delay and to have waived their right to any form of appeal insofar as such waiver can validly be made.

25.3 Any award made shall be complied with by the parties in good faith. The Board shall moreover lend its good offices to facilitate the enforcement of awards made under these Rules.

25.4 In case one party refuses to comply voluntarily with an arbitral award any of the other parties to the arbitration may, when necessary, ask the competent authorities of the place where the award is to be enforced, to grant enforcement in accordance with the law and procedure which are in force in that place.

Article 26

Non-institutional Arbitration

26.1 Whenever under the Rule of the United Nations Commission on International Trading Law (UNCITRAL), the Arbitration Board of the Euro–Arab Arbitration System has been chosen or designated as the appointing authority, the Arbitration Board of the Euro–Arab Arbitration System shall proceed to make such appointments according to the UNCITRAL Rules, and particularly the provisions of Articles 6, 7, and 8 thereof.

Moreover, and in case the parties so decide, the arbitral tribunal shall be invested with the powers and authorities laid down in these Rules, in addition to the powers and authorities conferred on it by the contract or the arbitration agreement.

26.2 Where the parties have agreed to settle their disputes by way of arbitration without referring to any rules of arbitration, they may, if they decide so whether their contract is concluded or afterwards, choose the Arbitration Board of the Euro–Arab Arbitration System as the appointing authority of the sole arbitrator and, if need be, the other arbitrators forming the arbitral tribunal, including the third arbitrator.

Moreover, and in case the parties so decide, the arbitral tribunal shall be invested with the powers and authorities laid down in these Rules, in addition to the powers and authorities conferred on it by the contract or the arbitration agreement.

26.3 If the parties agree to settle their dispute through an ad hoc arbitration, they may send a written request to the Registrar to assist in providing such arbitration proceedings whenever needed.

26.4 Any request presented in accordance with this Article shall contain sufficient information to enable the Arbitration Board to proceed knowingly with the appointment of an arbitrator.

26.5 When the Euro–Arab Arbitration System has been requested by the parties, or by any other authority, to undertake the administration of an arbitration, it will be allowed to collect administrative charges, costs and fees in accordance with the scale annexed to these Rules.

SECTION THREE
EXPERTISE

Article 27

Expertise before Conciliation or Arbitration

27.1 Independently of any Request for conciliation or arbitration and even before any such Request is made, but provided the contracting parties had expressly provided for this possibility, any of those parties may request from the Secretariat-Registry the appointment at that party's expense of one or more individuals acting as an expert or experts whose mission is the finding of facts and/or opinion.

27.2 Once the matter is referred by a party to the Secretariat-Registry the latter shall immediately inform the other party of its request. Thereafter the Secretary-General shall appoint an expert, indicating the subject-matter, the extent and the terms of his mission. Any inquiry for the purpose of the finding of facts and/or opinion shall take place either in the presence of the parties or after they have been duly invited to attend.

27.3 The party against whom or in respect of whom the finding of facts and/or opinion are requested may in turn request through an application filed with the Secretariat-Registry that the same expert makes further findings or gives a further opinion, or that another expert be appointed.

27.4 The expert appointed under the present Article may request the parties to submit documents and answer questions which he deems in keeping with his mission.

27.5 The report on findings of fact or opinion shall state the grounds for such findings. It shall be communicated to the Secretariat-Registry and the parties without delay.

SECTION FOUR

ADMINISTRATIVE CHARGES, COSTS AND FEES FOR CONCILIATION, ARBITRATION AND EXPERTISE

Article 28

Conciliation

28.1 Administrative charges, costs for conciliation and fees of the conciliator shall be fixed by the Secretary-General by reference to the scale applicable to arbitration and at his discretion whenever a claim does not involve a sum of money.

28.2 Parties to a conciliation shall bear administrative charges, general costs and fees in equal shares unless otherwise agreed. They shall be directly and totally liable to the conciliator for payment of his fees.

28.3 Each party to a conciliation shall bear its own costs unless otherwise agreed.

Article 29

Arbitration

29.1 Administrative charges, costs and fees to arbitrator payable in relation to an arbitration shall include:

(a) administrative charges and costs incurred by the System, including the fee for registration of the Request; and
(b) arbitrators' fees and their disbursements.

29.2 At the discretion of the Arbitration Board, and except for the registration fee which must be paid outright, first and subsequent deposits on account of administrative charges, estimated costs and fees may be either remitted in full whenever required, or paid in instalments with a first demand bank guarantee.

29.3 *Registration fee*
A registration fee shall be payable at the time the Request is filed with the Secretariat-Registry. In default of payment, the file shall be returned to the claimant. The initial payment to the Secretariat-Registry is non-refundable.

29.4 *Administrative charges and costs*
Administrative charges and costs relating to any Request for arbitration made under these Rules shall include:

(a) administrative charges assessed in relation to each matter by the Board by reference to the scale annexed hereto or assessed by the Board at its discretion where a claim does not involve a sum of money, and also in view of the complication of the case; and
(b) the reimbursement of costs incurred in relation to each set of proceedings, such as secretarial costs, postage and fax charges, copying, translation costs, hire of rooms etc.

29.5 *Agreed Lump sum*
Notwithstanding the above provisions, the Board may seek the agreement of the parties to a lump sum to cover all administrative charges and costs. This amount must be paid before the file is given to the arbitrator.

29.6 *Arbitrators' fees*
29.6.1 Each arbitrator's fees shall be fixed according to the amounts in dispute, by reference to the scale applicable to the date on which the Request for arbitration is submitted.
Where the parties have not specified the amounts in dispute when submitting their requests or where a claim does not involve any sum of money or where the case seems complicated, the Board shall fix at its discretion, the amount of the deposit to be paid on account of fees and, where necessary, the final fee.

29.6.2 As an exception to the above provisions, the arbitrator's fees may be calculated at an hourly rate, according to the amount of time spent by him in the matter, provided the parties have so requested to the Board at the start of the arbitration procedure or at the time of the appointment of the sole arbitrator or of the nomination of an arbitrator by each party, pursuant to Article 21. A request for the calculation of the arbitrator's fee on an hourly rate, may subsequently be presented by the parties jointly on behalf of the arbitrator.

29.6.3 Fees shall be determined by taking into account, more particularly, the complexity of the case and any other significant factors.

29.7 *Repayment of the arbitrator's disbursements*
Disbursements incurred by the arbitrator relating directly to the arbitration proceedings shall be reimbursed them from the sums advanced by the parties or from the lump sum amount, provided for in Article 29.5 above, on presentation of proof of expenditure and in accordance with the guidelines given by the Secretariat-Registry, which the arbitrator will receive on his appointment.

29.8 *Experts' fees and costs of expert investigation in arbitratoin's proceedings*
If the arbitral tribunal – whether on its own or as the result of the request of one of the parties – appoints an expert, the fee of the latter shall be paid and his disbursements repaid as follows:

29.8.1 the amount of the fees shall be fixed by the Arbitration Board on the recommendation of the arbitral tribunal based on the expert's quotation and the parties' views; this amount shall take account of the reputation of the expert and the difficulty and length of his task.

29.8.2 the expert's fee and estimated disbursements must be entirely covered by deposits or a bank guarantee presented by the parties or one of them, before the expert starts his mission.

29.9 *General provisions*
29.9.1 The Board shall fix the amount of the deposits for the estimated administrative charges, costs and fees as well as the final amounts of the administrative charges, costs and arbitrator's fees. The decision of the Board in that respect shall be final.

29.9.2 The payment of the deposit for the estimated administrative charges, costs and fees shall be made before the file is given to the arbitrator, in accordance with the provisions of

Article 23.5 of the Rules. The Board may subsequently require payment of further deposits as the arbitration proceedings progress.

29.9.3 Where the respondent files a counter-claim, the parties will receive a request for a separate payment on account.

29.9.4 Each party shall be liable for one half of the payments on account. Should, however, one party fail to pay its share, the other party shall disburse it within thirty days of being notified by the Secretariat-Registry of the failing. If no payment is made by that other party, the Request for arbitration will be deemed as having been withdrawn. In that case, the first payment on account, or the balance after finalizing the accounts shall be returned to the party which has paid it, excluding however the registration fee which shall be non-refundable under Article 29.3 above.

29.9.5 The arbitral award shall determine the apportionment between the parties of the total amount of the administrative charges, costs and fees in relation to the arbitration. The parties shall be jointly and severally liable to the Euro–Arab Arbitration System for the administrative charges and to the arbitrator for payment of all his disbursements and fees arising out of arbitration proceedings. The arbitrator shall have a right of action against the parties, but not the System, for the recovery of his disbursements and fees.

29.9.6 The arbitral tribunal shall determine the right of any party to recover its legal costs and shall determine the sum to be recovered, which shall be specified in the award.

Article 30

Expertise

30.1 The fees payable to each expert appointed under Article 27 of these Rules shall be fixed by the Secretary-General, based on the expert's quotation and the view of the contracting party which has requested the appointment of the expert.

30.2 The disbursements payable to the expert appointed under Article 27 of these Rules shall be assessed and released by the Secretary-General on the production of evidence of expenditure which shall be passed to the contracting parties.

30.3 The expert's fee and estimated disbursements must be entirely covered by deposits or a bank guarantee presented by the party which requested the appointment of the expert, before the latter starts with his mission.

30.4 The decision of the Secretary-General regarding the expert's fees and his disbursements confers on the expert a right of action against the party which requested his appointment, not against the System.

30.5 The fees and estimated disbursements of the expert appointed by the arbitral tribunal shall be agreed upon and covered pursuant to the provisions of Article 29.8 above.

Part III
General and Transitional Provisions

Article 31

Accepting the Rules

Including in a contract an arbitration clause referring to these Rules or putting in motion procedures under these Rules shall imply acceptance by the parties of the entirety of these Rules.

Article 32

Notices

32.1 All notices or communications between any of the parties, the Secretary-General, the Registrar, the Secretariat-Registry and the arbitrator shall be deemed to have been validly made if they are handed to the addressee(s) against a duly signed receipt, or if they are sent to the addressee(s) by recorded mail, with advice of delivery unless otherwise provided in the municipal law of the country in which the award is likely to be enforced.

32.2 Notice given by fax or telex should be deemed to have validly been given on the date of such fax or telex provided that either the recipient acknowledges receipt or the sender confirms the notice by letter sent by recorded mail with advice of delivery.

Article 33

Languages

33.1 These Rules have been drawn up in three official languages – French, Arabic and English. The texts in all three languages have equal force.

33.2 In the event of any construction dispute arising from the three official texts of the Rules, the Arbitration Board shall be empowered finally to resolve such dispute.

33.3 Translations into other working languages may be carried out at the initiative of the Arbitration Board or any of the Arbitration Committees. They shall be filed with the Secretariat-Registry and given to the Arbitration Board which may proceed with the necessary corrections after consulting with the initiator of the translation.

Article 34

Transitional Provisions

34.1 Arbitration, conciliation and/or expertise clause(s) adopted before the effective date of the present Rules, in contracts which refer to the Rules of Arbitration of the Franco–Arab Chamber of Commerce, the Arab–Swiss Chamber of Commerce and Industry and the Euro–Arab Chamber of Commerce in their successive versions which became effective on 10th January 1983, 28th November 1990 and 18th December 1994 shall continue to be fully effective.

34.2 When a dispute arises after these Rules have come into effect, the parties to that dispute shall be invited by the Secretariat-Registry to substitute these Rules for the rules mentioned in the preceding paragraph. This shall include the new scale of administrative charges, costs and fees of conciliation, arbitration and expertise.

34.3 The parties concerned shall be deemed to have accepted the substitution unless either of them expresses his refusal within the thirty-day period stipulated in Article 20.3 of these Rules.

34.4 In the event of a disagreement between the parties regarding such substitution, the dispute shall be determined in accordance with the arbitration rules referred to in the contract, with the exception, however, of the scale of administrative charges, costs and fees which shall be the one laid down by the present Rules.

To this date the following Euro–Arab Chambers of Commerce have subscribed to these Rules. These Chambers are (by alphabetical order of the European country concerned):

– The Arab–Austrian Chamber of Commerce
– The Arab–Belgium–Luxembourg Chamber of Commerce
– The Arab–British Chamber of Commerce
– The Franco–Arab Chamber of Commerce
– The Arab–German Chamber of Commerce
– The Arab–Hellenic Chamber of Commerce and Development
– The Arab–Irish Chamber of Commerce
– The Italo–Arab Chamber of Commerce
– The Arab–Portuguese Chamber of Commerce
– The Arab–Swiss Chamber of Commerce and Industry

Appendix 1
SCALE OF ADMINISTRATIVE CHARGES

In addition to the registration fee the administrative charges payable when implementing these Rules shall be determined as a percentage of the value of the subject-matter as below:

Value of the sum in dispute $ (in US dollars)	Charges per percentage
Registration fee and up to $50,000	$1,500
$50,001 to $100,000	2.00%
$100,001 to $300,000	1.50%
$300,001 to $500,000	1.00%
$500,001 to $1,000,000	0.80%
$1,000,001 to $2,000,000	0.30%
$2,000,001 to $5,000,000	0.15%
$5,000,001 to $10,000,000	0.08%
$10,000,001 to $50,000,000	0.05%
$50,000,001 to $100,000,000	0.03%
Over $100,000,000	0.01%

Appendix II

SCALE OF CONCILIATORS', ARBITRATORS' AND EXPERTS' FEES

The fees of the Conciliators, Arbitrators and Experts appointed or nominated under these Rules shall be based upon an hourly rate of $250–$350 per hour and or a percentage of the value of the subject-matter, as follows:

Value of the sum in dispute $ (in US dollars)	Minimum % Percentage	Maximum % Percentage
up to $50,000	2.50%	12.00%
$50,001 to $100,000	1.00%	7.00%
$100,001 to $300,000	0.70%	5.00%
$300,001 to $500,000	0.60%	2.50%
$500,001 to $1,000,000	0.40%	2.00%
$1,000,001 to $2,000,000	0.25%	1.50%
$2,000,001 to $5,000,000	0.15%	0.75%
$5,000,001 to $10,000,000	0.08%	0.40%
$10,000,001 to $50,000,000	0.03%	0.10%
$50,000,001 to $100,000,000	0.02%	0.08%
Over $100,000,000	0.01%	0.05%

Egypt
Law on Investment Guarantees and Incentives
(Law No. 8 of 1997)*

In the name of the People;
The President of the Republic;
The People's Assembly has passed the following Law and we have promulgated it.

Article 1

The provisions of the attached Law on Investment Guarantees and Incentives shall come into force.

Article 2

Without prejudice to the provisions of Article 18 of the attached Law, the provision of this Law shall not derogate the privileges and tax exemptions as well as the other guarantees and incentives prescribed for the companies and establishments existing at the time the Law comes into force. These companies and establishments shall maintain those privileges, exemptions, guarantees and incentives until their respective periods expire according to legislations and treaties from which they derive.

Article 3

The administrative Authority concerned with implementing the provisions of the attached law shall replace the General Authority for Investment, the Authority's Board of Directors, and the Head of its Executive body. A decree of the President of the Republic shall be issued determining this Administrative body and indicating its authorities as well as regulating its activity and setting the regulations related to personnel rules therein without being restricted by governmental rules.

Pending issue of this decree, the General Authority for Investment shall be considered the Competent Administrative Authority under the provisions of the Attached Law, and the rules regulating personnel affairs in this authority shall remain in force.

---

* Translated by Kosheri, Rashed & Riad.

Article 4

Without prejudice to the provisions of the previous article, the Investment Law promulgated by Law No. 230 of the year 1989 shall be abrogated, except for the Third Clause or Article 20 of the afore-mentioned Law. Articles 5 and 5-bis of Law No. 1 of the year 1973 concerning Hotels and Tourist Establishments, Articles 21, 24 and 25 of Law No. 59 of the year 1979 concerning New Urban Communities, and article 30 of Law No. 95 of the year 1995 concerning Financial Leasing. All other provisions contrary the provisions of the attached Law, shall also be abrogated.

Article 5

The Prime Minister shall issue the Executive regulation of the attached Law within three months from the date of its coming into force, and pending issue of this regulation, the regulations and decisions applicable at the date this law comes into force shall continue to apply where they do not contradict its provisions.

Article 6

This Law shall be published in the Official Journal and shall come into force effective the day following the date of its publication.[1]

---

[1] This Law was published in No. 16 bis of the Official Journal dated 11 May 1997.

PART I

GENERAL PROVISIONS

Article 1

The provisions of this Law shall apply to all companies and establishments, whatever the legal system they are subject to, that are established after the date of its entry into force, in order to exercise their activity in any of the following fields:

- Reclamation and cultivation of barren and desert lands or either of them.
- Animal, poultry and Fish Production.
- Industry and Mining.
- Hotels, Motels, Boarding Houses, Touristic Villages, and Touristic Transportation.
- Transport of Goods in Cooling Vans, Cold refrigerators for Preservation of agricultural Products, Industrial Products and food stuffs, container Stations, and Grain Silos.
- Air transport and the services directly connected therewith.
- High seas Maritime Transport.
- Oil Services supporting digging and exploration operations, and Transport and delivery of gas.
- Housing projects, the units of which are wholly leased empty for non-administrative housing purposes.
- The infrastructure comprising drinking water, drainage, electricity, roads and communications.
- Hospitals and medical and Treatment Centres which offer 10% of their capacity free of charge.
- Financial leasing.
- Guaranteeing subscription to securities.
- Risk Capital.
- Production of computer software and systems.
- Projects funded by the Social Fund for Development.

The Council of Ministers may add other fields needed by the country.

The Executive regulation of this law shall determine the conditions and limits of the above-mentioned fields.

Article 2

Enjoyment of the investment Guarantees and incentives including tax exemptions by companies and establishments of multiple purposes and activities shall be restricted to their activities in the fields determined in the previous article and in those added by the Council of Ministers.

Article 3

The provisions of this Law shall not derogate any better privileges, tax exemptions, or other guarantees and incentives prescribed in other legislation or treaties.

Article 4

The competent Administrative Authority shall be concerned with verifying the Articles of Association and the Statutes of Companies.

The data of the Articles of Association and the statutes shall indicate the names of the contracting parties, the legal form of the Company, its name, the subject of its activity, its duration period, its capital, the percentages of partnership by Egyptian and non-Egyptian parties, the methods of subscription thereto, and the partners' rights and obligations.

The preliminary Contracts and the statutes of Joint Stock Companies, Partnerships Limited by Shares, and Limited Liability Companies shall be drawn up according to the models to be issued by a decision of the Prime Minister.

The partners' signatures to the Companies Contracts whatever is their legal form shall be legalized against a legalization fee amounting to one fourth of one per cent of the paid up Capital, with a ceiling of five hundred Egyptian Pounds, or their equivalent in foreign currency as the case may be, whether such legalization is made in Egypt or with the Egyptian Authorities abroad.

A decision of the Competent Administrative Authority shall be issued licensing the foundation of Companies that are established according to this Law and that enjoy its privileges, and they shall have the juristic personality as from the date of their registration in the Commercial Register, and the Statutes and the Articles of Association of the Company shall be published according to the rules and procedures determined in the Executive regulation of this Law.

The foregoing provisions shall apply to all amendments to the Company's statute.

Article 5

The Administrative Authority, determined by the Executive Regulation of this Law, shall allocate the lands owned by the State or by public juristic persons, that are necessary for the Companies and establishments and shall conclude their respective contracts on behalf of the Concerned Authorities. These authorities shall provide the said Authority with all maps and data concerning the lands that are available for that purpose, along with the conditions and rules of conclusion of contracts related thereto.

This Authority shall also obtain from the concerned authorities, on behalf of the owners of companies and establishments, all licenses required for their establishment, management, and operation.

Article 6

The request for bringing the criminal action in connection with the crimes prescribed in Articles 124 of the Customs Law promulgated by Law No. 66 of the year 1963, Article 191 of the Law on Income Taxes promulgated by Law no. 157 of the year 1981, Article 45 of the Law on General Sales Tax promulgated by Law No. 11 of the year 1991 and Article 9 of Law No. 38 of the year 1994 concerning the organization of dealing in foreign currencies, shall be submitted after consulting the view of the Competent Administrative Authority, if the person accused of committing the crime is in the service of one of the companies or establishments subject to the provisions of this Law.

The Competent Administrative Authority has to give its view, in this respect, within fifteen days from the date of receipt of the letter requesting its view, otherwise the request may be submitted for bringing the action.

Article 7

The investment disputes concerning implementation of the provisions of this Law may be settled in the manner agreed upon with the investor.

Agreement may also be reached between the concerned parties on settling these disputes within the context of the treaties in force between the Arab Republic of Egypt and the state of the investor, or within the context of the treaties on Settlement of investment disputes signed between states and nationals of the other states to which the Arab Republic of Egypt has adhered by virtue of Law No. 90 of the year 1971, according to the conditions and terms, and in the cases in which these treaties apply, or according to the provision of the Law on Arbitration in Civil and Commercial Matters promulgated by Law No. 27 of the year 1994. Agreement may also be reached on settling the aforementioned disputes by means of arbitration at the Cairo Regional Centre for International Commercial Arbitration.

PART II
INVESTMENT GUARANTEES

Article 8

The Companies and Establishments may not be nationalized or confiscated.

Article 9

The Companies and Establishments may not be subject by administrative method to sequestration, attachment of their assets, or their seizure, guarding, freezing or confiscation.

Article 10

No Administration Authority may interfere in pricing the Companies' and establishments' products, nor in determining their profits.

Article 11

No Administrative Authority may cancel or suspend the licence granted to the Company or the establishment to use real estates wholly or partially, except in cases of infringement of the licence conditions.

The decision to cancel or suspend the licence shall be issued by the Prime Minister upon the proposal of the Competent Administrative Authority, and the concerned party shall have the right to contest such decree before the Judicial Administrative Court within thirty days from the date of notifying it to him or of the date of his learning of it.

Article 12

The Companies and establishments shall have the right to own the building lands and built real estates that are necessary for exercising their activities and for their expansion, whatever is the nationality, place of residence, or the percentages of partnership of the partners.

Article 13

Without prejudice to the provisions of the Laws, regulations and decisions organizing import, the Companies and establishments shall have the right to import by themselves or via third parties whatever they need, for their establishment, expansion or operation, of production inputs, materials, machines, equipment, spare parts, and means of transport that are suitable to the nature of their activities, and without need for registration in the Register of Importers.

The companies and establishments shall also have the right to export their products by themselves or through middlemen without need for license and without need for their registration in the Register of Exporters.

Article 14

The Joint Stock Companies, Partnerships Limited by Shares or Limited Liability Companies whose activities are restricted to the scopes referred to in Article 1 of this Law, shall not be subject to the provisions of Articles 17, 18, 19 and 41, as well as the first and fourth paragraphs of Article 77, and Articles 83, 92 and 93 of the Law on Joint Stock Companies, Partnerships Limited by Shares and Limited Liability Companies, promulgated by Law No. 159 of the year 1981.

The foundation parts and shares may be circulated during the first two financial years of the Company with the approval of the Prime Minister or his representative.

The Competent Administrative Authority shall replace the Companies Administration in applying the provisions of the above mentioned Law No. 159 of the year 1981, and its Executive regulation concerning the above mentioned companies.

The Joint Stock Companies shall not be subject to the provisions of Law No. 73 of the year 1973 specifying the conditions and procedures of election of the Workers' Representatives in the Board of Directors of Public Sector Units, Joint Stock Companies, and private associations and foundations. The company's statute shall indicate the mode of worker's participation in the administration thereof as determined by the Executive regulation of this Law.

Article 15

Joint Stock Companies shall be exempted from applying the provisions of Law No. 113 of the year 1958 concerning Appointment in positions of the Joint Stock Companies and Public Organizations. They shall also be exempted from applying Article 24 of Labour Law promulgated by Law No. 137 of the year 1981.

PART III
INVESTMENT INCENTIVES
CHAPTER 1: TAX EXEMPTIONS

Article 16

The profits of Companies' and establishments' and of the partners' shares therein shall be exempted from the tax on the Revenues of Commercial and Industrial Activity, or the tax on profits of Corporations.

The exemption shall be for a period of ten years for companies and establishments set up within the new industrial Zones, new urban communities and the remote areas which are determined by a decision of the Prime Minister, and also for the new projects financed by the Social Fund for Development.

Article 17

Profits of companies and establishments exercising their activities outside the Old Valley, and the partners shares therein, whether the establishment is outside that Old Valley or is transferred therefrom, shall be exempted from the tax on Revenues of Commercial and Industrial Activity or from the Tax on profits of Corporations, as the case may be for a period of twenty years, starting from the first financial year following the start of the production or exercise of the activity.

A decision of the Council of Ministers shall determine the areas to which this provision applies.

Article 18

Companies, establishments and projects financed by the Social Fund for Development, existing at the time this Law comes into force which exercise their activity in the fields referred to in Article 1 of this Law shall complete the periods of exemption prescribed in the two previous articles, if the exemption periods prescribed for them have not been completed at that date.

Article 19

In applying the provisions of the previous articles, the first year of the exemption shall include the period from the date of start of production or exercise of activity, as the case may be, up to the end of the following financial year. The Company or the Establishment shall notify the competent administrative Authority of the date of start of production or exercise of activity within one month from that date.

Article 20

The Articles of incorporation of companies and establishments and loan and mortgage contracts connected with their activities shall be exempted from the stamp tax and the notarization and registration duties, for a period of three years from the date of registration in the Commercial Register.

The contracts of registration of lands which are necessary for establishing the companies and establishments shall also be exempted from the aforementioned tax and duties.

Article 21

An amount equivalent to a percentage of the paid up capital determined at the Central Bank of Egypt's lending and discount rate for the year of the account, shall be exempted from the tax on the profits of corporations, providing the Company is a Joint Stock Company and its stocks are registered in one of the stock exchanges.

Article 22

Yields of bonds, finance share warrants, and of other similar securities issued by Joint Stock Companies shall be exempted from the tax on revenues of movable capitals, provided they are offered for public subscription and are registered in one of the stock exchanges.

Article 23

The provisions of Article 4 of the Law regulating Customs Exemptions promulgated by Law No. 186 of the year 1986 regarding the collection of a customs tax at a unified rate of 5% of the value, shall apply to all machines, equipment, and instruments imported by the companies and establishments, which are necessary for their establishment.

Article 24

Profits resulting from the merger, division or transformation of the companies' legal forms, shall be exempted from the taxes and duties due by reason of the merger, division or change of the legal form.

Article 25

The merging and merged companies and establishments and the companies and establishments which are divided, or whose legal form is transformed shall enjoy the exemptions prescribed therefore before the merger, division, or transformation of their legal form, until their relevant exemption periods expire. The merger, division or the transformation of the legal form shall not result in any new tax exemptions.

Article 26

The result of evaluation of the parts in kind participating in the foundation of Joint Stock Companies, partnership limited by shares, or limited liability companies, or in their capital increase, shall be exempted from the tax on revenues of commercial and industrial activity as the case may be, or the tax on profits of corporations.

Article 27

The executive regulation of this Law shall determine the conditions, rules and procedures concerning enjoyment of tax exemptions, automatically and without depending on an administrative approval, providing the exemption shall be cancelled in case of violation of those conditions and rules.

A decision of the Prime Minister upon the proposal of the competent administrative authority shall be issued concerning cancellation of the exemption, and the concerned party may contest this decision, before the judicial administrative court, within thirty days from the date such decision is announced thereto, or from his learning of it.

CHAPTER 2: LAND ALLOCATION

Article 28

A decision of the Council of Ministers, upon the proposal of the concerned Minister, may allocate state-owned lands or lands owned by public juristic persons, to the companies and establishments set up in defined areas, in the fields determined in Article 1 of this Law, free of charge, and according to the procedures prescribed in the executive regulation of this Law.

CHAPTER 3: FREE ZONES

Article 29

The free zone which covers a whole city shall be established by virtue of a Law.

Public free zones shall be established by virtue of a decision of the Council of Ministers upon the proposal of the Competent Administrative Authority, in view of establishment of licensed projects, whatever is their legal form.

A decision of the Competent Administrative Authority may be issued concerning the establishment of private free zones, each of which is confined to a single project, if its nature so necessitates. The Competent Administrative Authority may also approve changing one of the projects which are set up inside the country, into a private free zone, in the light of the rules determined in the executive regulation of this Law.

The decision establishing the free zone shall comprise an indication of its site and limits.

The Public Free Zone shall be managed by a Board of Directors to be formed and its Chairman appointed by a decision of the Competent Administrative Authority.

The Board of Directors shall be responsible for implementing the provisions of this Law, its executive regulation, and the decisions issued by the aforesaid Authority.

Article 30

The Competent Administrative Authority shall set the policy to be followed by the Free Zones. It shall have the power to issue whatever decisions it considers necessary for realizing the purpose for which these zones are set up for and in particular the following:

(a)   Setting up the systems and regulations necessary of managing the free zones.
(b)   Setting up the conditions for granting the licences, occupation of the lands and real estates, the rules on entry and exit of goods, the provisions of recording them, the charges for occupying the places in which they are deposited in and for examination and verification of the documents, and the system concerning control and guard of those zones, as well as the collection of duties due to the State.

Article 31

The Board of Directors of the Public Free zone shall be responsible for licensing the establishment of projects. Licensing the project to exercise the activity shall be granted by virtue of a decision issued by the Chairman of the Board of Directors of the Zone.

The licence shall comprise an indication of the purposes for which it is granted, its validity period, and the amount of the financial guarantee payable by the licencee. The licence shall not be assignable wholly or partially except with the approval of the Authority issuing it. Refusal to grant the licence or refusal of its assignment shall be issued by a motivated decision. The concerned party may complain against it to the Competent Administrative Authority according to the rules and procedures prescribed in the Executive regulation of this Law.

The licencee shall not enjoy the exemptions or privileges prescribed in this Law except within the limits of the purposes indicated in the licence.

Article 32

Without prejudice to the provisions prescribed in the Laws and Regulations concerning prohibition of dealing in certain goods or materials, goods which are exported abroad by the Zone projects or imported to exercise their activity shall not be subject to the rules on imports and exports, nor to the customs procedures for exports and imports. Nor shall they be subject to the Customs Taxes, the General Sales Tax and to other taxes and duties.

All articles, equipment, machines, and means of transport which are necessary for exercising the activity licensed for the projects inside the free Zones shall be exempted from Customs Taxes, the General Sales Tax, and other taxes and duties, with the exception of passenger cars.

The Executive regulation of this Law shall determine the procedures for transport of goods and their insurance, from start of unloading them until their arrival at the free zones, and vice versa.

The Competent Administrative Authority may allow entry of local and foreign goods, materials, parts and raw materials owned by the project or by third parties from inside the country to the free zone temporarily for their repair or for carrying out industrial processes on them then returning them into the country, without being subject to the applicable import rules, as indicated in the Executive regulation of this Law.

The Customs Tax shall be collected on the repair value according to the provision of the Customs Laws.

The provisions of Article 33 of this Law shall apply to the industrial processes.

Article 33

Import into the country from the free zones shall be in accordance with the general rules concerning import from abroad, and Customs Taxes shall be payable on goods which are imported form the free zone to the local market as though they were imported from abroad.

With regard to the products imported form the free zones projects which comprise local as well as foreign components, the Customs Tax basis in their respect shall be the value of the foreign components at the price ruling at the time of their exit from the free zone into the country, providing the Customs Tax due on the foreign components do not exceed the tax payable on the final product imported from abroad.

The foreign components are constituted in the imported foreign parts and materials according to their condition at their entry into the free zone, without taking into account the operating costs in this zone.

The free zone, with regard to the freight, shall be considered the country of origin concerning the products manufactured in it.

Article 34

The Customs director of the free zone shall notify the Chief of the Zone about the unjustified "Under and Over" cases other than what is indicated in the Bill of Lading, in the number of parcels or their contents, or the conserved or dispersed goods, if they are imported in the name of the free zone.

A decision of the Competent Administrative Authority shall be issued regulating the responsibility in the cases mentioned in the previous clause and the percentage of tolerance in them.

Article 35

Projects which are established in the free zones, and the profits which they distribute shall not be subject to the provisions of tax and duties Laws applicable in Egypt.

However, these projects shall be subject to an annual duty of 1% (one per cent) of the value of goods on their entry, concerning storage projects and of the value of commodities on their exit, concerning manufacturing and assembly projects. Transit goods trade whose destination is determined shall be exempted from this duty. Projects whose main activity does not require entry or exit of goods shall be subject to an annual duty of 1% (one per cent) of the total revenues which they realize, based on the accounts approved by a certificate of an accountant.

In all cases, the projects shall pay the services' charges determined in the executive regulation of this Law.

Article 36

Companies exercising their activities in the public free zones shall not be subject to the provisions prescribed in Laws No. 73 of the year 1973 and No. 159 of the year 1981.

Article 37

Maritime Transport Projects which are established in the free zones shall be exempted form the conditions on it, prescribed in the Maritime Trade Law, and in Law No. 84 of the year 1949 Concerning Registration of Merchant Ships.

Ships which are owned by these projects shall be exempted from the provisions of Law No. 12 of the year 1964 concerning the establishment of the Egyptian General Organization for Maritime Transport.

Article 38

The Licencee shall be obliged to insure the buildings, machines and equipment against all accidents, and he shall also remove them, at his own costs, within the period determined by the Board of Directors of the Zone, according to the rules set up by the Competent Administrative Authority.

Article 39

Entering or residing in the free zones shall be in accordance to the conditions and terms determined by the Executive Regulation of this Law.

Article 40

The provisions of Law No. 173 of the year 1958 stipulating obtainment of a work permit before taking up a job with foreign organizations and Law No. 231 of the year 1996 concerning certain provisions regulating the work of Egyptians with foreign organizations shall not apply to Egyptian workers in the projects set up in the free zones.

Article 41

No person may exercise a permanent trade or profession in the Public free zone, for his own account except after obtaining a permit therefore from its Board of Directors chairman according to the terms and conditions determined in the Executive Regulations of this Law and after paying the fees that are determined in this regulation, which shall not exceed five hundred pounds per year.

Article 42

The Labour Contract with the workers in the free zones shall be drawn up in quadruplicate of which one copy shall be handed to each one of the two parties, a copy shall be deposited with the Free Zone Department, and another with the Labour Office in the Zone, and if the contract is drawn up in a foreign language, an Arabic translation thereof shall be attached to each copy of these two copies.

Article 43

Projects set up in the Public Free Zones shall not be subject to the provisions of Law No. 113 of the year 1958, and to Article 24 and Chapter 5 of Part III of the Labour Law.

The Board of Directors of the Competent Administrative Authority shall set up the rules regulating personnel affairs in those projects.

Article 44

The provisions of the Social Insurance Law, promulgated by Law No. 79 of the year 1975 shall apply to the Egyptian workers employed in projects exercising their activities in the Free Zones.

Article 45

Whoever violates the provisions of Article 41 of this Law shall be liable to a fine penalty of not less than two thousand pounds, and not more than five thousand pounds.

The criminal action may only be brought concerning these crimes except upon a written request from the competent administrative authority.

A settlement may be concluded by the said Authority with the violator during the course of the action, in return for payment of a sum equivalent to the minimum amount of the value of the fine, and the settlement shall result in termination of the criminal action.

Article 46

The Provisions of Articles 8, 9, 10, 11 and 20 of this Law shall apply to the investment in free zones.

Egypt

Law Amending some Rules of the Law Concerning Joint Stock Companies, Partnerships Limited by Shares and Limited Liability Companies Promulgated by Law No. 159 of 1981 (Law No. 3 of 1998)

In the name of the People,
The President of the Republic
The People's Assembly has decided the Law whose text is as follows and we have promulgated it.

ARTICLE ONE

Articles 17, 18, 19, the first paragraph of Article 21, Articles 32, 33, 37 , 39, 48 and 64 of the Law concerning Joint Stock Companies, partnerships limited by shares, and Limited Liability Companies, promulgated by Law No. 159 of 1981, shall be replaced by the following texts:

Article 17

The founders or their representatives have to notify the Competent Advisory Authority about the formation of the Company. The following documents have to be enclosed with the notification.

A. The preliminary contract and the statute of the Company concerning Joint Stock Companies and partnerships limited by shares and the foundation contract concerning of the Limited Liability Companies.
B. The approval of the Council of Ministers of the foundation of the Company if its aim or one of its aims is to operate in the field of satellites, issue of newspapers or remote

* Translated by Kosheri, Rashed & Riad.

sensors or any activity concerning an aim or activity forming part of the aims or activities mentioned in the Law of associations and foundations.

C.   An attestation of an authorized bank confirming the subscription in the totality of the shares or parts of the Company, payment of the minimum value that has to be paid of the monetary shares or parts and that they have been put under the disposition of the Company until its acquisition of the juristic personality.

D.   A receipt of payment of a duty amounting to one over a thousand of the issued Capital of Joint Stock Companies and partnerships limited by shares and of the paid up capital of Limited Liability Companies and of a minimum of One Hundred Pounds and a maximum of One Thousand Pounds.

The competent Administrative Authority has to certify the above to the person who has made the notification if all the documents mentioned in the preceding subsections were rightly attached to it, and the Company shall be inscribed in the Commercial Register on presentation of this certificate without need for any other condition or procedure and whatever is the percentage of non Egyptian participation in it.

The Company shall be registered and shall acquire the juristic personality after fifteen days from its inscription in the Commercial Register.

Article 18

The competent Administrative Authority may within ten days from its notification of foundation of the Company object to its foundation by a registered letter sent to the address of the Company as stated in the documents attached to the notification, and a copy of this letter shall be sent to the Commercial Register of its notation on the data relating to the inscription of the Company.

The reason for the objection has to be stated and must contain the procedures that have to be followed in order to remove the reasons for the objection.

The Administrative Authority may only object to the foundation of the Company for the following reasons:

A.   The preliminary contract the foundation Contract or the statute of the Company's contravention of the obligatory data included in the model or its inclusion of illegal matters.

B.   If the aim of the Company was contrary to the Law or to public order.

C.   If one of the founders did not have the necessary capacity to found the Company.

Article 19

The Company has, within fifteen days of being informed of the objection, to remove its reasons or present a complaint about it to the Minister of Economy, otherwise the Competent Administrative Authority has to take a decision to strike out the inscription of the Company in the commercial register.

The expiry of fifteen days from the date of presentation of the complaint without deciding upon it, shall be considered an acceptance of it which removes the effects of the objection.

In case the complaint of the Company is rejected, it has to be informed about it by registered letter in order to remove the reasons for the objection, and if it does not remove them within ten days from the date of its notification of refusal of the complaint, the competent Administrative Authority shall take a decision to strike out the Company from the commercial register.

In all cases the juristic personality of the Company shall be terminated from the day of issue of the decision to strike out, and the concerned parties may challenge this decision before the Court of Administrative jurisdiction, within sixty days from the date of their being given notice of it or of their knowledge of it, and the Court has to decide on an urgent basis, upon the challenge.

The founders shall be responsible jointly and severally in their own funds for the results and damages to third parties due to striking out the Company from the commercial register, without prejudice to the applicable penal sanctions.

Article 21

(Paragraph 1)

The executive regulation shall prescribe the procedures relating to publication of the contract and statute of the Company in the Egyptian Gazette or in the special bulletin that is issued for this purpose or in any other way.

Article 32

The Company shall have an issued capital and the statute may provide for an authorized capital that exceeds up to ten times the issued capital.

The executive regulation may provide for a minimum issued capital in relation to companies exercising certain types of activity and the part of it that has to be paid on foundation.

The issued capital has to be fully subscribed and each subscriber has to pay at least 10% of the nominal value of the monetary shares which has to be increased to 25% within not more than three months from the date of foundation of the Company, and the rest of this value has to be paid within not more than five years from the date of foundation of the Company.

The executive regulation shall prescribe the procedures of circulation of shares before full payment of their value.

Article 33

The extraordinary general assembly may decide to increase the issued or the authorized capital.

The board of directors may also increase the issued capital within the limits of the authorized capital in case it exists.

In all cases the issued Capital may not be increased before its full payment, except by a decision of the extraordinary general assembly and a condition that the subscribers in the increase pay not less than the percentage of the issued Capital that has been decided to be paid before its increase and that they pay the rest of the value on the same dates as those decided for payment of the rest of the value of the issued Capital.

The increase in the issued Capital has to be actually made within the three years following the issue of the decision authorizing the increase or within the duration of payment of the issued Capital before its increase, whichever is longer, otherwise the decision authorizing the increase shall be null and void.

Article 37

Offer of the shares of the Company for public subscription has to be made through one of the banks authorized by the Ministry of Economy to receive subscriptions or by Companies authorized to deal in stocks, after approval of the money market General Authority.

In case the subscription is not covered within its due date, the banks or the Companies which received the subscription may – if so authorized – cover all or part of the shares offered for subscription which have not been covered.

They may reoffer to the public what they have subscribed to without being restricted by the procedures and constraints relating to circulation of shares, provided in this Law.

The executive regulation shall prescribe the proceedings and conditions of application of this Article.

Article 39

The Company shall have a financial year as decided in the statute.

It shall prepare for it, financial statements according to the accounting criteria decided upon by the Minister of Economy.

The statute of the Company may provide for the preparation of periodical financial statements for it whose duration is not less than three months.

On the other hand the Company whose aim is to participate in the foundation of other Companies or to participate in them in any way, has to prepare joint financial statements concerning those Companies.

Article 48

If the Company acquires by any means parts of its shares, it has to dispose of those shares to third parties within a maximum of one year from the date of its acquisition of them, otherwise it shall be obliged to lower its Capital by the nominal value of those shares and to follow the procedures decided upon in this respect.

The Company may purchase part of its shares in order to distribute them to its employees as part of their shares in the profit

Article 64

The board of directors has to prepare for each financial year – on a date that allows holding the generally assembly of the shareholders within not more than three months for the date of its expiry – the financial statements of the Company and a report concerning its activity during the financial year and its financial situation at the end of this year.

ARTICLE TWO

A new paragraph shall be added to Article 40 of the above-mentioned Law concerning Joint Stock Companies, partnerships limited by shares and limited liability Companies, as follows:

The statute of the Company may provide that the general Assembly has the right to distribute all or part of the profits as shown by the periodical financial statements made by the Company and on condition of attaching to them a report about them prepared by the auditor.

ARTICLE THREE

The word "notification" in the first paragraph of Article 14 shall be replaced by the sentence "request for the authorization", the sentence "except for reasons approved by the Committee mentioned in Article 18" mentioned in subsection "B" of Article 68 shall be replaced by the sentence "except for reasons approved by the Competent Administrative Authority" and the second paragraph of Article 158 shall be replaced by the following:

The request shall be presented to the Minister of Economy, and he shall form a Committee to examine the request whose membership shall include a supervisor from the Central Auditing Agency.

ARTICLE FOUR

Articles 21 bis, 22, 23, 36 and 92 shall be abrogated as well as the sentence "except with the approval of the Committee mentioned in Article 18 of this Law" in Article 16, and the sentence "after approval of the Committee mentioned in Article 18" in the two Articles 130 and 136 of the above-mentioned Law concerning Joint Stock Companies, partnerships limited by shares and Limited Liability Companies.

ARTICLE FIVE

The Minister of Economy shall issue the decisions necessary for implementation of this Law.

ARTICLE SIX

This Law shall be published in the official journal and shall come into force on the day following the date of its publication.

Palestine
The Palestinian Authority
Ministry of Justice
Rule of Law Strategic Development Plan
August 1996*

Since the establishment of the Palestinian Authority Ministry of Justice in 1994, much has already been achieved in restoring the legal infrastructure of Palestine. Still, many more challenges urgently need to be addressed. The responsibility of developing neoteric unified legislation for the West Bank and Gaza, standardising judicial and prosecution procedures and improving court buildings and facilities is a high priority of the Ministry.

The requirement for the Ministry to establish itself, to create responsible public service departments, to re-establish procedures that were lost under the period of Israel's occupation and the need for it to address and answer new demands, has also presented my staff and I with a series of great challenges. Assisted by the development priorities issued by the Palestinian Authority and aided by the generous assistance of the international donor community, the Ministry of Justice has developed a dynamic strategic plan to meet these challenges.

This plan has been devised after an intense study of the existing judicial and legal systems and close scrutiny of the Ministry's procedures and future requirements. The plan is designed to harmonize our legal procedures and to effectively coordinate donor assistance in this field.

The Strategic Development Plan outlines the manner in which the Ministry of Justice intends to modernize and improve the Palestinian legal and judicial system. It provides a framework for the activities of the Ministry, its supporting agencies and donor assistance. It clearly demonstrates the comprehensive and integrated strategies the Ministry plans to implement over the next 36 months.

The contribution of the international donor community in assisting our legal development programme has already been significant. I look forward to their future assistance and cooperation in creating a just and effective legal system for the Palestinian people.

Mr Ibrahim Aldaghma	Freih Abu Middein
General Counsel	Minister of Justice
Ministry of Justice	Palestinian Authority
August 1996	August 1996

---

* The Rule of Law Strategic Development Plan was compiled by the Ministry of Justice, Diwan Al-Fatwah Wal Tachri'e. The Ministry of Justice gratefully acknowledges the contribution of Australian International Legal Resources in the drafting, compiling and publishing of this document.

STATEMENT OF MISSION

The Rule of Law Strategic Development Plan provides the means to achieve a modern, comprehensive and effective Legal and Judicial System for the Palestinian people.
The Plan provides the following necessary management tools:

- Identification and definition of tasks
- Allocation of tasks
- Synchronization of tasks
- Coordination of resources
- Definition of channels of communication and liaison

EMERGING CHALLENGES

We recognize the need for the Ministry to be attuned to factors which may effect and reflect socio-economic changes to thePalestinian community. Four major strategic challenges we are now addressing are:

Government Policies and Priorities

Progressive Government policies regarding the criminal justice system and the government's approach to public management will require increased flexibility and responsiveness to change on the part of the Ministry.

International and Public Funding

In light of the increasing demand for the use of international donor and public funds, the Ministry of Justice, to be competitive and deserving of assistance, will need to demonstrate, on a continuing basis, the value of its contribution to the developmetn of a democratic Palestine.

Technological Developments

In a rapidly changing technological environment, new possibilities regarding delivery and access to information will require adaptation of the Ministry's systems and services.

Public Perceptions

Closer scrutiny of the courts by the media, the international community and the Palestinian public, coupled with changing community views and attitudes, will further raise public awareness of the court system and place increased demands on the Ministry, its activities and its services.

PRIMARY OBJECTIVES

The primary objectives of the Strategic Development Plan are:

– Unifying existing laws governing the West Bank and Gaza Strip
– Improve court buildings and facilities
– Unify judicial systems and procedures
– Standardize prosecution procedures and improve buildings and facilities
– Develop a computerized legal and judicial data base
– Develop an independent forensic science capability.

The strategies required to achieve each objective are outlined in Table 1.

OBJECTIVES	STRATEGIES
1 Unify Existing Laws Governing the West Bank and Gaza Strip	1.1 Compile in hard copy the existing laws having application in the West Bank and Gaza Strip.
	1.2 Establish subject based Law Commissions to review the existing laws. Diwan Al Fatwa Wal Tachri'e to draft new legislation.
	1.3 Submit proposed new legislation to the Executive Council.
	1.4 Palestinian Legislative Council Legal Committee review proposed new legislation.
	1.5 Legislation enacted by the Palestinian Legislative Council and authorized by the President of the Executive Council.
	1.6 Legislation published in the Official Gazette.
	1.7 Establish a dedicated computer section for populating, updating and maintaining the Computer Legal and Judicial Data Base.
2 Improve Court Buildings and Facilities	2.1 Construct new and renovate existing Court Buildings.
	2.2 Establish a Court Building Construction Working Group.
	2.3 Identify suitable locations for new Court Buildings and obtain necessary permissions.

2.3a Identify existing Courts in need of renovation.

2.4 Design new Court Buildings and Facilities including Computer Network and Audio Visual Technology.

2.4a Design a standard layout for renovation of existing Courts.

2.5 Construct new Court Buildings.

2.5a Renovate existing Court Buildings.

2.6 Furnish Court Buildings and distribute computer hardware and software. Existing laws to be made available until new legislation is enacted.

2.7 Staff employed and trained in Court duties and new technology and data processing techniques.

2.8 Existing and new Court Buildings opened.

3 Unify judicial systems and procedures

3.1 Conduct a survey of the existing Judicial Systems and Procedures of the West Bank and Gaza.

3.2 Commence Judicial Studies Seminars and Workshop Programme.

3.3 Draft new standardized Judicial Trial Procedures.

3.4 Establish Judicial Education Committee. Select and train Judge-Instructors and Judicial Educators.

3.5 New Judicial Procedures ratified by the Palestinian Legislative Council.

3.6 Develop Judicial Studies Program.
Conferences:
(a)   National Judicial Conference;
(b)   Continuing Workshop Program;
(c)   Induction Orientation Course.
Publications:
(a)   Court Bench Books;
(b)   Digest of Cases;

(c)   Journal of Conference Articles.

3.7 Judges undertake continuing Workshop Program. Induction Orientation Courses conducted as required.

3.8 Judicial Studies Institute located in newly constructed Court Buildings.

4 Standardize prosecution procedures and improve buildings and facilities	4.1 Conduct a study of the existing Prosecution Procedures, Buildings and Facilities.

4.2 Commence Prosecutor Training Seminars and Workshop Program.

4.3 Draft new standardized Prosecution Procedures.

4.3a Establish new computerized administrative procedures.

4.4 Establish Prosecutor Training Committee. Select and train Prosecutor-Instructors as Prosecution Educators.

4.5 New Prosecution Procedures ratified by the Palestinian Legislative Council.

4.6 Develop Prosecution Training Program. Conferences:
(a)   National Prosecutors Conference;
(b)   Continuing Workshop Program;
(c)   Induction Orientation Course
 Publications:
(a)   Prosecutors Manual;
(b)   Digest of Cases;
(c)   Journal of Conference Articles.

4.7 Prosecutors undertake continuing Workshop Program. Induction Orientation Courses conducted as required.

4.8 Renovate existing Gaza City Court Building for occupation by Attorney General's Department.

4.9 Attorney General's Department move to renovated Gaza City Court Building.

5 Develop a computerized legal and judicial data base

5.1 Construct a working model of a Computerized Legal and Judicial Data Base to understand operational concepts (English language).

5.2 Complete a detailed systems analysis. Draw up design specifications for a fully Computerised Legal and Judicial Data Base. Select hardware and software platforms. Develop software for conversion to Arabic.

5.3 Populate the Fully Functional Data Base with the existing laws.

5.4 Train users of the system and distribute technology to the Ministry of Justice, Judiciary and Legal Community.

5.5 Populate the data base with the new Palestinian Law Code which then takes precedence over previous laws.

5.6 Service and update the Computer Legal and Judicial Data Base.

NOTE: Developed concurrently with this program is the establishment of the Government Computer Centre.

6 Establish a TCP/IP Wide Area Network to all required locations

6.1 Allocate hardware and software to support the Rule of Law Computer Project.

6.2 Assist designated agenices in the development of the computerised Legal and Judicial Data Base.

6.3 Purchase computers and software for Judicial Officers, Ministry of Justice and Administration staff.

6.4 Train personnel in necessary computing and system maintenance skills.

7 Develop an Independent Forensic Science Capability

7.1 Conduct a study of existing Forensic Science Procedures, Capability and Facilities.

7.2 Train Forensic Medicine Centre staff in Forensic Science skills.

7.3 Construct a new Forensic Medicine Centre co-located with Al-Quds University's Faculty of Medicine.

7.3a Renovate existing morgues to include a post-mortem facility at 7 major hospitals throughout West Bank and Gaza.

74 Design Forensic Medicine Centre.

74a Design a fit-out for renovated morgues.

7.5 Construct Forensic Medicine Centre.

7.5a Renovate existing morgues.

7.6 Equip Forensic Medicine Centre and train staff on laboratory equipment and procedures.

7.7 Forensic Medicine Centre opened to complement Palestinian Civil Police Forensic Crime Laboratory.

Palestine
Palestinian National Authority
Ministry of Justice
Legal Development Project Advisory Board
Rules and Regulations
May 1998

1 DEFINITIONS AND TERMINOLOGY

Rules and Regulations	The Rules and Regulations described in this document are the Rules and Regulations which are to govern the actions of the Legal Development Project Advisory Board.
Palestinian National Authority (PNA)	
Ministry of Justice (MOJ)	The PNA ministry designated responsible for the planning and implementation of the World Bank funded Legal Development Project.
Diwan Al Fatwah Wal Tashri (Diwan)	The MOJ agency responsible for supervising the Legal Development Program Implementation.
The Steering Committee (SC)	The SC is responsible to the PNA for the management of the Legal Development Program. The SC is also responsible for providing direction to the Project Implementation Unit and the supervision of that agency. The Steering Committee is to consist of the Minister of Justice (Chairman), the Chief Justice of the High Court of Gaza, the Attorney General of Gaza and the Head of the Diwan.

The Advisory Board (AB)	The Advisory Board is a collection of PNA officials, legal luminaries, academics and senior business people. The AB is to consist of sixteen (16) members. The role of the AB is to provide technical advice to the Legal Development Program Steering Committee to assist in the planning, implementation and review of the Legal Development Program.
The Project Implementation Unit (PIU)	The Project Implementation Unit consists of the Project Director, Head of the Diwan Al Fatwah Wal Tashri, the Project Manager and the Finance Manager. The PIU is responsible to the SC for the planning, implementation and the reporting of the Legal Development Project.
The Legal Development Program	The World Bank title given to the seven (7) legal sector reform components contained within the MOJ's Rule of Law Strategic Development Plan. The term Legal Development Program refers to both the funded and unfunded components of the Rule of Law Strategic Development Plan. The funded components are:

       – Unification and Development of Legislation
       – Court Administration
       – Judicial and Prosecutor Training
       – Alternative Dispute Resolution Training
       – Legal Information

       The components still to be funded are:

       – Court Construction and Renovation
       – Full Text Data Base

The Legal Development Project (LDP)	The World Bank term used to describe those components of Rule of Law Strategic Development Plan which are funded by the World Bank.
Australian Legal Resources International (ALRI)	An Australian Non Governmental Organisation contracted by the MOJ as the Technical Adviser to the PIU for LDP planning and implementation.

2 LDP HISTORICAL BACKGROUND

In October 1996, the MOJ with the assistance of ALRI developed an investment program titled the Rule of Law Strategic Development Plan whose main objectives included the modernisation of the legal framework, the strengthening of the Judiciary and the Attorney General's Department, the construction of new courthouses and improvement of judicial infrastructure, the development of a legal and judicial database and the development of an independent forensic science capability. The Plan is to be implemented over several phases and will require international as well as local assistance. The Plan has been disseminated to the Executive Council, the Palestinian Legislative Council, the Judiciary and all elements of the Palestinian legal profession as well as the donor community, with consensus being reached about the areas and priority of reform to be undertaken.

The LDP is the first step toward the long-term goal of further developing the Rule of Law in Palestine, an undertaking that will require assistance well beyond what is proposed under the LDP. The LDP contains those components of the Legal Development Program which have been nominated by the PNA as the highest priorities which can be achieved with the funding made available by the World Bank.

The five (5) components of the LDP are funded through a World Bank trust fund credit. The project implementation, which is expected to be completed after four (4) years is based on the World Bank's rules and implementation procedures.

3 LDP AIM

3.1 The Aim of the LDP is to unify, modernise and harmonise the laws governing Palestine.

4 LDP OBJECTIVES

4.1 The Objectives of the LDP are to create a legal framework adequate to support a market economy and encourage private sector growth, and to improve the efficiency and predictability of the judicial process.

5 LDP DESCRIPTION

5.1 The legal framework will be improved by unifying and developing legislation and disseminating needed legal information. The Judiciary will be strengthened by providing judges and court personnel with new case management techniques, information technology and mediation procedures which will allow cases to be resolved in an efficient and effective manner and by improving the quality of judicial and prosecutor training. Through these components, the Judiciary will experience efficiency gains and improvements in the quality of service delivered to the public, while improvements in the legal framework will provide greater clarity to the Judiciary as well as investors.

5.2 The LDP will support the PNA's efforts to:

(i)   unify and develop the existing legal framework to help provide a hospitable environ-
        ment for market-oriented activities
(ii)   improve the Judiciary's administrative and case management procedures and reduce
        case backlog
(iii)   introduce selected training programs for judges and prosecutors
(iv)   expand the use of alternative dispute resolution mechanisms within the Judiciary, Bar
        Association and business communities
(v)   disseminate legislation and court precedents to the judicial, legal, academic and busi-
        ness communities, and the public at large.

5.3 The five LDP components are summarized as follows.

(a) Unification and Development of Legislation

Building on the compilation of existing legislation in WBG, the PIU will establish a Law
Commission Task Force Secretariat who will work with the MOJ to develop a legislation
review strategy and co-ordinate the work of the proposed five (5) Law Commission Task
Forces (LCTF).

The LCTF will consist of international, regional, and local experts in the subject under
review.

The trust fund credit will finance the services of outside legal experts who will as members of the LCTF assist in the review of existing legislation and advise on the substance of subject matters.

This component will also finance the preparation of diagnostic and other studies and the
conduct of related ancillary activities.

The LCTF will on a case by case basis, research legislation, propose new draft legislation
(or amendments to existing legislation) and hold workshops to discuss the new proposed legislation.

Areas of law to be covered by this activity cover both civil and criminal codes.

(b) Court and Administration

The Court Administration component will be a fundamental element in the overall strategy
of improving the capacity of the Judiciary. The aim of the component is to improve the
central administrative functions of the courts, the Attorney General's Department and the
Civil Police, establish a planning function, establish a personnel classification system, improve
record management, improve judicial statistics and management information systems, and
develop standard legal forms.

(c) Judicial and Prosecutor Training

The main objective of the Judicial and Prosecutor Training component is to support an impartial, effective, competent and efficient Judiciary and Attorney General's Department.
This component will support the development of a judicial and prosecutor education structure and curricula under the guidance of a Judicial Education Committee and Prosecutor

Training Committee, establish legal resource centres, develop judicial and prosecutor education and training standards, train judicial and prosecutor educators, develop long term training plans, establish internal and external programs and develop teaching materials and codes of ethics.

(d) Alternative Dispute Resolution Mechanisms

The main objective of the Alternative Dispute Resolution Mechanisms (ADR) is to identify and address some of the principal case management problems confronting the judiciary, as well as provide legal practitioners and the private sector with an introduction to modern ADR techniques used to settle commercial disputes.

   This component will include education of legal professionals about alternatives to judicial dispute resolution, a pilot mediation program within the judiciary for commercial cases in Gaza and Ramallah.

   The issue of legislation to support arbitration will be addressed by the Law Commission Task Forces.

(e) Legal Information

The main objectives of the Legal Information component will be to improve access to legal information for the public and legal community through the development of legal libraries in the MOJ, the Judiciary, and Attorney General's Department to serve as reference centres for the MOJ, the Judiciary, the Attorney General's Department, the Palestinian Bar Association, academics, the business sector, and the public at large; support the publication and dissemination of court decisions and laws, develop judicial bench books for judges and court support staff and prosecutor manuals, provision of electronic medium legal information to the legal community, assistance towards the further development of a legal data base to support the dissemination of legislation.

6 MEMBERSHIP, ESTABLISHMENT AND PURPOSE OF THE ADVISORY BOARD

6.1 The Advisory Board (AB) will consist of four (4) permanent members (LDP SC members), the Minister for Justice (Chairman) and the Head of the Diwan Al Fatwah Wal Tashri, the Chief Justice of the High Court of Gaza, and the Attorney General and twelve (12) members selected from a cross-section of the Palestinian political, legal and business communities.

6.2 The AB will be chaired by the Minister of Justice or in the Minister's absence, his deputy, Head of the Diwan.

6.3 Due regard is to be given to achieving balanced representation in terms of geographic distribution (West Bank and Gaza). AB members should be equipped and willing to take on the responsibilities designated to the AB, and will be selected based on the following criteria:

(a)   a member should enjoy good standing in the community
(b)   a member must display the ability to make decisions objectively, without imposing or pursuing their own personal, political or religious interests
(c)   a member should be able and willing to participate in collective discussion and consensus decision making
(d)   a member must be able and willing to attend regular AB meetings in both West Bank and Gaza

The LDP Project Manager will be an ex-officio member of the AB.

6.4 The AB will provide assistance and technical advice to the Legal Development Program Steering Committee to fulfil the determined aims and objectives of the LDP.

6.5 A member will be invited to participate on the AB by formal written request from the Minister of Justice or his designate.

6.6 The tenure of an AB member is for a period of four (4) years.

6.7 Resignation of a member from the AB, for whatever reason, is to be requested in writing from the Minister of Justice.

6.8 If the services of a particular member on the AB are no longer required, that member will be notified formally in writing by the Minister of Justice.

7 FUNCTIONS OF THE ADVISORY BOARD

7.1 The functions of the Advisory Board are as follows:

(a)   Assist the SC in the development of LDP strategy and policies.
(b)   Along with and in co-ordination with the PIU Director, representing to any authority, organisation or individual the guiding principles, aims, and objectives of the LDP and establishing and maintaining good co-operative relations with the local and international community, representing the interests of the Palestinian community, in pursuit of the goals of the LDP.
(c)   Monitor areas where policy and legislative actions are required within the context and scope of the LDP and report such actions to the SC.
(d)   Ensure timely and effective dissemination of information about LDP and Legal Development Program activities to public and private institutions, and the public at large.
(e)   Review LDP implementation progress and offer constructive assistance and criticism where appropriate.
(f)   Nominate and/or select members of the AB or an appropriate institution for various LDP sub-committees.

8 MEETINGS

8.1 The AB will meet at least four (4) times a calendar year.

8.2 The date of the next meeting will be determined at the previous meeting.

8.3 The agenda shall be prepared for each meeting by the Chairman in consultation with the PIU Director and circulated to all members at least ten (10) days before the scheduled date of the meeting. AB members who wish to add items to the agenda are to inform the Chairman or his delegate.

8.4 Clear record (minutes) of all AB meetings are to be taken by a qualified person appointed for this purpose by the AB.

8.5 Previous meeting minutes are to be read and approved at the commencement of the next AB meeting.

8.6 Additional rules and procedures may be developed by the AB as necessary to enable efficient functioning of its meetings.

9 LOGISTICS

9.1 Board membership is a voluntary assignment without any compensation. Transport, meals and accommodation (when required) will be provided/paid for by the LDP.

Oman
Law of Arbitration in Civil and Commercial Disputes*
(Royal Decree 47/97)

We, QABOOS BIN SAID, Sultan of Oman after perusal of:

Royal Decree No. 101/96, issuing the Basic Law of the State; and

Royal Decree No. 79/81 establishing the Commercial Court and its amendments and the system for supervising requests for arbitration before the Commercial Court promulgated by Royal Decree No. 32/84 and its amendments; and

The Commercial Law promulgated by Royal Decree 55/90 and its amendments;

And according to that which is in the public interest,

Have decreed as follows:

Article 1

There shall be a Law of Arbitration in Civil and Commercial Disputes as set out below.

Article 2

The Minister of Justice, Awqaf and Islamic Affairs shall issue all the necessary decisions for the implementation of this law.

Article 3

Everything which contravenes the provision of this law is cancelled.

---

* Unofficial translation provided by Trowers & Hamlins.

Article 4

This decree shall be published in the Official Gazette and shall be effective from the date of its issue.

Qaboos bin Said
Sultan of Oman
Issued on 22 Safar 1418 H
corresponding to 28 June 1997

ROYAL DECREE NO. 47/97
THE LAW OF ARBITRATION IN CIVIL AND COMMERCIAL DISPUTES

CHAPTER I
GENERAL RULES

Article 1

Without prejudice to the provisions of international agreements applicable in the Sultanate, the regulations of this law are applicable to all arbitration between parties consisting of matters of Public Law or Private Law and irrespective of the nature of the legal relationship which the dispute involves, and whether the arbitration takes place in the Sultanate, or whether the arbitration is an international commercial one which takes place abroad and its parties agree to subject it to the provisions of this law.

Article 2

According to this law, arbitration is considered commercial if a dispute arises over a legal relationship of an economic nature regardless whether it is contractual or non contractual. This includes, for example, but is not limited to the supply of goods or services, commercial agencies, construction contracts, engineering or technical expertise, the granting of industrial or tourism licences or others, the transfer of technology, investment, development contracts, operations concerning banks, insurance and transport operations concerning exploration and mining of natural resources, the supply of energy and the installation of gas or oil pipes, the building of roads and tunnels, reclamation of agricultural land, protection of the environment and the establishment of nuclear reactors.

Article 3

According to this law, arbitration is considered international if its subject is a dispute concerning international trade in the following situations:

1. If the head office of each of the two parties to the arbitration is located in two different countries upon the entering into of the arbitration agreement. If one of the parties has many business centres, the centre which is most closely related to the subject of the arbitration will be taken into consideration. If either of the parties to the arbitration does not have a centre of business, then his place of residence will be taken into consideration.

2. If the two parties to the arbitration agree to resort to a permanent arbitration organisation or an arbitration centre based in the Sultanate of Oman or outside it.
3. If the subject of the dispute, which is included in the arbitration agreement, is linked to more than one country.
4. If the principal centre of business of one of the parties to the arbitration is located in the same country at the time the arbitration agreement is entered into and one of the following places is located outside the country:
A. The place of arbitration is specified by the arbitration agreement or if it specifies the way for choosing the place of arbitration.
B. The place of implementing a substantive obligation resulting from the commercial relations between the two parties.
C. The place which is most closely related to the subject of the dispute.

Article 4

1. According to this law, the word "arbitration" refers to arbitration agreed upon by the parties to the dispute by their own free will regardless of whether the body entrusted with the arbitration proceedings pursuant to the parties' agreement is an organisation, a permanent centre for arbitration or otherwise.
2. The term "Arbitration Authority" refers to the authority which consists of one arbitrator or more in order to settle the dispute under arbitration. The term "Court" refers to the Commercial Court or the Court of Appeal within it.
3. The term "parties to the arbitration" in this Law refers to the parties to the arbitration regardless of their number.

Article 5

In cases where this law permits the parties to the arbitration shall choose the necessary proceedings regarding a certain issue; both of them can licence a third party to choose these proceedings. The third party in this regard is any organisation or centre for arbitration in the Sultanate of Oman or abroad.

Article 6

1. The parties to the arbitration shall have the freedom to specify the law which should be applied to the dispute by the arbitrators.
2. If the parties to the arbitration agree to make the legal relationship between them subject to the provisions of a standard contract, an international agreement or any other document, the provisions of this document including the provision specific to the arbitration shall be enforced.

Article 7

1. Unless there is a special agreement between the parties to the arbitration, any letter or notification should be delivered to the addressee personally at his place of work, place of residence or postal address known to the parties or specified in the arbitration agreement or the document which organises the legal relations which are the subject of the arbitration.

2.   If it is not possible to establish any of the addresses after conducting the necessary en-
       quiries, the delivery will be considered valid if the registered notification is served to
       the last work place, place of residence, or the addressee's known address.
3.   The provisions of this article do not apply to judicial notifications before the Court.

Article 8

If one of the parties to the arbitration continues with the arbitration proceedings with knowledge of the existence of a violation of one of the conditions of the arbitration agreement or
any of the provisions of this law, and if he does not present an objection to this violation within
the agreed period of time or within sixty days with effect from the date of knowledge of the
non-agreement, this is considered as a relinquishment of his right to object.

Article 9

The Commercial Court is the relevant authority responsible for the consideration of arbitration issues referred by this law to the Omani judiciary. If the arbitration is commercial
and international regardless of whether it is in Oman or abroad, the Court of Appeal is the
authority responsible for this issue.

CHAPTER II
ARBITRATION AGREEMENT

Article 10

1.   The Arbitration Agreement is the agreement in which its parties agree to resort to
       arbitration in order to settle all or some of the disputes which may arise between
       them on the occasion of a certain legal violations whether contractual or non-
       contractual.
2.   It is permitted that the arbitration [referral to arbitration] be included as a condition
       of arbitration before the dispute arises, and mentioned in a certain contract or in-
       cluded in a separate agreement entered into after the commencement of the dispute
       even if there was a case about it before a judicial authority and in this situation the agree-
       ment should specify the issues which the arbitration comprises, otherwise, the agree-
       ment will be null and void.
3.   Any reference in a contract to another document which includes an arbitration condi-
       tion will mean that that contract is considered to be an Arbitration Agreement if the
       reference makes it clear that this condition is part of the contract.

Article 11

Only a natural or legal person who can claim rights is permitted to agree to arbitration. It is
not permitted to arbitrate issues which are not capable of being the subject of reconciliation.

Article 12

The Arbitration Agreement should be in writing otherwise it will be considered null and void. The Arbitration Agreement is considered to be in writing if it comprises a document signed by both parties or an exchange of letters, telegrams or other correspondence.

Article 13

1. The Court to which a dispute related to an Arbitration Agreement is referred should rule that the case cannot be accepted if the defendant requests this before any request or defence regarding the case is raised.
2. The commencement of proceedings mentioned in the previous paragraph will not hinder the commencement and continuation of arbitration proceedings or the issuing of an arbitration judgment.

Article 14

The Court mentioned in Article 9 of this law and upon the request of one of the parties to the arbitration can order temporary or precautionary measures before or after the commencement of arbitration proceedings.

CHAPTER III
THE ARBITRATION AUTHORITY

Article 15

1. The Arbitration Authority is formed with the agreement of all the parties. The authority consists of one arbitrator or more unless they do not agree on the number of arbitrators, then the number will be three.
2. If there are many arbitrators, their number should be an odd number; otherwise, the arbitration will be null and void.

Article 16

1. The arbitrator should not be a minor placed under guardianship or deprived of his civil rights because of being sentenced in a felony or misdemeanour which violates his honour or honesty or because of bankruptcy unless he is reformed.
2. It is not stipulated that the arbitrator should belong to a certain sex or nationality unless the arbitration parties agree or the law states otherwise.
3. The arbitrator should accept his assignment in writing. He should disclose upon accepting the assignment, any circumstances which might cast doubts over his independence or impartiality. The arbitrator should reveal any such circumstances which may arise after his appointment or during the arbitration process, to the parties to the arbitration and other arbitrators.

Article 17

1. The parties to the arbitration can agree on the selection of arbitrators and how and when they are selected. If they cannot agree on this, the following measures will be taken:
   (a) If the Arbitration Authority consists of one arbitrator, the head of the Commercial Court will select him upon the request of one of the parties.
   (b) If the Arbitration Authority consists of three arbitrators, each party will choose one arbitrator, then the two arbitrators will agree on the third arbitrator. If one of the parties does not appoint his arbitrator within 30 days with effect from receiving the request of the other party, or if the two arbitrators cannot agree on choosing the third arbitrator within 30 days with effect from the date of appointing the second one then the head of the Commercial Court will choose the arbitrator upon the request of one of the parties.
   The arbitrator chosen by the appointed arbitrators or the one chosen by the head of the Court will be the President of the Arbitration Authority. These regulations are valid in case of forming an Arbitration Authority which consists of more than three arbitrators.
2. If one of the parties violates the regulations concerning the selection of arbitrators which have been agreed upon or not, if the two appointed arbitrators do not agree on an issue on which they should agree, or if the third party does not honour his duty in this regard, then the head of the Commercial Court and upon the request of one of the parties, will undertake the necessary step or action unless it is stated in the agreement that there is another way to complete this step or action.
3. The head of the Court should bear in mind while choosing the arbitrator, the conditions required by the law and what has been agreed by the parties. The head of the Court issues his decision to choose the arbitration as soon as possible. Without prejudice to the regulations at Articles 18, 19 of this law, this decision cannot be contested.

Article 18

1. The arbitrator cannot be rejected unless there are circumstances which cast serious doubts over his impartiality or independence.
2. It is not permitted for any of the parties to the arbitration to reject the arbitrator appointed by him or if he participates in his appointment unless there is a reason which is discovered after the appointment.

Article 19

1. The application to reject is presented to the Arbitration Authority in writing in which the reasons for the rejection should be mentioned. It should be presented within 15 days with effect from the date of the applicant's knowledge concerning the formation of this authority or the circumstances which justify the rejection. If the arbitrator does not step down, the Arbitration Authority will settle the request.
2. The application to reject by a party which has previously applied for the rejection of the same arbitrator in the same arbitration will not be accepted.
3. The applicant for the rejection can appeal the judgment which rejects his request within 30 days with effect from the date of his notification in this regard before the Court mentioned in Article 9 of this law; this later judgment cannot be contested at all.

4.   The issuing of the rejection application on appealing the arbitration judgment which rejects the application does not result in the stoppage of the arbitration process. If there is a judgment to reject the arbitration issued by the Arbitration Authority or the Court upon considering the appeal, this results in considering the arbitration process, including the judgment of the arbitrators, as if they did not take place.

Article 20

If the arbitrator cannot carry out his duty, did not start doing it, or discontinues carrying out his duty which may result in unnecessary delay in arbitration process and if he does not step down or the parties cannot agree on his sacking, the head of the Commercial Court is permitted to terminate his appointment upon the request of both parties.

Article 21

If the assignment of the arbitrator ends through sacking, stepping down, rejection judgment or any other reason, a replacement should be appointed according to the steps which have been used in choosing the arbitrator.

Article 22

1.   The Arbitration Authority issues a decision with regard to pleas about its lack of jurisdiction including the pleas based on the absence of Arbitration Agreement, its failure, nullity or if it does not include the subject of dispute.
2.   These pleas should be maintained until a date, which should not exceed the date of presenting the defence of the defendant referred to in the second paragraph of Article (30) of this law. The fact that one of the arbitration parties has appointed an arbitrator or has participated in appointing one, does not mean that he loses his right to present any of these pleas. As for the plea concerning the issues that the arbitration agreement does not mean that he loses his right to present any of these pleas. As for the plea concerning the issue that the Arbitration Agreement does not include the issues which are raised by the second party during the consideration of the dispute, this should be maintained immediately, otherwise, the related right will be lost. In all cases, the Arbitration Authority can accept the delayed plea, if it comes to the decision that there is an acceptable reason behind the delay.
3.   The Arbitration Authority issues a decision with regard to the pleas mentioned in the first paragraph of this article before the settlement of the dispute. It can also join it to the dispute in order to settle them jointly. If it decides to reject the plea, it cannot be maintained unless through raising a case claiming the nullity at the arbitration judgment which ends the whole dispute pursuant to Article 53 of this law.

Article 23

The arbitration condition is considered as an agreement independent from other conditions of the contract. The nullity, revocation or termination of the contract does not affect the arbitration condition included in it, if the condition is valid in its own right.

Article 24

1. The parties to the arbitration can agree to allow the Arbitration Authority, upon the request of either of them, to order either of them to take the necessary temporary or precautionary measures required by the dispute. It can also order either of them to present a guarantee adequate to cover the costs of the proceedings ordered by it.
2. If any one party does not carry out an order issued to it, the Arbitration Authority and upon the request of the other party, can allow that party to take the measures necessary for implementation without prejudice to the right of the party to request the head of the Commercial Court to order its implementation.

CHAPTER IV
ARBITRATION PROCEEDINGS

Article 25

The parties to the arbitration can agree on the proceedings applied by the Arbitration Authority including their right to make these proceedings subject to the rules enforced in any organisation or arbitration centre in Sultanate of Oman or abroad. If there is no such agreement, the Arbitration Authority, in accordance with the provisions of this law, can choose the arbitration proceedings which it deems suitable.

Article 26

The parties to the arbitration are treated equally and each one of them has a complete and equal opportunity to present his case.

Article 27

The arbitration proceedings commence with effect from the date on which the defendant receives the arbitration application from the plaintiff unless the two parties agree on another date.

Article 28

The parties to the arbitration can agree on the place of arbitration inside Oman or abroad. If there is no agreement, the Arbitration Authority will specify the place of arbitration bearing in mind the circumstances of the case and the suitability of the place to the parties.

The power of the Arbitration Authority is undiminished irrespective of whether it assembles in any place it deems suitable to conduct any arbitration proceedings such as the hearing of the parties to the dispute, witnesses, experts, or the perusal of documents, the examining of goods or money, or the conducting of deliberations among its members or other than this.

Article 29

1. Arbitration will be conducted in Arabic, unless the two parties or the Arbitration Authority decides to use another language or languages. The agreement or decision will

be valid with regard to the language of written statements, memoranda and verbal pleadings. It also includes any decision letter, judgment given by the authority unless the agreement of the parties or the decision of the Arbitration Authority states otherwise.

2. The Arbitration Authority can demand a translation of all or some of the documents presented with regard to the case. The translation should be in the language or languages used in the arbitration. In case there are many languages, it is possible to restrict the translation to some of them.

Article 30

1. The plaintiff sends to the defendant and each of the arbitrators during the period agreed upon by the parties or during the time specified by the Arbitration Authority, a written statement of his claim which includes name, address, name of the defendant, address, explanation of the incidents of the case, the specification of the issues which are the subject of dispute, requests and any other issues which should be written in the statement according to the agreement of the parties.

2. The defendant sends to the plaintiff and each of the arbitrators during the period agreed upon by the parties or during the time specified by the Arbitration Authority a written statement of defence in reply to the statement of claim. He can include in the statement any incidental requests related to the subject of the dispute or he may preserve the right to order to plea for compensation. He can do so even at a later stage in the proceedings, if the Arbitration Authority decides that the circumstances justify the delay.

3. Each party shall enclose with the statements of claim or defence copies of supporting documents and to refer to all or some of the documents and evidence which he plans to present, and this does not diminish the right of Arbitration Authority at any stage of the case to ask for the originals of these supporting documents.

Article 31

A copy of the documents, statements or any other papers presented by one of the parties to the Arbitration Authority, should be sent to the other party. The parties should receive a copy of all the experts' reports, documents and other evidence presented to the said authority.

Article 32

The parties to the arbitration can amend or complete their pleas or defence during the arbitration proceedings unless the Arbitration Authority decides not to accept this in order to prevent any delay in settling the dispute.

Article 33

1. The Arbitration Authority holds pleading sessions to enable both parties to explain their claim, their arguments and evidence. The Authority can decide that it is adequate to present written documents unless the parties agree otherwise.

2. The parties to the arbitration should be notified of the dates of sessions and meetings specified by the Arbitration Authority in sufficient time, which is fixed by the authority according to circumstances.

3. The Summary of the minutes of each session held by the Arbitration Authority is written down and copied to all parties unless they agree otherwise.
4. The hearing of witnesses and experts is undertaken without oath.

Article 34

1. If the plaintiff does not present a written statement of claim pursuant to the first paragraph of Article 30 of this law without acceptable excuse, the Arbitration Authority should order the termination of the arbitration process unless the parties agree otherwise.
2. If the defendant does not present his statement of defence pursuant to the second paragraph of Article 30 of this law, the Arbitration Authority should continue with the arbitration proceedings without considering this as an acknowledgement of the plaintiff's case by the defendant, unless the parties agree on otherwise.

Article 35

If one of the parties does not attend any of the sessions or does not present the required documents, the Arbitration Authority can continue with the arbitration proceedings and issue a judgment regarding the dispute based on the evidence available.

Article 36

1. The Arbitration Authority can appoint one expert or more to present a written or verbal report which will be written in the minutes of the session regarding certain issues specified by the authority. The authority sends to the parties a copy of its decision to specify the assignment given to the expert.
2. The parties should present to the expert the information concerning the dispute. They should enable him to examine such documents as he requests, or goods and money related to the dispute. The Arbitration Authority settles each dispute which may arise between any of the parties and the expert in this regard.
3. The Arbitration Authority sends a copy of the expert's report when lodged to all the parties. They will be given the opportunity to present their view about this. All parties have the right to study and examine the documentation on which the expert based his report.
4. The Arbitration Authority can decide by itself and after the presentation of the expert's report or upon the request of any of the parties to the arbitration regarding the holding of a session to hear the statement of the expert, while giving the parties the opportunity to hear and discuss the contents of his report. All parties can present in this session one expert or more to present their views regarding the issues discussed by the report of the expert appointed by the Arbitration Authority unless the arbitration parties agree otherwise.

Article 37

The Commercial Court has the jurisdiction upon the request of the Arbitration Authority to do the following:

A. order those witnesses who do not attend or refuse to answer to pay a fine, the value of which shall not be less than RO 5/- and not more than RO 20/-. This decision cannot be contested and carries the same weight as other judgments [i.e. judgments of the Commercial Court].

B.   order the appointment of an attorney.

Article 38

The dispute will be terminated before the Arbitration Authority in cases and conditions specified by the law.

CHAPTER V
THE ARBITRATION JUDGMENT AND THE TERMINATION OF PROCEEDINGS

Article 39

1.   The Arbitration Authority shall apply the principles which the parties agreed upon to the subject of dispute. If it was agreed to apply the law of a certain country, they must adhere to those principles in the dispute without recourse to the particular principles concerned with the conflict of laws unless it is agreed otherwise.
2.   If the two parties cannot agree on the legal principles which should be applied to the subject of the dispute, the Arbitration Authority will apply the substantive principles of the law which relates most closely to the dispute.
3.   The Arbitration Authority should have regard to the settlement of the dispute, the conditions of the contract, the subject of the dispute and the current customs.
4.   The Arbitration Authority, if the two parties agree clearly to authorise it to conduct reconciliation can settle the subject of the dispute according to the principles of justice and equity without abiding by the regulations of the law.

Article 40

The judgment of the Arbitration Authority which consists of more than one arbitrator is issued according to the majority of their views after discussions undertaken as specified by the Arbitration Authority, unless the parties to the arbitration agree otherwise.

Article 41

If the parties agree during the arbitration proceedings to settle the dispute, they can request the registration of the settlement before the Arbitration Authority which should issue a decision in this case. The said decision shall include the conditions of the settlement and enforcement measures. This decision will carry the same weight as [a decision issued by the arbitrators, pursuant to their appointment].

Article 42

It is permitted for the Arbitration Authority to issue intermediate judgments with regard to part of the dispute before the issuing of the judgment which will end the whole dispute.

Article 43

1. The arbitration judgment is issued in writing and signed by the arbitrators, and in case of the Arbitration Authority consisting of more than one arbitrator, the signatures of the majority of arbitrators will be enough, provided that the reasons behind the non-signing of the minority are recorded in the judgment.
2. The arbitration judgment should mention the reasons unless the arbitration parties agree otherwise or if the law which should be applied to the arbitration proceedings does not stipulate the mentioning of the reasons of the judgment.
3. The arbitration judgment should include the names of the parties [Note: the Arabic uses the word, 'adversaries'], addresses, names of arbitrators, addresses, nationalities, status, the text of the arbitration agreement, the summary of the requests, statements and documents of the parties, the text, date and place of issue of the judgment in addition to the reasons of the judgment if necessary.

Article 44

1. The Arbitration Authority delivers to all parties a copy of the arbitration judgment signed by the arbitrators which they agreed upon within 30 days with effect from the date of issue.
2. It is not permitted to publish the arbitration judgment or parts of it without the approval of the parties to the arbitration.

Article 45

1. The Arbitration Authority should issue the judgment which ends the dispute within the period agreed upon by the parties. If there was agreement, the judgment should be issued within 12 months with effect from the date of the commencement of the arbitration proceedings. In all cases the Arbitration Authority can extend the period for up to a maximum period of six months unless they agree on a period which exceeds this.
2. If the arbitration judgment is not issued during the period mentioned in the previous paragraph, the parties to the arbitration can request the head of the Commercial Court to issue a decision specifying an additional date or to terminate the arbitration proceedings. All parties can refer their cases to the appropriate Court.

Article 46

If during the arbitration proceedings, there is a forgery claim regarding one of the papers presented to it or there are criminal proceedings regarding this forgery or any other criminal act (beyond the jurisdiction of the Arbitration Authority), the Arbitration Authority can continue to consider the subject of the dispute, if it believes that the settlement of this issue of forgery or the other criminal act is not necessary for the settling of the dispute, otherwise, the proceedings will be suspended pending the issuing of a final judgment in this regard [i.e. the case of forgery]. This will result in setting aside of the relevant period for the issuing of the arbitration judgment.

Article 47

The party, in favour of which, the arbitration judgment is issued, should lodge the original judgment, a signed copy using the issuing language or an Arabic translation ratified by an approved authority if issued in a foreign language at the Secretariat of the Court mentioned in Article (9) of this law. The Secretary of the Court writes a record concerning this and each party to the arbitration can obtain a copy of the record.

Article 48

The arbitration proceedings [shall end], and by the issuing of the judgment or by the issuing of an order terminating the arbitration proceedings according to the second paragraph of Article 45 of this law, shall end the whole dispute. They may also be ended by the issuing of a decision from the Arbitration Authority terminating the proceedings in the following cases:

A.   If the parties agree to terminate the arbitration;
B.   If the plaintiff abandons the dispute unless the Arbitration Authority decides upon the request of the defendant that he has a serious interest in the continuation of the proceeding until the settlement of the dispute;
C.   If the Arbitration Authority decides for any reason that there is no use in continuing the arbitration proceedings or if it is impossible to do so; and
D.   Taking into consideration the regulations of Article 49, 50, 51 of this law, the assignment of the Arbitration Authority ends by the end of the arbitration proceedings.

Article 49

1.   The parties to the arbitration can request the Arbitration Authority within 30 days with effect from receiving the arbitration judgment to explain any vagueness in the text. The party requesting the explanation should notify the other party with this request before presenting it to the Arbitration Authority.
2.   The explanation is issued in writing within 30 days with effect from presenting the request for an explanation to the Arbitration Authority. The said Authority can extend this period for another 30 days if it deems necessary.
3.   The judgment concerning the explanation is considered as complementary to the arbitration judgment.

This judgment explains the later judgment and the regulations which are applied to it.

Article 50

1.   The Arbitration Authority is in charge of correcting any material, written or accounting mistakes within its judgment by a decision issued by the Authority and by itself or upon the request of one of the parties. The Arbitration Authority conducts the correction process without pleadings within 30 days with effect from the date of the issuing of the judgment or the lodging of the correction application as appropriate. It can extend the date for an extra 30 days if it deems necessary.
2.   The correction decision is issued by the Arbitration Authority in writing and it is notified to the parties within 30 days with effect from the date of issue. If the Arbitration Authority exceeds its authority in correcting, it is allowed to adhere to the nullity

of this decision by raising a nullity claim, on which the regulations of Articles 53 and 54 of this law are applied.

Article 51

1. The parties to the arbitration even after the end of the arbitration date, can request the Arbitration Authority within 30 days with effect from receiving the arbitration judgment to issue an additional arbitration judgment regarding requests which were presented during the proceedings and which were ignored by the arbitration judgment. This request should be notified to the other party before presenting it.
2. The Arbitration Authority issues its judgment within 60 days with effect from the date of presenting the application. It can extend this date from extra 30 days if it deems necessary.

CHAPTER VI
THE NULLITY OF THE ARBITRATION JUDGMENT

Article 52

1. Arbitration judgments which are issued pursuant to the regulations of this law cannot be contested by any legal means.
2. It is permitted to raise a case concerning the nullity of an arbitration judgment pursuant to the regulations mentioned in the following two articles.

Article 53

1. A case concerning the nullity of an arbitration judgment is not acceptable except in the following cases:
   (a) If there is no Arbitration Agreement or if the agreement was null and void or was liable for nullity or if it lapsed by the end of its period;
   (b) If one of the parties to the Arbitration Agreement was at the time of entering into the Agreement incapacitated or suffering from a deficiency according to the law which governs capacity;
   (c) If any of the parties to the arbitration could not present his defence because he was not notified correctly regarding the appointment of an arbitrator or the arbitration measures or for any other reason beyond his control;
   (d) If the arbitration judgment rules out the application of the law which it was agreed by the parties to apply to the subject of dispute;
   (e) If the Arbitration Authority is formed and the arbitrators appointed in a way which contravenes the law or the agreement of the parties;
   (f) If the arbitration judgment settles issues which are not included in the Arbitration Agreement or which are beyond the limits of this agreement. Even so, if it is possible to separate the parts of the judgments concerning issues which are subject to arbitration from the parts concerning issues which are not subject to arbitration, the nullity will apply on the latter parts only; and
   (g) If there is nullity in the arbitration judgment, or if the arbitration proceedings are null in a way which affects the judgment.

2.   The Court which considers the nullity case judges that the arbitration judgment will be null if it includes anything which may contravene the general law of the Sultanate of Oman.

Article 54

1.   A case concerning the nullity of the Arbitration Agreement is raised within 90 days with effect from the date of notifying the arbitration judgment to the judgment debtor. The party claiming the nullity relinquishes his right to raise the nullity case before the issuing of the arbitration judgment and does not hinder the acceptance of the nullity case.
2.   The Court of Appeal at the Commercial Court mentioned in Article 9 of this law has the jurisdiction regarding the nullity case.

CHAPTER VII
THE CONCLUSIVENESS OF THE JUDGMENTS OF THE ARBITRATORS AND THEIR IMPLEMENTATION

Article 55

The judgment of the arbitrators which is issued pursuant to this law is conclusive and should be enforced in accordance with the regulations mentioned in this law.

Article 56

The Head of the Commercial Court or any of its judges assigned by him can issue the order concerning the enforcement of the arbitrator's judgment. The application concerning the enforcement of the judgment should be presented along with the following documents:

1.   The original judgment and a signed copy;
2.   A copy of the Arbitration Agreement;
3.   A translation into Arabic of the arbitration judgment unless it is issued in Arabic. This translation should be certified by an approved authority; and
4.   A copy of the record which indicates the lodging of the judgment pursuant to Article 47 of this law.

Article 57

The raising of the nullity case does not mean suspending the enforcement of the arbitration judgment. Even so, the court can order a suspension of the enforcement, if the plaintiff requests this in his statement of claim and the request is based on serious reasons. The Court should settle the application to suspend the enforcement within 60 days with effect from the date of the first session specified for the consideration of this request. If the court orders the suspension of enforcement, it can order the presentation of a surety or financial guarantee. If it orders the suspension of the enforcement, it should settle the nullity case within six months with effect from the date of issue of the order.

Article 58

1. It is not permitted to enforce the arbitration judgment unless the period concerning the raising of a judgment of a nullity case has come to an end.
2. It is not permitted to enforce the judgment of the arbitration according to this law unless it ensures the following :
    (a) that it does not contradict any judgment previously issued by the Omani Courts regarding the subject of the dispute.
    (b) that it should not include anything which contravenes the general law of the Sultanate of Oman.
    (c) that it has been notified to the judgment debtor correctly.
3. It is not permitted to submit a grievance regarding the order concerning the enforcement of the arbitration judgment. As for the order concerning the rejection of the enforcement, an appeal can be submitted in this regard to the court mentioned in Article (9) of this law within 30 days with effect from the date of issue.

Oman
The New Arbitration Act of the Sultanate of Oman: Comment

*Abdul Hamid El-Ahdab**

Oman issued a new Arbitration Act on 27 July 1997. It was published in the Official Gazette No. 602.

The new Act is a close copy of the provisions of the latest Egyptian Arbitration Act 1994, itself based on the UNCITRAL Model Law.

We shall set out hereafter some differences with the Egyptian Act.

Until about ten years ago, arbitration in Oman was not codified. It was governed by the Moslem *Ibadite* doctrine (which is the same as the other four *sunnite* doctrines) which recognizes that arbitration agreements are valid but not binding, contrary to arbitral awards, which it holds to be binding on the parties.[1]

This gap was filled, however, by incorporating precise provisions which organized and governed arbitration, into the Sultanate Decree of 1984. This laid down the Statutes of the Board for Settlement of Commercial Disptues. An entire chapter (Articles 59 to 68) is devoted to arbitration, which thus advanced by a large step in Omani law. As the law-makers thought that the absence of a neutral body to settle disputes in international commercial contracts could be an obstacle to the development of investment in Oman, they preferred to welcome arbitration to Oman and grant national and international guarantees to foreign investments, by providing for means to resort to arbitration. Thus they conceived a modern and advanced arbitration Act, which applies a fundamental rule of Moslem law, i.e. "it must be possible to make easy what is difficult".[2]

Omani law thus implemented an arbitration system where the religious courts were no longer seized of the case. The Board for Settlement of Commercial Disputes oversaw arbitration in such a manner that the Board became a party to the arbitration: a member of the Board necessarily was the chairman of the arbitral tribunal appointed by the parties. The other members of the tribunal were appointed by the President of the Board if the parties themselves failed to appoint them. As a result, all commercial disputes were actually under the Board's jurisdiction.

Thus, under this system, the situation was as follows. When the parties to the dispute wished to resort to arbitration, the Board itself participated somewhat in hearing the case since

---

* Laywer, LLD and member of the Paris and Beirut Bars, who resides in Paris. He is also the president of the Arab Association for International Arbitration (AAAI) and secretary general of the Euro–Arab Council for International Arbitration. This commentary is reprinted from the December 1997 issue of Mealey's International Arbitration Report.

[1] Art. 14 of Sultanate Decree No. 32/84.

[2] Art. 17 of the *Majalla*.

the Chairman of the Arbitral Tribunal was a member of the Board, and the other arbitrators were chosen by the parties. If the parties had not agreed on arbitration, the Board heard the case without any participation of other arbitrators appointed by the parties.

Thus, when first approaching arbitration, Omani law chose to let the judicial character of arbitration prevail over the contractual character thereof.

On 28 July 1997, a new Act on civil and commercial arbitration[3] was issued, which repeals all earlier provisions.

This new Act is a close copy of the Egyptian Act on Arbitration in civil and commercial matters issued in 1994, and based on the UNCITRAL Model Law on arbitration.

The main differences between the Omani and the Egyptian Acts are as follows:

1. The court having jurisdiction over those (arbitration) matters which the law refers to the court:

    In the Egyptian Act, the court having jurisdiction in national arbitration is the court that originally had jurisdiction over the dispute. If this is a court of first instance, the matters which the law refers to the court are referred to this court. This is also true for the commercial court. The competent court will then be the commercial court of Cairo, Port Saïd or Alexandria, as the case may be.

    If it is an international arbitration, as determined by the Egyptian Law, the case is referred to the Cairo Court of Appeal.[4]

    The new Omani Act refers, in matters of national arbitration, to the commercial court which replaced the Board for Settlement of Commercial Disputes, under Decree No. 13/97 published in the Official Gazette No. 596. Thus, in matters of civil or commerical national arbitration, those matters that the law reserves for the courts are referred to the commercial court.

    In international arbitration, the competent court is the "appeal division" of the commercial court.

2. Under Egyptian law, the parties may appoint another appeal court than the Cairo Court of Appeal, since Article 9 of the Egyptian Act mentions "unless the parties agreed on another Egyptian Court of Appeal".

    The Omani law does not mention such a possibility, which is logical since there is only one single appeals division in commercial matters.

3. In the Egyptian Act, if one of the parties to the dispute continues the arbitration after it became aware of the fact that the other party breached one of the conditions of the agreement to arbitrate or of those provisions of the law which the parties can validly waive, and if this party does not object against this in the agreed time (or within a reasonable time failing an agreement in this respect), then it is held to have waived its objection against such a breach.[5]

    Under Omani law, if the parties have not agreed on a time for making such an objection, the time is specified to be sixty days.[6]

4. The Egyptian Act does not directly mention the parties' right to choose the law applicable to the dispute. It only mentions this indirectly, as it provides that an award "which does not apply the law that the parties had agreed upon for the dispute" may be set aside.[7]

---

[3] Published in the Omani Official Gazette, no. 602.
[4] Egyptian Arbitration Act, Art. 9(1).
[5] Egyptian Arbitration Act, Art. 8.
[6] Omani Arbitration Act, Art. 8.
[7] Egyptian Arbitration Act, Art. 53(1)d.

Omani law also has such a provision, but it adds a rule unknown in the Egyptian Act as it explicitly allows the parties to choose the applicable law. Indeed, Article 6 of the Act provides that "the parties may determine the law which they wish the arbitrators to apply to the dispute".

5.   Egyptian law prevents those persons convicted of a crime from being arbitrators.[8] Omani law also forbids this for persons having been convicted with a penalty involveing the loss of civil right.[9] The question is whether this addition is not superfluous!

6.   The Egyptian Act provides that "... when the arbitrator accepts (the mission) he must point out all circumstances which might give rise to a doubt as to his lack of bias or independence".[10] The Omani Act adds "If such a circumstance arises after his appointment or during the arbitral proceedings, the arbitrator must point this out to the parties and the other arbitrators."[11] Here, the Omani Act is stricter than the Egyptian Act and is close to the UNICTRAL Model Law which, in Article 12, provides: "An arbitrator, from the time of his appointment and throughout the arbitral proceedings, shall without delay disclose . . .".

7.   We have already pointed out that Article 9 of the Egyptian Act set out the courts competent over those matters which the law reserves for the courts (i.e. the court that originally had jurisdiction in national arbitration, or the Cairo Court of Appeal, or a Court of Appeal chosen by the parties, in international arbitration).

     Omani law does not refer to any court, but to the President of the court (President of the commercial court in national arbitration, the President of the "appeal division" in international arbitration). Thus, the President of the commercial court, in national arbitration (or the President of the appeals division in international arbitration):

(a)   appoints the sole arbitrator if there is only one;[12]
(b)   appoints an arbitrator if a party fails to do so when there are three members to the arbitral tribunal;[13]
(c)   appoints the chairman of the arbitral tribunal if the other arbitrators fail to agree on an appointment.[14] When doing so, he must respect the conditions imposed by the law and those agreed by the parties;[15]
(d)   terminates an arbitrator's mission if the conditions for this are not met;[16]
(e)   decides on the enforcement of provisional or conservatory measures decided by the Arbitral Tribunal if one of the parties requests this;[17]
(f)   fines witnesses;[18]
(g)   fixes a new time period for the arbitration, upon request of one of the parties, if the arbitrators do not make their award within the time granted to them;[19]

---

[8] Egyptian Arbitration Act, Art. 16(1).
[9] Omani Arbitration Act, Art. 16(1).
[10] Egyptian Arbitration Act, Art. 16(3).
[11] Omani Arbitration Act, Art. 16(3).
[12] Omani Arbitration Act, Art. 17.
[13] Omani Arbitration Act, Art. 17.
[14] Omani Arbitration Act, Art. 17.
[15] Omani Arbitration Act, Art. 17, para. 3.
[16] Omani Arbitration Act, Art. 20.
[17] Omani Arbitration Act, Art. 24.
[18] Omani Arbitration Act, Art. 37.
[19] Omani Arbitration Act, Art. 45(2).

   (h) orders enforcement of the arbitral award.[20] An appeal against a decision refusing enforcement lies before the entire commercial court (a decision granting leave to enforce is not subject to appeal);[21]

   (i) the court having jurisdiction over an appeal against an award in national arbitration is the entire commercial court. In international arbitration, it is the entire "appeal division" thereof.[22]

8.   In th Egyptian Act, the proceedings are interrupted in those cases foreseen in the Code of Civil Procedure.

Omani Law does not refer to such a code, which does not exist in Oman. There is the Commercial Courts Act, which replaced the Act on the Board for Settlement of Commerical Disputes. Under the Omani Arbitration Act, the arbitral proceedings are stayed in the conditions provided for in the Moslem *shari 'a* and the Commercial Courts Act.[23]

The provisions of the new Omani Arbitration Act only apply to arbitrations taking place in Oman or those taking place abroad and applying Omani Law. They do not apply to arbitral awards made abroad in proceedings applying another law.

In such a case, the law that applies to the enforcement of the award in Oman will not be the new Arbitration Act but the Commercial Court Act, as the provisions of this act relating to foreign arbitral awards were not repealed.

The new Act applies to all commercial arbitrations. It gives a wide interpretation to the notion of commerce (Article 3). This is also true for the notion of international arbitration. It differs from the model law in that, when distinguishing between international and national arbitration, the test is the "main seat of activity of each of the parties", whereas the model law mentions "the parties' place of business".

A new point in the Omani Act is that Article 3, paragraph 2 provides that an agreement to resort to a permanent arbitration centre is sufficient to make the arbitration international. Thus, an award issued by the Arbitration Centre of Bahrain Gulf Co-operation Centre, is international.

As a general rule, the new Act adopts a geographical test to distinguish between national and international arbitrations. The criterion is based on the differing nationalities of the parties and places (place of signature, of performance, of arbitration, or residence of the parties) but also takes account of the economic aspect, which is mentioned as follows: "Under this act, any arbitration over a dispute relating to international commerce, is international . . .".[24] Then it takes into account the geographical criterion, i.e. the fact that the arbitration has links with more than one country.

The distinction between national and international arbitration has important consequences on several points:

   (a) in national arbitration, the courts often control the substance of the award. This is not true in international arbitration, sometimes this is even prohibited by international conventions, and the law.

   (b) In "civil law" countries, the field of international arbitration is much larger than in national arbitration since some kinds of disputes (labour disputes, civil disputes) are not arbitrable in national matters, but may be arbitrated in international matters. This distinction is not so marked in Anglo-Saxon law countries.

---

[20] Omani Arbitration Act, Art. 56.
[21] Omani Arbitration Act, Art. 54.
[22] Egyptian Arbitration Act, Art. 38.
[23] Omani Arbitration Act, Art. 38.
[24] Omani Arbitration Act, Art. 3.

      Likewise, the question of arbitration dipsutes with the state or state departments is different: the state and state departments may be party to an international arbitration, but not to a national arbitration.

(c) The courts apply the national rules to national arbitration and may set aside awards breaching these rules. Foreign arbitral awards are not subject to the national rules, they must only comply with the rules of public order.

(d) Finally, public order, which limits the parties' will and makes awards viodable, is different in national and international matters. It will be International Public Order in international arbitrations and National Public Order in national arbitrations.

Curiously enough, however, while Omani law distinguishes between national arbitration and international arbitration, with a clean test for distinguishing between them, it has given no consequence to this difference, as was done by other arbitration Acts which also make this distinction. The only consequence is the difference in the courts having jurisdiction for appointing the arbitrators if one of the parties fails to do so, and the court having jurisdiction over appeals against the award, and granting leave to enforce.

Malaysia
Syariah Criminal Offences (Federal Territories) Act
(Laws of Malaysia Act 559, 1997)

An Act to provide for Syariah criminal offences, and matters relating thereto.

BE IT ENACTED by the Seri Paduka Baginda Yang di-Pertuan Agong with the advice and consent of the Dewan Negara and Dewan Rakyat in Parliament assembled, and by the authority of the same, as follows:

PART I
PRELIMINARY

1(1) This Act may be cited as the Syariah Criminal Offences (Federal Territories) Act 1997 and shall come into force on such date as the Yang di-Pertuan Agong may, by notification in the *Gazette* , appoint.

(2) This Act shall apply only
   (a)   to the Federal Territories of Kuala Lumpur and Labuan; and
   (b)   to persons professing the religion of Islam.

2(1) In this Act, unless the context otherwise requires:
   "Administration Act" means the Administration of Islamic Law (Federal Territories) Act 1993;
   "approved home" means any place or institution appointed as such under section 54;
   "approved rehabilitation centre" means any place or institution appointed as such under section 54.
   "*baligh*" mans having attained the age of puberty according to Islamic Law;
   "Court" means the Syariah Subordinate Court, the Syariah High Court, or the Syariah Appeal Court, as the case may be, constituted under section 40 of the Administration Act;
   "Enactment" means the Administration of Muslim Law Enactment 1952 of the State of Selangor:

    (a)   in relation to the Federal Territory of Kuala Lumpur, as modified by the Federal Territory (Modification of Administration of Muslim Law Enactment) Orders 1974, 1981 and 1988 made pursuant to subsection 6(4) of the Constitution (Amendment) (No. 2) Act 1973 and in force in the Federal Territory of Kuala Lumpur by virtue of subsection 6(1) of that Act and the Administration of Muslim Law (Amendment) Act 1984; and

    (b)   in relation to the Federal Territory of Labuan, as modified and extended by the Federal Territory of Labuan (Modification and Extension of Administration of Muslim Law Enactment) Order 1985 made pursuant to section 7 of the Constitution (Amendment) (No. 2) Act 1984;

"fatwa" means any fatwa made under section 34 of the Administration Act;

"Federal Territories" means the Federal Territories of Kuala Lumpur and Labuan;

"incest" means sexual intercourse between a man and a woman who are prohibited from marrying each other under Islamic Law;

"Islamic Law" means Islamic Law according to any recognized *mazhab*;

"Judge" means a judge of the Syariah Appeal Court, the Syariah High Court and the Syariah Subordinate Court appointed under sections 41, 42 and 43 respectively, of the Administration Act;

"*li'an*" means an allegation made by a man under oath in accordance with Islamic Law that his wife has committed *zina*;

"*liwat*" means sexual relations between male persons;

"*Majlis*" means the *Majlis Agama Islam Wilayah Persekutuan* established under subsection 4(1) of the Administration Act;

"*Mufti*" means the person appointed to be the *Mufti* for the Federal Territories under section 32 of the Administration Act, and includes the Deputy *Mufti*;

"*muncikari*" means a person who acts as a procurer between a female and male person for any purpose which is contrary to Islamic Law;

"*musahaqah*" means sexual relations between female persons;

"*qazaf*" means making false allegation on any person;

"*takfir*" means to regard a Muslim as a non-Muslim;

"*zina*" means sexual intercourse between a man and a woman out of wedlock.

(2)   All words and expressions used in this Act and not herein defined in the Interpretation Acts 1948 and 1967 shall have the meanings thereby assigned to them respectively to the extent that such meanings do not conflict with Islamic Law.

(3)   For the avoidance of doubt as to the identity or interpretation of the words and expressions used in this Act that are listed in the Schedule, reference may be made to the Arabic script for those words and expressions as shown against them therein.

PART II
OFFENCES RELATING TO '*AQIDAH*

3(1) Any person who worships nature or does any act which shows worship or reverence of any person, animal, place or thing in any manner contrary to Islamic Law shall be guilty of an offence and shall on conviction be liable to a fine not exceeding three thousand ringgit or to imprisonment for a term not exceeding two years or to both.

 (2) The Court may order that any device, object or thing used in the commission of or related to the offence referred to in subsection (1) be forfeit and destroyed, notwithstanding that no person may have been convicted of such offence.

4(1) An person who teaches or expounds in any place, whether private or public, any doctrine or performs any ceremony or act relating to the religion of Islam shall, if such doctrine or ceremony or act is contrary to Islamic Law or any fatwa for the time being in force in the Federal Territories, be guilty of an offence and shall on conviction be liable to a fine not exceeding five thousand ringgit or to imprisonment for a term not exceeding three years or to whipping not exceeding six strokes or to any combination thereof.

(2) The Court may order that any document or thing used in the commission of or related to the offence referred to in subsection (1) be forfeited and destroyed, notwithstanding that no person may have been convicted of such offence.

5. Any person who propagates religious doctrines or beliefs other than the religious doctrines or beliefs of the religion of Islam among persons professing the Islamic faith shall be guilty of an offence and shall on conviction be liable to a fine not exceeding three thousand ringgit or to imprisonment for a term not exceeding two years or to both.

6. Any person who —

(a) declared himself or any person a prophet, *Imam Mahadi* or *wali*; or
(b) states or claims that he or some other person knows of unnatural happenings,

such declaration, statement or claim begin false and contrary to the teachings of Islam, shall be guilty of an offence and shall on conviction be liable to a fine not exceeding five thousand ringgit or to imprisonment for a term not exceeding three years or to both.

PART III
OFFENCES RELATING TO THE SANCTITY OF THE RELIGION OF ISLAM AND ITS INSTITUTION

7. Any person who orally or in writing or by visible representation or in any other manner—

(a) insults or brings into contempt the religion of Islam;
(b) derides, apes or ridicules the practices or ceremonies relating to the religion of Islam; or
(c) degrade or brings into contempt any law relating to the religion of Islam for the time being in force in the Federal Territories,

shall be guilty of an offence and shall on conviction be liable to a fine not exceeding three thousand ringgit or to imprisonment for a term not exceeding two years or to both.

8. Any person who, by his words or acts, derides, insults, ridicules or brings into contempt the verses of *Al-Quran* or *Hadith* shall be guilty of an offence and shall on conviction be liable to a fine not exceeding five thousand ringgit or to imprisonment for a term not exceeding three years or to both.

9. Any person who acts in contempt of religious authority or defies, disobeys or disputes the orders or directions of the Yang di-Pertuan Agong as the Head of the religion of Islam, the *Majlis* or the *Mufti*, expressed or given by way of fatwa, shall be guilty of an offence and shall on conviction be liable to a fine not exceeding three thousand ringgit or to imprisonment for a term not exceeding two years or to both.

10. Any person who defies, disobeys, disputes, degrades, brings into contempt any order of a Judge or Court shall be guilty of an offence and shall on conviction be liable to a fine not exceeding three thousand ringgit or to imprisonment for a term not exceeding two years or to both.

11(1) Any person who teaches or professes to teach any matter relating to the religion of Islam without a *tauliah* granted under section 96 of the Administration Act shall be guilty of an offence and shall on conviction be liable to a fine not exceeding five thousand ringgit or to imprisonment for a term not exceeding three years or to both.

(2) Subsection (1) shall not apply to—
   (a) any person or class of persons exempted by the *Majlis* under section 98 of the Administration Act; or
   (b) any person who teaches or professes to teach any matter relating to the religion of Islam in his own residence to members of his own household only.

12. Any person who give, propagates or disseminates any opinion concerning Islamic teachings, Islamic Law or any issue, contrary to any fatwa for the time being in force in the Federal Territories shall be guilty of an offence and shall on conviction be liable to a fine not exceeding three thousand ringgit or to imprisonment for a term not exceeding two years or to both.

13(1) Any person who—
   (a) prints, publishes, produces, records, distributes or in any other manner disseminates any book, pamphlet, document or any form of recording containing anything which is contrary to Islamic Law; or
   (b) has in his possession any such book, pamphlet, document or recording,
   shall be guilty of an offence and shall on conviction be liable to a fine not exceeding three thousand ringgit or to imprisonment for a term not exceeding two years or to both.

(2) The Court may order that any book, pamphlet, document or recording referred to in subsection (1) be forfeited and destroyed, notwithstanding that no person may have been convicted of an offence connected therewith.

14. Any male person, being *baligh*, who fails to perform the Friday prayers in a mosque within his *kariah* for three consecutive weeks without *uzur syarie* or without any reasonable cause shall be guilty of an offence and shall on conviction be liable to a fine not exceeding one thousand ringgit or to imprisonment for a term not exceeding six months or to both.

15. Any person who during the hours of fasting in the month of *Ramadan*—

(a) sells to any Muslim any food, drink, cigarette, or other form of tobacco for immediate consumption during such hours; or
(b) openly or in a public place is found to be eating, drinking or smoking,

shall be guilty of an offence and shall on conviction be liable to a fine not exceeding one thousand ringgit or to imprisonment for a term not exceeding six months or to both, and for a second or subsequent offence to a fine not exceeding two thousand ringgits or to imprisonment for a term not exceeding one year or to both.

16. Any person, who, being liable to pay *zakat* or *fitrah*—

(a) refuses or wilfully fails to pay the *zakat* or *fitrah*; or
(b) refuses or wilfully fails to pay the *zakat* or *fitrah* through an *amil* appointed, or any other person authorized, by the *Majlis* to collect *zakat* or *fitrah*,

shall be guilty of an offence and shall on conviction be liable to a fine not exceeding one thousand ringgit or to imprisonment for a term not exceeding six months or to both.

17(1) Any person who instigates or induces any Muslim not to attend mosque or religious teachings or any religious ceremony shall be guilty of an offence and shall on conviction be liable to a fine not exceeding one thousand ringgit or to imprisonment for a term not exceeding six months or to both.

   (2) Any person who in any manner prevents another person from paying *zakat* or *fitrah* shall be guilty of an offence and shall on conviction be liable to a fine not exceeding two thousand ringgit or to imprisonment for a term not exceeding one year or to both.

18(1) Any person who gambles, or is found in a gaming house, shall be guilty of an offence and shall on conviction be liable to a fine not exceeding three thousand ringgit or to imprisonment for a term not exceeding two years or to both.

   (2) In this section, "gaming house" means any premises, including a room, an office or a stall, whether open or enclosed, used or kept for the purpose of any game of chance or a combination of skill and chance, whether permitted by any other law or otherwise, for money or money's worth.

19(1) Any person who in any shop or other public place, consumes any intoxicating drink shall be guilty of an offence and shall on conviction be liable to a fine not exceeding three thousand ringgit or to imprisonment for a term not exceeding two years or to both.

   (2) Any person who makes, sells, offers or exhibits for sale, keeps or buys any intoxicating drink shall be guilty of an offence and shall on conviction be liable to a fine not exceeding five thousand ringgit or to imprisonment for a term not exceeding three years or to both.

PART IV
OFFENCES RELATING TO DECENCY

20. Any person who commits incest shall be guilty of an offence and shall on conviction be liable to a fine not exceeding five thousand ringgit or to imprisonment for a term not exceeding three years or to whipping not exceeding six strokes or to any combination thereof.

21(1) Any woman who prostitutes herself shall be guilty of an offence and shall on conviction be liable to a fine not exceeding five thousand ringgit or to imprisonment for a term not exceeding three years or to whipping not exceeding six strokes or to any combination thereof.

   (2) Any person who—
     (a) prostitutes his wife or a female child under his care; or
     (b) causes or allows his wife or a female child under his care to prostitute herself,
     shall be guilty of an offence and shall on conviction be liable to a fine not exceeding five thousand ringgit or to imprisonment for a term not exceeding three years or to whipping not exceeding six strokes or to any combination thereof.

22. Any person who acts as a *muncikari* shall be guilty of an offence and shall on conviction be liable to a fine not exceeding five thousand ringgit or to imprisonment for a term not exceeding three years or to whipping not exceeding six strokes or to any combination thereof.

23(1) Any man who performs sexual intercourse with a woman who is not his lawful wife shall be guilty of an offence and shall on conviction be liable to a fine not exceeding five thousand ringgit or to imprisonment for a term not exceeding three years or to whipping not exceeding six strokes or to any combination thereof.

(2) Any woman who performs sexual intercourse with a man who is not her lawful husband shall be guilty of an offence and shall on conviction be liable to a fine not exceeding five thousand ringgit or to imprisonment for a term not exceeding three years or to whipping not exceeding six strokes or to any combination thereof.

(3) The fact that a woman is pregnant out of wedlock as a result of sexual intercourse performed with her consent shall be *prima facie* evidence of the commission of an offence under subsection (2) by that woman.

(4) For the purpose of subsection (3), any woman who gives birth to a fully developed child within a period of six *qamariah* months from the date of her marriage shall be deemed to have been pregnant out of wedlock.

24. Any person who does an act preparatory to sexual intercourse out of wedlock shall be guilty of an offence and shall on conviction be liable to a fine not exceeding three thousand ringgit or to imprisonment for a term not exceeding two years or to both.

25. Any male person who commits *liwat* shall be guilty of an offence and shall on conviction be liable to a fine not exceeding five thousand ringgit or to imprisonment for a term not exceeding three years or to whipping not exceeding six strokes or to any combination thereof.

26. Any female person who commits *musahaqah* shall be guilty of an offence and shall on conviction be liable to a fine not exceeding five thousand ringgit or to imprisonment for a term not exceeding three years or to whipping not exceeding six strokes or to any combination thereof.

27. Any—

(a) man who is found together with one or more women, not being his wife or *mahram*; or

(b) woman who is found together with one or more men, not being her husband or *mahram*,

in any secluded place or in a house or room under circumstances which may give rise to suspicion that they were engaged in immoral acts shall be guilty of an offence and shall on conviction be liable to a fine not exceeding three thousand ringgit or to imprisonment for a term not exceeding two years or to both.

28. Any male person who, in a public place, wears a woman's attire and poses as a woman for immoral purposes shall be guilty of an offence and shall on conviction be liable to a fine not exceeding one thousand ringgit or to imprisonment for a term not exceeding one year or to both.

29. Any person who, contrary to Islamic Law, acts or behaves in an indecent manner in any public place shall be guilty of an offence and shall on conviction be liable to a fine not exceeding one thousand ringgit or to imprisonment for a term not exceeding six months or to both.

PART V
MISCELLANEOUS OFFENCES

30(1) Any person who gives false evidence or fabricates evidence for the purpose of being used in any stage of a judicial proceedings in the Court shall be guilty of an offence and shall on conviction be liable to a fine not exceeding three thousand ringgit or to imprisonment for a term not exceeding two years or to both.

(2) Any person who knowing or having reason to believe that an offence has been committed under this Act or under any other written law relating to the religion of Islam, gives any information relating to such offence which he knows or believes to be false shall be guilty of an offence and shall on conviction be liable to a fine not exceeding three thousand ringgit or to imprisonment for a term not exceeding two years or to both.

31(1) Subject to subsection (2), any person who alleges or imputes by words, either spoken or written, or by sign or visible representation, or by any act, activity or conduct, or by organizing, promoting or arranging any activity or otherwise in any manner, that any person professing the religion or Islam or person belonging to any group, class or description of persons professing the religion of Islam—

   (a) is or are *kafir*;

   (b) has or have ceased to profess the religion of Islam;

   (c) should not be accepted, or cannot be accepted, as professing the religion of Islam; or

   (d) does not or do not believe in, follow, profess, or belong to, the religion of Islam,

shall be guilty of an offence and shall on conviction be liable to a fine not exceeding five thousand ringgit or to imprisonment for a term not exceeding three years or to both.

(2) Subsection (1) shall not apply to—

   (a) anything done by a Court or religious authority established, constituted or appointed by or under any written law and empowered to give or issue any ruling or decision on any matter relating to the religion of Islam; and

   (b) anything done by any person pursuant to or in accordance with any ruling or decision given or issued by such Court or religious authority, whether or not such ruling or decision is in writing or, if in writing, whether or not it is published in the *Gazette*.

32. Any person who destroys, damages or defiles any mosque or *surau* or other place of worship or any of its equipment with the intention of thereby insulting or degrading the religion of Islam shall be guilty of an offence and shall on conviction be liable to a fine not exceeding three thousand ringgit or to imprisonment for a term not exceeding two years or to both.

33. Any person who collects *zakat* or *fitrah* or causes to be collected *zakat* or *fitrah* without having been appointed as *amil* or otherwise authorized by the *Majlis* shall be guilty of an offence and shall on conviction be liable to a fine not exceeding three thousand ringgit or to imprisonment for a term not exceeding two years or to both, and the Court shall order such collection to be confiscated and paid into the Fund established under section 60 of the Administration Act.

34. Any person who pays or causes to be paid payment of *zakat* or *fitrah* to any person not lawfully authorized to collect *zakat* or *fitrah* shall be guilty of an offence and shall on conviction be liable to a fine not exceeding one thousand ringgit or to imprisonment for a term not exceeding six months or to both.

35. Any person who promotes, induces or encourages another person to indulge in any vice shall be guilty of an offence and shall on conviction be liable to a fine not exceeding five thousand ringgit or to imprisonment for a term not exceeding three years or to both.

36. Any person who entices a married woman or takes her away from or in any manner influences her to leave the matrimonial home determined by her husband shall be guilty of an offence and shall on conviction be liable to a fine not exceeding five thousand ringgit or to imprisonment for a term not exceeding three years or to both, and the Court shall order the said woman to return to her husband.

37. Any person who prevents a married couple from cohabiting as a legally married couple shall be guilty of an offence and shall on conviction be liable to a fine not exceeding two thousand ringgit or to imprisonment for a term not exceeding one year or to both, and the Court shall order the couple to cohabit as a legally married couple.

38. Any person who instigates, forces or persuades any man or woman to be divorced or to neglect his or her duties and responsibilities as a husband or wife shall be guilty of an offence and shall on conviction be liable to a fine not exceeding five thousand ringgit or to imprisonment for a term not exceeding three years or to both.

39. Any person who entices or induces or persuades any female person to run away from the custody of her parents or guardian shall be guilty of an offence and shall on conviction be liable to a fine not exceeding three thousand ringgit or to imprisonment for a term not exceeding two years or to both, and the Court may make such order as it deems appropriate in respect of the female person.

40. Any person who sells, gives away or delivers his child or a child under his care to any person who is not a Muslim shall be guilty of an offence and shall on conviction be liable to a fine not exceeding three thousand ringgit or to imprisonment for a term not exceeding two years or to both, and the Court may make such order as it deems appropriate in respect of the child.

41. Except in cases of *li'an*, any person who accuses another person of committing *zina* without procuring four male witnesses or an *iqrar* of the accused person in accordance with Islamic Law shall be guilty of an offence and shall on conviction be liable to a fine not exceeding five thousand ringgit or to imprisonment for a term not exceeding three years or to both.

42. Any person who displays, on or in respect of any food or drink which is not *halal*, any sign which indicates that such food or drink is *halal*, shall be guilty of an offence and shall on conviction be liable to a fine not exceeding five thousand ringgit or to imprisonment for a term not exceeding three years or to both.

PART VI
ABETMENT AND ATTEMPT

43. A person abets the doing of a thing who—

(a) instigates any person to do that thing;
(b) engages with one other person or more in any conspiracy for the doing of that thing, if an act or illegal omission takes place in pursuance of that conspiracy, and in order to the doing of that thing; or

(c) intentionally aids, by any act or illegal omission, the doing of that thing;

Explanation 1— A person who, by wilful misrepresentation, or by wilful concealment of a material fact which he is bound to disclose, voluntarily causes or procures, or attempt to cause or procure, a thing to be done is said to instigate the doing of that thing.

Explanation 2— Any person who, either prior to or at the time of the commission of an act, does anything in order to facilitate the commission of that act, and thereby facilitates the commission thereof, is said to aid the doing of that act.

44. A person abets an offence within the meaning of this Act, who, in the Federal Territories, abets the commission of an act outside the Federal Territories which would constitute an offence if committed in the Federal Territories.

45. Any person who abets any offence shall, if the act abetted is committed in consequence of the abetment, be punished with the punishment provided for the offence.

46. Where an act is abetted and a different act is done, the abettor is liable for the act done in the same manner and to the same extent as if he had abetted the act done if the act done—

(a) was a probable consequence of the abetment; and
(b) was committed under the influence of the instigation, or with the aid or in pursuance of the conspiracy which constituted the abetment.

47(1) Any person who attempts—
(a) to commit an offence under this Act or under any other written law relating to Islamic law; or
(b) to cause such an offence to be committed,
and in such attempt does any act towards the commission of such offence, shall, where no express provision is made by this Act or by such other written law, as the case may be, for the punishment of such attempt, be punished with such punishment as is provided for the offence.
(2) Any term of imprisonment imposed as a punishment for an attempt to commit an offence or to cause an offence to be committed shall not exceed one half of the maximum term provided for the offence.

PART VII
GENERAL EXCEPTIONS

48. Nothing is an offence which is done by a Judge when acting judicially in the exercise of any power which is, or which in good faith he believes to be, given to him by law.

49. Nothing is an offence which is done in pursuance of, or which is warranted by the judgment or order of, a Court if done whilst such judgment or order remains in force, notwithstanding that the Court may have no jurisdiction to pass such judgment or order, if the person doing the act in good faith believes that the Court had such jurisdiction.

50. Nothing is an offence which is done by a person who is justified by law, or who by reason of a mistake of fact and not by reason of mistake of law in good faith believes himself to be justified by law, in doing.

51. Nothing is an offence which is done by a child who is not *baligh*.

52(1) Nothing is an offence which is done by a person who at the time of doing it, by reason of unsoundness of mind, is incapable of knowing the nature of the act or that what he is doing is wrong and contrary to law.

  (2) For the purpose of this section, if a person was in a state of intoxication at the time of the act or omission complained of and—

    (a) the state of intoxication was such that he did not know that the act or ommission was wrong or he did not know what he was doing; and

    (b) the state of intoxication was caused without his consent by the malicious or negligent act of another person,

  he shall be deemed to be a person of unsound mind.

  (3) In this section, "intoxication" shall be deemed to include a state produced by drugs.

53(1) Nothing is an offence which is done by a person who is compelled to do it by threats, which at the time of doing it reasonably caused the apprehension that instant death to the person will otherwise be the consequence.

  (2) The exception under subsection (1) shall not apply if the person doing the act placed himself, of his own accord, in the situation by which be became subject to such constraint.

PART VIII
GENERAL MATTERS

54. The *Majlis* may, by notification in the *Gazette*, appoint any place or institution to be an approved rehabilitation centre or an approved home for the purposes of this Act.

55. Where the Court has convicted any person of an offence under Part II or under section 7, 8, 9 or 31, such Court may, in lieu of or in addition to any punishment specified for such offence, order any such person to be committed to an approved rehabilitation centre to undergo such counselling or rehabilitation for any period not exceeding six months as may be specified in the order; but where any sentence of imprisonment is imposed together with the counselling or rehabilitation the period thereof shall not in the aggregate exceed three years.

56. Where the Court has convicted any female person of an offence under Part IV, such Court may, in lieu of or in addition to any punishment specified for such offence, order any such person to be committed to an approved home for such period not exceeding six months as may be specified in such order; but where any sentence of imprisonment is imposed together with such committal the period thereof shall not in the aggregate exceed three years.

57(1) Part IX of the Enactment, other than sections 164 and 165, shall cease to apply to the Federal Territories and shall to that extent be deemed to have been repealed.

  (2) Notwithstanding the repeal of Part IX of the Enactment (the "repealed Part") all proceedings under that repealed Part, including any appeal from any Court under the repealed Part, shall be continued as if this Act had not been passed.

58. Section 164 of the Enactment in its application to the Federal Territories is amended by substituting for the words "34 of this Enactment" the words "28 of the Administration of Islamic Law (Federal Territories) Act 1993".

Part IV

Selected Cases

International Court of Justice
Year 1998

Libyan Arab Jamahiriya v. United States of America

1998
27 February
General List
No. 89

Case Concerning Questions of Interpretation and Application of the 1971 Montreal Convention Arising from the Aerial Incident at Lockerbie

PRELIMINARY OBJECTIONS

Objection to jurisdiction — Montreal Convention of 23 September 1971 — Treaty in force between the Parties — Article 14, paragraph 1, of the Convention.

Grounds for lack of jurisdiction invoked in the provisional measures phase — Arguments repeated in passing in the present phase of the proceedings — Negotiations — Request for arbitration — Six-month period before the Court can be seised.

Contention that no legal dispute exists concerning the interpretation and application of the Montreal Convention — Dispute of a general nature as to the legal régime applicable to the destruction of the Pan Am aircraft over Lockerbie — Specific disputes concerning the interpretation and application of Article 7 of the Convention, read in conjunction with Articles 1, 5, 6 and 8, and the interpretation and application of Article 11 of the Convention.

Contention that it is not for the Court to decide on the lawfulness of actions instituted by the Respondent to secure the surrender of the two alleged offenders — Jurisdiction of the Court to decide on the lawfulness of those actions in so far as they would be at variance with the provisions of the Montreal Convention.

Security Council resolutions 748 (1992) and 883 (1993) — Adoption after filing of the Application — Jurisdiction to be determined at the date of filing of the Application.

Objection to admissibility — Contention that the dispute between the Parties is governed by Security Council resolutions 748 (1992) and 883 (1993) and not the Montreal Convention —

Admissibility to be determined at the date of filing of the Application — Adoption of the resolutions after the filing of the Application.

Objection that there is no ground for proceeding to judgment on the merits — Contention that the Applicant's claims have become moot because Security Council resolution 748 (1992) and 883 (1993) have rendered them without object — Article 79, paragraph 1, of the Rules of Court — "Preliminary" Objection — Formal conditions for presentation — Article 79, paragraph 7, of the Rules of Court — 1972 Revision — Objection which is "not exclusively" preliminary containing "both preliminary aspects and other aspects relating to the merits" — Rights on the merits constituting the very subject-matter of a decision on the objection.

Request submitted in the alternative that the Court should "resolve the case in substance now" — By raising preliminary objections, the Respondent has made a procedural choice the effect of which, according to the express terms of Article 79, paragraph 3, is to suspend the proceedings on the merits.

Fixing of time-limits for the further proceedings.

JUDGMENT

Present: *Vice-President* WEERAMANTRY, *Acting President*; *President* SCHWEBEL; *Judges* ODA, BEDJAOUI, GUILLAUME, RANJEVA, HERCZEGH, SHI, FLEISCH-HAUER, KOROMA, VERESHCHETIN, PARRA-ARANGUREN, KOOIJ-MANS, REZEK; *Judge* ad hoc EL-KOSHERI; *Registrar* VALENCIA-OSPINA.

In the case concerning questions of interpretation and application of the 1971 Montreal Convention arising from the aerial incident at Lockerbie,

between

the Great Socialist People's Libyan Arab Jamahiriya,

represented by

H.E. Mr. Hamed Ahmed Elhouderi, Ambassador, Secretary of the People's Office of the Great Socialist People's Libyan Arab Jamahiriya to the Netherlands,

as Agent;

Mr. Mohamed A. Aljady,
Mr. Abdulhamid Raeid,

as Counsel;

Mr. Abdelrazeg El-Murtadi Suleiman, Professor of Public International Law, Faculty of Law, University of Benghazi,
Mr. Ian Brownlie, CBE, QC, FBA, Chichele Professor of Public International Law, University of Oxford,
Mr. Jean Salmon, Professor of Law emeritus, Université libre de Bruxelles,
Mr. Eric Suy, Professor of International Law, Catholic University of Louvain (KU Leuven),
Mr. Eric David, Professor of Law, Université libre de Bruxelles,

as Counsel and Advocates;

Mr. Nicolas Angelet, Principal Assistant, Faculty of Law, Catholic University of Louvan (KU Leuven),

Mrs. Barbara Delcourt, Assistant, Faculty of Social, Political and Economic Sciences, Université libre de Bruxelles, Research Fellow, Centre of International Law and Institute of European Studies, Université libre de Bruxelles,

Mr. Mohamed Awad,

as Advisers.

and

the United States of America,

represented by

Mr. David R. Andrews, Legal Adviser, United States Department of State,

as Agent;

Mr. Michael J. Matheson, Principal Deputy Legal Adviser, United States Department of State,

as Co-Agent;

Mr. John R. Crook, Assistant Legal Adviser, United States Department of State,
Mr. Sean D. Murphy, Counsellor for Legal Affairs, United States Embassy, The Hague,
Mr. Oscar Schachter, Professor at the Columbia University School of Law,
Ms. Elisabeth Zoller, Professor at the University of Paris II,

as Counsel and Advocates;

Mr. John J. Kim, Office of the Legal Adviser, United States Department of State,
Mr. Brian Murtagh, United States Department of Justice,

as Counsel.

THE COURT,

composed as above,

after deliberation,

delivers the following Judgment,

1. On 3 March 1992, the Government of the Great Socialist People's Libyan Arab Jamahiriya (hereinafter called "Libya") filed in the Registry of the Court an Application instituting proceedings against the Government of the United States of America (hereinafter called "the United States") in respect of a "dispute between Libya and the United States concerning the interpretation or application of the Montreal Convention" of 23 September 1971 for the Suppression of Unlawful Acts against the Safety of Civil Aviation (hereinafter

called "the Montreal Convention"). The Application referred to the destruction, on 21 December 1988, over Lockerbie (Scotland), of the aircraft on Pan Am flight 103, and to charges brought by a Grand Jury of the United States in November 1991 against two Libyan nationals suspected of having caused a bomb to be placed aboard the aircraft, which bomb had exploded causing the aeroplane to crash. The Application invoked as the basis for jurisdiction Article 14, paragraph 1, of the Montreal Convention.

2. Pursuant to Article 40, paragraph 2, of the Statute, the Application was immediately communicated to the Government of the United States by the Registrar; pursuant to paragraph 3 of that Article, all States entitled to appear before the Court were notified of the Application.

3. Pursuant to Article 69, paragraph 3, of the Rules of Court, the Registrar addressed to the Secretary General of the International Civil Aviation Organization the notification provided for in Article 34, paragraph 3, of the Statute.
Pursuant to Article 43 of the Rules of Court, the Registrar also addressed the notification provided for in Article 63, paragraph 1, of the Statute to all States which, on the basis of information obtained from the depository Governments, appeared to be parties to the Montreal Convention.

4. Since the Court included upon the Bench no judge of Libyan nationality, Libya exercised its right under Article 31, paragraph 2, of the Statute to choose a judge *ad hoc* to sit in the case: it chose Mr. Ahmed Sadek El-Kosheri to do so.

5. On 3 March 1992, immediately after the filing of its Application, Libya submitted a request for the indication of provisional measures under Article 41 of the Statute.
By an Order dated 14 April 1992, the Court, after hearing the Parties, found that the circumstances of the case were not such as to require the exercise of its power to indicate provisional measures.

6. By an order of 19 June 1992, the Court, having regard to the requests of the Parties, fixed 20 December 1993 as the time-limit for the filing by Libya of a Memorial and 20 June 1995 as the time-limit for the filing by the United States of a Counter-Memorial.
Libya duly filed its Memorial within the prescribed time-limit.

7. Within the time-limit fixed for the filing of its Counter-Memorial, the United States filed Preliminary Objections to the jurisdiction of the Court and the admissibility of the Application.
Accordingly, by an Order of 22 September 1995, the Court, noting that by virtue of Article 79, paragraph 3, of the Rules of Court the proceedings on the merits were suspended, fixed 22 December 1995 as the time-limit within which Libya might present a written statement of its observations and submissions on the Preliminary Objections.
Libya filed such a statement within the time-limit so fixed, and the case became ready for hearing in respect of the Preliminary Objections.

8. By a letter dated 19 February 1996, the Registrar, pursuant to Article 34, paragraph 3, of the Statute, communicated copies of the written pleadings to the Secretary General of the International Civil Aviation Organization and, referring to Article 69, paragraph 2, of the Rules of Court, specified that, if the Organization wished to present written observations to the Court they should be limited, at that stage, to questions of jurisdiction and admissibility.
By a letter of 26 June 1996, the Secretary General of the International Civil Aviation Organization informed the Court that the Organization "ha[d] no observations to make

for the moment" but wished to remain informed about the progress of the case, in order to be able to determine whether it would be appropriate to submit observations later.

9. The President of the Court, being a national of one of the Parties to the case, was unable, by virtue of Article 32, paragraph 1, of the Rules of the Court, to exercise the functions of the presidency in respect of the present case. It therefore fell to the Vice-President, in accordance with Article 13, paragraph 1, of the Rules of the Court, to exercise the functions of the presidency in the case.

10. In accordance with Article 53, paragraph 2, of its Rules, the Court decided to make accessible to the public, on the opening of the oral proceedings, the Preliminary Objections of the United States and the written statement containing the observations and submissions of Libya on the Objections, as well as the documents annexed to those pleadings.

11. Public sittings were held between 13 and 22 October 1997, at which the Court heard the oral arguments of:

For the United States: Mr. David Andrews,
                             Mr. Sean D. Murphy,
                             Mr. John R. Crook,
                             Mr. Oscar Schachter,
                             Ms. Elisabeth Zoller,
                             Mr. Michael J. Matheson.

For Libya: H.E. Mr. Hamed Ahmed Elhouderi,
                             Mr. Abdelrazeg El-Murtadi Suleiman,
                             Mr. Jean Salmon,
                             Mr. Eric David,
                             Mr. Eric Suy,
                             Mr. Ian Brownlie.

At the hearings, Members of the Court put questions to the Parties, who answered in writing after the close of the oral proceedings.

12. In the Application, the following requests were made by Libya:

"Accordingly, while reserving the right to supplement and amend this submission as appropriate in the course of further proceedings, Libya requests the Court to adjudge and declare as follows:

(a) that Libya has fully complied with all of its obligations under the Montreal Convention;
(b) that the United States has breached, and is continuing to breach, its legal obligations to Libya under Articles 5(2), 5(3), 7, 8(2) and 11 of the Montreal Convention; and
(c) that the United States is under a legal obligation immediately to cease and desist from such breaches and from the use of any and all force or threats against Libya, including the threat of force against Libya, and from all violations of the sovereignty, territorial integrity, and the political independence of Libya."

13. In the written proceedings, the following submissions were presented by the Parties:

On behalf of the Government of Libya,

in the Memorial:

"For these reasons, while reserving the right to supplement and amend these submissions as appropriate in the course of further proceedings, Libya requests the Court to adjudge and declare as follows:

    (a) that the Montreal convention is applicable to this dispute;
    (b) that Libya has fully complied with all of its obligations under the Montreal Convention and is justified in exercising the criminal jurisdiction provided for by that Convention;
    (c) that the United States has breached, and is continuing to breach, its legal obligations to Libya under Article 5, paragraphs 2 and 3, Article 7, Article 8, paragraph 3, and Article 11 of the Montreal Convention;
    (d) that the United States is under a legal obligation to respect Libya's right not to have the Convention set aside by means which would in any case be at variance with the principles of the United Nations Charter and with the mandatory rules of general international law prohibiting the use of force and the violation of the sovereignty, territorial integrity, sovereign equality and political independence of States."

On behalf of the Government of the United States:

in the Preliminary Objections:

"The United States of America requests that the Court uphold the objections of the United States to the jurisdiction of the Court and decline to entertain the case."

On behalf of the Government of Libya:

in the written statement of its observations and submissions on the Preliminary Objections:

"For these reasons, and reserving the right to complement or modify the present submissions in the course of the proceedings if necessary, Libya requests the Court to adjudge and declare:

    — that the preliminary objections raised by the United States must be rejected and that, as a consequence:
        (a) the Court has jurisdiction to entertain the Application of Libya,
        (b) that the Application is admissible;
    — that the Court should proceed to the merits."

14. In the oral proceedings the following submissions were presented by the Parties:

On behalf of the Government of the United States:

at the hearing on 20 October 1997:

"The United States of America requests that the Court uphold the objections of the United States to the jurisdiction of the Court and decline to entertain the case concerning *Questions of Interpretation and Application of the 1971 Montreal Convention arising from the Aerial Incident at Lockerbie (Libyan Arab Jamahiriya v. United States of America)*."

On behalf of the Government of Libya:

at the hearing on 22 October 1997:

"The Libyan Arab Jamahiriya requests the Court to adjudge and declare:

— that the Preliminary Objections raised by ... the United States must be rejected and that, as a consequence:
   (a) the Court has jurisdiction to entertain the Application of Libya;
   (b) that the Application is admissible;
— that the Court should proceed to the merits."

15. In its most recent arguments in the present case, the United States raised three objections: the first to the Court's jurisdiction, the second to the admissibility of the Application and the third alleging that the Libyan claims had become moot as having been rendered without object. For the United States, each of these objections is "genuinely preliminary in character". The United States contended moreover, in the alternative, that, should the Court nonetheless hold that it had jurisdiction and decide to exercise that jurisdiction, it could and should "resolve the case in substance now" by deciding, as a preliminary matter, that the relief sought by Libya is precluded.

16. The Court will first consider the objection raised by the United States to its jurisdiction.

17. Libya submits that the Court has jurisdiction on the basis of Article 14, paragraph 1, of the Montreal Convention, which provides that:

"Any dispute between two or more Contracting States concerning the interpretation or application of this Convention which cannot be settled through negotiation, shall, at the request of one of them, be submitted to arbitration. If within six months from the date of the request for arbitration the Parties are unable to agree on the organization of the arbitration, any one of those Parties may refer the dispute to the International Court of Justice by request in conformity with the Statute of the Court."

18. The Parties agree that the Montreal Convention is in force between them and that it was already in force both at the time of the destruction of the Pan Am aircraft over Lockerbie, on 21 December 1988, and at the time of filing of the Application, on 3 March 1992. However, the Respondent contests the jurisdiction of the Court because, in its submission, all the requisites laid down in Article 14, paragraph 1, of the Montreal Convention have not been complied with in the present case.

19. The United States contests the jurisdiction of the Court mainly on the basis of Libya's failure to show, firstly, that there exists a legal dispute between the Parties, and secondly, that such dispute, if any, concerns the interpretation or application of the Montreal Convention and falls as a result within the terms of Article 14, paragraph 1, of that Convention.

However, at the hearings, the United States also made reference, in passing, to the arguments it had advanced, in the provisional measures phase of the proceedings, as to whether the dispute that, in the opinion of Libya, exists between the Parties could be settled by negotiation, whether Libya had made a proper request for arbitration and whether it had respected the six-month period required by Article 14, paragraph 1 of the Convention.

20. The Court observes that in the present case, the Respondent has always maintained that the destruction of the Pan Am aircraft over Lockerbie did not give rise to any dispute between the Parties regarding the interpretation or application of the Montreal Convention and that, for that reason, in the Respondent's view, there was nothing to be settled by negotiation under the Convention; the Court notes that the arbitration proposal contained in the letter sent on 18 January 1992 by the Libyan Secretary of the People's Committee for Foreign Liaison and International Cooperation to the Secretary of State of the United States met with no answer; and it notes, in particular, that the Respondent clearly expressed its intention not to accept arbitration — in whatever form — when presenting and strongly supporting resolution 731 (1992) adopted by the Security Council three days later, on 21 January 1992.

Consequently, in the opinion of the Court the alleged dispute between the Parties could not be settled by negotiation or submitted to arbitration under the Montreal Convention, and the refusal of the Respondent to enter into arbitration to resolve that dispute absolved Libya from any obligation under Article 14, paragraph 1, of the Convention to observe a six-month period starting from the request for arbitration, before seising the Court.

21. As recalled by the Parties, the Permanent Court of International Justice states in 1924 that "A dispute is a disagreement on a point of law or fact, a conflict of legal views or of interests between two persons" (*Mavrommatis Palestine Concessions, 1924, P.C.I.J., Series A, No. 2*, p. 11). The present Court for its part, in its Judgment of 30 June 1995 in the case concerning *East Timor (Portugal v. Australia)* emphasized the following:

"In order to establish the existence of a dispute, 'It must be shown that the claim of one party is positively opposed by the other' (*South West Africa, Preliminary Objections, Judgment, I.C.J. Reports 1962*, p. 328; and further, 'Whether there exists an international dispute is a matter for objective determination' (*Interpretation of Peace Treaties with Bulgaria, Hungary and Romania, First Phase, Advisory Opinion, I.C.J. Reports 1950*, p. 74)." (*I.C.J. Reports , 1995*, p. 100.)

22. In its Application and Memorial, Libya maintained that the Montreal Convention was the only instrument applicable to the destruction of the Pan Am aircraft over Lockerbie, for the following reasons:

(a) the Respondent and Libya are bound by the Montreal Convention which is in force between the Parties;
(b) the Montreal Convention is specifically aimed at preventing that type of action (third paragraph of the Preamble);
(c) the actions ascribed to the Libyan nationals are covered by Article 1 of the Montreal Convention;
(d) "the system of the Montreal Convention, as compared to he system of the Charter, is both a *lex posterior* and a *lex specialis*; [consequently,] for matters covered by that Convention, it must *a priori* take precedence over the systems for which the Charter provides"; and
(e) there is no other convention concerning international criminal law in force which is applicable to these issues in the relations between Libya and the United States.

23. The United States does not deny that, as such, the facts of the case could fall within the terms of the Montreal Convention, However, it emphasizes that, in the present case, from the time Libya invoked the Montreal Convention, the United States has claimed that it was not relevant because it was not a question of "bilateral differences" but one of "a threat to international peace and security resulting from State-sponsored terrorism".

24. Consequently, the Parties differ on the question whether the destruction of the Pan Am aircraft over Lockerbie is governed by the Montreal Convention. A dispute thus exists between the Parties as to the legal régime applicable to this event. Such a dispute, in the view of the Court, concerns the interpretation and application of the Montreal Convention, and, in accordance with Article 14, paragraph 1, of the Convention, falls to be decided by the Court.

25. Furthermore, in its Application and Memorial, Libya stressed the following six points, in particular in support of the submissions set forth, respectively, in paragraph 12 (subparagraphs (a) and (b)) and paragraph 13 (subparagraphs (b) and (c)), above:

(a)   the actions which brought about the destruction of the Pan Am aircraft over Lockerbie constitute one of the offences covered by Article 1 of the Montreal Convention and therefore the Montreal Convention must be applied to those facts;

(b)   Libya has complied with the obligation imposed by Article 5, paragraph 2, of the Montreal Convention of establishing its jurisdiction over the alleged offenders in the destruction of the aircraft, and it has the right to exercise the jurisdiction so established;

(c)   Libya has exercised its jurisdiction over the two alleged offenders on the basis of its Penal Code, and the Respondent should not interfere with the exercise of that jurisdiction;

(d)   Libya has exercised the rights conferred by Article 6 of the Montreal Convention by taking all necessary measures to ensure the presence of the two alleged offenders, making preliminary enquiries, notifying the States concerned and indicating that it intended to exercise jurisdiction, but according to Libya the Respondent, by its actions and threats, is attempting, according to Libya, to prevent the application of the Convention;

(e)   Libya having decided not to extradite the two alleged offenders, Article 7 of the Montreal Convention gives its the right to submit them to its competent authorities for the purpose of prosecution in accordance with Libyan law; and

(f)   on the basis of Article 8, paragraph 3, of the Montreal Convention, it has the right not to extradite the two alleged offenders because they are Libyan nationals and the Libyan Constitution does not permit their extradition.

26. The Respondent disputes that the Montreal Convention confers on Libya the rights it claims to enjoy. It contends, moreover, that none of the provisions referred to by Libya imposes obligations on the United States. Finally, it recalls that it never itself invoked the Montreal Convention, and observes that nothing in that Convention prevented it from requesting the surrender of the two alleged offenders outside the framework of the Convention.

27. Article 1 of the Montreal Convention provides as follows:

"Article 1

1. Any person commits an offence if he unlawfully and intentionally:
(a)   performs an act of violence against a person on board an aircraft in flight if that act is likely to endanger the safety of that aircraft; or

(b)   destroys an aircraft in service or causes damage to such an aircraft which renders it incapable of flight or which is likely to endanger its safety in flight; or

(c)   places or causes to be placed on an aircraft in service, by any means whatsoever, a device or substance which is likely to destroy that aircraft, or to cause damage to it which renders it incapable of flight, or to cause damage to it which is likely to endanger its safety in flight; or

(d)   destroys or damages air navigation facilities or interferes with their operation, if any such act is likely to endanger the safety of aircraft in flight; or

(e)   communicates information which he knows to be false, thereby endangering the safety of an aircraft in flight.

        2. Any person also commits an offence if he:

(a)   attempts to commit any of the offences mentioned in paragraph 1 of this Article; or

(b)   is an accomplice of a person who commits or attempts to commit any such offence."

Article 5 provides:

"Article 5

        1. Each Contracting State shall take such measures as may be necessary to establish its jurisdiction over the offences in the following cases:

(a)   when the offence is committed in the territory of that State;

(b)   when the offence is committed against or on board an aircraft registered in that State;

(c)   when the aircraft on board which the offence is committed lands in its territory with the alleged offender still on board;

(d)   when the offence is committed against or on board an aircraft leased without crew to a lessee who has his principal place of business or, if the lessee has no such place of business, his permanent residence, in that State.

        2. Each Contracting State shall likewise take such measures as may be necessary to establish its jurisdiction over the offences mentioned in Article 1, paragraph 1(a), (b) and (c), and in Article 1, paragraph 2, in so far as that paragraph relates to those offences, in the case where the alleged offender is present in its territory and it does not extradite him pursuant to Article 8 to any of the States mentioned in paragraph 1 of this Article.

        3. This Convention does not exclude any criminal jurisdiction exercised in accordance with national law."

Article 6, for its part, states:

"Article 6

        1. Upon being satisfied that the circumstances so warrant, any Contracting State in the territory of which the offender or the alleged offender is present, shall take him into custody or take other measures to ensure his presence. The custody and other mea-

sures shall be as provided in the law of that State but may only be continued for such time as is necessary to enable any criminal or extradition proceedings to be instituted.

2. Such State shall immediately make a preliminary enquiry into the facts.

3. Any person in custody pursuant to paragraph 1 of this Article shall be assisted in communicating immediately with the nearest appropriate representative of the State of which he is national.

4. When a State, pursuant to this Article, has taken a person into custody, it shall immediately notify the States mentioned in Article 5, paragraph 1, the State of nationality of the detained person and, if it considers it advisable, any other interested State of the fact that such person is in custody and of the circumstances which warrant his detention. The State which makes the preliminary enquiry contemplated in paragraph 2 of this Article shall promptly report its findings to the said States and shall indicate whether it intends to exercise jurisdiction."

Article 7 is worded in the following terms:

"Article 7

The Contracting State in the territory of which the alleged offender is found shall, if it does not extradite him, be obliged, without exception whatsoever and whether or not the offence was committed in its territory, to submit the case to its competent authorities for the purpose of prosecution. Those authorities shall take their decision in the same manner as in the case of any ordinary offence of a serious nature under the law of that State."

Finally, in the words of Article 8:

"Article 8

1. The offences shall be deemed to be included as extraditable offences in any extradition treaty existing between Contracting States. Contracting States undertake to include the offences as extraditable offences in every extradition treaty to be concluded between them.

2. If a Contracting State which makes extradition conditional on the existence of a treaty receives a request for extradition from another Contracting State with which it has no extradition treaty, it may at its option consider this Convention as the legal basis for extradition in respect of the offences. Extradition shall be subject to the other conditions provided by the law of the requested State.

3. Contracting States which do not make extradition conditional on the existence of a treaty shall recognize the offences as extraditable offences between themselves subject to the conditions provided by the law of the requested State.

4. Each of the offences shall be treated, for the purpose of extradition between Contracting States, as if it had been committed not only in the place in which it occurred

but also in the territories of the States required to establish their jurisdiction in accordance with Article 5, paragraph 1(b), (c) and (d)."

28. In view of the positions put forward by the Parties, the Court finds that there exists between them not only a dispute of a general nature, as defined in paragraph 24 above, but also a specific dispute which concerns the interpretation and application of Article 7 — read in conjunction with Article 1, Article 5, Article 6 and Article 8 — of the Montreal Convention, and which, in accordance with Article 14, paragraph 1, of the Convention, falls to be decided by the Court.

29. Moreover, Libya maintained in its Application and Memorial that, once it had commenced its judicial investigation of the two alleged offenders, the Respondent was, according to Article 11, paragraph 1, of the Montreal Convention, under an obligation to hand over to the Libyan authorities all the evidence in its possession regarding the offence. In Libya's opinion, this obligation was not duly complied with, because the United States "has supplied *no* information".

30. In this regard, the United States acknowledges that "Article 11 is the only provision among those listed in Libya's complaint, that arguably addresses any obligation of any State other than Libya". However, it claims that "the obligation expressed in Article 11 is very general in nature" and that it had "satisfied [this] general obligation". It states in this connection that "on 21 November 1991, the United States transmitted to Libya through the authorities of the Government of Belgium copies of the grand jury indictment of the two Libyans". It also maintains that "Article 11 preserves the right of the United States, under United States law, to refuse to disclose additional details regarding the investigation, such as evidence derived from confidential sources". The United States, in addition, makes the following observations:

"As a practical matter, it is difficult to see how the Court can define specific forms of additional assistance that must be provided under Article 11. For the Court to try to inject into Article 11 specificity as to the level of assistance that is required — such as the provision of witness statements or other information — would simply be unworkable and could inhibit co-operation in an area that the drafters of the Montreal Convention deliberately did not seek to regulate".

31. Article 11 of the Montreal Convention is worded as follows:

"Article 11

1. Contracting States shall afford one another the greatest measure of assistance in connection with criminal proceedings brought in respect of the offences. The law of the State requested shall apply in all cases.

2. The provisions of paragraph 1 of this Article shall not affect obligations under any other treaty, bilateral or multilateral, which governs or will govern, in whole or in part, mutual assistance in criminal matters."

32. Having taken account of the positions of the Parties as to the duties imposed by Article 11 of the Montreal Convention, the Court concludes that there equally exists between them a dispute which concerns the interpretation and application of that provision, and which, in accordance with Article 14, paragraph 1, of the Convention, falls to be decided by the Court.

33. Libya, in the latest version of its submissions, finally asks the Court to find that

"The United States is under a legal obligation to respect Libya's right not to have the [Montreal] Convention set aside by means which would in any case be at variance with the principles of the United Nations Charter and with the mandatory rules of general international law prohibiting the use of force and the violation of the sovereignty, territorial integrity, sovereign equality and political independence of States".

34. The United States maintains that it is not for the Court, on the basis of Article 14, paragraph 1, of the Montreal Convention, to decide on the lawfulness of actions which are in any event in conformity with international law, and which were instituted by the Respondent to secure the surrender of the two alleged offenders. It concludes form this that the Court lacks jurisdiction to hear the submissions presented on this point by Libya.

35. The Court cannot uphold the line of argument thus formulated. Indeed, it is for the Court to decide, on the basis of Article 14, paragraph 1, of the Montreal Convention, on the lawfulness of the actions criticized by Libya, in so far as those actions would be contrary to the provisions of the Montreal Convention.

36. In the present case, the United States has contended, however, that even if the Montreal Convention did confer on Libya the rights it claims, those rights could not be exercised in this case because they were superseded by Security Council resolutions 748 (1992) and 883 (1993) which, by virtue of Articles 25 and 103 of the United Nations Charter, have priority over all rights and obligations arising out of the Montreal Convention. The Respondent has also argued that, because of the adoption of those resolutions, the only dispute which existed from that point on was between Libya and the Security Council; this, clearly, would not be a dispute falling within the terms of Article 14, paragraph 1, of the Montreal Convention and thus not one which the Court could entertain.

37. The court cannot uphold this line of argument. Security Council resolutions 748 (1992) and 883 (1993) were in fact adopted after the filing of the Application on 3 March 1992. In accordance with its established jurisprudence, if the Court had jurisdiction on that date, it continues to do so; the subsequent coming into existence of the above-mentioned resolutions cannot affect its jurisdiction once established (cf. *Nottebolm, Preliminary Objection, Judgment, I.C.J. Reports 1953*, p. 122; *Right of Passage over Indian Territory, Preliminary Objections, Judgment, I.C.J. Reports 1957*, p. 142).

38. In the light of the foregoing, the Court concludes that the objection to jurisdiction raised by the United States on the basis of the alleged absence of a dispute between the Parties concerning the interpretation or application of the Montreal Convention must be rejected, and that the Court has jurisdiction to hear the disputes between Libya and the United States as to the interpretation or application of the provisions of that Convention.

39. The Court will now turn to consider the objection of the United States according to which the Libyan Application is not admissible.

40. The United States emphasizes that the measures which Libya opposes are those taken by the Security Council under resolutions 731 (1992), 748 (1992) and 883 (1993):

(a)　　determining that Libya's failure to respond fully and effectively to the requests that Libya surrender the two accused for trial in the United States or the United Kingdom constitutes a threat to international peace and security;

(b)   deciding that the Government of Libya must comply with those requests; and
(c)   imposing economic sanctions and other measures to compel Libya to comply with
       those requests.

According to the United States, by seising the Court, Libya was endeavouring to "undo
the Council's actions". The United States argues that, even if Libya could make valid claims
under the Montreal Convention, these are "superseded" by the relevant decisions of the Security Council under Chapter VII of the Charter, which impose different obligations. The
said decisions thus establish the rules governing the dispute between Libya and the United
States. Those rules — and not the Montreal Convention — define the obligations of the
Parties; and the claims of Libya based on the Convention are therefore inadmissible. The
United States further contends that if the Court should see fit to "assert [its] jurisdiction to
examine on the merits, by way of objection, the validity of Security Council resolutions 731
(1992), 748 (1992) and 883 (1993), the Libyan Application should nonetheless be dismissed
at the preliminary objections stage because it is not admissible".

41. For its part, Libya argues that it is clear from the actual terms of resolutions 731 (1992),
748 (1992) and 883 (1993) that the Security Council has never required it to surrender its nationals to the United States or the United Kingdom; it stated at the hearing that this remained
"Libya's principal argument". It added that the Court must interpret those resolutions "in accordance with the Charter, which determined their validity", and that the Charter prohibited
the Council from requiring Libya to hand over its nationals to the United States or the United
Kingdom. Libya concludes that its Application is admissible "as the Court can usefully rule on
the interpretation and application of the Montreal Convention ... independently of the legal effects of resolutions 748 (1992) and 883 (1993)".

Libya also observes that the arguments of the United States based on the provisions of the
Charter raise problems which do not possess an exclusively preliminary character, but appertain to the merits of the dispute. It argues, in particular, that the question of the effect of
the Security Council resolutions is not of an exclusively preliminary character, inasmuch as
the resolutions under consideration are relied upon by the United States in order to overcome
the application of the Montreal Convention, and since Libya is justified in disputing that these
resolutions are opposable to it.

42. Libya furthermore draws the Court's attention to the principle that "[t]he critical date
for determining the admissibility of an application is the date on which it is filed" (*Border and
Transborder Armed Actions, (Nicaragua v. Honduras), Jurisdiction and Admissibility, I.C.J. Reports 1988*, p. 95, para. 66). It points out in this connection that its Application was filed on 3
March 1992; that Security Council resolutions 748 (1992) and 883 (1993) were adopted on
31 March 1992 and 11 November 1993, respectively; and that resolution 731 (1992) of 21
January 1992 was not adopted under Chapter VII of the United Nations Charter and was only
a mere recommendation. Consequently, Libya argues, its Application is admissible in any event.

43. In the view of the Court, this last submission of Libya must be upheld. The date, 3
March 1992, on which Libya filed its Application, is in fact the only relevant date for determining the admissibility of the Application. Security Council resolutions 748 (1992) and 883 (1993)
cannot be taken into consideration in this regard, since they were adopted at a later date. As to
Security Council resolution 731 (1992), adopted before the filing of the Application, it could not
form a legal impediment to the admissibility of the latter because it was a mere recommendation without binding effect, as was recognized moreover by the United States. Consequently,
Libya's Application cannot be held inadmissible on these grounds.

44. In the light of the foregoing, the Court concludes that the objection to admissibility derived by the United States from Security Council resolutions 748 (1992) and 883 (1993) must be rejected, and that Libya's Application is admissible.

45. The Court will now consider the third objection raised by the United States. According to that objection, Libya's claims have become moot because Security Council resolutions 748 (1992) and 883 (1993) have rendered them without object; any judgment which the Court might deliver on the said claims would thenceforth be devoid of practical purpose.

The Court has already acknowledged, on several occasions in the past, that events subsequent to the filing of an application may "render an application without object" (*Border and Transborder Armed Actions, (Nicaragua v. Honduras), Jurisdiction and Admissibility, I.C.J. Reports 1988*, p. 95, para. 66) and "therefore the Court is not called upon to give a decision thereon" (*Nuclear Tests (Australia v. France), Judgment, I.C.J. Reports 1974*, p. 272, para. 62) (cf. *Northern Cameroons, Judgment, I.C.J. Reports 1963*, p. 38).

Thus formulated, the Respondent's objection is that there is no ground for proceeding to judgment on the merits, which objection must be examined within the framework of this jurisprudence.

46. The Court must satisfy itself that such an objection does indeed fall within the provisions of Article 79 of the Rules, relied upon by the Respondent. In paragraph 1, this Article refers to "Any objection ... to the jurisdiction of the Court or to the admissibility of the application, or *other objection*" (emphasis added); its field of application *ratione materiae* is thus not limited solely to objections regarding jurisdiction and admissibility. However, if it is to be covered by Article 79, an objection must also possess a "preliminary" character. Paragraph 1 of Article 79 of the Rules of Court characterizes as "preliminary" an objection "the decision upon which is requested before any further proceedings". There can be no doubt that the objection envisaged here formally meets this condition. The Court would also recall that, in this instance, the Respondent is advancing the argument that the decisions of the Security Council could not form the subject of any contentious proceedings before the Court, since they allegedly determine the rights which the Applicant claims to derive from a treaty text, or at least that they directly affect those rights; and that the Respondent thus aims to preclude at the outset any consideration by the Court of the claims submitted by the Applicant and immediately terminate the proceedings brought by it. In so far as the purpose of the objection raised by the United States that there is no ground for proceeding to judgment on the merits is, effectively, to prevent, *in limine*, any consideration of the case on the merits, so that its "effect [would] be, if the objection is upheld, to interrupt further proceedings in the case", and "it [would] therefore be appropriate for the Court to deal with [it] before enquiring into the merits" (*Panevezys-Saldutiskis Railway, Judgement, P.C.I.J., Series A/B No. 76*, p. 16), this objection possesses a preliminary character and does indeed fall within the provisions of Article 79 of the Rules of Court.

Moreover, it is incontrovertible that the objection concerned was submitted in writing within the time-limit fixed for the filing of the Counter-Memorial, and was thus submitted in accordance with the formal conditions laid down in Article 79.

47. Libya doe not dispute any of these points. It does not contend that the objection thus derived by the United States from Security Council resolutions 748 (1992) and 883 (1993) is an objection on the merits, which does not fall within the provisions of Article 79 of the Rules of Court; nor does it claim that the objection was not properly submitted. What Libya contends is that this objection — like the objection of inadmissibility raised by the United States, and for the same reasons (see paragraph 41 above) — falls within the category of those which Article

79, paragraph 7, of the Rules of Court characterizes as objections "not possess[ing], in the circumstances of the case, an exclusively preliminary character".

On the contrary, the United States considers that the objection concerned possesses an "exclusively preliminary character" within the meaning of that provision. It contends, in particular, in support of this argument, that this objection does not require "the resolution of disputed facts or the consideration of evidence".

Thus it is solely on the question of the "exclusively" or "non-exclusively" preliminary character of the objection under consideration that the Parties are divided and on which the Court must now make a determination.

48. The present wording of Article 79, paragraph 7, of the Rules of Court was adopted by the Court in 1972. The Court has had occasion to examine its precise scope and significance in the Judgments it delivered in the case concerning *Military and Paramilitary Activities in and against Nicaragua (Nicaragua v. United States of America)*, on 26 November 1984 (*Jurisdiction and Admissibility, Judgment, I.C.J. Reports 1984*, pp. 425–426) and on 26 June 1986 (*Merits, Judgment, I.C.J. Reports 1986*, pp. 29–31), respectively. As the Court pointed out in the second of those Judgments,

"Under the Rules of Court dating back to 1936 (which on this point reflected still earlier practice), the Court had the power to join an objection to the merits 'whenever the interests of the good administration of justice require it', (*Panevezys-Saldutiskis Railway, Judgement, P.C.I.J., Series A/B No. 75*, p. 56), and in particular where the Court, if it were to decide on the objection, 'would run the risk of adjudicating on questions which appertain to the merits of the case or of prejudging their solution' (*ibid.*)." (*I.C.J. Reports 1986*, pp. 29–30, para. 39)

However, the exercise of that power carried a risk,

"namely that the Court would ultimately decide the case on the preliminary objection, after requiring the parties to fully plead the merits — and this did in fact occur (*Barcelona Traction, Light and Power Company, Limited, Second Phase, I.C.J. Reports 1970*, p. 3). The result was regarded in some quarters as an unnecessary prolongation of an expensive and time-consuming procedure" (*Ibid.* p. 30, para. 39.)

The Court was then faced with the following choice: "to revise the Rules so as to exclude ... the possibility of joinder to the merits, so that every objection would have to be resolved at the preliminary stage, or to seek a solution which would be more flexible" (*ibid.*, p. 30, para. 40). The solution adopted in 1972 was ultimately not to exclude the power to examine a preliminary objection in the merits phase, but to limit the exercise of that power, by laying down the conditions more strictly. The Court concluded, in relation to the new provision thus adopted:

"It thus presents one clear advantage: that it qualifies certain objections as preliminary, making it clear that when they are exclusively of that character they will have to be decided upon immediately, but if they are not, especially when the character of the objections is not exclusively preliminary because they contain both preliminary aspects and other aspects relating to the merits, they will have to be dealt with at the stage of the merits. This approach also tends to discourage the unnecessary prolongation of proceedings at the jurisdictional state." (*Ibid.*, p. 31, para. 41.)

49. The Court must therefore ascertain whether, in the present case, the United States objection considered here contains "both preliminary aspects and other aspects relating to the merits" or not.

That objection relates to many aspects of the dispute. By maintaining that Security Council resolutions 748 (1992) and 883 (1993) have rendered the Libyan claims without object, the United States seeks to obtain from the Court a decision not to proceed to judgment on the merits, which would immediately terminate the proceedings. However, by requesting such a decision, the United States is requesting, in reality, at least two others which the decision not to proceed to judgment on the merits would necessarily postulate: on the one hand a decision establishing that the rights claimed by Libya under the Montreal Convention are incompatible with its obligations under the Security Council resolutions; and, on the other hand, a decision that those obligations prevail over those rights by virtue of Articles 25 and 103 of the Charter.

The Court therefore has no doubt that Libya's rights on the merits would not only be affected by a decision not to proceed to judgment on the merits, at this stage in the proceedings, but would constitute, in many respects, the very subject-matter of that decision. The objection raised by the United States on that point has the character of a defence on the merits. In the view of the Court, this objection does much more than "touch[ing] upon subjects belonging to the merits of the case" (*Certain German Interests in Polish Upper Silesia, Jurisdiction, Judgment No. 6, 1925, P.C.I.J. Series A, No. 6*, p. 15); it is "inextricably interwoven" with the merits (*Barcelona Traction, Light and Power Company, Limited, Second Phase, I.C.J. Reports 1970*, p. 46).

The Court notes furthermore that the United States itself broached many substantive problems in its written and oral pleadings in this phase, and pointed out that those problems had been the subject of exhaustive exchanges before the Court; the United States Government thus implicitly acknowledged that the objection raised and the merits of the case were "closely interconnected" (*Barcelona Traction, Light and Power Company, Limited, Second Phase, I.C.J. Reports 1970*, p. 46, and the reference to *Pajzs, Csáky, Esterházy, P.C.I.J., Series A/B, No. 66*, p. 9).

If the Court were to rule on that objection, it would therefore inevitably be ruling on the merits; in relying on the provisions of Article 79 of the Rules of Court, the Respondent has set in motion a procedure the precise aim of which is to prevent the Court from so doing.

The Court concludes from the foregoing that the objection of the United States according to which the Libyan claims have become moot as having been rendered without object does not have "an exclusively preliminary character" within the meaning of that Article.

50. Having established its jurisdiction and concluded that the Application is admissible, the Court will be able to consider this objection when it reaches the merits of the case.

51. Lastly, the United States requested the Court, in the alternative, in the event that, notwithstanding the United States' objections, it should declare that it has jurisdiction and deem the Application admissible, to "resolve the case in substance now" by deciding, as a preliminary matter, that the relief sought by Libya is precluded.

As the Court has already indicated, it is the Respondent which sought to rely, in this case, on the provisions of Article 79 of the Rules. By raising preliminary objections, it has made a procedural choice the effect of which, according to the express terms of Article 79, paragraph 3, is to suspend the proceedings on the merits. The Court cannot therefore uphold the claim of the United States.

52. In accordance with Article 79, paragraph 7, of the Rules of Court, time-limits for the further proceedings shall be fixed subsequently by the Court.

53. For these reasons:

THE COURT

(1)(a) by thirteen votes to two, *rejects* the objection to jurisdiction raised by the United States on the basis of the alleged absence of a dispute between the Parties concerning the interpretation or application of the Montreal Convention of 23 September 1971;

IN FAVOUR: *Vice-President* Weeramantry, *Acting President; Judges* Bedjaoui, Guillaume, Ranjeva, Herczegh, Shi, Fleischhauer, Koroma, Vereshchetin, Parra-Aranguren, Kooijmans, Rezek; *Judge* ad hoc El-Kosheri;

AGAINST: *President* Schwebel; *Judge* Oda;

(b) by thirteen votes to two, *finds* that it has jurisdiction, on the basis of Article 14, paragraph 1, of the Montreal Convention of 23 September 1971, to hear the disputes between Libya and the United States as to the interpretation or application of the provisions of that Convention;

IN FAVOUR: *Vice-President* Weeramantry, *Acting President; Judges* Bedjaoui, Guillaume, Ranjeva, Herczegh, Shi, Fleischhauer, Koroma, Vereshchetin, Parra-Aranguren, Kooijmans, Rezek; *Judge* ad hoc El-Kosheri;

AGAINST: *President* Schwebel; *Judge* Oda;

(2)(a) by twelve votes to three, *rejects* the objection to admissibility derived by the United States from Security Council resolutions 748 (1992) and 883 (1993);

IN FAVOUR: *Vice-President* Weeramantry, *Acting President; Judges* Bedjaoui, Guillaume, Ranjeva, Shi, Fleischhauer, Koroma, Vereshchetin, Parra-Aranguren, Kooijmans, Rezek; *Judge* ad hoc El-Kosheri;

AGAINST: *President* Schwebel; *Judge* Oda, Herczegh;

(b) by twelve votes to three, *finds* that the Application filed by Libya on 3 March 1992 is admissible.

IN FAVOUR: *Vice-President* Weeramantry, *Acting President; Judges* Bedjaoui, Guillaume, Ranjeva, Shi, Fleischhauer, Koroma, Vereshchetin, Parra-Aranguren, Kooijmans, Rezek; *Judge* ad hoc El-Kosheri;

AGAINST: *President* Schwebel; *Judge* Oda, Herczegh;

(3) by ten votes to five, *declares* that the objection raised by the United States according to which the claims of Libya became moot because Security Council resolutions 748 (1992) and 883 (1993) rendered them without object, does not, in the circumstances of the case, have an exclusively preliminary character.

IN FAVOUR: *Vice-President* Weeramantry, *Acting President; Judges* Bedjaoui, Ranjeva, Shi, Koroma, Vereshchetin, Parra-Aranguren, Kooijmans, Rezek; *Judge* ad hoc El-Kosheri;

AGAINST: *President* Schwebel; *Judge* Oda, Guillaume, Herczegh, Fleischhauer.

Done in French and in English, the French text being authoritative, at the Peace Palace, The Hague, this twenty-seventh day of February, one thousand nine hundred and ninety-eight, in three copies, one of which will be placed in the archives of the Court and the others transmitted to the Government of the Great Arab Libyan Jamahiriya and the Government of the United States of America, respectively.

(*Signed*) Christopher G. WEERAMANTRY,
Vice-President

(*Signed*) Eduardo VALENCIA-OSPINA,
Registrar

(3) by ten votes to six, *declares* that the objection raised by the United Kingdom according to which Security Council resolutions 748 (1992) and 883 (1993) have rendered the claims of Libya without object does not, in the circumstances of the case, have an exclusively preliminary character.

IN FAVOUR: *Vice-President* Weeramantry, *Acting President*; *Judges* Bedjaoui, Ranjeva, Shi, Koroma, Vereshchetin, Parra-Aranguren, Kooijmans, Rezek; *Judge* ad hoc El-Kosheri;

AGAINST: *President* Schwebel; *Judges* Oda, Guillaume, Herczegh, Fleischhauer; *Judge* ad hoc Sir Robert Jennings.

Done in French and in English, the French text being authoritative, at the Peace Palace, The Hague, this twenty-seventh day of February, one thousand nine hundred and ninety-eight, in three copies, one of which will be placed in the archives of the Court and the others transmitted to the Government of the Great Arab Libyan Jamahiriya and the Government of the United Kingdom of Great Britain and Northern Ireland, respectively.

(*Signed*) Christopher G. WEERAMANTRY,
Vice-President

(*Signed*) Eduardo VALENCIA-OSPINA,
Registrar

Judges BEDJAOUI, GUILLAUME and RANJEVA append a joint declaration to the Judgment of the Court; Judges BEDJAOUI, RANJEVA and KOROMA append a joint declaration to the Judgment of the Court; Judges GUILLAUME and FLEISCHHAUER append a joint declaration to the Judgment of the Court; Judge HERCZEGH appends a declaration to the Judgment of the Court.

Judges KOOIJMANS and REZEK append separate opinions to the Judgement of the Court.

President SCHWEBEL, Judge ODA and Judge *ad hoc* Sir Robert JENNINGS append dissenting opinions to the Judgment of the Court.

(*Initialled*) C.G.W.

(*Initialled*) E.V.O.

Where a declaration or opinion has been submitted in the two official language of the Court, both texts are reproduced hereafter.

Where a declaration or opinion has been submitted in one of the two official languages of the Court, its translation by the Registry into the other official language will appear in the printed version of the Judgment.

Yemen

Republic of Yemen v. Baron, Smith and Omar

REPUBLIC OF YEMEN
MINISTRY OF JUSTICE
COURT OF FIRST INSTANCE

A public trial was held at the Sana'a Court of First Instance on 7 June 1998. The session was presided over by Chief Justice Judge Haikal Ahmed Othman and was attended by Mr Ali Abdullah al-Ansi (the Deputy Prosecutor for Press and Publications) and Mr Najeeb Mohammed al-Samhi (the Court Secretary). Following due deliberations, the Court issued the following judgment.

This has reference to the Criminal case No. 92/1419 forwarded to the said Court by the office of the Public Prosecutor in Sana'a and substantiated by the accusatory clause No. 10/1998 submitted by the office of the Deputy Prosecutor for Press and Publications. Within the jurisdiction of subject matter of the Court of First Instance, the Public Prosecutor pressed on 27 May 1998 the following charge sheet against:

(i)   Mr Robin John Baron (Age: 24 years; Profession: Journalist; Nationality: British; Professional Affiliation: British Broadcasting Corporation (BBC); Place of Work: London; Educational Qualifications: Masters Degree);
(ii) Mr Francis Andro Smith (Age: 29 years; Profession: Journalist; Nationality: British; Professional Affiliation: British Broadcasting Corporation (BBC); Place of Work: London; Educational Qualifications: Masters Degree);
(iii) Mr Raji Abdullah Omar (Age: 30 years; Profession: Journalist; Nationality: British; Professional Affiliation: British Broadcasting Corporation (BBC); Place of Work: London; Educational Qualifications: Masters Degree).

The said charge sheet pressed the following charges:

(1)   That all three defendants were in violation of the Law in attempting to gather information via illegal means. Specifically, the defendants travelled to Bani Dhabian in clear defiance of the advice and instructions of the Ministry of Information. The information gathered is detailed in the attached charge sheet.
(2)   That the second defendant unilaterally introduced into the Yemen a telecommunication device capable of sending and receiving telephone and facsimile messages worldwide via satellite. The said device was not listed among the items submitted by the

603

defendant for clearance purposes either to the Embassy of the Republic of Yemen in London or to the Ministry of Information. For more details, see attached charge sheet.

In view of the above, the Public Prosecutor demanded that the suspects receive punishment in accordance with the provisions of Article 30(2) and Article 140 of the Press and Publications Law No. 25 issued in 1990.

To look into the charges cited above, the Court of First Instance held a public trial on 6 June 1998 in the presence of all defendants. The Court appointed Mr Hassan Abu al-'Aula (Nationality: British; Passport No. 500225562) to act as Court Interpreter under oath during the said trial. The defendants were asked whether they had an attorney at law to represent them in Court. Their response was "yes". They named Sheikh Tariq Abdulla as their defence attorney.

At the beginning of the Court session, the charge sheet, including accusatory clause No. 10/1998, was read in the presence of all defendants and their Defence Attorney. The Defence Attorney requested full access to the case file and a duplicate copy of it in order to defend his clients properly. The Court then asked the suspects to present their defence in view of the charges pressed by the Prosecutor. The first and second suspects insisted that they were *not* guilty. The third suspect, Mr Raji Omar added "not only that he was *not* guilty but he categorically rejected all charges subsumed in the charge sheet". In view of this, the Prosecutor asked to be allowed to furnish evidence in support of all charges pressed against the defendants. He added that the two charges detailed in the Accusatory Clause were substantiated by confessions extracted from the defendants at the office of the Public Prosecutor. He asked the Court to refer to page 41 of the Public Prosecutor's interrogations where the First Defendant voluntarily confessed that he was in violation of the Law in view of the first charge pressed against him in the charge sheet. Furthermore, he expressed regret and offered an apology. The First Defendant confessed that he decided to travel to Bani Dhabian but he had no ill intentions towards Yemen nor did he intend to engage in any sabotage activity. He added that apparently there was some sort of misunderstanding about Yemeni Laws and regulations. It was because of this, he said he would offer his regret and apology. When faced with all charges, the First Defendant rejected them on grounds that he was unaware of the Yemeni Press and Publications Law. The Prosecutor concluded that *ignoratina legis meminem excusat*. As for the Second Defendant, the Prosecutor asked the Court to consider the confessions given by the Defendant on pages 15 and 17 of the Public Prosecutor's interrogations where he acknowledged that the satellite communication device was not included in the inventory of items submitted to the Yemen Embassy in London on 13 May 1998. When asked why the item was not included, he answered that he was *not* fully aware of the provisions of the said Law. The Prosecutor reiterated the legal dictum that says: *ignoratina legis meminem excusat*. The Prosecutor argued that the Third Defendant, Mr Raji Omar, acknowledged that the Yemen Embassy in London advised them to proceed through legal channels and warned them against all other alternative approaches (see pp. 14 and 45 of the Public Prosecutor's interrogations). Likewise, the Third Defendant expressed regret for violating the Law. He added, however, that he did neither mean nor did he intend to violate applicable Laws since he was *not* aware of the existence of such Laws. At this point, the Public Prosecutor reiterated once again the legal dictum that says *ignoratina legis meminem excusat*. The Prosecutor argued that the defendants resorted to dubious means to achieve their objectiveness. They used certain tactics to camouflage hotel authorities of their whereabouts – as they posted a "Do Not Disturb" signal on the doors of their hotel rooms at a time when they had already left for Bani Dhabian. Furthermore, they rented a small van (Dabbab) to meet their contact who was supposed to take them to Bani Dhabian. They took the small van instead of the Mercedes limousine they used to hire to mislead local authorities. The defendants travelled to their destination without Sheikh Ahmed Ali al-Dharhiri (who was supposed to accompany them to Bani Dhabian). Sheikh

al-Dharhiri however joined the group later in a mountainous area past all military and security check points. The defendants continued their journey to Bani Dhabian despite their
full knowledge of the objection of the Ministry of Information to the visit. While in Bani
Dhabian, the defendants took a great number of pictures and shot many films. They also
conducted televised interviews with the public. During the interviews, the defendants repeatedly asked questions about military bases and installations in clear violation of Article
30(2) of the Press and Publications Law.

In view of the above, the Public Prosecutor demanded that the defendants receive the punishment stipulated in Article No. 104 of the Press and Publications Law as well as the punishment required in accordance with Article No. 103 of the Penal and Criminal Code No.
12 which was issued in 1994. The Prosecutor also demanded confiscation of the films, videotapes and the telecommunication device in the defendant's possession as was detailed in the
charge sheet.

During the Court session, the Prosecutor furnished the Court with six video cassette tapes
allegedly containing all televised interviews and media coverage conducted by the defendants in Bani Dhabian. The Prosecutor argued that irrespective of the content of these videotapes, the filming was executed in violation of the Law and without prior approval of the Ministry of Information. The Prosecutor noted that the video tapes submitted to the Court
were *not* the original tapes but rather duplicate copies of the originals. The Prosecutor added
that the defendants were fully aware of the Laws and regulations which require them to inform the Ministry of Information in advance of all items and equipment they intended to
bring to Yemen. The fact that a list of items was submitted to the Ministry of Information
on 3 May 1998 was cited as evidence of the defendant's prior knowledge and awareness of
such Laws and regulations. Despite this, the defendants acted in defiance of the Law and
brought with them a satellite communication device which was not included in the list of
items submitted in advance to the Ministry of Information.

The defendants were asked by the Court as to whether they had in fact appointed Sheikh
Tariq Abdullah as their defence attorney. The defendants collectively responded by saying
"yes". The Defence Attorney then asked the Prosecutor whether he could furnish additional
evidence or call in to the witness stand eye witnesses to support the charges submitted in
the accusatory clause and the charge sheet. The Prosecutor responded by saying that he did
not understand the wisdom underlying such a question and added that the Prosecution had
already submitted all relevant evidence in accordance with the Law. The Defence Attorney
responded by saying that it was evident that the Prosecution had failed to provide more evidence other than what had already been furnished. He added that the file of the case at Bar,
however, featured other factual events providing sufficient evidence which could lead to the
acquittal of all defendants. The Defence Attorney added that he could call to the witness
box sufficient defence witnesses to prove that the charges pressed by the Prosecution were
false, inaccurate and inapplicable to the case at bar.

The Defence Attorney then requested the Court to adjourn the session until the next
day so that he could prepare his defence in connection with the case in question. At this point,
the Prosecutor intervened saying that the video films shot by the defendants in Bani Dhabian
were sent through a local resident to the home address of Mr David Pierce (the Deputy Head
at the British Embassy in Sana'a) whose address was 38 Baghdad Street, Sana'a, Yemen.
The person who was assigned to deliver the tapes confessed that the said tapes would ultimately be shipped to Britain via the diplomatic pouch. The Prosecutor added that it was
clear that the defendants did expect that the tapes could be detected and seized either at Sana'a
International Airport or any other place and, therefore, decided to secure safe passage for
the shipment with a person enjoying diplomatic immunity. The Prosecutor called upon the
Court to draw the necessary conclusions and inferences from the episode. In a rebuttal, the
Defence Attorney challenged that there was nothing on the tapes which would warrant concealment and that the Court could easily reach this conclusion once the tapes were reviewed.

The Defence Attorney once again reiterated his request and asked the Court to adjourn the session until the next morning so as to prepare his pleadings. He then asked the Court whether the defendants were still under arrest. The answer was no. The Court then sustained the Defence Attorney's request and granted him full access to the file of the case at Bar. The Court then ordered all evidence by inspection to be kept intact in Court and prohibited any publication of the Court proceedings pending a Court ruling.

On 7 June 1998, the second session of the public trial was held in the presence of all defendants and Mr Hassan Abu-al-'Aula who was appointed by the Court to act as a Court interpreter during the trial. The session was primarily held to call the Defence Attorney to present his preemptory plea in response to the charges brought about by the Prosecution. The Defence Attorney, Skeikh Tariq 'Abdullah, then requested the Court to grant the defendants the right to present their plea in view of the charges and the accusatory clause pressed by the Prosecution. The First Defendant, Mr Robin John Baron, then had the floor. He denied offering an apology and requested the Court to refer to page 41 of the Prosecutor's interrogation where he expressed regret. He said that if he had offered an apology at any point in time it would have been out of courtesy. He categorically rejected all charges pressed by the Prosecution. He expressed wonder at the Prosecutor's allegations that he acknowledged acting in violation of the Law. He said that the two statements were irreconcilable: he could *not* categorically reject all charges and at the same time offer an apology for violating the Law on the ground of ignorance. He upheld the legal dictum which affirms that *ignoratina legis meminem excusat*. He said that when he applied as a journalist for an entry visa to Yemen neither the Ministry of Information nor any other authority informed or advised him – at any point in time – of restricted zones or whether there were certain areas which could be off limits. He added that neither brochures nor booklets had been offered to help them understand rules and regulations governing the work of press and mass media professionals in Yemen.

The Second Defendant, Mr Francis Andro Smith, then had the floor. He said that the satellite telecommunications device cited in the charge sheet was added to the list at a later stage. He added that the most important fact was that the said device as well as all other items were declared to customs authorities in the United Kingdom as well as in Yemen. He argued that, "Had I intended to conceal the satellite telephone, I would have not declared it to customs authorities in both countries". He went on to say that it was a matter of fact that the fax facility of the said satellite telephone could not be activated in Yemen for technical reasons (lack of compatible cable systems). He brought to the attention of the Court that the video tapes submitted to the Court were *not* originals but rather duplicate copies made by the prosecution. He added that he had reasons to cast doubts about the contents of these tapes.

The Third Defendant, Mr Raji Omar, then had the floor. He disputed the Prosecutor's claim (on page 14 of the charge sheet) that the defendants were advised by the Embassy to approach legal channels in conducting their business in Yemen. He said that was *not* true. The advice given by the Embassy was never of a legal nature. Nor did the Embassy call for the necessity to secure a special permit to access certain areas. He also disputed the Prosecutor's claim (on page 45 of the charge sheet) that he apologized for violating the Law. He said that this was totally untrue. He confirmed that there was certainly some sort of misunderstanding for which he did express regret but *not* an apology. He added that this should not be construed as an acknowledgement of guilt in any form. He concluded by saying that it could not be logical on his part to categorically reject all charges and to acknowledge guilt at the same time as the Prosecution claimed.

Following this, the Defence Attorney started presenting his pleading. He said that it was evident that the Prosecution had failed throughout this case to present a single competent or concrete evidence to lend credibility to the charges cited in the charge sheet. None of the defendants admitted violation of any of the Laws and/or regulations currently in effect within the Republic of Yemen, though they had acknowledged with great honesty some of the events and episodes cited in the charge sheet. The Defence Attorney then listed the following. First, Robin John Baron and Francis Andro Smith secured their entry visa from London and Raji Omar from Amman. They had all explicitly indicated the purpose of their proposed visit to Yemen upon submission of their visa applications. He added that it is a well known fact that embassies of the Republic of Yemen abroad grant entry visas to journalists only after thorough investigation of the purpose and the proposed programmes underlying such visits. Second, all items and equipment brought about by the defendants were duly declared and cleared by customs authorities in Britain and Yemen. Third, the Ministry of Information was informed well in advance before the defendants left Amman and London. Fourth, immediately upon arrival, the First Defendant paid a visit to the Ministry of Information and kept concerned officials fully informed of the team's proposed plans. Fifth, on the morning of 20 May 1998, the defendants visited Sheikh Mohammed al-Rowaishan who managed to arrange a meeting at his house for the visiting journalists and an estimated number of fifty Sheikhs from Bani Dhabian. During the said meeting, the First Defendant explained to all those who were present the purpose of the visit which was to produce a reportage film about the area, people and the landscape. Sixth, following al-Rowaishan's visit, the Second and Third Defendants paid a visit to the Ministry of Information and reviewed with concerned officials their plans. The Ministry of Information did neither object to the proposed plan nor did the Ministry instruct the team *not* to visit Bani Dhabian. Seventh, on the same day, the Prime Minister gave clearance to the defendants and approved their plans to travel to Bani Dhabian at his own personal responsibility. The Prime Minister's approval was communicated through Mr Abdul-Hadi al-Hamdani. The Defence Attorney said that the Court may at its own discretion, summon Mr Abdul-Hadi al-Hamdani should the Prosecution refuse to admit this fact and event. He added that the witness (translator: Ikhlas al-Qirshi) confirmed during investigation that the Prime Minister did give his approval to the team. Eighth, there are no restricted or off limit areas in Yemen. Any person granted an entry visa is automatically allowed to visit any area in Yemen. There are no Laws and/or regulations in Yemen restricting freedom of mobility. The Defence Attorney concluded that the Prosecution had failed to furnish evidence to support its claim that concerned officials did object to the defendants' visit to Bani Dhabian. The Prosecution neither identified the person who objected to the visit nor explained the manner according to which the objection was made (whether verbal or written). Furthermore, the Prosecution had failed to tell the Court whether the objection, if true, was in fact executed within the framework of the Law. The Prosecution had failed to provide any concrete evidence or to call in credible witnesses to substantiate the claims subsumed in this charge sheet.

As to the Prosecution's claim that the defendants managed to smuggle the video films through a local resident to a villa located on 38 Baghdad Street, the Defence Attorney asked the Prosecution to identify the person with whom the tapes were allegedly smuggled and to explain his whereabouts. The Defence Attorney added that in fact the tapes were never sent to that address nor were they delivered to any person. He posed a question saying that, if the Prosecution's account of this event were true, why then did it neither arrest the person who attempted to smuggle the tapes nor did it call upon that person to come forward to Court as a prosecuting witness. Following this, the Defence Attorney requested the Court to adjourn the session so as to allow Ms Ikhlas al-Qirshi to present her testimony to Court. The Prosecution commented that Ms Ikhlas al-Qirshi was not in fact a witness for the Prosecution. He added that when Ms Ikhlas al-Qirshi was summoned by the Prosecution it was only for the purpose of confronting the First Defendant, the Defence Attorney and Mr Ahmad al-Dhahiri with allegations that the Defendants were somewhat linked to the British Secret Service. The Prosecution requested the Court to summon Mr Hassan Dhaif-Allah abu al-'Aula (the Prosecution's interpreter) to give his testimony in connection with the defendants' confession and avoidance. The Prosecution also asked the Court to hold the Third

Defendant, Mr Raji Omar, accountable for saying that the charges pressed by the Prosecution were all false or otherwise to ask him to withdraw such a statement. In view of this, the Court called upon Hassan Abu al-'Aula to give his testimony. In connection with the statement in question, Mr Abu al-'Aula testified that the word "false" may carry different sense components and may suggest different meanings, but with reference to the context in focus, the word "false" was used to mean "untrue".

Following this, the Court decided to adjourn the session for half an hour to allow Ms Ikhlas al-Qirshi to come forward to the witness box in order to give her testimony. The Public trial Court session was resumed on time and as scheduled in the presence of the defendants, the Court Interpreter and Ms Ikhlas Abdul-Habeeb Saleh al-Qirshi (ID No. 2684, issued in Sana'a, on 29 August 1994). The Court asked Ms al-Qirshi to come forward to the witness box to give her testimony. Then Ms al-Qirshi had the floor. She said that she works for the Ministry of Information and that her place of residence is Sana'a. She added that she was thirty-eight years old. Under oath, Ms al-Qirshi gave the following testimony. She said that she was invited to a banquet held at the Taj-Sheba hotel in Sana'a (she could *not* remember the exact date) where senior members of the government were also present, namely Mr Ahmad al-Beshari, Mr Abdul Wahab al-Hajri and Mr Abdul-Hadi al-Hamdani. She said that at the time she was keen on securing a permit from the Ministry of Information to launch a documentary film in collaboration with the defendants. In connection with this, she said that she had a meeting with Mr al-Hajri and explained to him the purpose of the proposed project and requested his assistance. Mr al-Hajri said that he would discuss the matter with Mr Abdul-Hadi al-Hamdani who may offer to resolve the stand-off. She said that Mr al-Hajri did explain to Mr al-Hamdani the matter and that the latter requested the former to call him in fifteen minutes were he would be chewing qat with Mr Abdul-Kareem al-Iryani. Ms al-Qirshi confirmed that in fifteen minutes she called Mr al-Hamdani who in turn requested her to call back in ten minutes. She said that at the agreed time she once again called Mr al-Hamdani who informed her that Mr al-Iryani had no objection to the proposed project even though he was informed of the fact that they had no permit from the Ministry of Information. Ms al-Qirshi said that she did communicate the substance of her conversation with Mr al-Hamdani to the defendants. At this point, the Prosecution asked Ms al-Qirshi to explain to the Court the nature of her relationship with the defendants. In response, Ms al-Qirshi said that she works for the Yemen TV Corporation in Sana'a. She added that it was in view of this and because of her professional experience her name has been listed with the British Broadcasting Corporation (BBC) as a documentary film expert. She added that it was against this background that the defendants contacted her and solicited her assistance. Ms al-Qirshi was then asked by the Prosecutor whether what she offered was paid service or not. Ms al-Qirshi confirmed that she did agree with defendants on a particular payment but she received nothing from them because of these complications. She added that she coordinated with Sheikh al-Rowaishan in connection with the BBC team's mission because he is a prominent tribal Sheikh and a social dignitary and because the BBC's team intended to launch a documentary on tribal and social traditions in Yemen. She added that Sheikh al-Rowaishan welcomed the idea and expressed readiness to provide the necessary protection for the team and to ensure the team's security and safety. Ms al-Qirshi added that when she went to secure the necessary permit from the Ministry of Information, she was asked by concerned officials there about the measures taken to ensure the security and safety of the team. She answered that Sheikh al-Rowaishan undertook to provide that. She added that the BBC's team, in the meantime, kept on waiting pending the arrival of other photographers (from Britain). The Prosecution then solicited clarification from al-Qirshi in connection with her statement that the Ministry of Information refused to grant permission to the team to travel to Bani Dhabian. In particular, the Prosecution asked Ms al-Qirshi to tell the Court of the date and the person who communicated the refusal of the Ministry of Information. The Defence Attorney objected to the question and added that Ms al-Qirshi did *not* state in her testimony that the Ministry of Information refused to grant the necessary permit to the team. The Court however, saw no reason to sustain the objection raised by the Defence Attorney. Indeed, the Court asked the witness (Ms al-Qirshi) to continue presenting the testimony to Court. In connection with the issue under dispute, Ms al-Qirshi confirmed that the Ministry of Information did *not* actually refuse but rather expressed concern about the safety and security of the team and on such grounds only the Ministry objected to the mission. Ms al-Qirshi said that Mr Robin John Baron had remained in Sana'a for three days pending the arrival of the photographer and editor who were expected to arrive on Sunday evening. In the meantime, she said that Sheikh al-Rowaishan called her and asked her to request the team *not* to travel to Bani Dhabian for security reasons. She added that Sheikh al-Rowaishan, however, asked her to contact the Minister of Information, in person, and to explain to him the purpose of the mission and to try to convince him that Skeikh al-Rowaishan had undertaken to guarantee the safety and security of the team. Based on this, Ms al-Qirshi said that she tried desperately to reach the Minister but the office Secretary told her that the Minister was sick and could not return her call. She said that she then contacted Mr Mohammed Handhal (from the Department of Public Relations, the Ministry of Information) and asked him whether the Ministry had any objection with the reference to the BBC's team mission. He categorically denied that there was any objection. In fact Mr Handhal said that the Minister was personally enthusiastic about the mission and asked him on a number of occasions about this. He said that he informed the Minister that the team was still waiting for the photographer and editor to arrive. Following this, Ms al-Qirshi said that she contacted the Minister of Information who refused to discuss the subject with her. She added that the Minister told her that his objection to the mission was driven by safety considerations. The Minister added that he was in receipt of clear instructions (from an unidentified source) not to grant permission to the team to travel to Bani Dhabian. Ms al-Qirshi continued to say that she informed the Minister that Sheikh al-Rowaishan guaranteed the safety and security of the team. She said that she even suggested to the Minister to meet the team so as to explain the situation to them. Ms al-Qirshi said that the Minister of Information promised to reconsider the case and to call her back. Unfortunately, she said, the Minister did not call back. The next day Ms al-Qirshi said that she had the opportunity to meet with Dr Abdul-Hadi al-Hamdani at the Taj-Sheba Hotel. After explaining the whole subject matter to Mr al-Hamdani, Ms al-Qirshi said that al-Hamdani informed her that Mr Abdul-Kareem al-Iryani had no objection to the team's plans. Accordingly, Ms al-Qirshi concluded, the BBC's team travelled to Bani Dhabian.

The Defence Attorney then had the floor but said that he had nothing to add other than his previous rebuttal to the Prosecution's charge sheet. At this point, the Prosecutor stepped in and requested the Court to allow him to present to Court some duplicate copies of pieces of evidence the origins of which were included in the case file. The Defence Attorney objected to this on grounds that no new evidence should be allowed in Court unless under very exceptional and justifiable circumstances. He warned against further engagement in excessive details on grounds that such a course would prolong the case to an indefinite time. The Court then asked the Prosecutor to explain the manner according to which the BBC's team was granted permission to come to Yemen. In response to this, the Prosecutor said that Mr Raji Omar was granted permission to come to Yemen in response to a letter from the Ministry of Foreign Affairs explaining the purpose of the visit which was to conduct interviews with some Yemeni officials. In addition, the Embassy of the Republic of Yemen in London sent a letter on 12 May 1998 to the Deputy Foreign Minister requesting his permission for a BBC mission to come to Yemen to hold interviews with Yemeni officials, representatives of international organizations operating in Yemen and the local business community in preparation for a documentary which would focus on recent developments in Yemen. Thirdly, the Prosecutor added, there was a letter from the Ministry of Information addressed to the Deputy Foreign Minister for Political Affairs. The said letter cited a request for a visit issued by the

Embassy of the Republic of Yemen in Amman in connection with the BBC team's proposed mission. In this letter, the Ministry of Information requested the Yemen Embassy in Amman to forward details of the proposed visit and to inform the Ministry, in due course, of the of the team's arrival date. The Prosecutor added that there was another letter which was sent to the Yemen Embassy in London requesting concerned officials there to forward a detailed list of the people the BBC's team would like to interview, together with a list of the items and equipment the BBC's mission would like to bring to Yemen. In response to the above cited letter, the Yemen Embassy in London wrote back explaining that the BBC's team would like to meet with Mr Abdul-Kareem al-Iryani and Skeikh Abdullah al-Ahmar. The Embassy also enclosed a list of items the BBC's team proposed to bring to Yemen. Furthermore, there was a letter from the Minister of Information requesting concerned officials to extend courtesy and to cooperate with the BBC mission and the accompanying Ministry's officials in filming non-restricted areas in both Sana'a and Ma'rib. The letter was dated 21 May 1998. Put differently, the said letter was issued following the Ministry's refusal (either verbal or in writing) to grant the BBC's team permission to travel to Bani Dhabian. The Prosecutor went on to say that the only item which was cited on a passport of one of the defendants was a TV camera with all accessories. He added that the BBC's team attempted to travel to Shibam but it was denied access at one check point for not having the necessary permit to visit such area. The Prosecution concluded that based on the above cited episode it was clear the at the BBC team knew of the regulations in Yemen which call for the provision of the necessary permit in order to photograph and execute documentary films. The Prosecutor added that even the Defence witness confirmed that the Ministry of Information changed its permission with reference to the team's visit to Bani Dhabian. The fact that no permission was granted was clear evidence of the Ministry's objection to the proposed visit. As to the date that Dr Abdul-Kareem al-Iryani gave his permission to the team to travel to Bani Dhabian, the Prosecutor argued that the Republic of Yemen is governed by Law and order and that it was *not* within the jurisdiction of the Deputy Prime Minister to issue such permits. He added that the Ministry of Information is the only branch of the government with administrative jurisdiction to grant permits of this nature. The Prosecution went on to say that the BBC team came to Yemen primarily to conduct interviews with two prominent figures and *not* to shoot a film about Bani Dhabian as was clear from the list of correspondence cited above. The satellite telephone the team brought with them to Yemen was introduced into the country in clear violation of the Law. The prosecution added that the government body with jurisdiction to issue entry permits for such items and under such circumstances is the Ministry of Information, *not* the Passport Department. Furthermore, there was *no* proof in any of the defendant's passports that the satellite telephone was seen by the passport authority at the port of entry.

Based on the above, the Prosecution demanded punishment for the defendants in accordance with Article No. 14 of the Press and Publications Law and in compliance with the Provisions of Article No. 103 of the Republic of Yemen Penal Code. The Prosecution also called for the seizure of the defendant's videotapes and satellite telephone. The Prosecutor also demanded dismissal of the Defence attorney's pleading and the defendant's testimonies as they were all groundless.

In a rebuttal, the Defence Attorney asked whether travelling in Yemen requires prior permission by the Law. If this was true, the Defence Attorney asked the Prosecution to name the Law in question or any other written by-laws issued by the Ministry of Information or any other competent authority regarding this matter. The Defence Attorney argued that to the best of his knowledge there is no such Law. He added that if the Ministry was the government body with administrative jurisdiction over such matters, it could have objected in writing to the team's proposed visit to Bani Dhabian. He concluded that since there was no clear objection in writing this should *not* be construed as "denial of permission to travel". He went on to say that it was evident that no clear instructions were given to the team. As to the Prosecution's claim that the defendants' visit to Bani Dhabian was in violation of the Law, the Defence Attorney asked whether it would be logical to assume that the Prime Minister was ignorant of the Laws and regulations currently in effect in the Republic of Yemen knowing that he was one of the most high ranking and competent government officials. The defendants did not dare to travel until they were assured of the Prime Minister's approval. As to the Prosecution's claim that the defendants submitted to the Embassy's officials in London a definitive programme, the Defence Attorney argued that there was nothing wrong should the defendants decide to introduce certain changes to their proposed programme specially that the charges were *not* kept secret and were made public to a prominent Sheikh who guaranteed the safety and security of the team. Based on all these events and episodes, the Defence Attorney argued it was evident that the defendants were never in violation of the Law at any point in time. Contrary to this, he added the defendants showed maximum respect for the Laws of the Republic of Yemen. In conclusion, the Defence Attorney demanded the Court to non-suit the case against the defendants and to exonerate them from all charges pressed by the Prosecution. The Defence Attorney added that the professional career of the defendants would certainly be at stake if the defendants were convicted. He went on to say that this was the first case of this nature to be reviewed by a Yemeni Court following unification. He added that the trial would put to test the integrity and credibility of the judicial system in Yemen. Furthermore, the whole world would be looking forward to the outcome of this trial. The Court ruling would have far reaching implications for the future of judicial reforms in Yemen. In concluding his pleading, the Defence Attorney urged the Court to rehabilitate the defendants by allowing them to reclaim all items seized and to permit them to proceed with their mission which would certainly be of value to Yemen. He concluded by saying that The British Broadcasting Corporation issued a statement and expressed regret for any inconvenience the BBC's team may have caused to Yemeni authorities. The statement added that the BBC's team planned to produce an unbiased media coverage (of certain events in Yemen). The team was keen on entering the country via legal channels and with clear permits from concerned Yemeni authorities. Furthermore, the statement said that the BBC's team had demonstrated willingness to comply with local Laws and regulations. The statement added that the BBC's team did not realize that visiting a particular area (considered by certain authorities as unsafe) would be in violation of the Press and Publications Law.

After the Defence Attorney's pleading, the Court decided to adjourn the session for one hour to arrive at a verdict. At the scheduled time, the Court reconvened and the following Court Ruling was issued.

LEGAL CONSIDERATIONS UNDERLYING THE COURT RULING

After hearing the pleadings, it was clear to the Court that the Prosecution demanded punishment for all defendants (Mr Robin John Baron, Mr Francis Andro Smith and Mr Raji Abdullah Omar) in accordance with the Provisions of Article No. 30(2) and Article No. 104 of the Press and Publications Law No. 25 which has been in effect since 1990. Based on the defendants' testimonies cited in the Prosecution's investigations of the case and the items seized by the Prosecution (six videotapes and a satellite telephone), the Prosecution demanded punishment of the defendants in accordance with the provisions of the above cited Articles.

On the other hand, the defendants together with the Defence Attorney categorically denied all charges subsumed in the charge sheet pressed by the Prosecution. The defendants insisted consistently that they were *not* guilty of any wrong doing and demanded a Court ruling acquitting them from all charges in view of the testimonies they brought forward to Court and the pleading of their Defence Attorney.

In view of the above, it was evident to the Court that the defendants were affiliates of the British Broadcasting Corporation (BBC). They came to Yemen through legal channels as was evidenced in a whole series of correspondence and communications as was detailed by the Prosecution (see communication documents 1–7). These documents clearly indicated that the defendants were able to secure official permission to visit Yemen. There was also a letter dated 21 May 1998 (document No. 7) where the Ministry of Information requested concerned authorities to extend all possible assistance to the BBC's team whose mission was to shoot a documentary film about the Republic of Yemen with focus on the country's tourism potential. The team was granted permission to film and photograph permissible zones in Sana'a and Ma'rib governorates. It was also a well known fact that Bani Dhabian falls within the vicinity of Sana'a governorate. It was also evident to the Court that the defendants had held extensive talks (during qat chew sessions) with Sheikh al-Rowaishan for a number of days. As a result of these meetings, a tribal Sheikh agreed to accompany the defendants to Bani Dhabian where they stayed for three days. This was confirmed by the witness Ms Ikhlas al-Qirshi. In consideration of all these facts, the defendants' testimonies – as was furnished by the prosecution that the defendants expressed regret for violating the Law – would sound inconsistent with all evidence established here in Court. Therefore, the charge sheet and the Accusatory Clause pressed by the Prosecution could hardly sound plausible in view of the facts and conclusive evidence established during Court hearings. The Accusatory Clause did not establish sufficient evidence leading to conviction.

The case under consideration was a clear manifestation of issues which became increasingly pressing as a result of technological advancements in the fields of communications and information processing. The information age revolutionizes our view of the world and makes cross cultural contacts virtually inevitable. Freedom of the Press is a prerequisite to viable contacts among nations and across cultures. Countries with real democracies understand and appreciate the value of press freedom where information, ideas and facts are pursued in earnest irrespective of political boundaries. There are no constraints on the freedom of the press other than respect for human rights and human freedom as well as respect for each country's Law and order. Yemen has charted a course for itself where human freedom is respected and human rights are protected. It was because of this, among other factors, that the BBC's team decided to come to Yemen.

Furthermore, after reviewing the videotapes which were filmed in Bani Dhabian, the Court arrived at a more profound understanding of the content of these tapes which focused on the daily life of people in that part of the country. There was nothing in these films which was not permissible by Law. In fact the Press and Publications Law in letter and spirit aims at consolidating freedom of speech and safeguarding the flow of information among nations of different cultural backgrounds.

As to the second major charge subsumed in the Accusatory Clause, the Court found after close scrutiny that the equipment brought by the BBC's team were in fact indispensable to a professional journalist. The equipment was introduced into the country through legal channels (via an official port of entry). The Law does *not* incriminate possession of such equipment. In Law, man is originally innocent and the defendant should always be given the benefit of doubt.

Therefore, in accordance with the provision of Articles 2, 3 and 321 of the Criminal Procedure Law for 1994, the Court ordered in the presence of all parties that:

First: Mr Robin John Baron, Mr Francis Andro Smith and Mr Raji Abdullah Omar were *not* guilty of any wrong doing.

Second: Recovery of all items seized (by the Prosecution) which consisted of six videotapes and a satellite telephone.

Issued in the Court on 7 June 1998

Judge Haykal Ahmad Othman
Court of First Instance Sana'a

Najeeb Mohammed al-Samhi
Court Secretary

Part V

Book Reviews, Notes and News

Book Reviews

Feminism and Islam: Legal and Literary Perspectives, edited by Mai Yamani, Ithaca Press, London, 1996, hb 392pp, £30, pb 400pp, £12.95

This book, with its fascinating title, is derived from a series of lectures delivered at the School of Oriental and African Studies at the University of London under the auspices of the Centre of Islamic and Middle Eastern Law (CIMEL), and under the chairmanship of Mai Yamani.

The series engendered much interest and was a great success. It will be welcomed by not only those who were able to attend the lectures but also by those who were not present.

The title may seem, to many, to be almost a contradiction in terms, as Islam is not seen as a religion which affords, or even seeks to afford, equal rights to women in any sense understood by Western ideology. Yet it must not be forgotten that at its inception, Islam was a religion of innovation and which, at the time, greatly improved the status of women within the family and in society in general, by according them rights which previously they did not possess. For example, the *shari'a*, within this instance its source in the Qur'an itself, requires that women be paid a dowry on marriage over which they alone have control. It also gave them the right of inheritance, which previously had been denied them.

But what is the position of women in Islam today, as the twenty-first century approaches? Many chapters of the book seek to show how the women of the Muslim world are endeavouring to play a more dynamic role in the life of their country, and the difficulties which are faced by women who are rebelling against their status of second class citizens are aptly illustrated.

Of particular interest in this context is the chapter on women in Saudi Arabia, which examines how, because of legal and customary restrictions in the kingdom, women are unable to exercise many of the rights which they possess.

The contributors to the book are all women of different nationalities, and from different disciplines. The topics covered are varied and, of course, not all will be of equal interest to every reader. For me, the most interesting of the chapters are those which deal with legal issues and the status of women under the law. These chapters show how difficult it is for women to achieve any degree of equality while remaining in an Islamic framework.

Although the *shari'a*, in the early days of Islam, elevated the position of women, the book illustrates how little their status has further improved in the intervening centuries. With few exceptions, polygamy is still permitted; the husband still retains the right of unilateral repudiation, even though most countries have now imposed certain formalities upon its exercise. The law of inheritance also remains largely unchanged. It must be difficult for a Muslim woman not to doubt her own worth and to regard herself as the equal of her brother,

617

when her share of inheritance is half that of his, and in many countries where her testimony is deemed worth only half that of a man, no matter how educated the woman might be and how uneducated the man.

It is perhaps surprising to find the view expressed in the chapter "Women in Islamic Law" that the verse of the Qur'an regarding testimony does not mar or degrade the intellectual status of women, and that the rule should be retained in the twentieth century, soon to be the twenty-first century, because of the more fragile personality of women.

This chapter illustrates the development of the law within the framework of the religion of Islam, and the interaction is ever present between the two sciences. However, the chapter contains several sweeping statements which, from a purely legal point of view, are inaccurate and misleading. Thus the author states that to ensure stability in family life, Islam assigned to marriage the status of a contract, "dissoluble if either party develops grievances against the other". This statement ignores the fact that the Hanifi school of law, the largest of the Sunni schools, gives a woman no right to seek a judicial dissolution of her marriage no matter how harmed she is by it. Changes in this regard have had to be made, in countries where Hanifi doctrine prevails, by legislation.

Again, the statement made later in the same chapter, that a woman has a completely independent personality and can make any contract in her own name, is also far too general in nature. It ignores the doctrine of the Maliki school, which denies an unmarried woman any contractual capacity, no matter what her age and which curtails the right of even married women to make gratuitous dispositions of their property.

One of the most interesting and, indeed, shocking chapters of the book, is that which deals with so-called "honour killing". The chapter reviews the position which still pertains in several countries of the Muslim world to the phenomenon of honour killing as a defence to homicide. From the lawyer's point of view, this chapter would have benefited from careful pruning, the legal content being retained and the sociological/anthropological content being removed and perhaps forming a separate chapter.

Despite its imperfections, *Feminism and Islam* is perhaps the first volume to attempt to examine the thoughts of the women of the Muslim world on their position and their future within Islam as the millennium approaches. This book will certainly engender much thought and controversy. It makes a substantial contribution to the literature on Islam in all its aspects.

Doreen Hinchcliffe

The Qadi and the Fortune Teller, by Nabil Saleh, Quartet Books, 1996, 148pp, £9.00

It is a distinct pleasure to review the first novel by a colleague who, for years, has hidden his talent at novel writing. Obviously, the first question that arises is why a yearbook on law should interest itself in reviewing a novel. The answer is not the distinguished position of the author as a practising lawyer and expert on Islamic law; it is rather the lucid, compact, frequently elegant and informative manner in which the author introduces numerous complex Islamic law concepts and practices as well as jurisdictional and political conflicts in the middle of the nineteenth century between the Ottoman Islamic Caliphate and Western powers, the period of the Capitulations.

The novel takes the form of a diary of a Qadi, a *shari'a* judge, in the year 1843. The "diary" is a clever invention of the author, and the choice of a Qadi as its author enabled Mr Saleh to introduce the legal concepts, types of problems, conflicts of jurisdiction and political intriguing of the period in a most readable and enlightening manner. Local conflicts, prejudices and animosities, social habits, differences in outlooks and behaviour are smoothly touched upon in a narrative of elegant, sometimes poetical, outstanding prose. To a large extent, the author has succeeded in transforming lecture subjects into short inspiring sentences.

The Qadi's personality, fortunes and misfortunes, connections with the various Lebanese religious and political sects (which were mercilessly in conflict), the political games played by the various Western powers to enhance intervention in local affairs are carefully and artistically painted and transformed through events and forces beyond the Qadi's control, as befits a person who believes in man's God ordained destiny. At every level of this transformation of fortune, the Qadi finds solace in a Qur'anic verse that the author quotes with maximum propriety. As if with an eye to the present, the downfall of a relatively liberal judge was engineered by conservative self-interested bigots under the pretext of the rule of *shari'a*, assisted by mobs who were carefully manipulated by these bigots.

The author's ability, in a first novel, to condense so much in 147 eminently readable pages is commendable. One senses that another "diary" of a different nature is in the making; this time the diary of the Lebanese journalist's mistress who was the last owner of the Qadi's diary before it reached the hands of the author. Perhaps, this new diary will tell the circumstances under which that mistress has passed the Qadi's diary to the author. It will be another diary worth waiting for.

Anis Al-Qasem

From Occupation to Interim Accords: Israel and the Palestinian Territories, by Raja Shehadeh, foreword by Ian Brownlie, foreword by Edward Said, Kluwer Law International, 1997, 320pp, £82.00

The author, Mr Raja Shehadeh, is a Palestinian lawyer practising in Jerusalem, a human rights activist and author of *Occupiers' Law: Israel and the West Bank*. He was involved, for a year (November 1991 to September 1992), in the Palestinian–Israeli negotiations in Washington as a legal advisor to the Palestinian Delegation. He left the Delegation because he "came to the conclusion that mine was an impossible mission".

The "impossible mission" was to convince the Palestinian leadership of the need for a legal advisor and legal strategies in the negotiations. The consequences of the absence of proper legal advice and strategies on the Palestinian side are felt in the Palestinian–Israeli agreements of Oslo I, the Declaration of Principles, and the other agreements concluded so far between the parties.

The book, as noted by Edward Said in his foreword, "is a milestone in the history and interpretation of the Middle East peace process". Through a careful analysis of the interim agreements, Mr Shehadeh shows how they have realized identifiable Israeli interim diplomatic objectives, while no interim Palestinian objectives, other than obtaining recognition of the PLO, were identifiable.

The book is divided into five chapters, a conclusion and nineteen appendices with recommended further reading. Chapters 1 and 2 discuss the two main agreements signed between Israel and the PLO: the Declaration of Principles on Interim Self-Governing Arrangements (DOP) of 13 September 1993 and the Interim Agreement on the West Bank and the Gaza Strip of 28 September 1995. The guiding principle of the Interim Agreement, as perceived by the author, was the separation between the administrative affairs of the Palestinians and those of the Israeli settlers living in the Occupied Territories.

This separation process was taking place since Israeli occupation through a restructuring of the legal system of the Territories. Chapter 3 deals with the legal changes which preceded the Interim Agreement, affecting, for example, jurisdiction, land registration, town planning and administration and, of course, security. These changes, which were, in most aspects, detrimental to the Palestinians, were to a large extent consolidated in the Interim Agreement. The only breakaway was in the economic field.

The course of the negotiations which led to these results of consolidation of Israeli changes is discussed in Chapter 4. From the Palestinian view, these negotiations fall into two phases, and the author discusses both: the first extends from the beginning of the talks in Washington DC and ends with the start of the secret talks in Oslo; the second ends with the signing of the DOP on 13 September 1993. In this chapter, the author provides first hand information and analysis of the Washington negotiations which is not generally known, while of course he had to rely on available literature regarding the second phase.

The effect of Oslo I was to give Israel a respite and open the door to normalization with the Arab states, while the major issues of conflict, such as Jerusalem, the settlements, the refugees, security etc. have been left to the final status negotiations. That represented great gain to Israel without comparable success for the Palestinians. The reviewer may note that Middle Eastern politics are rarely static. The Israeli gain is being eroded under the present Israeli government policies and may be lost if these policies continue.

In the last and fifth chapter, the author discusses post-agreements legislation in an attempt to analyse the indication of the legal instruments made by both sides as to the development of the relationship between Israel and the areas under the jurisdiction of the Palestinian Authority and the Israeli settlements in the West Bank and the Gaza Strip. On the Israeli side, the author considers Military Proclamation No. 7, "Proclamation Regarding the Implementation of the Interim Agreement" and the Israeli Bill on Implementing the Agreement Concerning the Gaza Strip and Jericho Area (Amendment of Legislation) of 25 July 1944 which was never passed as a Bill but was divided into a number of implementation laws. On the Palestinian side, the author refers to the amendment of the Palestinian Covenant, the creation of a fatwa and legislation department and the elected Palestinian Council. However, no Palestinian law was passed implementing the Interim Agreement and Palestinian legislation remained confused with very serious lacunae. The handling of this situation forms the subject of the conclusion.

The appendices are extremely useful since one can find in one place the most relevant documents on the subject from the UN Partition Resolution of 1947 to the Protocol Concerning the Redeployment in Hebron of 1997.

This book is a significant contribution to the Palestinian–Israeli debate and instructive not only for the Palestinians but also as to the art and strategy of negotiations. It also serves as a warning to those negotiators who belittle the role of legal strategies in negotiations. The author is pessimistic about the future. Nevertheless, his work justifies the conclusion that there is Palestinian legal talent of quality which is still not being utilized by the Palestinian leadership to improve the performance of the Palestinian negotiator.

Anis Al-Qasem

Citizenship and the State: A Comparative Study of Citizenship Legislation in Israel, Jordan, Palestine, Syria and Lebanon, by Uri Davis, Ithaca Press, 1997, 224pp, £30.00

This is not a law book designed to analyse the details of citizenship or nationality legislation in the countries under survey. Rather, it is a book in which the author applies his philosophy of citizenship to such legislation. This philosophy is discussed in the preface and first chapter. "The purpose of this study", writes the author, "is to make a contribution towards the constitution of an academic as well as political narrative on the subject of citizenship that does not implode into a conceptual and moral self-contradiction" (p. 2).

The author draws a distinction between "nationality" and "citizenship". "Nationality" is defined as "identity" (a fact of consciousness, and imagined community), while "citizenship" is "a *datum*, a certificate". He also draws a distinction between *jinsiyya*, which he terms as "passport" citizenship and *muwatana*, "democratic" citizenship, and finds the italicized Arabic terms illuminating particularly since, in English, the distinction between "nationality" and "citizenship" is blurred. The institution of this two-tier citizenship has made it possible for many states, including Jordan and Israel as far as the Palestinian citizens are concerned, to skirt around the requirement of equality in the enjoyment of human rights, which, to the author, is the foundation of democratic citizenship.

The distinction between "citizenship" and "nationality" implies a definition of "nation". In his definition, he "advisedly" excluded language as one of the defining elements while included is "common Deity (or religious tradition)". It is doubtful whether Protestants, for example, consider themselves as a "nation" with the right to "national" self-determination. One suspects that the introduction of religious confession was inspired by the Israeli example, while the intentional exclusion of language was inspired by the author's vision of the Middle East.

The author advocates the transformation of the League of Arab States into a Middle Eastern and North African Union in which Arabic is an official or one of the official languages so as to include Israel and remove the concepts of "Arabism", "Arab nationalism" and "Arab identity" from the definition of state and citizenship and the relegation of these terms to cultural discussions. In his view, this step is necessitated by democratic principles. It is questionable whether such a step is a necessity for "democratic" citizenship which grants equal rights to all citizens of the state. For example, in the case of Syria, the author rightly notes that once Syrian citizenship is recognized to a person, there is no discrimination as to the enjoyment of rights based on concepts of Arabism. The system may be undemocratic, but the rights of the citizens, whatever they are, are the same. His interpretation of the law of nullification of citizenship is not supported by the text which is of a general nature and not limited to Jews of Syrian citizenship. There is no intrinsic reason why the Arab states should shed their Arab identity or for them to include Israel in any regional organization they may decide to have. Again, there is no apparent reason why there could not be, in the future, an Arab citizenship created through a decision of the League of Arab States without its transformation into a Middle Eastern North African Union, which, in any event, is no guarantee that a common citizenship would emerge.

The author, in this important first chapter, is advancing a number of novel definitions, including definitions of sovereignty and independence, people, nation, secularism, etc., which, in my judgment, require further elaboration and great cohesion to show the relevance of each to a theory of citizenship. Certainly, with all the changes in the composition of populations and in concepts, there is a need for a reconsideration of traditional thinking. This need is obviously felt by the author and his first chapter is a contribution in meeting that need. The study demonstrates how traditional concepts have, in some instances and in varying degrees, most glaringly in the case of Israel, influenced citizenship legislation in the countries covered by the study. Preconceived undemocratic ideas have produced discrimination, and the book is a contribution to the clarification of thinking on the subject.

In his five case studies, the author is on solid factual ground. The treatment of Palestinians, whether as citizens or refugees, is constantly on his mind. This is no surprise for a determined activist for Palestinian rights. He deals with the discrimination against them in Israel through the adoption of two-tier citizenship, although through his acceptance of religious confession as a basis for the concept of Nation may appear supportive of the concept of "Jewish" people which is at the heart of Israeli Zionist philosophy – a philosophy which the author does not accept.

The fluctuation of the rights of Palestinians because of ever-changing Jordanian policies is carefully attended to, as well as the discriminatory exclusion of Jews who were Palestinian citizens from citizenship of the state. The position of Palestinian refugees in Syria, is different. They are not Syrian citizens, but enjoy all the rights of Syrian citizens. The author advocates their naturalization. In Lebanon, Palestinian refugees are classified as foreigners. With that classification, employment opportunities are extremely limited. With understanding, he notes the absence of definition of a "Palestinian" in the draft Basic Law whose preparation this reviewer has supervised. The omission was, of course, intentional, but does not make Palestinians under the authority of the PNA stateless, as concluded by the author. The PNA recognizes them as its own citizens and they enjoy democratic citizenship in the areas under its control. *Ad hoc* definitions have started appearing in legislation, such as the Elections Law.

Apart from his study of citizenship legislation, the author makes a relevant contribution to the study of the legal status of the Palestinians in the countries covered by the study. In his concluding chapter, he makes a number of recommendations. His solution is the creation of a Middle East on the model of the European Union, particularly Union citizenship and the rights attached to it. It is a vision worth pursuing for the elimination of discriminatory legislation and practices and equal enjoyment of rights.

The author has opened a serious discussion of importance for a re-definition of citizenship in the Middle East, which should attract attention and, hopefully, more contributions.

Anis Al-Qasem

Business Laws of Yemen, edited by Abdulla M. A. Maktari and John McHugo, Graham & Trotman, 1995, 312pp, £150.00

A publication which comprises most business statutes of a given country would certainly be welcomed by foreign lawyers who deal, or may one day deal, with that country. It is definitely a plus when it is distant Yemen which is concerned and statutes are translated into English which, as a matter of fact, is the nternational language of the day.

Business Laws of Yemen should find a place in the law library of lawyers and businessmen who may find themselves looking for an answer to a problem, the solution of which is in the business laws of Yemen. True, the editors, in a note at the beginning of the book, have warned the reader that ". . . translation always involves an element of interpretation on the part of the translator. In case of doubt, recourse should be had to the original Arabic which alone is authoritative." But a translated text is far better than none – whether or not coupled with the warning.

Among the translated statutes, the Law of Commercial Companies and the Arbitration Law call for attention. The Law of Commercial Companies follows the same pattern as the companies laws of the region which are nearly all of Franco–Egyptian inspiration. The Arbitration Law applies to both national and international arbitration and Article 7 allows the parties, when at least one of them is a non-Yemeni, to agree the law to which arbitration is to be subject, both as regards procedure and substance as well as the language and place of arbitration.

Article 23 states the limited cases whereby an arbitrator can be removed. This article is of great relevance, for it neutralizes a rule of Islamic *fiqh* which deems that the appointment of an arbitrator is akin to the appointment of any attorney and therefore revocable at will. That is no more the case, due to Article 23.

Nabil Saleh

Islamic Law and Finance: Religion, Risk and Return, by Frank E. Vogel and Samuel L. Hayes III, Kluwer Law International, 350pp, £60.00

Until about thirty years ago the practice of Islamic law was, other than for acts of worship and ritual, limited to family matters. Most, if not all Muslims married, divorced and bequeathed their estates which were divided among the heirs, according to rules found in the Qur'an and the *Sunnah* and expounded in confirmed law treatises.

At that time, Islamic law did not apply to any significant transactions concluded in the Arab world. Indeed, transactions conducted in remote or poor areas were still governed by the *shari'a*, but richer and more populated regions had been the subject of a pervasive Western influence which brought with it a set of foreign legislation that replaced the indigenous one.

Faced with this cultural onslaught, scholars such as Sanhuri and Mahmassani tried – particularly after the Second World War and onwards – to keep the *shari'a*'s light burning if not glowing. These scholars had received a Western education, but they were also aware of their own legal heritage and so they followed the only course available to them. They attempted to align the principles and rules of the *shari'a* with those of the imported system of law. To achieve this they chose and brought out from the vast corpus of the teaching of the Islamic schools of law, rules and principles that bore most resemblance to their Western counterparts and focused on them. They deemed it necessary, owing to the circumstances prevailing at the time, to play down the differences which necessarily exist among system of law – more particularly when one of them is deeply rooted in religion.

The admirable work of these pioneers has the effect of keeping interest alive in the *shari'a* as a law which could govern transactions whenever circumstances will allow it. The opportunity presented itself in the early 1970s when the oil-rich countries took the exploitation of their natural resources into their own hands. The cosy but one-sided arrangement between the indigenous and foreign systems of law had to change. As it happened, until they took control of their own destiny these countries were the more backward and poorer among the Arab states – one or two cases excepted. In a matter of years the voices and requirements of the newly enriched states had to be heard. Holding the purse-strings, they demanded that contracts with their Western partners be governed by the local law, with the *shari'a* forming an integral part.

Puzzled Western lawyers had to agree to negotiated contracts being governed by a legal system about which they knew very little. In turn, Western scholars who had until then confined their attention to family law – the one division of the *shari'a* which had continued to receive actual application – felt compelled to start getting more acquainted with the other divisions regarding transactions.

The time of my settling in England coincided with the revival period of the *shari'a*. Because of the raging war in Lebanon – fuelled in part, as it happened, with oil revenues – the late Sobhi Mahmassani's forgotten lessons regained tremendous importance for me and I launched myself into the studies of *shari'a* with obsessive interest. In 1986, my *Unlawful Gain and Legitimate Profit in Islamic Law: Riba, Gharar and Islamic banking* was published first by the Cambridge University Press and in 1992 by Graham & Trotman. It was Frank Vogel who wrote the foreword to the second edition.

After the passage of twelve years I was delighted to be given for review Vogel and Hayes' *Islamic Law and Finance: Religion, Risk and Return*. At first it was surprising to realize that the analyses of the same instruments of Islamic financing are repeated in the first two parts of the book. These parts are written separately by each of the authors, while the latter part is by both.

The one explanation that comes to mind after reading this extraordinarily well-researched book is that the two authors may have distinct views about the future of Islamic financing. While Vogel seems to suggest that the answer to the shortcomings of Islamic financing is in the emergence of Islamically correct markets of adequate volume (p. 178), Hayes makes the following sweeping conclusion: "Ultimately, no financial system can survive in the contemporary world unless it is in harmony with the dominant global financial market forces" (p. 200).

What appears to be different conclusions drawn by each author must have been of benefit to Part III which they have produced together. Their suggestions for innovation in Islamic finance, based on what I believe to be different approaches, are remarkably bold and imaginative, and stem from an in-depth knowledge of the theory and practice of Islamic finance. The field interviews conducted by the authors, and their own studies and researches, have allowed them not only to be descriptive, but to go further and make fresh propositions for the development of Islamic financing, which points the way for the entangled system to evolve.

One could also find in the book the answers to some baffling questions; why, for example, does Saudi Arabia – which is supposed to be the most traditionally Islamic among Arab countries – discourage a distinct Islamic banking sector? The reasons is that to single out certain banks as Islamic would imply that the others are not. In Iraq and Syria, Islamic banking is wholly absent for the opposite reason: these countries are fearful of the symbols of Islamic identity.

One may reflect, however, whether devices, stratagems and ingenious structures are what Muslims expect from genuine Islamic banks and investment companies. Viewed from a religious standpoint, would it not be more appropriate for the providers of Islamic banking and financial services to refrain from trying to mimic all the conventional services and confine themselves to those services which are Islamically acceptable, with no need to resort to "ducking and diving"? And yet the actual course followed by banks and financial institutions which have characterized themselves as Islamic does not signal the possibility for such an occurrence.

The situation being such, *Islamic Law and Finance* will be of tremendous value for the forces behind the Islamic banks and investment companies, as well as for their users. Moreover, the "new" instruments developed by the authors would necessarily incite deep reflection and generate interest among the religious scholars who form the advisory boards attached to banks and investment companies. These scholars often lack real knowledge of the law and of the economic systems as practised in the West. This book provides them with the necessary data and directions on which they could base new imaginative opinions.

Nabil Saleh

Islamic Law: Theory and Practice, edited by Robert Gleave and Eugenia Kermeli, I. B. Tauris, 256pp, £50.00

In recent years, there has been a slow but rising interest in the study of Islamic law. Be it the formative, classical or modern period of Islamic law, works of *furu' al-fiqh* or *usul al-fiqh*, *fatawa* compilations or modern legal systems in the Muslim world, Islamicists are discovering the huge significance and contribution of "law" to the Muslim intellectual and social traditions. The book, *Islamic Law: Theory and Practice*, is an attempt to reflect the diversity of themes and approaches currently of interest to emerging scholars within this field. It is a collection of eleven papers, of which one by Eric Chaumont is in French, originally delivered at a conference entitled, "Islamic law: Theory and Practice".

The book has been divided into four sections: legal theory, *ifta'*, *fatwas* and *muftis*, minorities under Islamic law and finally, modern Islamic law. Many of the articles are concerned with exploring the nature and relevance of *ijtihad* towards the elaboration and development of Islamic law. They look at isolated cases or particular problems to draw general theories about the nature and applicability of Islamic law in today's societies. Chaumont's article on *ijtihad* and history in classical sunni Islam reflects a common concern among many scholars regarding the issue of *ijtihad* and the applicability of *fiqh* in society. He uses two eleventh-century scholars, Juwayni and Shirazi, to show that the nature of Islamic law has always been one of a connection between *fiqh* and *ijtihad*, that every problem of *fiqh* is a problem of *ijtihad*. "The closing of the door of *ijtihad*", he concludes, is "imaginary", and one of the ways this can be shown is by examining the *fatwa* collections where *muftis* have used *ijtihad* to find new solutions to varying problems throughout history.

Arguing for caution in drawing general conclusions on law with the use of only fatwa literature, is the article on *darura* or necessity in modern Islamic law and the issues of organ transplantation by Birgit Krawietz. Krawietz accuses Western scholarship on this subject of neglecting important aspects of legal theory in relation to its discussions about *maslaha/darura*, need and necessity, when it comes to medical ethics. Quoting from Rispler-Chaim, *Islamic Medical Ethics in the Twentieth Century*, in which the author states that "Islamic law permits all organ transplants", Krawietz addresses the importance of *hurma* or respect for the sanctity of the human body within law. She argues that the Qur'an itself allows certain concessions when it is a matter of saving of human life, a principle which would arguably confirm the necessity for many transplants, but the issues become far more complex when the aim of a transplant is no longer to save a life but merely prolong a life for a short while. Interference with the corpse then becomes more problematic as there is no certainty of full recovery and this calls for examining the restrictions of necessity or *shurut al-darura*. The principle of *hurma* is that if life is sacred, so is death. Krawietz is right to call for recognition and use of secular expertise and knowledge on issues of medical and scientific ethics, by the *muftis*. It is only by working together that the notion of *ijtihad* can continue to be of relevance in Muslim societies and offer solutions to contemporary dilemmas.

Yitzhak Reiter's article on *qadis* in Israel highlights an interesting social and political development whereby the Islamic courts have retained their powers in areas of personal law, even though the Muslim judicial system has been integrated into the general juridical system of Israel. This inevitably leads to certain tensions between civil authorities and *shari'a* courts. Reiter does not dwell too much on this, as he appears more concerned with the lack of higher Islamic education in Israel which has resulted in poorly qualified *qadis*, generally perceived as the applicators of Islamic law. As there are no minimum educational criteria for *qadis*, and the *shari'a* judiciary has not received adequate funding, as it has "for many years been the object of discrimination vis-à-vis the Jewish religious judiciary", this has led to a decline in Muslim public confidence in the competence of the *qadis*.

Reiter examines the reforming policies of Sheikh Ahmed al-Natur, *qadi* of Jaffa and Beersheva. Through a brief examination of some of his rulings, Reiter shows why and how Natur, who himself is an example of an academically trained *qadi*, objects to the use of Israeli law, but urges other *qadis* to refer to Islamic legal sources and interpret these in the "spirit of the law". Reiter sees that the *shari'a* courts are the only official Islamic institution that Muslims still retain in Israel, and the overriding tone of his article is sympathetic to the need for recognition and amelioration of these courts.

The above have been selected as examples of the type of discussions presented in the book. They provide some interesting reading but no great systematic analysis of the various aspects of *fiqh* literature. The articles are not textual examinations of the development of laws and the nature of the law books themselves; they are rather concerned with giving case examples to reflect the fluidity of Islamic law and the tensions between *shari'a* as an immutable ideal and *shari'a* as interpretative and normative practice. The variety of approaches reflects the growing appeal of *fiqh* literature in contemporary scholarship, but the concern with law and practice followed by the rather hurried conclusions of some of the articles, overlook a significant characteristic of Islamic law, namely, form and creativity within the literary process.

Mona Siddiqui

Human Rights, Self-Determination and Political Change in the Occupied Territories, edited by Stephen Bowen, Martinus Nijhoff, incorporated under the publishing programme of Kluwer Law International, 1997, £68.00

Both these volumes are collections of papers, and both deal with various aspects of human rights, but the style and presentation of the two are substantially different. The first constitutes the publication of a number of papers by international legal scholars presented originally at the International Colloquium on Human Rights and Political Change convened in the summer of 1994 by the Gaza Centre for Rights and Law when it was under the directorship of Raji Sourani, now director of the Palestinian Centre for Human Rights. The editor, Stephen Bowen, explains that the book "attempts to examine, from the standpoint of international law, the implications of the [1993] Declaration of Principles [on Interim Self-Government Arrangements] and the extent to which the agreements negotiated during this period of rapid political change provide for the realisation of self-determination for the Palestinian people and for the protection and promotion of human rights and fundamental freedoms."[1] The papers have been amended and updated – to varying degrees – to take account of developments up to 1 June 1996, including the conclusion of the Israeli–Palestinian Interim Agreement on the West Bank and the Gaza Strip in September 1995,[2] the assassination of Yitzhak Rabin in November 1995,[3] the elections for the Palestinian Legislative Council in January 1996, and Israel's "Grapes of Wrath" attack on Lebanon and the Likud victory in Israel's general election in the spring of that year, along with more general developments in the human rights situation under the Palestinian National Authority. In general, the articles stand the test of time well and some indeed are of immediate significance in light of the delay in commencement of final status negotiations and of the anticipated declaration of statehood which Yasser Arafat has said he will be making in the spring of 1999.

The ten papers in the volume cover a variety of topics and each can be read alone. Read as a volume, the book presents a coherent overview of related law-based concerns for the transitional period and in this sense would have benefited from a rather more substantial and thematic introduction drawing the papers together. There is some overlap, but only Catriona Drew and Iain Scobbie appear to cross-reference other contributions in the volume. Surprisingly, there is no contribution from any of the Palestinian experts and legal scholars who were at the Colloquium, although some of the papers – notably those by Hilary Charlesworth and Stephen Marks – make specific reference to the content of some of those contributions in their papers, and with the exception of the contribution by Hans Peter Gasser of the International Committee of the Red Cross, all make reference to published work by Palestinian experts and/or organizations.

The first paper in the volume is by Richard Falk, Professor of International Law and Practice at Princeton. Entitled "Some international law implications of the Oslo/Cairo framework for the PLO/Israeli peace process", the article is a wide-ranging, compelling and eminently readable analysis of the international and domestic political context of the peace process, the role of "legitimacy" and third parties, and the implications of all this for the future of the Oslo/Cairo framework in specific reference to its legal ramifications for Palestinian rights. True to form, Falk scrutinizes a number of uncomfortable truths about the practical politics and power play involved in the conclusion of the agreements and draws forward-looking conclusions with judiciously chosen references to other contexts including Algeria and France,

---

[1] Bowen (ed.), Introduction xiii.
[2] Variously short-handed in this volume as "Oslo II"(see Iain Scobbie's contribution) and the "Interim Agreement"(see John Quigley's contribution).
[3] A typing error has this as November 1996 in the article by Richard Falk, p. 11.

Vietnam, South Africa and Indonesia/East Timor. He begins with a fascinating discussion of "what sort of peace process?" setting out the particular disparity in strength and domestic circumstance between the PLO and Israel in the lead-up to the 1993 Declaration of Principles peace process and its implications for the content and sustainability of the subsequent agreements. A main contention is that

[I]f this peace process is ever to eventuate in "peace", then it will need strong reinforcement from time to time by external actors, especially by the United States, but also by European states, as well as by Arab countries in the region, by the European Union and possibly by the United Nations. More than this, at the level of implementation, NGOs, transnational citizens associations, and private diplomacy will turn out to be indispensable.[4]

This last theme, the role of NGOs and transnational citizens associations, is one picked up in later contributions. Falk's basic theme of the vulnerability of the Palestinian position is examined with regard to a set of five aspects central to the agreements:

- deference (i.e. the "strong tendency in international law to respect whatever framework parties to an agreement can agree upon to resolve their differences, especially if their accord is undertaken against a background of prolonged warfare, and with the encouragement of influential members of the international community"[5] and what happens when this deference is assailed by issues of "legitimacy" – as compared to "legality" raised by the results of excessive disparities in power);
- the *sui generis* nature of the agreements (i.e. "[t]here is little relevant precedent"[6] – another point on which there is general agreement);
- status ("[a]s never before, the state of Israel operationally accepted the PLO and Arafat as diplomatic equals, as "parties". Yet formally and textually, as well as in substantive arrangements, inequality of status was enshrined throughout the process");[7]
- self-determination (here Falk picks up a point reiterated by later contributors, "remarkably, the right of self-determination for the Palestinian people is never explicitly and unconditionally affirmed in the arrangements negotiated to date");[8]
- implementation: here Falk opines that "the informal roles of NGOs in reinforcing governmental and inter-governmental procedures are likely to be crucial"; and in regard to the claims of those not yet 'included' in the process, suggests that "[i]t might be appropriate at this point to urge the General Assembly to request an Advisory Opinion from the International Court of Justice on such outstanding matters as the status of Jerusalem, the rights of Palestinians living outside the Gaza Strip and the West Bank, and the distribution of water rights."[9]

As part of his conclusion, Falk reminds his readers that:

No matter how one-sided the agreed texts, Palestinian rights of self-determination are intrinsic and inalienable. Their application may be ignored, or even repudiated, for a time, but never truly lost.[10]

---

[4] Falk in Bowen, p. 4.
[5] *Ibid.* p. 9.
[6] *Ibid.,* p. 12.
[7] *Ibid.,* pp. 9–10.
[8] *Ibid.,* p. 17.
[9] *Ibid.,* p. 21.
[10] *Ibid.,* p. 22.

This is a theme that informs, to a certain extent, the second paper in the collection. "The PLO-Israeli interim arrangements and the Geneva Civilians Convention", by Professor John Quigley, Professor of Law and Political Science at Ohio State University, concentrates on the continuing applicability of the body of international humanitarian law to the territories during the transitional period. In particular, the focus is on the continuing applicability of the Fourth Geneva Convention Relative to the Protection of Civilian Persons in Time of War[11] for so long as and in so far as Israel continues to exercise any of the "functions of government" therein.[12] The focal article of the Convention for Quigley's analysis is Article 47:

Protected persons who are in occupied territory shall not be deprived, in any case or in any manner whatsoever, of the benefits of the present Convention by any change introduced, as the result of the occupation of a territory, into the institutions or government of the said territory, nor by any agreement concluded between the authorities of the occupied territories and the Occupying Power, nor by any annexation by the latter of the whole or part of the occupied territory.

Quigley's basic premise is that "[a]ny provision of the Israel–PLO agreements that contemplates a diminution of the obligations of Israel as the occupying power is invalid".[13] Having rehearsed, in brief, the arguments on the applicability of the Convention and rightly dismissed as irrelevant in this regard the fact that none of the PLO–Israel agreements refer explicitly to the Fourth Geneva Convention, or indeed to belligerent occupation, Quigley proceeds to consider "features of the Declaration of Principles and the interim instruments, namely, the provisions addressing the settlements, the status of Jerusalem, and Israel's military orders, [which] raise apparent inconsistencies with the manner in which these matters are treated by the Geneva Civilians Convention."[14] The inconsistencies having been competently established, Quigley reaffirms that the Convention prevails in the event of any conflict, but concedes that:

A serious danger in the Declaration of Principles is that the international community may assume that the situation of the Palestinians is now a bilateral matter between Israel and the PLO, and therefore that international action is unnecessary. Even if this view were not taken in a formal way, the international community might be less inclined than before to intervene to protect the Palestinians.[15]

In terms of law-based enforcement action to uphold the protections guaranteed in the Convention, this is of course precisely what has happened. Quigley draws attention to the third-party state responsibility under Article 1 of the Convention under which all states party undertake to "respect and ensure respect for the present Convention in all circumstances", and to the ground-breaking call made by the Security Council in December 1990 for states to take action in accordance with that responsibility (SCR 681). He contrasts this with US insistence, in the Madrid stage of the peace process, that there would be no "competing or parallel process in the United Nations Security Council", and the express abstention by the US in a Security Council resolution in 1994, following the massacre of Palestinian worshippers at the Ibrahimi mosque in Hebron by an Israeli settler, on the preambular

---

[11] Referred to in short by Quigley as the Geneva Civilians Convention, although more usually shortened to the Fourth Geneva Convention or Geneva IV.
[12] See Article 6 of the Fourth Geneva Convention.
[13] Quigley in Bowen, p. 28.
[14] *Ibid.*, p. 32.
[15] *Ibid.*, pp. 43–44.

clause reaffirming the applicability of the Fourth Geneva Convention to East Jerusalem. There are other striking examples both before and since of the retreat of influential international parties – particularly the US but to some extent also the European Union states – from international law-based positions and certainly from international law-based action in support of those positions.[16] Nevertheless, Quigley's conclusion, that it is "incumbent upon the international community, acting collectively, to fulfil the responsibilities it has assumed by drafting and adopting the Geneva Civilians Convention"[17] finds resonance in the more recent efforts in the United Nations General Assembly where a series of emergency session resolutions dating from the summer of 1997 calls for preparations for a conference of High Contracting Parties to the Convention to discuss measures of enforcement in the Occupied Palestinian Territories.[18] Just as the ground-breaking Security Council resolution 681 (1990) was taken against the exceptional political backdrop of Iraq's invasion of Kuwait and the build-up to operation "Desert Storm" at the beginning of 1991, so these General Assembly resolutions reflect a wide concern at the deterioration of the peace process and specifically at the intransigence of the Netanyahu government. The particular issues around which the first of the resolutions was adopted was the decision by Israeli authorities to build a settlement at Jabal Abu Ghneim south of Jerusalem ("'Har Homa"), and measures to deny Palestinian residency rights in Jerusalem.

Guy Goodwin-Gill's contribution, "The West Bank and Gaza: free and fair elections, human rights and the transition to democracy", is a lucid and informative exposition of "election rights", their relation to the expanded concept of self-determination, and the democratic process. Professor of Law at Carleton University, Ottawa and of Asylum Law at Amsterdam, Goodwin-Gill makes particularly good use of the post-Colloquium update period by including an account and assessment of the Palestinian Legislative Council (PLC) elections in January 1996. Of particular interest in the beginning of the article is his exposition of "the centrality of self-determination":

Of all the human rights at stake in the context of representative government, and therefore also of elections, the right of self-determination can be considered fundamental.[19]

This section is a succinct examination of the concept of self-determination, a concept that other writers in the volume (Chinkin and Drew in particular) similarly note has remained ambiguous. Goodwin-Gill considers the "internal" or "political self-determination" aspect, and states that:

in its internal aspect, self-determination can be read as stating the same objective as is reflected in the principle of free and fair or genuine elections – that the will of the people shall be the basis of the authority of government.[20]

---

[16] See papers by the current reviewer, "International protection and international diplomacy: policy choices for third-party states in the occupied territories", and "Consensual intervention: a case study on the temporary international presence in Hebron", pp. 225-314 in CIHRE , *International Human Rights Enforcement: The Case of the Occupied Palestinian Territories in the Transitional Period*, Ramallah 1996, and more recently "International humanitarian law and the Middle East peace process: aspects of EU policy", *Journal of Armed Conflict Law* 2(2), 1997, pp. 177–192.

[17] Quigley in Bowen, p. 46.

[18] UN General Assembly resolutions ES-10/2 25/4/97; ES-10/3 15/7/97; ES-10/4 13/11/97; ES-10/5 17/3/98.

[19] Goodwin-Gill in Bowen, p. 48.

[20] *Ibid.,* p. 50.

There follows a clarification of "election rights" in the human rights instruments, an exposition of the criteria for free and fair elections, and finally an assessment of the Palestinian elections of January 1996. Here Goodwin-Gill takes note of a number of the concerns voiced by a variety of groups – Palestinian and international – regarding the process, noting in the end that the Palestinian elections were "widely hailed, and with reason, as a significant success" while pointing out that:

At the same time, an appreciation of the broader context, including Israel's visible and invisible presence and an uncertain background of political repression, justify a measure of caution in assessing their overall impact.[21]

In concluding, Goodwin-Gill points out that there is as yet no provision for periodic elections, and leaves the final judgement to history: "whether those elections did indeed produce a lasting, representative and responsible government".[22] The chapter is followed by useful annexes on standards and criteria for free and fair elections.

The three articles by women contributors come together in the middle of the volume, two concerned particularly with women and the third leading on to the following articles. In "International human rights law: prospects and problems for Palestinian women", Hilary Charlesworth, Professor of Law at the University of Adelaide, sets out to:

explain and attempt to justify the claim that the international law of human rights has generally delivered very little to women: that it has developed as a gendered regime.[23]

In examining how one might negotiate a path "between essentialism and relativism in discussing the relevance of international human rights law to Palestinian women",[24] Charlesworth posits that "an 'imagined community' of women may find international legal intervention a useful strategy in particular, limited contexts".[25] A brief history of Palestinian women's involvement in the political struggle and activism is set in the comparative context of the non-representation of women in political decision-making as "one manifestation of the limited agenda of liberation movements".[26] The writer then considers the international human rights regime, in particular the marginalisation of women's human rights and the Women's Convention:[27]

The area of human rights in international law rests on, and reinforces, a distinction between public and private spheres which operates to the disadvantage of women. In effect, human rights are defined by the criterion of what men fear will happen to them.[28]

Charlesworth points up, with good cause, the UNRWA rules relating to refugee status as "based on both sexist and 'orientalist' stereotypes", holding that they violate the guarantees of non-discrimination on grounds of gender in both the ICCPR and the CEDAW. For Charlesworth, the question is whether or not it is worthwhile for Palestinian women to participate in the marginalised women's human rights system during the transitional period and indeed beyond, or whether they could more usefully invest their efforts elsewhere. With a degree of prescience, Charlesworth points out that

---

[21] *Ibid.*, p. 64.
[22] *Ibid.*, p. 66.
[23] Charlesworth in Bowen, p. 79.
[24] *Ibid.*, p. 80.
[25] *Ibid.*, p. 81.
[26] *Ibid.*, p. 83.
[27] Convention for the Elimination of All Forms of Discrimination Against Women.
[28] Charlesworth in Bowen, p. 88: footnote suppressed.

Times of political change frequently disadvantage women. Their interests are seen as subordinate to those of a male-defined "community" and invocation of women's human rights as divisive and confrontational.[29]

The culmination in the spring of 1998 of the campaign on women's rights around the Palestinian Model Parliament: Women and Legislation, which raised very publicly the whole range of women's rights in Palestine during the transitional period and looking to statehood, met with just these charges and with a large degree of hostility on the part of certain identifiable sectors of the Palestinian community. Charlesworth's article is challenging and compelling, and her concluding sentence is worth quoting for the attention of all those who concern themselves with human rights in Palestine and elsewhere:

An important task for all Palestinians and human rights organizations during transition to self-government will be to ensure that the human rights observed during the transition and in the new entity are genuinely universal.[30]

The second article, of similar high quality, to address the subject of Palestinian women in particular is "The potential and pitfalls of the right to self-determination for women", by Christine Chinkin, at the time Professor of Law at Southampton and now at the London School of Economics. Chinkin begins with an overview of the "right to self-determination", noting at the outset that it embraces a number of separate strands:

Taken together these strands seems to underpin the right to a secure existence within a democratically chosen political framework. The linkage of the right to self-determination to the entire spectrum of political, civil, economic, social and cultural rights contained within the two UN Covenants underscores its importance for the attainment of all human rights.[31]

Examining the characterization of self-determination as a group right as compared to an individual one, Chinkin examines some of the uncertainties that arise in its implementation before going on to examine the concept of "internal self-determination" and the link that has been made to the argument for an emerging international norm of the right to democratic governance.[32] Having noted the complexities and ambiguities associated with this right, she proceeds to consider the Palestinian situation, noting at the outset the general absence of explicit references to the right to self-determination in any of the international or bilateral instruments that establish the framework for the peace process, and questioning the implications of this omission.

Chinkin's focus, having set this framework, turns to Palestinian women and what self-determination can and might mean for them. She notes some of the particularities of the impact of the Israeli occupation upon women as well as the more general role of women within national liberation struggles, moving on to look at the challenge presented by Palestinian women's struggle for gender equality:

An important aspect of asserting national identity is the retention of the national cultural heritage. The family unit and the role of women within the family are symbols of the societal identity that the people as a whole are committed to preserving in the face of its intended destruction by the occupier . . . Maintaining the social parameters within which the family unit operates can be seen as part of the commitment to national identity, but these same assumptions also preserve patriarchy.[33]

---

[29] *Ibid.*, p. 91.
[30] *Ibid.*
[31] Chinkin in Bowen, p. 93.
[32] *Ibid.*, p. 96.
[33] *Ibid.*, p. 102. Paragraph break suppressed and footnotes removed.

Chinkin finishes this section with a consideration of the impact on the women's struggle of the growth in influence of Hamas and other conservative religious groupings in the Occupied Territories. The next three sections of the article deal with political self-determination, social and cultural self-determination, and economic self-determination, with examination of what each means, or might mean, with reference to the Vienna Declaration and Programme of Action from the 1993 World Conference on Human Rights, the Report of the International Conference on Population and Development in Cairo 1994, the Beijing Platform for Action from the 1995 Fourth World Conference on Women, and the Convention on the Elimination of All Forms of Discrimination Against Women. In her conclusion, she notes the use made by women of "transnational issues networks":

This emergence of an international civil society has been lauded as a counter-balance to the statism of international law.[34]

The sixth article in the volume is by Catriona Drew, Lecturer in law at Glasgow. "Self-determination, population transfer and the Middle East Peace Accords" is one of two articles in the book – the other being Iain Scobbie's contribution – which look at a particular area of international law in the light of the Oslo II (or Interim) Agreement with a view to the final status negotiations. Both articles examine the history of their respective legal topics and critically examine legal arguments that have been or may in the future be put up by the Israeli side of the argument; they are both extensively researched and comprehensively referenced, and very lengthy.

Drew's contribution begins with an extensive review of the right of self-determination under international law, in far more detail than is attempted in previous articles — for example, teasing out "political goals" from "the language of legal entitlement" in distinguishing between the right to self-determination and the right to establish an independent state[35] — and with frequent comparative references. The core of the article leads on from this to a treatment of a most thorny topic: "the relationship between the right of self-determination and population transfer, and the consequences for the international legal position of the Israeli settlers."[36] Drew considers first population transfer as violating the right of self-determination in a variety of settings, but "[m]ost irreparably [. . . when] undertaken for the specific purpose of altering the demographic balance in a self-determination unit or with a view to annexing land."[37] The presence of over 140,000 Israel settlers in the Palestinian territories she finds prima facie to provide "one of the most striking contemporary examples of a people's right to self-determination".[38] Having considered the various angles of this argument, Drew suggests that there are advantages in framing arguments in the context of the bilateral final status negotiations which establish the illegality of Israel's settlements under international law (as a violation of the right to self-determination) rather than simply reiterating their established illegality under the law of belligerent occupation and in particular the Fourth Geneva Convention. It is here that she turns to the likelihood of an argument for the dismantling of the settlements (on the basis of their illegality under international humanitarian law) being "met with a counter claim based on the human rights of the Israeli settlers."[39]

This part of the article is fascinating reading on the subject of the legality — or otherwise — of requiring the Israeli settlers to leave as part of the political settlement. Drew introduces the problem as follows:

---

[34] *Ibid.*, p. 116.
[35] *Ibid.*, p. 117.
[36] Drew in Bowen, 121.
[37] *Ibid.*, p. 142.
[38] *Ibid.*, p. 144.
[39] *Ibid.*, p. 154.

It is clear that population transfers which have the aim or the effect of defeating the right of self-determination contravene international law. A question arises, however, as to the legality of a population transfer carried our for the purpose of *promoting* the right of self-determination. For example, would it also be illegal to carry out a reverse population transfer of Israeli settlers in the West Bank in order to facilitate the exercise of Palestinian self-determination?[40]

Drew's consideration ranges through concepts such as the "critical date", the "overtly lawful regime", and the human rights consequences for the respective populations, and includes comparative references to the situations in New Caledonia, Western Sahara, Tibet, Estonia and other areas. Her conclusion is that it would be lawful to carry out a reverse transfer of Israeli settlers subject to four caveats:

(a)   responsibility for reversing the transfer lies with Israel not with the Palestinians;
(b)   settlers must be dealt with on an individual rather than a collective basis;
(c)   adequate provision should be made for compensation; and
(d)   the methods employed to facilitate the reverse population transfer must not violate fundamental human rights.[41]

Although Iain Scobbie's contribution is placed later in the volume, it would seem more logical for it to follow that of his colleague Catriona Drew. Dr Scobbie, Senior Lecturer in International Law at the University of Glasgow, looks mostly at the issue of water rights in his lengthy and scholarly article on "Natural resources and belligerent occupation: mutation through permanent sovereignty". Complete with Internet and CD-ROM references, the piece begins with an examination of "what is belligerent occupation" in order to consider the traditional law on the Occupying Power's ability to exploit the natural resources of the territory it is occupying. Having established that "practice and legal opinion has consistently adhered to the position that the occupant can only act as usufructuary"[42] he goes on to consider the standards of treatment of natural resources. This part includes a particularly interesting discussion of the arguments around Israel's oil exploration in the Gulf of Suez and the Sinai during its occupation of these areas of Egypt.

Scobbie's premise is that the traditional law has been modified by the doctrine of permanent sovereignty over natural resources, which he explains as "the economic aspect of self-determination".[43] A discussion of this doctrine leads to the conclusion that permanent sovereignty over natural resources in the West Bank and Gaza remains vested in the population as a corollary or accompaniment of its right to self-determination. Scobbie then proceeds to a legal assessment of Israel's use of water resources in Gaza and the West Bank, having established that

The Palestinian Authority does not possess the exclusive governmental powers which are characteristic of sovereignty . . . Thus the status of the Occupied Territories is not changed by Oslo II: this can only be determined by the outcome of the final status negotiations.[44]

A detailed analysis of the changes introduced by Israel into the water law of the West Bank and Gaza is followed by consideration of water use in each of the two areas. In examining the impact of the peace process on the issues at hand, Scobbie takes note of the "the most momentous provision on water reached by the parties in the Oslo II negotiations" in which Israel "recognizes the Palestinian water rights in the West Bank". [45]

---

[40] *Ibid.*
[41] *Ibid.*, p. 162.
[42] Scobbie in Bowen, p. 234.
[43] *Ibid.*, p. 247.
[44] *Ibid.*, p. 259. Quote and notes suppressed.
[45] Annex III, Appendix I, Article 40, as cited in Scobbie p. 283.

Scobbie points out that this and other provisions on water in Oslo II are only applicable during the interim period. Of the Israeli recognition of Palestinian water rights he notes

Undoubtedly this recognition was an important political breakthrough, but legally it adds nothing. Palestinian rights to water resources in the Occupied Territories pre-existed this recognition as a matter of customary international law. Oslo II simply reiterates this legal status quo.[46]

Scobbie concludes with a consideration of the multilateral track of the Middle East peace process and the Israel–Jordan negotiations in so far as they have produced agreement on the management and utilization of water resources.

The contributions by Stephen Marks and Paul Hunt both deal with the domestic implementation by the Palestinian Authority of international human rights standards. Dr Marks, of the School of International and Public Affairs at Columbia University, addresses "Criminal justice and public security under Palestinian self-government".

Dr Marks' chapter considers what might be done in the interim/transitional period by the Palestinian authorities towards incorporating the standards of international law in criminal justice and public security despite the constraints of the Oslo formula on the legislative powers of the Palestinian Council. His starting point is the complexity and general repressiveness of the relevant laws currently applicable in the two areas, and the consequent need for transitional legislation. He pays much attention to the "remarkable text" of the Draft Basic Law for the National Authority in the Transitional Period, originally drafted by the Palestinian National Council's Legal Committee, and containing some real commitments to human rights standards. At the time Marks was writing, the original draft had been through four versions as a result of consultation and discussion in civil society before coming under the purview of the newly-elected Palestinian Legislative Council's Legal Committee and going through further amendments. Throughout the article Marks refers to the fourth draft and the later version formally introduced to the PLC's Legal Committee dated July 1996.[47]

Marks bases his suggestions for provisional legislation on the standards identified by the United Nations for criminal justice and public security:

An advantage of incorporating these standards into local law applicable in all areas under Palestinian authority is that decades of experience elsewhere can be reflected in a provisional text that does not have to await the lengthy legislative codification.[48]

The particular experience on which Marks draws in this regard is that of the UN Transitional Authority in Cambodia, where he sees a number of similarities with the situation in Palestine.[49] He considers a number of specific areas giving a useful outline of what the laws currently are in the West Bank and Gaza, with some examples of human rights violations that had already occurred under the PA when he was writing, and then proposing draft texts to cover those areas drawn from the UN standards. The specific areas with which he deals are arrest and detention, fair trial, the correctional system and the position of UN instruments as law during the interim period. In his concluding observations, Marks notes that:

The definition and application of law relating to the administration of justice and public security are essential elements of self-government. There are clear signs that many NGOs and the Palestinian people want self-government to be based upon the rule of law and a

---

[46] Scobbie in Bowen, p. 284.
[47] He calculates this to be the eighth version, citing information from Anthony Chase. Marks in Bowen, p. 171 and note 9.
[48] Marks in Bowen, p. 175.
[49] Marks in Bowen, pp. 176–177.

regime protective of human rights. It is not so clear that this desire is shared by the PA. The Palestinian Council could fill the gap by adopting interim provisions as a prefigurement of a democratic constitution to be elaborated following the final status negotiations.[50]

Two years after Marks was writing, it is no secret that the relationship between the legislature and the executive in Palestine since the 1996 elections has been problematic. In its third annual report, the Palestinian Independent Commission for Citizens' Rights noted that:

The PICCR found that the PLC's ability to legislate continued to be greatly circumscribed during 1997, owing to the lack of a clearly structured legal relationship between the PLC and the Executive Branch. This situation stems from the Executive Branch's control over the implementation of legislation, as well as its abstention, without any official justification, from participating in the process of legislative development, and its failure to act on legislation submitted to it for comment or for either ratification or veto.[51]

Far from being able to adopt the interim provisions suggested by Marks, the PLC has been unable to get the Basic Law itself rendered into legislation. The Council completed its third and final reading of the Basic Law on 2 October 1997. At the time this review was being written, in the early autumn of 1998, President Arafat had still not passed the bill into law, although under the Standing Orders for the PLC he is supposed to ratify or veto within 30 days of the third reading being finished.[52] One can conclude without going too much out on a limb that President Arafat seems to have no intention of signing the bill into law. Regarding the areas of particular concern to Marks, in September 1998 Amnesty International reported, five years after the Oslo Agreement, that

Political arrest and detention under the PA has seen the stabilization of a system of prolonged detention without charge or trial. There has been virtually no attempt by the PA to follow local laws regulating arrest and detention with regard to political prisoners.[53]

In similar vein Paul Hunt, Senior Lecturer at the University of Waikato, Hamilton, addresses "Economic and social rights: issues of implementation" – although it is worth noting, as the writer himself concedes, that there is hardly any mention of economic rights apart from in the title: "[g]enerally the same points arise in relation to the implementation of both social and economic rights."[54] Hunt begins with an attempt to describe the relationship between the Palestinian authorities and social rights:

The Gaza–Jericho Agreement requires both parties to exercise their responsibilities "with due regard to internally-accepted norms and principles of human rights". Presumably, these norms and principles include the provisions of the International Bill of Rights, an integral component of which is the International Covenant on Economic, Social and Cultural Rights (ICESCR). Thus, in this indirect way, the Palestinian authorities have obligations in respect of the social rights enshrined in ICESCR.[55]

---

[50] Marks in Bowen, p. 197.
[51] PICCR, Third Annual Report 1 January 1997 to 31 December 1997 (n.d.) xii in the Director-General's Introduction.
[52] LAW – Palestinian Society for the Protection of Human Rights and the Environment, *Basic Law Draft Resolution*, unofficial translation, Jerusalem n.d., p. 5.
[53] Amnesty International, *Five Years after the Oslo Agreement: Human Rights Sacrificed for "Security"*, September 1998, p. 24.
[54] Hunt in Bowen, p.203.
[55] *Ibid.*, p. 200.

Following this with a reference to the Palestinian Independent Commission for Citizens Rights as "a mechanism by which the Palestinian authorities may – and should – be held to account in relation to social rights", Hunt seems to be rather straining the point in a desire to "show that the Palestinian authorities have responsibilities in relation to economic and social rights".[56] It is a fact that they have responsibilities under Oslo, as Hunt points out, but his initial overview obscures the very real and complex legal issues around the appropriate addresses and mechanisms of scrutiny and redress during the transitional period, and the "accountability gap" that has been left in regard to the protection of some very basic human rights.

This said, Hunt's main argument is a general one, that "social rights are much more amenable to legal protection than the prevailing orthodoxy suggests".[57] He goes through the issues around economic and social rights, commenting on the marginalisation of social rights, through the issues of justiciability and multi-layered obligations, state abstention versus state intervention and 'the policy objection' raised to appearing to give the judiciary power over decisions seen more as matters of policy than as law. His proposal is that the Palestinian authorities "implement basic social rights by enshrining them in legislation and making them justiciable".[58]

The final contribution to the volume is "The Geneva Conventions and the Autonomous Territories in the Middle East", by Hans-Peter Gasser, editor-in-chief of the International Review of the Red Cross. Gasser gives the customary disclaimer, that "the views expressed are personal and do not necessarily reflect those of the International Committee of the Red Cross".[59] That said, the piece is a fairly standard reflection of the ICRC position on the question he poses: "Does the Fourth Geneva Convention with its international rules on the protection of the civilian population in armed conflict continue to apply under the new circumstances and, if so, to what extent?"[60] He stresses, as have other contributors, that the situation of the "Autonomous Territories" is *sui generis*, but that the Autonomous Territories lack essential elements of sovereignty.[61] Clearly, where Israel exercises any of the functions of government in the Palestinian territories, in accordance with the terminology of Article 6 of the Fourth Geneva Convention, international humanitarian law continues to govern its conduct. Gasser's answer to his own question is thus quite simply that:

humanitarian law steps in when a problem arises in a domain over which Israel continues to exercise its powers. The international rules on belligerent occupation therefore remain partially applicable to the Autonomous Territories.[62]

Gasser then deals with a point not covered directly in Quigley's article on the Convention: the activities of the ICRC in the areas under PA rule. He points out that in the first place the ICRC maintains its presence because Israel continues to exercise functions of an Occupying Power, so the ICRC will monitor its compliance with the Convention – and "such presence is also warranted by the continued presence of Israeli settlers in the Gaza Strip and the West Bank".[63] Secondly, he notes that the ICRC visits detainees held by the Palestinian Authority and carries out tracing activities:

---

[56] *Ibid.* note 75 p. 220.
[57] *Ibid.,* p. 204.
[58] *Ibid.,* p. 220.
[59] Gasser in Bowen, p. 291.
[60] *Ibid.,* p. 293.
[61] It is worth noting here that Gasser appears to be the only contributor to employ the phrase "autonomous territories/areas", otherwise generally avoided.
[62] *Ibid.,* p. 296.
[63] *Ibid.,* p. 298.

Such activities in the Autonomous Areas do not derive from the 1949 Geneva Conventions. However, the Statutes of the International Red Cross and Red Crescent Movement, which have been approved by all States party to the 1949 Geneva Conventions, confer on the ICRC the prerogative to offer its services in situations not covered by the Conventions, if needs of a humanitarian nature call for such services.[64]

This statement passes over a most complex legal discussion about the nature of the transfer of authorities from the Occupying Power to the Palestinian Authority and the issues of accountability, and thus, regrettably, stands as a statement of position rather than an explanation thereof.

The volume is competently edited, with minor copy-editing irritations only — the occasional missed or misplaced word or repeated sentence, the rendering of UNRWA as UNWRA, and inconsistencies in upper case/lower case usage (Peace Process, Permanent Status negotiations). As noted above, a rather more thematic introduction would have been useful, and the varying lengths and to a certain extent nature or style of the contributions suggests that editorial instructions were not extensive. It contains, as set out above, a number of thought-provoking and highly significant articles, and some which represent real scholarly investment. It is, in short, a collection that is well worth having, or, if the price is too high, worth finding access to, for all those interested in the legal implications of the interim agreements, the transitional period, and the allegedly imminent permanent status negotiations.

Lynn Welchman

---

[64] *Ibid.*, p. 299.

The Role of the Judiciary in the Protection of Human Rights, edited by Eugene Cotran and
Adel Omar Sherif, CIMEL Book Series, Kluwer Law International, 1997, 400pp, £105.00

Edited by Judge Eugene Cotran and Judge Adel Omar Sherif, this book has its origins in
the conference on the role of the judiciary in the protection of human rights co-sponsored
in Cairo in December 1996 by the Supreme Constitutional Court of Egypt and the British
Council. This was the second major effort focusing international attention on the role of
the Supreme Court, the first being the book *Human Rights and Democracy: the Role of the
Supreme Constitutional Court of Egypt* co-edited by Judge Omar Sherif and Professor Kevin
Boyle of the Human Rights Centre at the University of Essex and published the previous year
in the CIMEL series. In December 1997, a second conference was convened in Cairo on
the theme of Democracy and the Rule of Law, from which a publication is also forthcoming. The Court is certainly worthy of this attention, and the institutionalization of the Cairo
meetings, in whatever form, it is a welcome development in view of its aim to "provide a regional forum for scholarly, expert and technical debate about constitutional and human rights
themes."[1]

The editors note that they have "not attempted to substantially edit the papers even though
this has resulted in a certain amount of repetition".[2] The book is divided not thematically but
geographically into four parts, containing papers on the role of the judiciary in the protection of human rights in Egypt; in Arab and African countries other than Egypt; and in the
United States, Europe and Brazil; with the final section collecting together papers with an international or comparative dimension. The twenty-five contributors include senior members
of the judiciary in their various countries (including Egypt, the Sudan, Ireland, Lesotho, Germany, Brazil), academic and practising lawyers, and legal advisers; they include three women.
The volume includes a short foreword by Chief Justice Awad al-Murr, who retired from his
post as President of the Supreme Constitutional Court of Egypt in the summer of 1998. Each
section of the book is prefaced with a summary of the papers included, which serves as quite
a useful guide to the contents.

In contrast to the book edited by Stephen Bowen reviewed in this volume of the *Yearbook*,
these papers have clearly been finalized fairly quickly after the conference was held, with
publication less than a year after the event. The first section, concentrating on Egypt, provides articles with a wealth of summaries of recent rulings by the Supreme Constitutional
Court and their relation to international human rights standards. The second section includes
a consideration of judicial protection of human rights in the Lebanon – with an interesting
focus on the application of international human rights instruments by the judiciary; an
overview of the rule of law in Palestine; and reviews of the role of the judiciary in the protection of human rights in Lesotho – historically and to the present – and the Sudan. The
latter chapter annexes a note by Justice Farida Ibrahim Hussein on "Religion and universality of human rights", which addresses the portrayal of "penalties derived from Islamic *shari'a*
as cruel and degrading punishments" on the basis of what she considers to be erroneous interpretations of the international instruments.[3]

In the third section, there are papers on the state of victims' rights and on the independence of federal judges in the US, and on the role of the judiciary and the rule of law in Ireland,
the UK, Germany and Brazil. As in the other sections, some very interesting case material is
included. The final section includes eight papers on a variety of related topics from international and comparative perspectives, including comparisons between Egypt and the US on
the topics of judicial review, constitutional analysis and freedom of expression, and meth-

---

[1] Cotran and Sherif, Preface, xiii.
[2] *Ibid,*. p. xiv.
[3] Farida Ibrahim Hussein in Cotran and Sherif, p. 132.

ods of reviewing the constitutionality of government action. There is a comparative analysis of constitutional law in the Middle East, a consideration of "*supra*-legislative norms" with reference to Egypt and France, and a discussion of how the judiciary might reconcile "the demand for cultural and individual freedoms in a plural society with the daily functions of society". Another contribution examines the "privatization of administrative authority" in the US permitting private individuals and groups to help enforce laws, and advocates a limited adoption of the system in Egypt.

The volume has a useful index, although a table of cases referred to in the various papers would have been welcome. The articles are of differing lengths and vary in style, as is to be expected, but there is plenty of fascinating material.

Given the specific focus in the book on the protection of human rights by the Egyptian judiciary, this would seem to be a fitting place to pay tribute to the life and memory of Hisham Mubarak, one of Egypt's leading human rights advocates, who died in Cairo in January 1998 at the age of 35. The founder and director of the Centre for Human Rights and Legal Aid, Hisham Mubarak was a lawyer by training and an activist and thinker by nature. Passionate about justice and tolerance, and tireless in his efforts, Hisham Mubarak defended victims of human rights violations across the breadth of Egypt's complicated political spectrum. *The New York Times*' obituary quoted Hanny Megally, director of Human Rights Watch/Middle East, as saying "He was remarkable in that he was truly independent and fought for all whose rights were denied, no matter what their political perspective . . . Because he was always ready to help new activists in the field and stood aloof from the human rights movement's in-fighting, he was seen as a role model by many younger Egyptians. He will be sorely missed."[4] Those who knew Hisham Mubarak were stunned by his early death, a great loss to the region's human rights movement in general, and the NGO movement in particular.

Lynn Welchman

---

[4] Judith Miller, "Hisham Mubarak dies at 35; rights campaigner in Egypt", *The New York Times* , 15 January 1998.

British Extra-Territorial Jurisdiction in the Gulf 1913–1971: An Analysis of the System of British Courts in the Territories of the British Protected States of the Gulf During the Pre-independence Era, by Husain M. Al-Baharna, Archive Editions, 1998, 192pp, £60.00

Dr Husain Al-Baharna, former Minister of Legal Affairs of Bahrain, gained his doctorate at Cambridge in 1961 as a result of a thesis on the "Legal problems of the Persian Gulf states". It was first published in 1968 by the Manchester University Press under the title *The Legal Status of the Arabian Gulf States*, with a revised edition in 1975 with the title *The Arabian Gulf States: Their Legal and Political Status and their International Problems* (Beirut, Librarie du Liban 1975, reprinted in Singapore, 1978).

He has now produced a book on a subject included in his Cambridge thesis (and considerably expanded, but not covered in the two previous publications. The contents of the book are best described by Dr Al-Baharna's preface, viz:

The book comprises nine chapters, the first of which is in the nature of background. It reviews the evolution of political institutions in the Gulf countries and describes their juridical status in international relations. For this chapter, I have drawn extensively on the introductory chapter of my book, *The Arabian Gulf States: Their Legal and Political Status and their International Problems*, Beirut, 1975. It explains the context and indeed constitutes a background for the exercise of British extra-territorial jurisdiction in the Gulf.

Chapter 2 describes the historical antecedents in the form of Capitulations, the institution of Consular Courts and Mixed Courts that bear a relationship to the present study. They present, as it were, an historical perspective to the study.

Chapter 2 explains the juridical basis for the exercise of British extra-territorial jurisdiction in the Gulf. As the question engages international law as much as municipal law, it has been examined from both points of view. The importance of the interaction between international law and municipal law for the subject has also been pointed out in this chapter.

Chapter 4 depicts the territorial and personal aspects of extra-territorial jurisdiction which explain the nature and scope of British foreign jurisdiction in the Gulf. The chapter also explains the changing character of this jurisdiction.

Chapter 5 sets out the sources of law that the British Courts were called upon by the British Crown's Orders-in-Council to apply in the settlement of cases that came up before them. It would seem that considerable latitude was given to the British Political Agency in the adaptations of English law to individual circumstances. More importantly, the British courts were authorized to apply the principles of justice, equity and good conscience in certain circumstances. Not to be forgotten, in this connection, is the authorization of the Orders-in-Council to apply the "local customs" of the Gulf countries in certain situations.

Chapter 6 explains the structure of the courts set up by the British Government for the Gulf countries and their relation to one another. The differences between these courts and those in England are brought out in this chapter.

Chapter 7 describes the jurisdiction in criminal cases, specifying the penalties to be imposed and the discretion to be enjoyed by the judges in the matter of penalties. The chapter also points to the relationship between the local government of the country concerned and the British Court in the matter of conduct of trials and execution of sentences.

Chapter 8 on civil jurisdiction is by far the largest chapter in the study. It depicts the wide range of matters and cases to be dealt with by the British courts in the area and the way they actually exercised their functions. Like the earlier chapter, it reflects the nature of cooperative relationship between the local institutions and the British courts. By and large, the British Court for Bahrain, for example, exercised most useful functions and, indeed, was a powerful agency for the promotion of law and justice in Bahrain.

The last chapter reviews the legal position as regards the so-called mixed cases, cases involving persons subject to the Orders in Council and others not subject to the Orders. These cases were to be decided by the so-called Joint Courts which comprised a British Judge and the Ruler of the State or his appointee. Unhappily, except in Bahrain, the provisions in the Orders in Council as regards the mixed cases did not get off the ground. Even in Bahrain, the role of the Joint Court was limited to mixed civil cases. The factors behind the limited role of the Joint Courts are explained in this chapter.

I have included in the book, for the benefit of readers, appendices containing the full texts of the following relevant documents: the Foreign Convention of 1861 between the Ruler of Bahrain and the British Government; the Transfer of Jurisdiction and Termination of Jurisdiction Regulations of 1972; and the Bahrain Removal of Prisoners Orders of 1956.

The study undertaken in this book is both empirical and comparative in its approach. It is based on original law cases decided by the British Political Agents' Courts in the territories of the Arab States of the Gulf over which the British Government exercised a virtual protectorate regime during the pre-independence period. For the first time case law is used to construct a picture of the law in the various territories of the Arab States of the Gulf region at the time. Such law, though based on a foreign legal system, was, nevertheless, acknowledged by the Muslim Rulers of the Arab States of the Gulf.

The book demonstrates, in general, the impact of the Indian–British judicial system on the evolution of the juridical and legal history of the Arab States of the Gulf, formerly described as the British Protected States of the Gulf. To the best of my knowledge, this is the first book of its kind to make an attempt to canvass, within a single volume, the various case law problems arising from the exercise of British foreign jurisdiction in the area.

There is also a useful select bibliography and a good index and table of cases.

It is refreshing and greatly welcome for English-trained lawyers to read a work in a legal language they understand by a member of the English Bar – what better than of Lincoln's Inn! The stress on case law is not only familiar but very well done.

When one looks at the great heritage of the English common law one tends to look at and get publication after publication on the spread of the common law and traditions into the ex-colonial territories of Britain – now constituting the Commonwealth. In Arab countries we look to the influence of France, Egypt and Islamic law.

The Gulf States, of course, provide an exception which Dr Al-Baharna has demonstrated in an admirable way. In his Introduction to the book, Professor Ian Brownlie says:

Dr Al-Baharna, my friend and colleague on the International Law Commission, has had a significant role in expounding the legal problems of the Gulf States. His original monograph was published in 1968, and a substantially revised second edition was published in 1975. In these studies the legal status of the Gulf States was carefully examined and a number of territorial disputes and boundary problems were analysed.

These studies are now rounded out and complemented by this new enterprise. The author provides a detailed account of the unusual milieu of British extraterritorial jurisdiction in the Gulf States. The exposition is enriched by frequent reference to the case law. Many points of interest arise. Apart from the issues of jurisdiction, the system involved interesting problems of law-finding and ascertainment of the applicable law. Thus, for example, in a tort case heard in the British Court for Bahrain, reference was made to Britain, Indian and United States authorities.

Dr Al-Baharna has produced a most fascinating study of a complex system of jurisdiction.

I fully agree and commend the book as essential reading to all historians and lawyers inter-ested in the export of the English system of law and its heritage to foreign countries gener-ally and the Arab Gulf area specifically.

Eugene Cotran

Jerusalem Today: What Future for the Peace Process?, Ghada Karmi (ed.), 1996,
Ithaca Press, hb 256pp, £25.00, pb 214pp, £12.95

This volume is the first product of an independent body of "ordinary people who . . . cared about the fate of Jerusalem", known as the International Campaign for Jerusalem (ICJ), headed by the editor of this book, Dr Ghada Karmi, who also wrote its introduction. In June 1995, a conference was held in London to discuss Jerusalem from various aspects. Professor Edward Said gave the keynote address to the audience. With his usual eloquence and thought provoking essays, Said first turns to lament the collective incompetence of Palestinians who have failed to record the story of Jerusalem's loss in 1948 and 1967. He noted that there has been no Palestinian narrative of 1948 and after to challenge the dominant Israeli narrative (p. 5). It seems that Said was echoing Israel Shahak's thoughts on Israel's falsification of the history of Jerusalem and Palestine (p. 127) that need to be challenged by the other party.

Correctly so, one may note that there is not a single Arab university or a research institute that has built a special department specializing in Jerusalem's history, geography, religious sites, archaeology, etc. to counter Israel's narrative. Israel has at least a dozen of such institutes that only deal with Jerusalem.

Edward Said, and rightly so, noted that "Palestinian leaders have always been misunderstood, particularly at times like this, when Israel depends so heavily on the virtual absence of Palestinian voices, counter representations, and strategies" (p. 16). It is no wonder, one may add, that Israel's aggressive colonization process in and around Jerusalem in particular has coincided with the Oslo process when the Israelis discovered that the Palestinian negotiators in Oslo had no strategic approach in those negotiations.

Said emphasized that Jerusalem is so central to Palestine itself and central to the ideological struggle against Zionism. If it is lost, he warned, "then peace in this generation is not at hand" (p. 21).

The editor categorized the papers presented into four major parts. The first part, dealing with the legal status of Jerusalem, incorporates two papers presented by two experienced lawyers. John Quigley, professor of law at Ohio State University, presented a well researched and carefully documented paper entitled "Jerusalem in international law". As in his previous works, Quigley does not truncate the issue of Jerusalem as separate and distinct from the entire spectrum of the conflict. Title to Jerusalem and the legal status of Jerusalem are not viewed as separate from the Palestinian people's claim to the territory of Palestine including Jerusalem. Quigley asserts that the Palestinian territory is a territory that fell under Israel's military occupation, by the belligerent occupation authority. Hence, Israel's thin techniques of annexing parcels of that occupied territory under the pretext of expanding the municipal boundaries of Jerusalem, does not undermine the legal status of Jerusalem as an integral part of an occupied territory.

Professor Quigley demolishes Israel's argument that because it was acting in the June 1967 war in self-defence it has gained legitimate title to the territory it occupied including Jerusalem. Quigley argues persuasively that international law does not recognize the right of any belligerent occupant to the territory it occupies whether in defensive or aggressive war. In neither situation does the occupying power gain sovereignty over that territory. This prescription applies to the occupied Palestinian territory including Jerusalem.

Mr Rodwan Bundy's article on "Legal approaches to the question of Jerusalem" has arbitrarily reduced the entire issue to "a question of demarcation" of boundaries (p. 45). One should recall that soon after the June war of 1967, President L. B. Johnson asked Prime Minister Levy Eshkol to define the boundaries that Israel wanted to be secured. He received no reply. One should also recall the debate that the representatives of the Jewish settlers in Palestine had two days before they declared a "Jewish State" on 15 May 1948. In that debate, Ben Gurion refused to identify the boundaries of the new state, and refused to accept the delimitation set out in the Partition Resolution of 1947. In that meeting, Moshe Shertok (later Sharette), supporting Ben Gurion's position said: "we do not, in fact, intend to observe that resolution in all its details".[1] In the last fifty years, the evasive position of Israel on the definition of its boundaries is still intact. In summary, it is not, as Bundy attempted to simplify it, a question of boundary. It is a relentless drive for expansion and creeping annexation.

Another over simplified issue raised by Mr Bundy is his support to the idea of arbitrating the status of Jerusalem as in the Taba arbitration. Yet he doubts that Israel would ever agree to the idea but without explaining to us why. Mr Bundy is probably aware that all attempts to solicit an advisory opinion of the International Court of Justice on the Palestinian Question were systematically frustrated by the major powers, with the influence of the Jewish Agency representatives, ever since the Partition Resolution of 1947 was debated in the UN General Assembly. Furthermore, Bundy must be also aware that when Israel acceded to the ICJ's jurisdiction it did so with the exclusion of virtually all matters relating to the Palestinian Question. This move establishes a fact that Israel would not accept the rule of law on any aspect of its conflict with the Palestinians.

Mr Bundy examines briefly the traditional roots of title to territory known in international law such as occupation and control, state succession, prescriptive rights, historical claims, etc. He found that none of these is supportive of Israeli claim. Yet, he concludes that the deficiency in Israel's claim does not necessarily mean that the Palestinian claim is any better. This is a perplexing conclusion indeed.

Part II deals with the ownership of Jerusalem viewed from three different angles. Uri Avneri, an Israeli peace activist and founder of the Gush Shalom (Peace Block), presented an Israeli view. Like other contributors to this part, he argues that Jerusalem should be "Our Jerusalem", meaning that it is a city for all Palestinians and Israelis, Muslims, Christians and Jews. In his views, Jerusalem should be the capital of two states: Jewish and Palestinian. Adnan Abu Odeh who served as Jordan's representative to the United Nations, presented a Jordanian view. While presenting an articulate thesis about Jerusalem, Abu Odeh fell inadvertently into the Israeli trap. Israel's position on Jerusalem has been consistently held that Jerusalem as a political question is not open for debate; however, from a religious point of view, Jerusalem is open. Mr Abu Odeh argues that the Old City, having incorporated all the holy shrines, should be separated form the rest of the city. It should be open for all "for it belongs only to the One God". This thesis will ossify the burning political issue of Jerusalem into a religious myth – a thesis which fits squarely with Israel's.

Rami Abdul Hadi, the Director of PASSIA, presents a Palestinian view. While he elaborated on the ten basic elements of the Jerusalem question, two points, in particular, are worthy of further elaboration. The enlargement of the Jerusalem boundaries is not only intended by Israel to change the character of these additional territories from being "occupied territory" into an "Israeli territory", it is also intended to dissect the Palestinian territory into more but less viable pockets. At present, no Palestinian can travel from Nablus or Ramallah to Hebron or Bethlehem without passing through Jerusalem. This passage needs an Israeli permit. The second point which deserves more elaboration was the issue of the *waqf* properties. While Abdul Hadi touched lightly on this type of property in Western Jerusalem (p. 71), he did not say a word about the *waqf* property in East Jerusalem. In one estimate, 80 per cent of the property in East Jerusalem is a Muslim or Christian *waqf*, a fact which establishes beyond any doubt who really owns Jerusalem.

Part III deals with the changing character of Jerusalem. The three articles falling under this part are well written and documented by three leading experts. Geoffrey Aronson, who publishes an excellent "Report on Israeli settlement in the Occupied Territories", Michael

---

[1] See the text in *The Palestinian Yearbook of International Law*, 4, 1987–1988, p. 265 at pp. 279–281.

Dumper, a scholar who has researched and written extensively on Jerusalem and Tim Llewellyn, a seasoned correspondent for the BBC in the Middle East. While they share similar data, analyses and perceptions, the reader cannot help but ascertain that there are no strategic differences between the Likud and Labour policies with respect to Jerusalem. All the papers under review were written and presented (June 1995) when the Labour government was in office. When the Netanyahu government assumed office in June 1996, the confiscation and expropriation policies have continued as they were under Rabin and Peres governments. The three papers furthermore emphasized the discriminatory policies of the Israeli governments. Llewellyn quoted the Jerusalem Councillor, Anat Hoffman, of the Meretz Party as saying that discrimination against Arabs is ingrained in Israel's political culture, at least as far as Jerusalem is concerned. Hoffman said "My file cabinets are literally overflowing with examples in every sphere: economics, housing, employment, taxation, education, welfare, health, city planning, construction roads, buses, sewerage, street lights" (p. 102). A third conclusion that can be ascertained is that the Oslo Agreements have been utilized by Israel to speed up the judaization of Jerusalem.

Part IV deals with the significance of Jerusalem to Judaism, Christianity and Islam. The article by Professor Israel Shahak is probably the most interesting and revealing. Shahak emphasizes that Jerusalem, or in fact the site of the Temple in particular, has a meaning for religious Jews who are a minority; and that Zionist leaders from Weizmann to Ben Gurion through Begin, Rabin and Peres had little interest in that religious aspect of Jerusalem. Yet, their intention was "to manipulate the real feelings of religious Jews for their own [political] purposes . . .", (p. 122). He further emphasized the continuous process of falsification of the history of Jerusalem and Palestine as being taught in the secular education curriculum in Israel. The education process tends to ignore or minimize the role of non-Jews who inhabited Palestine or played a role in its history (p. 127). This process has developed into building a chauvinistic attitude in the minds of the Israeli Jews.

Without subtracting from the value of this handsome volume, it would have been necessary to have a study on the "cleansing operation" that the Israeli government, aided and supported by its High Court of Justice, has intensified against the non-Jewish residents of Jerusalem.[2] The Jerusalemite Arabs have been subject to a systematic campaign of denying them the right to live in Jerusalem if their "centre of life", as invented by the High Court, is a few hundred yards away from the Jerusalem boundaries as defined by Israel. Another topic that deserved special attention was the Klugman Report which is an official document that elaborates on money laundering-like apparatus that operates inside Jerusalem to confiscate Arab properties.[3]

If this volume is the first product of the ICJ, it should be warmly congratulated on this valuable and comprehensive treatise. The expectation now runs high for more products with no less quality and objectivity.

Anis F. Kassim

---

[2] See Tsemel, "The continuing exodus: the ongoing expulsion of Palestinians from Jerusalem", *The Palestinian Yearbook of International Law*, 9, 1996–1997, p. 39.

[3] *Ibid.*, at p. 317.

Notes and News

OBITUARY OF DR NORMAN CALDER (1950–1998)

The doctoral student is lonely. More often than not, a doctoral dissertation, which takes at least three years to complete, is a hard, arid, endeavour. This is a long time in a person's life. Sometimes the supervisor has no time. Often, the supervisor's area of expertise, especially in such a vast field as Islamic law, does not match the student's doctoral topic, and the student finds himself in a niche outside the supervisor's interest or competence. This can be compensated with method, and with friendship, but the latter is a matter of luck. All I can say is that the hour or so in the defence of my doctoral thesis brought to me more precious insights than three years of supervision in the SOAS law department. That was thanks to the presence of Norman Calder on the examining panel.

I had the occasion to see him regularly thereafter, including for an all too brief stay in his kind hospitality in Manchester. His works became staple references in my classes on Islamic law. His *Studies in Early Islamic Jurisprudence* I liked so much that I quoted them in an article on contemporary Arab literature even before the manuscript (which was passed on to me by John Wansbrough) was published at Oxford University Press in 1993.

Nor is an obituary capable of accounting for the tremendous contribution he brought to the field. First, his doctoral dissertation under John Wansbrough, which deserves to be made accessible to a larger public than university library visitors, was a major semantic endeavour in classical Shi'i law, long the *parent pauvre* in the field to the benefit of Sunni lawyers. Then came articles of Norman Calder's with a "modern" ring. His study of the concept of *wilayat al-faqih* in Ansari's *Makaseb* has to date remained unmatched ("Accommodation and revolution in Imami Shi'i jurisprudence: Khumayni and the classical tradition", *Middle East Studies*, 1982, 3–20).

Norman was also a superb lecturer, and I had two occasions to see him operating, once in London, in an excellent conference on the Qur'an, the other a few years later in Copenhagen. That was the last time I saw him, but we kept in touch, and I eagerly followed his many articles in important journals and in major encyclopaedias.

Beyond the personal attachment, and my regret that he never joined us during my tenure at SOAS, there is in Norman Calder's death a major problem for Islamic law scholarship in the twentieth century. This is because, in between the access to teaching and research of my generation, and that of the late Joseph Schacht and Noel Coulson, there was a huge gap with no scholar – outside the work of strict historians, whose approach is fundamentally different – to carry on the mantle. Except for Norman Calder, who died so very prematurely. The generation gap will continue for years to come.

Chibli Mallat

Index